Keys for
Writers

SIXTH EDITION

Keys for Writers

ANN RAIMES

with
MARIA JERSKEY

LaGuardia Community College,
City University of New York

WADSWORTH
CENGAGE Learning

Australia • Brazil • Japan • Korea • Mexico • Singapore • Spain
United Kingdom • United States

WADSWORTH
CENGAGE Learning™

Keys for Writers,
Sixth Edition
Ann Raimes
with Maria Jerskey

Publisher: Lyn Uhl

Acquisitions Editor:
Kate Derrick

Development Editor:
Renee Deljon

Senior Assistant Editor:
Kelli Strieby

Media Editor:
Cara Douglass-Graff

Marketing Manager:
Christina Shea

Marketing Coordinator:
Ryan Ahern

Marketing Communications
Manager: Stacey Purviance

Content Project Manager:
Rosemary Winfield

Art Director: Jill Ort

Print Buyer: Betsy Donaghey

Text Permissions Editor:
Margaret Chamberlain-
Gaston

Production Service, Text
Design, and Compositor:
Nesbitt Graphics, Inc.

Photo Manager: John Hill

Cover Designer: Walter
Kopec

Cover Image: Mark Viker /
Getty Images

For product information and technology assistance,
contact us at **Cengage Learning Customer & Sales
Support, 1-800-354-9706.**

For permission to use material from this text
or product, submit all requests online at
www.cengage.com/permissions.
Further permissions questions can be e-mailed to
permissionrequest@cengage.com.

Library of Congress Control Number: 2009940454

ISBN-10: 0-495-79982-3

ISBN-13: 978-0-495-79982-5

Wadsworth
20 Channel Center Street
Boston, MA 02210
USA

Cengage Learning is a leading provider of customized
learning solutions with office locations around the globe,
including Singapore, the United Kingdom, Australia,
Mexico, Brazil and Japan. Locate your local office at
international.cengage.com/region.

Cengage Learning products are represented in Canada
by Nelson Education, Ltd.

For your course and learning solutions, visit
www.cengage.com.

Purchase any of our products at your local college store
or at our preferred online store **www.ichapters.com.**

Printed in China
1 2 3 4 5 6 7 13 12 11 10 09

Preface

In these days of texting, tweeting, blogging, e-mailing, posting to Facebook, and firing off IMs, we can all claim to be writers—much more so than when I was a college student and wrote only handwritten letters, an embarrassingly personal diary, and school assignments. Now, for most of us, daily writing is brief, purposeful, and informal, so much so that students facing a formal writing task raise all kinds of questions of what is expected and what to do to meet expectations—especially to get an A! Recent technological changes and our present-day culture of rapid written communications have certainly made writing less of an unfamiliar and scary enterprise than it was once, but when much is at stake—such as a grade or a promotion at work—the specter of what instructors and bosses expect looms large.

This new edition of *Keys for Writers* aims to help student writers bridge the gap between what they already know and do in their everyday writing and what academic readers, as well as readers in work settings, expect. This handbook still helps students plan and edit their writing and make it fit into academia. There are still many examples that show how to construct effective sentences, paragraphs, and essays. (In chapter 3, a manuscript page from Philip Roth's novel *Patrimony* points out dramatically that even professional writers make many changes as they revise their work.) And to follow the tradition of earlier editions, the needs of multilingual writers are taken into account both in Part 9, Writing across Cultures, and throughout in the many Notes for Multilingual Writers.

However, in keeping with the emphasis on technology in our Internet age, this sixth edition pays more attention to showing how to search online for academic sources, how to cite them accurately, and how to select and use visuals that enliven and dramatize written work. The eight Source Shots in Parts 3 and 4 display what sources look like when students access them on a page or screen and show how to use the information in a citation list in a paper. The use of technology in academic writing is highlighted, notably in dozens of Tech Notes. In addition, chapter 21 includes screenshots of Word 2007 for PC and Word 2008 for Mac that illustrate how to insert specific text features in a research paper. Part 5 has been updated with new visuals, a new sample brochure, new material on multimedia presentations, and more on PowerPoint.

Research papers often determine a large part of a course grade, so this edition devotes new sections to how to get the most out of Google, advanced searches, and online alerts (7c); finding appropriate visuals (7g); and using bibliographical software, databases, and Word to help keep records and avoid plagiarism (9f). Illustrating the variety of sources available today, The Key Points box in 12g shows nine different sources for the song "Pray" by Jay-Z, with examples of how to cite each one in a research paper.

Feedback from users has indicated how useful samples of student writing are, so this sixth edition includes authentic student writing from various stages throughout the process—annotated drafts, brainstorming lists, and outlines; a passage annotated and revised for style; a working bibliography; an online portfolio; a student-generated Web site; and a student-designed brochure. This edition also showcases actual student essays in MLA style (an argument, a literature paper, and an analysis of the cultural symbol of the smiley face), a complete APA paper, and excerpts from a CSE paper and a Chicago paper. Most of these papers include visuals, a way of communication familiar to most students.

But although the story of this sixth edition is based on dramatic global and technological shifts, I continue to believe that the best handbook is one that students will use. It is one that not only keeps pace with writers' changing needs but also invites use and is easy to use. The success of the previous editions of *Keys for Writers* tells me to keep this handbook's distinctive navigation and its two (yes, only two) color-coded, numbered, and descriptively labeled rows of tabs; the coaching tone that students see as lively but respectful; and the concise explanations and examples of grammar and style that have guided and delighted many users. Yet *Keys for Writers* has also changed because both teachers and students have conveyed in person, mailed, and e-mailed invaluable suggestions to help the book keep pace with current trends in writing and be as accurate and timely as a handbook should be. I am grateful for those shared ideas and am happy to incorporate them.

So you have in your hand a handbook that provides solid instruction and lively examples in an updated design, keeps up with change, insists on authentic examples of student writing, and conveys the challenges of writing for multiple audiences in multiple settings. I'd like to hear your reactions. You can write to me in care of (c/o) Kate Derrick at Cengage Learning, 20 Channel Center Street, Boston, MA 02210.

Wadsworth has prepared the following expanded summary of what's new to the sixth edition, a summary of the features that have been hallmarks of this book and that continue in the new edition, and a guide to its comprehensive supplements package, which includes several exciting additions and is described in this Preface beginning on page x.

New to the Sixth Edition

In addition to a dynamic new design, this edition of *Keys for Writers* offers the following new coverage and features:

2009 MLA and 2010 APA style updates The MLA documentation coverage reflects significant changes in the new *MLA Handbook for Writers of Research Papers,* Seventh Edition (published in March 2009), and the APA coverage reflects the new *Publication Manual of the American Psychological Association,* Sixth Edition (published in July 2009 and in full effect as of January 2010).

Revised, updated, and expanded coverage of many topics, including annotated bibliographies (9e); scratch and formal outlines (1h); how to use, integrate, and document sources (new chapter 10 in Part 2); and tips for multilingual writers (Part 9).

Thoroughly revised coverage of argument as well as design, media, and presentation Maria Jerskey, LaGuardia Community College, worked with Ann Raimes to provide thoroughly revised coverage of argumentation in chapter 4, including visual arguments, and academic paper formatting and design using Word for Mac and PC, hardcopy and electronic portfolios, multimedia presentations, and more throughout Part 5.

New Key Points boxes appear throughout the handbook, including one titled "Nine Ways to Document a Jay-Z Song" (CD, MP3 file, LP record, lyrics in print and online, DVD, video, live performance, and video of live performance). As often as possible, continuing Key Points boxes have been revised for even greater concision and improved quick-reference format.

More Source Shots, the majority of them new Part 3 (MLA) now includes five of the text's popular Source Shots, four of them new, including one featuring a government publication, and Part 4 (APA, CSE, and Chicago) now includes three Source Shots, two of them new.

New examples and models for essay outlines (1h); generation of thesis (1f); freewriting (1e); brainstorming (2e); writing and researching in the humanities, arts, and natural sciences (5f, 5g); annotated bibliography entries (9e); a student research paper in MLA style on the topic of the smiley face (chapter 13); a student research paper in APA style on savants (chapter 4); an excerpt from a student's research paper on the bristlecone pine tree in CSE style; and an excerpt from a student's research paper on Mondrian in *Chicago* style. All but one of these student samples include visuals.

Continuing Proven Features

This text's intuitive, color-coded two-part organization, laminated tabbed part dividers, customizable KeyTabs®, quick reference features such as Key Points boxes, abundant examples and models, friendly writing style, and uncluttered design continue in the sixth edition, making information easy for student writers to find, understand, and apply.

Two rows of color-coded divider tabs   The unusual simplicity and clarity of only two rows of tabs make it easy to find information quickly. The first row is red, for writing and research issues; the second row is gold, for sentence-level issues.

Unique KeyTabs®   Located at the back of the book, the eight blank, Do-It-Yourself (DIY)—customizable and moveable—KeyTab® notecards enable students to bookmark sections of the handbook that they refer to frequently, find relevant to comments on assignments, or otherwise find especially helpful. Students (and instructors) simply write their notes on a card and move it to its intended location, inserting it into the binding, with the top of the KeyTab® extending from the top of the book.

Practical "Key Points" boxes   These handy boxes open or appear within most major sections of the handbook to provide quick-reference summaries of essential information. Sixth edition Key Points boxes include When to Begin a New Paragraph (Part 1); Developing Your Junk Antennae: How to Evaluate Web Sites (Part 2); Guidelines for the MLA List of Works Cited (Part 3); Working with DOIs and URLs (Part 4); Guidelines for College Essay Format (Part 5); Checklist for Word Choice (Part 6); Form of Personal Pronouns (Part 7); Titles: Quotation Marks or Italics/Underlining (Part 8); and Articles at a

Glance: Four Basic Questions about a Noun (Part 9). A complete list of the Key Points boxes is provided on pages 608–609.

Bracketed labels on selected sample citations in all styles   These clearly labeled models show at a glance what types of information students need to include and how to format, arrange, and punctuate that information when documenting sources in all covered styles.

```
                                        print          print publication
    ┌─ author ─┐  ┌─ title of poem ─┐  ┌─ source ─┐  ┌── information ──┐
    Levine, Philip. "What Work Is." What Work Is. New York: Knopf, 1991.
                    ┌─ title of Web site ─┐  ┌─ sponsor of site ─┐
    N. pag. Internet Poetry Archive. U of North Carolina P., n.d. Web.
    date of
    ┌─ access ─┐
    19 Feb. 2009.
```

Thorough coverage of style   *Keys for Writers* continues to devote a full part (Part 6, Style: The Five C's) to the important area of style, covering sentence- and word-related style issues in a unified presentation. The popular coverage advises students in straightforward, memorable fashion to Cut, Check for Action, Connect, Commit, and Choose the Best Words.

Thorough, consolidated, and clear coverage of grammar   Part 7, Common Sentence Problems, gives students one central place to turn to when they have grammar questions. Grammar coverage is not divided confusingly over several parts, as in other handbooks. A section on students' frequently asked grammar questions begins Part 7.

Distinctive approach to English as a new language, Englishes, and vernaculars   Superior coverage for multilingual writers takes a "difference, not deficit" approach presented within Language and Culture boxes, an extensive Editing Guide to Multilingual Transfer Patterns, an Editing Guide to Vernacular Englishes, and Notes for Multilingual Writers integrated throughout the text. Complete lists of the Language and Culture boxes and Notes for Multilingual Writers are provided on page 609.

Helpful tips for using technology   Tech Note boxes provide useful ideas and resources for writing, using the Web, and researching with technology. Tech Notes in the sixth edition include "Taking Accessibility Issues and Disabilities into Account," "Using GoogleDocs," and "Exploring Data Visualization Tools." A complete list of the Tech Notes is provided on page 609.

Coverage of writing and communicating throughout and beyond college   *Keys for Writers* prepares students for a range of writing and communicating tasks they may meet in college as well as in the community and the workplace. With many model documents, Web pages, PowerPoints, tips for oral presentations, and other resources, Part 5 covers writing, communicating, and document design in a range of media for diverse audiences.

A Complete Support Package

The sixth edition of *Keys for Writers* is accompanied by a wide array of supplemental resources developed to create the best teaching and learning experience inside as well as outside the classroom, whether that classroom is on campus or online.

Enhanced InSite for *Keys for Writers*, Sixth Edition

With Enhanced InSite for *Keys for Writers*, Sixth Edition, instructors and students gain access to exceptional resources designed to best help students become more successful and confident writers, including access to Personal Tutor, an interactive e-book handbook with an integrated text-specific workbook and tutorials, as well as the proven, class-tested capabilities of Wadsworth's InSite for Writing and Research™, which includes electronic peer review, an originality checker powered by Turnitin®, an assignment library, help with common grammar and writing errors, fully integrated discussion boards, and access to InfoTrac® College Edition. Additionally, portfolio management gives you the ability to grade papers, run originality reports, and offer feedback in an easy-to-use online course management system, and using InSite's peer review feature, students can easily review and respond to their classmates' work. To learn more, please visit **www.cengage.com/insite.**

This book's support package also includes the following materials for instructors and students.

Supplemental Resources for Instructors

Instructor's companion Web site (www.cengage.com/english/ raimes) Access the password-protected *Keys for Writers,* Sixth Edition, Web site for instructors to find resources including the handbook's Instructor's Resource Manual. The online **Instructor's**

Resource Manual provides an overview of the handbook and ideas on how to use it, a section on teaching composition to multilingual students, advice on using the Internet both within the composition classroom and throughout the course, diagnostic test handouts on five main areas of grammar, and answers to numbered items in the online exercises.

Exercises to accompany *Keys for Writers*   The online exercises cover grammar, punctuation, usage, and style. The workbook combines exercises with clear examples and explanations that supplement the information and exercises found in the sixth edition of *Keys for Writers*.

Supplemental Resources for Students

Multimedia e-book for Raimes, *Keys for Writers*, **Sixth Edition**   An interactive, multimedia e-book provides your students with instant access to the reference material most used and needed in the composition course. The e-book includes interactive exercises, an integrated text-specific workbook, a highlighting and note-taking tool, a printing option, and a search tool.

Student's companion Web site (www.cengage.com/english/ raimes)   This Web site provides open access to companion learning resources for all aspects of the writing and research processes (including avoiding plagiarism)—such as additional writing samples, templates, exercises, quizzes, and up-to-date Web links.

It is also a gateway to premium resources, including the text's interactive, multimedia e-book and interactive activities, grammar podcasts, and a rich collection of citation examples.

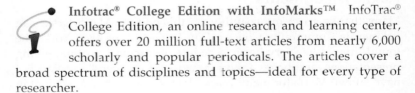

Infotrac® College Edition with InfoMarks™   InfoTrac® College Edition, an online research and learning center, offers over 20 million full-text articles from nearly 6,000 scholarly and popular periodicals. The articles cover a broad spectrum of disciplines and topics—ideal for every type of researcher.

Turnitin®   This proven online plagiarism-prevention software promotes fairness in the classroom by helping students learn to correctly cite sources and allowing instructors to check for originality before reading and grading papers. Visit **www.cengage.com/turnitin** to view a demonstration.

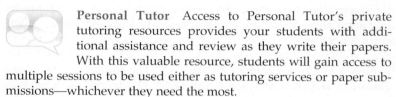 **Personal Tutor** Access to Personal Tutor's private tutoring resources provides your students with additional assistance and review as they write their papers. With this valuable resource, students will gain access to multiple sessions to be used either as tutoring services or paper submissions—whichever they need the most.

Merriam-Webster's Collegiate® Dictionary, Eleventh Edition Available only when packaged with a Wadsworth text, the new eleventh edition of America's best-selling hardcover dictionary merges print, CD-ROM, and Internet-based formats to deliver unprecedented accessibility and flexibility at one affordable price. This resource is also available in paperback.

Dictionary/Thesaurus Available only when packaged with a Wadsworth text, this dictionary and thesaurus is two essential language references in one handy volume. Included are nearly 60,000 alphabetical dictionary entries integrated with more than 13,000 thesaurus entries including extensive synonym lists, as well as abundant example phrases that provide clear and concise word guidance.

Ordering options for student supplements are flexible. Please consult your local Cengage Learning sales representative or visit us at **www.cengage.com** for more information, including ISBNs; to receive examination copies of any of these instructor or student resources; or for product demonstrations. Print and e-book versions of this text and many of its supplements are available for students to purchase at a discount at **www.cengagebrain.com**.

Acknowledgments

Many thanks go to my coauthor on this edition, Maria Jerskey of LaGuardia Community College, City University of New York. She found time in her very hectic schedule of teaching, writing, giving presentations, and being a mom to work on chapter 4 and Part 5. I have known Maria for many years. She was a remarkable student in my graduate courses and has since become a dear friend. I feel fortunate to have her working with me on the *Keys* series of books. We both acknowledge the contributions of Doug Eyman (George Mason University and senior editor of the journal *Kairos*), whose technological expertise was invaluable. We are both grateful to teachers and students across the country for their feedback and insightful suggestions that led us to rethink material in the book. Thanks again, too, to Tony Doyle, Hunter College librarian, for helping with finding successful student essays to include in this book.

I have always made a point of using authentic student writing in my handbooks. For giving me permission to use their work, I offer many thanks to the following, all of whom were responsive, helpful, and a pleasure to work with: Dana Alogna, Tiffany Brattina, Brian Cortijo, Yulanda Croasdale, Andrew Dillon, Mara Lee Kornberg, Charles Mak, Lynn McCarthy, Juana Mere, Maria Saparauskaite, Daniel Sauve, Jennifer Richards, Catherine Turnbull, Jared Whittemore, Natasha Williams, and Jimmy Wong.

The following composition instructors were instrumental in suggesting changes in this new edition. I am grateful to them for sharing their wisdom and experience in detailed reviews:

Candace Boeck, *San Diego State University*
Stephen Byars, *University of South Carolina*
Amber Carini, *San Diego State University*
Kathy Ford, *Lakeland Community College*
Janet Gerstner, *San Juan College*
Marshall Kitchens, *Oakland University*
Mary Nagler, *Oakland Community College*
Paul Walker, *Murray State University*

I am also grateful to the following dedicated instructors who completed a helpful survey:

Jennifer Banning, *Illinois State University;* Richard Beighey, *Community College of Allegheny County—North Campus;* Christina Pinkston Betts, *Hampton University;* Linda Brender *Macomb Community College;* Fahamisha Patricia Brown, *Metropolitan College of New York;* Vincent Bruckert, *Wright College;* Sherry Cisler, *Arizona State University;* Gene Crutsinger, *Tiffin University;* Amie Doughty, *State University of New York, Oneonta;* Bart Ganzert, *Forsyth Technical Community College;* Patricia Griffin, *Saint Joseph's University;* Leean Hawkins, *National Park Community College;* Karen Heywood, *Stephens College;* Clark Iverson, *Macomb Community College—Center Campus;* Lewis J. Kahler, *Mohawk Valley Comunity College;* Noel Kinnamon, *Mars Hill College;* Victoria Lannen, *Southwestern College;* Chad Littleton, *University of Tennessee at Chattanooga;* Orit Rabkin, *University of Oklahoma;* Susan Richardson, *Macomb Community College;* Michael E. Smith, *Western Carolina University;* Sandra Van Pelt, *Belhaven College;* Catherine Vedder, *Kentucky State University.*

In addition I extend my grateful thanks to the following, who helped at earlier stages of composition:

Joseph A. Alvarez, *Central Piedmont Community College;* Akua Duku Anokye, *University of Toledo;* Jennie Ariail, *University of South Carolina;* Janet Badia, *Marshall University;* Pamela J. Balluck, *University of Utah;* Lona Bassett, *Jones County Junior College;* Jennifer Beech, *Pacific Lutheran University;* B. Cole Bennett, *Abilene Christian University;* Robin A. Benny, *Chicago State University;* Linda Bergman, *Illinois Institute of Technology;* Clair Berry, *State Technical Institute at Memphis;* Curtis W. Bobbit, *College of Great Falls;* Candace A. Boeck, *San Diego State University;* Darsie Bowden, *Western Washington University;* Laurie Bower, *University of Nevada, Reno;* Terry Brown, *University of Wisconsin, River Falls;* Stephen M. Byars, *University of Southern California;* Jeffrey P. Cain, *Sacred Heart University;* Bettina Caluori, *DeVry Institute, New Brunswick;* Karen A. Carlton, *Humboldt State University;* Laura B. Carroll, *Abilene Christian University;* Gina Claywell, *Murray State University;* Linda Clegg, *Cerritos College;* Robert Cousins, *Utah Valley State College;* Ned Cummings, *Bryant and Stratton College;* Lisa Davidson, *Passaic County Community College;* Ben Davis, *Cuyahoga Community College;* Judith Davis, *Old Dominion University;* Virginia B. DeMers, *Ringling School of Art and Design;* Rob Dornsife, *Creighton University;* David A. Dzaka, *Messiah College;* Darlynn R. Fink, *Clarion University of Pennsylvania;* Murray A. Fortner, *Tarrant County College;* Katherine Frank, *University of Southern Colorado;* Muriel Fuqua, *Daytona Beach Community College;* David W. Furniss, *University of Wisconsin, River Falls;* Lynée Lewis Gaillet, *Georgia State University;* Philip Gaines, *Montana State University;* Dennis Gartner, *Frostburg State University;* Dorothy Gilbert, *California State University, Haywood;* Thomas Goodman, *University of Miami;* Katherine Green, *Albuquerque Technical-Vocational Institute;* John Gregorian, *Contra Costa Community College;* Claudia Gresham-Shelton, *Stanly Community College;* Elizabeth Grubgeld, *Oklahoma State University;* Keith Gumery, *Temple University;* Jane E. Hardy, *Cornell University;* D. Alexis Hart, *University of Georgia;* Beth L. Hewett, *Community College of Baltimore County, Essex;* Christopher Z. Hobson, *State University of New York, College at Old Westbury;* Franklin E. Horowitz, *Columbia University;* Michael Hricik, *Westmoreland City Community College;* Margaret Hughes, *Butte College;* Mary L. Hurst, *Cuyahoga Community College;* John Hyman, *American University;* Ernest H. Johansson, *Ohio University;* Ted E. Johnston, *El Paso Community College;* Karen Jones, *St. Charles Community College;* Mary

Kaye Jordan, *Ohio University*; Ann Judd, *Seward County Community College*; Susan Kincaid, *Lakeland Community College*; Martha Kruse, *University of Nebraska, Kearney*; Sally Kurtzman, *Arapahoe Community College*; Joseph LaBriola, *Sinclair Community College*; Lindsay Lewan, *Arapahoe Community College*; Daniel Lowe, *Community College of Allegheny County*; Kelly Lowe, *Mount Union College*; Dianne Luce, *Midlands Technical Community College*; Mike MacKey, *Community College of Denver*; Mary Sue MacNealy, *The University of Memphis*; Gina Maranto, *University of Miami*; Louis Martin, *Elizabethtown College*; JoAnne Liebman Matson, *University of Arkansas, Little Rock*; Ann Maxham-Kastrinos, *Washington State University*; Nancy McTaggart, *Northern Virginia Community College*; Michael G. Moran, *University of Georgia*; Marie Nigro, *Lincoln University, Pennsylvania*; Carolyn O'Hearn, *Pittsburgh State University*; Liz Parker, *Nashville State Technical Institute*; Sally Parr, *Ithaca College*; Kathy Parrish, *Southwestern College*; Jane Petersor, *Richland College*; Lillian Polak, *Nassau Community College*; Jeffrey Rice, *Wayne State University*; Nelljean M. Rice, *Coastal Carolina University*; Kenneth Risdon, *University of Minnesota at Duluth*; Mark Rollins, *Ohio University*; Julia Ruengert, *Pensacola Junior College*; Cheryl W. Ruggiero, *Virginia Polytechnic Institute*; Kristin L. Snoddy, *Indiana University at Kokomo*; James R. Sodon, *St. Louis Community College at Florissant Valley*; Ellen Sostarich, *Hocking College*; Eleanor Swanson, *Regis University*; Jami M. Taylor, *ECPI College of Technology*; Michael R. Underwood, *San Diego State University*; Amy Ulmer, *Pasadena City College*; Jane Mueller Ungari, *Robert Morris College*; Margaret Urie, *University of Nevada*; Thomas Villano, *Boston University*; Brian K. Walker, *Pulaski Technical College*; Colleen Weldele, *Palomar College*; Barbara Whitehead, *Hampton University*; Stephen Wilhoit, *University of Dayton*; Debbie J. Williams, *Abilene Christian University*; James D. Williams, *University of North Carolina, Chapel Hill*; James Wilson, *LaGuardia Community College, City University of New York*; Sallie Wolf, *Arapahoe Community College*; Randell Wolff, *Murray State*; Martin Wood, *University of Wisconsin, Eau Claire*; Randal Woodland, *University of Michigan, Dearborn*; Pamela S. Wright, *University of California, San Diego*; Pavel Zemliansky, *James Madison University*; Laura W. Zlogar, *University of Wisconsin, River Falls*.

The publisher plays a large role in the development and publication of a new edition. Thanks go to Lyn Uhl, Publisher, and Kate Derrick, Acquisitions Editor, for their support and encouragement throughout the process; to Renee Deljon, Development Editor, and to Frank Hubert, Copy Editor, for their contributions to the manuscript; and to both Rosemary Winfield, Content Project Manager, and Aaron Downey, Project Manager at Nesbitt Graphics, Inc., for coping so ably with production schedules, snags, and deadlines. Grateful acknowledgments are also due to others on the *Keys* team for their help and expertise: at Cengage Learning, Kelli Strieby, Jake Zucker, Amy Gibbons, Judy Fifer, and Christina Shea, and all at Nesbitt Graphics, Inc., especially Jerilyn Bockorick and Alisha Webber.

And as always, thanks go to my family, who fortunately have the right attitude—that "living well is the best revenge" and that being together, having fun, and eating great meals are the main goals. Throughout the editions of this book, my husband, James, who volunteers to take on many chores, has become a terrific cook. I only hope this edition is as delectable as his dinners.

Ann Raimes

PART **1**

The Writing Process

1 Ways into Writing   3

2 Developing Paragraphs and Essays   27

3 Revising, Editing, and Proofreading   40

4 Writing and Analyzing Arguments   51

5 Writing in All Your Courses   80

@ | **ONLINE RESOURCES**
    www.cengage.com/english/raimes
Companion online resources are available for sections throughout this part. We invite you to visit the book's Web site for more information and direct access.

PART 1

The Writing Process

1 Ways into Writing 3
1a Writing for readers 3
1b Everyday writing and college writing 4
1c Reading words and images critically 5
1d Purpose, audience, voice, and media 8
1e Ways to generate a topic and ideas 11
1f Ways to present your thesis or claim 18
1g Writing with others 23
1h Tips for drafting and outlining (with sample outlines) 23

2 Developing Paragraphs and Essays 27
2a Paragraph basics 27
2b Unified paragraphs and topic sentences 28
2c Using transitions and links for coherence 29
2d Eight examples of paragraph development 31
2e Writing introductions and conclusions 36

3 Revising, Editing, and Proofreading 40
3a Strategies for revising 42
3b Giving and getting feedback 43
3c Drafting and revising a title 45
3d Editing 45
3e A student's annotated drafts 46
3f Proofreading 50

4 Writing and Analyzing Arguments 51
4a Thinking critically about arguments 52
4b Formulating and constructing a good argument 52
4c Structuring an argument essay 53
4d Topic and claim (thesis) 55
4e Supporting a claim with reasons and evidence 59
4f Four questions for constructing an argument (Toulmin) 61
4g Appeals, common ground, and opposing views 62
4h Logical reasoning, logical fallacies 66
4i Using and analyzing visual arguments 69
4j Sample paper 1: A student's argument essay 73

5 Writing in All Your Courses 80
5a Writing under pressure: Essay exams and short-answer tests 81
5b Writing about literature 82
5c Sample paper 2: A student's literature paper 87
5d Writing about community service 90
5e Writing and researching across the curriculum 91
5f Writing and researching in the humanities and arts 92
5g Writing and researching in the natural sciences (with student samples) 92
5h Writing and researching in the social sciences 95

1 🔑

Ways into Writing

1a Writing for readers

Getting started can be hard if you only think of a piece of writing as a permanent document that others can judge you on. A blank page or an empty screen with its blinking cursor can be daunting, but the act of writing offers an advantage over speaking: You can go back and make changes. You are not locked into what you have written until you decide to turn your finished work over to readers. You can also present whatever image of yourself you choose. You have the freedom to invent yourself anew. As journalist Adam Gopnik says fondly of writing, "It's you there, but not quite you." One of the pleasures of writing is taking advantage of that freedom.

When you write, you take on many roles. You're a writer, yes, but you're also a reader and critical thinker, a participant in the formation of ideas and reactions to ideas, and an analyzer of the many kinds of texts (written, visual, auditory) produced by others. What you write is influenced by your knowledge and experience and by what you read and learn as you prepare to write.

How you write is also influenced by the expectations of the audience you are writing for; while in college, that's usually academic readers. Academic readers want to know not just what you've found in what you've read, observed, or experienced but also what you have to say about what you found. After all, regardless of their different knowledge and life experiences, your readers can easily find the exact same books, articles, and Web sites! That means an important question to bear in mind when writing is always this: What is your take on an issue, idea, or event?

It's a good thing then that writing itself helps you have ideas, make connections, and raise questions. That is, in writing, you do not just *display* what you know; you also *discover* what you know and think. How is that possible? It's possible because writing is not a linear or step-by-step procedure but a frequently messy *process*—a sort of adventure, one that you control but that often surprises you with your own insights as you progress through the relatively set sequence of several overlapping and recurring activities that comprise the writing process:

Given that most of us multitask as a matter of course in today's world, what composition scholar Ann Berthoff called the "all-at-onceness" of writing will probably be familiar to you.

1b Everyday writing and college writing

Academic writing such as reports, essays, research papers and everyday writing such as letters, lists, and online messages are *genres,* or types, of writing. Other genres include creative writing (novels, poems, etc.) and business writing (memos, proposals, etc.). An awareness of the genre of writing you're working in is important because it is tightly tied to your purpose for writing, your understanding of the audience for your writing, the voice or tone you use, and the medium through which you present your writing. It puts your writing task into perspective and often dictates a set of conventions, both of which may make it seem more manageable and even save you time.

What makes academic writing different from the everyday writing we do when we fill out a form, compose a letter to an elected official, text or e-mail friends, post comments on Twitter or Facebook, or post a blog online? Essentially, writing for college involves more of everything: more time, more thought, more knowledge, more revision, more care, more attention to your readers' formal expectations.

Your everyday correspondents generally don't care about your spelling, punctuation, or even your phrasing. Your online or texted messages are ephemeral, read quickly and deleted. But more is at stake with college writing—in a word, grades! Nobody grades your online messages, but an essay for a college course dashed off in a short time will likely earn you a D.

All writers need to pay attention to *conventions*—the customs associated with a genre. The following passage shows abbreviations, current expressions, shortcuts, and code words that constitute some of the conventions attached to texting and IM conversations:

> Smiley 123: hey sup?
>
> Nicagalxoxo: wut r u doin l8ter?
>
> Smiley 123: goin 2 the movies 2nite 2 c iron man
>
> Nicagalxoxo: OMG I wanna c that—wut time r u going?
>
> Smiley 123: dunno ttyl

Students generally know this code from using it in daily life. If that same exchange were written in academic language, it would sound faintly ridiculous. Similarly, there is a code for academic writing, which leads to very different and more formal texts. The later chapters in this book will help you become familiar with the conventions for academic writing.

However, while the worlds are different, they are not entirely distinct. Using the spontaneity, immediacy, and desire to get an idea across to a real reader will always stand you in good stead in college writing.

1c Reading words and images critically

When we read and write, we engage in a process of locating and entering an ongoing discussion about an issue, examining critically the ideas expressed by others and asking questions about those ideas. For example, we may find ourselves nodding and agreeing with or even admiring a text or an image. Or we may be triggered to use the word "but . . ." as we read—either saying it in our head or writing it in the text or in our notes. This marks our entry into the swirl of ideas around the topic. As we read, we scrutinize the ideas we find and adjust our own ideas accordingly. During the process of writing, we think critically about our own position and the positions others take. That critical thinking helps shape our writing, and then others can respond to what *we* write and continue the conversation.

Thinking critically does not mean criticizing others. Instead, it means questioning, discussing, and looking from a number of sides at what others say in their words and images, as when we respond mentally to what we hear, see, or read with reactions like, "Well, yes, but," "On the other hand," or even "No way." It also means looking for points of connection and agreement with someone else's views, responses such as, "I agree" and "In addition . . . ."

Looking at the following image, for example, may prompt several questions:

Brooklyn street scene, April 2009.

- Why did the photographer choose to photograph this scene? What attracted him or her to it? Was the writing on the newspaper box important to the photographer?
- When was this photo taken, and why aren't any people in it?
- What does the camera angle accomplish? What does it include and exclude?
- What are the white objects that appear to be the photo's focal point? Why are they on the street?
- What, if any, social implications does the scene have? Does it suggest a commentary on urban Brooklyn? What does the scene suggest about the neighborhood?

Reflecting on these or similar questions constitutes critical reading of this image. For more on thinking critically about arguments, see 4a. See 4i for more on using visual arguments in a paper.

KEY POINTS

How to Be a Critical Reader of Text and Images

- **Do close readings.** Read more than once; examine a text or an image slowly and carefully, immersing yourself in the work and annotating to record your reactions.

to furnish with notes

- **Look for common ground.** Note where you nod in approval at points made in the text or image.

- **Question and challenge.** Take on the role of a debater in your head. Ask yourself: Where does this idea come from? What biases does the writer reveal? What interesting information does the writer or creator provide—and is it convincing? Does the writer use sound logic? Is the writer fair to opposing views? Does the writer even take opposing views into account?

- **Write as you read.** Write comments and questions in the margins of a page, between the lines in an online document saved to your word processor, on a blog, or on self-stick notes. In this way, you start a conversation with anything you read. If you have made the text you are reading look messy, that's a good sign.

- **Remember that readers will read critically what you write.** It is not enough just to *read* critically. Be aware that your own writing has to stand up to readers' careful scrutiny and challenge, too.

Critical reading in action: A "conversation" with a text   While reading the following passage about the Ultimatum Game, a student annotates the passage as she reads it. Her comments, questions, and challenges establish her role in the conversation about fair play.

I like the direct approach!

Imagine that somebody offers you $100. All you have to do is agree with some other anonymous person on how to share the sum. The rules are strict. The two of you are in separate rooms and cannot exchange information. A coin toss decides which of you will propose how to share the money. Suppose that you are the proposer. You can make a single offer of how to split the sum, and the other person—the responder—can say yes or no. The responder also knows the rules and the total amount of money at stake. If her answer is yes, the deal goes ahead. If her answer is no, neither of you gets anything. In both cases, the game is over and will not be repeated. What will you do?

Critical point
Ha! Why anonymous?

Authors use feminine pronoun here

Daring or greedier

Instinctively, many people feel they should offer 50 percent, because such a division is "fair" and therefore likely to be accepted. More daring people, however, think they might get away with offering somewhat less than half the sum.

Have the authors researched this assumption?

Before making a decision, you should ask yourself what you would do if you were the responder. The only thing you can do as the responder is say yes or no to a given amount of money. If the offer were 10 percent, would you take $10 and let someone walk away with $90, or would you rather have nothing at all? What if the offer were only 1 percent? Isn't $1 better than no dollars? And remember, haggling is strictly forbidden. Just one offer by the proposer; the responder can take it or leave it.

But the organizers will know what I offer, so it's not entirely between two anonymous people.

So what will you offer?

—Karl Sigmund, Ernst Fehr, and Martin A. Nowak,
"The Economics of Fair Play"

1d Purpose, audience, voice, and media

The genre of writing you are undertaking influences your purpose, audience, voice, and often the delivery medium you choose.

Your purpose   Ask yourself what is your main purpose for writing in a particular writing situation, beyond aiming for an A in the course! Here are some possibilities:

- to explain an idea or theory or explore a question (expository writing)
- to report on a process, an experiment, or lab results (technical or scientific writing)
- to provide a status update on a project at work (business writing)
- to persuade readers to understand your point of view, change their minds, or take action (persuasive or argumentative writing)
- to record and reflect on your own experiences and feelings (expressive writing)
- to create a work of art such as a play or short story (creative writing)

The purpose of your writing will determine your ways of presenting your final text. Formal academic writing generally concerns the first four purposes just listed, and less formal, more personal writing concerns the last two.

Your audience   A good writer keeps readers in mind at all times, as if in face-to-face communication. Achieving this connection, however, often proves challenging because not all readers have the same characteristics. Readers come from different parts of the world, regions, communities, ethnic groups, organizations, and academic disciplines, all with their own linguistic and rhetorical conventions.

This means that "you" as a writer have several shifting selves depending on your audience. In other words, you write differently when you text a friend, present yourself on MySpace or Facebook, post a blog, write an essay for a college instructor, or apply for a grant, an internship, or a job.

For success in academic writing, consider the questions in the Language and Culture box.

LANGUAGE AND CULTURE

Assessing Your Readers' Expectations

- **What readers do you envision for your writing?** Write a list of what those readers will expect in terms of length, format, date of delivery, use of technical terms, and formality of language.

- **Which characteristics do you share with your readers?** Consider for example nationality, culture, race, class, ethnicity, gender, profession, interests, and opinions. Write down how any common ground (see 4g for more on this) could influence the style, tone, dialect, words, and details you may use and include.

- **Is your instructor your main reader?** If so, find out about the expectations of readers in his or her academic discipline. In most cases, regard your instructor as a stand-in for an audience of general readers, and ask yourself what background information you need to include for a general reader. Ask to see a model paper.

TECH NOTE

Taking Accessibility Issues and Disabilities into Account

For documents you prepare for online viewers or for oral and multimedia presentations, issues of accessibility are important.

- Consider whether readers have a dialup or a broadband connection before you post large image files online.

- For any vision-impaired viewers, increase type size, provide a zoom function, and limit the number of visuals or describe them in words.

- Pay attention to color in visuals. Contrasting shades work better for some viewers than different colors.

- Use online sites such as WebAim and Bobby to test your documents for accessibility.

Your voice   Academic writing, as well as business writing and news reporting, is characterized by an unobtrusive voice. The writer is obviously there, having confronted ideas and sources and come up with what to say about them, avoiding slang, contractions, and personal references. However, the person behind the paper does not need to come across as cute or aggressive or extreme but rather as someone who knows what he or she is writing about and expresses the ideas with an authority that impresses the reader. The content takes precedence.

Your voice in writing is how you come across to readers. What impression do you want them to form of you as a person, of your values and opinions? One of the first considerations is whether you want to draw attention to your opinions as the writer by using the first person pronoun "I" or whether you will try the seemingly more objective approach of keeping that "I" at a distance. Even if you do the latter, though, as is often recommended for academic and especially for scientific writing, readers will still see you behind your words. Professor Glen McClish at San Diego State University has pointed out how the voice—and consequently, the effect—of a text such as the one below changes significantly when the first fourteen words, including the first person pronouns, are omitted:

> *In the first section of my paper, I want to make the point that* the spread of technology is damaging personal relationships.

The *I* phrases may be removed to make the sentence seemingly more objective and less wordy. However, the voice also changes: What remains becomes more forceful, proffered confidently as fact rather than as personal opinion.

LANGUAGE AND CULTURE
Using "I" in Academic Writing

When readers read for information, it is the information that appeals to them, not the personality of the writer. Views differ on whether "I" should be used in academic writing, and if so, how much it should be used. Scholarly journals in the humanities some forty years ago used to edit out uses of "I." Not any more. In the sciences and social sciences, however, an objective voice is still preferred. To be safe, always ask your instructor whether you can use "I."

However, even if the word "I" never appears in a college research paper, beware of the leaden effect of using I-avoiding phrases such as "it would seem" or "it is to be expected that" and of overusing the pronoun "one." William Zinsser in *On Writing Well* points out that "good writers are visible just behind their words," conveying as they write "a sense of I-ness." He advises at least thinking "I" as you write your first draft, maybe even writing it, and then editing it out later. It's worth a try.

Your use of media   What are you working toward? A printed document? Print and images? An online document with hyperlinks, images, sound, or video? A presentation of your work using the bells and whistles available in presentation software, such as bulleted items appearing one by one or flying onto the screen? As you work through the process of choosing and developing a topic (1e) for a defined purpose and audience, consider simultaneously the communication means available to you, especially if you are presenting your work online or with the help of presentation software. Always bear in mind how you can enhance your ideas with the design of your document and the use of images, graphs, or multimedia tools (covered in chapters 21, 22, 24, 26, and 29).

1e   Ways to generate a topic and ideas

Whether you have to generate your own idea for a topic or have had a topic assigned, you need strategies other than staring at the ceiling or waiting for inspiration to fly in through the window. Professional writers use a variety of prewriting techniques to generate ideas at various stages of the process. In her article "Oh Muse! You Do Make Things Difficult!" Diane Ackerman reports that the poet Dame Edith Sitwell used to lie in an open coffin, French novelist Colette picked fleas from her cat, statesman Benjamin Franklin soaked in the bathtub, and German dramatist Friedrich Schiller sniffed rotten apples stored in his desk.

Perhaps you have developed your own original approach to generating the mess of ideas that will help you write a draft. Perhaps you were taught a more formal way to begin a writing project, such as by constructing an outline. If what you do now does not seem to produce good results, or if you are ready for a change, try some of the following methods and see how they work.

Generating a topic "What on earth am I going to write about?" is a question frequently voiced or at least thought, especially when students are free to write about any topic that interests them.

The strategies in this section will help you find topics. In addition, think about what matters to you. Reflect on issues raised in your college courses; read newspapers and magazines for current issues; consider campus, community, city, state, and nationwide issues; and look at the Library of Congress Subject Headings to get ideas (see also 7e). If you can, begin with an idea that has caught your interest and has some connection to your life.

TECH NOTE

Using Web Directories to Find a Topic

Academic Web directories assembled by librarians and academic institutions provide reliable sources for finding good academic subjects. The *Librarians' Index to the Internet, Academic Info,* and *Voice of the Shuttle,* a University of California at Santa Barbara directory for humanities research, are among the best.

The directories offered by Yahoo! and Google offer subject categories such as "Education" or "Science" that you can browse and narrow down to a topic suitable for an essay. They will also include links to sites with bibliographies—a useful start to research.

Adapting to an assigned topic that does not interest you This can happen, but don't panic. First read as much as you can on the topic until something strikes you and captures your interest. You can try taking the opposite point of view from that of one of your sources, challenging the point of view. Or you can set yourself the task of showing readers exactly why the topic has not grabbed people's interest—maybe the literature and the research have been just too technical or inaccessible? If you can, find a human angle.

For more on topics, see 4d.

TECH NOTE

Web Sites for Generating Ideas and Planning

The *Purdue University Online Writing Lab* and other online resources include information on generating ideas and planning.

Drawing from journals, blogs, and online conversations *Your own daily journal* can be far more than a personal diary. Many writers carry a notebook, either paper or electronic, and write in it every day, jotting down observations, references, quotations, questions, notes on events, and ideas about assigned texts or topics, as well as specific pieces of writing in progress. Your journal can also serve as a review for final examinations or essay tests, reminding you of areas of special interest or subjects you did not understand.

The *double-entry journal* provides a formalized way for you to think critically about readings and lectures. Two pages or two columns or open windows in your word processor provide the space for interaction. On the left side, write summaries, quotations, and accounts of readings, lectures, and class discussions. The left side, in short, is devoted to what you read or hear. On the right side, record your own comments, reactions, and questions about the material. In this way, the conversation with sources becomes visual.

A *blog* also gives you the opportunity to think aloud in public. Not only can others read your posting, but they can respond to it as well. A blog is easy to set up by using an automated publishing system. Blogs are posted in reverse chronological order but otherwise function similarly to a writer's journal, but with responses. The unedited blog entitled "The *Life* of a Salesman" (p. 14) was posted on a writing course blog site by Tiffany Brattina, a student at Seton Hill University. Here she works out a personal, original, and critical point of view as, after a missed class, she considers an interpretation of the character Willie Loman in Arthur Miller's play *Death of a Salesman*. Brattina largely avoids the colloquial nature of instant messaging and informal e-mail and begins to move to the conventions of public discourse suitable for her academic audience, the students in her class.

A student's blog on a course site

March 16

The *Life* of a Salesman

Ok. So, I'm sure during class today everyone talked about how crazy Willie was, and I am the first to agree. Willie was insane, in the end. However, what about his life?

In *Death of a Salesman* we see the end of Willie's life as a salesman. He went through his entire life working on the road selling things to buyers, he didn't know how to do anything else. Don't you think that would make you go crazy? If a company you worked for your entire life took you off of salary and put you on commission like you were just starting out wouldn't you feel like you were unworthy? Then there is the fact that Willie and his family didn't really have any money to their names at all. Willie kept borrowing money from Charley so that Linda wouldn't know that he wasn't getting paid anymore. Then the company he worked for fired him! I feel bad for Willie, I really do. His kids thought that he was insane and wanted nothing to do with him. The people he worked for his entire life turned him away. Willie was old, tired, and worn out and people including his family turned their backs on him.

Let me make this personal for a minute. My dad recently went through something very similar at his place of work. The company he worked for came into new management and they tried to put my dad on commission. My dad has major tenure where he works considering he is now 56 and has been working there for 40 years making him the longest member still working at the company. He took the new management to court and won his case. I know that while my dad was going through that time he was a total mess, so seeing my dad I can understand what Willie was going through.

What do you guys think? Do you feel bad for Willie or do you think he was just a jerk? Why or why not?

Posted by Tiffany Brattina at March 16, 06:49 PM

Comments

Do you remember Greek Tragedy? I do, and let me say that Willie is the tragic hero. I kept wanting him to succeed, and he didn't. I really felt that there was a chance for him to make something of himself, and couldn't. I had the feeling that Willie was going to kill himself, but something kept telling me that he was going to get out of the severe skid that he was in.

Posted by The Gentle Giant at March 16, 08:58 PM

Never thought of that Jay ... you are right though. I did feel like he was going to succeed, especially there at the end ... Oh well.
Tiff

Posted by Tiffany at March 16, 09:57 PM

Freewriting   If you do not know what to write about or how to approach a broad subject, try doing five to ten minutes of *freewriting* either on paper or on the computer. When you freewrite, you let one idea lead to another in free association without concern for correctness. The important thing is to keep writing. If you cannot think of a word or phrase while you are freewriting, simply write a note to yourself inside square brackets, or put in a symbol such as #. On a computer, use the Search command to find your symbol later, when you can spend more time thinking about the word.

Jimmy Wong did some unedited freewriting on the topic of uniforms (an excerpt from a classmate's paper appears in 3e):

> When I think of uniforms I think of Derek Jeter and A-Rod and how cool they look as they leap for a baseball, spin around and throw it straight to first to get someone out. But does the uniform add anything to the skill? I'd say not, but it probably adds a lot of other stuff. Baseball is a team game so a uniform can work as a reminder that the game is about the team winning, not just one player scoring well and earning a place in the Hall of Fame.

Just this short piece, done very quickly, gave Wong an indication that he could develop a piece of writing focused on the unity-building effect that uniforms can have on those wearing them and on outsiders.

Brainstorming   Another way to generate ideas is by *brainstorming*—making a freewheeling list of ideas as you think of them. Brainstorming is enhanced if you do it collaboratively in a group, discussing and then listing your ideas (see also 1g, Writing with others). You can then, by yourself or with the group, scrutinize the ideas, arrange them, reorganize them, and add to or eliminate them.

Before they were assigned a chapter from *Uniforms: Why We Are What We Wear* by Paul Fussell, a group of students working collaboratively made the following brainstorming list on the topic of what uniforms signify:

> Pink for girls, blue for boys—perpetuating stereotypes
>
> Uniforms in parochial schools and in many British schools
>
> Men's suits and ties
>
> Uniforms for prisoners and wardens
>
> Team uniforms; nurse uniforms
>
> Municipal employee uniforms
>
> The uniform of fashion—ripped jeans fashionable
>
> George Bush and Mission Accomplished
>
> Official vs. nonofficial uniforms
>
> Advantages of uniforms—but for whom?

Keep them in line. Keep them recognizable.

Armed services

How do we treat uniforms—respect, contempt, pity, indifference?

Once the students had made the list, they reviewed it, rejected some items, expanded on others, and grouped items. Thus, they developed subcategories that led them to possibilities for further exploration and essay organization:

Uniforms for spectators

Uniforms that command respect

Uniforms that mark occupations

Fashion as a uniform of social markers—part of an "in-group"

Mapping   *Mapping,* also called *clustering,* is a visual way of generating and connecting ideas. It can be done individually or in a group. Write your topic in a circle at the center of a page, think of ideas related to the topic, and write those ideas on the page around the central topic. Draw lines to make connections. For a writing assignment that asked for a response to a chapter in Paul Fussell's book *Uniforms* (see pp. 180–181), a student created the following map. She saw that it indicated several possibilities for topics, such as the increasing casualness of American society and the power of uniforms to both camouflage and identify their wearers. You can see an excerpt from her draft in 3e.

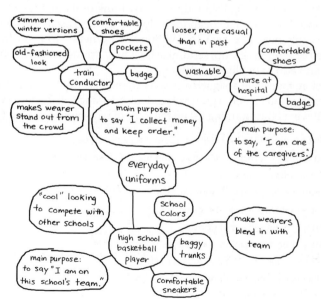

Using journalists' questions Journalists check the coverage of their stories by making sure they answer six questions—though not in any set order: Who did it? What happened? When did it happen? Where did it occur? Why did it happen? How did it turn out? If you are telling the story of an event, either as a complete essay or as an example in an essay, asking the journalists' six questions will help you think comprehensively about your topic.

Using prompts Sometimes, you might find it helpful to use a formal set of directions (known as *prompts*) to suggest new avenues of inquiry. Write down responses to any of the prompts that apply to your topic, and note possibilities for further exploration. A topic assigned by your instructor may also include these terms, sometimes in combination. See 2d for examples of ideas developed in these and other ways.

Define your terms Look up key words in your topic (like *success, identity, ambition,* and *ethnicity*) in the dictionary, and write down the definition you want to use. Consider synonyms, too.

Give examples or facts Think of facts and stories from your reading or experience that relate to your topic.

Include descriptions Whatever your topic, make your writing more vivid with details about color, light, location, movement, size, shape, sound, taste, and smell. Help your reader "see" your topic, such as a person, place, object, or scientific experiment, exactly as you see it.

Make comparisons Help your reader understand a topic by describing what it might be similar to and different from. For example, how is learning to write like learning to ride a bike—or isn't it?

Assess cause and effect Convey information on what causes or produces your topic and what effects or results emerge from it. For example, what are the causes and effects of dyslexia? inflation? acid rain? hurricanes? salmonella? asthma?

Respond to what you read If you are assigned a response to something you have read, use whichever of the following types of responses seem appropriate to help you evaluate the reading:

▶ When I read X, I think of my own experience . . .

▶ When X says . . . , I don't agree because . . .

▶ Generally, X makes good points but misses the fact that . . .

▶ When X tells us that . . . , I immediately think of a very different example: . . .

▶ **The evidence that X presents for her views could be interpreted differently: . . .**

▶ **I find X's arguments convincing because . . .**

1f Ways to present your thesis or claim

You might be given any of the following essay assignments, arranged here from the broadest in scope to the narrowest:

- a free choice of subject
- a broad subject area, such as "genetic engineering" or "social networking sites"
- a focused and specific topic, such as "the city's plans to build apartments on a landfill" or "the effect of a bad economy on students' lives"
- an actual question to answer, such as: "What are the arguments made against same-sex marriage in California?" or "What are the dangers participants in social networking sites may face?"

If you are given a free choice of subject, you will need to narrow your focus to a specific subject area, to a topic, or to a question. After that, still more narrowing is necessary to formulate a thesis.

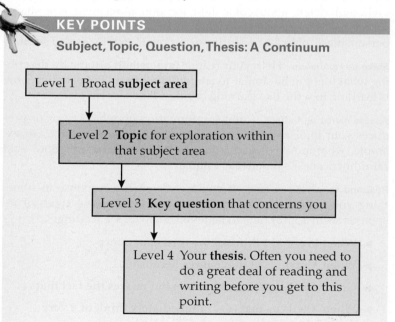

KEY POINTS

Subject, Topic, Question, Thesis: A Continuum

Level 1 Broad **subject area**

Level 2 **Topic** for exploration within that subject area

Level 3 **Key question** that concerns you

Level 4 Your **thesis**. Often you need to do a great deal of reading and writing before you get to this point.

Your thesis, or claim, is your statement of opinion, main idea, or message that unifies your piece of writing, makes a connection between you and the subject area, lets your reader know where you stand in relation to the topic, and responds to the question posed.

From subject to topic to thesis   After analyzing some readings, discussing Web sites, and making notes, students were given the task of working together in groups to formulate a progression from subject to thesis. This is what one group produced:

Subject: Social networking spaces

Topic: Use of Facebook and MySpace by teens

Question: What hazards do teens need to be aware of when they enter a social networking site?

Thesis: When teens enter the world of Facebook and other social networking spaces, they may gain friends but they also expose themselves to rejection, ridicule, and worse, to online predators.

See 1h for essay outlines that students developed on this topic.

If you choose a topic and a question that are too broad, you will find it difficult to generate a thesis with focused ideas and examples. Whenever you find yourself thinking, for instance, "There's so much to say about social life online that I don't know where to start," narrow your topic. If you begin by choosing a topic and a question that are too narrow, you probably will not find enough material and will end up being repetitive. Whenever you feel you have enough material to fill only a page and can't imagine how you will find more ("What else can I say about my sister's friend Henry on MySpace?"), broaden your topic. Above all, stay flexible. You may want to change your topic or your question as you discover more information.

Progressing from topic to thesis   It is not enough to say, "I am writing about Facebook," though that may be what you start with. However, this simply names your topic. It does *not* indicate what you might explore about Facebook. Are you going to address Facebook as a tool for communication or as a fad for teens? As a temporary craze or as a social leveler? As a way for young people to communicate or as a place where predators lurk? Are you going to analyze Facebook postings? Its effects on teenage interaction? Which readers will you regard as your primary audience? Which geographical areas will you discuss? Will you be concerned with teens or twenty-somethings or what? In short, work toward considering the most important point you want to make about which aspect of a social networking tool and for which readers. Maybe you will compare Facebook with MySpace, or perhaps you will interview parents to get their reactions to their children's participation. Maybe you will do online and print research to find out the dangers that lurk for teens within social networking sites. Or you could explore how the networks provide outlets for students who need an alternative to parental authority. Whichever road you take, play with your first general idea until it gels more for you and you find something that makes a point you know you can describe, explain, and support.

Start drafting what point you want to make, or start with three or four statements that you would like to explore more.

Knowing what a thesis statement looks like—and why you need one　Suppose someone were to ask you, "What is the main idea that you want to communicate to your reader in your piece of writing?" The sentence you would give in reply is your *thesis statement*, also known as a *claim*. Your claim tells readers what stand you are going to take on a topic. It won't take you far to say, for instance, "I am interested in writing about social networking sites" if you stop right there and hope that somehow ideas will shoot right out at you. What aspects of the sites interest you and what are the issues? Which readers do you regard as your primary audience? Which geographical areas will you discuss? Will you be concerned with the present or the future? What do you intend to propose about the area of social networking you have selected? In short, what point will you end up making and for which readers? You don't have to know exactly where to put your thesis statement in your essay right now, but having a thesis will focus your thoughts as you read and write. (4d gives more help with the thesis in an argument paper.)

A good thesis statement may be one or more of the following:

1. a generalization needing support

   ▶ **Facebook gives students a real reason to write and real readers a reason to read what is written.**

2. a strong, thought-provoking, or controversial statement

   ▶ **Even though social networking sites such as Facebook encourage people to write, their practices may actually work against helping students improve their academic writing.**

3. a call to action

> ▶ **Students who genuinely want to improve their writing for college and the business world would be well advised to stop participating in IM, Facebook, MySpace, and other social networking sites.**

4. an analytical statement that sets up the structure of the essay

> ▶ **Social networking sites offer two things that college essays can never offer: a nonthreatening environment and readers who genuinely respond to the ideas writers express.**

Keep a working thesis in front of you on a self-stick note or an index card as you write your first draft, but be flexible. You are the boss as you write. You can change and narrow your thesis whenever you like. Many readers will expect to discover your point within the introductory paragraphs of an essay, but your thesis may, in fact, not take shape in your mind until you have read, written, and revised a great deal. Sometimes, a clear thesis may not emerge for you until the end of your first draft, pointing the way to the focus and organization of your next draft.

KEY POINTS

A Good Working Thesis

- **narrows your topic** to a single main idea that you want to communicate
- **makes your point** clearly and firmly in one sentence or two
- **states not simply a fact but rather an opinion or a summary conclusion** from your observation
- **makes a generalization that can be supported** by details, facts, and examples within the assigned limitations of time and space
- **stimulates curiosity and interest in readers** and prompts them to wonder, "Why do you think that?" and read on

Seeing your thesis as a signpost or indication of where you have been In most academic writing in the humanities and social sciences, a thesis is stated clearly in the essay, usually near the beginning. See your thesis statement as a signpost—both for you as you write your draft and, later, for readers as they read your essay. A clear thesis prepares readers well for the rest of the essay. If you use key words from your thesis as you write, you will keep readers focused on your main idea.

Sometimes, though, particularly in descriptive, narrative, and informative writing, you may choose to imply your thesis and not explicitly state it. In such a case, you make your thesis clear by the examples, details, and information you include. An essay that details all the beneficial—or harmful—changes to a neighborhood may not need a bald statement that, for example, the South Congress area of Austin has made great strides. You may also choose to state your thesis at the end of your essay instead of the beginning, presenting all the evidence to build a case and then making the thesis act as a climax and logical statement about the outcome of the evidence.

On not falling in love with your thesis Many writers begin with a tentative working thesis and then find that they come to a new conclusion at the end of the first draft. If that happens to you, start your second draft by focusing on the thesis that emerged during the writing of the first draft. Be flexible: It's easier to change a thesis statement to fit new ideas and newly discovered evidence than to find new evidence to fit a new thesis. Note that your final thesis statement should take a firm stand on the issue. Flexibility during the writing process is not the same as indecision in the final product.

LANGUAGE AND CULTURE

Language, Identity, and the Thesis Statement

Often, writers who have developed their writing skills in one language notice distinct differences in the conventions of writing in another language, particularly with respect to the explicit statement of opinion in the thesis. In 1989, when China was more rural than it is now, a Chinese writer, Fan Shen, regarded the explicit thesis statement favored in Western writing as "symbolic of the values of a busy people in an industrialized society, rushing to get things done" (*College Composition and Communication* [Dec. 1989]: 462). It is difficult to determine how much of a role one's culture plays in the way one writes and to separate culture's role from the roles of gender, socioeconomic status, family background, and education. However, always consider what approaches your anticipated readers are likely to be familiar with and to value.

1g Writing with others

Writing is not necessarily a solitary process. In the academic or business world, you will often have to work collaboratively with one or more classmates or colleagues. You might be part of a group, team, or committee assigned to draft a proposal or a report. You might be expected to produce a document reflecting the consensus of your section or group. Or you might need to draft and circulate a document and then incorporate into it the comments of many people, as is the case with the student drafts in 3e and in chapter 35.

In group settings, make sure that every member of the group contributes. You can do this by assigning each person a set of specific tasks, such as making lists of ideas, drafting, analyzing the draft, revising, editing, assembling visuals, and preparing the final document. Schedule regular meetings, and expect everyone to come with a completed written assignment. Build on strengths within the group. For example, ask the member skilled in document design and computer graphics to prepare the visual features of the final document.

However, make sure that you work collaboratively only when doing so is expected. An instructor who assigns an essay will not always expect you to work on it with your sister, classmate, or tutor. If collaborative peer groups are encouraged, try using the peer response form in 3b.

TECH NOTE

Writing Collaboratively on the Computer

Word processing programs and e-mail provide useful tools for collaboration. You can work on a text, make and highlight changes, and attach the revised text to an e-mail message to a colleague, who can then accept or reject the changes. GoogleDocs also provides a useful tool for working with others, allowing you to upload a document that others can then access, change, and add to. See 7c for more on how Google can help writers.

1h Tips for drafting and outlining (with sample outlines)

Drafting Writing provides what speech can never provide: the opportunity to revise your ideas and the way you present them.

Writing drafts allows you to work on a piece of writing until it meets your goals.

KEY POINTS

Tips for Writing Drafts

- **Plan the steps and set a schedule (6b).** Work backward from the deadline, and assign time in days or hours for each of the following: deciding on a topic, generating ideas, making a scratch outline, writing a draft, getting feedback, analyzing the draft, making large-scale revisions, finding additional material, editing, proofreading, formatting, and printing.

- **Manage "writer's block."** If you feel yourself suffering from what is called "writer's block," try to ignore any self-imposed rigid rules that hinder you, such as, "Always stick with a complete outline," or "Check everything and edit as you write." Editing too early may lock you into rigid and unhelpful rules and may prevent you from thinking about ideas and moving forward.

- **Don't start at the beginning.** Don't automatically begin by writing the introduction. Begin by writing the essay parts for which you already have some specific material. Then you will know what you need to introduce.

- **Pace yourself.** Write in increments of twenty to thirty minutes to take advantage of momentum.

- **Put your first draft to work.** Write your first draft as quickly and fluently as you can and print it triple-spaced. Write notes to yourself in capitals or surrounded by asterisks to remind yourself to add or change something or to do further research.

- **Consider making an outline.** You may find a scratch outline useful to get you started. A formal outline may be helpful as a check on what you have done in an early draft, to see what gaps you need to fill, or what revisions you need to make.

- **Be specific.** Avoid obvious, vague, or empty generalizations (such as "All people have feelings"). Be specific, and include interesting supporting details.

- **Resist the lure of Copy and Paste.** Copying a passage from an online site and pasting it into your own document may seem like a good solution when you are facing a looming deadline and surfing for good Web sources. However, the penalties for plagiarism are far worse than those for lateness (see 9a). So the bottom line here is *don't do it.*

TECH NOTE

Using Comment and AutoCorrect

Word processing programs have a Comment function that allows you to type notes that appear only on the screen, not in a printout, provided you set the Print options to ignore them. These notes are easily deleted from later drafts. In addition, if you use a term frequently (for example, the phrase "bilingual education"), abbreviate it (as "b.e.") and use a tool like AutoCorrect and Replace to substitute the whole phrase throughout your draft as you type.

Outlining   Outlining often supports drafting stages of the writing process. Alternatively, in the initial stages of a research project, a purpose statement or a proposal may work better for you than a scratch outline (see 6f).

The following table is a guide to two frequently used types of outlines, *scratch* and *formal*, with samples following.

Using Outlines while Drafting

	Scratch Outline	Formal Outline
What it is	a rough list of numbered points that you intend to cover in your essay	spells out, in order, what points and supportive details you will use to develop your thesis and arranges them to show the overall form and structure of the essay
What it helps you do	lets you see what ideas you already have, how they connect, what you can do to support and develop them, and what further planning or research you still need to do	serves as a check on the logic and completeness of what you have written, revealing any gaps, repetition, or illogical steps in the development of your essay
When you use it	early in the process and at midpoints if integrating major revisions	before you begin to write, but you are likely to find that making an outline with a high level of detail is more feasible after you have written a draft
Starting point	chosen topic	thesis statement

Scratch outline One student in a class discussing social networking sites (see 1f, p. 19) made the following scratch outline:

> **Topic:** Social networking sites
>
> **Question:** Are there any dangers for subscribers to social networking sites?
>
> **Possible thesis:** Users face the dangers of rejection, ridicule, and predators.
>
> **Points:**
>
> 1. Feelings of rejection and inferiority can occur when people don't respond to an invitation and do not want to be a friend.
> 2. Some old friendships get restarted and then fizzle out. Two examples from Facebook experience.
> 3. People get reminded of who they were in the past: the ninth-grade fat kid, the hopeless basketball player, the acned nerd (me!).
> 4. The worst danger is probably from people who lurk on the Web looking for people to latch on to and begin a relationship with. Sex offenders have registered on Facebook and MySpace and posted naked pictures (articles in *NY Times*, *Chronicle of Higher Ed.*, and *MSNBC.com*).
>
> **Possible directions:** The role of school, parents, regulatory agencies; education of teens; monitored registration?

Formal outline When the same student began to work on a new draft, however, he developed a more nuanced and more focused thesis. Note how to structure an outline:

> **Main points:** I, II, III, etc.
>
> **2nd level:** A, B, C, etc.
>
> **3rd level:** 1, 2, 3, etc.
>
> **4th level:** a, b, c, etc.

The student used only three levels in the following outline, with complete sentences for the first two levels. When you create your own outline, be sure you have at least two items in each of the levels: an "a" must have a "b," for example.

> **Thesis:** While dangers may lurk in some major social networking sites, subscribers gain the opportunity to renew old friendships and make new ones, to span the world without paying for travel, to pursue special interests, and to expand business opportunities.
>
> I. Dangers exist, but careful subscribers can avoid them.
>
>   A. Subscribers can be discriminating about the people they contact: Classmates they didn't like in high school are not likely to have changed much.

  B. They can immediately sever contact with an old acquaintance who belittles or offends them.
     1. Story of Eduardo being reminded of his obesity
     2. Story of Nancy whose so-called "friend" broadcast to everyone the tales of her sexual exploits in high school
  C. They can refuse to continue contact with people they don't know or are not connected to through others, however harmless they appear at first.
II. The advantages outweigh the disadvantages.
  A. Friendships can be renewed and new ones can develop and flourish with frequent networking.
     1. Ease of connection
     2. Contact not just in words but in pictures, music, and so on
  B. Networks are worldwide, so they can inform subscribers about making contacts in other countries (for example, the site *Couchsurfing*) and learning about communities through photo sharing.
  C. Networking makes it easy to connect with others sharing the same interests and passions.
     1. Networks for hobbies: music, books, athletics, even knitting and crochet (*Ravelry* site)
     2. Networks for intellectual pursuits, such as literature, art, politics, environmental issues
  D. Networks provide information about business and career opportunities.
     1. Job information available on *LinkedIn*
     2. Sites for scientists, language learning, finance

2 🔑

Developing Paragraphs and Essays

Paragraphs form the building blocks of essays.

2a Paragraph basics

A good paragraph makes a clear point, supports your main idea, and focuses on one topic. Some paragraphs, however, may have more to do with function than with content. They serve to take readers from one point to another, making a connection and offering a smooth transition from one idea to the next. These transitional paragraphs are often short.

To indicate a new paragraph, indent the first line a half-inch from the left margin or, in business and online documents, begin it at the left margin after a blank line.

For introductory and concluding paragraphs, see 2e.

KEY POINTS
When to Begin a New Paragraph

1. To introduce a new point (one that supports the claim or main idea of your essay)

2. To expand on a point already made by offering new examples or evidence

3. To break up a long discussion or description into manageable chunks that are easier to read

Both logic and aesthetics dictate when it is time to begin a new paragraph. Think of a paragraph as something that gathers together in one place ideas that connect to each other and to the main purpose of the piece of writing.

2b Unified paragraphs and topic sentences

Just as a thesis statement helps readers of an essay keep your main idea in mind, a *topic sentence* in a body paragraph lets readers know explicitly what the main idea of the paragraph is. Readers should notice a logical flow of ideas as they read through a paragraph and as they move from one paragraph to another through an essay.

When you write a paragraph, imagine a reader saying, "Look, I don't have time to read all this. Just tell me in one sentence (or two) what point you are making here." Your reply would express your main point. Each paragraph in an academic essay generally contains a controlling idea expressed in a sentence (called a *topic sentence*) and does not digress or switch topics in midstream. Its content is unified. A *unified paragraph*, in academic writing, includes one main idea that the rest of the paragraph explains, supports, and develops.

The following paragraph is devoted to one broad topic—tennis—but does not follow through on the topic of the *trouble* that the *backhand* causes *average* players (key terms highlighted). The unity of the paragraph could be improved. What is Grand Slam winner Serena Williams doing in a paragraph about average players? What relevance does her powerful serve have to the average player's problems with a backhand? The writer would do well to revise by cutting out the two sentences about Serena Williams (sentences highlighted).

> The backhand in tennis causes average weekend players more trouble than other strokes. Even though the swing is natural and free flowing, many players feel intimidated and try to avoid it. Serena Williams, however, has a great backhand, and she often wins difficult points with it. Her serve is a powerful weapon, too. When faced by a backhand coming at them across the net, midlevel players can't seem to get their feet and body in the best position. They tend to run around the ball or forget the swing and give the ball a little poke, praying that it will not only reach but also go over the net.

Where to put the topic sentence   When placed first, as it is in the paragraph on the troublesome backhand, a topic sentence makes a generalization and serves as a reference point for the rest of the information in the paragraph. When placed after one or two other sentences, the topic sentence focuses the details and directs readers' attention to the main idea. When placed at the end of the paragraph, the topic sentence serves to summarize or draw conclusions from the details that precede it.

Some paragraphs, such as the short ones typical of newspaper writing or the one-sentence paragraphs that make a quick transition, do not always contain a topic sentence. Sometimes, too, a paragraph contains such clear details that the point is obvious and does not need to be explicitly stated. However, in academic essays, a paragraph in support of your essay's claim or thesis (main point) will usually be unified and focused on one clear topic, whether or not you state it in a topic sentence.

2c   Using transitions and links for coherence

However you develop your individual paragraphs, readers expect to move with ease from one sentence to the next and from one paragraph to the next, following a clear flow of argument and logic. When you construct an essay or paragraph, do not force readers to grapple with "grasshopper prose," which jumps suddenly from one idea to another without obvious connections. Instead, make your writing *coherent*, with all the parts connecting clearly to one another with transitional expressions, context links, and word links. (See also 40j for examples of the contribution of parallel structures to coherence.)

Transitional words and expressions Make clear connections between sentences and between paragraphs either by using explicit connecting words like *this, that, these,* and *those* to refer to something mentioned at the end of the previous sentence or paragraph or by using transitional expressions.

KEY POINTS

Transitional Expressions

Adding an idea also, in addition, further, furthermore, moreover

Contrasting however, nevertheless, nonetheless, on the other hand, in contrast, still, on the contrary, rather, conversely

Providing an alternative instead, alternatively, otherwise

Showing similarity similarly, likewise

Showing order of time or order of ideas first, second, third (and so on), then, next, later, subsequently, meanwhile, previously, finally

Showing result as a result, consequently, therefore, thus, hence, accordingly, for this reason

Affirming of course, in fact, certainly, obviously, to be sure, undoubtedly, indeed

Giving examples for example, for instance

Explaining in other words, that is

Adding an aside incidentally, by the way, besides

Summarizing in short, generally, overall, all in all, in conclusion

For punctuation with transitional expressions, see 47e.

Though transitional expressions are useful to connect one sentence to another or one paragraph to another, do not overuse these expressions. Too many of them, used too often, make writing seem heavy and mechanical.

Context links A new paragraph introduces a new topic, but that topic should not be entirely separate from what has gone before. Let readers know the context of the big picture. If you are writing about the expense of exploring Mars and then switch abruptly to the hazards of climbing Everest, readers will be puzzled. You need to state clearly the connection with the thesis: "Exploration on our own planet can be as hazardous and as financially risky as space exploration."

Word links   You can also provide coherence by using repeated words or connected words, such as pronouns linked to nouns; words with the same, similar, or opposite meanings; or words linked by context. Note how Deborah Tannen maintains coherence not only by using transitional expressions (*for example, furthermore*) but also by repeating words and phrases (blue) and by using certain pronouns (red)—*she* and *her* to refer to *wife*, and *they* to refer to *Greeks*.

> Entire cultures operate on elaborate systems of indirectness. For example, I discovered in a small research project that most Greeks assumed that a wife who asked, "Would you like to go to the party?" was hinting that she wanted to go. They felt that she wouldn't bring it up if she didn't want to go. Furthermore, they felt, she would not state her preference outright because that would sound like a demand. Indirectness was the appropriate means for communicating her preference.
>
> —Deborah Tannen, *You Just Don't Understand*

2d   Eight examples of paragraph development

Whether you are writing a paragraph or an essay, you will do well to keep in mind the image of a skeptical reader always inclined to say something challenging, such as, "Why on earth do you think that?" or "What could possibly lead you to that conclusion?" Show your reader that your opinion is well founded and supported by experience, knowledge, logical arguments, the work of experts, or reasoned examples and provide vivid, unique details. Here are illustrations of some rhetorical strategies you can use to develop ideas in paragraphs and essays. They may serve as prompts to help you generate ideas.

Give examples   Examples that develop a point make writing interesting and informative. The following paragraph about Harry S. Truman (president of the United States 1945–53) as a young boy follows an account of his happy childhood. It begins with a topic sentence that announces the controlling idea: "Yet life had its troubles and woes." The author then gives examples of some "troubles and woes" that young Harry faced. Beginning with a generalization and supporting it with specific illustrative details is a common method of organizing a paragraph known as *deductive organization*.

> Yet life had its troubles and woes. On the summer day when his Grandfather Truman died, three-year-old Harry had rushed to the bed to pull at the old man's beard, trying desperately to wake him. Climbing on a chair afterward, in an attempt to comb his hair

in front of a mirror, he toppled over backward and broke his collar-
bone. Another time he would have choked to death on a peach
stone had his mother not responded in a flash and decisively, pushing the stone down his throat with her finger, instead of trying to
pull it out. Later, when Grandpa Young [Harry's mother's father]
lay sick in bed and the little boy approached cautiously to inquire
how he was feeling, the old pioneer, fixing him with a wintry stare,
said, "How are you feeling? You're the one I'm worried about."

—David McCullough, *Truman*

In addition, you may decide to illustrate an idea in your text by
using a visual image as an example.

Tell a story   Choose a pattern of organization that readers will
easily grasp. Organize the events in a story chronologically so that
readers can follow the sequence. In the following paragraph, the
writer tells a story that leads to the point that people with disabilities often face ignorance and insensitivity. Note that she uses *inductive organization*, beginning with background information and the
specific details of the story in chronological order and ending with
a generalization.

> Jonathan is an articulate, intelligent, thirty-five-year-old man
> who has used a wheelchair since he became a paraplegic when he
> was twenty years old. He recalls taking an able bodied woman out
> to dinner at a nice restaurant. When the waitress came to take their
> order, she patronizingly asked his date, "And what would he like to
> eat for dinner?" At the end of the meal, the waitress presented
> Jonathan's date with the check and thanked her for her patronage.
> Although it may be hard to believe the insensitivity of the waitress,
> this incident is not an isolated one. Rather, such an experience is a
> common one for persons with disabilities.

—Dawn O. Braithwaite, "Viewing Persons with Disabilities as a Culture"

Describe with details appealing to the senses   To help readers
see and experience what you feel and experience, describe people,
places, scenes, and objects by using sensory details that re-create those
people, places, scenes, or objects for your readers. In the following
paragraph from a memoir about growing up to love food, Ruth Reichl
tells how she spent days working at a summer camp in France and
thinking about eating. However, she does much more than say, "The
food was always delicious" and much more than "I looked forward to
the delicious bread, coffee, and morning snacks." Reichl appeals to
our senses of sight, smell, touch, and taste. We get a picture of the

campers, we smell the baking bread, we see and almost taste the jam, we smell and taste the coffee, and we feel the crustiness of the rolls. We feel that we are there—and we wish we were.

> When we woke up in the morning the smell of baking bread was wafting through the trees. By the time we had gotten our campers out of bed, their faces washed and their shirts tucked in, the aroma had become maddeningly seductive. We walked into the dining room to devour hot bread slathered with country butter and topped with homemade plum jam so filled with fruit it made each slice look like a tart. We stuck our faces into the bowls of café au lait, inhaling the sweet, bitter, peculiarly French fragrance, and Georges or Jean or one of the other male counselors would say, for the hundredth time, *"On mange pas comme ça à Paris."* Two hours later we had a *"gouter,"* a snack of chocolate bars stuffed into fresh, crusty rolls. And two hours later there was lunch. The eating went on all day.
>
> —Ruth Reichl, *Tender at the Bone: Growing Up at the Table*

Develop a point by providing facts and statistics   The following paragraph supports with facts and statistics the assertion made in its first sentence (the topic sentence) that the North grew more than the South in the years before the Civil War.

> While southerners tended their fields, the North grew. In 1800, half the nation's five million people lived in the South. By 1850, only a third lived there. Of the nine largest cities, only New Orleans was located in the lower South. Meanwhile, a tenth of the goods manufactured in America came from southern mills and factories. There were one hundred piano makers in New York alone in 1852. In 1846, there was not a single book publisher in New Orleans; even the city guidebook was printed in Manhattan.
>
> —Geoffrey C. Ward, *The Civil War: An Illustrated History*

Here, too, visuals such as tables, charts, and graphs would help present data succinctly and dramatically.

Define key terms   Sometimes, writers clarify and develop a topic by defining a key term, even if it is not an unusual term. Often, they will explain what class something fits into and how it differs from others in its class; for example, "A duckbilled platypus is a mammal that has webbed feet and lays eggs." In his book on diaries, Thomas Mallon begins by providing an extended definition of his basic terms. He does not want readers to misunderstand him because they wonder what the differences between a diary and a journal might be.

The first thing we should try to get straight is what to call them. "What's the difference between a diary and a journal?" is one of the questions people interested in these books ask. The two terms are in fact hopelessly muddled. They're both rooted in the idea of dailiness, but perhaps because of *journal*'s links to the newspaper trade and *diary*'s to *dear*, the latter seems more intimate than the former. (The French blur even this discrepancy by using no word recognizable like *diary*; they just say *journal intime*, which is sexy, but a bit of a mouthful.) One can go back as far as Dr. Johnson's *Dictionary* and find him making the two more or less equal. To him a diary was "an account of the transactions, accidents, and observations of every day; a journal." Well, if synonymity was good enough for Johnson, we'll let it be good enough for us.

—Thomas Mallon, *A Book of One's Own: People and Their Diaries*

Analyze component parts Large, complex topics sometimes become more manageable to writers (and readers) when they are broken down for analysis. The *Columbia Encyclopedia* online helps readers understand the vast concept of life itself by breaking it down into six component parts:

Although there is no universal agreement as to a definition of *life*, its biological manifestations are generally considered to be organization, metabolism, growth, irritability, adaptation, and reproduction. . . . Organization is found in the basic living unit, the cell, and in the organized groupings of cells into organs and organisms. Metabolism includes the conversion of nonliving material into cellular components (synthesis) and the decomposition of organic matter (catalysis), producing energy. Growth in living matter is an increase in size of all parts, as distinguished from simple addition of material; it results from a higher rate of synthesis than catalysis. Irritability, or response to stimuli, takes many forms, from the contraction of a unicellular organism when touched to complex reactions involving all the senses of higher animals; in plants response is usually much different than in animals but is nonetheless present. Adaptation, the accommodation of a living organism to its present or to a new environment, is fundamental to the process of evolution and is determined by the individual's heredity. The division of one cell to form two new cells is reproduction; usually the term is applied to the production of a new individual (either asexually, from a single parent organism, or sexually, from two differing parent organisms), although strictly speaking it also describes the production of new cells in the process of growth.

—Available from infoplease.com

Classify into groups Dividing people or objects into the classes or groups that make up the whole gives readers a new way to look at the topic. In the following paragraphs, the writer develops his essay on cell phones by classifying users into three types and devoting one paragraph to each.

> Cell phone use has far exceeded practicality. For many, it's even a bit of an addiction, a prop—like a cigarette or a beer bottle—that you can hold up to your mouth. And each person is meeting a different psychological need by clinging to it.
>
> As I see it, the pack breaks down something like this: Some users can't tolerate being alone and have to register on someone, somewhere, all of the time. That walk down [the street] can be pretty lonely without a loved one shouting sweet nothings in your ear.
>
> Others are efficiency freaks and can't bear to lose 10 minutes standing in line at Starbucks. They have to conduct business while their milk is being steamed, or they will implode. The dividing line between work and home has already become permeable with the growth of telecommuting; cell phones contribute significantly to that boundary breakdown.
>
> Then there are those who like to believe they are so very important to the people in their personal and professional lives that they must be in constant touch. "Puffed up" is one way to describe them; "insecure" is another.
>
> —Matthew Gilbert, "All Talk, All the Time"

Compare and contrast When you examine similarities and differences among people, objects, or concepts, different types of development achieve different purposes.

1. You can deal with each subject one at a time in a block style of organization, perhaps summarizing the similarities and differences at the end. This organization works well when each section is short and readers can easily remember the points made about each subject.

2. You can select and organize the important points of similarity or difference in a point-by-point style of organization, referring within each point to both subjects.

The following example uses the second approach in comparing John Stuart Mill, a British philosopher and economist, and Harriet Taylor, a woman with whom Mill had a close intellectual relationship. The author, Phyllis Rose, organizes the contrast by points of difference, referring to her subjects' facial features, physical behavior, ways of thinking and speaking, and intellectual style. (A block organization would deal first with the characteristics of Taylor, followed by the characteristics of Mill.)

John Stuart Mill

You could see how they complemented each other by the way they looked. What people noticed first about Harriet were her eyes—flashing—and a suggestion in her body of mobility, whereas his features, variously described as chiselled and classical, expressed an inner rigidity. He shook hands from the shoulder. He spoke carefully. Give him facts, and he would sift them, weigh them, articulate possible interpretations, reach a conclusion. Where he was careful, she was daring. Where he was disinterested and balanced, she was intuitive, partial, and sure of herself. She concerned herself with goals and assumptions; he concerned himself with arguments. She was quick to judge and to generalize, and because he was not, he valued her intellectual style as bold and vigorous where another person, more like her, might have found her hasty and simplistic.

—Phyllis Rose, *Parallel Lives: Five Victorian Marriages*

Harriet Taylor

2e Writing introductions and conclusions

Introductions   Readers like to know a little about a topic, about why it is even worth discussing, before you pronounce your opinion on it. Think of your introduction as providing a necessary social and intellectual function between writer and reader, presenting ideas to readers in context and not out of the blue. If you find it difficult to write an introduction because you are not yet clear about your thesis or how you will support it, wait until you have written the body of your essay. You may find something concrete easier to introduce than something you have not yet written.

When you write an essay in the humanities, keep the following points in mind. (For other disciplines, see 5g and 5h.)

KEY POINTS

How to Write a Good Introduction

Options

- Make sure your first sentence stands alone and does not depend on readers' being aware of the essay title or an assigned question. For instance, avoid beginning with "This story has a complex plot."

- Provide context and background information to set up the thesis.

- Indicate what claim you will make in your essay, or at least indicate the issue on which you will state a claim.

- Define any key terms that are pertinent to the discussion.

- Establish the tone of the paper: informative, persuasive, serious, humorous, personal, impersonal, formal, informal.

- Engage the interest of your readers to make them want to explore your topic with you. Tell them something they may not know or something to surprise them, such as an unlikely fact or statistic, a challenging question, a pithy quotation, interesting background details, a joke, an intriguing opinion, a startling verbal image, or a description of a problem.

What to Avoid

- Avoid being overly general and telling readers the obvious, such as "Crime is a big problem" or "In this fast-paced world, TV is a popular form of entertainment" or "Since the beginning of time, the sexes have been in conflict."

- Do not refer to your writing intentions, such as "In this essay, I will . . . ." Do not make extravagant claims, such as "This essay will prove that bilingual education works for every student."

- Do not restate the assigned essay question.

Consider these attention-grabbing beginnings of books or chapters:

> ▶ "You gonna eat that?" The woman is eyeing the tray the flight attendant has just set before me. I can't tell if she wants reassurance that I find it as repellent as she does or if she is simply hungry and hopeful that I will hand my food over. I loosen my seatbelt, swivel in my narrow seat, and see that her face holds a challenge. Is she *daring* me to eat the food?
>
> —Ruth Reichl, *Garlic and Sapphires*

▶ Faced with working-class life in towns such as Winchester, I see only one solution: beer.
—Joe Bageant, *Deer Hunting with Jesus: Dispatches from America's Class War*

▶ It is a truth universally acknowledged, that a single man in possession of a good fortune, must be in want of a wife.
—Jane Austen, *Pride and Prejudice*

▶ It was a bright cold day in April, and the clocks were striking thirteen.
—George Orwell, *1984*

▶ Every day in the United States, roughly 200,000 people are sickened by a foodborne disease, 900 are hospitalized, and fourteen die.
—Eric Schlosser, *Fast Food Nation*

Brainstorming may help you come up with catchy openings. A brainstorming session, for example, produced the following openers for an essay on fashion:

A DESCRIPTION
Everyone stared at him as he walked in. His jeans were torn, his sneakers stained and ripped, his jacket a shapeless rag, his tee shirt sweaty. He was the coolest guy in the room.

A MEMORABLE QUOTATION
The flamboyant author Oscar Wilde advises, "One should either be a work of art or wear a work of art."

A STARTLING FACT
How far obedience to fashion can be taken was shown in China when for hundreds of years women were truly fashionable when they had undergone the torture and permanent disfigurement of having their feet bound so they could fit into unnaturally tiny shoes.

AN ANECDOTE
I keep clothes I have rarely worn for a time when they might come back into fashion and I can maybe wear them again. I still have bright green pants with vast bell bottoms and a purple jacket with football-quarterback shoulders in my closet. The sad thing is that a fashion never returns in exactly the same style or colors. When I put on the pants, my friends just laugh and say "So nineties!"

A QUESTION | "Who are you wearing?" Such a question, the one most often heard on the red carpet before the Oscars, would have been unintelligible a few decades ago.

AN INTERESTING OBSERVATION | Identical twins can live apart for twenty years without ever having been in touch and yet at any moment can be wearing the same colored dress, shoes of the same make, hair cut in the same style.

Conclusions   Think of your conclusion as completing a circle. You have taken readers on a journey from presentation of the topic in your introduction, to your thesis, to supporting evidence and discussion, with specific examples and illustrations. Remind readers of the purpose of the journey. Recall the main idea of the paper, and make a strong statement about it that will stay in their minds. Readers should leave your document feeling satisfied, not turning the page and looking for more.

When you write an essay in the humanities, keep the following points in mind. (For other disciplines, see 5g and 5h.)

KEY POINTS

How to Write a Good Conclusion

Options

- Frame your essay by reminding readers of something you referred to in your introduction and by reminding readers of your thesis.

- End on a strong note: a quotation, a question, a suggestion, a reference to an anecdote in the introduction, a humorous insightful comment, a call to action, or a look to the future.

- Leave readers with a sense of completion of the point you are making.

What to Avoid

- Do not use the obvious "In conclusion."

- Do not apologize for the inadequacy of your argument ("I do not know much about this problem") or for holding your opinions ("I am sorry if you do not agree with me, but . . .").

- Do not repeat the identical wording you used in your introduction.

- Do not introduce a totally new direction. If you raise a new point at the end, readers might expect more details.

(Continued)

(Continued)

- Do not contradict what you said previously.
- Do not be too sweeping in your conclusions. Do not condemn the whole medical profession, for example, because one person you know had a bad time in one hospital.

A long article on the health care system and insurance (or lack of it) in the United States concludes with a paragraph that summarizes the complex issues discussed in the article. The author condenses the issues to several rhetorical questions, ending by reiterating strongly his thesis concerning the assumptions made about health care in the United States and in the rest of the world.

> The issue about what to do with the health-care system is sometimes presented as a technical argument about the merits of one kind of coverage over another or as an ideological argument about socialized versus private medicine. It is, instead, about a few very simple questions. Do you think that this kind of redistribution of risk is a good idea? Do you think that people whose genes predispose them to depression or cancer, or whose poverty complicates asthma or diabetes, or who get hit by a drunk driver, or who have to keep their mouths closed because their teeth are rotting ought to bear a greater share of the costs of their health care than those of us who are lucky enough to escape such misfortunes? In the rest of the industrialized world, it is assumed that the more equally and widely the burdens of illness are shared, the better off the population as a whole is likely to be. The reason the United States has forty-five million people without coverage is that its health-care policy is in the hands of people who disagree, and who regard health insurance not as the solution but as the problem.
>
> —Malcolm Gladwell, "The Moral-Hazard Myth"

3

Revising, Editing, and Proofreading

Always allow time in your writing schedule for putting a draft away for a while before you look at it with a critical eye.

Revising—making changes to improve a piece of writing—is an essential part of the writing process. It is not a punishment inflicted on inexperienced writers. Even Leo Tolstoy, author of the monumental Russian novel *War and Peace,* commented: "I cannot understand how anyone can write without rewriting everything over and over again."

Take a look at one manuscript page from Philip Roth's *Patrimony,* a nonfiction account of the life and death of his father. Although a bit hard to read, the page shows how Roth, the author of more than thirty books, revised and edited a page near the end of the book.

TECH NOTE

Computer Tools for Revising an Essay

- **Copy and paste first sentences.** Select the first sentence of each paragraph, and use the Copy and Paste features to move the sequence of sentences into a new file. Then examine these first sentences to check for logical progression of ideas, repetition, or omission.
- **Use different file names.** Write multiple drafts and save every draft under a separate file name, one that clearly labels the topic and the draft. Some people prefer to save deleted sections in a separate "dump" file so that they can retrieve deleted parts.
- **Use the "Find" feature.** The Find feature helps you find words and phrases that you tend to overuse. Use it to look for instances of "there is" or "there are," for example, and you will see if you are using either phrase too often.
- **Use the "Insert Comment" feature.** The Insert Comment feature allows you to write a note to yourself in the middle of a draft and see it highlighted on your screen. You can then choose to print your document with or without the comments showing.

3a Strategies for revising

It is often tempting just to correct errors in spelling and grammar and see the result as a new draft, but revising entails more than fixing errors. Legitimate new drafts have been revised for ideas, interest, and logic. Use these proven strategies to improve your writing in substantial ways:

- **Wait.** Don't start revising until you have completed a significant part of your draft.
- **Create distance and space.** Put a draft away for at least a few hours or days, and then read it again with fresher, more critical eyes.
- **Make room.** Write a triple-spaced draft so that if you print it out, you can easily write in changes and comments.
- **Consider your reader.** Consider a reader's reaction to your thesis and title, and rethink your approach to the topic.
- **Highlight key words in the assignment.** Then mark passages in your draft that address those key words. If you fail to find any, that could signal where you need to revise.
- **Read your draft aloud.** Mark any places where you hesitate and have to struggle to understand the point. Go back to them later. Alternatively, ask somebody else to read a copy of the draft and to note where he or she hesitates or seems confused.

- **Make an outline.** Outlining what you have written will help you to discover gaps or repetitions (see 1h).
- **Use the "Triggers for Revision" Key Points box.** These points will alert you to things to look for as you read your draft.
- **Remember documentation requirements.** Check all quotations and citations for accurate use of your style guide conventions (see chapters 11–20).

KEY POINTS

Triggers for Revision

Any of the following should alert you to a need for revision:

1. A weak or boring introductory paragraph

2. A worried frown, a pause, or a thought of "Huh? Something is wrong here" in any spot as you read your draft

3. A paragraph that never makes a point

4. A paragraph that seems unrelated to the thesis of the essay

5. A phrase, sentence, or passage that you cannot immediately understand (if you have trouble grasping your own ideas, readers surely will have trouble, too)

6. Excessive use of generalizations—*everyone, most people, all human beings, all students/lawyers/politicians,* and so on (use specific examples: *the students in my political science course this semester*)

7. A feeling that you would have difficulty summarizing your draft (maybe it is too vague?)

8. An awareness that you have just read the same point earlier in the draft

9. Failure to find a definite conclusion

3b Giving and getting feedback

Ask a friend, colleague, or tutor to read your draft with a pencil in hand, placing a checkmark next to the passages that work well and a question mark next to those that do not. Ask your reader to tell you what main point you made and how you supported and developed it. This process might reveal any lack of clarity or indicate gaps in the logic of your draft. Your reader does not have to be an expert English teacher to give you good feedback. If you notice worried frowns (or worse, yawns) as the person reads, you will know that something in your text is puzzling, disconcerting, or boring. Even that simple level of feedback can be valuable. See section 3e and chapter 35 for examples of student writing revised after feedback.

If you are asked to give feedback to a classmate or colleague, use the following guidelines.

KEY POINTS
Giving Feedback to Others

1. Don't think of yourself as an English teacher armed with a red pen.

2. Read for positive reactions to ideas and clarity. Look for parts that make you think, "I agree," "I like this," or "This is well done."

3. As you read, put a light pencil mark next to one or two passages that make you pause and send you back to reread.

4. Try to avoid comments that sound like accusations ("You were too vague in paragraph 3"). Instead, use *I* to emphasize your reaction as a reader ("I had a hard time visualizing the scene in paragraph 3").

Here is a sample peer response form that can be used to provide feedback.

Peer Response Form

Draft by _____   Date _____

Response by _____   Date _____

1. What do you see as the writer's main point in this draft?

2. What part of the draft interests you the most? Why?

3. Where do you feel you would like more detail or explanation? Where do you need less?

4. Do you find any parts unclear, confusing, or undeveloped? Mark each such spot with a pencil question mark in the margin. Then write a note to the writer with questions and comments about the parts you have marked.

5. Give the writer **one** suggestion about one change that you think would improve the draft the most.

TECH NOTE

Using Track Changes or GoogleDocs

The Track Changes feature in Word (Tools [2003] or Review/Tracking [2007]) allows you to see and keep track of changes you make to your own document or one that you receive electronically to work on collaboratively. This feature lets you see clearly on the screen and on the printed page the changes you have made. Settings allow you to choose the color of your text inserts and label your comments with whatever initials or name you specify. The Accept Changes and Reject Changes options allow you to automatically accept or reject all the changes at once or individually. You can also use GoogleDocs for collaborative projects (see 7c).

3c Drafting and revising a title

A good title captures the reader's attention, makes the reader want to read on, and lets the reader know what to expect in a piece of writing. You might have a useful working title as you write, but after you finish writing, brainstorm several titles and pick the one you like best.

WORKING TITLE   **The Benefits of Travel**

REVISED TITLE   **From Katmandu to Kuala Lumpur: A Real Education**

WORKING TITLE   **How Bad Weather Affects New Orleans**

REVISED TITLE   **After Hurricane Katrina, Did "Brownie" Really Do a "Heck of a Job"?**

3d Editing

Examine your draft for grammar, punctuation, and spelling errors. Often, reading your essay aloud will help you find sentences that are tangled, poorly constructed, or not connected. If you pay attention to your own reading, your hesitations and restarts will alert you to possible problem areas that are not well constructed or gracefully phrased. Looking carefully at every word and its function in a sentence will alert you to grammatical problem areas. Part 7 will help you with Standard English and methods for correcting common errors.

TECH NOTE

Computer Tools for Editing

■ A **spelling checker** will flag any word it does not recognize, and it is very good at catching typographical errors such as *teh* for *the* or *responsability* for *responsibility*. However, it will not identify grammatical errors that affect only spelling, such as missing plural or *-ed* endings. Nor will it flag an omitted word or find a misspelled word that forms another word, such as *then* for *than*, *their* for *there*, or *affect* for *effect*.

■ An online **thesaurus** will prompt you with synonyms and words close in meaning to a highlighted word; check suggested words in a dictionary for their connotations.

■ The **Word Count** feature of word processing programs is handy when you are given a word limit; it provides an immediate, accurate count.

NOTE FOR MULTILINGUAL WRITERS

Beware of Grammar-Check Programs

Never make a change in your draft at the suggestion of a grammar-check program before verifying that the change is really necessary. A student from Ukraine wrote the grammatically acceptable sentence "What he has is pride." Then, at the suggestion of a grammar-check program, he changed the sentence to "What he has been pride." The program had not recognized the sequence "has is."

See 37b for more on the uses and dangers of grammar-check programs.

3e A student's annotated drafts

With her class, student Catherine Turnbull was assigned to read a chapter of Paul Fussell's book *Uniforms: Why We Are What We Wear* and respond to it. After she wrote a first draft, she read it aloud to a group of classmates and took note of their comments. She also received feedback from her instructor in a conference. Turnbull's first rough draft of her first two paragraphs and her conclusion shows her notes and annotations for revision. Following that is her second draft, in which she moved material from the end to the beginning for a clearer thesis statement; fine-tuned her style, sentence structure, word choice, and accuracy; and cited her source. Her major changes are noted. She did not include MLA identification format (see 21a) or works-cited information until she was ready to write her final edited draft.

FIRST DRAFT

Shift from self to topic— get readers interested

Reader Response Essay: Nonmilitary Uniforms   *Think up better title*

I read the wedding gown chapter from Paul Fussell's assigned book. This chapter covered the history of the white tradition, cost, fanciness, and saving the dress afterwards, etc. This chapter and the idea of the book made me look at the uniforms of people around me. While wedding dresses are intended to be incredibly special and are basically heavy, tight, and uncomfortable, many "real" uniforms are intended to be comfortable, casual, and are team- or job-related.

—Say how?
Move to end?
Expand this point.

Change this

My first example is my aunt, a nurse at a hospital. She wears colorful, baggy, easy-wash scrubs most days, like pajamas with pockets, badge, and a stethoscope. Her name and credentials (RN) are on her badge. She wears super-comfortable shoes because she has to walk miles in the course of making her rounds, day or night. Her uniform says, I am part of the hospital team and am hear to help you.

add More details
sp

[Two more paragraphs were included: on her brother's basketball uniform and a train conductor's uniform.]

Move to beginning.
Make Stronger

In sum, Paul Fussell writes on wedding dresses in his uniform book, but they are not really uniforms in the sense most working people mean the term. More commonly, uniforms are functional and comfortable garments, symbolizing an active day-to-day role played for the larger good. They make you one with your team and also stand out from the rest of the general populace. Unlike a wedding dress, an average uniform is not so special that it needs special storage. It is what people do and their roles in society that are special.

thesis
choppy

SECOND DRAFT

Comfortable Shoes: Everyday Uniforms
and the People Who Fill Them

How many people would call a bridal gown a uniform?

Paul Fussell makes this somewhat startling claim in a chapter in a recent book in which he examines the so-called uniform of the formal wedding gown, its history, cost, and traditions, particularly the way it is often stored carefully away for future generations (167–69). He may justify his classification of the wedding dress as a uniform, but that is not the way most people mean the term. Surely it is more common to see uniforms as functional and comfortable garments, symbolizing an active day-to-day role played for a larger good.

My aunt, for instance, a nurse at Boston City Hospital, wears colorful, baggy, cotton medical scrubs to work, like pajamas with pockets, a badge, and a stethoscope. She says this outfit is easy to wash, which is important in the hygienic hospital setting. She wears the most comfortable rubber-soled shoes she can find since her job involves a lot of walking in the course of a day, making her rounds. Her name and credentials (RN) are on her badge, letting people know her official status and role as well-trained caregiver. In the past, nurses might have had to dress in white or wear more formal outfits and hats, but today the code is relaxed, with an emphasis on comfort and ease of laundering. Still, no matter how casual, her uniform definitely communicates the message, "I am an experienced member of the hospital team. I am here to help you."

Annotations:

- Title revised to include word *everyday*
- New intro: third person voice (1d)
- Cites author and page
- Thesis moved here from last ¶ of first draft (1f)
- Deletes reference to "my first example" (30c)
- Has added descriptive details of uniforms

[Turnbull included two more paragraphs.]

Paul Fussell stretches the definition of uniform when he includes wedding gowns. He correctly points out that wedding dresses conform to many set features, but even so they are meant to be as out of the ordinary and beautiful as possible. They are usually expensive, heavy, and snugly fitting, made with impractical fabrics and beads. In contrast, however, most everyday uniforms are loose, comfortable, and inexpensive; they identify wearers as part of a particular team with a particular mission, thus making them stand out from the crowd. Unlike a wedding dress, an average uniform is not so valuable that it needs to be preserved in a special garment bag. It is what people *do* in their uniforms and the roles they have taken on within their larger community that has special value.

Makes a strong point about Fussell

Synthesis of role of uniforms in 3 adjectives

Ends with a strong claim

3f Proofreading

Even after editing carefully with help from computer tools and this handbook, you still need to write a final draft and format it according to the conventions of the discipline you're in or your instructor's directions. Sections 21a and 21b show how to format a document for page or screen, and chapter 22 shows how to include visuals.

Before you submit or post a paper, give it one more careful proofreading to make sure no errors remain.

KEY POINTS
Proofreading Tips

All of these tips will help you spot remaining errors.

- Do not try to proofread on the computer screen. Print out hard copy.

- Make another copy of your manuscript, and read it aloud while a friend examines the original as you read.

- Use proofreading symbols to mark typographical and other errors (see page 610).

- Put a blank piece of paper under the first line of your text. Move it down line by line as you read, focusing your attention on one line at a time.

- Read the last sentence first, and work backward through your text. This strategy will not help you check for meaning, logic, pronoun reference, fragments, or consistency of verb tenses; but it will focus your attention on the spelling, punctuation, and grammatical correctness of one sentence at a time.

- If possible, put your manuscript away for a few hours or longer after you have finished it. Proofread it when the content is not so familiar.

Once you have revised, edited, and checked your work thoroughly, you can turn your attention to how you will present it to readers. For how to format and design your document for print or online presentation, see part 5, chapters 21, 22, and 24–29.

4

Writing and Analyzing Arguments

In an argument, you present your opinions on an issue as clearly and convincingly as you can. A well-formed argument—one that will persuade readers that your point of view is based on solid evidence—presents a carefully chosen and developed claim (a thesis) with persuasively compelling reasons and evidence to support that claim. A good argument is strategically arranged to appeal to an audience's inherent logical, ethical, and emotional inclinations. The best arguments establish common ground as they consider and address opposing views in a manner that allows those who may have been opposed to save face as they change their minds. With such tact and strategy, it is no wonder that argument is called the *art* of persuasion.

But it is also a *science* of persuasion when you consider that behind a good argument is a writer who has gone through the rigorous process of considering and weighing his or her own assumptions, biases, and quick conclusions. In his introduction to John Brockman's *What Have You Changed Your Mind About?* Brian Eno points out that as an intellectual invention, science is "a construction designed to neutralize the universal tendency to see what we expected to see and overlook what we didn't expect." Although the brilliance of the human brain, he continues, allows us to discern "complex ideas from insubstantial data," the downside is that it all too easily allows us to reach a familiar but wrong conclusion rather than an unfamiliar but right conclusion.

When you write and analyze arguments, you challenge that tendency in yourself and invite others to do the same through a careful weighing of evidence and reason.

Understanding the process of constructing a well-formulated argument goes beyond writing essays for your composition class. As you become more practiced in the process of writing and analyzing arguments in your humanities and social science courses, you become more aware of the arguments all around you—in magazine articles, advertisements, blogs, visually displayed information, letters to publishers, scientific explanations, political opinions, newsletters, and business reports. Discerning the structures and strategies that form arguments is the very essence of what it means to be a critical thinker, reader, and writer.

4a Thinking critically about arguments

Whatever your topic, approach it by thinking critically as you read and do research and as you write (see 1c). Remember, thinking critically means keeping an open mind and asking probing questions.

It is a good habit to step back and read an argument critically, whether it is your own or somebody else's, to identify its merits and faults. As you read, develop a system of inquiry. Do not assume that because something is in print, it is accurate. Assume that readers will use the same care when they read an argument that *you* write. So put yourself in a critical reader's shoes when you evaluate your own arguments. Here are questions to ask while analyzing an argument:

1. **What am I reading?** A statement of fact, an opinion, an exaggeration, an attack, an emotional belief?
2. **Where does the information come from?** Can I trust the sources?
3. **How reliable are the writer's statements?** Are they measured, accurate, fair, and to the point? Do I feel the need to interject a challenge, using "but ..."?
4. **Can I ascertain the writer's background, audience, and purpose?** What biases does the writer reveal?
5. **What assumptions does the writer make?** If a writer argues for a college education for everyone, would I accept the underlying assumption that a college education automatically leads to happiness and success? (For more on assumptions, see 4f.)
6. **Does the writer present ideas in a convincing way?** Is the writer relying on extreme language or name-calling rather than presentation of evidence?

For more on critical thinking, go to 5b (literary texts) and 4i (visual arguments).

4b Formulating and constructing a good argument

When you are writing an argument, the goal is to persuade readers to adopt your point of view on your chosen or assigned topic. We often associate the word *argument* with combat and confrontation, but the Latin root of the word *argue* means "to make clear." The Greek word *persuasion* derives from the verb "to believe." So, in the process of formulating and constructing a good argument, your work lies in making your claim so clear to your readers that they will come to believe what you do. Your readers need to recognize that the claim you make about your topic rests on solid, reliable evidence and that you have provided a fair, unbiased approach to this evidence. In reading your argument, your readers will discover that you have good reasons for your position.

KEY POINTS

The Features of a Good Argument

A good argument

- deals with an arguable issue (4d)
- is not based on strong gut reactions or beliefs but on careful analysis of reliable information (4d)
- stands up to a critical reading (4a)
- takes a position on and makes a clear claim about the topic (4d)
- supports that position with detailed and specific evidence (such as reasons, facts, examples, descriptions, and stories) (4e)
- establishes common ground with listeners or readers and avoids confrontation (4g)
- takes opposing views into account and either refutes them or shows why they may be unimportant or irrelevant (4g)
- presents reasons logically (4h)
- is engaged and vital, a reflection of your careful, critical thinking rather than just a collection of others' opinions

4c Structuring an argument essay

Essay arguments are typically structured to follow one of four basic patterns: (1) general to specific, (2) specific to general, (3) problem and solution, and (4) cause and effect.

General to specific The general-to-specific structure is used frequently in the humanities and arts. It moves from the thesis to support and evidence. Obviously, writers find many variations on this structure, but it is one you can use as a reliable starting point.

KEY POINTS

Basic Structure for a General-to-Specific Argument

- **Introduction:** Provide background information on the issue, why it is an issue, and what the controversies are. After you have introduced your readers to the nature and importance of the issue, announce your position in a general statement of your claim or thesis statement (4d), perhaps at the end of the first paragraph or in a prominent position within the second paragraph depending on the length and complexity of your essay.

- **Body:** Provide evidence in the form of supporting points for your thesis, with concrete and specific details (4e). For each new point, start a new paragraph.

- **Acknowledgment of opposing views:** Use evidence and specific details to describe and logically refute any opposing views (4g).

- **Conclusion:** Return to the topic as a whole and your specific claim. Without repeating complete phrases and sentences, remind readers of the point you want to make. End on a strong note.

Specific to general   Alternatively, you might choose to begin with data and points of evidence first and then draw a conclusion from that evidence, provided that the evidence is relevant and convincing. A basic specific-to-general argument on the topic of driving with a cell phone looks like this:

Introduction: background, statement of problem and controversy

Data:

1. Cell phone users admit to being distracted while driving (cite statistics).

2. Many accidents are attributable to cell phone use (cite statistics).

3. Several states have passed a law against using a handheld cell phone while driving.

4. NPR talk show hosts Click and Clack (Tom and Ray Magliozzi) criticize the small sample size used by the AAA (only forty-two cases) to claim that only very few (8.3 percent) car crashes are caused by driver distraction, with even fewer of those distractions (1.5 percent of 8.3 percent) attributable to cell phone use (<http://www.newsfactor.com/perl/story/12502.html>).

Conclusion: Discussion of data and presentation of thesis (generalization formed from analysis of the data): All states should pass laws prohibiting use of handheld cell phones while driving.

In an argument in the sciences or social sciences (as in sample paper 4 in chapter 16), writers often begin with a hypothesis that they can test. They list their findings from experimentation, surveys, facts, and statistics. Then, from the data they have collected, they draw conclusions to support, modify, or reject the hypothesis.

Problem and solution If your topic offers solutions to a problem, you probably will find it useful to present the details of the problem first and then offer solutions. Think about the strongest position in your paper for placing the solution: at the beginning of your solutions section or at the end? Do you want to make your strong point early, or would you rather lead up to it gradually?

Cause and effect Writers of arguments in history, art history, and social movements often examine the causes and effects of events and trends to enhance their point of view. The reasoning behind an analysis of causes and effects is far from simple, involving many variables and interpretations. Take care not to reduce your analysis to one simple cause, and avoid the logical fallacy of assuming that one event causes another simply because it precedes it (see 4h).

4d Topic and claim (thesis)

A good argument begins with choosing a topic, clearly defining it, and formulating it into an arguable claim. The topic should be significant and debatable, such as in what grade should homework be assigned to children rather than how many schools assign homework in kindergarten. The former issue can lead to an arguable claim such as, "Homework should not be assigned to children before fourth grade," rather than a truism (a statement that is obviously true and is not debatable) such as, "Many schools assign homework to children in kindergarten."

Choosing a topic Choose an issue that is fresh. Avoid topics such as the death penalty, drug laws, and abortion, which have been written about so often that original or interesting arguments are hard to develop. Beware of saying that you intend to write about "global warming and the environment," "the church and morality," or "racial prejudice." Such issues might mean a great deal to you personally, but you will have difficulty structuring a logical argument around them.

Brainstorming; reading books, magazines, and newspapers; and browsing online in search directories, informational sites, or social networking sites can help you discover novel and timely issues. When you find an interesting issue and your instructor has approved it (if necessary), begin by writing the issue as a question and then considering the arguments on both or all sides.

Student Mara Lee Kornberg decided to tackle the issue of the health effects of a vegan diet. As a vegan, she was interested in examining the facts of a case in which a child who had been fed a vegan diet had to be hospitalized. Envisioning her classmates, instructor, and a wider general audience as her readers, she began with a topic and a focused research question:

> **Topic:** A vegan diet for children
>
> **Research question:** Does a vegan diet supply adequate nutrition for children?

As she read and researched, took notes, and discussed her topic, she eventually developed her working thesis, which guided her further research and the content and organization of her argument. (Her paper is in section 4j.)

Formulating an arguable claim (thesis)   The position you take on a topic constitutes your thesis or claim. Kornberg knew that the claim in her argument paper should be debatable, so after some reading and research, she formulated a preliminary working thesis on her topic, though she remained prepared to change it if her research led her in a different direction.

> **Working thesis:** A vegan diet is a healthy diet for children.

Avoid using any of the following as claims because they are not debatable:

- a neutral statement, which gives no hint of the writer's position
- an announcement of the paper's broad subject
- a fact, which is not arguable
- a truism (statement that is obviously true)
- a personal or religious conviction that cannot be logically debated
- an opinion based only on your own feelings
- a sweeping generalization

Here are some examples of nondebatable claims, each with a revision that makes it more debatable.

NEUTRAL STATEMENT	**There are unstated standards of beauty in the workplace.**
REVISED	**The way we look affects the way we are treated at work and the size of our paychecks.**

TOO BROAD	This paper is about violence in video games.
REVISED	Violence in video games has to take its share of blame for the violence in our society.

FACT	*Plessy v. Ferguson,* an 1896 Supreme Court case that supported racial segregation, was overturned in 1954 by *Brown v. Board of Education.*
REVISED	The overturning of *Plessy v. Ferguson* by *Brown v. Board of Education* has not led to significant advances in integrated education.

TRUISM	Bilingual education has advantages and disadvantages.
REVISED	A bilingual program is more effective than an immersion program at helping students grasp the basics of science and mathematics.

PERSONAL CONVICTION	Racism is the worst kind of prejudice.
REVISED	The best weapon against racism is primary and secondary education.

OPINION BASED ONLY ON FEELING	I think jet-skiing is a dumb sport.
REVISED	Jet-skiing should be banned from public beaches.

SWEEPING GENERALIZATION	Women understand housework.
REVISED	The publication of a lengthy guide to housekeeping and its success among both men and women suggest a renewed interest in the domestic arts.

Avoiding loaded terms In your claim, avoid sweeping and judgmental words—for instance, *bad, good, right, wrong, stupid, ridiculous, moral, immoral, dumb,* and *smart.*

Modifying or changing your claim Sometimes, you will have an instant reaction to an issue and immediately decide which position you want to take. At other times, you will need to reflect and do research before you take a stand. Whenever you decide what your position is, formulate a position statement that will serve as your working thesis—for example, "Undocumented aliens should (or should not) have to pay higher college tuition fees than citizens or other immigrants." However, keep an open mind. Be prepared to find out more about an issue so that you can make an educated claim with concrete support, and be prepared to modify, qualify, or even change your original claim as you do your research.

Mara Lee Kornberg began with a working thesis that guided her research. However, as she did more reading and research and as she examined her assumptions (see 4f) and got feedback on her ideas, she began to refine her thesis to take counterarguments into account. The following shows how she progressed in her planning:

> **Topic:** A vegan diet for children
>
> **Research question:** Does a vegan diet supply adequate nutrition for children?
>
> **Working thesis:** A vegan diet is a healthy diet for children.
>
> **Revised thesis:** A vegan diet can be healthy for children provided that it is supplemented with vitamins and minerals.

You can read a draft of her essay in 4j to see how she supports her claim with evidence, appeals to her readers, establishes common ground, and discusses opposing views.

 LANGUAGE AND CULTURE

Arguments across Cultures: Making a Claim and Staking a Position

The types of arguments described in this section are those common in academic and business settings in North America and the Western world. Writers state their views directly, arguing for their viewpoints. The success of their arguments lies in the credibility and strength of the evidence they produce in support. But such an approach is not universal. Other cultures may prefer a less direct approach, one that begins by exploring and evaluating all options rather than by issuing a direct claim. One of the basic principles of writing well—know your audience's expectations—is especially relevant to writing arguments in cultures different from your own.

4e Supporting a claim with reasons and evidence

Supporting your claim means telling your readers what reasons, statistics, facts, examples, and expert testimony bolster and explain your point of view. If a reader asks, "Why do you think that?" about your claim, then the support you offer answers that question in detail.

Reasons Imagine someone saying to you, "OK. I know your position on this issue, but I disagree with you. What led you to your position?" This is asking you to provide the reasons for your conviction. To begin to answer the question, add at least one "because clause" to your claim.

> **Claim:** Colleges should stop using SAT scores to determine admissions.
>
> **Reason:** (because) High school grades predict college success with more accuracy.
>
> **Claim:** Organized hunting of deer is necessary in suburban areas.
>
> **Reason:** (because) With a diminishing natural habitat, deer are becoming an otherwise uncontrollable hazard to people and property.
>
> **Claim:** A large coal-fired cement factory in a rural scenic region could be an ecological disaster.
>
> **Reason:** (because) Its operation would threaten water, wildlife, and the residents' health.

Once you have formulated a tentative claim, make a scratch outline listing the claim and developing and expanding your reasons for supporting it. As you work more on your argument, you will then need to find specific and concrete evidence to explain and support each reason. Here is an example of a scratch outline (see 1h) developed to argue against building a cement factory in a rural scenic region. Note the revised, more detailed claim, the expanded list of reasons, and the inclusion of visual arguments to make a strong point.

> **Claim:** Although a large, coal-fired cement factory on the Hudson River would satisfy the increased demand for building materials and might help boost the local economy, the danger is that it could not only

pollute air and water but also threaten the wildlife and the natural beauty of the area.

Reasons:

1. Drilling, blasting, and mining pose dangers to the local aquifer and to the nearby city's water supply.
2. Every year, a 1,800-acre coal-burning plant with a 406-foot stack would emit just under 20 million pounds of pollution, including arsenic, lead, and mercury.
3. Smokestack emissions could affect birds; barge traffic and discharge into the river could affect fish.
4. Views portrayed by the Hudson River school of painters would be spoiled.

Billboards sponsored by Scenic Hudson, Inc., and Columbia Action Now to oppose the plans for a cement plant.

Concrete evidence   You need reasons, but reasons are not enough. You also need to include specific evidence that supports, illustrates, and explains your reasons. Imagine a reader saying, after you give one of your reasons, "Tell me even more about why you say that." Your details will make your essay vivid and persuasive.

Add to the outline any items of concrete evidence you will include to illustrate and explain your reasoning. What counts as evidence? Facts, statistics, stories, examples, and testimony from experts can all be used as evidence in support of your reasons.

LANGUAGE AND CULTURE

Evidence Used to Support an Argument

The way arguments are structured, the concept of *expertise*, and the nature of evidence regarded as convincing may vary from one culture to another. In some cultures, for example, the opinions of religious or political leaders may carry more weight than the opinions of a scholar in the field. Be sure to consider the readers you will be writing for and the type of evidence they will expect.

4f Four questions for constructing an argument (Toulmin)

The four questions in the Key Points box, derived from Stephen Toulmin's *The Uses of Argument*, will provide you with a systematic way to construct a logical argument.

KEY POINTS

Four Questions to Ask about Your Argument

1. **What is your point?** (What are you claiming?)

2. **What do you have to go on?** (What support do you have for your claim in the form of reasons, data, and evidence?)

3. **How do you get there?** (What assumptions—Toulmin calls them *warrants*—do you take for granted and expect readers to take for granted, too?)

4. **What could prevent you from getting there?** (What qualifications do you need to include, using *but, unless,* or *if* or adding words such as *usually, often, several, mostly,* or *sometimes*, to provide exceptions to your assumptions?)

Here is an example showing how the Toulmin questions can be used to develop the claim and supporting reasons introduced in 4e:

CLAIM
Colleges should stop using SAT scores in their admissions process.

SUPPORT
(because) High school grades and recommendations predict college success with more accuracy.

ASSUMPTION/
WARRANT
Colleges use SAT scores to predict success in college.

QUALIFIER
. . . unless the colleges use the scores only to indicate the level of knowledge acquired in high school.

REVISED CLAIM
Colleges that use SAT scores to predict college success should use high school grades and recommendations instead.

Examine your assumptions   Pay special attention to examining assumptions that link a claim to the reasons and evidence you provide. Consider whether readers will share those assumptions or whether you need to explain, discuss, and defend them. For example, the claim "Telemarketing should be monitored because it preys on the elderly and the gullible" operates on the assumption that monitoring will catch and reduce abuses. The claim "Telemarketing should be encouraged because it benefits the economy" operates on the assumption that benefiting the economy is an important goal. These different assumptions will appeal to different readers, and some may need to be persuaded of the assumptions before they attempt to accept your claim or the reasons you give for it.

Note that if your claim is "Telemarketing should be encouraged because it is useful," you are saying little more than "Telemarketing is good because it is good." Your reader is certain to object to and reject such circular reasoning. That is why it is important to ask question 3 from the Key Points box. That question leads you to examine how you get from your evidence to your claim and what assumptions your claim is based on.

4g   Appeals, common ground, and opposing views

Ask who your readers are   Consider the readers you are writing for. Assess what they might know, what assumptions they hold, what they need to know, how they can best be convinced to accept your position, and what strategies will persuade them to respect or accept your views.

If you are writing for readers with no specific prior knowledge, biases, or expertise—a *general audience*—remember to include background information: the place, the time, the context, the issues. Do not assume that a general reader knows a great deal more than you do. For more on audience, see section 1d.

Appeal to readers Aristotle classified the ways that writers appeal to readers in arguments. Your profile of readers will help you decide what types of appeal to use. Within one extended argument, you may find it necessary to use more than one type of appeal to reach all readers' needs. The examples of the appeals that follow, for example, were used by Peggy Orenstein in a *New York Times Magazine* article in which she argued against a trend in U.S. kindergartens toward increased instruction and testing ("Kindergarten Cram: Toss Out the No. 2 Pencils and Let Them Play." 3 May 2009. 13).

Rational appeal (Logos) A rational appeal bases an argument's conclusion on facts, examples, and authoritative evidence. Such an appeal is appropriate for educated readers and useful when readers are uninformed or hostile.

Sample rational appeal:
Orenstein presents authoritative evidence that assigning homework and testing young children neither predicts nor improves their academic success. In addition, instruction and testing in reading and math take up the time previously allotted to free play, which has proven instrumental not only in children's intellectual development but also in their emotional, psychological, social, and spiritual development. To underscore just how much of a decline in play there is, Orenstein cites a survey of kindergarten teachers. It

TELLING TIME
Average number of minutes spent daily on **literacy, math, test prep** and **free play** in 112 Los Angeles kindergarten classes:

89
47
21
19

SOURCE: "Crisis in the Kindergarten," Alliance for Childhood, March 2009 <http://www.nytimes.com/2009/05/03/magazine/03wwln-ede-t.html>

found that kindergartners spent less than 30 minutes a day playing in comparison to two to three hours a day being instructed or tested in math and reading. In a visual illustration of survey results, a simple, colorful graph effectively displays the shrinking free play of Los Angeles kindergarten classes. (For more on the use of visual arguments, see 4i. For more on creating and using tables, charts, and graphs, see chapter 22.)

Ethical appeal (Ethos) You make an ethical appeal to readers when you represent yourself or any sources you refer to as reliable, experienced, thoughtful, objective, and fair, even when considering opposing views. Such an appeal is appropriate for formal situations in business and academic worlds. In advertising, too, ethical appeals often include testimony from famous people, whether they are experts or not—for example, American Express uses Tina Fey to promote its credit card.

Sample ethical appeal: Orenstein presents as experts in early childhood education the Alliance for Childhood, a nonprofit research and advocacy group and draws from their report, "Crisis in Kindergarten." She cites as a reliable source Daniel Pink, a writer on the changing world of work who argues that without the "imagination economy" fostered by among other things, "playfulness," the United States' continued viability in the twenty-first century is at risk. She addresses and refutes opposing views by invoking Jean Piaget, the twentieth century's groundbreaking child psychologist, who famously challenged the American penchant for speeding up children's development.

Emotional appeal (Pathos) You make an emotional appeal when you try to gain the empathy and sympathy of your readers by assessing their values and to persuade them by using descriptions, anecdotes, case studies, and visuals to appeal to those values. Such an appeal is less common in academic writing than in journalism and the other media. It is appropriate when readers are regarded as either already favorable to particular ideas or apathetic toward them.

Sample emotional appeal: Orenstein shares personal anecdotes to establish a bond with her readers. She wants for her child what the *New York Times Magazine*'s readers want for their children. Although she and her readers want their children to grow up ethical, thoughtful, and responsible, they are concerned with how their early education will impact their ability to compete in a future job market. She confesses to her readers, "I wonder how far I'm willing to go in my commitment to the cause: would I embrace the example of Finland—whose students consistently come out on top in international assessments—and delay formal reading instruction until age 7?" Orenstein ends her article on a note that will seal her readers' empathy: her daughter, now enrolled in a school that does not assign homework until fourth grade, has complained that she doesn't have homework like "all the other kids."

Within one extended argument, you will probably find it necessary to use all types of argument to reach the maximum number of readers, each with individual expectations, preferences, and quirks. See 4j for examples of these appeals in student Mara Lee Kornberg's argument essay.

Establish common ground Remember that readers turned off by exaggerations or extreme language have the ultimate power to stop reading and ignore what you have to say.

KEY POINTS

Ways to Establish Common Ground with Readers

1. **Avoid extreme views or language.** Do not label someone's views as *ridiculous, ignorant, immoral, fascist,* or *crooked,* for example.

2. **Write to convince, not to confront.** Recognize shared concerns, and consider the inclusive use of *we*.

3. **Steer clear of sarcastic remarks** such as, "The company has come up with the amazingly splendid idea of building a gigantic cement factory right in the middle of a natural beauty spot."

4. **Use clear, everyday words** that sound as if you are speaking directly to your readers.

5. **Acknowledge valid arguments from your opponents,** and work to show why the arguments on your side carry more weight.

6. **If possible, propose a solution** with long-term benefits for everyone.

Refute opposing views It is not enough to present your own reasons and evidence for your claim. When you take into account any opposing arguments and the reasons and evidence that support those arguments, you present yourself as objective and evenhanded, furthering your ethical argument. Examine opposing arguments; describe the most common or convincing ones; evaluate their validity, applicability, and limitations; and explain what motivates people to take those positions. Then discuss why you see your reasons and evidence as more pertinent and convincing than those in opposing arguments.

Be careful to argue logically and rationally without insulting your opponents. Take pains to explain rationally why your views differ from theirs. You may choose to do this by following each one of your own points with a discussion of an opposing view. Or you may prefer to devote an entire section of your essay to dealing with opposing views.

4h Logical reasoning, logical fallacies

Reasoning logically   As you evaluate the logic of your arguments, assess whether they are valid examples of deductive or inductive reasoning and ensure that they do not fall prey to logical fallacies.

Deductive reasoning   The classical Aristotelian method of constructing an argument is based on a reasoning process (a syllogism) that moves from true premises to a certain and valid conclusion.

MAJOR PREMISE   **Coal-fired factories can cause significant damage to the environment.**

MINOR PREMISE   **The proposed cement plant will use coal for fuel.**

CONCLUSION   **The proposed cement plant could cause significant damage to the environment.**

Even if the major premise is not stated, readers must nevertheless accept it as the truth:

MAJOR PREMISE   **Since the new proposed cement plant will be coal-**
NOT STATED   **fired, it could cause significant damage to the environment.**

The premises must be true for a conclusion to be valid.

Inductive reasoning   An inductive argument begins with details that lead to a *probable* conclusion. Inductive arguments are used often in the sciences and social sciences. Researchers begin with a tentative hypothesis. They conduct studies and perform experiments; they collect and tabulate data; they examine the evidence of other studies. Then they draw a conclusion to support, reject, or modify the hypothesis. The conclusion, however, is only probable and not necessarily certain. It is based on the circumstances of the evidence. Different evidence at a different time could lead to a different conclusion. Conclusions drawn in the medical field change with the experiments and the sophistication of the techniques—eggs are called good for you one year, bad the next. That is because the nature of the evidence changes.

Recognizing logical fallacies   Faulty logic can make readers mistrust you as a writer. Watch out for some common flaws in logic (called *logical fallacies*) as you write and check your drafts.

Sweeping generalization   Generalizations can sometimes be so broad that they fall into stereotyping. Avoid them.

▶ **All British people are stiff and formal.**

▶ **The only thing that concerns students is grades.**

The reader will be right to wonder what evidence has led to these conclusions. Without any explanation or evidence, they will simply be dismissed. Beware, then, of the trap of words like *all, every, only, never,* and *always.*

Hasty conclusion with inadequate support   To convince readers of the validity of a generalization, you need to offer enough evidence—usually more than just one personal observation. Thoughtful readers can easily spot a conclusion that is too hastily drawn from flimsy support.

▶ **My friend Arecelis had a terrible time in a bilingual school. It is clear that bilingual education has failed.**

▶ **Bilingual education is a success story, as the school in Chinatown has clearly shown.**

Non sequitur   *Non sequitur* is Latin for "it does not follow." Supporting a claim with evidence that is illogical or irrelevant causes a non sequitur fallacy.

▶ **Maureen Dowd writes so well that she would make a good teacher.** [The writer does not establish a connection between good writing and good teaching.]

▶ **Studying economics is a waste of time. Money does not make people happy.** [Here the writer does not help us see any relationship between happiness and the study of a subject.]

Causal fallacy   You are guilty of a causal fallacy if you assume that one event causes another merely because the second event happens after the first. (The Latin name for this logical flaw is *post hoc, ergo propter hoc:* "after this, therefore because of this.")

- ▶ **The economy collapsed because a new president was elected.** [Was the election the reason? Or did it simply occur before the economy collapsed?]

- ▶ **The number of A's given in college courses has increased. This clearly shows that faculty members are inflating grades.** [But does the number of A's clearly show any such thing? Or could the cause be that students are better prepared in high school?]

Examine carefully any statements you make about cause and effect.

Ad hominem attack   *Ad hominem* (Latin for "to the person") refers to unfair ethical appeals to personal considerations rather than to logic or reason. Avoid using arguments that seek to discredit an opinion through criticizing a person's character or lifestyle.

- ▶ **The new curriculum should not be adopted because the administrators who favor it have never even taught a college course.**

- ▶ **The student who is urging the increase in student fees for social events is a partygoer and a big drinker.**

Argue a point by showing either the logic of the argument or the lack of it, not by pointing to flaws in character. However, personal considerations may be valid if they pertain directly to the issue, as in, "The two women who favor the abolition of the bar own property on the same block."

Circular reasoning   In an argument based on circular reasoning, the evidence and the conclusion restate each other, thus proving nothing.

- ▶ **Credit card companies should be banned on campus because companies should not be allowed to solicit business from students.**

- ▶ **That rich man is smart because wealthy people are intelligent.**

Neither of these statements moves the argument forward. They both beg the question; that is, they argue in a circular way.

False dichotomy or false dilemma Either/or arguments reduce complex problems to two simplistic alternatives without exploring them in depth or considering other alternatives.

▶ **After September 11, New York could do one of two things: increase airport security or screen immigrants.**

This proposal presents a false dichotomy. These are not the only two options for dealing with potential terrorism. Posing a false dilemma like this will annoy readers.

TECH NOTE

Logical Fallacies on the Web

Go to the *Logical Fallacies* Web site at <http://www.logicalfallacies.info/> for lists of many more types of logical fallacies (including the "No True Scotsman" Fallacy and the Fallacist's Fallacy) with explanations, examples, and real-world examples.

4i Using and analyzing visual arguments

We commonly think of arguments as spoken or written, and sections 4a–4h deal largely with the features of written arguments. However, visual arguments are widespread. Because of their immediacy and subtle appeals to a viewer's reason, emotions, and morals (see 4g), they can be as compellingly persuasive—if not more so—as written arguments. Whether it's to strengthen an argument or to illustrate an argument in its complexity, writers often choose to supplement their essays with visuals. When you write an argument, consider adding to the impact of your thesis by including a visual argument.

TECH NOTE

Images on the World Wide Web

A comprehensive Web site, constructed by librarian Heidi Abbey for the University of Connecticut Libraries, provides demystifying information on digital image formats; a primer on basic copyright issues; links to search engines; and best of all, links to several annotated image Web sites, including image resources for specific subjects.

Using visuals in arguments　You can supplement your written arguments with visual arguments: maps, superimposed images, photographs, charts and graphs, political cartoons—vivid images that will say more than many words can to your readers.

An argument essay on the media, for example, would make a strong visual impact if its argument included an image such as the example from *Adbusters.org*.

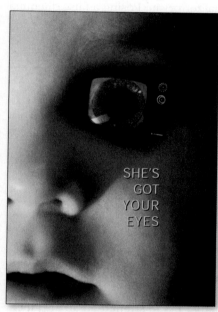

SHE'S
GOT
YOUR
EYES

From Adbusters.org.

It says that children see what their parents watch and challenges us to consider how much the media dictate what we see.

Visual arguments make their appeals in ways similar to written arguments by appealing to logic, showcasing the character and credentials of the author, or appealing to viewers' emotions. But unlike written arguments, which present arguments, reasons, and evidence in a linear and logical manner, arguments made in cartoons, advertisements, and works of art can simultaneously pit our logic against our ethics while moving us emotionally. Note how the two visuals shown in 4e offer strong visual arguments to support a writer's stand against a concrete factory; their depiction of sinister, polluting industrial plants pushing smoke into the sky has a strong emotional impact as well. To see how a student uses a visual in her written argument on a vegan diet, see 4j.

KEY POINTS

Using Visuals

1. Use visuals in your argument when:

- The visual serves to strengthen or illustrate your argument
- Your paper focuses on a visual topic (an analysis of an ad, a cartoon, a work of art)

- Your paper relies on visual images for its evidence and support of your argument
2. Choose an appropriate visual in your argument that:

- Has a concrete connection to your argument
- Appeals to your readers' reason, emotions, and/or ethics
3. Integrate the visual into your paper by:

- Connecting the visual to your text with a comment
- Locating the visual close to the text that describes it
- Including a caption with the figure number and title or a brief description (see chapters 13 and 16 for examples)
- Providing complete documentation in your works cited page

Analyzing visual arguments Photographs of hurricane devastation or of starving children in Africa are carefully chosen to appeal for donations and can distract viewers from asking important questions like: What exactly will my money be used for? Analyzing a visual for its unspoken argument or point of view is part of the critical thinking process that underlies good reading and writing.

Consider, for example, the image on the cover of the July 21, 2008, *New Yorker* magazine depicting then-presidential nominee Barack Obama as a Muslim and his wife Michelle Obama as a Black radical. A color cartoon easily found online, the image shows the couple fist bumping in the Oval Office while an American flag burns in the fireplace and a portrait of Osama bin Laden hangs on the wall behind them. Its ambiguity created media controversy as soon as it was published: Did the cartoonist want viewers to believe that the Obamas would take over the White House with radical and fundamentalist ideals? Did he want to turn a mirror on his viewers' unspoken misgivings in electing the first African American president? Did he want to illustrate and satirize the unfounded arguments of Obama's opponents? Just as written arguments challenge readers to question assumptions and implications, visual arguments push viewers to think critically about the implications and intended effects of images. If a picture is worth a thousand words, it is still up to us to interpret what those words are.

Using visuals as tools for analysis Visuals can be used as tools for analysis (for more on visuals like charts and graphs, see chapter 22). Using word clouds, for example, the *New York Times* analyzed the language of presidential inaugural addresses by visually depicting word frequency in the inaugural address (indicated by the size of each word) and word frequency compared to other presidential inaugural addresses (indicated in yellow highlight). The word clouds here show George W. Bush's 2005 inaugural address (left) and Barack Obama's 2009 inaugural address (right).

<table>
<tr><td>

freedom America
liberty nation American country world
time free citizen hope history people day human right
seen ideal work unite justice cause government move choice
tyranny live act life accept defend duty generation great question honor
states president fire character force power fellow enemy century witness excuse
soul God division task define advance speak institution independence society serve

</td><td>

nation America people
work generation world common
time seek spirit day American peace crisis hard
greater meet men remain job power moment women
father endure government short hour life hope freedom carried
journey forward force prosperity courage man question future friend
service age history God oath understand ideal pass economy care
promise children Earth stand demand purpose faith hand found interest

</td></tr>
</table>

SOURCE: <http://www.nytimes.com/interactive/2009/01/17/washington/20090117_ADDRESSES.html>

TECH NOTE

Exploring Data Visualization Tools

IBM's Many Eyes project <http://manyeyes.alphaworks.ibm.com/manyeyes/> provides a wide range of data visualization examples that allow you to see how you might use visuals to show relationships among data points (plots and network diagrams), comparisons (bar charts), changes over time (line graphs), ratios (pie charts), textual relationships (word clouds and word trees), and maps. You can also use the Many Eyes site to create visualizations using your own data.

Creating multimedia arguments   Present-day technology allows for a new way to express ideas. No longer limited to using type on a page, writers now can use screens to present an interaction of words, color, music, sound, images, and movies to tell a story and make a point.

In preparing a multimedia presentation, consider, then, the effectiveness of juxtaposing images and conveying emotion and meaning through colors and pictures as well as through words. If you use media imaginatively, you can do what writing teachers have long advised: Show, don't just tell.

An outstanding example of a multimedia visual argument was created by undergraduates at the University of Southern California for a course in Near Eastern and Mediterranean archeology. The students chose the ancient city of Troy as the subject of their presentation. Using excavation records, archeological findings, and Homer's texts (as well as architectural modeling software, audio, and virtual reality techniques), the students reconstructed "the citadel as it may have appeared at the time of the Trojan War in the 13th century B.C."

4j Sample paper 1: A student's argument essay

Here is a draft of Mara Lee Kornberg's argument paper on a vegan diet, annotated to point out the strategies in her argument. Note how she presents her thesis, supports it, considers and refutes opposing views, and varies appeals to readers. As this was an early draft, she did not include an identification (her name, professor's name, course, and date) or any page headers; see 21a for instructions on how to include these in a final draft.

Dispelling the Media Myth: Vegan Diet Is Safe for Children

Several years ago, a Queens couple was convicted of assault and related charges for nearly starving their young daughter to death by feeding her only vegan foods. Silva and Joseph Swinton placed their daughter on a strict, meat- and dairy-free diet shortly after her birth. By the time Ilce Swinton was fifteen months old, she weighed only ten pounds, had no teeth, had suffered broken bones and internal injuries, and was diagnosed as being severely malnourished. She was then taken into foster care, and almost immediately the media swarmed, focusing not on the fact that this child had obviously been abused and neglected and never once given medical care, but on the fact that she had been fed—when she was fed at all—a vegan diet. Before long, the case was being referred to in newspapers as "the Vegan Baby Diet" (Retsinas).

Emotional appeal: story of a sick child

Definition of term

A vegan is defined as a "strict vegetarian who consumes no animal food or dairy products" ("Vegan"). While it is not uncommon to be a vegetarian nowadays, "knowledge of adequacy and nutritional effects of vegan diets is still limited," according to the German Vegan Study (GVS) of 154 vegans, a scholarly study conducted in 2003, which has greatly helped in shedding light on this still widely unknown way of eating (Waldmann et al. 947). Because it is uncommon, the practice of veganism was not received well by the general public when the Swinton case became headline news. As is often the case, a way of life was perceived as problematic simply because it was not well understood, and this vegan diet was very quickly assumed to be the cause of the baby's medical problems. However, veganism can be a very healthful dietary choice for parents to make for their children, provided they see to it that the diet is properly employed and therefore sufficient in vitamins and minerals.

Claim—with qualifier (4f)

While the mainstream media, in the wake of the Swinton case, has painted a portrait of veganism as a risky alternative lifestyle, it is for the most part simply a dietary decision a person makes, similar to the decision one may make to eat kosher. While the choice to observe a kosher diet is almost certainly a religious one, those who observe a vegan diet tend to fall into two schools of reasoning. Of the 154 vegans participating in the GVS, more than 90 percent of them admitted to becoming vegan for one of the following two reasons: ethics or health (Waldmann et al. 951). Those who subscribe to the first set of reasons choose to eliminate animal by-products because of moral concerns. They feel that animals should not be used to feed human beings. Often, people who subscribe to this belief also choose to eliminate leather, wool, and other animal-based materials from their wardrobes. According to a Web page devoted to teaching respect for animals, veganism is "an integral component of a cruelty-free lifestyle" ("Cruelty-Free Living").

Scholarly research cited

The second group of vegans excludes animal products for health reasons. Many people are lactose intolerant and therefore choose not to consume animal milk or similar products that may act as allergens upon their systems. Others eliminate foods such as red meat and cheese from their diets because of their high fat content. These vegans tend to regard veganism as a dietary option only and do not usually eliminate animal products from their wardrobes. Vegans who employ such a diet for their children tend to see the diet as a moral choice. Similar to those who encourage a kosher diet in their offspring because of their religious beliefs, these vegans attempt to pass down their set of beliefs and moral concerns to their children.

Veganism has gained exposure in recent years, especially after the details of the Swinton case brought it to the forefront of debates among nutritionists. The debate extends outside the medical field as well and has brought to society's attention both an opposition to and advocacy of veganism. Many celebrities, including singer Moby and Olympic gold-medal runner Carl Lewis, have claimed to be vegans. During the filming of the movie *Gladiator*, actor Joaquin Phoenix insisted that his costumes be made entirely of synthetic materials, as he not only excludes animals from his diet but from his wardrobe as well ("Joaquin Phoenix"). Restaurants serving vegan items are becoming more numerous and more popular, such as *Wild Ginger* in New York City and the *Happy Cow* restaurants in Los Angeles, with the latter chain providing lists online of vegetarian and vegan restaurants and health food stores across North and Central America and other continents as well as recipes for the home cooks (*Happy Cow Compassionate Eating Guide*).

> Ethical appeal: testimony from well-known people

For children, the diet rightly comes under more scrutiny. For a child's diet to be a healthy one in the eyes of pediatric medicine, it should take direction from the federal recommendations made in the food guide pyramids proposed in 1992 and revised in 2005 by the United States Department of Agriculture. According to medical journalist Karen Sullivan, the diet should be balanced and include at the very least "the required number of fruits and vegetables" as well as "good sources of protein and carbohydrates" (76). Sullivan lists some of what she calls "good quality protein" as including "fish, lean meat, chicken, turkey, cheese, milk, yogurt, tofu, nuts, nut butters, seeds, and legumes" (77). Perhaps most important in a child's diet is variety, which is precisely the problem that many nutritional experts express with the practice of veganism. "The keyword is balance," writes Sullivan (76). As long as a child eats a fair amount of foods from each group in the food guide pyramid and consumes a balanced group of nutrients and minerals, there should be no harm done to his or her general health. Almost half of the twelve items on Sullivan's list of proteins are appropriate for the very strictest vegan diet. Were a parent to eliminate meat, dairy, and fish from the sum of protein-rich foods he or she serves a child, there would still be a number of healthy proteins to choose from, as

> Expert testimony to support thesis

Use of image to make a visual argument (4i)

is shown in the legumes and nuts section of the vegan pyramid in Figure 1.

Fig. 1 The vegan food pyramid (Source: *Vegsource.com* at Univ. of Chicago Vegan Soc. Web. 18 May 2009).

While veganism is gaining some acceptance in today's society in spite of opposition, a stigma still attaches to those who choose to raise their children this way. This is evident in the way the media has focused on young Ilce Swinton's vegan diet, despite the fact that she was obviously otherwise neglected and abused. Such a restrictive diet appears on the surface to be dangerous for young, developing bodies; however, if the diet is applied properly, a baby or toddler can live a perfectly healthy young life eating only vegan foods. *Dr. Spock's Baby and Child Care*, a text long regarded as the foremost authority on parenting and pediatric health, plainly states that "children can thrive on vegetarian and vegan diets" (Spock and Needleman 338), with the cautionary note that children should also receive vitamin and mineral supplements.

1st opposing argument about diet

Authority to refute opposing view—with qualifier

In fact, adequate amounts of vitamins and minerals are a concern often associated with veganism. A mother's breast milk is allowed on even the strictest of vegan diets, but there have been cases in which babies fed breast milk of mothers on vegan diets suffered from malnutrition and/or vitamin B12 deficiency. Vitamin B12 "occurs naturally only in animal products" (Lawson). However, according to Maria Elena Jefferds, an epidemiologist who worked with the Centers for Disease Control in monitoring the babies involved in the aforementioned cases, vitamin B12 deficiency is a problem "that doesn't just affect vegetarians" (Lawson). Amy Joy Lanou, the nutrition director of Physicians for Responsible Medicine, who in fact testified during the 2003 Swinton case, warns that a vitamin B12 deficiency "is becoming more common among infants of vegan and vegetarian as well as meat-eating parents." She notes, however, that families who are vegetarians or vegans "generally take in much higher levels of important vitamins and minerals." And the GVS researchers found that only a few vitamins and minerals (calcium, iodine, and cobalamin) needed to be supplemented in the diets of the vegans they studied (Waldmann et al. 954).

2nd opposing argument about vitamin deficiency

Refutation of 2nd opposing argument

Logical appeal of facts from research

Those who oppose implementing vegan diets in children worry not only about what is lacking in the diet but also about the unnecessary additives that may interrupt a child's system. Soy milk, a staple of a vegan diet, may contain added sugar or artificial sweeteners, which can be disruptive to a child's body chemistry. Soy milk also contains phytoestrogens, hormonal compounds that, though helpful in preventing some cancers in adults, are unnecessary for children and may adversely affect their hormones (Sullivan 350). In addition, just as a child can develop an allergy to cow's milk, too much soy milk can lead to similarly unfavorable reactions.

3rd opposing argument about additives

However, these problems that could potentially arise from a vegan diet are easily remedied. Sugar-free soy milks are available, and as long as they are not used as a child's sole source of protein and calcium, there is no problem with their inclusion in a pediatric diet plan. As to the lack of vitamin B12 and other important vitamins and minerals in a vegan diet, "parents need to take special care that their children are getting enough," advises Dr.

Solutions to counter 3rd opposing argument

Spock, which he thinks is easily achieved: "A multivitamin and mineral supplement can offer the needed insurance" (Spock and Needleman 338). Lucy Moll, author of *The Vegetarian Child*, agrees: "Including B12 in your diet is easy . . . the solution is as simple as a bowlful of fortified breakfast cereal" (18).

Support for thesis: vegan diet is healthy

Not only does a vegan diet satisfy a child's health needs; it also "offers significant protection from many health complications" (Lanou). Many sources of traditional proteins, the food group most often lacking in a vegetarian or vegan diet, are very high in saturated and trans fats, which can lead to obesity in children, which in turn can lead to a variety of other medical ailments. Soy proteins are generally lower in fat and cholesterol than their animal-based counterparts, and there is some evidence that soy proteins actually help lower levels of bad cholesterol, a substance in the blood that, in abundance, can lead to such medical conditions as heart disease (Sullivan 350).

Dr. Spock has alerted parents to the dangers of animal milks: "Milk may actually pose health risks" (Spock and Needleman 340). Traditional animal milk is high in saturated fat and low in iron and essential fats. These healthy fats are more often found in vegetable sources, such as avocados, vegetable oils, and nut butters. Furthermore, cow milk is a common allergen in children, and just as many adults avoid animal milks because of lactose intolerance, it may be safest for children to avoid cow milk as well. Milk-based products can contribute to headaches and stomach ailments like diarrhea and constipation and can increase the risk of developing genetic diseases such as asthma, eczema, and juvenile onset diabetes (Spock and Needleman 341). Sullivan also addresses issues surrounding pediatric milk consumption. The recent use of genetically engineered bovine somatotrophin, a hormone naturally present in cow milk, to increase milk production in dairy cows has led to concern about human consumption of such chemically enhanced milk (29). While this hormone was banned in Canada and the United Kingdom more than ten years ago, it is still in use in the United States, though some large chain stores ban the sale of milk from cows treated with the hormone. Because

Support: dangers of dairy products

children generally take in a much greater amount of milk than their parents, the youngest Americans make up the group most at risk.

Although most of the blame for Ilce Swinton's poor health was laid on the vegan diet her mother and father fed her, it should be noted that although Silva Swinton admitted in court to feeding her daughter according to a vegan diet plan, she was not applying the diet properly. Because breast milk is not derived from animals, and none are harmed in its production, it is perfectly acceptable for a vegan baby to consume. Mrs. Swinton, however, chose not to feed Ilce with breast milk and chose instead to mix homemade soy formulas, which were obviously inadequately prepared. If a vegan diet is sensibly employed, it can be perfectly healthy, both for adults and children. In fact, vegans generally lead much healthier lifestyles than meat-eaters. The GVS reports that only three percent of the vegans studied were smokers (Waldmann et al. 949), and just one-quarter of participants regularly drank alcohol. The implication here is that vegans possess a greater awareness than the general population as to what are the building blocks of a healthy lifestyle. The GVS study concludes reassuringly with this: "Our data show that the participants of the GVS had an above average healthy lifestyle" (Waldmann et al. 955). Moreover, according to Dr. Spock, a meat-free diet, when set up with care, may be able to "offer even more long-term health benefits to you and your children" (Spock and Needleman 338). It is important that parents instill in their young children a sense of what is and what is not healthful so that they will make educated diet and lifestyle choices throughout their lives.

In light of the issues surrounding animal foods and the proven benefits of a meat-free diet, a viable dietary choice is to eliminate animal sources of nutrition from one's diet. This is especially true in the case of children, who are considerably more susceptible to the ills of poor nutrition and obesity. While there is still a great deal of opposition to veganism for children, much of it derived from society's general ignorance of the diet, raising a child as a vegan, with careful supplements of necessary vitamins and minerals, can be a safe and healthy choice.

Lead-in to conclusion: a return to the introductory story

Strong logical appeal of data from research study

Conclusion

Reiteration of thesis

Works Cited

"Cruelty-Free Living." *The Animal Spirit*. Homeless Animal Lifeline, 2009. Web. 15 May 2009.

Happy Cow Compassionate Eating Guide. Happy Cow's Vegetarian Guide, 2009. Web. 21 May 2009.

"Joaquin Phoenix." *IMDb. Internet Movie Database*, n.d. Web. 17 May 2009.

Lanou, Amy Joy. "Vegan's Bad Wrap." *Psychology Today* Sept./Oct. 2003: 6. *Academic Search Premier*. Web. 17 May 2009.

Lawson, Willow. "Brain Food." *Psychology Today* May/Jun. 2003: 22. *Academic Search Premier*. Web. 19 May 2009.

Moll, Lucy. *The Vegetarian Child*. New York: Perigee, 1997. Print.

Retsinas, Greg. "Couple Guilty of Assault in Vegan Case." *New York Times* 5 Apr. 2003, late ed.: A1. *LexisNexis*. Web. 19 May 2009.

Spock, Benjamin, and Robert Needleman. *Dr. Spock's Baby and Child Care*. 8th ed. New York: Pocket, 2004. Print.

Sullivan, Karen. *The Parent's Guide to Natural Health Care in Children*. Boston: Shambala, 2004. Print.

United States. Dept. of Agriculture. *MyPyramid.gov*. 7 May 2009. Web. 18 May 2009.

"Vegan." *Medline Plus. Merriam-Webster Medical Dictionary*, 2003. Web. 16 May 2009.

Waldmann, A., J. W. Koschizke, C. Leitzmann, and A. Hahn. "Dietary Intakes and Lifestyle Factors of a Vegan Population in Germany: Results from the German Vegan Study." *European Journal of Clinical Nutrition* 57.8 (2003): 947–55. *Academic Search Premier*. Web. 18 May 2009.

Annotations (left margin):

List includes *only* works actually cited in the paper

"n.d." used to indicate that no date was given for the site

Annotations (right margin):

New page for list of works cited

Documented in MLA style: chapters 11 and 12

5 🔑

Writing in All Your Courses

Writing is required in many, if not most, college courses. In fact, colleges and universities that emphasize the importance of writing often have initiatives or programs commonly referred to as Writing

Across the Curriculum (WAC) that encourage instructors in a broad array of disciplines to require writing in their courses. Specific guidelines for writing under pressure (a mainstay of college!), writing about literature, writing about community service, and common forms of writing in disciplines across the curriculum follow.

5a Writing under pressure: Essay exams and short-answer tests

Essay exams and short-answer tests are a challenge because you have to organize your thoughts and write quickly on an assigned topic.

For short-answer tests In short-answer tests, use your time wisely. So that you know how long you should spend on each question, count the number of questions and divide the number of minutes you have for taking the test by the number of questions (add 1 or 2 to the number you divide by, to give yourself time for editing and proofreading). Then, for each answer, decide which points are the most important ones to cover in the time you have available. You cannot afford to ramble or waffle during short-answer tests. Get to the point fast, and show what you know. To increase your confidence, answer the easiest question first.

For essay exams and short-answer tests Always read the questions carefully, and make sure you understand what each question asks you to do. Test writers often use the following verbs when specifying writing tasks:

analyze: divide into parts and discuss each part

argue: make a claim and point out your reasons

classify: organize people, objects, or concepts into groups

compare: point out similarities

contrast: point out differences

define: give the meaning of

discuss: state important characteristics and main points

evaluate: define criteria for judgment and examine good and bad points, strengths and weaknesses

explain: give reasons or make clear by analyzing, defining, contrasting, illustrating, and so on

illustrate: give examples from experience and reading

relate: point out and discuss connections

KEY POINTS
Guidelines for Essay Exams

1. **Prepare.** Prior to a content-based essay test, review assigned materials and notes; assemble facts; underline, annotate, and summarize significant information in your textbooks and other assigned materials; predict questions on the basis of the material your instructor has covered in detail in class; and draft some answers.

2. **Highlight or underline key terms in the assigned questions** (see the list on p. 81).

3. **Think positively about what you know.** Work out a way to emphasize the details you know most about. Stretch and relax.

4. **Make a scratch outline (see 1h) to organize your thoughts.** Jot down specific details as evidence for your thesis.

5. **Focus on providing detailed support for your thesis.** In an exam, this is more important than an elaborate introduction or conclusion.

6. **Check your essay for content, logic, and clarity.** Make sure you answered the question.

5b   Writing about literature

Pay careful attention to the content and form of the work of literature by reading the work more than once and highlighting significant passages. Then use the Key Points box on pages 83–84 to help you analyze the work systematically.

Here are some basic guidelines for writing about literature, followed by more specific guidelines for analyzing fiction, nonfiction, poetry, and drama.

- **Assume a larger audience than your instructor.** Think of your readers as people who have read the work but have not thought of the issues you did.

- **Make sure that you formulate a thesis.** Do not devote a large part of your essay to summary; assume that readers have read the work. Occasionally, though, you may need to include a brief summary of the whole or of parts to orient readers. Make sure you tell them not just what is in the work but also how you perceive and interpret important aspects of the work.

■ **Turn to the text for evidence, and do so often.** Text references, in the form of paraphrase or quotation, provide convincing evidence to support your thesis. But do not let your essay turn into a string of quotations.

KEY POINTS

Ten Ways to Analyze a Work of Literature

1. **Plot or sequence of events** What happens and in what order? What stands out as important?

2. **Theme** What is the message of the work, the generalization that readers can draw from it? A work may, for example, focus on making a statement about romantic love, jealousy, sexual repression, courage, ambition, revenge, dedication, treachery, honor, lust, greed, envy, social inequality, or generosity.

3. **Characters** Who are the people portrayed? What do you learn about them? Do one or more of them change, and what effect does that have on the plot or theme?

4. **Genre** What type of writing does the work fit into—parody, tragedy, love story, epic, sonnet, haiku, melodrama, comedy of manners, or mystery novel, for example? What do you know about the features of the genre, and what do you need to know? How does this work compare with other works in the same genre? What conventions does the author observe, violate, or creatively vary?

5. **Structure** How is the work organized? What are its major parts? How do the parts relate to each other?

6. **Point of view** Whose voice speaks to the reader and tells the story? Is the speaker or narrator involved in the action or an observer of it? How objective, truthful, and reliable is the speaker or narrator? What would be gained or lost if the point of view were changed?

7. **Setting** Where does the action take place? How are the details of the setting portrayed? What role, if any, does the setting play? What would happen if the setting were changed?

8. **Tone** From the way the work is written, what can you learn about the way the author feels about the subject matter and the theme? Can you, for example, detect a serious, informative tone, or is there evidence of humor, sarcasm, or irony?

(Continued)

(Continued)

9. **Language** What effects do the following have on the way you read and interpret the work: word choice, style, imagery, symbols, and figurative language?

10. **Author** What do you know, or what can you discover through research, about the author and his or her time and that author's other works? Does what you discover illuminate this work?

Writing about prose   As you read novels, short stories, memoirs, and biographies or autobiographies, consider these basic questions for thinking about what you read: What happened? When and where did it happen? Who did what? How were things done? Why? Then extend your inquiry by considering the ten options for analyzing literature in the preceding Key Points box in addition to the following:

- **Narrator** What is the author's attitude to and depiction of the narrator: omniscient, deceived, observant, truthful, biased, crazy?

- **Style** What do you notice in regard to the author's word choice, sentence length and structure, significant features?

- **Imagery** What effect do the figures of speech, such as similes, metaphors, and others, have on you? (see pp. 85–86 and section 34e)

- **Symbols** Are there objects or events with special significance or with hidden meanings?

- **Narrative devices** How, if at all, does the author use foreshadowing, flashback, leitmotif (a recurring theme), alternating points of view, turning point, and dénouement (outcome of plot)?

Writing about poetry   In addition to using some of the suggestions relating to prose, consider the following factors when you analyze a poem.

stanza: lines set off as a unit of a poem

rhyme scheme: system of end-of-line rhymes that you can identify by assigning letters to similar final sounds—for example, a rhyme scheme for couplets (two-line stanzas), *aa bb cc;* and a rhyme scheme for a sestet (a six-line stanza), *ababcc*

meter: number and pattern of stressed and unstressed syllables (or *metric feet*) in a line. Common meters are trimeter, tetrameter, and pentameter (three, four, and five metric feet). The following line is written in iambic tetrameter (four metric feet, each with one unstressed and one stressed syllable):

Whŏse woŏds/thĕse aŕe/Ĭ thínk/Ĭ knów.　　—Robert Frost

foot: unit (of meter) made up of a specific number of stressed and unstressed syllables

Writing about drama　As you prepare to write about a play, use any of the relevant points listed for prose and poetry, and in addition, focus on the following dramatic conventions:

structure of the play: acts and scenes

plot: episodes, simultaneous events, chronological sequence, causality, climax, turning point

characters: analysis of psychology, social status, relationships

setting: time, place, and description

time: real time depicted (all action takes place in the two hours or so of the play) or passage of time

stage directions: details about clothing, sets, actors' movements, expressions, and voices; information given to actors

scenery, costumes, music, lighting, props, and special effects: purpose and effectiveness

presentation of information: recognition of whether the characters in the play know things that the audience does not or whether the audience is informed of plot developments that are kept from the characters

Figurative language　The writers of literary works often use figures of speech to create images and intensify effects.

metaphor: implied comparison, with no *like* or *as*

　　The still, sad music of humanity　　　—William Wordsworth

　　The quicksand of racial injustice　　　—Martin Luther King, Jr.

simile: type of metaphor, but with two sides stated

　　Like as the waves make towards the pebbled shore,
　　So do our minutes hasten to their end.
　　　　　　　　　　　　　　　　—William Shakespeare

> The weather is like the government, always in the wrong.
> —Jerome K. Jerome

> Playing for teams other than the Yankees is "like having a crush on Cinderella but dating her ugly stepsisters."
> —David Wells (when Yankees pitcher)

irony: mismatch of words and meaning, meaning the opposite

> Yet Brutus says he was ambitious;
> And Brutus is an honourable man.
> —William Shakespeare, *Julius Caesar*

metonymy: substitution of one term for another closely associated with it

> *Washington* has set in motion a huge bailout. (that is, the U.S. government)

> The *pen* is mightier than the *sword*.

synecdoche: use of part for whole or whole for part

> The ranch owner rode into town with thirty *head* of cattle and two hired *guns*.

oxymoron: contradiction, as in "clean coal"

alliteration: repetition of consonant sounds

> He bravely breach'd his boiling bloody breast.
> —William Shakespeare

assonance: repetition of vowel sounds

> And feed deep, deep upon her peerless eyes   —John Keats

onomatopoeia: sound of word associated with meaning

> murmuring of innumerable bees   —Alfred, Lord Tennyson

personification: description of a thing as a person

> rosy-fingered dawn   —Homer

zeugma: use of a word with two or more other words, forming different and often humorous logical connections

> The art dealer departed in anger and a Mercedes.

> He came out in a top hat and a rash.

For more on using figurative language, see 34e.

Common Conventions in Writing about Literature

- **Tense** Use the present tense to discuss works of literature even when the author is no longer alive (41e).

- **Authors' Names** Use an author's full name the first time you mention it: "Stephen King." Thereafter, and always in parenthetical citations, use only the last name: "King," not "Stephen," and certainly not "Steve."

- **Author/Narrator Distinction** Make a clear distinction between author and narrator. The narrator is the person telling a story or serving as the voice of a poem and does not necessarily express the author's views. Often, the author has invented the persona of the narrator. Keep the terms distinct.

- **Titles of Works** Underline or italicize the titles of books, journals, and other works published as an entity and not as part of a larger work. Use quotation marks to enclose the title of a work forming part of a larger published work: short stories, essays, articles, songs, and short poems.

- **Quotations** Integrate quotations into your text, and use them to help make your point (10e). Avoid a mere listing and stringing together: "Walker goes on to say, . . . Then Walker states, . . ." When quoting two or three lines of poetry, separate lines with a slash (/). When using long quotations (more than three lines of poetry or four typed lines of prose), indent one inch, but do not add quotation marks; the indentation signals a quotation.

5c Sample paper 2: A student's literature paper

The following essay draft was written by sophomore Brian Cortijo for a course on multicultural American literature. The assignment was to compare and contrast two collections of stories according to the way they present a concept of identity and to focus on the texts themselves without turning to secondary sources. Cortijo was writing for his instructor and classmates, all of whom were familiar with the stories, so summary was unnecessary. He decided to focus on three of the ten areas in the Key Points box on pages 83–84: theme, setting, and language, specifically symbols. The draft is documented according to MLA 2009 style; in a later draft, the writer added a paper identification and a page break for the works-cited list. For more on this and MLA format for a final draft, see 21a and chapters 11–13.

Identity and the Individual Self

While distinct in their subject matter, the collections of stories presented in Sherman Alexie's *The Lone Ranger and Tonto Fistfight in Heaven* and Edwidge Danticat's *Krick? Krack!* are strikingly similar in the responses they evoke and in their ability, through detached or seemingly detached narratives, to create a sense of collective selfhood for the peoples represented in those narratives. Through connected stories, repetition of themes and events, shifting of narrative voice and honest, unapologetic discussion of the problems and the beauty of their personal experiences, Danticat and Alexie provide frank, cohesive portrayals of a Haitian and Native American peoplehood, respectively.

While it may not be the intention of these authors to address such a collective identity, it is clear that each is working from some conception of what that identity is, if not what it should be. Each author has symbols and characters that are used to display the identity in all its glory and shame, all its beauty and horror. For Alexie, both characters and objects are used, each for its own purpose. Most notable among these are Thomas Builds-the-Fire, a symbol of spirituality; Norma, who remains uncorrupted by the life imposed on the Indian peoples; and the seemingly ubiquitous drum, a symbol of religion that, if played, "might fill up the whole world" (23). Danticat, by contrast, concentrates more on objects than on characters to embody the ideals and the fears of the identity she is constructing through her narrative. The most prominent among these symbols are the bone soup, braids, and, more generally, hair.

Danticat's use of the bone soup in her last story, "Caroline's Wedding," and of the braids in her "Epilogue: Women Like Us" is of paramount importance to any claim of Haitian peoplehood, or Haitian womanhood, that she might try to make. The use of these elements is indicative of the loving imposition and inclusion of past generations into one's own, as well as the attempt to pass down all that has gone before to those who will one day bear the burden of what that past means. Thus, Hermine's soup is her daughter Gracina's soup as well, not because she eats of it but because

Introduces the works with complete names of authors

States thesis, emphasizing similarity

Refers to setting and theme

Now uses last names only

Points out how theme is addressed

Integrates quotation

Uses present tense

Analyzes symbols

Provides specific references to the text and to characters

those bones—that ancestry—are a part of her and she will one day be responsible for passing them (and it) on. Likewise, Danticat's reader in the epilogue must know her history and her lineage, not only to know how to braid her daughter's hair but for whom those braids are tied.

Returns to similarities in theme

Not surprisingly, as both books deal greatly with ancestry, they also deal with the transition and maintenance of an identity over time. Both authors assert that the collective self represented by the past is part and parcel of that embodied by the future—bound to it and inseparable. The one serves to define the other. Likewise, there is a call to make the efforts and struggles of the past worthwhile—to do better, if simply for the sake of one's ancestors.

Gives specific references

In *Tonto*, Alexie goes as far as to suggest that time is unimportant, if even existent, with respect to reality. Watches and keeping track of time are of no consequence. One's past will always be present, and the future always ahead, so there is no need to dwell on either, but that does not mean that they do not matter. A person lives in the now, but every "now" was once the future and will become the past (22). Alexie makes extensive use of the period of five hundred years, as though that is a length of time perceptible to the human consciousness, if appreciated more by the Indian.

Focuses on structure of work

Danticat's twisting of time is less blatant than Alexie's, but that may be because it is not necessary to speak of things in terms of hundreds of years. A few generations suffice, and the connections between her characters rely so heavily on the similarities between their stories that their relations are obvious. The suicide of the new mother in the first story is mirrored perfectly in the last, though they might take place fifty years apart. The question and answer game played by the sisters forces one to wonder whether Caroline and Grace's mother went through an experience similar to Josephine's mother's. Then there is Marie, who finds and claims the dead baby Rose, who very well may be the daughter of Josephine, who is connected to at least two of the other tales. Beyond the characters themselves, the reuse of the symbols of hair and the bloody water is striking. The Massacre River, which took the lives of many who attempted to cross it, is named (44), but it is also implied in the bloody stream

Provides specific details about characters

Points out relevance of symbols

of Grace's dream with her father, even though the character may know nothing of it. After years, generations, and physical separation, the events at that river seem to pervade the collective consciousness of the Haitian people.

Draws threads together with term "collective identities"

Clearly, these authors make no attempt to glorify the identity that they are helping to define. What is vital to the presentation of these collective identities is that they are transcendent of both time and location and that they are honest, if not visceral, in their telling. As beautifully told as these pieces of fiction are, they aim for truth and are unapologetic in presenting the faults and difficulties inherent in that truth. By telling these tales honestly and without pretense, Alexie and Danticat help to reveal what many may not be willing to admit or acknowledge about others or about themselves—the importance, beauty, and complexity of a collective selfhood.

Ends on a strong note, affirming thesis of "peoplehood"

New page in final MLA draft

Works Cited

Alexie, Sherman. *The Lone Ranger and Tonto Fistfight in Heaven.* New York: HarperCollins, 1994. Print.

Danticat, Edwidge. *Krick? Krack!* New York: Vintage-Random, 1996. Print.

Follows MLA for citing books (12a, 12c)

5d Writing about community service

Service learning projects link a college to the community. For such projects, students volunteer for community service, often related to the content of a discipline or a particular course. They then must demonstrate what they learned from the service experience. You'll probably do three main types of writing for community service projects:

1. You'll work with the site supervisor to outline the goals, activities, and desired outcomes of the service project.

2. During the service work, you'll prepare reports to a supervisor, daily records, summaries of work completed, and documents such as flyers and brochures (chapter 26).

3. In the course, you'll write reflective reports that describe the service objectives and your experiences and that assess the project's success.

To reflect fully on the work you do, keep an ongoing journal of your activities so that you can provide background about the setting and the work, and give specific details about the problems you encounter and their solutions. Link your comments to the goals of the project.

Section 24e shows an example of a Web site designed by a student in a course devoted to community service.

5e Writing and researching across the curriculum

One semester you may be writing about *Hamlet*, and the next semester you may move to exploring the census, writing about Chopin's music, discussing geological formations, researching the history of the civil rights movement, or preparing a paper on Sigmund Freud and dreams. You may be expected to write scientific laboratory reports or to manipulate complex statistical data and to use a style of documentation different from one you learned in an English course.

Find out which style of writing and documenting is expected in each of your courses.

LANGUAGE AND CULTURE
The Cultures of the Academic Disciplines

When you take a course in a new discipline, you are joining a new academic community with established conventions and ways of thinking and writing. Use the following strategies to get acquainted with the discipline's conventions.

- Listen carefully to lectures and discussion; note the specialized vocabulary used in the discipline. Make lists of new terms and definitions.

- Read the assigned textbook, and note the conventions that apply in writing about the field.

- Use subject-specific dictionaries and encyclopedias to learn about the field. Examples include *Encyclopedia of Religion* and *Encyclopedia of Sociology*.

- Subscribe to e-mail discussion lists (23b) in the field to discover what issues people are concerned about.

- When given a writing assignment, make sure you read samples of similar types of writing in that discipline.

- Talk with your instructor about the field, its literature, and readers' expectations.

TECH NOTE

Useful Sites for Writing Across the Curriculum

Try these Web sites for useful advice on writing in all your courses and for more links to other sites:

- The Dartmouth College site with advice to nonmajors on writing in the humanities, sciences, and social sciences

- The George Mason University Writing Center site on writing in public affairs, management, psychology, biology, and history

---

5f Writing and researching in the humanities and arts

Guidelines

- Consult primary sources, such as original works of literature, or attend original performances, such as plays, films, poetry readings, and concerts.

- Form your own interpretations of works. The first person *I* is used in personal and expository writing more than in other disciplines.

- Use secondary sources (works of criticism) only after you have formed your own interpretations and established a basis for evaluating the opinions expressed by others.

- Look for patterns and interpretations supported by evidence, not for one right answer to a problem.

- Use the present tense to refer to what writers have said: *Emerson points out that . . .*

- Use MLA guidelines (chapters 11–13) or *The Chicago Manual of Style* (chapter 19) for documentation style.

You will find examples of students' humanities and arts research papers in sections 4j, 5c, and chapters 13 and 20.

5g Writing and researching in the natural sciences

Most writing in the natural sciences (such as astronomy, biology, chemistry, and physics) and applied sciences (agriculture, engineering, environmental studies, computer science, and nursing, for example) concerns itself with empirical data—that is, with the explanation and analysis of data gathered from a controlled laboratory experiment or from detailed observation of natural phenomena. Frequently, the study will be a replication of a previous experiment, with the new procedure expected to uphold or refute the hypothesis of that previous experiment.

Guidelines

- Focus on empirical data.
- Avoid personal anecdotes.
- Report firsthand original experiments and calculations.
- Present a hypothesis.
- Give background information in the introductory section of your paper, a section sometimes called "Review of the Literature."
- Use the present perfect tense to introduce a survey of the literature: *Several studies have shown that . . .*
- Use the past tense for details of specific studies: *Cocchi et al. isolated the protein fraction . . .*
- Use the passive voice more frequently than in other types of writing: *The muscle was stimulated . . .*
- Be prepared to write according to a set format, using sections with headings such as Abstract, Method, Results, Discussion, Conclusion.
- Use APA (chapters 14–16) or CSE (chapter 17) documentation style, or follow specific style manuals in scientific areas.

KEY POINTS

A Model for the Organization of an Experimental Paper in the Sciences

1. **Title page:** running head, title, author's name, institution
2. **Table of contents:** necessary for a long paper or for a paper posted online
3. **Abstract:** a summary of your research and your conclusions (about 100 to 175 words)
4. **Title, followed by background information:** why the study is necessary, your hypothesis, review of other studies
5. **Method:** with headed subsections on participants, apparatus, procedures

(Continued)

(Continued)

6. **Results:** backed up by statistics or survey data, with tables, charts, and graphs where appropriate

7. **Discussion:** evaluation of the results from the perspective of your hypothesis

8. **Conclusion and recommendations:** implications of the results of the study and suggestions for further research

9. **References:** a list of the works cited in the paper

10. **Tables and figures:** check with your instructor about placing these at the end or within your text.

Abstract Here is student Jennifer Richards' abstract for her paper "Leroy, the 'Go Fishin' Robot," written at the University of Florida in a computer engineering course. She accompanied the paper with a photograph of Leroy the robot. You can find the complete paper at <http://mil.ufl.edu/imdl/papers/IMDLFall2000.html>.

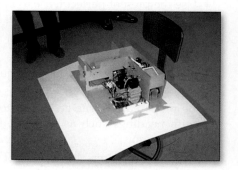

    This report outlines the complete design of Leroy and describes the desired behaviors and actions necessary for him to complete the set objectives. These objectives include the ability to accept and manage a hand of cards to play a game of "Go Fish" with human counterparts. In order to interact, Leroy and the players must communicate using pushbuttons and LEDs. Figures detailing the construction and arrangement of these critical components are included in this report. Other key parts include the recirculation mechanism where Leroy's cards are kept, the "fishpond" that holds the deck, and the "body" platform that encompasses all moving parts. This report also describes a model test of Leroy's desired behaviors and functions. This test involves a real time investigation into the ability of Leroy to perform a set of critical tasks.

Excerpt from a student's lab report The following annotated excerpt is from Natasha Williams's lab report on microbial genetics conjugation, written for a cell biology course.

Discussion	Major section heading centered
Conjugation involves transfer by appropriate mating types. F+ and Hfr are donor cells with respectively low and high rates of genetic transfer. F- cells are recipients. Contact between the cell types is made by a conjugation bridge called an F pilus extending from the Hfr cell. The donor chromosome appears to be linearly passed through the connecting bridge. Sometimes this transfer is interrupted. The higher the frequency of recombination, the closer the gene is to the beginning of the circular DNA. In this way one can determine the sequence of genes on the chromosome.	Passive voice common in lab reports Use of *one* for general reference
Table 1 shows consistently that histidine is the last amino acid coded with the smallest number of recombinants, and arginine is the second to last coded with the next smallest number of recombinants. However, the results obtained for proline and leucine/threonine vary.	Discussion of table included in paper

5h Writing and researching in the social sciences

The social sciences (anthropology, business, economics, geography, political science, psychology, and sociology) examine how society and social institutions are constructed, how they work (or don't work), and what the ramifications of structures, organizations, and human behavior are.

Two types of writing prevail in the social sciences. Some writers use empirical scientific methods similar to those used in the natural sciences to gather, analyze, and report their data, with a focus on people, groups, and their behavior. Then there are writers in the social sciences who are more social philosophers than scientists. In fields such as public policy and international relations, researchers examine trends and events to draw their conclusions. Ethnographic studies are common, too, with researchers taking detailed notes from observing a situation they want to analyze—the behavior of fans at a baseball game, for example.

When you are given a writing assignment in the social sciences, find out whether your instructor expects an empirical study or a more philosophical, interpretive essay.

Guidelines

- Understand that the research method you choose will determine what kind of writing is necessary and how you should organize the writing.
- Decide whether your purpose is to describe accurately, measure, inform, analyze, or synthesize information.
- Decide what kind of data you will use: figures and statistics from experimental research, surveys, the census, or questionnaires; observational data from case studies, interviews, and on-site observations; or your reading.
- For an observational study, take careful field notes that describe accurately everything you see. Concentrate on the facts rather than interpretations. Save the interpretive possibilities for the sections of your paper devoted to discussion and recommendations.
- Examine research studies in the field, evaluate their methodology, compare and contrast results with those of other studies, and draw conclusions based on the empirical evidence uncovered. Devote a section of the paper to a review of the literature. (If your field is public policy, international relations, or ethnography, however, your writing will examine trends and draw conclusions, an approach closer to the humanities than to the natural sciences.)
- Look for accurate, up-to-date information, and evaluate it systematically against stated criteria.
- Use sections and headings in your paper. See the APA paper in chapter 16 written as the research paper in a first-year composition course.
- Report facts and data. Add comments and expressions such as "I think" only when this is a specific requirement of the task.
- Use the past tense to refer to another researcher's work: *Smith's study (2004) showed that . . .*
- Use the passive voice when it is not important for readers to know the identity of the person performing the action: *The participants were timed . . .*
- Present statistical data in the form of tables, charts, and graphs whenever possible (chapter 22).
- Follow the APA *Publication Manual* or whichever style manual is recommended.

Turn to chapter 16 for an example of a complete documented paper in the social sciences.

PART 2

Research/Sources/ Documentation

6 The Research Process: A Conversation with Sources 99

7 Searching for Sources 110

8 How to Evaluate Sources 126

9 How to Avoid Plagiarizing 133

10 How to Use, Integrate, and Document Sources 145

ONLINE RESOURCES

www.cengage.com/english/raimes

Companion online resources are available for sections throughout this part. We invite you to visit the book's Web site for more information and direct access.

PART 2

Research/Sources/Documentation

6 **The Research Process: A Conversation with Sources** 99

6a What's involved in a research paper 99
6b Set a schedule 102
6c Use primary and secondary sources 104
6d Consult print and online reference works to get you started 105
6e Move from research question to working thesis 107
6f Write a purpose statement or a proposal 108
6g Tips for writing, revising, and editing a research paper 109

7 **Searching for Sources** 110

7a Starting the search for sources on a topic 111
7b Search engines and keyword searching 113
7c Getting the most out of Google, advanced searches, and online alerts 116
7d Databases 118
7e Print sources: Books and articles 120
7f Web sources 123
7g Visual sources 124

8 **How to Evaluate Sources** 126

8a Read sources critically 126
8b Recognize a scholarly article in print 127
8c Recognize a scholarly article online 128

8d Evaluate works originating in print 129
8e Evaluate Web sources and learn to recognize junk 130

9 **How to Avoid Plagiarizing** 133

9a The seven sins of plagiarism 134
9b How to avoid even the suspicion of plagiarism 135
9c Know why, how, and what to cite 136
9d Keep track of sources 138
9e Record information and set up a working bibliography (with sample) 140
9f Use bibliographical software, databases, and Word 2007 to help you keep records 143

10 **How to Use, Integrate, and Document Sources** 145

10a Interact with your sources: Annotate and make notes (with sample) 145
10b Put yourself in your paper, and synthesize sources 146
10c Organize your essay by ideas, not sources 146
10d Summarize and paraphrase 147
10e Quote accurately 150
10f Indicate the boundaries of a source citation in your text 154
10g Introduce and integrate source material 155
10h Document to fit the discipline 156
10i One source, four systems of documentation 157

6 🔑

The Research Process: A Conversation with Sources

What is research and why do it? You think you might have swine flu, and you try to find out what the symptoms are and the best way to treat them. That's research. You want to buy an XM satellite radio player, but you don't know anything about the features, brands, and prices. You order catalogs, talk to salespeople, go to stores, ask friends what they recommend, read consumer magazines, and surf the Web. That's research, too. And when your English professor asks you to write a paper on, say, the role of government in protecting the environment, research helps you as you interview experts, find reliable print and online sources, consult government documents, and get help from librarians. Doing research is finding out as much as possible about an issue, formulating a research question, and then attempting to find answers to that question. Entering into the ongoing debates around an issue is a vital part of daily life; contributing to the discussion is an essential part of academic and scholarly work.

6a Know what's involved in a research paper

1. Know the requirements, and set a realistic schedule   Find out what the demands of the assignment are, such as length, due date, information to include, number and types of sources, documentation style, and manuscript format. Set a week-by-week or day-by-day schedule for the steps in the process (see 6b).

2. Assemble the tools you will need   Have on hand a research notebook, a flash drive, printer cartridges, index cards, highlighting pens, folders, paper clips, a stapler, self-stick notes, and a card for the library copier. Set up computer folders for all your research files, such as "Drafts," "Notes from Sources," and "Works Cited."

3. Do preliminary research to establish your topic   Make sure you understand and answer the assigned question or address the assigned topic. If you select your own topic, check with your instructor to make sure it is appropriate. Do preliminary research in reference works to browse for topics and understand the issues. Narrow the topic so that it is manageable for the number of pages you intend to write (see 1e). Also be sure to choose a topic that will engage and sustain not only readers' interests but also your own, with connections to your own experience whenever possible. If your topic is assigned, make sure you understand the terms used in the assignment (5a). Chapter 7 shows you how to go about searching.

4. Develop your research question   For a full-scale research paper, design a research question that establishes what you know and what you want to discover. The answer you find as you do research is likely to become your thesis (see 1f and 6e).

5. Write a statement of purpose or a proposal   Section 6f explains how to write both.

6. Determine types of sources and how to find them   Decide which types of primary and secondary sources will give you the best results (use section 6c and chapter 7 to help you with this stage); then draw up a plan of action. Allow large blocks of time for locating sources. You'll see from chapter 7 that this work cannot be done in just an hour or two.

7. Look for and evaluate sources, make copies, and keep full and accurate records   Select only reliable sources (see chapter 8). Record full bibliographical information for every source you consult (9e). Download, print, or make photocopies of your source material whenever possible so that you can annotate and make notes later. There are several computer applications and online tools that can help you save, tag, and annotate resources (such as EndNote and Zotero); see 9f for more on reference tools.

8. Take precise notes   Paraphrase and summarize as often as possible while taking notes (10d). Be sure to use your own words and write down why the information is useful or how you might integrate it into your paper (10g). Make sure you copy quotations exactly as they are written (10e), using quotation marks or a colored font. In your notes, record all page numbers of print sources. Copy and save Web addresses in a Favorites file or a specially named file for your paper; be sure to also record the date of access along with the address.

9. Establish your thesis or hypothesis   Digest your material, and determine your focus. Your paper should not simply string together what others have said with no commentary from you. Especially in the humanities, use your research to help form opinions and arrive at conclusions about your topic. Readers want to find *you* and your ideas in your paper (6f, 10b). Develop a working thesis as soon as you can, and make lists of supporting evidence and specific details from what you know and what you read. In the sciences and social sciences, it is more usual to form a hypothesis, present the evidence, and then draw conclusions (5g and 5h).

At some point here, when you decide you have something to say about what you think and what your sources say, make a plan or a map, and start a rough first draft (1h).

10. Write drafts: Revise, revise, revise   Write more than one draft. As with almost all writing for college and beyond, revision is an essential step in the writing process. You should not expect to produce a perfect first draft. Make an outline of each draft to check on your coverage of the main points and the logic of your argument (1h).

11. Organize your drafts   Be sure to save copies of each draft as a new file so you can keep a record of the changes you have made. It's a good idea to develop a consistent naming convention so you can quickly see which file includes your most recent draft. You can also distinguish among your earliest rough drafts, your later revisions, and your final copyedited versions by using keywords like "rough," "revised," and "edited" along with numbers, as shown in this sample course folder:

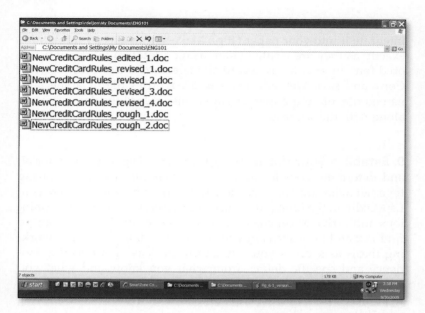

Be sure to follow any file-naming conventions that your instructor provides if you will be turning in your work electronically.

12. Acknowledge and document all your sources   Avoid plagiarism by providing information in your text every time you not only quote but also refer to the ideas you find in a source (10d, 10e).

13. Prepare a list of works cited   Follow a clear and consistent set of conventions (spacing, indentation, names, order, and punctuation of entries) when you prepare a list of works cited (see chapters 12–13 and 15–20). Then compare your citations with your list. Make sure that every item on your list appears in your paper and that every work referred to in your paper appears on your list. Use a system of checkmarks in both places as you read a draft.

6b   Set a schedule

Get started as early as you can. As soon as a project is assigned, set a tentative schedule for searching, evaluation, and drafting, working backward from the date the paper is due and splitting your time so that you know when you absolutely must move on to the next step. On the next page is a sample time block schedule that you can download, print, or adapt. You will find that in reality, several tasks overlap and the divisions are not neat. If you finish a block before the deadline, move on and give yourself more time for the later blocks.

RESEARCH SCHEDULE

Starting date:

Date final draft is due:

Block 1: Getting started

Understand the requirements.

Select a topic or narrow a given topic.

Determine the preliminary types of sources to use.

Do preliminary research to discover the important issues.

Organize research findings in computer files.

Write a research question.

Complete by _____

Block 2: Reading, researching, and evaluating sources

Find and copy print and online sources.

Annotate and evaluate the sources.

Write summaries and paraphrases and make notes.

Set up a working bibliography.

Complete by _____

Block 3: Planning and drafting

Formulate a working thesis.

Write a purpose statement, proposal, and/or an outline.

Write a first draft.

Complete by _____

Block 4: Evaluating the draft and getting feedback

Put the draft away for a day or two—but continue collecting useful sources.

Outline the draft and evaluate its logic and completeness.

Plan more research as necessary to fill any gaps.

Get feedback from instructor and classmates.

Complete by _____

Block 5: Revising, preparing list of works cited, editing, presenting

Revise the draft.

Prepare a list of works cited.

Design the format of the paper.

Edit.

Proofread the final draft.

Complete by _____
(final deadline for handing in)

6c   Use primary and secondary sources

First-year college writing assignments often ask student writers to engage with and write about *primary sources*—a poem, a short story, a
historical document, scientific data, or a photograph. First-year research
assignments typically require students to consider and include *secondary sources*—a literary analysis of a work of literature or a historical
event, an interpretation of data, an art critic's commentary on a photograph—to expand, enrich, and challenge the writer's ideas.

Primary sources   Primary sources are the firsthand, raw, or original
materials that researchers study and analyze, such as historical documents, visuals, journals and letters, autobiographies, memoirs, government statistics, and speeches. You can examine works of art, literature,
and architecture or watch or listen to performances and programs. You
can study or initiate case studies or scientific experiments and take
extensive field notes. You can also conduct interviews and use data collected from questionnaires. The use of such primary sources can bring
an original note to your research and new information to your readers.

Interviews   Interview people who have expert knowledge of your
topic. Plan a set of interview questions, but do not stick so closely to
your script that you fail to follow up on good leads in your respon-
dent's replies. Ask permission to tape-record the interview; otherwise, you will have to take quick and accurate notes, particularly if
you want to quote. Check the functioning of your tape recorder be-
forehand. Make note of the date, time, and place of the interview.
While it is possible to conduct interviews via e-mail or instant messaging, the development of good questions and performing the background research on your interviewee will be just as important.

Surveys and questionnaires   Designing useful questionnaires is tricky
because much depends on the number and sample of respondents
you use, the types of questions you ask, and the methods you employ to analyze the data. Embark on survey research only if you have
been introduced to the necessary techniques in a college course or
have consulted experts in this area. You may also need permission to
conduct research on human subjects. You can also use low-cost, user-
friendly online survey applications, such as *SurveyMonkey*.

Secondary sources   Secondary sources are analytical works that
comment on and interpret other works, such as primary sources.
Common in the humanities, examples include reviews, discussions,
biographies, critical studies, analyses of literary or artistic works or

events, commentaries on current and historical events, class lectures, and electronic discussions.

6d Consult print and online reference works to get you started

Reference works provide basic factual information and lead to other sources. You can access many standard reference works online. However, use reference works only to get started with basic information and to help you explore a topic and find out what issues the topic involves. Then quickly move beyond them. Check to see if your library subscribes to the huge online database for reference works *xreferplus*.

Encyclopedias Encyclopedias provide an overview of the issues involved in a complex topic. Some may also provide extensive bibliographies of other useful sources, so they can help you develop your research and formulate a research proposal if you are asked to provide one.

General print and online encyclopedias such as *Columbia Encyclopedia, Encyclopaedia Britannica,* and subject-specific encyclopedias such as the *Internet Encyclopedia of Philosophy* or *Berkshire Encyclopedia of World History* can help you get started.

TECH NOTE

Using *Wikipedia*

Be aware that while the online *Wikipedia* can be useful in getting you started with information on a topic, it is a work in progress and constantly subject to error and revision. So check any information you find there, and do not include it as a source. In addition, your instructor may not recommend using it. Even the founder of *Wikipedia*, Jimmy Wales, has said, "You're in college; don't cite the encyclopedia."

Bibliographies (also known as *guides to the literature*) You can find lists of books and articles on a subject in online bibliographical databases such as the following: *Books in Print, International Medieval Bibliography, MLA International Bibliography of Books and Articles on the Modern Languages and Literature, New Books on Women and Feminism,* and *Political Science Bibliographies.*

Biographies Read accounts of people's lives in biographical works such as *Who's Who, Dictionary of American Biography, Biography Index: A Cumulative Index to Biographic Material in Books and Magazines,*

Contemporary Authors, Dictionary of Literary Biography, African American Biographies, Chicano Scholars and Writers, Lives of the Painters, and *American Men and Women of Science.*

Directories   Directories provide lists of names and addresses of people, companies, and institutions. These are useful for setting up interviews and contacting people when you need information. Examples are *Jane's Space Directory* and *Communication Media in Higher Education: A Directory of Academic Programs and Faculty in Radio-Television-Film and Related Media.*

Dictionaries   For etymologies, definitions, synonyms, and spelling, consult *The American Heritage Dictionary of the English Language,* 4th edition; *Oxford English Dictionary* (multiple volumes—useful for detailed etymologies and usage discussions); *Facts on File* specialized dictionaries; and other specialized dictionaries such as *Dictionary of Literary Terms* and *Dictionary of the Social Sciences.*

Dictionaries of quotations   For a rich source of traditional quotations, go to *Bartlett's Familiar Quotations;* for more contemporary quotations, searchable by topic, go to *The Columbia World of Quotations* (both are available online). Also consult specialized dictionaries of quotations, such as volumes devoted to chess, law, religion, fishing, women, and Wall Street.

Collections of articles of topical interest and news summaries   *CQ (Congressional Quarterly)* weekly reports, *Facts on File* publications, and *CQ Almanac* are available in print and online by subscription. *Newsbank* provides periodical articles on microfiche, classified under topics such as "law" and "education," and *SIRS (Social Issues Resources Series)* appears in print and online.

Statistics and government documents   Among many useful online sources are *Statistical Abstract of the United States, Current Index to Statistics, Handbook of Labor Statistics, Occupational Outlook Handbook,* U.S. Census publications, *GPO Access, UN Demographic Yearbook, Population Index,* and *Digest of Education Statistics.*

Almanacs, atlases, and gazetteers   For population statistics and boundary changes, see *The World Almanac, Countries of the World,* or *Information Please.* For locations, descriptions, pronunciation of place names, climate, demography, languages, natural resources, and industry, consult a gazetteer such as *Columbia-Lippincott Gazetteer of the World* and the *CIA World Factbook* series.

General critical works Read what scholars have to say about works of art and literature in *Contemporary Literary Criticism* and in *Oxford Companion* volumes (such as *Oxford Companion to Art* and *Oxford Companion to African American Literature*).

Indexes Indexes of articles appearing in periodicals will start you off in your search for an article on a specific topic. Print indexes, such as *Readers' Guide to Periodical Literature*, list works published before 1980. More recent publications are listed in online indexes, such as *Applied Science and Technology Index, Engineering Index, Art Index*, and *ERIC* (Educational Resources Information Center). An index will provide a complete citation: author, title, periodical, volume, date, and page numbers, often with an abstract, but no complete text. Then you have to locate the periodical in a library or use a database to find the actual article. Note that the *Readers' Guide* is now available online in a mega edition, including full texts of recent articles.

6e Move from research question to working thesis

Designing a research question For a research paper, design a research question that gets at the heart of what you want to discover. Your question should contain concrete keywords that you can search (see 7b) rather than general terms or abstractions. The answer you find as you do research is likely to become your thesis. If you find huge amounts of material on your question and realize that you would have to write a book (or two) to cover all the issues, narrow your question.

Questions Needing Narrowing	Revised Questions
How important are families? *Too broad: important to whom and for what? No useful keywords to search.*	In what ways does a stable family environment contribute to an individual's future success?
What problems does the Internet cause? *Too broad: what types of problems? What aspects of the Internet?*	What types of Internet controls would protect individual privacy?
What are the treatments for cancer? *Too wide-ranging: volumes could be and have been written on this.*	For which types of cancer are the success rates of radiation therapy the most promising?

Formulating a working thesis If your research question is "Should Internet controls be established to protect individual privacy?" as you read and do research, you will probably move toward either a "yes" or "no" answer to the question. At this point, you will formulate a working thesis in the form of a statement of opinion, which will help drive the organization of your paper (see also 1f).

KEY POINTS
Writing a Working Thesis

1. **Make sure it is a statement.** A phrase or a question is not a thesis: "Internet controls" is a topic, not a thesis statement. "Are Internet controls needed?" is a question, not a thesis statement.

2. **Make sure it is not merely a statement of fact.** "About 50 percent of U.S. residents are active users of the Internet" is a statement that cannot be developed and argued. A statement of fact does not let readers feel the need to read on to see what you have to say.

3. **Make sure it does more than announce the topic.** "This paper will discuss Internet controls" is inadequate because your thesis statement should give information about or offer an informed opinion on the topic: "Service providers, Internet users, and parents share the responsibility of establishing Internet controls to protect an individual's privacy."

4. **Be prepared to change and refine your thesis as you do more research.** Changes and refinements are essential as you discover more about what your topic entails.

6f Write a purpose statement or a proposal

Begin with "what do I know about this topic?" And then ask "what do I want to find out?" Write a simple statement of purpose after you have done some preliminary research. This statement may become more developed or later even change completely, but it will serve to guide your first steps in the research process. Here is an example:

> The purpose of this documented paper is to persuade general adults that films based on historical events—such as *Frost/Nixon*—should give precedence to a good story over historical accuracy because adults expect entertainment rather than education when they go to the movies.

Your instructor may also ask for an outline (1h) or for a fuller proposal with a working bibliography attached (9e). Once you have your brief purpose statement, you can use it as a basis for a proposal in narrative or list form, covering background information, establishing your connection to the topic, addressing what you regard as your purpose and audience, and including your research question.

6g Tips for writing, revising, and editing a research paper

WHAT NOT TO DO

- Do not expect to complete a polished draft in one sitting.
- Do not write the title and the first sentence and then panic because you feel you have nothing left to say.
- Do not constantly imagine your instructor's response to what you write.
- Do not worry about coherence—a draft by its nature is something that you work on repeatedly and revise for readers' eyes.
- Do not necessarily begin at the beginning, and especially do not think you must first write a dynamite introduction. That is why you need to set aside time to revise!

WHAT TO DO

- Wait until you have a block of time available before you begin writing a draft of your paper.
- Turn off your cell phone, log out of Facebook, close the door, and tell yourself you will not emerge from the room until you have written several pages.
- Promise yourself a reward when you meet your target—a refrigerator break or a trip to a nearby ice cream store, for instance.
- Assemble your copy of the assignment, your purpose statement and thesis statement, all your copies of sources, your research notebook and any other notes, your working bibliography, and your proposal or outline. Yes, that's a lot! So start early.
- Write the parts you know most about first.
- Write as much as you can as fast as you can. If you only vaguely remember a reference in your sources, just write what you can remember—but keep writing, and don't worry about gaps: *As so*

and so (who was it? Jackson?) has observed, malls are taking the place of city centers (check page reference).

- Write the beginning—the introduction—only after you have some ideas on paper that you feel you can introduce.
- Write at least something on each one of the points in your outline. Start off by asking yourself: What do I know about this point, and how does it support my thesis? Write your response in your own words without worrying about who said what in which source. You can check your notes and fill in the gaps later.
- Write until you feel you have put down on the page or screen your main points and you have made reference to most of your source material.

If you can, set your draft aside and do not look at it for a while. In the meantime, follow up on research leads, find new sources, discuss your draft with your instructor, classmates, or a tutor at your campus writing center, and continue writing ideas in your research notebook. To revise your draft, make an outline of what you have written and ask these questions:

- Have I covered the most important points?
- When I read the paper aloud, where do I hesitate to try to sort out the meaning? (Watch for those worried frowns!)
- Do I come across as someone with ideas on this topic? What opinions do I offer?
- Have I cited sources accurately and used summary, paraphrase, and quotation responsibly? (See chapters 9 and 10 for more on this important point.)
- Where do I need to provide more evidence from sources?

7 ⚷

Searching for Sources

Doing research involves looking for and collecting information on a topic to develop and refine your own views. When you conduct research for an academic paper, you gather information that you need to evaluate as valid, reliable, and relevant. Then you cite this source information in your paper in ways that are specific to the discipline.

No matter how many sources you find and use, your paper should be a synthesis of the main issues you come across in your research. In the sciences, the structuring of information is more important than the personal opinion of the writer. In the humanities, the writer is often more in evidence, so avoid the danger of listing an abundance of sources without coming to some conclusion or without presenting your point of view. A good research paper is not simply a mindless compilation of sources. Rather, let your paper establish your place in the ongoing conversation about the topic. Let it present you in interaction with your topic and engaged with the ways others have addressed that topic.

Once you find a good source, always make sure it is readily available to you again for rereading, summarizing, discussing, and so on. Section 9f provides information about online sites that help with saving and organizing the sources you find.

7a Starting the search for sources on a topic

General reference sources in print or online   Ask librarians for their recommendations of useful reference sources, bibliographies, databases, indexes, and when appropriate, serious informational Web sites. Encyclopedias, specialized dictionaries, bibliographies, and government documents may be helpful starting points (see 6d). These sources will give you a sense of the field and the issues, but be sure to move beyond them to more substantial sources.

Web directories   Libraries, colleges, and other organizations provide valuable subject directories for researchers. These allow you to start with a subject area and drill down until you get to specific sites on specific topics.

- *Research Quickstart* at the University of Minnesota with lists of sources in many academic subjects

- *Michigan Electronic Library* (MeL), a University of Michigan site

- *Internet Public Library*, run by librarians, offering a guide to subject collections and an "Ask an IPL Librarian" feature, which allows you to e-mail a question about a research project to librarians for evaluation and possible response within three days

- *INFOMINE*, a University of California, Riverside, site, with scholarly resources in medical sciences, business, and visual arts, along with general references

- *Voice of the Shuttle*, a University of California, Santa Barbara, site, listing research sources in the humanities
- *Library of Congress*, important for the listing of its own collections
- *Librarians' Index to the Internet*, which includes useful links to sites in cross-disciplinary subject areas, some presenting a specific viewpoint
- *Intute*, an easy-to-use database published by seven universities, with sources in science and technology, arts and humanities, social sciences, and health and life sciences
- *The WWW Virtual Library*, providing a common access point to Web catalogs/directories maintained by different institutions across the world
- *MLA International Bibliography*, providing "a classified listing and subject index for books and articles published on modern languages, literatures, folklore, and linguistics"

Online library subscription databases   Databases of abstracts and full-text general and scholarly articles are a good place to start serious online searching on topics not demanding the most recent data. They provide abstracts and full texts of works previously published in print. Material is best accessed by keyword searching (7b). Examples of databases with full texts of scholarly articles (most of which are also available in print) include EBSCO *Academic Search Premier* and many other databases; Wilson *Readers' Guide to Periodical Literature*; Gale Cengage *Expanded Academic ASAP*; Gale Cengage *InfoTrac College Edition*; *JSTOR*; databases sponsored and searched by OCLC *FirstSearch*; LexisNexis *Academic*; *ERIC* (for education); *PsycINFO* (for psychology); *PAIS* (for public affairs); Sage *Sociology Collection*; *Art Index*; *ScienceDirect*; and *ISI Web of Science*. In addition, some databases specialize in images (for example, *ARTstore*) or quantitative statistics (for example, *Social Explorer*).

Visit the Web site of your college library to find out what is available at your school. For more on databases, see 7d.

Online literary texts   Complete works that are out of copyright are available for downloading at, for example, *Project Bartleby*, *Project Gutenberg*, *Oxford Text Archive*, and *University of Virginia Electronic Text Center*; *The Internet Archive* <http://www.archive.org> also includes literary and nonliterary texts as well as audio and moving-image archives.

7b Search engines and keyword searching

Researchers can access vast resources on the Web and in libraries. Search engines such as Google and Ask.com find their results in different ways, so if one does not work for you, try another. Also useful to researchers are Web directories (7a) and meta-search engines such as Dogpile and MetaCrawler, which search the results of other search engines. For college researchers, licensed library databases also offer options of searching by author, title, subject, and other features and are likely to produce the full texts of reliable sources.

KEY POINTS

Tips on Using Search Engines

1. **Don't mistake popularity for quality.** Though the exact methods commercial search engines use to find and rank sources are trade secrets, the number of links and visits to a page play a large role in determining which sites get listed first. However, the popularity of a Web site is not necessarily an indication of quality. Search engines do not assess the quality of the content. So make your search string as specific as possible to exercise greater control of what you get on the first page. Few people have the patience to look at subsequent pages!

2. **Be aware of "sponsored links."** These sites often appear on the very top of a Google result list (against a pale yellow background, which may be hard to notice on some monitors) and are in addition to the easily spotted "sponsored links" in the sidebar or the right side of the screen. The site's owner pays for it to appear at the top of the page, so its inclusion there is no indication of either quality or popularity.

3. **Try using search engines that are intended for academic work.** You probably use a search engine such as Google for everyday Web searches using keywords or to search for images and videos. For your academic work, branch out and use Google Scholar and Book Search, the directories listed earlier in 7a, and your library's online licensed databases, where no paid advertisements appear on the screen. For finding material in journal and newspaper articles, use databases such as *Academic Search Premier, InfoTrac, LexisNexis,* and specialized subject-area databases; there you can find

(Continued)

(Continued)

abstracts (when available) or full articles. See 7d for more on searching databases.

4. Persist and be resourceful. If a search yields only a few hits, try new keywords in new combinations. Also try variant spellings for names of people and places (such as *Chaikovsky, Tchaikovsky, Tschaikovsky*), and/or try a different search engine.

After you have decided which search engines to use for your particular task, you then have to decide on how best to do the search. Here are some tips.

Tips on how to do efficient keyword searches for academic purposes

- **Know the system of the database or search engine.** Use Search Tips or Help to learn how to conduct a search. (In Google, you need to scroll to the bottom of a page to find the Search Tips link.) Some systems search for any or all of the words you type in, some need you to indicate whether the words make up a phrase, and others allow you to exclude search terms or search for alternatives.

- **Learn how to do Boolean searches.** Many database searches operate on the Boolean principle; that is, they use the "operators" *AND, OR,* and *NOT* in combination with keywords to define what you want the search to include and exclude. Imagine that you want to find out how music can affect intelligence. A search for "music AND intelligence" would find sources in the database that include both the word *music* and the word *intelligence.*

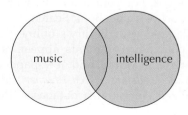

A search for "music AND (intelligence OR learning)" would expand the search. You would find sources in the database that included both the word *music* and the word *intelligence* or the word *learning*.

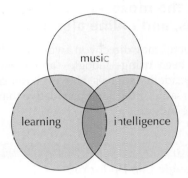

Some search engines let you use terms such as *NEAR* and *ADJ* (adjacent to) to find phrases close to each other in the searched text.

- **Know how to expand or narrow a search.** Many search engines, including Google, let you use signs such as + or – to include or prohibit a term, thereby expanding or narrowing your search. You do not need to insert the word *and*.

- **Use a wildcard character (* or ?) to truncate a term and expand the search.** The truncated search term *podiatr** will produce references to *podiatry*, *podiatrist*, and *podiatric*. In Google, however, the wildcard character * is used to stand for a whole word only, as in "Foot doctor is a *," but Google automatically uses "stemming" and searches for "podiatrist" as well as "podiatry" if you have entered the latter term only.

- **Narrow a search by grouping words.** Enclose search terms in quotation marks (or in some cases, parentheses) to group the words into a phrase; this is a useful technique for finding titles, names, and quotations. A half-remembered line from a poem by Wordsworth ("the difference to me") entered as a Google search without quotation marks does not produce a Wordsworth poem on the first page of hits. However, putting quotation marks around this phrase produces a hit to the full text of Wordsworth's "Lucy" poem as the first result.

▪ **Be flexible.** If you don't get good results, try using synonyms: In Google, for example, type a tilde (~) immediately before the search term, as in ~ *addiction*. Or try a different search engine or database.

7c Getting the most out of Google, advanced searches, and online alerts

Your college instructor may direct you away from the popular search engine you have been using—Google—and toward engines more geared to finding academic sources. However, remember that Google can be far more versatile, direct, and productive than the results in its basic search engine indicate.

KEY POINTS
What Google Can Do for You

Google provides the following useful functions for researchers. Use them.

Google Tools for Searching

▪ **Google Advanced Search** provides many options for tailoring your search to your precise needs (see the screenshot on p. 117).

▪ **Google Scholar,** an excellent resource for researchers, searches scholarly sources (such as research studies, dissertations, peer-reviewed papers) across many disciplines. You may also be able to customize the program to provide links to the full text of articles in your college library. Click "Scholar preferences" and enter the name of the library. You can then import local links into bibliographical programs your college may own, such as EndNote or RefWorks.

▪ **Google Book Search** helps you find books and provides details of the contents, even allowing you to search the full text of many books for specific content.

▪ **Google Earth** allows you to search for maps, detailed satellite images, and 3D images.

Other Google Tools

▪ **Google Reader Alerts** will send you regular e-mail updates as it checks your favorite news sites or blogs for new content on any topic you specify.

- **Google Docs** allows you to create or upload existing online materials, such as documents, presentations, and spreadsheets. Others can then access the material and make comments and changes, recording their contribution. This is a useful tool for collaborative projects.

- **Google Notebook** allows you to make clippings from Web pages, save and organize them, and add your own notes, clearly separated so that you know exactly what comes from the Web clip and what comes from you. You can use this feature from any computer, and you can share your notebooks with others—another useful tool for collaborative projects.

Using advanced searches   Whenever you can, use a search engine's advanced search feature. This will allow you to specify results that use all the keywords in any order, the exact phrase, or only one of the words, or that exclude unwanted words. Databases also often provide an advanced search feature that allows you to limit your search to retrieve only full-text or "peer-reviewed" articles (scholarly articles, scrutinized and approved for publication by reviewers familiar with the field). The screenshot on page 119 shows this feature.

In addition, a Google Advanced Search allows you to be specific about the order and number of keywords, number of results, language of the source, and the file type (Word, Excel, PowerPoint, Acrobat, and so on).

Google Advanced Search

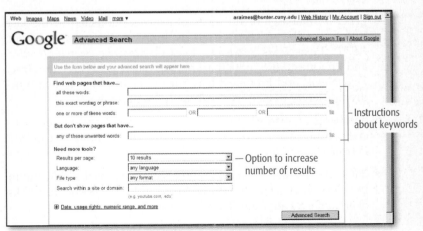

How to get information to come to you—research in your pajamas Not only can you find a vast amount of source material online, but you can also arrange to be notified when materials on your specific topic become available. For example, Google Alerts will e-mail search results directly to you, and Google Reader allows you to keep up with Web sites' RSS (Really Simple Syndication or Rich Site Summary) feeds by notifying you of the latest news items, events, or discussion postings on a given topic at the time interval you specify. In addition, several journal databases, such as those sponsored by EBSCO, SAGE, and CSA, will run a search on a topic you specify as often as you request, even daily, and alert you via e-mail to articles that meet the criteria you establish. These RSS feeds mean that you get full-text research articles brought to you 24/7 without your having to remember to redo a search.

7d Databases

Online databases of journal articles provide sources that have been previously published and referred to by experts.

Online databases and citation indexes owned or leased by libraries can be accessed in the library itself. Many libraries also make the databases they subscribe to available on the Internet through their home pages. For example, many libraries provide online access to the following:

- databases of abstracts in specific subject areas, such as *ERIC* (for education), *PAIS* (for public affairs), *PsycINFO* (for psychology), and *SocIndex* (for sociology)

- general databases of full texts of articles published in the last twenty or thirty years, such as InfoTrac *Expanded Academic ASAP,* LexisNexis *Academic,* EBSCO *Academic Search Premier,* and ProQuest *SIRS* (note that sponsors such as EBSCO, InfoTrac, LexisNexis, and ProQuest may each offer from ten to one hundred different databases covering different fields)

- databases of abstracts (with some full texts) of general, nonspecialized magazine articles, such as the Wilson *Readers' Guide to Periodical Literature*

- databases devoted to quantitative statistics, such as the Millennium Development Goal Indicators Database, or to images such as works of art at the J. Paul Getty Trust Web site.

- the *JSTOR* database, providing access to less recent sources

- open-access databases, freely available online but often easier to find via the library catalog. These databases may include full-text scholarly or scientific articles (*PubMed Central*), catalogs of government documents, and collections of bibliographies.

Access to databases in university library Web sites, from both library and home computers, is often limited to enrolled students, who need to verify their status when they log on. Check with your college library to learn which databases it subscribes to. Articles that you find in a database have for the most part been previously published in print, so evaluate them as print sources for currency, objectivity, and author's reputation (see 8cb–8d).

Before you begin a search, read the instructions on the database to learn how to perform a simple search and an advanced search. Knowing what you are doing can save you a great deal of frustration. Generally, begin a search by using keywords or subject terms if you know them. Use what the database provides to limit a search as to type of source, date, full-text articles or not, and scholarly, peer-reviewed articles, as shown in the accompanying screenshot.

Advanced Search Screen: EBSCO *Academic Search Premier* Database

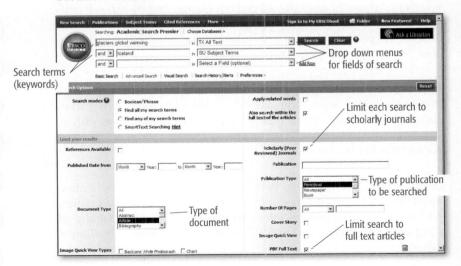

7e Print sources: Books and articles

For library catalogs and periodical databases, decide whether to search by title, author, subject, or keyword (7b). Exact wording and exact spelling are essential for all these searches.

Subject searches   To find sources focused on one topic, try subject searching. For that, you need to know the specific subject headings the catalogers used to identify and classify material, so consult a reference source such as *Library of Congress Subject Headings*, or ask a librarian for help. For example, you won't find *cultural identity* or *social identity* in *Library of Congress Subject Headings*, but you can look up *culture* and find a list of thirty-two associated headings, such as "language and culture" and "personality and culture."

In addition, these subject headings show related terms, which can suggest ways to narrow or broaden a topic and can help you in other searches, particularly in electronic keyword searches. The term *bilingualism,* for example, takes you to topics such as "air traffic control," "code switching," and "language attrition." An entry in a library catalog will appear with the subject descriptors, so if you find one good source, use its subject classifications to search further. A search in a library online catalog using the keywords *bilingual, education,* and *politics* comes up with fifty records. One of these sources (shown on p. 121) provides some subject terms to help with further searching: *education and state, educational change,* and *educational evaluation.* Similarly, a keyword search of an online database of full-text articles will produce articles with subject terms attached, as in Source Shot 3 in section 12e, page 193.

Finding books   Keep in mind that, if your college library does not own a book you want, you have the option of asking a librarian about an interlibrary loan. This option is helpful, of course, only if you begin your search early. Use the following guides to find the books your library does have.

Online library catalogs The Web gives you access to the online resources of many libraries (actual and virtual) and universities, which are good browsing sites. Some useful sites are *Library of Congress, LibWeb, New York Public Library,* and *Smithsonian Institution Libraries.*

Call number Most college libraries use the Library of Congress classification system, which arranges books according to subject area and often the initial of the author's last name and the date of publication. The call number tells you where a book is located in the library stacks (the area where books are shelved). Write this number down immediately if a book looks promising, along with the book's title and author(s) and publication information (9d). If a library has open stacks, you will be able to browse through books on a similar topic on the same shelf or on one nearby. Many library catalogs now offer the option of seeing other books on the same shelf as an extension of your search. Whether browsing online or in the stacks, being open to discovering new sources can reward you with options you might not have otherwise found.

Information in the catalog The screens of electronic catalogs vary from one system to another, but most screens contain the name of the system you are using; the details of your search request and of the search, such as the number of records found; and detailed bibliographical information, which is useful for evaluating whether the book will be helpful in your research.

Library Catalog Screen: Library of Congress

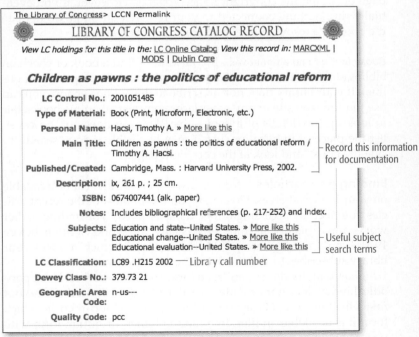

The Library of Congress> LCCN Permalink

LIBRARY OF CONGRESS CATALOG RECORD

View LC holdings for this title in the: LC Online Catalog *View this record in:* MARCXML | MODS | Dublin Core

Children as pawns : the politics of educational reform

LC Control No.:	2001051485	
Type of Material:	Book (Print, Microform, Electronic, etc.)	
Personal Name:	Hacsi, Timothy A. » More like this	
Main Title:	Children as pawns : the politics of educational reform / Timothy A. Hacsi.	⎱ Record this information for documentation
Published/Created:	Cambridge, Mass. : Harvard University Press, 2002.	
Description:	ix, 261 p. ; 25 cm.	
ISBN:	0674007441 (alk. paper)	
Notes:	Includes bibliographical references (p. 217-252) and index.	
Subjects:	Education and state--United States. » More like this Educational change--United States. » More like this Educational evaluation--United States. » More like this	⎱ Useful subject search terms
LC Classification:	LC89 .H215 2002 — Library call number	
Dewey Class No.:	379.73 21	
Geographic Area Code:	n-us---	
Quality Code:	pcc	

The screen shown on page 121 shows publication information and the library call number, as well as all the essential information you will need to document the source at the end of your paper: the author, the title, the place of publication, the publisher, and the year of publication. It also lets you know the number of pages in the book, including the number of pages (ix: nine) of introductory material and shows that the book contains a bibliography and an index, both of which are useful research tools. In addition, the subject terms shown here indicate the subjects the book addresses; these can help you structure further searches.

Once you find a book that seems related to your topic, you do not have to read the whole book to use it for your paper. Learn what you can from the catalog entry; then skim the table of contents, chapter headings, and bibliography. Your best timesaver here is the index. Turn to it immediately, and look up some key words for your topic. Read the section of the book in which references to your topic appear, take notes, and annotate a photocopy of the relevant pages (see 10a for a sample annotated text). A book's bibliography and references are useful, too. The research the author has done can help you in your search. It is a good idea to make a copy of the title page and the page on which the copyright notice appears. However, if you eventually find nothing connected to your research question, do not cite the book as a resource, even though you looked at it.

***Books in Print* and alternatives**　If you want to find a book or check on bibliographical details, use *Books in Print* (available in print and online). If your library does not subscribe to the online version, you can use the Amazon site or any other large commercial online bookseller to look up the details of a book—free. Amazon does not, however, list the place of publication, but it may be visible if you "search inside the book" and look at the copyright page.

Finding print articles　New issues of periodicals will be available on your library shelves. However, you'll find most of the recent articles you need by accessing online databases (7d). For finding earlier works for a historical study—especially for works written before 1970—you'll need to use print indexes. Check which services your library subscribes to and the dates the indexes cover.

Search methods are similar to those in book searches. If the periodical index does not provide the full text, you will need to find out first whether your library owns the periodical and then in which form it is available: in files, in bound volumes, or in film form with pages shown in a strip (microfilm) or on a sheet (microfiche), which you will need to read with a special machine. The catalog for your library will tell you on the screen which issues are available in the library and in which format and location. For articles in journals not available in your library, ask about interlibrary loan.

7f Web sources

The democratic nature of the Internet means that many Web pages have no editorial control, so although you will probably find a great deal of material, much of it could be mindless and inaccurate. On the plus side, you will find vast resources, current material, and frequent updates—all without leaving your computer. As you plan your research, consider which of the following Internet resources might be the most appropriate for your topic. A reference librarian can help you decide.

Online magazines and online scholarly journals   Online magazines and journals are proliferating. Online scholarly journals will acknowledge their process of having all articles read and approved by experts (peer reviewers), whereas online magazines will typically have editors but no scholarly peer reviewers. You'll find a useful directory at Librarians' Internet Index. Some scholarly journals have no print versions. Some online journals and magazines are available free; others allow you to view only the current issue at no cost. Many, however, require a subscription through your library computer network or a personal subscription. Several university libraries, such as Albany and Houston, include a directory of journals in their sites.

Online literary texts   Literary texts that are out of copyright and in the public domain are increasingly available online. Try *Project Bartleby*, *Project Gutenberg*, *University of Virginia's Electronic Text Center*, or *The Internet Archive*.

E-books   Many books are becoming available as e-books that can be read online at a computer or downloaded and read in an e-book reader. If your library subscribes to e-book databases, check their offerings when you are looking for a book.

Online news sites   The Web sites of major newspapers, magazines, and television networks provide up-to-date news information; some offer archived information but often only to subscribers. The *New York Times* and *CNN* are among the sources to offer open archives. *LexisNexis* also provides access to articles from many newspapers.

Nonprofit research sites Some nonprofit sites offer valuable and objective information. For example, see *Public Agenda Online, American Film Institute, Follow the Money*, and *San Francisco Bay Bird Observatory*. Others such as *Wikipedia* are less accurate and reliable.

Web home pages and hypertext links Universities and research institutes provide information through their own Web home pages, with hypertext links that take you with one click to many other sources. Individual Web pages can provide useful information, too, but they need careful evaluation because anyone can publish anything on the Web (see 8e for more on how to evaluate a Web site). Be sure to pay attention to context as well; sites don't always warn you when links go out to other sites that may be less authoritative.

E-mail discussion groups With e-mail, you have access to many discussion groups. Messages go out to a list of people interested in specific topics. Without charge, you can join a list devoted to a topic of interest (23b). However, most of the lists are not refereed or monitored, so you have to evaluate carefully any information you find.

For academic research, personal blogs, Usenet newsgroups, and chat rooms may provide little that is substantive. Evaluating the reliability of a contributor's comments can be difficult.

Using URLs If you already know the Web address (the uniform resource locator, or URL) of a useful site, type it exactly, paying attention to underscores, dots, symbols, and capital or lowercase letters. Leave no spaces in a URL. Just one small slip can prevent access. Whenever you can, copy and paste a URL from a Web source so that you do not make mistakes when typing. If you ever get a message saying "site not found," check your use of capital and lowercase letters (and avoid inserting spaces as you type an address), and try again. Or try adding "l" to an .htm suffix or deleting "l" from .html. You may find, however, that the site really is no longer available. If a good resource appears to no longer exist, try putting the URL into the search engine at the Internet Archive, which keeps a permanent archive of a series of snapshots of the Web that begin in 1996.

7g Visual sources

In a research paper, consider where tables and charts could present visual data concisely and clearly. Images may also help you strengthen an argument (see 4i). Use visuals to illustrate and enhance a point or to present information clearly and economically. Do not use visuals merely to fill space or to look trendy (more on this in chapter 22).

If you look at sections 4e and 4i, as well as the sample papers in 4j and in chapters 13 and 16, you'll see how photographs and Web visuals work well to highlight or illustrate specific information or to capture the essence of an argument and thus make a point convincingly. Visuals can also be used effectively to convey quantitative information in a readily comprehensible form in tables, graphs, and charts (see chapter 22 for more on visuals of this type).

Finding appropriate visuals   Several of the major search engines, including Google, AltaVista, and Yahoo!, offer specific image searches, and by using the advanced search forms there, you will be able to narrow your search to certain types of images, including those that are licensed for noncommercial use; adding that to your search parameters means you won't have to worry about copyright or whether to ask permission to use the image. Another useful source is Flickr, which is now owned by Yahoo!. Flickr is a depository for photos only, and people can put their photos in this database independent of any Web site. This is, therefore, a complementary site providing access to a large number of amateur photos.

Searching for images can often be difficult and frustrating because many "hits" may not interest you. Image searches use keywords or tags attached to the image, and often, these are not very accurate or do not describe the image the same way you would describe it. So rather than doing a general image search, it may be more productive to look for images at the Web sites where you find relevant textual information in the first place. Many Web sites, including government sites like the U.S. Bureau of the Census or nonprofit organizations like Public Agenda, make great efforts to present the information on their sites in a visually attractive form. In addition, the National Telecommunications and Information Administration is a good source for tables and charts analyzing Internet use; and the College Board and the UCLA Higher Education Research Institute provide annual studies of first-year students using many tables and graphs.

As a general rule, whichever style of documentation you use, you need to identify and label a visual source such as a figure or a table where you include it in your paper. See section 4j and chapters 13, 16, and 18 for examples of documenting visuals in MLA, APA, and CSE styles.

8

How to Evaluate Sources

How can you identify good, relevant sources? Use the following guidelines.

8a Read sources critically

Reading what others write always provides ideas, but not just the ideas you absorb from the page or screen. If you read critically, you will generate ideas of your own as you read and make your own contributions to the issues under discussion. The principles of critical analysis discussed in 1c and 4a can be extended to the critical reading of sources.

KEY POINTS
Reading Sources Critically

- Ask questions about the credentials and reputation of the author and the place of publication. What do you learn about the writer's purpose and the audience whom the author is addressing? Make sure you subject any material you find on Web pages to especially careful scrutiny (8e).

- Ask questions about the ideas you read. An easy way to do this is to write your annotations in the margin. If you find yourself thinking "but . . ." as you read, go with that sense of doubt, and make a note of what troubles you. Examples of annotated readings are in 1c and 10a.

- Be on the lookout for assumptions that may be faulty. If you are reading an article on home-schooling and the writer favors home-schooling because it avoids subjecting students to violence in schools, the unstated assumption is that all schools are violent places. For more on the logic of argument, see 4f and 4h.

- Make sure the writer's evidence is adequate and accurate. For example, if the writer is making a generalization about all Chinese students based on a study of only three, you have cause to challenge the generalization as resting on inadequate evidence.

- Note how the writer uses language. Which terms does the writer use with positive—or negative—connotations, signaling the values the writer holds? Does the writer flamboyantly denigrate the views of others with such phrases as "a ridiculous notion" or "laughably inept policies"?

- Be alert for sweeping generalizations, bias, and prejudice: "Women want to stay home and have children." "Men love to spend Sundays watching sports."

Do your reading when you can write—not on the treadmill or while watching TV. Note any questions, objections, or challenges on the page, as in the annotated text shown in 10a, on self-stick notes, on index cards, in a response file on your computer, or in a journal. Your critical responses to your reading will provide you with your own ideas for writing.

8b Recognize a scholarly article in print

A scholarly article is not something you are likely to find in a magazine in a dentist's office. A scholarly article does the following—the first point being the most important.

KEY POINTS
How to Recognize a Scholarly Article in Print

1. It is reviewed by other scholars (peer reviewers) for their approval before publication.

2. It refers to the work of other scholars and includes notes, references, and/or a list of works cited, footnotes, or endnotes.

3. It names the author and may describe the author's affiliation and credentials

4. It deals with a serious issue in depth.

5. It uses academic or technical language for informed readers.

6. It generally appears in journals that do not include colorful advertisements or eye-catching pictures.

(*Note:* Not all scholarly articles will include all six of these criteria.)

Periodicals such as *Time, Newsweek,* and *The Economist* are serious but not scholarly periodicals. Note that a scholarly article may appear in a publication for the general population, such as *Psychology Today.* Source Shot 2 on page 189 shows an example of a scholarly print article.

8c   Recognize a scholarly article online

Online articles in HTML or other digital formats, unlike PDF articles, do not necessarily provide the immediate signals of color, illustrations, and varied advertisements that would identify nonscholarly work in print publications. For print articles replicated online, use the PDF version. Otherwise, examine Web-based articles with care using the following guidelines:

- Look for evidence of peer review (if the article is in an online journal, it should be relatively easy to find information about the journal and its policies).

- Look for a list of references.

- Follow links from the author's name (if available) to find a résumé and more information.

- In Google Scholar, use the author's name as a search term to see publications and citations by others (7c).

- Examine any article you find online as you would a print article. In addition, do a search for the title of the periodical in which the article appears to find out that periodical's purpose and its requirements for submitting and publishing articles. In some library databases (EBSCO's, for example), you can limit your search to articles that are peer-reviewed; that is, they are read by other scholars working on similar topics and are found to contribute new and important knowledge before they are accepted for publication.

TECH NOTE

Databases of Journal Information

- Genamics JournalSeek provides links to the Web sites of journals to help you identify journals as scholarly or not.

- The Cornell University Web site *Distinguishing Scholarly Journals from Other Periodicals* provides definitions and examples of four categories of periodical literature: scholarly, substantive news and general interest, popular, and sensational.

8d Evaluate works originating in print

Before you make detailed notes on a book or an article that began its life in print, be sure it will provide suitable information to help answer your research question.

Print books Check the date of publication, notes about the author, table of contents, and index. Skim the preface, introduction, chapter headings, and summaries to give yourself an idea of the information in the book and the book's theoretical basis and perspective. Do not waste time making detailed notes on a book that deals only tangentially with your topic or on an out-of-date book (unless your purpose is to discuss and critique its perspective or examine a topic historically). Ask a librarian or your instructor for help in evaluating the appropriateness of sources you discover. If your topic concerns a serious academic issue, readers will expect you to consult books and not limit your references to popular magazines, newspapers, and Internet sources.

Periodical articles in print Take into account the type of periodical, any organization with which it is affiliated, and the intended audience. Differentiate among the following types of articles (listed in descending order of reliability, with the most reliable first):

- scholarly articles (see 8b and 8c)
- articles, often long, in periodicals for nonspecialist but serious, well-educated readers, such as *New York Review of Books, Atlantic Monthly, Economist, Scientific American,* and *Nation*
- shorter articles, with sources not identified, in popular magazines for a general audience, such as *Ebony, Time, Newsweek, Parents, Psychology Today,* and *Vogue,* or in newspapers
- articles with dubious sources, written for sensational tabloid magazines, such as *National Enquirer, Globe,* and *Star*

KEY POINTS
Questions to Evaluate a Print Source

1. **What does the work cover?** It should be long enough and detailed enough to provide adequate information.
2. **How objective is the information?** The author, publisher, or periodical should not be affiliated with an organization that has an ax to grind—unless, of course, your topic entails reading critically and making comparisons with other points of view.

(Continued)

(Continued)

3. **How current are the views?** Check the date of publication. The work should be up-to-date if you need a current perspective.

4. **How reputable are the publisher and author?** The work should be published by a reputable publisher in a source that is academically reliable, not one devoted to gossip, advertising, propaganda, or sensationalism. Check *Books in Print, Literary Market Place,* or ACQWEB's *Directory of Publishers and Vendors* for details on publishers. The author should be an authority on the subject. Find out what else the author has written (in Google, in *Books in Print,* or at Amazon.com) and what his or her qualifications are as an authority.

Newspaper articles and news articles online   The *New York Times, Washington Post,* and *Los Angeles Times,* for example, provide mostly reliable accounts of current events; daily editorial comments; and reviews of books, film, and art. Be aware that most newspapers (as well as televised news reports such as Fox News and MSNBC) have political leanings, so perspectives on the same event may differ.

8e   Evaluate Web sources and learn to recognize junk

What makes the Internet so fascinating is that it is wide open, free, and democratic. Anyone can "publish" anything, and anyone can read it. For anyone looking for well-presented facts and informed opinion among the more than 625 million domain names registered as of January 2009 (ISC Internet Domain survey), however, the Internet can pose a challenge.

Conventional library sources available online   An article in a subscription database (*InfoTrac* or *LexisNexis,* for example), has probably already been published in print, so you can use the criteria for print works (8d) to evaluate it. If an article has been published in a reputable periodical or in an online journal sponsored by a professional organization or university, you can assume it is a valid source for a research paper. You do need to make sure that any electronic version of a literary book is based on a reliable, authoritative edition of the text. Usually, you can safely assume the reliability of scholarly sources accessible online in databases such as those sponsored by professional institutions or government agencies—*ERIC* for education, for instance—but other items (for example, newspaper articles) are not necessarily of high quality. Always corroborate information given in a media source.

Postings found in e-mail discussion lists, blogs, and wikis
Discussion list postings, blogs (Web logs), and wiki entries (addition to or editing of a Web text appearing in a wiki) will often appear in a list of a search engine's findings. Many professionally moderated lists and other targeted discussion lists can be useful sources of information, though quality can vary considerably. Treat with caution postings in e-mail bulletin boards, newsgroups, blogs, or synchronous (real-time) communications such as chat rooms.

Web sites   Evaluate Web sites with particular care. Individuals on a rant, as well as serious government or research agencies, can establish a site. Because anyone can "publish" anything, and thousands or millions can read it, finding reliable information and well-presented, informed opinions on Web pages can pose a challenge. Learn to separate good information from junk.

Note: For more on the features to look for, evaluate, and record in Web sites, see the screenshot and examples of documentation in 10i: "One source, four systems of documentation."

TECH NOTE

Finding Out about a Site

If you can't readily find information on the actual Web site, a good way to begin an evaluation is to look the site up on <http://www.betterwhois.com>. This site will provide information on the author, date, sponsor, and address, and so provide clues to the reliability of the site.

KEY POINTS

Developing Your Junk Antennae: How to Evaluate Web Sites

1. **Scrutinize the domain name of the URL.** Reliable information can usually be found on .gov and .edu addresses that are institutionally sponsored (but also see item 2). With .com ("dot com"), .net, .info, or .org sources, always assess whether the source provides factual information or advocates a specific point of view on an issue.

(Continued)

(Continued)

2. **Assess the originator of an .edu source.** Is the educational institution or a branch of it sponsoring the site? A tilde (~) followed by a name in the URL generally indicates a posting by an individual, with no approval from the institution. So follow up by finding out what else the individual has published.

3. **Determine the author, and discover what you can about him or her.** Look for a list of credentials, a home page, a résumé, or Web publications. In Google or Google Scholar, use the author's name as a search term to see what else the person has published on the Internet or if anybody has cited the author. When no individual is named as an author, look for an organization, agency, or business that sponsors the site. Do not confuse the Web site manager with the author of the information on the site.

4. **Check the About page or the Home page.** If you find your way to a Web page, always go to Home or About (if available) to find out about the larger site. Look for the title of the site, its stated purpose, and sponsor. Check, too, for bias. For instance, does the site aim to persuade, convert, or sell? If you reach a page via a search engine and no site name is visible or shown in About, delete the URL progressively back to each single slash, and click to see which part of the site you access.

5. **Investigate the purposes of a Web page author or sponsor.** Objectivity and rationality are not necessarily features of all Web pages. Even if the message is not obviously biased and extreme, be aware that most authors write from some sense of conviction or purpose. (Note, though, that a Web site can be oriented toward a specific view without necessarily being irresponsible.)

6. **Evaluate the quality of the writing.** A Web page filled with spelling and grammatical errors should not inspire confidence. If the language has not been checked, the ideas probably haven't been given much time and thought, either. However, postings to discussion lists, though often written spontaneously, can contain useful ideas to stimulate thinking on your topic.

7. **Follow the links.** See whether the links in a site take you to authoritative sources. If the links no longer work (you'll get a 404 message: "Site Not Found"), the home page with the links has not been updated in a while—not a good sign.

8. **Check for dates, updates, ways to respond, and ease of navigation.** A well-managed site will have recent updates, clear organization, up-to-date links, and easy-to-find contact information.

9. **Corroborate information.** Try to find the same information on another reliable site. If you find contradictory information, beware, and do some follow-up work.

9

How to Avoid Plagiarizing

The convenience and comfort of researching online are not without a downside. The ease of finding, copying, and downloading information from the screen has its attendant dangers: that researchers lose sight of what is theirs and what isn't, that they forget where they read something, that information seems so abundant that surely it must be there for the taking. Unfortunately, though, that is not the case, especially in the academic world, where presenting somebody else's words or ideas without acknowledging where those words and ideas come from is a punishable offense.

The word for the offense, *plagiarism*, is derived from a Latin verb meaning "to kidnap," and if you use someone else's words and ideas without acknowledging them, you are in effect cheating by kidnapping or stealing those words and ideas. Readers do not want to be fooled into thinking that the ideas and words that you wrote actually originated someplace else. For all audiences, but especially for academic readers, honesty counts for a great deal, so much so that many colleges encourage professors and students to run papers through a plagiarism-checking program such as Turnitin.com to ensure that no passages in the text match any in the database of the service.

This chapter describes the various types of plagiarism, and it stresses that acknowledging the research you have done by accurately citing your sources (who said it, where, and when) is always the way to go.

9a The seven sins of plagiarism

KEY POINTS

Plagiarism's Seven Sins

1. **Intentional grand larceny** Presenting as your own work a whole essay bought from paper mills, "borrowed" or commissioned from a friend, or intentionally copied and pasted from an online source.

2. **Premeditated shoplifting** Taking passages from a book, article, or Web site and intentionally inserting them in your paper without indicating who wrote them or where you found them. This type of plagiarism differs from intentional grand larceny only because passages, not the entire paper, are copied.

3. **Tinkering with the evidence** Making only a few word changes to source material and inserting the slightly altered version into your paper as if you wrote it, with no acknowledgment of the source, and trusting that those changes are enough to avoid charges of plagiarism.

4. **Idea kidnapping** Using ideas written by others (even if you do use your own words) and neglecting to cite the source of the ideas.

5. **Unauthorized borrowing of private property** Citing your source but following its sentence structure and organization too closely or not indicating with quotation marks any of your source's exact words.

6. **Trespassing over boundaries** Failing to indicate in your paper where ideas from a source end and your ideas take over (see 10f for more on this).

7. **Writing under the influence** Being too tired, lazy, or disorganized, or facing an imminent deadline, and turning to any of the six previous sins in desperation or ignorance.

Consequences Obviously, these "sins" vary in their severity and in the intention to deceive. The types of plagiarism described in items 4 through 6 of the Key Points box sometimes occur unintentionally, but they may be perceived as plagiarism nevertheless. You have to work hard at avoiding them, especially since the consequences of plagiarism can be severe, ranging from an F on a paper or an F in a course to disciplinary measures or expulsion from college.

In the world at large, plagiarism can lead to lawsuits and ruined careers. Those are reasons enough to do your own work and learn to document your sources fully and correctly.

LANGUAGE AND CULTURE

Ownership Rights across Cultures

The Western view takes seriously the ownership of words and text. It respects both the individual as author (and authority) and the originality of the individual's ideas. In some cultures, memorization and the use of classic texts are common in all walks of life. And worldwide, the ownership of language, texts, music, and videos is being called into question by the democratic, interactive nature of the Internet. In short, therefore, plagiarism is not something universal and easy to define. In Western academic culture, basic ground rules exist for the "fair use" of another writer's writing without payment, but easy access to music and media sources poses interesting questions about intellectual property and the opportunities to create and remix culture.

TECH NOTE

A Web Site on Plagiarism

For more on the topic of plagiarism, use the link to the excellent Georgetown University Web site *What Is Plagiarism?*

9b How to avoid even the suspicion of plagiarism

Research and clear documentation open a channel of communication between you and your audience. Readers learn what your views are and what has influenced those views. They will assume that anything not documented is your original idea and your wording.

Remember that citing any words and ideas that you use from your sources works to your advantage. Citing accurately reveals a writer who has done enough research to enter ongoing conversations in the academic world. In addition, citations show readers how hard you have worked, how much research you have done, and how the points you make are supported by experts. So be proud to cite your sources.

KEY POINTS

How to Avoid Plagiarizing

- Start your research early enough to avoid panic mode.
- Make a record of each source so that you have all the information you need for appropriate documentation.
- Set up a working annotated bibliography (9e).
- Take notes from the sources, with a systematic method of indicating quotation, paraphrase, and your own comments. For example, use quotation marks around quoted words, phrases, sentences, and passages; introduce a paraphrase with a tag, such as "Belkin makes the point that . . . "; in your notes about a source, write your own comments in a different color. Then, later, you will see immediately which ideas are yours and which come from your source.
- Always acknowledge and document the source of any passage, phrase, or idea that you have used or summarized from someone else's work.
- Never use exactly the same sequence of ideas and organization of argument as your source.
- When you use a single key word from your source or three or more words in sequence from your source, use the appropriate format for quoting and documenting.
- Be aware that substituting synonyms for a few words in the source or moving a few words around is not enough to counter a charge of plagiarism.
- Don't use passages in your paper that have been written or rewritten by a friend or a tutor.
- Never even consider buying, downloading, or "borrowing" a paper or a section of a paper to turn in as your own work.

9c Know why, how, and what to cite

Why you need to cite sources

- Citing sources shows your audience that you have done your homework on an issue; you will get respect for the depth and breadth of your research and for having worked hard to make your case.

- Citing responsible and recent sources lets your audience know that your arguments are both weighty and current.

- Citing sources draws your readers into the conversation about the issue and educates them. It also allows them to see you as engaged in the ongoing intellectual conversation around the issue you are writing about. With full and accurate citations, they can follow up on the same sources you used and so can learn more.

- Citation can be used to strengthen your argument, protect against counterclaims, or align your thinking with a particular scholar or institutional perspective. In other words, careful use of citations can make your writing and research stronger and more persuasive.

- Citing all sources fully and accurately is essential if you are to avoid even the suspicion of plagiarizing.

How to cite sources   Citing a source means letting readers know whose words or ideas you are quoting, summarizing, or paraphrasing; where you found the information; and in the case of Web sites, when you found the material and when it was published or posted online. Styles of documentation vary in whether they ask initially for author and page number (MLA) or author and year of publication (APA), with a detailed list at the end of the paper of all the sources cited. Other systems (*Chicago* and CSE) use numbering systems in the paper, with a listing of source details at the end. See comparisons of a citation in each system in 10i, and follow the detailed models in parts 3 and 4 for each of these systems.

How to cite visuals   Provide a number and a source note for all tables and figures you include in your paper. In MLA style, put the visual close to the text it illustrates, with a credit line immediately beneath it. For APA papers, consult with your instructor. Some recommend including visuals within the text of a college paper; others adhere to strict APA style, with tables and figures placed at the end of the paper. See chapters 4, 13, 16, and 18 for student papers with visuals.

What to cite   Intentionally presenting another person's work as your own may be the most deceptive kind of plagiarism, but the effect is the same if you neglect to acknowledge your sources because of sloppy research and writing practices. In both cases, readers will not be able to discern which ideas are yours and which are not.

Always provide full documentation of sources, with a citation in your text and an entry in your list of sources. The following Key Points box shows you what you must always cite and also points out when citing is not necessary. If you are in doubt about whether you need to cite a source, it is always safer to cite it.

KEY POINTS
Sources to Cite or Not to Cite

What to Cite

- exact words, even facts, from a source, enclosed in quotation marks
- somebody else's ideas and opinions, even if you restate them in your own words in a summary or paraphrase
- each sentence in a long paraphrase if it is not clear that all the sentences paraphrase the same source
- facts, theories, and statistics

What Not to Cite

- common knowledge, especially when it is available in many sources—such as the dates of the Civil War, birth and death dates, chronological events in the lives of authors and public figures, or allusions to nursery rhymes or folktales handed down through the ages

Note how James Stalker, in his article "Official English or English Only," does not quote directly but still cites Anderson as the source of the specialized facts mentioned in the following passage:

> By 1745 there were approximately 45,000 German speakers in the colonies, and by 1790 there were some 200,000, nine percent of the population (Anderson 80).

9d Keep track of sources

The first step toward avoiding plagiarism is keeping track of what your sources are and which ideas come from your sources and which from you. You will find that one of the frustrating moments for you as a researcher occurs when you find a note about an interesting point you read—but cannot remember where you found the passage or who wrote it or whether your notes represent an author's exact words. Avoid this frustration by keeping track as you go along.

- **Keep a working bibliography.** Some options: Make a bibliography card (one for each source; use one side only); save screens or printouts from a library catalog, database listing, or Web site; or use as a research organizing tool any bibliographical software provided by your library, such as EndNote or RefWorks (9f). Record all the relevant information for each source you read and plan to use, including reference works, and remember to record inclusive page numbers for all print sources and the date on which you access Web sites. You may want to include annotations (notes of varying length that provide more detail) in your working bibliography either for your own benefit or to fulfill assignment requirements that include an annotated bibliography. You'll find a sample entry from an annotated bibliography in 9e.

- **Make copies of print material.** While you are in the library, scan or photocopy complete journal or magazine articles and a periodical's table of contents (which will provide date and volume number). Then you will be able to devote more library time to locating new sources and work on your copies later at home. Scan or copy book sections or chapters, too, along with the title page and copyright page of the book. You will need this information for your list of works cited.

- **Make a copy of every Web source you may use.** Material you find online can be volatile, so always print a source, e-mail it to yourself, add it to your bibliographical software file (9f), or save it on a flash drive, making sure you use highlighting or a special font to distinguish your own comments and notes from the material you have copied and saved.

- **Use your browser's Bookmark or Favorites feature.** Save all the links to useful sites so that you can easily find them again. If you work on a networked computer in a lab where you cannot save your work on the hard drive, export your bookmarks to your own computer or CD, or use a free online bookmark manager such as del.icio.us.

- **Record complete online document information, the URL, and the date of your access.** Bookmarking will not always last with the URLs of subscription databases. If you do not copy the whole site, record the name of the author, title, and date posted or updated (this information is sometimes available via the Properties or Page Info commands in your browser). Copy and paste to save the URL exactly on your hard drive or flash drive, and note the date on which you access the online material.

- **Make use of Google Notebook.** With Google Notebook, you can save, organize, label, and comment on clippings from Web sites from any computer, at home or at school. In addition, Google Notebook provides different fonts, different size fonts, and highlighting in an obvious place on the screen so that you can ensure you differentiate the words of the source from your own words (see also 7c).

- **Highlight, copy, and paste.** As you read material on the Web, highlight a passage you find, copy it, and then paste it into your own file. Make sure that you indicate clearly in your new document that you have included a direct quotation. Use quotation marks and/or a bigger or colored font or highlighting along with an author/page citation, as in the following example:

  > Novelist John Lanchester has made a telling point about our image of self by having his narrator declare that we **"wouldn't care so much what people thought of us if we knew how seldom they did"** (62).

Save as much information as you can about the original document in your working bibliography (9e).

9e Record information and set up a working bibliography

From the first steps of your research, keep accurate records of each source in a working bibliography, with or without annotations about each source. Record enough information so that you will be able to make up a list of references in whichever style of documentation you choose, though not all the points of information you record will be necessary for every style of documentation.

Sort your sources into four categories: print books, print articles, Web sources, and online database sources. The table on source essentials summarizes what you should record.

Source Essentials: What to Record

	Print Book	Print Article	Web Source	Online Database Source
Author(s), editor(s), translator(s), or name of company or government agency	✓		✓ (if available on site)	✓
Title and subtitle	✓	✓	✓ (if available on site)	✓
Print publication information	✓	✓		✓
Volume/edition/issue	✓	✓		
Call number	✓	✓		
Page numbers of document		✓	✓ Only for PDF documents; include number of paragraphs only if numbers appear on screen	✓ Only for PDF documents; otherwise, include start page if given
Title of Web site			✓	✓ Title of database
Other essential information to include	Place; Publisher, date	**Scholarly article:** Include volume number, issue number, date of publication, inclusive page numbers **Article in a book:** Include title, editor, place, publisher, year of publication, inclusive page numbers of the article	**Web site:** Include name of sponsor, date of online publication or update, URL, and date of access **Article in online journal:** Include volume and issue number; always include URL and note your date of access **E-mail message or discussion list posting:** Include name of sender, subject line, date of posting, name of list, and your date of access to the list	**Article in a database:** Include volume, issue number, and date of print publication; also include URL of home page of database or digital object identifier (DOI) of article and your date of access

Important Essential information to note for a Web source is the sponsor or publisher of the site, the date the site was established or updated, the URL, and the date on which you access the material. Since many online sources exist at more than one URL, and there may be differences depending on location, it is critical to keep track of where you found your sources. Noting the URL will help you access the source again. In addition, although the URL is not needed for MLA documentation, it is for the three other documentation styles covered in this handbook. See 10i for a screenshot and the information you need to look for on a Web site.

For information you need to record for visual, performance, multimedia, and miscellaneous sources, see 12g, 15f, 17f, and 19g.

Keep your list of sources in a form that you can work with to organize them alphabetically, add and reject sources, and add summaries and notes. Note cards, computer files, or your own files kept in licensed bibliographical software such as RefWorks or EndNote (9f) have the advantage over sheets of paper or a research journal. They don't tie you to page order.

Here is a sample bibliographical record in a computer file for an article accessed in an online subscription database.

> Belkin, Lisa. "When Whippersnappers and Geezers Collide." *New York Times* 26 July 2007, late ed.: G2. *LexisNexis*. Web. 30 Mar. 2009.

For handwritten index cards, use underlining to represent italics.

Sample annotated bibliography entry Here is a sample from Jared Whittemore's annotated bibliography that he prepared for a paper on the community college system in California. He writes the bibliographical details for future reference and ease of relocating the source, adding also useful comments about the content of the source and its relevance to his purpose in including it in his paper.

> *Significant Historical Events in the Development of the Public Community College*. American Association of Community Colleges. 13 Feb. 2001. Web. 23 Mar. 2009.

> This site provides a timeline charting the significant events in the history of community colleges, from 1862 to 2001. The timeline includes historical events, such as the founding of the first community college in 1901, and tracks important legislation and publications relating to the development and improvement of the community college system. It provides a historical

perspective on the implementation and advancements made in the system in more than a century.

TECH NOTE

Annotated Bibliographies

For more information on how to prepare an annotated bibliography, along with examples, go to the Purdue Online Writing Lab.

Use bibliographical software, databases, and Word 2007 to help you keep records

Bibliographical software When you are asked to write research papers, you may find that your college library owns special software (such as EndNote or RefWorks) to help you search databases, store the results of your database searches, organize your research, insert citations while you write, and prepare a bibliography in one of many styles available.

KEY POINTS

What Bibliographical Software Can Do

- It can provide a way for you to record and easily save citations for sources you find in online databases.
- It will automatically create a bibliographical list or endnotes either in Cite While You Write (CWYW) mode or after completion of your text.
- It can prepare these lists in a variety of documentation styles, including those commonly required in college courses and covered in this handbook: MLA, APA, *Chicago*, and CSE. In fact, EndNote claims to offer 3,000 styles—more than enough for anyone.
- It does a lot but not everything. Take the time to learn the program. Using these programs requires a considerable initial investment of time and patience, but the investment will pay off eventually by making citations in research papers much easier to manage. Read the documentation and consult the Help menu whenever you need to.

(Continued)

(Continued)

■ It needs to be supplemented by your informed knowledge of the system you are using. Do not let the program take over *all* the chores of recording the results of your research, inserting your citations, and preparing your list of works cited. You still need to be able to check citations for general accuracy and completeness, fix glitches, insert your anchors and hyperlinks in online papers, and handle the occasional abstruse reference yourself.

If you have no library access to EndNote, RefWorks, ProCite, or similar licensed software, you can sign up for a free service such as Connotea or Zotero (only for Firefox). Zotero especially is recommended by many as a reason to switch to the Firefox browser as it too allows you to "cite while you write" and lets you file and keep citations and some texts of academic papers, articles, and copies of Web sites in your own personal file.

Databases   Several database screens, such as the heading of those sponsored by EBSCO, shown here, include useful features for writers of research papers.

From the Citation screen for an article, clicking on the third icon from the right ("Cite This Article") will take you to a screen that shows you how to cite the article in several documentation styles, including AMA, APA, *Chicago,* and MLA. The second icon from the right allows you to "Export to Bibliographic Manager." This feature enables you to save citations in a file for export to EndNote, RefWorks, and other bibliographical software. Try out these features with the article shown in Source Shot 3 on page 193.

Word 2007   In Word 2007, you can keep a master list of the sources you consult, and then Word will prepare and insert a citation in your paper for the sources you actually cite (in the style you choose) and will also construct a list of all the sources from your list that you have used in your bibliography.

For an example of how this useful Word feature works, go to <http://office.microsoft.com/en-us/word/HA102904981033.aspx>.

10 🔑

How to Use, Integrate, and Document Sources

10a Interact with your sources: Annotate and make notes

Printing and saving from online sources make a source text available for you to annotate. You can interact with the author's ideas, asking questions, writing comments, and jotting down your own ideas. Here is a passage from an article by Ellen Laird on plagiarism. As Laird, a college professor, discusses the case of Chip, a student who has plagiarized, she is considering her own role and her student's explanation. The passage shows the annotations that student Juana Mere made as she gave the article a critical reading.

But what if her instructions weren't as clear as she thought?

To save face with myself, I must assume that Chip understood that downloading an essay and submitting it as his own was an egregious act. Why, then, did he do it? *Can she ever really know?*

Look up

Chip explained he had been "mentally perturbed" the weekend before the paper was due and that the essay he had written failed to meet his high standards. But I sensed that Chip felt he had made a choice akin to having a pizza delivered. He had procrastinated on an assignment due the next day, had no time left in which to prepare his work from scratch, and had to get on to those pressing matters that shape the world of an 18-year-old. He dialed his Internet service provider, ordered takeout, and had it delivered.

But it's speculation on her part

Sounds like a very general excuse

Is this condescending? *Nice analogy* *Good quotation*

Source: Laird, Ellen. "Internet Plagiarism: We All Pay the Price." *Chronicle of Higher Education* 13 July 2001: 5. *Academic Search Premier*. Web. 30 Mar. 2009.

Annotating is useful for comments, observations, and questions. You also will need to make notes when you do not have a copy that you can write on or when you want to summarize, paraphrase, and make detailed connections to other ideas and other sources. Write notes on the computer, on legal pads, in notebooks, or on index cards—whatever works best for you. On the computer, you can use Word's Comment function to annotate a text or insert your own comments within a text and highlight them in a color. Index cards—each card with a heading and only one note—offer flexibility: You can shuffle and reorder them to fit the organization of your paper. In your notes, always include the author's name, a short version of the title of the work, and any relevant page number(s). Include full source information in your working bibliography (9e). Then, when you write your paper, you will have at your fingertips all the information necessary for a citation.

10b Put yourself in your paper, and synthesize sources

Large amounts of information are no substitute for a thesis with relevant support. Your paper should *synthesize* your sources, not just tell about them one after the other. When you synthesize, you connect the ideas in individual sources to create a larger picture, to inform yourself about the topic, and to establish your own ideas on the topic. So leave plenty of time to read through your notes, think about what you have read, connect with the material, form responses to it, take into account new ideas and opposing arguments, and find connections among the facts and the ideas your sources offer. Avoid sitting down to write a paper at the last minute, surrounded by library books or stacks of photocopies. In this scenario, you might be tempted to lift material, and you will produce a lifeless paper. Remember that the paper is ultimately your work, not a collection of other people's words, and that your identity and opinions as the writer should be evident.

10c Organize your essay by ideas, not sources

Let your ideas, not your sources, drive your paper. Resist the temptation to organize your paper in the following way:

 1. What points Smith makes

2. What points Jones makes

3. What points Fuentes makes

4. What points Jackson and Hayes make in opposition

5. What I think

That organization is driven by your sources, with the bulk of the paper dealing with the views of Smith, Jones, and the rest. Instead, let your thesis and its points of supporting evidence determine the organization:

1. First point of support: what ideas I have to support my thesis and what evidence Fuentes and Jones provide

2. Second point of support: what ideas I have to support my thesis and what evidence Smith and Fuentes provide

3. Third point of support: what ideas I have to support my thesis and what evidence Jones provides

4. Opposing viewpoints of Jackson and Hayes

5. Common ground and refutation of those viewpoints

6. Synthesis

To avoid producing an essay that reads like a serial listing of summaries or references ("Crabbe says this," "Tyger says that," "Tyger also says this"), spend time reviewing your notes and synthesizing what you find into a coherent and convincing statement of what you know and believe.

- Make lists of good ideas your sources raise about your topic.
- Look for the connections among those ideas: comparisons and contrasts.
- Find links in content, examples, and statistics.
- Note connections between the information in your sources and what you know from your own experience.

If you follow these guidelines, you will take control of your material instead of letting it take control of you.

10d Summarize and paraphrase

Summaries are useful for giving readers basic information about the work you are discussing. To summarize a source or a passage in a source, select only the main points as the author presents them, without your own commentary or interpretation. Be brief, and use your own words at all times. A good thing to remember is to not have the original source in front of you as you write. Read, understand, and put the passage away before writing your summary. Then, if you find that you absolutely need to include some particularly apt words from the original source, put them in quotation marks.

Use summaries in your research paper to let readers know the gist of the most important sources you find. When you include a summary in a paper, introduce the author or the work to indicate where your summary begins. At the end of the summary, give the page numbers you are summarizing. Do not include page numbers if you are summarizing the complete work or summarizing an online source; instead, indicate where your summary ends and your own ideas return (see 10f). When you write your paper, provide full documentation of the source in your list of works cited at the end.

Here are a few paragraphs from a *New York Times* article by Lisa Belkin. A student's bibliographical citation for the article is shown in 9e on page 142.

Original (paragraphs 4–6 from a longer source)

> Summer is the season of culture shock in the working world, when the old guard comes face to face with a next wave of newcomers, and the result is something like lost tribes encountering explorers for the first time.
>
> Add to this the favorite fact of human resource managers everywhere: this is the first time in history that four generations—those who lived through World War II, Baby Boomers, Generation X and Generation Y—are together in the workplace.
>
> Managers tell stories of summer associates who come to meetings with midriffs exposed, baring a belly ring; of interns who walk through the halls engaged with iPods; of new hires who explain they need Fridays off because their boyfriends get Fridays off and they have a share in a beach house. Then there is the tale of the summer hire who sent a text message to a senior partner asking "Are bras required as part of the dress code?"
>
> —Lisa Belkin, "When Whippersnappers and Geezers Collide." *New York Times,* 26 July 2007, late ed.: G2, *LexisNexis,* 30 Mar. 2009.

No page number is needed in the following in-text citations as the article is only one page long and the page number will appear in the bibliographical citation. For longer articles, always include the page number(s) in parentheses before the final period.

Summary (recorded in a computer file)

Belkin   Summary

"When Whippersnappers and Geezers Collide"

Lisa Belkin points out that summer jobs for young people expose older managers to behavior they regard as unusual, even shocking.

A *paraphrase*, in contrast, is similar in length to the original material. It presents the details of the author's argument and logic, but *it avoids plagiarism by not using the author's exact words or sentence structure*. If you keep the source out of sight as you write a paraphrase, you will not be tempted to use any of the sentence patterns or phrases of the original. Even if you are careful to cite your source, your writing may still be regarded as plagiarized if your paraphrase resembles the original too closely in wording or sentence structure. You can use common words and expressions without quotation marks, but if you use longer or more unusual expressions from the source, always enclose them in quotation marks.

KEY POINTS

How to Paraphrase

- Keep the source out of sight as you write a paraphrase so that you will not be tempted to copy the sentence patterns or phrases of the original.

- Do not substitute synonyms for some or most of the words in an author's passage.

- Use your own sentence structure as well as your own words. Your writing will still be regarded as plagiarized if it resembles the original in sentence structure as well as in wording.

- Do not comment or interpret. Just tell readers the ideas that the author of your source presents.

- Check your text against the original source to avoid inadvertent plagiarism.

- Cite the author (and page number if a print source) as the source of the ideas, introduce and integrate the paraphrase, and provide full documentation. If the source does not name an author, cite the title.

You can use common words and expressions such as "managers" or "four generations," but if you use more unusual expressions from the source ("the next wave of newcomers," "lost tribes encountering explorers," or "baring a belly ring"), you need to enclose them in quotation marks. In the first sample paraphrase shown here, nothing is quoted, but the words and structure resemble the original too closely.

Paraphrase too similar to the original (similarities are highlighted)

Belkin   Paraphrase, paragraphs 4–6

Lisa Belkin describes the summer culture shock of the working world when the old timers see the generation Y newcomers as creatures they encounter for the first time. Summer interns shock managers by exposing their midriffs, listening to iPods, and wanting to take Fridays off to go to the beach.

Revised paraphrase

Lisa Belkin describes the clash in the workplace when the new young summer interns surprise—and shock—the managers with their behavior. They wear informal, even revealing clothes, listen to music through headphones, and ask for time off to be with friends.

10e Quote accurately

Readers should immediately realize why you are quoting a particular passage and what the quotation contributes to the ideas you want to convey. They should also learn who said the words you are quoting and, if the source is a print source, on which page of the original work the quotation appears. Then they can look up the author's name in the list of works cited at the end of your paper and find out exactly where you found the quotation.

The Modern Language Association (MLA) format for citing a quotation from an article by one author is illustrated in this chapter and in part 3. For the use of quotation marks, see chapter 49.

Decide what and when to quote Quote sparingly and only when the original words express the exact point you want to make and express it succinctly and well. Ask yourself: Which point of mine does the quotation illustrate? Why am I considering quoting this particular passage rather than paraphrasing it? What do I need to tell my readers about the author of the quotation?

Quote the original exactly Any words you use from a source must be included in quotation marks (unless they are long quotations) and quoted exactly as they appear in the original, with the same punctuation marks and capital letters. Do not change pronouns or tenses to fit your own purpose, unless you enclose changes in square brackets (see the examples on p. 152).

NOT EXACT QUOTATION **Belkin describes how "old-timers at work act like tribes seeing explorers for the first time" when the summer interns arrive.**

EXACT **When managers see the new summer interns, Belkin reports, they act like "lost tribes encountering explorers for the first time."**

If a quotation includes a question mark or an exclamation point, include it, and if a page number is necessary, put the final period after it: *An intern asked, "Are bras required as part of the dress code?" (G2).* However, a page number is not necessary for citing a one-page article.

How to indicate words omitted from a quotation

In the middle If you omit as irrelevant to your purpose any words or passages from the middle of a quotation, signal this by using the ellipsis mark, three dots separated by spaces, as in the first example that follows.

At the end If you omit the end of the source's sentence at the end of your own sentence, use three ellipsis dots and put the sentence period after any necessary parenthetical citation of page number.

▶ **Belkin makes the point that "summer is the season . . . when the old guard comes face to face with a next wave of newcomers . . ." (G2).**

If no citation in parentheses ends the sentence, put the sentence period, followed by three dots—four dots in all—as in the following example:

▶ **Belkin makes the point that "summer is the season . . . when the old guard comes face to face with a next wave of newcomers. . . ."**

At the beginning   If you omit any words from the beginning of a quoted sentence, do not use an ellipsis.

> ▶ **Belkin sees summer as the "season of culture shock."**

Omitting a sentence or a line of poetry   If you omit a complete sentence (or more), use three dots after the previous period. For an omitted line of poetry, use a line of dots (see 51g).

Note: In MLA style, if your source passage itself uses ellipses, place your ellipsis dots within square brackets to indicate that your ellipsis mark is not part of the original text: [. . .].

How to split a quotation   For variety, you may want to use your own words to split a quotation:

> ▶ **"Summer is the season" according to Belkin, "of culture shock in the working world."**

Don't rig the evidence   It should go without saying that quoting means quoting an author's ideas without omitting or adding any of your own contextual material that substantially changes the author's intent. For example, it would distort the author's views and present the evidence incorrectly to write this, even though the words that are quoted are in the original article:

> ▶ **Lisa Belkin sees new hires in summer jobs as being like "lost tribes."**

How to add or change words to fit into your sentence   If you add any comments or explanations in your own words or if you change a word of the original to fit it grammatically into your sentence or to spell it correctly, enclose the added or changed material in square brackets. Generally, however, it is preferable to rephrase your sentence because bracketed words and phrases make sentences difficult to read. The first example shows a word in the quotation changed to make it fit the quoter's sentence structure, and the second is a personal interjected comment; the revised example does away with the awkward square brackets.

AWKWARD   **Lisa Belkin's article shows summer interns as irresponsibly "[coming] to meetings with midriffs exposed, baring [to their managers' horror] a belly ring."**

REVISED   **Lisa Belkin reports how some summer interns in the workplace shock their managers when they "come to meetings with midriffs exposed, baring a belly ring."**

How to quote a long passage If you quote more than three lines of poetry or four typed lines of prose, do not use quotation marks.

- Begin the quotation on a new line.
- For MLA style, indent the quotation one inch or ten spaces from the left margin.
- For APA or *Chicago* style, indent the quotation a half inch from the left margin.
- Double-space throughout.
- Do not indent from the right margin.
- If you quote from more than one paragraph, indent the first line of a new paragraph an additional two or three spaces.
- Establish the context for a long quotation and integrate it into your text by stating the point you want to make and naming the author of the quotation in your introductory statement.

> Belkin's account of the clash between older managers and the brand-new summer interns gives specific examples of workplace culture shock:
>
>> Managers tell stories of summer associates who come to meetings with midriffs exposed, baring a belly ring; of interns who walk through the halls engaged with iPods; of new hires who explain they need Fridays off because their boyfriends get Fridays off and they have a share in a beach house.

Note: With a long indented quotation with a parenthetical page citation, put the period before the parenthetical citation, not after it.

Avoid a string of quotations Use quotations, especially long ones, sparingly and only when they help you make a good argument. Readers do not want a collection of passages from other writers; they could read the original works for that. Rather, they want your analysis of your sources and the conclusions you draw from your research. Quotations should not appear in a string, one after the other. If they do, your readers will wonder what purpose the quotations serve and will search for your voice in the paper.

Fit a quotation into your sentence   When you quote, use the exact words of the original, and make sure that those exact words do not disrupt the flow of your sentence and send it in another direction, with, for instance, a change of tense.

A BAD FIT   **In my last summer job, I too saw "interns who walk through the halls engaged with iPods" (Belkin).**

A BETTER FIT   **In my last summer job, I too saw new hires "walk through the halls engaged with iPods" (Belkin).**

10f   Indicate the boundaries of a source citation in your text

Naming an author or title in your text tells readers that you are citing ideas from a source, and citing a page number at the end of a summary or paraphrase lets them know where your citation ends. However, for one-page print or database articles and for Internet sources, a page citation is not necessary, so indicating where your comments about a source end is harder to do. You always need to indicate clearly where your summary or paraphrase ends and where your own comments take over. Convey the shift to readers by commenting on the source in a way that clearly announces a transition back to your own views. Use expressions such as *it follows that, X's explanation shows that, as a result, evidently, obviously,* or *clearly* to signal the shift.

Unclear citation boundary

> According to promotional material on a Sony Web site more than ten years ago, the company decided to release a cassette and a CD based on a small research study indicating that listening to Mozart improved IQ. The products showed the ingenuity of commercial enterprise while taking the researchers' conclusions in new directions.

Revised citation, with source boundary indicated

> According to promotional material on a Sony Web site more than ten years ago, the company decided to release a cassette and a CD based on research indicating that listening to Mozart improved IQ. Clearly, Sony's

strategy demonstrated the ingenuity of commercial enterprise, but it cannot reflect what the researchers intended when they published their conclusions.

Another way to indicate the end of your citation is to include the author's or authors' name(s) at the end of the citation instead of (or even in addition to) introducing the citation with the name.

Unclear citation boundary

For people who hate shopping, Web shopping may be the perfect solution. Jerome and Taylor's exploration of "holiday hell" reminds us that we get more choice from online vendors than we do when we browse at our local mall because the online sellers, unlike mall owners, do not have to rent space to display their goods. In addition, one can buy almost anything online, from CDs, cell phones, and books to cars and real estate.

Revised citation, with source boundary indicated

For people who hate shopping, Web shopping may be the perfect solution. An article exploring the "holiday hell" of shopping reminds us that we get more choice from online vendors than we do when we browse at our local mall because the online sellers, unlike mall owners, do not have to rent space to display their goods (Jerome and Taylor). In addition, one can buy almost anything online, from CDs, cell phones, and books to cars and real estate.

10g Introduce and integrate source material

Introduce quotations, summaries, and paraphrases, and integrate them into the flow of your writing. They should not just pop up with no lead-in.

Source not introduced and integrated

Summer interns can make life difficult. Managers are "like lost tribes encountering explorers for the first time" (Belkin).

Source introduced and integrated

In an article about summer interns in the workplace, journalist Lisa Belkin describes managers as being "like lost tribes encountering explorers for the first time."

If you quote a complete sentence, or if you paraphrase or summarize a section of another work, introduce the source material by providing an introductory phrase with the author's full name (for the first reference to an author) and a brief mention of his or her expertise or credentials, as in the preceding example. For subsequent citations, the last name is sufficient.

Ways to introduce source material

X has pointed out that	According to X,
X has made it clear that	As X insists,
X explains that	In 2008, X, the vice president
X suggests that	of the corporation, declared

Vary the introductory phrase   The introductory verbs *say* and *write* are clear and direct. Occasionally, use one of the following verbs to express subtle shades of meaning: *acknowledge, agree, argue, ask, assert, believe, claim, comment, contend, declare, deny, emphasize, explain, insist, note, point out, propose, speculate,* or *suggest.*

10h Document to fit the discipline

Documentation is an integral part of a research paper. Conventions vary from discipline to discipline and from style manual to style manual—as illustrated by the inclusion of MLA, APA, CSE, and *Chicago* styles in parts 3 and 4—but the various styles of documentation are not entirely arbitrary. The styles tend to reflect what the disciplines value and what readers need to know.

In the humanities, for instance, many research findings offer scholarly interpretation and analysis of texts, so they may be relevant for years, decades, or centuries. Publication dates in the Modern Language Association (MLA) style, therefore, occur only in the works-cited list and are not included in the in-text citation. Such a practice also serves to minimize interruptions to the text.

The endnote/footnote system of the *Chicago Manual of Style* and Council of Science Editors (CSE) citation-sequence and citation-name systems go further, requiring only a small superscript number in the text to send readers to the list of sources.

The American Psychological Association (APA) and the CSE name-year style include the date of the work cited right there in the text citation, emphasizing that timeliness of research is an issue in the sciences and social sciences. In addition, abbreviations used in all three CSE styles (chapter 17) reflect the fact that scientists are expected to be aware of the major sources in their field.

All systems, however, aim to give enough information in the text for readers to be able to find full details of the source in a bibliographical list at the end of the work or in footnotes or endnotes.

See also 5e on writing and researching across the curriculum.

10i One source, four systems of documentation

This section will take you through the details you should record of one source to be able to access it again when you need to and to document it in any of the four styles commonly used in college: MLA, APA, *Chicago*, and CSE. The source example selected here is a Web site. Such a source is often more fluid and variable than others; information may lurk in different places on the site or may not be present at all. Such sites consequently give researchers more difficulties with finding the information necessary for responsible documentation.

Scrutinize a Web site and record the details of as many of the following so that you will be able to document the source in whichever style you choose:

1. **Name(s) of author(s) or name of organization acting as author.**

2. **Title of a document on a site.** Some Web sites will contain documents with titles, and some will not. Check the title bar of your browser for the page title, but if there is a clear title in the page content, use that as the preferred title. Note any section name for information you may refer to in your paper; record page numbers only for PDF documents. Also note any prior print publication of the material.

3. **Title of Web site plus any version or edition number.** If this information is not visible on a Web page, check the Home or About pages for site information.

4. **Sponsor/publisher of the site.** This may appear on the last page of the site and may be the same as the Web site title. If it is not visible, check the root domain of the URL, immediately

before the first single slash. If no publisher/sponsor is named, use *n.p.* to record that fact.

5. **Date of posting/publication plus page numbers if available.** If no date is given, write *n.d.* in your records. Note page numbers *only* for PDF documents or for a source that appeared previously in print. (For CSE style, also record the place of the home page publication along with the date.)

6. **Your date of access and the URL.** Copy and paste the URL from your browser into your working bibliography. (MLA style calls for URLs only when a site is difficult to access. The other three styles call for the URL in the list of references.) Print or save the home page and any page that provides crucial information or is likely to change its content. Also, because Web sites come and go, always record the exact date on which you access the site.

Note: If you print or save the page, the URL and your date of access will appear on the printout or saved file. Set your browser to print out the site with the complete URL (with no "..." in the middle) and the date of access on each page.

Recognize the difficulties   Note that on many sites, you may have difficulty finding a date of posting, a document title as well as a Web site name, or an exact identification of the author of the material, whether an individual or an organization. Just record whatever you can find on a thorough search of the site, always scrolling down to the bottom of a page and consulting the Home or About pages, as well as the page properties or page info tools found in your browser. Also try using the root domain of the URL—the material just before the dot preceding the first single slash—to identify the owner, also referred to as the *publisher* or *sponsor,* of the site, who is responsible for its content. If the Home and About links provide no useful information, consider whether you should use a source if you are unsure about the identity of the author, the author's credentials, or the owner and purpose of the site. You can also do a search to see who links to a site and what those referrers have to say about it as an additional aid to evaluation. (When using a search engine, if you put "link:" followed by a URL in the Search field and hit Return, the results will show you which sites link to that URL.)

URL   Title of Web site

If you find and record as many of the indicated items of information as you can find, you will then be able to cite the source in the four different documentation styles covered in this book.

MLA STYLE

Boff, Leonardo. "Living Better or Living a 'Good Life'?" *Organic*
    Consumers Association. Organic Consumers Assoc.,
    27 Mar. 2009. Web. 31 Mar. 2009.

APA STYLE

Boff, L. (2009, March 27). Living better or living a "good life"?
    Retrieved from Organic Consumers Association website: http://
    www.organicconsumers.org/articles/article_17378.cfm

CSE STYLE

2. Boff L. Living better or living a "good life"? [Internet]. 2009. Finland
    (MN): Organic Consumers Assoc.; [cited 2009 Mar 31]. Available
    from: http://www.organicconsumers.org/articles/article_17378.cfm

***CHICAGO* STYLE NOTE**

    9. Leonardo Boff, "Living Better or Living a 'Good Life'?" Organic
Consumers Assoc., March 27, 2009, http://www.organicconsumers.org/
articles/article_17378.cfm (accessed March 31, 2009).

PART 3

MLA Documentation

11 Citing Sources in Your Paper, MLA Style 165

12 The MLA List of Works Cited 176

13 Sample Paper 3: A Student's Research Paper, MLA Style 209

 ONLINE RESOURCES

www.cengage.com/english/raimes

Companion online resources are available for sections throughout this part. We invite you to visit the book's Web site for more information and direct access.

PART 3

MLA Documentation

MLA AT A GLANCE INDEX

11 Citing Sources in Your Paper, MLA Style 165

11a Basic features of MLA style 165
11b How to cite sources in your paper 167
11c Explanatory footnotes and endnotes 175

12 MLA List of Works Cited 176

12a How to set up and organize the list 176
12b How to list authors 178
12c Sample listings: Print books, parts of books, pamphlets 179

12d Sample listings: Print works in periodicals 187
12e Sample listings: Works accessed in online library databases 191
12f Sample listings: Sources found on the Web 194
12g Sample listings: Visual, performance, multimedia, and miscellaneous sources (live, print, and online) 201

13 Sample Paper 3: A Student's Research Paper, MLA Style 209

AT A GLANCE: INDEX OF MLA STYLE FEATURES

11 Citing Sources in Your Paper, MLA Style 165

11a Basic features of MLA style 165
11b How to cite sources in your paper, MLA author/page style 167

CITING A WORK WITH INDIVIDUAL AUTHOR OR AUTHORS 167
A. One author named in your text 167
B. Author cited in parentheses 168
C. Work written by two or more authors 168
D. Work by an author with more than one work cited 168
E. Sequential references to a work by the same author 169
F. Two authors with the same last name 169
G. Author of work in an edited anthology 169
H. Author of work quoted in another source 169
I. More than one work in one citation 170

CITING A WORK WITH NO INDIVIDUAL AUTHOR NAMED 170
J. Corporation, government agency, or organization as author 170
K. No author or editor named 170

L. Unauthored entry in dictionary or encyclopedia 171

CITING A WORK WITH PAGE NUMBERS NOT AVAILABLE OR RELEVANT 171
M. Reference to an entire work 171
N. Work only one-page long 171
O. Web or electronic source with no page numbers 171

CITING MULTIMEDIA AND MISCELLANEOUS SOURCES 172
P. Multimedia or nonprint source 172
Q. Multivolume work 172
R. Lecture, speech, personal communication, interview 173
S. Frequently studied literary works: Fiction, poetry, and drama 173
T. The Bible and other sacred texts 174
U. Historical or legal document 174
V. A long quotation 175
W. A footnote 175

11c Explanatory footnotes and endnotes 175

12 MLA List of Works Cited 176

12a How to set up and organize an MLA list of works cited 176
12b How to list authors 178
12c Sample listings: Print books, parts of books, pamphlets 179

1. One author (Source Shot 1) 179
2. Two or more authors 180
3. Book with editor(s) 181
4. Author and editor 182
5. One work in an anthology (original or reprinted) 182
6. More than one work in an anthology, cross-referenced 183
7. Entry in a reference book 183
8. No author named 184
9. Corporation, organization, or government agency as author 184
10. Translation 184
11. Multivolume work 184
12. Book in a series 185
13. Publisher and imprint 185
14. Foreword, preface, introduction, or afterword 185
15. Republished book 185
16. Book not in first edition 185
17. Title including a title 186
18. Illustrated work (e.g., graphic novel) 186
19. The Bible and other sacred texts 186
20. Dissertation 186

12d Sample listings: Print works in periodicals (articles, reviews, editorials, etc.) 187

21. Scholarly journal article (Source Shot 2) 187
22. Magazine article 187
23. Newspaper article 188
24. Article that skips pages 189
25. Review 190
26. Unsigned editorial or article 190
27. Letter to the editor 190
28. Abstract in an abstracts journal 190
29. Article on microform 190

12e Sample listings: Works accessed in online library databases 191

30. Magazine article in an online database (Source Shot 3) 191
31. Scholarly article in an online database 192
32. Newspaper article in an online database 193

12f Sample listings: Sources found on the Web 194

33. Authored document on nonperiodical Web site, with no print version (Source Shot 4) 194
34. Web site document, no author named 194
35. Entire Web site, no author named 195
36. Article in an online scholarly journal 195
37. Article in an online magazine 195
38. Article in an online newspaper 195
39. Online review, editorial, letter, or abstract 196
40. Entry in an online encyclopedia, dictionary, or other reference work 197

(Continued)

41. Government publication online (Source Shot 5) 198
42. Scholarly project 198
43. Online book 198
44. Online poem 198
45. Personal Web site/home page 199

46. Course page 199
47. Online posting on a blog, discussion board, wiki, online mailing list 199
48. Forwarded document 200
49. Personal e-mail message 200

12g Sample listings: Visual, performance, multimedia, and miscellaneous sources (live, print, and online) 201

50. Documenting across media: Nine ways to document a Jay-Z song 201
51. Work of visual art 203
52. Cartoon 204
53. Advertisement, brochure, museum placard 205
54. Map or chart 205
55. Film or video 205
56. Television or radio program 206
57. Sound recording 206

58. Live performance 206
59. Podcast 207
60. Interview (personal, published, broadcast, or online) 207
61. Lecture or speech 207
62. Letter or personal communication 208
63. Legal or historical document 208
64. CD-ROM or DVD 208
65. Digital files

13 Sample Paper 3: A Student's Research Paper, MLA Style 209

For research papers and shorter documented essays, always provide detailed information about any books, articles, Web sites, or other sources that you cite. Many composition and literature courses ask you to follow the guidelines of the Modern Language Association (MLA) as recommended in the *MLA Handbook for Writers of Research Papers,* 7th edition (New York: MLA, 2009), and on the MLA Web site.

Your college may provide free access to bibliographical software that helps compile citations and bibliographies in any documentation style. Ask a librarian if a program such as EndNote or RefWorks is available. With these programs, you enter details in specific fields, and the program then formats your book or journal citations into a bibliography according to MLA, APA, or another documentation style. Some will also transfer the bibliographical references for titles found during a literature search directly into the user's Web-based account (9d, 9f). However, whether you use such a program or do the formatting yourself, you still have to find—and type—the information necessary for citations not directly transferred. The examples in the following chapters will help you find the information to include and the format to use.

11 ⌁

Citing Sources in Your Paper, MLA Style

When you refer to, comment on, paraphrase, or quote another author's material, you must indicate that you have done so by inserting what is called a *citation*. In MLA style, you give the name of the author(s) and the page number(s) where you found the material, if available. You can put the author's name in your own text to introduce the material, with the page number in parentheses at the end of the sentence; or especially for a source you have cited previously, you can put both author and page number in parentheses at the end of the sentence in which you cite the material. Then all of the more detailed information about your sources goes into a list of works cited at the end of the paper so that readers can themselves retrieve and read the same source.

Sections 11a–11b show you examples and variations on the basic principle of citation—for instance, what to do when no author is named or how to cite an online source that has no page numbers.

11a Basic features of MLA style

KEY POINTS

How to Cite and List Sources in MLA Style

1. *In your paper*

   - Include the **last name(s)** of the author (or authors). Give a title if no author is known.

   - Include the **page number(s)** where the information is located (except when the source is online or only one page long), but do not include the word "page" or "pages" or the abbreviation "p." or "pp." Omit a shared first digit in numbers over 100, such as 257–58.

   Both author and page can be given in parentheses at the end of the sentence that makes the reference. You can also give the name of the author in your text, with the page number in parentheses at the end of the sentence. *(Continued)*

(Continued)

2. At the end of your paper

■ Include a **list**, alphabetized by authors' last names or by title (in italics) if the author is not known, of all the sources you refer to in the paper. Also include information about publisher, date of publication, and the medium of publication of the source (Print, Web, Film, Television, Performance, CD, and so on). Begin the list on a new page and title it "Works Cited." Sections 12c–12g provide many examples of listing different types of sources.

Illustrations of the Basic Features (MLA)

Citation in Your Paper	Entry in List of Works Cited
Author of print book named in your text with page(s) in parentheses The renowned scholar of language, David Crystal, has promoted the idea of "dialect democracy" (168).	Crystal, David. *The Stories of English.* Woodstock: Overlook, 2004. Print.
Author and pages(s) of print book given in parentheses A renowned scholar of language has promoted the idea of "dialect democracy" (Crystal 168).	Crystal, David. *The Stories of English.* Woodstock: Overlook, 2004. Print.
Author of print article named in your text with page(s) in parentheses If indeed "anything goes" in art, Barry Gewen is right to question the role of an art critic (29).	Gewen, Barry. "State of the Art." *New York Times* 11 Dec. 2005, early ed. Book Rev. sec.: 28–32. Print.
Author and page(s) of print article provided in parentheses If indeed "anything goes" in art, the role of an art critic can be questioned (Gewen 29).	Gewen, Barry. "State of the Art." *New York Times* 11 Dec. 2005, early ed. Book Rev. sec.: 28–32. Print.
Author of article in an online database (no exact page numbers in HTML version) Barry Gewen questions the role of an art critic if "anything goes" in art.	Gewen, Barry. "State of the Art." *New York Times* 11 Dec. 2005: n. pag. *LexisNexis.* Web. 14 Jan. 2009. See also 12f, item 38, for the same source accessed on the Web.

Citation in Your Paper	Entry in List of Works Cited
Author of Web document named in your text According to William Saletan of *Slate* magazine, more and more researchers are exploring the ways in which the craving for junk food resembles drug addiction.	Saletan, William. "Is Food Addictive?" Human Nature: Science, Technology, and Life. *Slate*. Washington Post, 9 May 2008. Web. 10 Feb. 2009.

11b How to cite sources in your paper, MLA author/page style

You can get a great deal of help with the automatic "cite while you write" feature (CWYW) offered in bibliographical software programs such as EndNote and RefWorks. See 9f on the value of learning to use these programs often offered by college libraries.

CITING A WORK WITH INDIVIDUAL AUTHOR OR AUTHORS (MLA)

A. One author named in your text   You can cite an author in a sentence in your paper, or you can put the author and page number in parentheses at the end of your sentence. Naming the author as you introduce the source material allows you to supply information about the author's credentials as an expert and so increases the credibility of your source for readers. Another advantage of naming your source in your text is that readers then know that everything between the mention of the author and the cited page number is a reference to your source material and not your own ideas. Put a page number only within parentheses, not in the text of your paper.

For the first mention of an author, use the full name and any relevant credentials. After that, use only the last name. Generally, use the present tense to cite an author. See 12c, item 1, for the entry in a works-cited list.

> ┌─────── author and credentials ───────┐
> National Book Award winner Paul Fussell points out that even people in low-paying jobs show "all but universal pride in a uniform of any kind" (5).
>   ↖ page number

When a quotation ends the sentence, as in this example, close the quotation marks before the parentheses, and place the sentence period after the parentheses. (Note that this rule differs from the one for undocumented writing, which calls for a period before the closing quotation marks.)

When a quotation includes a question mark or an exclamation point, also include a period after the citation:

> Paul Fussell reminds us of our equating uniforms with seriousness of purpose when he begins a chapter by asking, "Would you get on an airplane with two pilots who are wearing cut-off jeans?" (85).

For a quotation longer than four lines, see 10e, page 110.

B. Author cited in parentheses If you have referred to an author previously or if you are citing statistics, you do not need to mention the author to introduce the reference. Simply include the author's last name before the page number within the parentheses, with no comma between them.

> The army retreated from Boston in disarray, making the victors realize that they had defeated the "greatest military power on earth"
>
> author and
> ⌐ page number ⌐
> (McCullough 76).

See 10e, page 147, for the punctuation of a citation after a long quotation.

C. Work written by two or more authors For a work with two or three authors, include all the names either in your text sentence or in parentheses.

> Lakoff and Johnson have pointed out . . . (42)
>
> (Baumol, Litan, and Schramm 18–20)

For a work with four or more authors, use only the first author's last name followed by "et al." (*Et alii* means "and others.") See 12c, item 2, for how to list a work with several authors in a works-cited list.

D. Work by an author with more than one work cited Include the author and title of the work in your text sentence.

> Alice Walker, in her book *In Search of Our Mothers' Gardens*, describes revisiting her past to discover more about Flannery O'Connor (43–59).

If you do not mention the author in your text, include in your parenthetical reference the author's last name followed by a comma, an abbreviated form of the title, and the page number.

comma ⟍
O'Connor's house still stands and is looked after by a caretaker (Walker,

abbreviated title ⎽page number
In Search 57)

E. Sequential references to a work by the same author If you rely on several quotations from the same page of your source within one of your paragraphs, one parenthetical reference after the last quotation is enough, but make sure that no quotations from other works intervene. If you are paraphrasing from and referring to one work several times in a paragraph, mention the author in your text. Then give the page number at the end of a paraphrase and again if you paraphrase from a different page. Make it clear to a reader where the paraphrase ends and your own comments take over (10f).

F. Two authors with the same last name Include each author's first initial or the complete first name if the authors' initials are the same.

> A writer can be seen as both "author" and "secretary," and the two
>
> roles can be seen as competitive (F. Smith 19).

G. Author of work in an edited anthology Cite the author of the included or reprinted work (not the editor of the anthology) and the page number(s) you refer to in the anthology. Mention the editor of the anthology only in the entry in the works-cited list, as shown in 12c, items 5 and 6.

> Saunders predicts that Bill Clinton will eventually be seen "as the
>
> embodiment of a certain strain of ornery, compassionate, complicated
>
> American energy" (300).

H. Author of work quoted in another source If the work you refer to quotes an author in a different source, use "qtd. in" (for "quoted in") in your parenthetical citation, followed by the last name of the author of the source in which you find the reference (the indirect source) and the page number where you find the quotation. List the author of the indirect source in your list of works cited. In the following example, the indirect source Hofstadter would be included in the list of works cited, not Harry Williams.

> Harry Williams argues that Lincoln waged the war "for the preservation of the status quo which had produced the war" (qtd. in Hofstadter 31).

See 12c, item 5, for the entry in the works-cited list.

I. More than one work in one citation Use semicolons to separate two or more sources in the same citation. Avoid making a parenthetical citation so long that it disrupts the flow of your text.

> The links between a name and ancestry have occupied many writers
> and researchers (Waters 65; Antin 188).

If sources refer to different points in your sentence, cite each one after the point it supports.

CITING A WORK WITH NO INDIVIDUAL AUTHOR NAMED (MLA)

J. Work by a corporation, government agency, or organization as author See 8e for help with finding the author of a Web site. When you use material authored not by an individual but by a corporation, government agency, or organization, cite the organization as the author, making sure it corresponds with the alphabetized entry in your works-cited list (Source Shot 5, p. 200). Use the complete name in your text or a shortened form in parentheses. The following examples cite a page number in the introduction of a PDF Web site document.

> ┌──────────── full name ────────────┐
> The United States Department of Education has projected an increase
> in college enrollment of 13% between 2006 and 2015 (Introd. 3).
>
> An increase in college enrollment of 13% between 2006 and 2015
>
> ┌──short name──┐
> has been projected (US Dept. of Educ. Introd. 3).

K. No author or editor named If no author or editor is named for a source, refer to the title of the book (italicized), the article title (within quotation marks), or the title of the Web site (italicized). Within a parenthetical citation, shorten the title to the first word alphabetized in the works-cited list (12c, item 8).

> According to *The Chicago Manual of Style*, writers should always
> "break or bend" rules when necessary (xiii).
>
> Writers should always "break or bend" rules when necessary (*Chicago* xiii).

If you need help with reading a Web site to determine its author, see 8e. For a site with no author indicated, use the name of the site.

L. Unauthored entry in a dictionary or encyclopedia   For an unsigned entry, give the title of the entry. A page number is not necessary for an alphabetized work. Begin the entry in the works-cited list with the title of the alphabetized entry (see 12c, item 7).

> Drypoint differs from etching in that it does not use acid ("Etching").

CITING A WORK WITH PAGE NUMBERS NOT AVAILABLE OR RELEVANT (MLA)

M. Reference to an entire work and not to one specific page
If you are referring not to a quotation or idea on one specific page, but rather to an idea that is central to the work as a whole, use the author's name alone. Include details of the work in your works-cited list.

> Mallon insists that we can learn from diaries about people's everyday
> lives and the worlds they create.

N. Work only one-page long   If a print article is only one page long, give the author's name alone in your text but include the page number in your works-cited list (12d, item 22). However, a page reference in parentheses indicates where a citation ends, so you may prefer to include the reference as a marker in your text.

O. Web or electronic source with no page numbers or author
Electronic database material and Web sources, which appear on a screen, have no stable page numbers that apply across systems or when printed, unless you access them in PDF (portable document format) files.

> Science writer Stephen Hart describes how researchers Edward Taub and
> Thomas Ebert conclude that for musicians, practicing "remaps the brain,"
> no page citation: online source has no numbered pages or paragraphs.
> thus maybe suggesting that it is better to start practicing at an early age.

If your source as it appears on the screen includes no visible numbered pages or numbered paragraphs, include "n. pag." in your works-cited list, as shown in 12f, item 36.

With no page number to mark where your citation ends (at "brain," above, or at the end of the sentence?), you need to define the point at which your citation ends and your own commentary takes

over, so it may be advisable to give the author's name in a parenthetical citation to mark the end of the reference:

> Researchers Edward Taub and Thomas Ebert conclude that for musicians,
> practicing "remaps the brain" (Hart), thus maybe suggesting that. . . .

Section 10f shows how to define the boundaries of a citation.

To document an online source with no author, give the title of
the Web page or the posting either in full or abbreviated to begin
with the first word you alphabetize (see 12f, item 35).

> A list of frequently asked questions about documentation and up-to-date
> instructions on how to cite online sources in MLA style can be found
> on the association's Web site (*MLA*).

With no page numbers to refer to, you may locate online scholarly material by the internal headings of the source (for example, *introduction, chapter, section*). Give paragraph numbers only if they are
supplied in the source and you see the numbers on the screen (use the
abbreviation "par." or "pars."). And then include the total number of
numbered paragraphs in your works-cited list (see 12f, item 36).

> Hatchuel discusses how film editing "can change points of view and
> turn objectivity into subjectivity" (par. 6).

> Film editing provides us with different perceptions of reality (Hatchuel, par. 6).

CITING MULTIMEDIA AND MISCELLANEOUS SOURCES (MLA)

P. Multimedia or other nonprint source   For radio or TV programs,
interviews, live performances, films, computer software, recordings,
works of art, and other nonprint sources, include only the author (or
contributor such as producer, actor, and so on) or title. Make sure that
your text reference corresponds to the first element of the information
you provide in the entry in your works-cited list. See 12g, item 58, for
examples of documenting the source cited that follows.

> The most moving theatrical experience of 2008 was the production of
> *Black Watch*.

> Linking the Vietnam war with a pub in Scotland was a tour de force for
> director John Tiffany.

Q. Multivolume work   If you refer to more than one volume in
your paper, indicate the volume number, followed by a colon, a
space, and the page number (Einstein 1: 25). Give the total number of

MLA ▼ (Modern Language Association)

volumes in your works-cited list. If you refer to only one volume in your paper, just give the page number in your in-text citation, and give the volume number in your list of works cited (see 12c, item 11, for examples in the list).

R. Lecture, speech, personal communication (letter, e-mail, conversation), or interview Give the name of the person delivering the communication. In your works-cited list, state the type of communication after the author's name or title of communication (see 12f, item 49, and 12g, item 60).

> According to Roberta Bernstein, professor of art history at the University of Albany, the most challenging thing about contemporary art is understanding that it is meant to be challenging. This may mean that the artist wants to make us uncomfortable with our familiar ideas or present us with reconceived notions of beauty.

S. Frequently studied literary works: Fiction, poetry, and drama For well-known works published in several different editions, include information so readers may locate material in whatever edition they are using. For a short story or novel with no divisions or chapters, simply give the author's name and page number. For other works, particularly classic works appearing in many editions, the following guidelines will allow your readers to find your reference in any edition. Include details about the edition you use in your works-cited list.

For a novel Give a chapter or section number in addition to the page number in the edition you used: (104; ch. 3).

For a poem Give line numbers, not page numbers: (lines 62–73). Omit the word *lines* in subsequent line references. Include up to three lines of poetry sequentially in your text, separated by a slash with a space on each side (/) (see 51f). For four or more lines of poetry, begin on a new line, indent the whole passage one inch from the left, double-space throughout, and omit quotation marks from the beginning and end of the passage (see 10e).

For classic poems, such as the *Iliad*, with divisions into books or parts Give the book or part number, followed by a period and then, with no space, line numbers, not page numbers, separated by a dash: (8.21–25).

For a play With dialogue, set the quotation off from your text, indented one inch with no quotation marks, and write the name of the character speaking in all capital letters, followed by a period. Indent subsequent lines of the same speech another quarter inch. Give act, scene, and line numbers in Arabic numerals.

For a new play available in only one published edition, cite author and page numbers as you do for other MLA citations.

For a classic work For classic plays published in several different editions (such as plays by William Shakespeare or Oscar Wilde), omit page numbers and cite in parentheses the act, scene, and line numbers of the quotation in Arabic numerals.

> Shakespeare's lovers in *A Midsummer Night's Dream* appeal to
> contemporary audiences accustomed to the sense of loss in love songs:
>> LYSANDER. How now, my love! Why is your cheek so pale?
>>> How chance the roses there do fade so fast?
>> HERMIA. Belike for want of rain, which I could well
>>> Beteem them from the tempest of mine eyes. (1.1.133–36)

In your works-cited list, list the bibliographical details of the edition you use.

For Shakespeare, Chaucer, and other classic literary works, abbreviate titles cited in parentheses, such as the following: *Tmp.* for *The Tempest*; *2H4* for *Henry IV, Part 2*; *MND* for *A Midsummer Night's Dream*; *GP* for the *General Prologue*; *PrT* for *The Prioress's Tale*; *Aen.* for *Aeneid*; *Beo.* for *Beowulf*; *Prel.* for Wordsworth's *Prelude*.

T. The Bible and other sacred texts In a parenthetical citation, give the title of the sacred text (italicized), along with the book (abbreviated), chapter, and verse. Note, though, that in a reference to a sacred text that is not directing readers to a specific citation in the list of works cited, the title of the sacred text is not italicized, as in the example that follows (see also section 52b).

> not a reference: no italics
> Of the many passages in the Bible that refer to lying, none is more apt
> today than the one that says that a wicked person "is snared by the
> transgression of his lips" (*Holy Bible*, Prov. 12.13).
>   italics for a reference   name of book abbreviated

See 12c, item 19, for this entry and others in a list of works cited.

U. Historical or legal document Cite any article and section number of a familiar historical document, such as the Constitution, in parentheses in your text (US Const., art. 2, sec. 4), with no entry in the works-cited list. Italicize the name of a court case (*Roe v. Wade*), but not the names of laws and acts. List cases and acts in your works-cited list (see 12g, item 63).

V. A long quotation   Indent a quotation of four or more lines one inch, without using quotation marks. See section 10e, page 110, for an example.

W. A footnote or footnotes   To cite a footnote in a source, give the page number followed by "n" or "nn" (as in "65n"). For a footnote in an annotated edition of a sacred text, give the edition (with any "The" omitted from your citation), book, chapter, and verse(s), followed by "n" or "nn" (*New Oxford Annotated Bible*, Gen. 35.1–4n). See 12c, item 19, for this entry in a works-cited list.

11c MLA explanatory footnotes and endnotes

The MLA parenthetical style of documentation uses a footnote (at the bottom of the page) or an endnote (on a separate numbered page at the end of the paper before the works-cited list) only for notes giving supplementary information that clarifies or expands a point. You might use a note to refer to several supplementary bibliographical sources or to provide a comment that is interesting but not essential to your argument. Indicate a note with a raised number (superscript) in your text after the word or sentence your note refers to.

- Begin the first line of each note one-half inch from the left margin.
- Do not indent subsequent lines of the same note.
- Double-space endnotes.
- Single-space within each footnote, but double-space between notes.

NOTE NUMBER IN TEXT

Ethics have become an important part of many writing classes.[1]

CONTENT FOOTNOTE OR ENDNOTE

half-inch   raised number followed by a space

[1] For additional discussion of ethics in the classroom, see Stotsky 799–806; Knoblauch 15–21; Bizzell 663–67; Friend 560–66.

The *MLA Handbook* also describes a system of footnotes or endnotes as an alternative to parenthetical documentation of references. This

(Modern Language Association) ▼ **MLA**

style is similar to the footnote and endnote style described in *The Chicago Manual of Style* (see chapter 19).

12 ⊙—

The MLA List of Works Cited

The references you make in your text to sources are brief—usually only the author's last name and a page number—so they allow readers to continue reading without interruption. For complete information about the source, readers use your brief in-text citation to direct them to the full bibliographical reference in the list of works cited at the end of your paper. For formatting instructions for books, articles, databases, Web sources, and multimedia sources, see the sample listings in 12c–12g.

12a How to set up and organize the MLA list

KEY POINTS

Guidelines for the MLA List of Works Cited

1. **What to list** List only works you actually cite in the text of your paper, not works you read but did not mention, unless your instructor requires you to include all the works you consulted as well as those mentioned in your text.

2. **Format of the list** Begin the list on a new numbered page after the last page of the paper or any endnotes. Center the heading (Works Cited) without quotation marks, italicizing, or a period. Double-space within and between entries. Do not number the entries.

3. **What to put first in an entry (author or title)** List works alphabetically by the author's last name (see 12b for more on how to list authors' names) or the name of an organization as author (12c, item 9). List works with no stated author by the first main word of the title (12c, item 8, and 12d, item 26).

4. **Indentation** To help readers find a source and to differentiate one entry from another, indent all lines of each entry—except the first—one-half inch. A word processor can provide these "hanging indents" (go to your Help menu). See the Tech Note on p. 178 on posting your paper online.

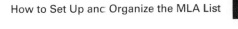

5. **Periods** Separate the main parts of an entry with a period, followed by one space.

6. **Capitals in titles** Capitalize the first letter of all words in titles of books and articles except *a, an, the,* coordinating conjunctions, *to* in an infinitive, and prepositions (such as *in, to, for, with, without, against*) unless they begin the title or subtitle.

7. **Italics, not underlining** Italicize the titles of books, periodicals, and Web sites, as well as the titles of films, performances, and so on. See the examples of specific sources in 12c–12g. *Note:* Prior to 2009, the MLA recommended underlining.

8. **Abbreviations** Use abbreviations for publishers' names; well-known religious and literary works; some common words in references, such as *fig., assn., ser., dept.,* and *introd.*; and common terms such as *e.g.* and *i.e.* When Web or other sources are missing information that MLA style usually requires, use "n.p." for "no publisher (or Web site sponsor)"; "n.p." for "no place" of publication given for a book; "n.d." for "no date" of publication; and "n. pag." for "no pagination" of a print or database work. See items 19, 31, 34, 42, 44, 45, and 53 for examples.

9. **Page numbers**
   - Give inclusive page numbers for print articles and sections of books.
   - Do not use "p." (or "pp.") or the word "page" (or "pages") before page numbers in any reference.
   - For page citations over 100 and sharing the same first number, use only the last two digits for the second number (for instance, 683–89, but 798–805).
   - For a work in print or in a database with no pagination information given, write "n. pag." (See items 31 and 44.)
   - Do not include page numbers for online works unless they are in PDF format or are provided on the screen as part of an original print source. If a Web source has sections, then providing the name of a section may help your readers locate the exact place in the source.

10. **Genre label** Include a label identifying the type of source if it will help your reader locate information. Labels include Advertisement, Afterword, Cartoon, Chart, Comic strip, Foreword, Home page, Interview, Introduction, Map, Online posting, and Preface.

(Continued)

(Continued)

11. **Publication medium**   Include in each entry the medium of publication of the source, such as Print, Web, Film, Television, CD, DVD, Lecture, MS, E-mail, MP3 file, Performance, and so forth or, for a work of visual art, the medium of composition (oil on canvas, encaustic, bronze, styrofoam, and so on). See the specific examples in 12c–12g.

12. **Scholarly journals**   Include the volume and issue number for all scholarly journals.

   NOTE on URLs   As of 2009, the *MLA Handbook* recommends using a URL only "when the reader probably cannot locate the source without it or when your instructor requires it" (182). If you need to include a URL, remove any automatically inserted hyperlinks. Then you will be able to enclose the URL in angle brackets, followed by a period. Break a URL for a new line only after a slash. Never insert a hyphen into a URL (see items 47 and 50 for examples).

TECH NOTE

Posting Your Paper Online

For an online list of works cited, do not use indentation, which HTML does not support well. Instead, keep all lines flush left and follow each entry with a line space.

12b How to list authors in the MLA list of works cited

Name of author(s)

- Put the last name first for a single author or the first author: *Fussell, Paul.*

- For two or more authors, reverse the names of only the first author: *Nichols, John, and Robert W. McChesney.*

- For four or more authors, use *et al.* after the reversed name of the first author (see 12c, item 2).

- When a corporation, agency, or organization is the author, begin your entry with that name (see 12c, item 9).

- Include a title such as *Jr.* or a numeral such as *II* after the first name, separated by a comma: *King, Martin Luther, Jr.*

Alphabetical order Alphabetize entries in the list by authors' last names. Note the following:

- Alphabetize by the exact letters in the spelling: *MacKay* precedes *McHam.*
- Let a shorter name precede a longer name beginning with the same letters: *Linden, Ronald* precedes *Lindenmayer, Arnold.*
- With last names using a prefix such as *le, du, di, del,* and *des,* alphabetize by the prefix: *Le Beau, Bryan F.*
- When *de* occurs with French names of one syllable, alphabetize under *D: De Man, Paul.* Otherwise, alphabetize by last name: *Maupassant, Guy de.*
- Alphabetize by the first element of a hyphenated name: *Sackville-West, Vita.*
- Alphabetize by the last name when the author uses two names without a hyphen: *Thomas, Elizabeth Marshall.*

Author not known For a work with no author named, alphabetize by the first word in the title of the work other than *A, An*, or *The* (see 12c, item 8, and 12d, item 26).

Several works by the same author(s) For all entries after the first, replace the name(s) of the author(s) with three hyphens followed by a period, and alphabetize according to the first significant word in the title. If an author serves as an editor or translator, put a comma after the three hyphens, followed by the appropriate abbreviation ("ed." or "trans."). If, however, the author has coauthors, repeat all authors' names in full and put the coauthored entry after all the single-name entries for the author.

Goleman, Daniel. *Destructive Emotions: A Scientific Dialogue with the Dalai Lama.* New York: Bantam-Dell, 2003. Print.

---. *Working with Emotional Intelligence.* New York: Bantam, 2000. Print.

Goleman, Daniel, Richard E. Boyatzis, and Annie McKee. *Primal Leadership: Learning to Lead with Emotional Intelligence.* Cambridge: Harvard Business School, 2004. Print.

Authors with the same last name Alphabetize by first names: *Smith, Adam* precedes *Smith, Frank.*

12c Sample MLA listings: Print books, parts of books, and pamphlets

1. Book with one author See Source Shot 1 (p. 180) for an example.

SOURCE SHOT 1

Listing a Book in MLA Style

Find the necessary information for documenting a book on its title page. If the date is not on the title page, look on the copyright page. Include the following:

❶ **Name of author(s)** Last name first for the first author

❷ *Title of Book: Subtitle* In italics, with capitals for main words (see p. 177), followed by a period

❸ **City of publication** The first city mentioned on the title page, followed by a colon

❹ **Name of publisher** The short form of the name (*Cengage*, not *Cengage Learning; Basic,* not *Basic Books; Abrams,* not *Harry N. Abrams*) followed by a comma. (*Note:* Omit words such as *Press* or *Books* and omit any abbreviations such as *Co.* and *Inc.*: *Simon,* not *Simon & Schuster, Inc.* For university presses, however, use the abbreviations "U" and "P" with no periods: *Columbia UP, U of Chicago P,* and so on.)

❺ **Year of publication** Available after © on the copyright page of the book, ending with a period. Give the most recent year if several are listed.

❻ **The medium of publication** For a book, "Print."

Items 1–19 give examples of and provide information on variations.

```
                    First name
       comma    ┌──period          ❷ Title: italicized        ❸ City of
❶ Last name/    │                   — and capitalized —          publication
       Fussell, Paul. Uniforms: Why We Are What We Wear. Boston:
                                                          period   colon

              ❹ Publisher  ❺ Year  ❻ Medium
    ◄────────►  Houghton, 2002. Print.
  Indented              comma  period
  ½ inch
```

2. Book with two or more authors

Use authors' names in the order in which they appear in the book. Separate the names with commas. Reverse the order of only the first author's name.

```
   comma              name(s) of last author(s) not reversed
Baumol, William J., Robert E. Litan, and Carl J. Schramm. Good Capitalism,
     Bad Capitalism, and the Economics of Growth and Prosperity. New
     Haven: Yale UP, 2007. Print.
```

MLA ▼ (Modern Language Association)

Title Page of Print Book

❷ Title and subtitle

UNIFORMS

Why We Are What We Wear

❶ Author

PAUL FUSSELL

❹ Name of publisher

Houghton Mifflin Company

BOSTON   NEW YORK

2002

❸ City of publication (the first one mentioned)

❺ Year of publication

❻ Medium of publication: Print

Copyright Page

❺ Year of publication

Copyright © 2002 by Paul Fussell
All rights reserved

information about permission to reproduce selections
his book, write Permissions, Houghton Mifflin Company,
215 Park Avenue South, New York, New York 10003.

Visit our Web site: www.houghtonmifflinbooks.com.

Library of Congress Cataloging-in-Publication Data
is available.
ISBN 0-618-06746-9

Printed in the United States of America

Book design by Victoria Hartman

QUM 10 9 8 7 6 5 4 3 2 1

ther is grateful for permission to quote from the following works:
oria," from *The Poems of Lincoln Kirstein*, by Lincoln Kirstein.
ght © 1987 by Lincoln Kirstein. Reprinted with the permission of
bner, an imprint of Simon & Schuster Adult Publishing Group.
a View to a Death, by Anthony Powell. Copyright © by Anthony
Powell. Reprinted by permission of Heinemann.

For a work with four or more authors, either list all the names or use only the first author's name followed by "et al." (Latin for "and others").

Bellah, Robert N., et al. *Habits of the Heart: Individualism and Commitment in American Life*. Berkeley: U of California P, 1985. Print.

3. Book with editor or editors Use the abbreviation "ed." or "eds.," preceded by a comma, after the name(s) of the editor or editors.

(Modern Language Association) ▼ MLA

Gates, Henry Louis, Jr., ed. *Classic Slave Narratives*. New York: NAL, 1987.

Print.

For a work with four or more editors, use the name of only the first, followed by a comma and "et al."

4. Author and editor When an editor has prepared an author's work for publication, list the book under the author's name if you cite the author's work. Then, in your listing, include the name(s) of the editor or editors after the title, introduced by "Ed." for one or more editors. "Ed." stands for "edited by" in the following entry.

author of
letters   name of editor
Bishop, Elizabeth. *One Art: Letters*. Ed. Robert Giroux. New York: Farrar,

1994. Print.

If you cite a section written by the editor, such as an introduction or a note, list the source under the name of the editor, and give the page numbers.

name of editor   editor   author of letters
Giroux, Robert, ed. Introduction. *One Art: Letters*. By Elizabeth Bishop. New

York: Farrar, 1994. vii–xxii. Print.

5. One work in an anthology (original or reprinted) For a work included in an anthology, first list the author and title of the included work. Follow this with the title of the anthology, the name of the editor(s), publication information (place, publisher, date), and then, after the period, the pages in the anthology covered by the work you refer to. End with the medium of publication: "Print."

author of article — title of article — title of book
Saunders, George. "Bill Clinton, Public Citizen." *The Best American*

Non-Required Reading. Ed. Dave Eggers. Boston: Houghton,

2008. 267–300. Print.   means "edited by"   name of editor
inclusive page numbers of article   medium of publication

title of play   title of anthology
Shepard, Sam. *True West*. *The Wadsworth Anthology of Drama*, 5th ed. Ed.

name of editor of anthology
W. B. Worthen. Boston: Wadsworth, 2006. 1139–1158. Print.

If the work in the anthology is a reprint of a previously published scholarly article or chapter, supply the complete information for both the original publication and the reprint in the anthology.

Hofstadter, Richard. "Abraham Lincoln and the Self-Made Myth."

> *American Political Tradition: And the Men Who Made It.*
>
> New York: Knopf, 1948. 119–174. Rpt. in *The Best American*
>
> *History Essays on Lincoln.* Ed. Sean Wilentz. New York:
>
> Palgrave-Macmillan, 2009. 3–40. Print.

6. More than one work in an anthology, cross-referenced If you refer to more than one work from the same anthology, list the anthology separately, and also list each essay with a cross-reference to the anthology. Alphabetize in the usual way, as in the following examples. Include the medium of publication only with the anthology entry.

editor of
⌐ anthology ⌐   ⌐———————— title of anthology ————————⌐
Eggers, Dave, ed. *The Best American Non-Required Reading 2008.* Boston:

> Houghton, 2003. Print.

```
                 title of work  editor of
author of        in anthology   anthology        page numbers
⌐—— work ——⌐    ⌐————————⌐   ⌐————⌐           / of work
King, Stephen. "Ayana." Eggers 200–15.
```

```
                                          editor of       page numbers
author of                                 anthology        of work
⌐——— work ———⌐  ⌐— title of work in anthology —⌐  ⌐————⌐   / 
Saunders, George. "Bill Clinton, Public Citizen." Eggers 267–300.
```

7. Entry in a reference book For a well-known reference book, such as a dictionary or encyclopedia, give title and author (if available), the title of the reference work, the edition number, and the year of publication with no editor or publication details. When entries are arranged alphabetically, omit volume and page numbers.

"Etching." *The Columbia Encyclopedia.* 6th ed. 2000. Print.

Kahn, David. "Cryptology." *Encyclopedia Americana.* Int. ed. 2001.

> Print.

For reference works that are not widely known, also give details of editors, volumes, place of publication, and publisher.

8. Book or pamphlet with no author named Put the title first. Do not consider the words *A, An,* and *The* when alphabetizing the entries. The following entry would be alphabetized under C.

The Chicago Manual of Style. 15th ed. Chicago: U of Chicago P, 2003. Print.

9. Book written by a corporation, organization, or government agency Alphabetize by the name of the corporate author or branch of government. If the publisher is the same as the author, include the name again as publisher.

Hoover's Inc. Hoover's Handbook of World Business. Austin: Hoover's Business,
     2008. Print.

If no individual author is named for a government publication, begin the entry with the name of the federal, state, or local government, followed by the agency. Note that you can use an abbreviated form for a term referring to a government agency (such as *dept.*, *natl.*, and *Cong. House*). See item 41 and Source Shot 5 (p. 200) for an online government publication.

United States. Natl. Commission on Terrorist Attacks upon the US. The 9/11
     Commission Report. New York: Norton, 2004. Print.

10. Translated book After the title, include "Trans." followed by the name of the translator, first name first.

Saviano, Roberto. Gomorrah: A Personal Journey into the Violent International
     Empire of Naples' Organized Crime System. Trans. Virginia Jewiss. New
     York: Farrar, 2008. Print.

11. Multivolume work If you refer to only one volume of a multivolume work, limit the information in the entry to that one volume, and give the author and page number in your in-text citation.

Richardson, John. A Life of Picasso. Vol. 2. New York: Random, 1996. Print.

If you refer to more than one volume of a multivolume work in your paper (as in 11b, item Q), give the number of volumes (abbreviated "vols.") after the title in your list of works cited.

Einstein, Albert. Collected Papers of Albert Einstein. 10 vols. Princeton: Princeton
     UP, 1987–2006. Print.

12. Book in a series End the entry with the medium of publication, followed by the name of the series.

Connor, Ulla. *Contrastive Rhetoric: Cross-Cultural Aspects of Second Language Writing.* New York: Cambridge UP, 1996. Print. Cambridge Applied Linguistics Ser.

13. Book published under a publisher's imprint State the names of both the imprint (the publisher within a larger publishing enterprise) and the larger publishing house, separated by a hyphen.

Atwood, Margaret. *Negotiation with the Dead: A Writer on Writing.* New York: Anchor-Doubleday, 2003. Print.

14. Foreword, preface, introduction, or afterword List the name of the author of the book element cited, followed by the name of the element (Foreword, Introduction, and so on), with no quotation marks. Give the title of the work; then use "By" to introduce the name of the author(s) of the book (first name first). After the publication information, give inclusive page numbers for the book element cited, and conclude with the medium of publication.

Trillin, Calvin. Foreword. *Eat Me: The Food and Philosophy of Kenny Shopsin.* By Kenny Shopsin and Carolynn Carreño. New York: Knopf, 2008. xiii–xxi. Print.

15. Republished book For a paperback edition of a hardcover book, give the original date of publication. Then cite information about the current publication.

King, Stephen. *On Writing.* 2000. New York: Pocket, 2002. Print.

For a book republished under a different title, give the date and publication facts of both titles.

Raimes, James. *An Englishman's Garden in America.* London: Frances Lincoln, 2007. Print. Rpt. of *Gardening at Ginger.* Boston: Houghton, 2006.

16. Edition after the first After the title, give the edition number, using the abbreviation "ed."

Raimes, Ann. *Pocket Keys for Writers.* 3rd ed. Boston: Wadsworth, 2010. Print.

17. Book title including a title Do not italicize a book title (or a journal name) included in the title of the work you list. (However, if the title of a short work, such as a poem or short story, is included, enclose it in quotation marks.)

title within title not in italics

Hays, Kevin J., ed. *The Critical Response to Herman Melville's* Moby Dick.

Westport: Greenwood, 1994. Print.

18. Illustrated work, such as graphic novel For collaborative graphic narratives, use labels to indicate roles (writer, illus., adapt., trans., and so on). Begin your entry with the name of the person(s) whose work you want to emphasize.

Pekar, Harvey, and Joyce Brabner, writers. *Our Cancer Year*. Illus. Frank Stack.

New York: Four Walls, 1994. Print.

Stack, Frank, illus. *Our Cancer Year*. By Harvey Pekar and Joyce Brabner. New

York: Four Walls, 1994. Print.

19. The Bible and other sacred texts Take the information from the title page and give the usual bibliographical details for a book. Also include the edition and the name of a translator or editor where appropriate. When no date of publication is given, use *n.d.* for "no date." Ignore any *The* in the title for alphabetizing purposes in the list: Put *The Holy Bible* under *H*. Put the name of a version at the end of the entry, as in the second example that follows.

Enuma Elish. Ed. Leonard W. King. Escondido: Book Tree, 1998. Print.

The Holy Bible. Peabody: Hendrickson, 2003. Print. King James Vers.

The Koran. Trans. George Sales. London: Warne, n.d. Print.

The New Oxford Annotated Bible. 3rd ed. Ed. Michael D. Coogan. Oxford:

Oxford UP, 2001. Print.

20. Dissertation Cite a published dissertation as you would a book, with place of publication, publisher, and date, but also include dissertation information after the title (for example, "Diss. U of California, 2006.").

If the dissertation is published by University Microfilms International (UMI), italicize the title and include "Ann Arbor: UMI," the year, and the medium of publication.

Jerskey, Maria. *Writing Handbooks, English Language Learners, and the*
Selective Tradition. Diss. New York U, 2006. Ann Arbor: UMI, 2006. Print.

For an unpublished dissertation, follow the title (in quotation marks) with "Diss." and then the university and year, ending with the medium of publication.

Hidalgo, Stephen Paul. "Vietnam War Poetry: A Genre of Witness." Diss. U of
Notre Dame, 1995. Print.

If you cite an abstract published in *Dissertation Abstracts International* (available in the ProQuest and FirstSearch databases), give the relevant volume number, issue number, year, item or page number, and end with the medium of publication.

Hidalgo, Stephen Paul. "Vietnam War Poetry: A Genre of Witness." Diss. U of
Notre Dame, 1995. *DAI* 56.8 (1995): item 0931A. Print.

12d Sample MLA listings: Print articles in periodicals

The conventions for listing print articles (or older articles preserved on microform) depend on whether the articles appear in newspapers, popular magazines, or scholarly journals. For distinguishing scholarly journals from other periodicals, see 8b.

21. Article in a scholarly journal   After the author, title, and year of publication, give the volume and issue numbers, the year in parentheses, page numbers, and the medium of publication (Print) (see Source Shot 2, p. 188).

22. Article in a magazine

- Do not include *The* in the name of a magazine: *Atlantic*, not *The Atlantic*.

- For a magazine published every week or biweekly, give the complete date (day, month, and year, in that order, with no commas between them).

- For a monthly or bimonthly magazine, give only the month and year, as in the first example that follows. In either case, do not include volume and issue numbers.

SOURCE SHOT 2

Listing a Scholarly Article in MLA Style

Include the following when listing a scholarly article:

❶ **Name of author(s)** Last name, first name, followed by a period

❷ **"Title of Article: Subtitle."** Followed by a period, within quotation marks

❸ *Name of journal or periodical* In italics, omitting any *A, An,* or *The*, with no period following, followed by **volume.issue number** (if available), separated by a period

❹ **Date of publication** The year—in parentheses, followed by a colon

❺ **Page number or range of pages** (such as 24–27; 365–72)

❻ **Medium of publication** Here, "Print" followed by a period.

❷ Title of article in quotation marks,
❶ Author: last name, first name   capitals for major words

Bhatia, Tej K. "Super-Heroes to Super-Languages: American Popular Culture through

South Asian Language Comics." *World Englishes* 25.2 (2006): 279–98. Print.

❸ Title of journal (italics) ❹ (Year) colon ❻ Medium
+ volume and issue number ❺ Inclusive page numbers

- If the article is on only one page, give that page number. If the article covers two or more consecutive pages, list inclusive page numbers.
- End with the medium of publication, "Print."

Mitchell, Luke. "Sick in the Head: Why America Won't Get the Health System It Needs." *Harper's* Feb. 2009: 33–44. Print.

Smith, Richard Norton. "The Ghosts of '33." *Time* 26 Jan. 2009: 39. Print.

23. Article in a newspaper After the newspaper title (omit the word *The*), give the date, followed by any edition given at the top of the first page (*late ed., natl. ed., intl. ed.*). For a newspaper that uses letters to designate sections, give the letter that appears on the page before the page number: "A23." For a numbered or titled section,

MLA ▼ (Modern Language Association)

Table of Contents of a Scholarly Journal

Vol. 25, No. 2   **WORLD ENGLISHES**   2006

❸ Journal, volume, and issue   ❹ Year

CONTENTS

❶ Author

❷ Title

SYMPOSIUM ON
WORLD ENGLISHES IN POP CULTURE
Guest editors: Jamie Shinhee Lee and Yamuna Kachru

JAMIE SHINHEE LEE and YAMUNA KACHRU: Introduction 191

TOPE OMONIYI: Hip-hop through the world Englishes lens: a response to
globalization 195

ANDREW J. MOODY: English in Japanese popular culture and J-Pop music . . 209

YAMUNA KACHRU: Mixers lyricing in Hinglish: blending and fusion in
Indian pop culture 223

JAMIE SHINHEE LEE: *Crossing* and *crossers* in East Asian pop music: Korea
and Japan. 235

ROBERT J. BAUMGARDNER: The appeal of English in Mexican commerce . . 251

IRINA P. USTINOVA: English and emerging advertising in Russia 267

TEJ K. BHATIA: Super-heroes to super-languages: American popular culture
through South Asian language comics 279

LIWEI GAO: Language contact and convergence in computer-mediated
communication 299

❺ Page span

Review

SALIKOKO S. MUFWENE: *The Ecology of Language Evolution* (Thomas
A. Klingler) 309

Publications Received 313

❻ Medium of publication: Print

write, for example, "sec. 2: 23" or "Arts and Leisure sec: 3+." End
with the medium of publication, "Print."

Rimer, Sara. "At M.I.T., Large Lectures Are Going the Way of the Blackboard."
New York Times 13 Jan. 2009, late ed., A12. Print.

For a newspaper editorial, see 12d, item 26.

24. Article that skips pages   When an article does not appear on
consecutive pages, give only the first page number followed by a
plus sign. The following article by Chris Baker is on pages 58–61 and
108 of the magazine *Wired*.

Baker, Chris. "Fantasy Island: Live Free or Drown." *Wired* Feb. 2009: 58+. Print.

25. Review   Begin with the name of the reviewer and the title of the review article if these are available. After "Rev. of," provide the title and author of the work reviewed, followed by publication information for the review and the word "Print."

Angell, Marcia. "Drug Companies and Doctors: A Story of Corruption." Rev. of
    Shyness: How Normal Behavior Became a Sickness, by Christopher Lane.
    New York Review of Books 15 Jan. 2009: 12. Print.

26. Unsigned editorial or article   Begin with the title. For an editorial, include the label "Editorial" after the title. In alphabetizing, ignore an initial *A, An,* or *The* in the title.

"Ready for Day One." *Economist* 17–23 Jan. 2009: 31–32. Print.

"A Respectful Homecoming." Editorial. *Washington Post* 1 Mar. 2009, late ed.:
    A16. Print.

27. Letter to the editor   Write "Letter" or "Reply to letter of . . ." after the name of the author (or after the title, if there is one).

Youmans, Gilbert. Letter. *Atlantic* Jan./Feb. 2009: 16. Print.

28. Abstract in an abstracts journal   For abstracts of articles, provide exact information for the original work, and add information about your source for the abstract: the title of the abstract journal, volume number, year, and item number or page number. End with the word "Print." For a dissertation abstract, see 12c, item 20.

Van Dyke, Jan. "Gender and Success in the American Dance World." *Women's*
    Studies International Forum 19 (1996): 535–43. *Studies on Women*
    Abstracts 15 (1997): item 97W/081. Print.

29. Article on microform (microfilm and microfiche)   To cite sources that are neither in hard copy nor in electronic form, provide as much print publication information as is available along with the name of the microfilm or microfiche and any identifying features. Some early newspaper and magazine articles still are available only in microfiche or microfilm, so you will need to use this medium for historical research; however, be aware that such collections may be incomplete and difficult to read and duplicate clearly. *Newsbank* offers large collections of microfiche indexed by subject area. In the example that follows, "FTV" stands for "Film and Television."

Bass, Alison. "Do Slasher Films Breed Real-Life Violence?" *Boston Globe* 19 Dec. 1988: 33. Microform. *Newsbank:* FTV (1989): fiche 5, grids B2-4.

12e Sample MLA listings: Works in online databases

Libraries subscribe to large information services to gain access to extensive databases of online articles (such as *Academic Search Premier, InfoTrac, LexisNexis, WorldCat,* and others) as well as to specialized databases (such as *ERIC, Contemporary Literary Criticism, JSTOR,* and *Project Muse*). You can use these databases to locate abstracts and full texts of thousands of articles. And because many of the articles will have been previously accepted for publication, you will be able to find reliable materials for your papers.

KEY POINTS

MLA Guidelines for Listing Works in Online Databases

Include the following:

- **Print publication details** Give information for the print publication of the work as shown in the examples in 12d, but omit the medium "Print."

- **Page numbers** Access a PDF version if possible so that you can include the inclusive page numbers. If no information about pagination is available, use "n. pag." Use a plus sign after the first page number if the database indicates that pagination is not continuous.

- **Database information** Italicize the name of the database. Do not include the name of the service providing the database, such as EBSCO, and do not include the name and place of the library system.

- **Medium and date of access** End with the word "Web" and the date on which you access the source. (Do not include the URL of the home page of the database.)

30. Magazine article in an online database See Source Shot 3 on page 192 for an example.

SOURCE SHOT 3

Listing a Magazine Article in an Online Database (MLA)

❶ **Name of author(s)** Last name, first name, followed by a period

❷ **"Title of Article: Any Subtitle."** In quotation marks

❸ **Print publication details, if available**
- ■ *Name of magazine* In italics, excluding any volume or issue number
- ■ date of publication
- ■ inclusive **page numbers** of the print document if given or shown on the screen. When no complete information about the page span appears, write "n. pag." (see item 31). When only the number of the first page is given, you may give that page number followed by a plus sign. Use page numbers from a printout only if you cite a PDF document.

❹ *Title of the database* In italics, for example, *Academic Search Premier*, followed by a period

❺ **The medium of publication** Here, "Web"

❻ **Your date of access** Day month (all abbreviated except May, June, July) year, as shown on a printout of the work, with a period at the end

See items 30–35 for examples.

❶ Author   ❷ "Title of article"   ❸ *Name of print magazine* (italics), date: page span
Lindsey, Brink. "Culture of Success." *New Republic* 12 Mar. 2008: 30–31.

    ❹ *Title of database* (italics)   ❺ Medium of publication   ❻ Your date of access
    Academic Search Premier. Web. 13 Aug. 2009.

31. Scholarly article in an online database

Lowe, Michelle S. "Britain's Regional Shopping Centres: New Urban Forms?"

    journal, volume and issue number (year): page span   *title of database*   medium
    Urban Studies 37.2 (2000): 261–74. *Academic Search Premier*. Web.
    4 Feb. 2009. —— date of access

If you access in a database a scholarly journal published only online, indicate the absence of page numbers with "n. pag."

Academic Search Premier Citation Page for a Magazine Article

The citation page indicates that the full text of the article is available in HTML or PDF. Always choose PDF as your source when available so that you can provide an exact page number for a citation.

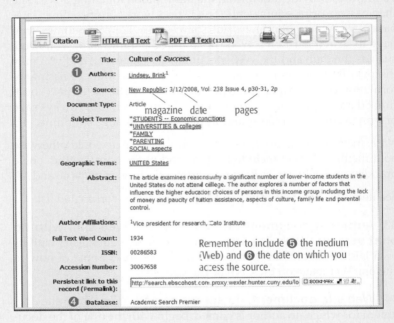

Apter, Emily. "Technics of the Subject: The Avatar Drive." *Postmodern Culture* 18.2 (2008): n. pag. *Project Muse*. Web. 22 Mar. 2009.

32. Newspaper article in a library database

Mehta, Seema. "Meaner Bullying Is Stirring New Tactics." *Los Angeles Times* 7 Mar. 2008: B1. *LexisNexis*. Web. 16 Feb. 2009.

12f **Sample MLA listings: Sources found on the Web**

With whatever system of documentation you use, the basic question is, "What information do readers need to access the same Web site and find the same information I found?" Source Shot 4 (p. 196) shows you how to provide and format the information for citing a Web site that has no print equivalent. (For listing works from online databases, with corresponding print sources, see 12e.) Sometimes, you have to search hard on a Web site to find the information you need, such as the date and the Web site publisher (sponsor), and you may discover that the information just isn't there to be found. Missing information could be a factor to persuade you not to use a site. (You'll find 8d and 8e helpful as you look for the information.) Always save or print a copy of a Web source as details may change over time.

Note: Include a URL in your citation only if a source would otherwise be difficult to locate. Include it at the end of the entry, within angle brackets, and split across lines only after a slash, as in items 46 and 47.

See items 33–49 for examples of Web sources in a works-cited list.

33. Authored document on nonperiodical Web site, with no print version   Web sites often comprise many pages, each with its own URL. Source Shot 4 on page 196 shows an example of how to cite one Web page on the CNNhealth.com site.

34. Web site document, no author named   For a Web site document for which no author is named, begin with the title of the document. Continue with other details of the site: sponsor/publisher, date of publication, medium of publication (Web), and your date of access.

"Freedom of Information Act." *Federal Relations and Information Policy.* Assn.
    of Research Libraries, 1 June 2005. Web. 22 Dec. 2005.

"Polar Bears Creaking under the Strain." *WWF.* Polar Bear Tracker, World
    Wildlife Fund, 12 Jan. 2009. Web. 5 Feb. 2009.

If you follow a specific path to reach the document, it may be helpful to readers to supply details of the path:

"Archaeologists Enter Tomb of King Tut." *History.com.* The History Channel,
    n.d. Web. 4 Feb. 2009. Path: This Day in History; November 26.

35. Entire Web site or professional site, no author named

Harvard University: The Office of Federal Relations. Harvard College, 2009. Web.
6 Feb. 2009.

MLA. Mod. Lang. Assn. of Amer. 17 Aug. 2009. Web. 19 Aug. 2009.

36. Article in an online scholarly journal Give the author, title of article, name of online journal, volume and issue numbers, and date of publication. Include page number or the number of paragraphs only if pages or paragraphs are numbered in the source, as they are for the first example. End with the medium of publication (Web) and your date of access.

```
┌── author ──┐  ┌──────────── title of article ────────────
Hatchuel, Sarah. "Leading the Gaze: From Showing to Telling in Kenneth
                                                    volume and
                                         name of    issue numbers
                      ──────── online journal ───────┐  ┌─┐
     Branagh's Henry V and Hamlet." Early Modern Literary Studies 6.1
     date of online   number of paragraphs   date of access
      publication    (numbered in the text)
     (2000): 22 pars. Web. 1 Aug. 2009.
```

```
┌── author ──┐  ┌──────────── title of article ────────────┐
Hart, Stephen. "Overtures to a New Discipline: Neuromusicology."
                          volume and       medium of
     title of online journal   issue numbers   publication    date of access
     21st Century 1.4 (1996): n. pag. Web. 3 Feb. 2009.
                          date of electronic publication   no numbered pages
                                                          or paragraphs
```

37. Article in an online magazine Give the title of the magazine, its sponsor, and date of posting. End with the medium of publication and your date of access.

Kazdin, Alan E., and Carlo Rotella. "No, You Shut Up! What to Do When Your
Kid Provokes You into an Inhuman Rage." *Slate.* Washington Post, 5 Feb.
2009. Web. 1 May 2009.

38. Article in an online newspaper Give author, title of article, title of the Web site (in italics), sponsor of the site, and date of online publication ending with the word "Web" and your date of access. Note that for a newspaper article on the Web, no page numbers for the print version are given and it is not necessary to include "n. pag." to indicate that.

Gewen, Barry. "State of the Art." *New York Times.* New York Times, 11 Dec.
2005. Web. 14 Jan. 2009.

SOURCE SHOT 4

Listing a Web Source (MLA)

Include these five basic items if they are available:

❶ **Name of author(s), editor, director, performer, etc.** Last name, first, middle initial; *or* name of corporation, institution, or government agency when it is the author; *or* title of document if you find no author credited on the site—ending with a period

❷ **"Title of the Work."** In quotation marks or in italics if the work is independent (such as an archive, a bibliography, or a scholarly project) and ending with a period plus any **print publication information**, if available.

❸ *Title of Web site* (italics) + any version or edition number, if available, ending with a period

❹ **Site information** Sponsor/publisher of the site (often found at bottom of Web page; if not available anywhere, use "n.p.") + comma + date of posting or update or "n.d." if no date is given. *Note:* A Webmaster is not the sponsor of the site (see 8e).

❺ **The medium of publication** Here, "Web" with a period after it

❻ **Your date of access** Day month (abbrev.) year, with a period at the end

If you make a copy of the Web page as soon as you find it or save it to your computer, your date of access will appear on your printout or with your saved file, as shown on page 197.

❶ Author ❷ "Title of work"

Vercammen, Paul. "Economic Troubles Bring Many to the Brink."

CNNhealth.com. Cable News Network, 28 Jan. 2009. Web.

22 Mar. 2009. ❹ Site information: ❺ Medium of publication
Sponsor, date of posting
❸ Title of Web site

❻ Access date

Ortutay, Barbara. "Facebook to Adopt New Rules despite Vote Shortfall." *SignOnSanDiego.com*. San Diego Union-Tribune, 24 Apr. 2009. Web. 25 Apr. 2009.

39. Online review, editorial, letter, or abstract   After author and title, identify the type of text: "Letter," "Editorial," "Abstract," or "Rev. of . . . by . . ." (see 12d, items 25–28). Continue with details of the electronic source, the word "Web," and your date of access.

An Authored Document on a Web Page

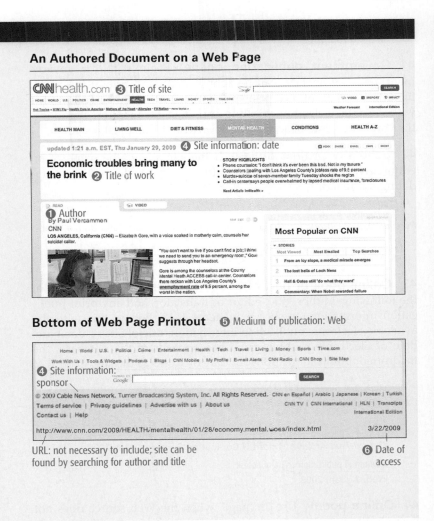

Bottom of Web Page Printout   ⑤ Medium of publication: Web

④ Site information: sponsor

URL: not necessary to include; site can be found by searching for author and title

⑥ Date of access

Raimes, Ann. Rev. of *Dog World: And the Humans Who Live There* by Alfred
Gingold. *Amazon.com.* Amazon.com, 18 Feb. 2005. Web. 1 May 2009.

40. Entry in an online encyclopedia, dictionary, or other reference work   When entries are not individually authored, begin with the title of the entry. Give the latest date of posting. Provide details of the publisher or sponsor, the medium of publication, and your date of access.

"Vicarious." *Cambridge Advanced Learner's Dictionary.* Cambridge UP, 2004.
    Web. 6 Feb. 2009.

41. Government publication online Begin with the government, name of agency (can be abbreviated), and title of the work. Include the date of any print publication, if available. Follow this with the date of electronic posting or update, the medium of publication, and your date of access (see Source Shot 5 on p. 200).

42. Scholarly project online If the site shows the name of an editor, give it after the title. If no date is given for site creation or updating, write n.d.

                                                        no date   medium of
                                                        for site   publication
┌──────── sponsor ────────┐   ┌─┐   ┌──────┐
Perseus Digital Library. Ed. Gregory Crane. Dept. of Classics, Tufts U., n.d. Web.
        date of
    ┌── access ──┐
    2 Feb. 2009.

43. Online book or part of book Give whatever is available of the following: author, title, editor or translator, and any print publication information, as shown in items 1–18. Follow this with the available electronic publication information: title of site or database, date of electronic posting, publisher/sponsor of the database, the medium of publication, and your date of access to the site.

                                                print publication
┌──── author ────┐ ┌──────── title of work ────────┐ ┌──── information ────┐
Darwin, Charles. *The Voyage of the Beagle.* New York: Collier, 1909.

                                        name of sponsor of
    ┌── title of database ──┐ ┌──────── site and date ────────┐
    Oxford Text Archive. Oxford U Computing Service, 1 May 2005.

    medium of publication date of access
    Web. 22 Jan. 2009.

44. Online poem Use "n. pag." when the Web source does not indicate the pages in a previous print source. Use "n.d." when no date is given for online publication.

                                        print   print publication
┌── author ──┐ ┌── title of poem ──┐ ┌── source ──┐ ┌──── information ────┐
Levine, Philip. "What Work Is." *What Work Is.* New York: Knopf, 1991.

            ┌──── title of Web site ────┐ ┌── sponsor of site ──┐
    N. pag. *Internet Poetry Archive.* U of North Carolina P., n.d. Web.
        date of
    ┌── access ──┐
    19 Feb. 2009.

45. Personal Web site/home page If a personal Web page has a title, supply it, in italics. Otherwise, use the genre designation "Home page." If no publisher/sponsor is named, write "n.p." Use "n.d." when no date of posting or updating is available. End with the medium (Web) and your date of access.

Gilpatrick, Eleanor. *Online Fine Art Gallery.* N.p., n.d. Web. 25 May 2008.

Pollitzer, Sally. Home page. *Architectural Glass.* N.p., 2006. Web. 22 Mar. 2009.

46. Course page For a course home page, give the name of the instructor and the course, the words *Course home page*, the dates of the course, the department and the institution, and then the medium of publication (Web) and your access date. The URL is included here as the site may otherwise be difficult to access.

Hammond, John. Work and Society. Course home page. Fall 2008. Dept. of
    Sociology, Hunter Coll., City U of New York. Web. 11 Dec. 2008. <http://
    hc.bbprod.cuny.edu/webapps/portal/frameset.jsp?tab=courses&url=
    %2Fbin%2Fcommon%2Fcourse.pl%3Fcourse_id%3D_40364_1>.

47. Online posting on a blog, discussion board, wiki, mailing list, and so on Give the author's name, the document title (as written in the subject line in an e-mail list or as the title of a blog), or the label "Online posting" if there is no document title. Continue with the name of the blog, mailing list, discussion board, or wiki; the name of the sponsor/publisher; the date of posting; the medium of publication; and the date of access. Add a URL if the source will be difficult for others to find. Include online postings as references in a paper only if you assess a source as reliable—always check the authors and their qualifications.

Jong, Erica. "J.U. and I." *The Huffington Post.* HuffingtonPost.com, Inc., 2 Feb.
    2009. Web. 3 Feb. 2009.

Saletan, William. "Body Parts from Trash." Human Nature: The Blog. *Slate.*
    Washington Post, 2 Feb. 2009. Web. 2 Feb. 2009.

Morales, Ariadna. Online posting. *Reflective Letter Portfolio 2.* Wikifish, Spring
    2008. Web. 23 Mar. 2009. <http://wikifish.org/wiki/ariadna_morales/
    reflective_letter_portfolio2?wikiPageId=1402708&searchresult=1402708>.

Here the URL is given as this wiki source would otherwise be difficult to find.

(Modern Language Association) ▼MLA

SOURCE SHOT 5

Listing Online Government Publications (MLA)

Include the following:

❶ **Name of government and name of agency** along with any office or institute posting the publication (abbreviated)

❷ *Title of the work* in italics, followed by "By . . ." if an author is named

❸ **Date of posting online** (or n.d. if no date is given)

❹ *Title of the Web site*

❺ **Medium** of publication, here Web

❻ **Your date of access**

❶ Government and name of agency   **❷** *Title of work*
United States. Dept. of Educ. Inst. of Educ. Sciences. *Digest of*

     ❸ Date of posting online   **❹** *Title of Web site*

     Education Statistics: 2007. Mar. 2008. *National Center for*

     Education Statistics. Web. 21 Jan. 2009.

    ❺ Medium of publication   **❻** Date of access

To make it easy for readers to find a posting in a discussion list, refer whenever possible to one stored in Web archives.

Kuechler, Manfred. "Google Docs: A New Tool for Collaborative Writing." 5 Dec.

    2007. Hunter-L Archives. Web. 22 Jan. 2009.

    <http://hunter.listserv.cuny.edu/scriptshc/

    wa-hc.exe?A2=ind0712A&L=HUNTER-L&P=R2013>.

48. Forwarded online document To cite a forwarded document in an online posting, include the author, title, and date, followed by "Fwd. by" and the name of the person forwarding the document. End with the date of forwarding, the name of the discussion group, the medium of publication, and your date of access.

Beaky, Lenore A. "Chronicle Article." 18 Mar. 2008. Fwd. by Jack Hammond. 18

    Mar. 2008. Hunter-L. Web. 20 Mar. 2008.

49. Personal e-mail message Provide the subject line heading and treat the communication like a letter (see item 62).

Bernstein, Roberta. "Challenges." Message to the author. 12 Feb. 2009. E-mail.

An Online Government Publication

❹ Title of Web site ❶ Name of government Name of agency

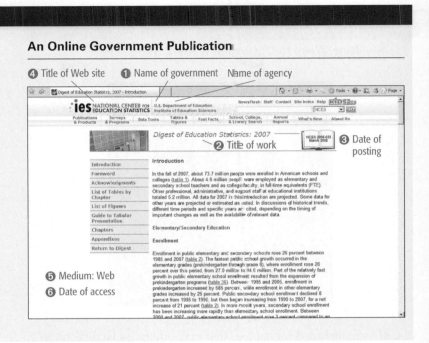

❷ Title of work
❸ Date of posting
❺ Medium: Web
❻ Date of access

12g Sample MLA listings: Visual, performance, multimedia, and miscellaneous sources (live, print, and online)

Identify online interviews, maps, charts, films and film clips, videos, television programs, radio programs, sound recordings, works of art, cartoons, and advertisements as you would sources that are not online, with the addition of electronic publication information (such as the date and site name), the word "Web," and your date of access.

Items 50, 51, 54, 55, and 59 include citations of online works.

50. Documenting across media The following box shows nine different publication sources of one song by rap artist Jay-Z, documented in MLA style. The sources include lyrics in print and online, CD, DVD, LP record, MP3 file, live performance, and videos. URLs are included for sources that may otherwise be difficult to find.

KEY POINTS
Nine Ways to Document a Jay-Z Song

URLs are included for sources that may otherwise be difficult to find.

CD

Jay-Z, and Beyoncé Knowles, perf. "Pray." *American Gangster*. Roc-A-Fella, 2007. CD.

MP3 file

Jay-Z, and Beyoncé Knowles, perf. "Pray." *American Gangster*. Roc-A-Fella, 2007. MP3 file. 20 Feb. 2009. <http://www.beemp3.com/download.php?file=687559&song=Pray>.

LP record

Jay-Z, and Beyoncé Knowles, perf. "Pray." *American Gangster*. Roc-A-Fella, 2007. LP.

Lyrics in print (print material with CD)

Jay-Z lyrics booklet. "Pray." *American Gangster*. Roc-A-Fella, 2007. Print.

Lyrics on Web

Jay-Z. "Pray" lyrics. *American Gangster*. Roc-A-Fella, 2007. Web. 15 Feb.
2009. <http://www.hiphopdx.com/index/lyrics/song.101542/
artistname.jay-z-f-beyonce/title.pray>.

DVD

Jay-Z, and Beyoncé Knowles, perf. "Pray." *American Gangster*. Roc-A-Fella,
2007. Universal Music Group. Dir. Jason Goldwatch. Prod. P. Diddy.
2008. DVD.

Video on Web

Jay-Z, and Beyoncé Knowles, perf. "Pray." *American Gangster*. Dir. Jason
Goldwatch. 2008. Web. 20 Feb. 2009. <http://www.youtube.com/
watch?v=SNevcnizZ4E>.

Live performance

Jay-Z, and Beyoncé Knowles, perf. "Pray." *American Gangster*. Heart of the
City Tour. Oracle Arena, Oakland CA. April 21, 2008. Performance.

Web video of live performance

Jay-Z, and Beyoncé Knowles, perf. "Pray." *American Gangster*.
Heart of the City Tour. Oracle Arena, Oakland CA. April 21, 2008.
Web. 21 Feb. 2009. <http://www.youtube.com/
watch?v=1begkrWD2L8>.

51. Work of visual art, slide, or photograph   List the name of
the artist; the title of the work (in italics); the date of the work—or
"n.d." if no date is available; the medium of composition used by the
artist; the name of the museum, gallery, site, or owner; and the
location.

Duchamp, Marcel. *Bicycle Wheel*. 1951. Metal wheel mounted on painted wood
stool. Museum of Mod. Art, New York. 23 Mar. 2009.

Johns, Jasper. *Racing Thoughts*. 1983. Encaustic and collage on canvas.
Whitney Museum of Amer. Art, New York.

Indicate a work of art accessed on the Web by including the medium
of publication (Web) before your date of access. Do not include the
medium of composition for works accessed on the Web.

MLA ▼ (Modern Language Association)

Christo and Jeanne-Claude. *The Umbrellas.* 1984–1991. Japan-USA. Web. 3 Nov. 2009.

For a reproduction in a book, give complete publication information, including the number of the page on which the photograph appears.

Johns, Jasper. *Racing Thoughts.* 1983. Whitney Museum of Amer. Art, New York. *The American Century: Art and Culture 1950–2000.* By Lisa Phillips. New York: Norton, 1999. 311. Print.

For a slide in a collection, include the slide number (as in "Slide 17").

52. Cartoon Include the label "Cartoon." Follow this with the usual information about the source and the medium of publication. Include the page number for a print source.

Chast, Roz. "A Heart-to-Heart Talk." Cartoon. *New Yorker* 21 Jan. 2008: 32. Print.

53. Advertisement, brochure, or museum wall placard   Give the name of the product or company, followed by the label "Advertisement." If a print page is not numbered, write "n. pag." Use "n.d." if the source is not dated.

Lincoln car. Advertisement. *Wired* Feb. 2008: 50–51. Print.

Geico car insurance. Advertisement. MSNBC. 24 Mar. 2009. Television.

Document a brochure as you would a book.

Titan Missile Museum. *Titan Missile Museum* Salmarita: Titan Missile Museum, n.d. Print.

For a placard such as a museum wall label, include the label "Placard" after the name of the work. Also give the museum and the dates of the show, followed by the medium of publication ("Print").

Rauschenberg, Robert. *Collection*. Placard. New York: Metropolitan Museum of Art, 20 Dec. 2005–2 Apr. 2006. Print.

54. Map or chart   Italicize the title of the map or chart, and include the genre designation of "Map" after the title. Also include the medium of publication (print, Web, etc.).

Auvergne/Limousin. Map. Paris: Michelin, 1996. Print.

For a Web source, include the date of posting and your date of access.

"Attack Map." *Remembering Pearl Harbor*. Multimedia map. *Nationalgeographic.com*. National Geographic Soc., 2001. Web. 1 May 2009.

San Francisco, CA. Map. *Google Maps*, Google, 24 Mar. 2009. Web. 24 Mar. 2009.

55. Film or video   List the title, director, performers, and any other pertinent information. End with the name of the distributor, the year of distribution, and the medium consulted.

Frost/Nixon. Dir. Ron Howard. Perf. Frank Langella. Imagine Entertainment and Working Title Films, 2008. Film.

For an online video, provide your date of access and indicate the medium of publication (Web).

Ndege, Yvonne (narr.). *Africa's Endangered Mountain Gorillas*. Video. *YouTube*. AlJazeeraEnglish, 25 Sept. 2007. Web. 1 May 2009.

When you cite a videocassette or DVD, include the date of the original film if relevant, the name of the distributor of the DVD or cassette, the year of the new release, and the medium of publication.

Casablanca. Dir. Michael Curtiz. Perf. Humphrey Bogart and Ingrid Bergman.
    1943. MGM, 1998. DVD.

56. Television or radio program   Give the title of the program episode or series, the title of the program (in italics), the network and local station if there is one, and the date of broadcast. End with the medium of publication. After the title of the episode or series, include any pertinent information about individual contributions, such as of a performer or narrator.

"The New Boss." *This American Life.* Narr. Ira Glass. Natl. Public Radio. WNYC,
    New York, 30 Jan. 2009. Radio.

If you listen to a podcast or MP3 recording of a radio program, end the entry with "Web" instead of "Radio" and add your date of access (see item 59).

To refer to the work of a particular person, begin the entry with the person's name and contribution (dir., narr., perf., etc.).

MacDonald, Iain B., dir. "Mansfield Park." By Jane Austen. Adapt. Maggie
    Wadey. *Masterpiece Theatre.* PBS. WNET, New York, 27 Jan. 2008.
    Television.

57. Sound recording   List the composer or author, the title of the work, the names of artists, the production company, the date, and the medium of publication, such as *CD, LP,* or *audiocassette.*

Brooks, Gwendolyn. "We Real Cool." *The Norton Anthology of African American
    Literature Audio Companion.* Disc 2. New York: Norton, 2004. CD.
Bustin, Dillon. *Willow of the Wilderness: Emersonian Songs.* Emerson Umbrella
    Center for the Arts, 2003. CD.
Walker, Alice. Interview with Kay Bonetti. Columbia: American Audio Prose
    Library, 1981. Audiocassette.

58. Live performance   Give the title of the play, the author, any pertinent information about the director and performers, the theater, the location, and the date of the performance. End with the word

MLA ▼ (Modern Language Association)

"Performance." If you are citing an individual's role in the work, begin your citation with the person's name, as in the second example that follows.

Black Watch. By Gregory Burke. Dir. John Tiffany. St Ann's Warehouse,
Brooklyn. 11 Nov. 2008. Performance.

Tiffany, John, dir. *Black Watch*. By Gregory Burke. St Ann's Warehouse,
Brooklyn. 11 Nov. 2008. Performance.

59. Podcast (online audio recording)

Krause, Marty, and Jim Canary. "On the Road Again." Indianapolis Museum
of Art. 18 July 2008. Web. 22 Feb. 2009 <http://www.imamuseum.org/
connect/podcast/59161>.

60. Interview (personal, published, broadcast, or Web) For a personal interview, include the type of interview (telephone, e-mail, personal, etc.).

Gingold, Toby. Telephone interview. 4 Apr. 2009.

For a published interview, give the name of the person interviewed, followed by the word "Interview" or "Interview with . . .". Include information about the print publication.

Parker, Dorothy. Interview with Marion Capron. *Writers at Work:* The Paris
Review *Interviews*. London: Secker and Warburg, 1958. 66–75. Print.

For a broadcast or online interview, provide information about the source and date of the interview.

Rossol, Monona. Interview with Leonard Lopate. *The Leonard Lopate Show:
Dangerous Household Chemicals*. Natl. Public Radio. WNYC, New York, 4
Feb. 2009. Radio.

For a Web replay of a radio or television interview, replace the term for the medium of publication such as "Radio" with the term "Web," followed by your date of access.

For a sound recording of an interview, see item 57.

61. Lecture, reading, speech, or address Give the author and title, if known. Also give the name of any organizing sponsor, the

venue, and the date. For the medium of publication, include an appropriate label at the end.

Muldoon, Paul. MFA Program in Creative Writing, Hunter College, New York. 26
Feb. 2009. Reading.

62. Letter or personal communication For a handwritten letter that you receive, include the phrase "Letter to the author" after the name of the letter writer, and give "MS" (manuscript) as the medium of publication. Describe the medium of any other personal communication ("Telephone call," "E-mail," or "TS"—typescript—for example). (See also 12f, items 47–49, for online messages.)

Rogan, Helen. Letter to the author. 3 Feb. 2009. TS.

Cite a published letter in a collection as you would cite a work in an anthology. After the name of the author, include any title the editor gives the letter and the date. Add the page numbers for the letter and end with the medium of publication, "Print."

Bishop, Elizabeth. "To Robert Lowell." 26 Nov. 1951. *One Art: Letters*. Ed. Robert
Giroux. New York: Farrar, 1994. 224–26. Print.

63. Legal or historical document For a legal case, give the name of the case with no italics or quotation marks, the number of the case, the name of the court deciding the case, the date of the decision, and the medium of publication and access date for a Web publication. (Note, however, that if you mention the case in the text of your paper, you should italicize it: "Chief Justice Burger, in *Roe v. Wade*, noted that . . .".)

Roe v. Wade. No. 70-18. Supreme Ct. of the US. 22 Jan. 1973. Web. 8 Feb. 2009.

Give the name of an act, its Public Law number, its Statutes at Large volume and page numbers, the date it was passed, and the medium of publication that you consulted.

USA Patriot Act. Pub. L. 107-56. 115 Stat. 272-402. 26 Oct. 2001. Web. 10 Feb.
2009.

Well-known historical documents should not be included in your works-cited list (see 11b, item U).

64. CD-ROM or DVD-ROM Cite material from a CD-ROM or DVD-ROM in the same way you cite an article in a book, but include any version or release number and end with the medium of publication.

Flanner, Janet. "Führer I." *New Yorker* 29 Feb. 1934: 20–24. *The Complete New Yorker.* New York: Random, 2005. DVD-ROM.

Keats, John. "To Autumn." *Columbia Granger's World of Poetry.* Rel. 3. New York: Columbia UP, 1999. CD-ROM.

If you access the source in an online database, end with database information (italicized title of the database, publisher, date of database) and your date of access.

65. Digital files For files that you create, receive, or download (such as a photograph, a sound recording, a book, or a typed word processing file), document the source according to the original work and cite as your medium of publication the type of file: PDF file, MP3 file, JPEG file, Word file, and so on, ending with the date on which you access the source.

Byrne, David. "A Walk in the Dark." *Uh-Oh.* Luaka Bop/Warner Bros., 1992. MP3 file. 22 Mar. 2009.

13 🔑

Sample Paper 3: A Student's Research Paper, MLA Style

Here is Dana Alogna's research paper written in an expository writing course at Hunter College, City University of New York. The assignment was to analyze a cultural artifact by tracing its history and development and assessing its societal and personal impact. The citations and the list of works cited are in the style recommended in the 2009 *MLA Handbook for Writers of Research Papers,* 7th edition.

Note: Annotations have been added here to point out features of her paper that you may find useful when you write your own research paper in MLA style. Blue annotations point out issues of content and organization. Red annotations point out MLA format issues.

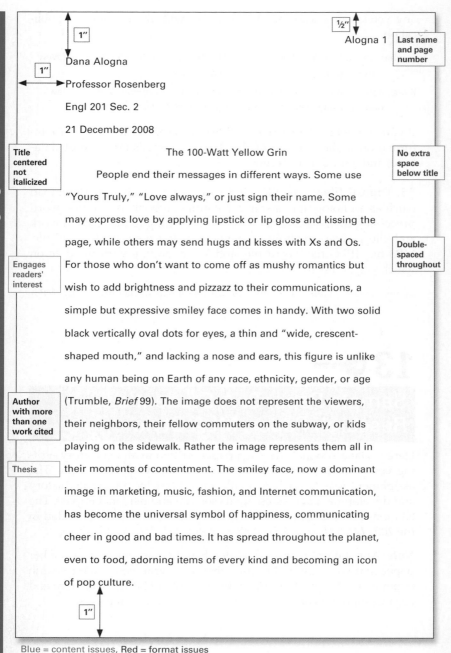

½"

Alogna 1 | **Last name and page number**

1"

1"

Dana Alogna

Professor Rosenberg

Engl 201 Sec. 2

21 December 2008

Title centered not italicized

The 100-Watt Yellow Grin

No extra space below title

People end their messages in different ways. Some use "Yours Truly," "Love always," or just sign their name. Some may express love by applying lipstick or lip gloss and kissing the page, while others may send hugs and kisses with Xs and Os.

Engages readers' interest

For those who don't want to come off as mushy romantics but wish to add brightness and pizzazz to their communications, a simple but expressive smiley face comes in handy. With two solid black vertically oval dots for eyes, a thin and "wide, crescent-shaped mouth," and lacking a nose and ears, this figure is unlike any human being on Earth of any race, ethnicity, gender, or age

Double-spaced throughout

Author with more than one work cited

(Trumble, *Brief* 99). The image does not represent the viewers, their neighbors, their fellow commuters on the subway, or kids playing on the sidewalk. Rather the image represents them all in

Thesis

their moments of contentment. The smiley face, now a dominant image in marketing, music, fashion, and Internet communication, has become the universal symbol of happiness, communicating cheer in good and bad times. It has spread throughout the planet, even to food, adorning items of every kind and becoming an icon of pop culture.

1"

Blue = content issues, Red = format issues

Alogna 2

When, exactly, two eyes and a mouth were drawn to represent a smiling face for the first time is unknown. Angus Trumble's history of the smile cannot pinpoint the origins exactly: "The smiley face was borrowed, copied, and recycled so frequently, in an effort to brighten so many different sorts of message[s]—deploying and exchanging it as a kind of currency of good cheer—that its origins are surprisingly difficult to locate" (*Brief* 100). Images of a simple happy face were used in the 1930s by Sunkist oranges, in the 1940s by a drug company, and in the 60s by an advertising agency. However, this smiley was not yellow and was not "as cleverly schematic as the classic logo that came later" (Trumble, "Yellow Fever").

I. Rise of smiley historically

Web source: no page number

In late 1963, the smiley face that we know today began to appear. Several people claim to have created it ("Exhibitions: Smiley Face"), but the most comprehensive documentation is provided by the town that claims the creator: Harvey R. Ball, a graphic artist who ran an advertising and public relations agency in Worcester, Massachusetts, designed the smiley face for a client, The State Mutual Life Assurance Company of America. When two of its companies were about to merge, Ball was paid forty-five dollars to create a pin that would cheer up employees during the merger (Cramoton). He designed a yellow disk with a smiling mouth and then added the eyes so the disk would not be turned upside-down and have its message reversed (Trumble, "Yellow Fever"). An order of 100 buttons was immediately increased to 10,000 (Nordin). Figure 1 shows Ball amidst spin-offs from his original creation.

Source with no author

Alogna 3

Fig. 1. Harvey Ball, Photograph by Michael Carroll, Worcester Historical Museum; <http://www.worcesterhistory.org/hb2007/HBall.jpg>.

Harvey Ball never tried to profit from the universal appeal of the smiley face or to trademark the image. It was left to Franklin Loufrani, a Frenchman, to see the business potential. Loufrani claimed to have first used the symbol in the *France Soir* newspaper to indicate positive news stories. He claimed that he "initially registered the design with the French trademark authorities in October 1971," eight years after Ball created his smiley face, and he proudly stated, "A prehistoric man probably invented the smiley face in some cave, but I certainly was the first to register it as a trademark" (qtd. in Crampton). Loufrani claims that he trademarked

Alogna 4

the symbol SMILEY® in more than a hundred countries ("Intellectual Property"), even naming his London-based company SmileyWorld Ltd. Of Harvey Ball's image, Loufrani is reported to have said, "I don't care if he designed the Smiley face. We promote, we own, we market" ("Still Smiling"). After SmileyWorld filed for the United States trademark of the smiley in 1997, a legal battle began with Wal-Mart Stores, which used the face to promote low prices (Nordin).

Harvey Ball did not enjoy this battle over the claim to his symbol. He became concerned about the "over-commercialization of his symbol, and how its original meaning and intent had become lost in the constant repetition of the marketplace" (*World Smile Day*). The Worcester Historical Museum tells the story of the controversy: "Riled up by 'the France guy' as he put it, Harvey in 1999 created World Smile Day®—the first Friday in October—to promote the true meaning of the Smiley Face. And he trademarked it" ("He Made the Whole World Smile"). He wanted one day to be designated for smiles and acts of kindness, with no commercialization: "The smiley face knows no politics, no geography, and no religion. Harvey's idea was that for at least one day each year, neither should we" (*World Smile Day*). Most of the profits of the World Smile Day® Foundation go to charities for children.

> **Quotation within a quotation**

Although Harvey Ball never wished to profit from the smiley face, the symbol still became a marketable fad in the United States, appearing on clothes, mugs, and all kinds of merchandise. One may say that the smiley face and its message

> **II. Smiley as a marketing symbol**

Alogna 5

were timed perfectly. "If the apparent calm of the 1950s and 1960s was shattered by dislocations and upheavals that followed in the wake of the Kennedy assassination in 1963, the restless search for happiness as pleasure and good feeling only intensified" (McMahon 463). That same year, Ball produced, without knowing it, a much-needed symbol, one that then became associated

Quotation integrated into the writer's sentence

with youthful hippies looking for hope and peace in their not-so-peaceful world. It cheered up the '70s and became "a light-hearted punctuation mark at the end of a tumultuous decade" (Hirsch C1).

III. Smiley in music and fashion

Toward the end of the '70s and early '80s the smiley face fad changed direction and became associated with "acid house" music, LSD, and Ecstasy. Acid house began in the states and traveled abroad

Part of the quotation omitted

to London in 1986. "In the summer of 1987, several London disk

Word added to quotation

jockeys took the music to Iviza, one of the Balearics. . . . [That] was where acid-house met and married with the colorful hippie fashion of the summer beach clothes, paisley prints and tie-dyed shirts with peace signs galore" (Hirsch C8). As the music caught on, the smiley face became popular in London, and then the fashion fad spread to American retailers, appearing on all types of apparel and accessories.

IV. Smiley in food

Since then, even the food industry has appropriated the symbol. To appeal to children, food manufactures have shaped their products into smiley faces or stamped smiley faces onto products. At a cheese tasting event, a child ignored all the gourmet cheeses and headed straight for "a block of white and yellow mild cheddar molded into a smiley face" (D'Agnese). The specialty

Alogna 6

foods manager at Delicious Orchards in Colts Neck proclaimed, "It's a nice way to introduce kids to cheese that's good for them" (D'Agnese). The McCain company brightens up its mashed potatoes by forming them into smiling faces (*McCain SMILES*®). Luring children in this way turns out to be an old ruse. As early as the 1940s, a drug company used a smiling face on its pills (Trumble, *Brief* 101). The smiley face was also used as early as 1936 in a book called *Manners Can Be Fun*, which Trumble regards as "a doomed attempt to trick small children into thinking that good table etiquette is irresistibly jolly" ("Yellow Fever").

Page number for print source

Today the smiley fad lives on in the Internet. The first Internet smiley faces were created with simple keystrokes using a colon, a dash, and a closing parenthesis :-). Although the Internet was not widely used in the '80s, the first keystroke smiley or emoticon was created in 1982 by Dr. Scott E. Fahlman, a computer scientist at Carnegie Mellon University. The emoticon was used on an online university bulletin board to differentiate between joking messages and serious ones. The marker soon caught on and was being used by Fahlman's colleagues ("Q & A with Mr. Smiley"). Now such handmade smileys are largely replaced by pictographs that span a gamut of emotions from confusion to anger.

V. Smiley on the Internet

Smileys are increasingly used to help express emotions when communicating quickly in electronic environments. However, is a symbol a good way to express yourself when you are already disconnected physically from the person with whom you are

VI. Views of emotions

Alogna 7

communicating? Smileys may be good to break the ice, but

Indirect source: Cites work in which quotation appears

they raise questions like Trumble's "What did people do before emoticons? What did people do before little signs like kisses and hugs?" (qtd. in Trumble, "In Search"). Scott E. Fahlman, a research professor of computer science at Carnegie Mellon University, and

Considers opposing views

one of the inventors of the Internet smiley face, has commented extensively on positive and negative reactions to the emoticon:

Long quotation indented

> Many people have denounced the very idea of the
> smiley face, pointing out that good writers should

Comment inserted into quotation

> have no need to explicitly label their humorous
> comments [or other feelings]. Shakespeare and
> Jonathan Swift and Mark Twain got along just fine

Title given when more than one work by author is cited

> without this. ("Smiley Lore :-)")

He reminds us, though, that not all writers who use emoticons have the literary skills that famous writers have. Trumble acknowledges that those of us who are not famous writers are nevertheless "a society of writing creatures in constant search of a convenient form of shorthand" to convey emotions (qtd. in Trumble, "In Search"). However, he also drives home the point that overusing smileys can be as annoying to readers as overusing exclamation points.

VII. Smiley as psychological tool

The smiley face has also been taken to the streets and used as a coping mechanism on a group level. On Wednesday May 28, 2003, a group that called itself Smile Mania put on a national event called the Great American Grump Out that aimed "to do for cantankerousness what the Great American Smoke-

Blue = content issues, Red = format issues

Alogna 8

Out did for tobacco addiction" (St. John). Janice Hathy, a stress management consultant, "headed a 'drive-by smiling' in which she and some local students stood at an intersection and flashed cardboard smiley-faces at passing motorists" (St. John). Similar to the '70s desire of wanting happier times, after September 11 America has once again craved the lighter side of things: "Since 2002, pyrotechnical smileys have appeared in the skies over New York on the Fourth of July—perhaps, as a statement of the city's resolve to keep up its spirits after September 11" (Kotchemidova 20).

Some complain that the smiley face is overused. If that is the case, then I am guilty as charged. Not only have I been using the smiley face since I was a child, but I seem to find the smiley everywhere. Before embarking on this cultural icon exploration I did not realize the numbers of little yellow smileys in my life. As I look around my room now, I see on the top of my boom box about twenty little smiley face stickers: yellow, blue, pink, and green. In September, I received a Hallmark birthday card from my two best friends. On the card there are about forty smiley faces of different colors looking as if they were drawn with a crayon, in metallic colors. Recently, too, I noticed that on every note my mother writes she puts a smiley face. She even adds the icon on notes where emotion is unnecessary, like "Pork For Stuffing ☺." Smileys are everywhere in my life and in the world around us. Even the Chinese food I ordered the other day came in a bag

VIII. Writer's experience with smileys, reinforcing thesis

Alogna 9

Fig. 2. Image on bag of food delivered by
Chinese restaurant

that had a smiley on it and said "Have a Nice Day, Thank You"

(Figure 2).

**IX.
Conclusion
shows the
universality
of the
cultural
artifact of
the smiley
face**

The smiley face is the happiness mascot of the world,

"the most recognizable symbol of good will and good cheer on

the planet" (*World Smile Day*). Its simple features make it so

that it can be used universally by anyone. It can be manipulated

to express any emotion and can be dressed as any object for

any occasion. As the smiley face ages it is adapted to the most

recent pop-culture fads of the world's youth. Some say that "a

**Reiterates
thesis:
Universality
of smiley**

picture is worth a thousand words." However, if the smiley face

is recognized worldwide, it can be worth up to 6,634,388,373

words expressing optimism, happiness, or hope from each being

on Earth ("US and World Population Clocks"). The world needs

its "100-watt" (Hirsch) yellow grin to light up our dark and scary

**Ends on a
strong note**

world with hope of peace and happiness.

Blue = content issues, Red = format issues

Alogna 10

Works Cited

Crampton, Thomas. "Smiley Face Is Serious to Company." *New York Times*. New York Times, 5 Jan. 2006. Web. 18 Nov. 2008.

D'Agnese, Joseph. "Smiling Cheese and Other Good Food." *New York Times* 29 Aug. 1999: New Jersey sec.: 12. *Historical New York Times*. Web. 11 Nov. 2008.

"Exhibitions: Smiley Face." *Worcester Historical Museum*. Worcester Historical Museum, 2006. Web. 20 Nov. 2008.

Fahlman, Scott E. Interview with Terrell Karlsten. "Q & A with Mr. Smiley Himself." *Yodel Anecdotal*. 10 July 2007. Web. 19 Nov. 2008.

- - -. "Smiley Lore :-)." Carnegie Mellon U, n.d. Web. 19 Nov. 2008.

Harvey Ball World Smile Foundation. Harvey Ball World Smile Foundation, 2006. Web. 20 Nov. 2008.

"He Made the Whole World Smile." *Worcester Historical Museum*. Worcester Historical Museum, 2006. Web. 18 Nov. 2008.

Hirsch, James. "The Happy Face Has a Nice New Day." *New York Times* 15 Feb. 1989: C1+. *Historical New York Times*. Web. 11 Nov. 2008.

"Intellectual Property." *Smiley Licensing*. 2007. Web. 19 Nov. 2008.

Kotchemidova, Christina. "From Good Cheer to 'Drive-By Smiling': A Social History of Cheerfulness." *Journal of Social History* 39.1 (2005): 5–37. *Project Muse*. Web. 5 Dec. 2008.

1"

Title centered not underlined

Organized alphabetically

Medium of publication and access date

Article in an online database

Title first: No author name

Medium of publication Date of access

Date of posting

Two works by same author

No page number for Web source

Published article in online database

MLA ▼ (Modern Language Association)

(Modern Language Association) ▼ MLA

Alogna 11

McCain SMILES®. 2007. McCain Foods. Web. 4 Dec. 2008.

McMahon, Darrin M. *Happiness: A History*. New York: Atlantic

    Monthly P, 2006. Print.

Nordin, Kendra. "Smiley Face: How an in-House Campaign

    Became a Global Icon." *Christian Science Monitor* 98.1

    (2006): 15–16. *Academic Search Premier*. Web. 9 Nov. 2008.

"Still Smiling." *People* Archive. 3 Aug. 1998. Web. 17 Nov. 2008.

St. John, Warren. "Defending the Right Not to Have a Nice Day."

    New York Times. New York Times, 25 May 2003. Web.

    5 Dec. 2008.

Trumble, Angus. *A Brief History of the Smile*. New York: Basic,

    2004. Print.

- - -. "In Search of the Smiley Face." Interview with Declan

    McCullagh. *CNET News*. CBS Interactive, 12 Mar. 2004.

    Web. 6 Dec. 2008.

- - -. "Yellow Fever." *I.D. Magazine* Mar.–Apr. 2004. Web. 20 Nov.

    2008.

"US and World Population Clocks: POPClocks." *US Census Bureau*.

    Nov. 2007. Web. 29 Nov. 2008.

World Smile Day®. Harvey Ball World Smile Foundation, 2007.

    Web. 20 Nov. 2008.

Date of posting

Date of access

List includes only sources actually cited in paper

PART 4

APA, CSE, and *Chicago* Documentation

14 Citing Sources in Your Paper, APA Style   225

15 APA List of References   232

16 Sample Paper 4: A Student's Research Paper, APA Style   251

17 CSE Style of Documentation   262

18 Sample Paper 5: Excerpt from a Student's Research Paper, CSE Style   268

19 *Chicago Manual of Style:* Endnotes, Footnotes, and Bibliography   273

20 Sample Paper 6: Excerpt from a Student's Research Paper, *Chicago* Style   285

PART 4 APA, CSE, AND CHICAGO DOCUMENTATION

ONLINE RESOURCES

www.cengage.com/english/raimes

Companion online resources are available for sections throughout this part. We invite you to visit the book's Web site for more information and direct access.

PART 4

APA, CSE, and *Chicago* Documentation

APA AT A GLANCE INDEX

14 **Citing Sources in Your Paper, APA Style** 225

14a Basic features of APA style 225
14b How to cite sources (author/year) in your paper 227
14c Notes, tables, figures, and headings 232

15 **APA List of References** 232

15a How to set up an APA list of references 232
15b How to list authors in the APA reference list 234
15c Sample listings: Print books, pamphlets, and parts of books 235
15d Sample listings: Print articles in periodicals 240
15e Sample listings: Online sources 243
15f Sample listings: Visual, multimedia, and miscellaneous sources (live, print, and online) 250

16 **Sample Paper 4: A Student's Research Paper, APA Style** 251

CSE AT A GLANCE INDEX

17 **CSE Style of Documentation** 262

17a Basic features of CSE style 263
17b How to cite sources in your paper 264
17c How to list CSE references 264

17d Sample listings: Print books and parts of books 265
17e Sample listings: Print articles 266
17f Sample listings: Online, electronic, and miscellaneous sources 266

18 **Sample Paper 5: Excerpt from a Student's Research Paper, CSE Style** 268

CHICAGO AT A GLANCE INDEX

19 ***Chicago Manual of Style:* Endnotes, Footnotes, and Bibliography** 273

19a Basic features of the *Chicago* note style 274
19b How to cite sources and prepare notes 274
19c How to format *Chicago* endnotes and footnotes 276
19d Sample notes: Print books and parts of books 277
19e Sample notes: Print articles in periodicals 279
19f Sample notes: Online sources 280
19g Sample notes: Visual, multimedia, and miscellaneous sources 282
19h A student's *Chicago* bibliography 283

20 **Sample Paper 6: Excerpt from a Student's Research Paper, *Chicago* Style** 285

AT A GLANCE: INDEX OF APA STYLE FEATURES

14 Citing Sources in Your Paper, APA Style 225

14a Basic features of APA style 225
14b How to cite sources (author/year) in your paper 227

CITING AN AUTHOR OR AUTHORS 227
A. Author named in your text 227
B. Author cited in parentheses 227
C. Author quoted or paraphrased 227
D. A work with more than one author 227
E. Author with more than one work published in one year 228
F. Author of work in an edited anthology 229
G. Author's work cited in another source (secondary source) 229
H. Entire work or idea in a work 229
I. More than one work in one citation 229
J. Two authors with the same last name 229

CITING A WORK WITH NO INDIVIDUAL AUTHOR NAMED 230
K. No author named 230
L. Work by a corporation, government agency, or organization 230

CITING VISUAL, MULTIMEDIA, AND MISCELLANEOUS SOURCES 230
M. Internet source 230
N. Visual, multimedia, or nonprint source 231
O. Multivolume work 231
P. Personal communication, such as a conversation, a letter, an interview, an e-mail, or an unarchived electronic discussion group 231
Q. A classical or religious work 231
R. A long quotation 231

14c Notes, tables, figures, and headings 232

15 APA List of References 232

15a How to set up an APA reference list 232
15b How to list authors in the APA reference list 234
15c Sample listings: Print books, pamphlets, and parts of books 235

1. Book with one author (Source Shot 6) 236
2. Book with two to seven authors 236
3. Edited book 237
4. Work in an edited collection or reference book 238
5. No author identified 238
6. Work by a corporation, government agency, or organization 238
7. Translated book 238
8. Multivolume work 239
9. Foreword, preface, introduction, or afterword 239
10. Revised, republished, or reprinted work 239
11. Technical report 239
12. Dissertation or abstract 240

15d Sample listings: Print articles in periodicals 240

13. Article in a scholarly journal 240
14. Magazine article (Source Shot 7) 241
15. Newspaper article 241
16. Article that skips pages 241

17. Review or interview 241
18. Unsigned editorial or article 242
19. Letter to the editor 243

15e Sample listings: Online sources 243

20. Online database journal article with a DOI (Source Shot 8) 245
21. Online database journal article with no DOI 246
22. Online article with a PDF print source 246
23. Article in an online journal with no print source available 247
24. Newspaper article retrieved from a database or Web site 248
25. Online abstract, review, editorial, or letter 248

26. Authored document on Web site 248
27. Web site document, no author identified 248
28. Entire Web site, no author 249
29. Report on a university or government site 249
30. Online book 249
31. Online reference work 249
32. Blogs, discussion boards, wikis, newsgroups, and archived mailing lists 249

15f Sample listings: Visual, multimedia, and miscellaneous sources (live, print, and online) 250

33. Personal communication (letter, telephone conversation, interview, e-mail) 250
34. Conference paper/conference proceedings 250
35. Poster session 250
36. Film, recording, or video 250

37. Television or radio program 250
38. Podcast or MP3 download 250
39. Video Weblog posting 251
40. Presentation slides 251
41. CD-ROM or DVD 251
42. Computer software 251

16 Sample Paper 4: A Student's Research Paper, APA Style 251

Part 4 covers documentation styles other than the MLA system. Chapters 14 and 15 focus on the style recommended for the social sciences by the *Publication Manual of the American Psychological Association*, 6th edition (Washington, DC: Amer. Psychological Assn., 2010), and on the APA Web site. A student's paper written in APA style is in chapter 16. Chapter 17 describes the citation-sequence and the citation-name styles recommended by the Council of Science Editors (CSE); chapter 18 shows an excerpt from a student's CSE research paper in the citation-sequence style. Chapter 19 illustrates the endnote and footnote style recommended in *The Chicago Manual of Style*, 15th edition (Chicago: U of Chicago P, 2003), for writing in the humanities, a style sometimes used as an alternative to MLA style. Chapter 20 includes an excerpt from a student's research paper in *Chicago* endnote style.

14 ⚷

Citing Sources in Your Paper, APA Style

14a Basic features of APA style

KEY POINTS
How to Cite and List Sources in APA Style

1. **In the text of your paper**, include at least two pieces of information each time you cite a source:

   - the last name(s) of the author (or authors) or first words of the title if no author's name is available
   - the year of publication or posting online

   Also give the page number for a quotation, summary, or paraphrase.

2. **At the end of your paper**, on a new numbered page, include a list titled "References," double-spaced and arranged alphabetically by authors' last names, followed by the initials of first and other names, the date in parentheses, and other bibliographical information. See sections 15c–f for forty-two sample entries.

Illustrations of APA style's basic features

In-Text Citation	Entry in List of References
Book, citation in parentheses	
The speed at which we live is seen as cause for concern and derision (Gleick, 1999).	Gleick, J. (1999). *Faster: The acceleration of just about everything.* New York, NY: Pantheon.
Author name introduces comment	
A renowned scholar of language, David Crystal, has promoted the idea of "dialect democracy" (2004, p. 168).	Crystal, D. (2004). *The stories of English.* Woodstock, NY: Overlook Press.
[Page number included for quotation]	
Print article: Author and year in your text	
According to Jeffrey Kluger (2005), ambition is seen as an impulse that "requires an enormous investment of emotional capital" (p. 59).	Kluger, J. (2005, November 14). Ambition: Why some people are most likely to succeed. *Time, 166*(20), 48–54, 57, 59.
[Page number included for quotation]	
or	
Kluger (2005, p. 59) sees ambition as an impulse that "requires an enormous investment of emotional capital."	
Article with digital object identifier (DOI) in an online database	
Research has shown that cross-cultural identification does not begin before 8 years of age (Sousa, Neto, & Mullet, 2005).	Sousa, R. M., Neto, F., & Mullet, E. (2005). Can music change ethnic attitudes among children? *Psychology of Music, 33*(3), 304–316. doi:10.1177/0305735605053735
[See 15e, item 20, for more on DOIs, and see 15d for when to include an issue number.]	

APA ▼ (American Psychological Association)

A document on a Web site

Hempel (2008) has reported on efforts to make social networking safe for young users.	Hempel, J. (2008, January 14). New effort to protect kids online. *Fortune*. Retrieved from http://money.cnn.com /2008/01/14/technology/hempel _myspace.fortune/index.htm

14b How to cite sources (author/year) in your paper

CITING AN AUTHOR OR AUTHORS [APA]

A. Author named in your text If you mention the author's name in your own text, include the year in parentheses directly after the author's name.

author   year
Wilson (1994) has described in detail his fascination with insects.

See 15c, item 1, and Source Shot 6 for this work in a reference list.

B. Author cited in parentheses If you do not name the author in your own text (maybe because you have referred to the author previously), include both the name and the year, separated by a comma, in parentheses.

The army retreated from Boston in disarray, making the rebels realize that

they had achieved a great victory (McCullough, 2001).

author   comma   year

C. Author quoted or paraphrased If you use a direct quotation or a paraphrase, include in parentheses the abbreviation "p." or "pp." followed by a space and the page number(s). Use commas to separate items within parentheses.

Memories are built "around a small collection of dominating images"

(Wilson, 1994, p. 5).

comma   comma   page number with
a quotation

D. A work with more than one author

Two authors For a work by two authors, name both in the order in which their names appear on the work. Within parentheses, use an ampersand (&) between the names in place of *and*. Use the word *and* for a reference made in your text.

> the word *and* in your text
>
> Kanazawa and Still (2000) in their analysis of a large set of data show that the statistical likelihood of being divorced increases if one is male and a secondary school teacher or college professor.

> Analysis of a large set of data shows that the statistical likelihood of being divorced increases if one is male and a secondary school teacher or college professor (Kanazawa & Still, 2000).
>
> ampersand in parentheses

See 15d, item 13, for this work in a reference list.

Three to five authors or editors   Identify all of them the first time you mention the work in your running text.

> Baumol, Litan, and Schramm (2007) posit the existence of several types of capitalist economies around the world.

In later references, use name of the first author, followed by "et al." (*et alii*—Latin for "and others") in place of the other names.

> In the United States, the dominant type of capitalism, called "entrepreneurial capitalism," shows significant differences from the capitalism in Japan and Europe, which tends to avoid "radical entrepreneurship" (Baumol et al., 2007, p. viii).

See 15c, items 2 and 9, for this work in a list of references.

Six or more authors   Cite the name of only the first author followed by "et al." both for all citations in your text and in a parenthetical citation. However, include the names of up to seven authors in your reference list; for eight or more authors, use ellipsis dots to indicate authors beyond the first seven, and then add the name of the last author (see 15b).

E. Author with more than one work published in one year
Identify each work with a lowercase letter after the year: (Schell, 2007a, 2007b). Separate the dates with commas. In the reference list, repeat the author's name in each entry, and alphabetize by the title. See 15b for how to order such entries in the list of references.

F. Author of work in an edited anthology In your text, refer to the author of the work, not to the editor of the anthology (but you will include information about the anthology in your list of references). The essay referred to next is in an anthology of writing about race.

> The voice of W. E. B. Dubois (2007) resonates today as soldiers return from a different war, hoping to find change in their country.

In the reference list, give the author's name, title of the work, and bibliographical details about the anthology, such as the editor, title, publisher, and date (see 15c, item 4).

G. Author's work cited in another source (secondary source) Give the author or title of the work in which you find the reference, preceded by "as cited in" to indicate that you are referring to a citation in that work. List that secondary source in your list of references. In the following example, *Smith* will appear in the list of references with details of the source; *Britton* will not.

> The words we use simply appear, as Britton says, "at the point of utterance" (as cited in Smith, 1982, p. 108).

H. Entire work or an idea in a work Use only an author and a year to refer to a complete work; for a paraphrase or a comment on a specific idea, a page number is not required but is recommended.

I. More than one work in one citation List the sources in alphabetical order, separated by semicolons. List works by the same author chronologically (earliest source first) or by the letters *a*, *b*, and so on if the works were published in the same year.

> Criticisms of large-scale educational testing are anything but new. They have been appearing for many years (Crouse & Trusheim, 1988; Nairn, 1978, 1980; Raimes, 1990a, 1990b; Sacks, 2003).

J. Two authors with the same last name Include the authors' initials, even if the publication dates of their works differ.

> F. Smith (1982) first described a writer as playing the two competitive roles of author and secretary.

For the order of entries in the list of references, see 15b.

CITING A WORK WITH NO INDIVIDUAL AUTHOR NAMED (APA)

K. No author named If a print or Web source has no named individual or organization as author, use the first few words of the title in your text (capitalizing major words).

> Many Hurricane Katrina survivors were located to trailers whose materials
> caused health problems from breathing disorders to cancer (*World Almanac*,
> 2009, p. 55).

> According to the Web page *Arthritis Facts* (2007), arthritis is a major cause
> of work disability.

See 15c, item 5, and 15e, item 27, for how to list these source items.

L. Work by a corporation, government agency, or organization

In the initial citation, use the organization's full name; in subsequent references, use an abbreviation if one exists.

> first mention: full name
>
> In its annual survey of college costs, the College Board gives examples of
> rapid increases in 2008. In 4-year colleges, for example, tuition and fees have
> increased 4.2% in the last decade (CB, 2008).
>
> abbreviation

Section 15c, item 6, shows how to list this work.

CITING VISUAL, MULTIMEDIA, AND MISCELLANEOUS SOURCES (APA)

M. Internet source Give the author's name, if it is available, or a short form of the title, followed by the year of electronic publication or update. Use "n.d." if no date is given. To locate a section of text you quote, paraphrase, or comment on in a source with no page or paragraph numbers visible on the screen, give any available section heading, and indicate the paragraph within the section: (Conclusion section, para. 2).

Be wary of citing e-mail messages (personal, bulletin board, discussion list, or Usenet group) because they are not peer-reviewed or easily retrievable. If you need to refer to an e-mail message, cite from an archived list whenever possible (see the example in 15e, item 32); otherwise, cite the message in your text as a personal communication (see 14b, item P), but do not include it in your list of references.

N. Visual, multimedia, or nonprint source For a film, television or radio broadcast, podcast, MP3 file, video recording, Web presentation, live performance, artwork, or other nonprint source, include in your citation the name of the originator or main contributor (such as the writer, interviewer, narrator, director, performer, or producer), along with the year of production.

> An Al Jazeera video highlights the plight of the African mountain gorillas (Ndege, 2007).

O. Multivolume work In your citation, give the publication date of the volume you are citing: (Einstein, 1987). If you refer to more than one volume, give inclusive dates for all the volumes you cite: (Einstein, 1998–2004). See 15c, item 8, for how to list this work.

P. Personal communication, such as a conversation, a letter, an interview, an e-mail, or an unarchived electronic discussion group Mention these sources only in your paper with the tag "personal communication"; do not include them in your list of references. Give the last name and initial(s) of the author of the communication and the exact date of posting.

> According to V. Sand, executive director of the Atwater Kent Museum of Philadelphia, "Museums engage our spirit, help us understand the natural world, and frame our identities" (personal communication, February 7, 2009).

For including archived postings in the list of references, see 15e, item 32.

Q. A classical or religious work If the date of publication of a classical work is not known, use in your citation "n.d." for "no date." If you use a translation, give the year of the translation, preceded by "trans." You do not need a reference list entry for the Bible or ancient classical works. Just give information about book, chapter, verse, and line numbers in your text, and identify the version you used in your first citation: Gen. 35: 1–4 (Revised Standard Version).

R. A long quotation If you quote more than forty words of prose, do not enclose the quotation in quotation marks. Start the quotation on a new line, and indent the whole quotation half an inch from the left margin. Double-space the quotation. Any necessary parenthetical citation should come after the final period of the quotation.

14c Notes, tables, figures, and headings (APA)

Notes　In APA style, you can use content notes to amplify information in your text. Number notes consecutively with superscript numerals. After the list of references, attach a separate page containing your numbered notes and headed "Footnotes." Use notes sparingly; include all important information in your text, not in footnotes.

Tables and figures　APA style for manuscripts submitted for publication asks for all tables and figures to be placed on separate pages at the end of the paper, after the references and any notes. However, college instructors may prefer you to insert tables and figures within your paper, as shown on pages 258–59 in the sample research paper in chapter 16. In either case, each table or figure should be numbered and provided with a caption. Consult with your instructor about the desired placement for tables and figures.

Headings　The headings "Abstract" and "References" are centered but not boldfaced. Use boldface centered headings for the sections within the main text of your paper, such as Method, Review of the Literature, Participants, Procedure, and Results. The next level of subheading should be boldface and flush left. See chapter 16 for a student's paper in APA style. A third level should be bold, indented to begin a new paragraph, and followed by a period.

15 ○━

APA List of References

15a How to set up an APA list of references

The APA *Publication Manual* (2010) and the association's Web site provide guidelines for submitting professional papers for publication, and many instructors ask students to follow those guidelines to prepare them for advanced work. This section follows APA guidelines. Check with your instructor, however, as to any specific course requirements for preparation of the paper and the reference list.

APA ▼ (American Psychological Association)

KEY POINTS
Guidelines for the APA List of References

- **What to list** List only the works you cited (quoted, summarized, paraphrased, or commented on) in the text of your paper, not every source you examined.

- **Format** Start the list on a new numbered page after the last page of the text of your paper. Center the heading "References," without quotation marks, not bold, underlined, or italicized, and with no period following it. Double-space throughout the list, with no additional space between entries. Place any tables and charts after the reference list, or consult with your instructor.

- **How to list works and authors** List the works alphabetically by last names of primary authors or by the name of a corporation or organization that acts as the author. Do not number the entries. Begin each entry with the author's name, last name first, followed by an initial or initials. Give any authors' names after the first in the same inverted form, separated by commas (but see 15b for more than seven authors). List works with no author by title, alphabetized by the first main word.

- **Date** Put the year in parentheses after the authors' names. For journals, magazines, and newspapers, also include the month and day, but do not abbreviate the names of the months.

- **Periods** Use a period and one space to separate the main parts of each entry.

- **Indentation** Use hanging indents. Begin the first line of each entry at the left margin; indent subsequent lines one-half inch. (Go to Page layout/Paragraph dialogue in Word 2007.)

- **Titles and capitals** In titles of books, reports, articles, and Web documents, capitalize *only* the first word of the title, any subtitle, and any proper nouns or adjectives. For magazines and journals, give the periodical name in full, using uppercase and lowercase letters.

- **Titles and italics** Italicize the titles of books, but do not italicize or use quotation marks around the titles of articles. Italicize the titles of newspapers, reports, and Web pages. For magazines and journals, italicize the title of the publication, the comma following it, and the volume number—but not the issue number (see an example in 15d, item 16).

(Continued)

(Continued)

- **Page numbers** Give inclusive page numbers for print articles and sections of books, using complete page spans, such as 251–259. Use the abbreviation "p." or "pp." only for newspaper articles and sections of books (such as chapters or anthologized articles).

- **Online sources** Include whatever is available of the following: author(s), date of work, title of work, any print publication information, and identification of the type of source in square brackets (for example, [Letter to the editor], [Abstract]). For an article accessed online, give the URL of the home page of the site, not of the actual document (as in 15e, item 23). Split a URL across lines only before a punctuation mark such as a period or a slash (except for the double slash that follows "http:"). Do *not* underline the URL as a hyperlink unless you are posting the paper online (see 21b), and do *not* put a period after a URL when it occurs at the end of an entry. Provide page numbers only for documents accessed as PDF files.

15b How to list authors in the APA reference list

Name of author(s) Put the last name first, followed by a comma and then the initials.

> Gould, S. J.

Reverse the names of all authors listed, except the editors of an anthology or a reference work (15c, item 4). Use an ampersand (&), not the word *and*, before the last author's name (15c, item 2). For eight or more authors, give the reversed names of the first six, then use three ellipsis dots before the name of the last author.

Alphabetical order Alphabetize letter by letter. Treat *Mac* and *Mc* literally, by letter.

> MacKay, M.   D'Agostino, S.
> McCarthy, T.   De Cesare, P.
> McKay, K.   DeCurtis, A.

A shorter name precedes a longer name beginning with the same letters, whatever the first initial: *Black, T.* precedes *Blackman, R.*

For a work with no known author, list by the first word in the title other than *A, An,* or *The.* Alphabetize numerals according to their spelling: 5 ("five") precedes 2 ("two").

Individual author(s) not known   If the author is a group, such as a corporation, agency, or institution, give its name, alphabetized by the first important word (15c, item 6). Use full names, not abbreviations. If no author or group is named, alphabetize by the first main word of the title (15c, item 5).

Several works by the same author   List the author's name in each entry. Arrange entries chronologically from past to present. Entries published in the same year should be arranged alphabetically by title and distinguished with lowercase letters after the date (*a, b,* and so on). Note that entries for one author precede entries showing the same author with coauthors.

> Goleman, D. (1996a, July 16). Forget money; nothing can buy
>   happiness, some researchers say. *The New York Times*,
>   p. C1.
> Goleman, D. (1996b). *Vital lies, simple truths.* New York, NY: Simon &
>   Schuster.
> Goleman, D. (2007). *Social intelligence: The new science of social
>   relationships.* New York, NY: Bantam.
> Goleman, D., Boyatzis, R. E., & McKee, A. (2004). *Primal leadership:
>   Learning to lead with emotional intelligence.* Cambridge, MA:
>   Harvard Business School Press.

Authors with the same last name   List alphabetically by first initial: Smith, A. precedes Smith, F.

15c Sample APA listings: Print books, pamphlets, and parts of books

- Look for the necessary information on the title page and the copyright page of a book.

(American Psychological Association) ▼ APA

SOURCE SHOT 6

Listing a Book (APA)

On the title page and copyright page of the book, you'll find the information you need for an entry in the list of references.

❶ **Author(s)** Last name, initials (see 15b on how to list multiple authors)

❷ **(Year of publication)** In parentheses, followed by a period; the most recent copyright (©) date or "n.d." if no date is supplied

❸ *Title of book: Any subtitle* In italics, with capital letters only for the first word of the title and subtitle and any proper names

❹ **Place of publication** City and state (two-letter U.S. Postal Service abbreviation), omitting the state when its name appears in the name of the publisher, as in "University of Illinois Press," followed by a colon

❺ **Publisher** In a short but intelligible form, including *Books* or *Press* but omitting *Publishers, Co.,* or *Inc.* and ending with a period

See also 15c, items 1–12 for more examples.

```
                   initials  periods
❶ Last name       /        / ❷ Year in parentheses
        / comma  /  /  /      period  ❸ Title italicized
Wilson, E. O. (1994). Naturalist. Washington, DC: Island Press.
                      ❹ Publication city   colon  ❺ Publisher   final period
                        and state
```

- Use the most recent copyright date or "n.d." if no date is given.
- Include the city (or the first city if two or more are given) and the state of publication (two-letter U.S. Postal Service abbreviation).
- Give the publisher's name in a shortened but intelligible form, including *Books* or *Press* but omitting *Publishers, Co.,* or *Inc.*

1. Book with one author   Give the last name first, followed by the initials. See Source Shot 6 for an example.

2. Book with two to seven authors   List all authors' names in the order in which they appear on the book's title page. Reverse the order of each name: last name first, followed by initials. Separate all names with commas, and insert an ampersand (&) before the last name.

Title Page

Copyright Page

③ Title

NATURALIST

EDWARD O. WILSON

① Author

⑤ Publisher

ISLAND PRESS / Shearwater Books
Washington, D.C. • Covelo, California

④ Place of publication

② Year of publication

A Shearwater Book
published by Island Press

Copyright © 1994 by Island Press
Illustrations copyright © 1994 by Laura Simonds Southworth

The excerpt from "Daybreak in Alabama" is from
Selected Poems by Langston Hughes, copyright © 1948
by Alfred A. Knopf Inc., and renewed 1976
by The Executors of the Estate of Langston Hughes.
Reprinted by permission of the publisher.

All rights reserved under International and Pan-American
Copyright Conventions. No part of this book may be
reproduced in any form or by any means without permission
in writing from the publisher: Island Press, 1718 Connecticut
Avenue, N.W., Suite 300, Washington, DC 20009.
SHEARWATER BOOKS is a trademark of
The Center for Resource Economics.

LIBRARY OF CONGRESS
CATALOGING-IN-PUBLICATION DATA
Wilson, Edward Osborne, 1929–
Naturalist / Edward O. Wilson.
p.   cm.
Includes index.
ISBN 1-55963-288-7 (cloth)
1. Wilson, Edward Osborne, 1929–   . 2. Naturalists—
United States—Biography. I. Title.
QH31.W64A3   1994
508'.092—dc20   94-13111
[B]   CIP

Printed on recycled, acid-free paper
Manufactured in the United States of America
10 9 8 7 6 5 4 3 2 1

ampersand

┌─────────all names reversed─────────┐
Baumol, W. J., Litan, R. E., & Schramm, C. J. (2007). *Good capitalism,*
indented   *bad capitalism, and the economics of growth and prosperity.*
a half inch
⟶ New Haven, CT: Yale University Press.

For eight or more authors, see 15b.

3. Edited book   Use "Ed." or "Eds." for one or more editors, in parentheses.

Gates, L., Jr., & Jarrett, G. A. (Eds.). (2007). *The new Negro: Readings*
on race, representation, and African American culture, 1892–1938.
Princeton, NJ: Princeton University Press.

4. Work in an edited collection or reference book   List the author, the date of publication of the edited book, and the title of the work. Follow this with "In" and the names of the editors (not inverted), the title of the book, and (in parentheses) the inclusive page numbers (preceded by "pp.") of the chapter. End with the place of publication and the publisher. If you cite more than one article in an edited work, include full bibliographical details in each entry.

DuBois, W. E. B. (2007). Returning soldiers. In L. Gates, Jr., & G. A. Jarrett
(Eds.), *The new Negro: Readings on race, representation, and African
American culture, 1892–1938* (pp. 85–91). Princeton, NJ: Princeton
University Press.

For a well-known reference book with unsigned alphabetical entries, begin with the title of the entry, and include the page number(s).

Antarctica. (2000). In *The Columbia encyclopedia* (6th ed., pp. 116–118).
New York, NY: Columbia University Press.

5. No author identified   Put the title first. Ignore *A, An,* and *The* when alphabetizing. Alphabetize the following under *W.*

The world almanac and book of facts 2009. (2009). Pleasantville, NY: World
Almanac Books.

6. Book, pamphlet, or brochure by a corporation, government agency, or other organization   Give the name of the corporate author first. If the publisher is the same as the author, write "Author" for the name of the publisher. For a brochure, include the word *brochure* in square brackets, [Brochure], after the title.

College Board. (2008). *Trends in college pricing 2008.* Washington, DC: Author.

If no author is named for a government publication, begin with the name of the federal, state, or local government department, followed by the agency.

U.S. Department of Homeland Security, Federal Emergency Management
Agency. (2004). *Preparing for disaster for people with disabilities and
other special needs.* Washington, DC: Author.

7. Translated book   In parentheses after the title of the work, give the initials and last name of the translator, followed by a comma and "Trans."

name of translator not reversed

Jung, C. G. (1960). *On the nature of the psyche* (R. F. C. Hull, Trans.).

Princeton, NJ: Princeton University Press.

8. Multivolume work   Give the number of volumes after the title, in parentheses. The date should indicate the range of years of publication, when appropriate.

Einstein, A. (1987–2006). *Collected papers of Albert Einstein* (Vols. 1–10).

Princeton, NJ: Princeton University Press.

If you cite only one volume, give only that volume number and its date.

9. Foreword, preface, introduction, or afterword   List the name of the author of the book element cited. Follow the date with the name of the element, the title of the book, and in parentheses, the page number or numbers on which the element appears, preceded by "p." or "pp."

Baumol, W. J., Litan, R. E., & Schramm, C. J. (2007). Preface. *Good*

capitalism, bad capitalism, and the economics of growth and

prosperity (pp. vii–viii). New Haven, CT: Yale University Press.

10. Revised, republished, or reprinted work   For a revised edition of a book, give the edition number after the title.

Raimes, A. (2010). *Pocket keys for writers* (3rd ed.). Boston, MA: Wadsworth.

For a republished work, give the most recent date of publication after the author's name and at the end in parentheses add "Original work published" and the date. Do not add a final period. In the citation in your paper, give both dates: (Smith, 1793/1976).

Smith, A. (1976). *An inquiry into the nature and causes of the wealth of*

nations. Chicago, IL: University of Chicago Press. (Original work

published 1793)

For a reprint, begin the details in the parentheses with "Reprinted from," followed by the title, page numbers, author or editor, date, place, and publisher of the original work.

11. Technical report   Give the report number (following "Report No.") after the title.

National Endowment for the Arts. (2007, November). *To read or not to read: A question of national consequence* (Report No. 47). Washington, DC: Author.

12. Dissertation or abstract   For a manuscript source, give the author, year, title, and description (in parentheses) followed by "Available from" and the name of the database, ending with any accession or order number.

Jerskey, M. (2006). *Writing handbooks, English language learners, and the selective tradition* (Doctoral dissertation). Available from ProQuest Dissertation and Theses database. (UMI No. 3235697)

For a microfilm source, also include in parentheses at the end of the entry the University Microfilms number. For a CD-ROM source, include "CD-ROM" after the title; then name the electronic source of the information and provide the access number.

For an abstract published in *DAI*, give author, date, and dissertation title (as in the previous example) followed by *Dissertation Abstracts International:* and the name of the section. After a comma, add the volume, (issue), and page number(s).

15d Sample APA listings: Print articles in periodicals

Do not use quotation marks around article titles or initial capitals for words in the titles, except for the first word and proper nouns or adjectives. After the title, include the italicized periodical name in uppercase and lowercase, then the italicized volume number, followed by inclusive page numbers. For a periodical with each issue paged separately, add the issue number immediately after the volume number, as shown in Source Shot 7, page 242.

13. Article in a scholarly journal   Give the year of publication and the volume number. Include an issue number only if each issue is paged separately and begins with page 1. Also, as in the following example, include a DOI (digital object identifier) if one has been assigned to the article, so that any readers can easily access the source online. (See page 244 for more information on DOIs.) Use capital letters only for the first word of an article title or subtitle and for proper nouns and adjectives. (See sections 3b and 8c on how to recognize scholarly articles.)

Do not use "p." or "pp." with page numbers. (See 15b for more on listing multiple authors.)

authors' names reversed, connected by ampersand (&)
no quotation marks around or capitals within title

Kanazawa, S., & Still, M. C. (2000). Teaching may be hazardous to your

journal title, comma, and volume number italicized

marriage. *Evolution and Human Behavior, 21*, 185–190.

doi:10.1016/S1090–5138(00)00026–X

DOI

no "p." or "pp." before page numbers

14. Magazine article Include the year and any exact date of publication in parentheses. Do not abbreviate months. Italicize the name of the magazine, the comma following it, and the volume number. Then give the issue number in parentheses and the page number(s). See Source Shot 7 (p. 242) for an example.

15. Newspaper article In parentheses, include the month and day of the newspaper after the year. Give the section letter or number before the page, where applicable. Use "p." and "pp." with page numbers. Do not omit *The* from the title of a newspaper or a magazine. For articles with no author, begin with the title.

Blakeslee, S. (2008, January 15). Monkey's thoughts propel robot, a step that may help humans. *The New York Times*, p. F3.

16. Article that skips pages When an article appears on discontinuous pages, give all the sequences of page numbers, separated by commas.

Baker, C. (2009, February). Fantasy island: Live free or drown. *Wired, 17*(2), 58–61, 108.

17. Review or interview After the title of the review article, add in square brackets a description of the work reviewed and identify the medium: book, film, or video, for example.

Angell, M. (2009, January 15). Drug companies and doctors: A story of corruption [Review of the book *Shyness: How normal behavior became a sickness*, by C. Lane]. *The New York Review of Books, 56*(1), 12.

SOURCE SHOT 7

Listing a Periodical Article (APA)

When listing a print periodical article, include the following:

❶ Author(s) Last name, initials (see also 15b on how to list authors)

❷ (Date of publication of article) In parentheses: year, month (not abbreviated), day, according to type of periodical, followed by a period

❸ Title of article: Any subtitle No quotation marks or italics; capitals only for first word of title, subtitle, and proper nouns or adjectives; ending with a period

❹ *Periodical Title, volume*(issue number) All italicized, except for issue number. For periodicals with each issue paged separately, put the issue number in parentheses immediately following the volume number, with no space between. Use a comma to separate an article title from the volume number and use another before the page numbers.

❺ Inclusive range of page numbers All digits included (as in 167–168). Do not use "p." or "pp." (except with pages of newspaper articles).

If an article has been assigned a DOI (see page 244), provide it after the page numbers.

Note the use of periods and commas.

| ❶ Author | ❷ Date | ❸ Title | ❹ *Name of magazine, volume* (issue) |

Bell, R. E. (2008, February). The unquiet ice. *Scientific American, 298*(2),

❺ Page numbers
60–67.

Give the title of the interview and the name of the person interviewed.

Jeffery, C. (2009, January/February). The Maddow knows [Interview with Rachel Maddow]. *Mother Jones, 34*(1), 72–73.

18. Unsigned editorial or article For a work with no author named, begin the listing with the title; for an editorial, add the label "Editorial" in square brackets after the title.

Ideas for a new era [Editorial]. (2009, January 12). *The Nation, 288*(2), 3–4.

Ready for day one. (2009, January 17–23). *The Economist, 390*(8614), 31–32.

Table of Contents of a Magazine (APA)

❹ Magazine name   ❷ Date   ❹ Volume and issue number

FEATURES

SCIENTIFIC AMERICAN February 2008 ■ Volume 298 Number 2

38 *SPECIAL REPORT*
The Future of Physics

39   The Discovery Machine
By Graham P. Collins
The Large Hadron Collider, the biggest and
most complicated particle physics experiment
ever seen, is nearing completion and is
scheduled to start colliding protons this year.

**46   The Coming Revolutions
in Particle Physics**
By Chris Quigg
No matter what the Large Hadron
Collider finds, it is going to take physics
into new territory.

Image by CERN and Phil Saunders / Space Channel Ltd.

**54 Building the
Next-Generation Collider**
*By Barry Barish, Nicholas Walker
and Hitoshi Yamamoto*
To further investigate the intricacies
of high-energy particle physics,
researchers must construct a more
powerful electron-positron collider.

CLIMATE CHANGE   ❸ Title
■ **60   The Unquiet Ice**
By Robin E. Bell   ❶ Author
Abundant liquid water discovered
underneath the great polar ice sheets could
catastrophically intensify the effects
of global warming on the rise of sea level
around the world.

❺ Page span

INNOVATIONS
68   RFID Powder
By Tim Hornyak
Radio-frequency identification (RFID) tags label
all kinds of inventoried goods and speed commuters
through toll plazas. Now tiny RFID components
are being developed with a rather different aim:
thwarting counterfeiters.

SHARE YOUR THOUGHTS
Post your comments about articles in this
issue for the benefit of other readers.
Go to www.SciAm.com/ontheweb

ON THE COVER
The Large Hadron Collider and a proposed International
Linear Collider should propel humankind into a pristine
realm of unknown particle physics. Image by Kenn Brown

www.SciAm.com   SCIENTIFIC AMERICAN **1**

19. Letter to the editor   Put the label "Letter to the editor" in
brackets after the date or the title of the letter, if it has one.

Youmans, G. (2009, January/February). [Letter to the editor]. *The Atlantic,*
    303(1), 16.

15e Sample APA listings: Online sources

The American Psychological Association supplements the sixth edition of its *Publication Manual* (2010) with its Web site <http://www
.apastyle.org>, which provides citation examples, periodic updates,
and tips.

(American Psychological Association) ▼ **APA**

Include in your citation whatever information is available of the following to enable your readers to locate your online source:

1. **Name(s) of author(s)** of online document, if available
2. **Year and date** of print publication or of online posting (use "n.d." if no date is available)
3. **Title of document and subtitle**, along with an identification of a special type of source in square brackets, such as [Review], [Abstract], or [Multimedia presentation]
4. **Source details**: any available print publication information for online books and journal articles (as in examples in 15c and 15d), such as name of journal, volume and issue number, and page numbers if they are shown; use a PDF version of a document when you can because it provides on-screen page numbers and figures for reference
5. **Retrieval statement**:

   DOI available If a work has been assigned a DOI (digital object identifier), copy and paste the DOI and use it as a retrieval statement, such as doi:10.1037/0022-3514.94.1.168 as in Source Shot 8 (p. 246). The DOI will never change even if the URL does. If you give the DOI, do not include any other retrieval information.

   DOI unavailable For online scholarly journal articles with no DOI, write "Retrieved from" followed by the home page URL. For a work in a database, use the home page or the menu page URL. If the content may be changed or updated, such as content on a wiki, also add your retrieval date (month + day, year).

Note: Write "Available from" in place of "Retrieved from" when a URL does not provide the actual source but tells how to retrieve it.

KEY POINTS
Working with DOIs and URLs

- Copy and paste a URL or a DOI from its site to be sure it is accurate. Many can be long and complex.
- In subscription databases such as the ones sponsored by EBSCO (Source Shot 8, p. 246), the DOI is easy to find on the

Citation page. On some sites, however, the DOI may lurk behind a button such as "Article," "CrossRef," or the name of a supplier of full-text articles. Remember to search the site fully for a DOI.

- If you give a DOI, a reader can then easily turn the DOI string into a URL by going to http://www.crossref.org or by appending the DOI string after http://dx.doi.org/ to access the work or the database in which it is located.

- APA recommends splitting a URL or a DOI across lines only before a slash, a period, or other punctuation mark.

- Do not underline a URL as a hyperlink unless you are preparing an online paper.

- Do not include a period after a DOI or a URL that appears at the end of your reference.

20. Online database journal article with a DOI Universities and libraries subscribe to large searchable databases of print publications, such as Gale *InfoTrac*, EBSCO *Academic Search Premier, ERIC, LexisNexis*, EBSCO *PsycARTICLES*, and WilsonWeb *Education Full Text*, providing access to abstracts and full-text articles. In addition to print source information, give the DOI for electronic retrieval information. Source Shot 8, page 246, shows the relevant part of the EBSCO *PsycARTICLES* database citation page that provides the information needed for the citation.

Do not give the name of the database when a DOI is available.

A reader attaching the DOI string to <http://dx.doi.org/> so that it became <http://dx.doi.org/10.1037/0022-3514.94.1.168> would be taken directly to a *PsycARTICLES* Web page containing the abstract and could then either purchase the full text or access it free by logging into a library database.

Note: Because the DOI leads to a URL, for college papers, it may be quicker and more convenient to give a persistent URL to a database the school has licensed. Consult with your instructor about this divergence from APA style recommendations.

APA ▼ (American Psychological Association)

SOURCE SHOT 8

Listing an Article (with a DOI) in an Online Database

Include the following information:

❶ **Author(s)** Last name, initials

❷ **(Date of work)** In parentheses, including whatever is necessary to identify the print source (items 13–15) and its date of print publication: year, month and day ("n.d." if no date is available)

❸ **Title of work: Subtitle** No quotation marks or italics; capitals only for first word of title and subtitle and for proper nouns and adjectives; period at the end

❹ **Source details** *Name of periodical* + *volume number* (both italicized), with issue number only for periodicals paged separately by issue + inclusive page numbers if shown on the screen

❺ **Retrieval statement** The DOI—with no final period

```
                              ❶ Authors                           ❷ Date
Papadatou-Pastou, M., Martin, M., Munafo, M. R., & Jones, G. V. (2008).
                              ❸ Title: Subtitle
     Sex differences in left-handedness: A meta-analysis of 144 studies.
     ❹ Source details: periodical name, volume, pages
        Psychological Bulletin, 134, 677–699. doi:10.1037/a0012814
                              ❺ DOI for retrieval, no period at end
```

21. Online database journal article with no DOI   Give the URL of the home page of the journal.

Cleary, J. M., & Crafti, N. (2007). Basic need satisfaction, emotional eating, and dietary restraint as risk factors for recurrent overeating in a community sample. *E-Journal of Applied Psychology, 3*(2), 27–39. Retrieved from http://ojs.lib.swin.edu.au/index.php/ejap

22. Online article with a PDF print source   Cite an article originally published in print and retrieved in PDF format as you would cite a print article, with the addition of "[Electronic version]" after the title of the article.

APA ▼ (American Psychological Association)

Online Database Citation Page (from EBSCO *PsycARTICLES* database)

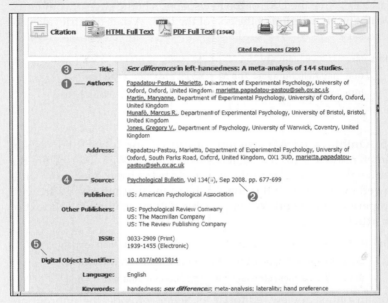

Jones, C. J., & Meredith, W. (2000, June). Developmental paths of

   psychological health from early adolescence to later adulthood

   [Electronic version]. *Psychology and Aging, 15,* 351–360.

23. Article in an online journal with no print source available

If only an HTML version is available, with information such as page numbers or figures missing, give journal information and the URL.

Svoboda, E. (2008, January/February). Scents and sensibility. *Psychology

   Today, 41*(1). Retrieved from http://www.psychologytoday.com

If you have a choice, always access the PDF version.

24. Newspaper article retrieved from a database or Web site
Newspaper articles, as well as journal articles, are often available from several sources, in several databases, and in a variety of formats, such as in the newspaper's database or a library subscription database. Give the URL of the newspaper's home page in your entry. Do not insert a period at the end of the URL. A date of retrieval is not necessary.

Blakeslee, S. (2008, January 15). Monkey's thoughts propel robot, a step

　　that may help humans. *The New York Times*. Retrieved from

　　http://www.nytimes.com　　no period at end when a URL ends the entry

25. Online abstract, review, editorial, or letter　For an abstract retrieved from a database or from a Web site, begin the retrieval statement with the words "Abstract retrieved from" followed by the URL of the home page of the journal's Web site, with no period at the end. When possible, however, cite the full text of an article.

Frith, H., & Gleeson, K. (2004). Clothing and embodiment: Men managing

　　body image and appearance. *Psychology of Men & Masculinity,*

　　5, 40–48. Abstract retrieved from http://content.apa.org/

For an online review, editorial, or letter, provide the appropriate term in the retrieval statement, such as "Review of . . .", and a date of retrieval if the content may change.

26. Authored document on Web site　Give the date of retrieval for content that may be changed or updated.

Cohen, E. (2008, January 31). Caring for Mom and Dad from afar. *CNN.com*

　　/health. Retrieved February 8, 2009, from http://www.cnn.com

27. Web site document, no author identified　Italicize the title of the document (the Web page). Alphabetize by the first major word of the title.

Arthritis facts. (2007). Retrieved January 22, 2009, from http://www

　　.arthritis.org/facts.php

28. Entire Web site, no author   Give the complete URL in the text of your paper, not in your list of references (14b, item M).

29. Report on a university or government site   Italicize the title of a technical or research report. In the retrieval statement, give the name of the university or government agency (and the department or division if it is named). Follow this with a colon and the URL.

McClintock, R. (2000, September 20). *Cities, youth, and technology: Toward a pedagogy of autonomy.* Retrieved from Columbia University, Institute for Learning Technologies website: http://www.iit.columbia .edu/publications/

30. Online book

Freud, S. (1923). *A young girl's diary.* New York, NY: Seltzer. Retrieved from http://books.google.com

31. Online reference work   Give your retrieval date for a work that is likely to be updated, especially a source such as *Wikipedia* that anyone can update and change at any time.

Hilgevoord, J., & Uffink, J. (2006). The uncertainty principle. In E. N. Zalta (Ed.), *The Stanford encyclopedia of philosophy.* Retrieved January 26, 2009, from http://plato.stanford.edu

Gardening. (n.d.). In Wikipedia. Retrieved August 18, 2009, from http://en .wikipedia.org/wiki/Gardening

32. Blogs, discussion boards, wikis, newsgroups, and archived mailing lists   Include in your list of sources only academic material posted on archived lists or blogs. If no archives exist, cite an entry on a discussion board or message board as a personal communication (15f, item 33). Always give the retrieval date for wiki pages, which may change constantly.

Baron, D. (2009, January 13). Read all about it: Reading on the rise as economy falters [Web log post to The Web of Language]. Retrieved from http://webtools.uiuc.edu/blog/view?blogId=25

Navia, J. (2008, January 19). Space travel by humans is not possible now [Newsgroup message]. Retrieved from http://groups.google.com /group/sci.space.policy/

15f Sample APA listings: Visual, multimedia, and miscellaneous sources (live, print, and online)

33. Personal communication (letter, telephone conversation, interview, personal e-mail, message on discussion board) Cite only in the body of your text as "personal communication." Do not include these communications in your list of references (see 14b, item P).

34. Conference paper/conference proceedings

Szenher, M. (2005, September). *Visual homing with learned goal distance information.* Paper presented at the Third International Symposium on Autonomous Minirobots for Research and Edutainment, Fukui, Japan. Retrieved from http://books.google.com

Cite a conference paper accessed in a print volume of conference proceedings as you would a work in an edited collection, as in 15c, item 4. If a DOI is available, include it.

35. Poster session

Szenher, M. (2005, September). *Visual homing in natural environments.* Poster session presented at the annual meeting of Towards Autonomous Robotic Systems, London, England.

36. Film, recording, or video Identify the medium (motion picture, videocassette, DVD, etc.) in brackets after the title. Give the country where a film was released, or give the city for other formats.

Berman, S. S., & Pulcini, R. (Directors). (2003). *American splendor* [Motion picture]. United States: Fine Line Features.

Jacquet, L. (Director). (2005). *The march of the penguins* [DVD]. Burbank, CA: Warner Home Video.

37. Television or radio program

Gazit, C. (Writer). (2004). The seeds of destruction [Television series episode]. In D. J. James (Producer), *Slavery and the making of America.* New York, NY: WNET.

38. Podcast or MP3 download Give author, producer, or interviewer; title; and as many other details as you can that will help a reader access the same source.

Bayoumi, M. (Author). (2008, December 5). *Being young, Arab, and Muslim in America.* [Audio podcast]. Retrieved from http://www.brooklyn .cuny.edu/pub/podcasts.php

Davis, A. (2007, October 2). Angela Davis speaks. *Panel discussion with Burnham, Mitchell, and Noble* [MP3 download]. Washington, DC: Folkways Records. Retrieved from http://www.amazon.com

Tanenhaus, S. (2008, January 12). *Book Update.* Interview with Anthony Lewis on his book *Freedom for the Thought that We Hate* [Audio podcast]. Retrieved from http://graphics8.nytimes.com/podcasts/2008/01/11/12bookupdate.mp3

39. Video Weblog posting Use a screen name if it is the only one available.

nnnicck. (2007, February 7). The march of the librarians [Video file]. Retrieved from http://www.youtube.com/watch?v=Td922I0NoDQ

40. Presentation slides

Norvig, P. (2000). *The Gettysburg PowerPoint presentation* [PowerPoint slides]. Retrieved from http://norvig.com/Gettysburg/index.htm

41. CD-ROM or DVD Identify the medium in square brackets after the title.

World of warcraft [CD-ROM]. (2004). Irvine, CA: Blizzard Entertainment.

Izzard, E. (2009). *Live from Wembley.* [DVD]. London, England: Ella Communications.

42. Computer software Do not use italics for the name of the software.

Snaglt (Version 9.0) [Computer software]. (2008). Okemos, MI: TechSmith.

16 🔑

Sample Paper 4: A Student's Research Paper, APA Style

The following paper was written by Maria Saparauskaite in a required first-year course at Hunter College. The assignment was to explore a current issue in the news. Using the APA style of documentation, she provides a title page, an abstract, and section headings. Her citations and the list of references at the end follow APA guidelines and serve to answer any questions readers may have about the authors, dates, and publication details of her source material. Her instructor asked for tables and figures to be included in the paper rather than attached separately at the end.

Note: Blue annotations point out issues of content and organization; Red annotations point out APA format issues.

Title Page (APA)

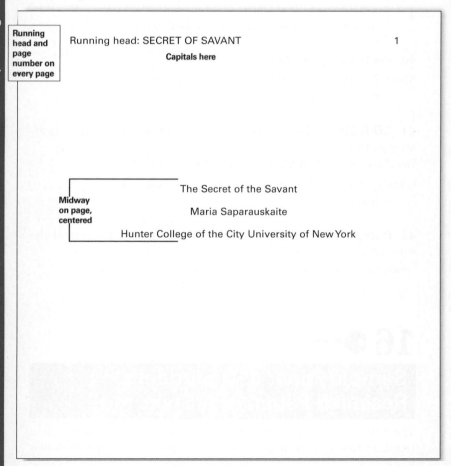

Running head and page number on every page

Running head: SECRET OF SAVANT   1

Capitals here

The Secret of the Savant

Midway on page, centered

Maria Saparauskaite

Hunter College of the City University of New York

Abstract Page (APA)

Heading centered Abstract

This paper investigates the phenomenon of savants, people with unusual mental talents, and describes some of their extraordinary feats. Theories of the development of the rare savant syndrome are explored, especially the connection between a savant's abilities and whether the effects of brain damage on the hemispheres of the brain cause savant talents to emerge spontaneously. A study by Snyder, Bahramali, Hawker, and Mitchell (2006) is explored in detail. The researchers wanted to examine how stimulation of the brain affected mental functions, with participants experiencing either brain stimulation or a sham session and then being asked to make judgments about what they saw. The study suggests that the savant condition could be stimulated, thus raising questions about not only whether rewiring of the brain is advisable but also to what ends any newfound intelligence may be applied.

Length:
137 words
(aim for
100–200)

Passive
voice
common
in APA

Summary
of findings

APA ▼ (American Psychological Association)

(American Psychological Association) ▼ APA

Essay (APA)

The Secret of the Savant

Many of us struggle with learning and memorization. We may long to be able to do math problems quickly in our heads, play a favorite song on the piano after hearing it only once, or recapture details from an event we have observed. We may wish we could learn a second language as easily as we did our first. For a few individuals among us, these talents are as natural as breathing. These individuals are *savants* and they are capable of unusual mental feats. Some recent studies have shown that there may be a savant within all of us, which means that our brains may be capable of the same abilities as savants. Through artificial means these talents can in some cases be accessed temporarily.

Background Review of the Literature

Savants and Their Accomplishments

Savants exhibit extraordinary talents. Researchers Treffert and Wallace (2004) have reported that at the age of 14, Leslie Lemke was able to play Tchaikovsky's *Piano Concerto No. 1* without a single mistake after hearing it only once. He had never had a piano lesson in his life but today he tours all over the world playing in concerts even though he is blind and developmentally disabled. Lemke even composes his own music. Another savant, Kim Peek, the inspiration for the Oscar-winning film *Rain Man*, has memorized more than 7,600 books. It would take him less than three seconds to tell you which day of the week your birthday fell on and which

Annotations (margin notes):
- Title centered, not bold or underlined
- 1" margin
- Area of research and hypothesis
- Main heading bold and centered
- Subhead bold and flush left
- Year in parentheses
- No extra space around headings

SECRET OF SAVANT   4

day of the week you will be collecting your first pension. Like

Lemke, Peek is also developmentally disabled. The artwork of

another savant, Richard Wawro, is known all over the world. His

childhood oil paintings left people speechless (Treffert & Wallace,

2004). He is an autistic savant, as is David Tammet, who can

calculate 37 to the power of four in his head (Heffernan, 2005).

The Savant Syndrome

The savant syndrome is an extremely rare condition, most

often found in people with IQs ranging from 40 to 70, though

sometimes it can occur in people with IQs up to 114 or higher

(Treffert & Wallace, 2004). Most savants are physically disabled or

suffer from autism, which is a "pervasive development disorder

[that] is characterized by a severe disturbance of communication,

social, and cognitive skills, and is often associated with mental

retardation" (Sternberg, 2004, p. 352). Despite that, savants exhibit

amazing mental superiority in specific areas, such as arithmetic,

drawing, music, or memory. However, their way of thinking is very

literal, and they have problems understanding abstract concepts.

Their abilities emerge spontaneously and cannot be improved

over time. Also savants cannot explain how they do what they do

(Snyder et al., 2006).

Theories of Development of the Syndrome

Scientists have only a vague idea of how the savant

syndrome develops. Recent studies have illustrated that

developmental problems in the left brain hemisphere are most

commonly seen in savants. Bernard Rimland of the Autism

SECRET OF SAVANT   5

Mentions authority of source

Research Institute has observed that most abilities in autistic savants are associated with the right hemisphere, whereas the abilities they are deficient in are associated with the left hemisphere (Treffert & Wallace, 2004). The left hemisphere is

Present perfect tense used to introduce source

thought to be responsible for forming hypotheses and concepts. This observation helps to explain why savants tend to be so literal. Another set of evidence for this theory is the occasional emergence of savantlike talents in people suffering from dementia.

Past tense for a research study

Bruce Miller of the University of California observed five elderly patients who spontaneously developed exceptional artistic skills in music and painting. All of these patients had what is called frontotemporal dementia (FTD). Miller discovered that most brain damage caused by FTD was localized in the left hemisphere (Treffert & Wallace, 2004). In another case of brain damage, psychologist T. L. Brink reported that a nine-year-old boy developed "unusual savant mechanical skills" (Treffert & Wallace, 2004, para. 18) after a bullet damaged his left hemisphere. According to Treffert and Wallace, these reports of spontaneous emergence of

Question for research

the savant syndrome in people with brain damage could point to a possibility that savant talents may be innate to everyone. So, as reporter Lawrence Osborne provocatively asked, "Could brain damage, in short, actually make you brilliant?" (2003, p. 40).

New section of paper: heading centered

Snyder's Experiment

Allan Snyder of the University of Sydney, "one of the world's most remarkable scientists of human cognition" (Osborne, 2003, p. 38), became interested in the prospect of hidden genius when

Credentials of researcher

Blue = content issues   Red = format issues

SECRET OF SAVANT   6

observing patients who underwent a procedure called transcranial

magnetic stimulation (TMS). TMS was "originally developed as

a tool for brain surgery: by stimulating or slowing down specific

regions of the brain, it allowed doctors to monitor the effects of

surgery in real time" (Osborne, 2003, p. 38). Interestingly enough,

this procedure had very noticeable side effects on the patients'

mental functioning. A patient would either temporarily lose his

ability to speak or make odd mistakes while speaking. But one

side effect intrigued Snyder the most: Some patients undergoing

TMS would gain savantlike intelligence for a limited amount of

time. With his colleague Mitchell, he came up with the theory

that savants have a privileged access to lower levels of cognition,   Claim of
                                                                       researchers
whereas normal persons do not (Snyder & Mitchell, 1999).

Participants and Method

        To test this theory, Snyder, along with Bahramali, Hawker,

and Mitchell, led an experiment (2006) which was based on the

finding that some savants are able to guess the exact number

of items, such as matches, just by glancing at them. He tells of

autistic twins who were able to estimate correctly the number

of matches (111) fallen on the floor. By using TMS on the brains of

12 volunteers, Snyder wanted to find out if a normal person could

accomplish the same thing. The goal was to create virtual lesions in

the left anterior temporal lobes of the volunteers, thus suppressing

mental activity in that region of the brain (see Figure 1).

        The participants underwent two sessions. During one   Description
                                                                      of the
of them, they received TMS stimulation, while during the other   experiment

SECRET OF SAVANT   7

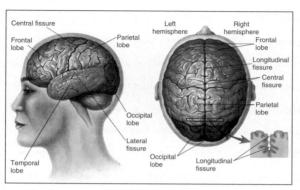

Figure 1. Diagram of the brain. From R. J. Sternberg, *Psychology*, 2004, p. 91.

"sham" session, they did not. The participants were not able to tell the difference. During each session, the participants were shown a random number of dots on a computer screen (as shown in Figure 2) and then told to estimate the number of dots they saw. They were asked to do this before the TMS stimulation, then 15 minutes afterward, and finally an hour later. The same procedure was used in both real and sham sessions.

Results of the Experiment

Purpose of figure explained

The results, summarized in Figure 3, are surprising. Eight of the 12 participants improved their ability to estimate the number of dots within an accuracy range of five after the TMS stimulation. The probability for this to happen merely by chance alone is less than 1 in 1,000. Clearly there is a significant increase in the number of correct estimations after the TMS stimulation. The sham session shows relatively little variation.

APA ▼ (American Psychological Association)

SECRET OF SAVANT   8

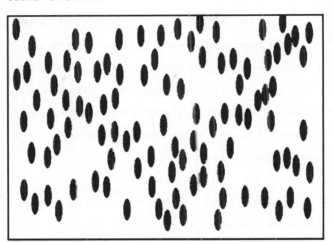

Figure 2. The task—to estimate the number of dots. From A. Snyder et al., 2006, p. 838.

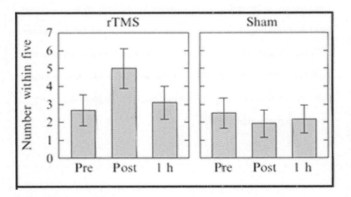

Figure 3. Participants' ability to make guesses within an accuracy range of 5, both with repetitive transcranial magnetic stimulation and without (the sham session). From A. Snyder et al., 2006, p. 841.

(American Psychological Association) ▼ APA

Confirmation of hypothesis

Snyder and the other researchers concluded that the experiment "demonstrated an enhanced ability of healthy normal individuals to guess the absolute number of discrete elements by attempting to artificially stimulate the savant condition" (2006, p. 842). They described savants as being able to see the parts of the holistic picture, thus having access to raw information, unlike normal healthy individuals.

Conclusion

Questions for further research

Thesis

The line separating a normal person from a savant may thus be less "hard wired" than previously assumed. If a person could become brilliant by having his or her brain rewired, how would this newfound intelligence be used? For personal gain or for selfless good? Whatever directions and possibilities such research may reveal, understanding the savant syndrome brings us closer to understanding the human brain. Perhaps, in the future, research on savants will not only teach us more about what intelligence is and where it lies but will also help people who are born mentally retarded or brain damaged. The research that is just beginning opens up many possibilities.

SECRET OF SAVANT   10

Organized alphabetically   References   New page, double-spaced

Heffernan, V. (2005, February 23). A savant aided by the sparks that

    he sees inside his head. *The New York Times*. Retrieved from

    http://www.nytimes.com

Osborne, L. (2003, June 22). Savant for a day. *The New York Times*

    Magazine. Retrieved from http://www.nytimes.com

Snyder, A., Bahramali, H., Hawker, T., & Mitchell, D. J. (2006).

    Savant-like numerosity skills revealed in normal people by

    magnetic impulses. *Perception, 35*, 837–845. doi:10.1068

    /p5539

Snyder, A. W., & Mitchell, D. J. (1999). Is integer arithmetic

    fundamental to mental processing? The mind's secret

    arithmetic. *Proceedings of the Royal Society B: Biological*

    Sciences, 266, 587–592. Retrieved from http://www.ncbi.nlm

    .nih.gov/pmc/journals/137

Sternberg, R. J. (2004). *Psychology* (4th ed.). Toronto, Ontario,

    Canada: Wadsworth.

Treffert, D. A., & Wallace, G. L. (2004, January). Islands of genius,

    [special issue]. *Scientific American, 14*(1), 14–23. Retrieved

    from http://scientificamerican.com

APA ▼ (American Psychological Association)

17 ⚷

CSE Style of Documentation

AT A GLANCE: INDEX OF CSE STYLE FEATURES

17a Basic features of CSE style 263
17b How to cite sources in your paper 264
17c How to list CSE references 264
17d Sample listings: Print books and parts of books 265

1. Whole book with one author 265
2. Part of a book 266
3. Book with two or more authors 266
4. Book with editor(s) 266

17e Sample listings: Print articles 266

5. Article in a scholarly journal 266
6. Newspaper or magazine article 266
7. Article with no author identified 266

17f Sample listings: Online, electronic, and miscellaneous sources 266

8. Electronic journal article with a print source 266
9. Online journal article with no print source 267
10. Article in an online database 267
11. Internet home page 267
12. Posting to a discussion list 267
13. DVDs, CD-ROMs, and other media 268

18 Sample Paper 5: Excerpt from a Student's Research Paper, CSE Style 268

This chapter describes the documentation style recommended for all scientific disciplines by the Council of Science Editors (CSE) in *Scientific Style and Format: The CSE Manual for Authors, Editors, and Publishers*, 7th edition (New York: Cambridge University Press, 2006). This edition describes three systems of documentation for citing the elements necessary to "ensure retrievability of the cited documents" (p. xii):

- a name-year system similar to APA style, in which the in-text citation includes author(s) and year of publication
- a citation-sequence system that numbers and lists sources in the order they are cited in the paper

■ a citation-name system that also gives numbers to citations but organizes and numbers the list of references alphabetically by author or title, differing from the citation-sequence only in the numbering of entries, not in the format of the list

This last option is the one used in *The CSE Manual* itself. Because the name-year system is so similar to APA and because citations for the citation-sequence and citation-name systems differ only in the numbering, this chapter concentrates on examples of entries for those last two citation systems.

17a Basic features of CSE style

Always check with your instructors about documentation style guidelines. Some may not specify one particular style but will ask you to select one and use it consistently.

KEY POINTS

How to Number and List Sources in the CSE Citation-Sequence or Citation-Name Style

1. **In the text of your paper**, number each reference with a superscript number in a smaller size than the type for the text, or place the reference number on the line within parentheses. Place punctuation *after* the superscript number (new to 7th edition).

2. **At the end of your paper**, list the references on a new page with the title "References."

For the *citation-sequence system*, arrange and number the references in your list in the order in which you cite them in your paper. The first citation that appears in your paper will be 1, and the first reference in your list (also number 1) will give information about that first citation. Therefore, an author's name beginning with Z could be number 1 and listed first if it is the first source cited in your paper.

For the *citation-name system*, arrange and number the references in your list alphabetically by author (or title when no author is known). The first citation number in your paper will then match the alphabetical placement. The citation numbered 1 in your text could appear anywhere in your text but the reference will appear first in your alphabetical list of references. An author's name beginning with Z is therefore likely to appear near the end of your list and numbered accordingly, wherever the citation appears in your paper.

(Council of Science Editors) ▼ CSE

Example of documenting a periodical article

In-text number citation	Numbered entry in list of references
The mutation may prevent degradation of unknown substrates leading to their accumulation in Lewy bodies in neuronal cells[6].	6. De Silva HR, Khan NL, Wood NW. The genetics of Parkinson's disease. Curr Opin Genet Dev. 2000; 10(3):292–298.

17b How to cite CSE sources in your paper (citation-sequence and citation-name styles)

Use superscript numbers to refer readers to the list of references at the end of your paper. Note that the superscript number goes before a punctuation mark.

superscript number

A recent fruit fly study has produced interesting results[2].

One summary of studies of the life span of the fruit fly[3] has shown . . .

Refer to more than one entry in the reference list as follows:

Two studies of the life span of the fruit fly[1,2] have shown that . . .

Several studies of the life span of the fruit fly[1–4] have shown that . . .

Studies of the fruit fly are plentiful[1–4], but the most revealing is . . .

17c How to list CSE references (citation-sequence and citation-name systems)

KEY POINTS

Setting Up the CSE List of Cited References

1. After the last page of your paper, attach the list of references, headed "References" or "Cited References."

2. Arrange and number the works either (1) consecutively in the order in which you mention them in your paper (citation-sequence system) or (2) alphabetically (citation-name system). Invert all authors' names, and use the initials of first and

middle names. Use no punctuation between last names and initials, and leave no space between initials.

3. Begin each entry with the note number followed by a period and a space. Do not indent the first line of each entry; indent subsequent lines to align beneath the first letter on the previous line.

4. Do not italicize, underline, or use quotation marks for the titles of articles, books, or journals and other periodicals.

5. Capitalize only the first word of a book or article title, and capitalize any proper nouns.

6. Abbreviate titles of journals, organizations, and words such as *volume* (vol.) or *series* (ser.).

7. Use a period between major divisions of each entry.

8. Put a semicolon and a space between the name of the publisher (not abbreviated in the 7th edition) and the publication year of a book. Use a semicolon with no space between the date and the volume number of a journal.

9. For books, you may give the total number of pages, followed by a space and "p." For journal articles, give inclusive page spans, using all the digits: 135–136.

10. For online sources, provide author, title, any print publication information, date and place of online publication, your date of access after the word "cited," and the URL or a DOI (see 15e).

17d Sample CSE listings: Print books and parts of books (citation-sequence or citation-name system)

1. Whole book with one author

no
punctuation ┌────── title not underlined, only first word capitalized ──────┐

1. Finch CE. Longevity, senescence and the genome. Chicago:

initials with no period between

┌────── publisher ──────┐ semicolon number of pages in book

The University of Chicago Press; 1990. 922 p. (optional)

Give the city of publication, and include the state if the city is not well known.

(Council of Science Editors) ▼ **CSE**

2. Part of a book Include inclusive page numbers for the excerpt, specific reference, or quotation.

2. Thomas L. The medusa and the snail. New York: Viking Press; 1979. On

cloning a human being; p. 51–56.

3. Book with two or more authors List all the authors.

all authors'
⌐ names inverted ⌐
3. Ferrini AF, Ferrini RL. Health in the later years. 2nd ed. Dubuque (IA):

Brown & Benchmark; 1993. 470 p.
semicolon after publisher

4. Book with editor(s)

4. Aluja M, Norrbom AL, editors. Fruit flies (tephritidae): Phylogeny and

evolution of behavior. Boca Raton (FL): CRC Press; 2000. 984 p.

17e Sample CSE listings: Print articles

5. Article in a scholarly journal

5. Kowald A, Kirkwood TB. Explaining fruit fly longevity. Science.

1993;260:1664–1665. —— complete page span
volume ⌐
⌐_____⌐
no spaces in information about journal

In a journal paginated by issue, include the issue number in parentheses after the volume number.

6. Newspaper or magazine article Give the full name of the newspaper, the edition, the date, and the first page and column number of the article.

6. Pollack A. Custom-made microbes, at your service. The New York Times

(Late Ed.). 2006 Jan 17;Sect F:1 (col. 5).

7. Article with no author identified Begin with the title of the article.

17f Sample CSE listings: Online, electronic, and miscellaneous sources

8. Online journal article with a print source Cite as for a print journal article, and include the type of medium in brackets after the journal title. Include any document number, the accession date "[cited (year, month, date)]," and an availability statement with the URL.

8. Jones CC, Meredith W. Developmental paths of psychological health from early adolescence to later adulthood. Psych Aging [Internet]. 2000 [cited 2009 Jan 18];15(2):351–360. Available from: http://www .psycinfo.com

9. Online journal article with no print source If no print source is available, provide an estimate of the length of the document in pages, paragraphs, or screens. Place the information in square brackets, such as "[about 3 p.]," "[5 paragraphs]," or "[about 6 screens]."

9. Holtzworth-Munroe A. Domestic violence: Combining scientific inquiry and advocacy. Prev Treatment [Internet]. 2000 Jun 2 [cited 2009 Jan 20];3 [about 6 p.]. Available from: http://journals.apa.org/prevention /volume3/pre0030022c.html

10. Article in an online database After author, title, and print publication information, give the name of the database, the designation in square brackets "[database on the Internet]," any date of posting or modification, or the copyright © date. Follow this with the date of access, the approximate length of the article, the URL, and any accession number.

10. Mayor S. New treatment improves symptoms of Parkinson's disease. BMJ. 2002;324(7344):997. In: PubMedCentral [database on the Internet]; c2002 [cited 2008 Jan 19]. [about 1 screen] Available from: http://www .pubmedcentral.gov/articlerender.fcgi?tool=pmcentrez&artid-1122999

11. Web page Give author (if available) and title of page followed by "[Internet]." Follow this with any available information about place of home page publication and sponsor, and then include date of publication or copyright date, along with any update. End with your date of citation and the URL.

11. Cohen E. Caring for Mom and Dad from afar [Internet]. Cable News Network; 2008 Jan 31 [cited 2009 Feb 7]. Available from http://www .cnn.com/2008/HEALTH/family/01/31/ep.long.distance.care/index.html

12. Posting to a discussion list After the author's name and the subject line of the message, give information about the discussion list, including name of list; place and sponsor, if available; year, date, and time of posting; date of citation; and approximate length of the posting. End with an availability statement of the address of the discussion list or the archive.

12. Bishawi AH. Summary: hemangioendothelioma of the larynx. In: MEDLIB-L [discussion list on the Internet]. [Buffalo (NY): State University of NY]; 2002 May 6, 11:25am [cited 2009 Jan 19]. [about 4 screens]. Available from: MEDLIBL@listserv.acsu.buffalo.edu; item 087177.

13. DVDs, CD-ROMs, and other media   Begin with the title and include the medium in brackets. Follow this with details of producer, author, or director; place; publisher; and date. Include a description, such as length (of a film), color (of a work of art), number of disks, and type of accompanying material.

18 ⚷

Sample Paper 5: Excerpt from a Student's Research Paper, CSE Style

The following excerpt from a paper titled "Longaeva: The Scientific Significance of the Ancient Bristlecone Pine" was written by Andrew Dillon for a first-year course on "Volcanoes of the Eastern Sierra Nevada" at Indiana University. He uses the CSE citation-sequence documentation style as required by his instructor, and divides his paper into sections with headings: Abstract, Introduction, Phenotype and Physiology, Natural Range and Growing Adversities, Contributions to Science, Conclusion, and References. He also illustrates his twenty-one-page paper with photographs and images that show some features and settings of the huge ancient trees. Dillon's title page, numbered page 1, provides the essay title, the running head—Bristlecone Pine—his name, name of the course, instructor, and date. Shown here are pages excerpted from the paper: the abstract, the beginning of the Phenotype and Physiology section, and the references, all of which demonstrate key features of the CSE citation-sequence system.

Note: Blue annotations point out issues of content and organization. Red annotations point out CSE format issues.

Abstract

Abstract

More than any other species of tree, the bristlecone pine (Pinus longaeva), of the White Mountains in California, helps scientists to understand the environmental conditions of the past. With some living specimens attaining ages nearing 5,000 years, and dead matter persisting for another several thousand, these ancient trees have provided climatologists, geologists, and dendrochronologists with a continuous tree-ring chronology that dates back to the last Ice Age. This paper examines the complex physiology and habitat of the species and considers what scientists have learned from the bristlecone about the earth's history. Research from the past half century illuminates the magnificence of bristlecone pines as living evidence of past millennia.

Running head and page number on every page (title page is page 1)

Section heading centered

Summary of paper

CSE ▼ (Council of Science Editors)

(Council of Science Editors) ▼ CSE

Excerpt from third section of paper, page 6

Phenotype and Physiology

1" margins

Like all pines, bristlecones belong to the phylum Coniferophyta:
the conifers. Classified within this phylum are almost 50 genera
and roughly 550 species. Evidence suggests that the Coniferophyta
developed some 300 million years ago in the Carboniferous
Period, developing the pine family after 165 million years.
Now approximately 135 million years old, this family includes
bristlecones and coastal redwoods, respectively holding records for
the oldest and tallest trees in the world[1].

Although maintaining easily identifiable conifer traits, the
bristlecone pine has a distinctive, even odd, appearance. Many of
these trees have been gnarled, bent, and twisted over time, resulting
in ghostly entangled forms of both living and dead material. Some
researchers believe that in fact, "over the millennia bristlecones
genetically programmed to twist may have been better adapted to
survive"[2], potentially explaining the unusual contortions, as shown
in Figure 1.

Section heading centered

Superscript number referring to #1 in references (citation-sequence style)

Punctuation mark after citation number

Includes data on age and size

Figure 1 Bristlecone Pine (*pinus aristata*), among the oldest
known trees (Lola B. Graham, The National Audubon Society
Collection/Photo Researchers).

Blue = content issues   Red = format issues

Bristlecone Pine   7

Deadwood colors range from white to dark gray or black, living from light to dark brown. Because these trees grow for so long and at such slow rates, wood tends to be tightly compact, resinous, and highly resistant to disease, infestation, or rot[3]. For their old age they are also remarkably small, hardly ever exceeding thirteen meters tall by four meters around[4].

List of references (selected here to match the excerpt)

Bristlecone Pine   20

References

1. Allaby M. Plants and plant life. Vol. 8, Conifers. Danbury (CT):
   Grolier; 2001. 49 p.

2. Little JB. Time line. Amer Forests [Internet] 2004 [cited
   2007 May 6];109(4):22–27. Available from https://
   www.americanforests.org/productsandpubs/magazine/
   archives/2004winter/feature1_1.php

3. Ferguson CW. Bristlecone pine: science and esthetics. Science
   New Ser. 1968;159(3817):839–846.

4. Gidwitz T. Telling time. Archaeology [Internet] 2001 [cited 2007
   May 4];54(2):36–41. Available from http://www.archaeology
   .org/0103/abstracts/time.html

19

Chicago Manual of Style: Endnotes, Footnotes, and Bibliography

AT A GLANCE: INDEX OF *CHICAGO* STYLE FEATURES

19a Basic features of the *Chicago* note style 274
19b How to cite sources and prepare notes 274
19c How to format *Chicago* endnotes and footnotes 276
19d Sample notes: Print books and parts of books 277

1. Book with one author 277
2. Book with two or three authors 277
3. Book with four to ten authors or more 277
4. Book with no author identified 277
5. Book with editor or translator 277
6. Work in an edited volume or anthology (essay, story, chapter, article, poem, letter) 277
7. Entry in a reference work 278
8. Preface, introduction. foreword, afterword 278
9. Author's work quoted in another work 278
10. Government document 278
11. Scriptures and classics 278
12. A multivolume work 279

19e Sample notes: Print articles in periodicals 279

13. Article in a scholarly journal, continuously paged 279
14. Article in a scholarly journal, each issue paged separately 279
15. Article in a magazine 279
16. Article in a newspaper 280
17. Editorial, no author identified 280
18. Letter to the editor 280
19. Review (of book, play, film, performance, etc.) 280

19f Sample notes: Online sources 280

20. Online reference work 281
21. Online book 281
22. Article retrieved from online database 281
23. Article in an online journal 281
24. Article in an online magazine 281
25. Article in an online newspaper 282
26. Government publication online 282
27. Web page/Web document 282
28. Personal home page 282
29. E-mail communication 282
30. Posting on electronic discussion list, wiki, or blog 282

19g Sample notes: Visual, multimedia, and miscellaneous sources 282

31. CD, CD-ROM, DVD, e-book 282
32. Interview 283
33. Lecture, speech, or debate 283
34. Film, slide, cassette, DVD 283
35. Other newer sources 283

19h A student's *Chicago* bibliography 283

20 Sample Paper 6: Excerpt from a Student's Research Paper, *Chicago* Style 285

A s an alternative to an author-year parenthetical system of references similar to the APA system, *The Chicago Manual of Style*, 15th ed. (Chicago: U of Chicago P, 2003), also describes a system in which sources are documented in footnotes or endnotes. This system is used widely in the humanities, especially in history, art history, literature, and the arts. For a *Chicago*-style paper, include an unnumbered title page, and number the first page of your paper "2."

19a Basic features of the *Chicago* note style

KEY POINTS
How to Number and Document Sources in the *Chicago* Endnote/Footnote Style

1. **In your text,** place a superscript numeral at the end of the quotation or the sentence in which you mention source material; place the number after all punctuation marks except a dash.

2. **On a separate numbered page at the end of the paper,** list all endnotes, and number the notes sequentially, as they appear in your paper. If you use footnotes, a word processing program will automatically place them at the bottom of a page (see 21a on using Word for endnotes and footnotes).

Example of an endnote or footnote for a book

In-text citation with numeral	Numbered endnote or footnote
Numeral only Mondrian planned his compositions with colored tape.[3]	
Source mentioned in your paper According to Arnason and Prather, Mondrian planned his compositions with colored tape.[3]	3. H. Harvard Arnason and Marla F. Prather, *History of Modern Art* (New York: Abrams, 1998), 393.

19b How to cite sources and prepare notes (*Chicago*)

To cite a source in your paper Use the following format and number your notes sequentially. If you use endnotes and not footnotes, mention the source in your text whenever possible so that readers do not have to flip to the end to find the source.

> George Eliot thought that *Eliot* was a "good, mouthfilling, easy to pronounce word."[1]

First note for a source when no bibliography is attached
Source notes can supply full details of a source, so a separate list of references is not necessary. However, if your instructor requires one, see the sample in 19h.

author's name in normal order   comma   book title italicized, all important words capitalized   place, publisher, and date in parentheses

1. Margaret Crompton, *George Eliot: The Woman* (London: Cox and Wyman, 1960), 123.——page number

comma

First note for a source if a bibliography is provided If you are required to attach a separate bibliography listing all the sources you cited or consulted, the note citation can be concise.

> 1. Crompton, *George Eliot*, 123.

For the format of a bibliography, see 19h.

Note referring to the immediately preceding source In a reference to the immediately preceding source, you may use "Ibid." (Latin *ibidem*, meaning "in the same place") instead of repeating the author's name and the title of the work. All the details except the page number must be the same as in the previous citation. If the page number is the same, too, omit it following "Ibid."

> 2. Ibid., 127.

However, avoid a series of "ibid." notes. These are likely to irritate your reader. Instead, place page references within your text: *As Crompton points out (127), . . .*

Any subsequent reference to a previously cited source For a reference to a source cited in a previous note but not in the immediately preceding note, give only the author and page number:

> 6. Crompton, 124.

However, if you cite more than one work by the same author, include a short title to identify the source.

19c How to format *Chicago* endnotes and footnotes

KEY POINTS

Guidelines for *Chicago* Endnotes and Footnotes

1. **Numbering** In the list of endnotes, place each number on the line (not as a superscript), followed by a period and one space. For footnotes, word processing software will often automatically make the number a superscript—just be consistent with whatever format you use.

2. **Spacing and indentation** Indent the first line of each note three or five spaces. Single-space within a note and double-space between notes unless your instructor prefers double-spacing throughout.

3. **Authors' names** Use the author's full name, not inverted, followed by a comma and the title of the work.

4. **More than one author** In section 19d, items 2–3 show how to cite multiple authors of books. Follow these examples for articles, online, multimedia, and miscellaneous works.

5. **Titles of works** Put quotation marks around article titles, and italicize titles of books and periodicals. Capitalize all first letters of words in the titles of books, periodicals, and articles except *a, an, the*; coordinating conjunctions, such as *and, but* and *so*; *to* in an infinitive; and prepositions.

6. **Publishing information** After a book title, give the city (and state if necessary for a city not well known), name of publisher, and year. Follow this with a comma and the page number(s), with no "p." or "pp." After an article title, give the name of the periodical and pertinent publication information (volume, issue, date, and page numbers where appropriate). Do not abbreviate months in the date of publication.

7. **Punctuation** Separate major parts of the citation with commas, not periods.

8. **Online sources** Provide the URL, and for time-sensitive material, end with the date on which you last accessed the source.

9. **Quotations and specific references** Provide the page number following the publication details and after a comma, as in item 1. No page number is required for a reference to a work as a whole.

19d Sample *Chicago* notes: Print books and parts of books

1. Book with one author

1. Robert A. Caro, *Master of the Senate: The Years of Lyndon Johnson* (New York: Knopf, 2002), 3.

A page number is included for a citation to a specific page of the book.

2. Book with two or three authors

2. George Lakoff and Mark Johnson, *Metaphors We Live By* (Chicago: University of Chicago Press, 1980).

List three authors in the order they appear on the title page, separated by commas.

3. Book with four to ten authors or more For a book with multiple authors, use the name of only the first author followed by "and others" in a note.

3. Randolph Quirk and others, *A Comprehensive Grammar of the English Language* (London: Longman, 1985).

Note: In a bibliography, for a reference to a work with ten authors or fewer, include all ten names; for a reference to a work with eleven or more authors, list only the first seven along with "et al."

4. Book with no author identified Begin with the title.

4. *Chicago Manual of Style*, 15th ed. (Chicago: University of Chicago Press, 2003).

5. Book with editor or translator

5. John Updike, ed., *The Best American Short Stories of the Century* (Boston: Houghton Mifflin, 1999).

For a translated work, after the title write "trans." and the name of the translator.

6. Work in an edited volume or anthology (essay, story, chapter, article, poem, letter) Begin with the author and title of the work, and follow this with the title of the anthology. Include "ed." for "edited by." For a letter, also include the addressee and the date (Elizabeth Bishop to Marianne Moore, January 5, 1945).

6. Adrienne Rich, "Split at the Root," in *The Art of the Personal Essay*, ed. Phillip Lopate (New York: Anchor/Doubleday, 1994), 649.

7. Entry in a reference work   Include no page number or date. Give the edition and indicate the alphabetical heading in the book with the abbreviation "s.v." (*sub verbo*: under the word).

7. *The Columbia Encyclopedia*, 6th ed., s.v. "Etching."

8. Preface, introduction, foreword, or afterword   Give the name of the writer of the material when this is different from the author of the book.

8. David Remnick, introduction to *Politics*, by Hendrik Hertzberg (New York: Penguin, 2004).

9. Author's work quoted in another work

9. E. M. Forster, *Two Cheers for Democracy* (New York: Harcourt, Brace, and World, 1942), 242, quoted in Phyllis Rose, *Woman of Letters, A Life of Virginia Woolf* (New York: Oxford University Press, 1978), 219.

Note, however, that *The Chicago Manual of Style* recommends that whenever possible a reference be cited from the original work.

10. Government document

10. U.S. Department of Education, National Center for Education Statistics, *The Condition of Education, 2008* (Washington, D.C.: GPO, 2008).

11. Scriptures and classics   Provide the reference in the text or in a note. For the Bible, include the book (in abbreviated form, along with chapter and verse, but no page number) and the version used (not italicized).

11. Gen. 27:29 (New Revised Standard Version).

For Greek and Roman works and for classic plays in English, locate by the number of book, section, and line or by act, scene, and line. Cite a classic poem by book, canto, stanza, and line, whichever is appropriate. Specify the edition used only in the first note referring to the work.

Do not include the Bible or classical works in a bibliography.

12. A multivolume work Give the number of any specific volume you cite, followed by the page number.

> 12. Albert Einstein, *Collected Papers of Albert Einstein* (Princeton, N.J.: Princeton University Press, 1987), 1:107.

If you refer to the work as a whole, the part of the citation after the title should look like this: *10 vols. (Princeton, N.J.: Princeton University Press, 1987–2006).*

19e Sample *Chicago* notes: Print articles in periodicals

Cite multiple authors for articles in the same way as for books: 19d, items 2–3.

13. Article in a scholarly journal, continuously paged If journal volumes are paged continuously through issues (for example, if issue 1 ends on page 188 and issue 2 of the same volume begins with page 189), give only the volume number and year, not the issue number. If you refer to a specific page, put a colon after the year in parentheses, and then add the page number(s). To cite an abstract, include the word *abstract* before the name of the journal. For more on scholarly journals, see 8b.

> 13. Warren Wilner, "The Lone Ranger as a Metaphor for the Psychoanalytic Movement from Conscious to Unconscious Experience," *Psychoanalytic Review* 92 (2005): 764.

14. Article in a scholarly journal, each issue paged separately When each issue of a journal begins on page 1, include "no." for "number" after the volume number, and follow it with the issue number, date in parentheses, and page number(s) cited.

> 14. Rami Ginat, "The Soviet Union and the Syrian Ba'th Regime: From Hesitation to Rapprochement," *Middle Eastern Studies* 36, no. 2 (2000): 160.

15. Article in a magazine Include the month for monthly magazines and the complete date for weekly magazines (month, day, year). Cite only a specific page number in a note (after a comma), not the range of pages. (In a bibliography, provide the range of pages of the whole article.)

> 15. Robin E Bell, "The Unquiet Ice," *Scientific American*, February 2008, 62.

See Source Shot 7 on page 243 for a screenshot of this source.

16. Article in a newspaper   Do not include an initial *The* in the name of a newspaper. Give any section number and edition, but not the page number.

> 16. Jimmy Wang, "Now Hip-Hop, Too, Is Made in China," *New York Times*, sec. C, January 24, 2009, late edition.

If the city is not part of the newspaper title, include it in parentheses: *Times* (London).

17. Editorial, no author identified   For editorials with no author, begin the note with the title of the article.

> 17. "A Respectful Homecoming," *Washington Post*, sec. A, March 1, 2009, late edition.

18. Letter to the editor

> 18. Gilbert Youmans, letter to the editor, *Atlantic*, January/February, 2009, 16.

19. Review (of a book, play, film, performance, etc.)

> 19. Marcia Angell, "Drug Companies and Doctors: A Story of Corruption," review of *Shyness: How Normal Behavior Became a Sickness*, by Christopher Lane, *New York Review of Books*, January 15, 2009, 12.

19f   Sample *Chicago* notes: Online sources

- To cite an online book, poem, article, government publication, or multimedia source in *Chicago* style, provide exactly the same available information as for a non-Internet source, adding the URL at the end.
- To split a URL across lines, do not insert a hyphen. Make the split after a slash (/) or before a period or any other punctuation mark.

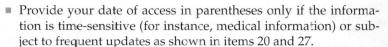

- Provide your date of access in parentheses only if the information is time-sensitive (for instance, medical information) or subject to frequent updates as shown in items 20 and 27.
- Put a period at the end of each entry, including an entry ending in a URL.

20. Online reference work   Cite an online dictionary or an encyclopedia in a note, but do not include it in a bibliography. Because reference works are frequently updated, you need to give the date on which you access the material. Precede the title of an alphabetized article with the initials "s.v." (Latin for *sub verbo*—"under the word").

20. *Columbia Encyclopedia*, 6th ed., s.v. "Bloomsbury group," http://www.bartleby.com/65/bl/Bloomsbury.html (accessed January 24, 2009).

21. Online book   For books in print and online, cite the source you consult. Include date of access only for online material that may be revised in new editions.

21. Mary Wollestonecraft Shelley, *Frankenstein, or, the Modern Prometheus* (London: Dent, 1912), http://ota.ahds.ac.uk.

22. Article retrieved from an online database   Give the URL of the entry page of the service and any other retrieval information. No date of access is necessary unless the material is time-sensitive or may exist in varying editions.

22. Geoffrey Bent, "Vermeer's Hapless Peer," *North American Review* 282 (1997), http://www.infotrac.galegroup.com.

See 19h for a bibliography entry for this source.

23. Article in an online scholarly journal

23. Brian Vickers, "Approaching Shakespeare's Late Style," *Early Modern Literary Studies* 13, no. 3 (2008), http://extra.shu.ac.uk/emls/13-3/revmcd.htm.

24. Article in an online magazine   Cite as for a print publication, but add the URL.

24. Elizabeth Svoboda, "Scents and Sensibility," *Psychology Today*, January/February, 2008, http://www.psychologytoday.com.

25. Article in an online newspaper   Cite as for a print publication, with the URL added at the end after a comma.

> 25. Ken Bensinger, "Chrysler's Hometown Tries to Retool," *Los Angeles Times*, January 24, 2009, http://www.latimes.com/business/.

26. Government publication online

> 26. U.S. Department of Education, National Center for Education Statistics, *The Condition of Education: Mobility of College Students*, 2008, http://nces.ed.gov/programs/coe/2008/section1/indicator10.asp.

27. Web page or document from a Web site   Give the author of the content, if known; the title of the document; the owner or sponsor of the site; the URL; and your date of access only if the material is frequently updated.

> 27. "MLA Style," Modern Language Association, February 27, 2009, http://www.mla.org/ (accessed March 1, 2009).

28. Personal home page   If a page does not have a title, use a descriptive phrase such as "home page."

> 28. Alfred Gingold, home page, http://www.alfredgingold.com.

29. E-mail communication

> 29. Toby Gingold, e-mail message to the author, February 17, 2009.

30. Posting on an electronic discussion list, wiki, or blog   Whenever possible, cite a URL for archived material. Otherwise, end the note after the date.

> 30. Charles Bazerman, "Raising the Stakes," online posting to WPA-L mailing list, May 1, 2008, https://lists.asu.edu/.

19g Sample *Chicago* notes: Visual, multimedia, and miscellaneous sources

31. CD, CD-ROM, DVD, e-book   Indicate the medium (compact disc, DVD, etc.) and any version number.

31. Ann Raimes, *Digital Keys 5.0* (Boston: Houghton Mifflin, 2007), CD-ROM.

32. Interview   Treat a published interview like an article or a book chapter, including the phrase "interview with."

32. Rachel Maddow, "The Maddow Knows," interview with Clara Jeffery, *Mother Jones,* January/February. 2009, 72–73.

For an unpublished interview, include in your text the type of interview (such as "telephone interview with the author") and the date.

33. Lecture, speech, or debate   In addition to the speaker(s) and title, provide the location and the date in parentheses.

33. Maria Jerskey, "At Their Point of Strength: Teaching Multilingual Writers of English," (paper presented at the 2009 Conference on College Composition and Communication, San Francisco, March 14, 2009).

34. Film, filmstrip, slides, videocassette, or audiocassette End the note with an indication of the type of medium, such as film, filmstrip, slide, videocassette, or audiocassette. For online multimedia, include the type of medium, such as MP3 audio file or MPEG.

34. *Citizen Kane*, produced, written, and directed by Orson Welles, 119 min., RKO, 1941, film.

35. Other newer sources   The 15th edition of *The Chicago Manual of Style* does not cover recent forms of online multimedia. Give author, title, and date, and include the type of medium, such as a podcast, MP3 file, or MPEG audio file, and indicate when you accessed the source and where. Give the URL.

19h A student's *Chicago* bibliography

Check whether your instructor wants you to include a bibliography of works cited (or a bibliography of works consulted) in addition to notes. If you do, you can use the short form for notes (19b, p. 274). Include complete page spans for articles.

(Chicago Manual of Style) ▼ **CHICAGO**

Note how the bibliography form differs from the note form:

Note form	Bibliography form
commas separate 3 major parts of note; note number, indented	periods separate 3 major parts of entry; no note number, indented after first line
7. Peter C. Sutton, *Pieter de Hooch, 1629–1684* (New Haven, Conn.: Yale University Press, 1988), 57. page number of exact citation publication; details in parentheses	Sutton, Peter C. *Pieter de Hooch, 1629–1684*. New Haven, Conn.: Yale University Press, 1988.

The following bibliography is from a student's paper on the seventeenth-century Dutch painter Pieter de Hooch.

Quinones   16

Bibliography

Bent, Geoffrey. "Vermeer's Hapless Peer." *North American Review* 282 (1997): 10–13. http://www.infotrac.galegroup.com.

Botton, Alain de. "Domestic Bliss: Pieter de Hooch Exhibition." *New Statesman*, October 9, 1998, 34–35.

Hollander, Martha. "Public and Private Life in the Art of Pieter de Hooch." *Nederlands Kunsthistorisch Jaarboek* 51 (2000), 272–293.

Sutton, Peter. *Pieter de Hooch: Complete Edition, with a Catalogue Raisonné*. Ithaca, N.Y.: Cornell University Press, 1980.

20 🔑

Sample Paper 6: Excerpt from a Student's Research Paper, *Chicago* Style

Here is the third paragraph (along with its corresponding endnotes) of an essay by Lynn McCarthy, written for Professor Roberta Bernstein's course in modern art at the State University of New York at Albany. Page 1 of her paper was a numbered title page. The assignment was to analyze a work of art by Piet Mondrian. In her paper, she included a visual image of the painting *Trafalgar Square*.

Paragraph on third page of essay (*Chicago* style)

McCarthy 3

Trafalgar Square, an oil on canvas measuring 145.2 by 120 cm, today is housed in the Museum of Modern Art in New York City. It is interesting to discover that Mondrian planned out his compositions with colored tape before he applied any paint.[3] Some tape actually still remains on his *Victory Boogie Woogie* (1942–44), which is an unfinished work he was involved in at the time of his death. But what is even more interesting is that although Mondrian preplanned the compositions, we know from x-rays that he reworked the paint on his canvases over and over again.[4] So as methodical and mathematical as we may think Mondrian was, he still felt constant inspiration and intuitive urges to make changes along the way. It is interesting, too, to note that he worked on a flat, horizontal table rather than at an easel.[5] Maybe he did this for practical or comfort reasons, but it also can be seen as a break from the conventional way artists created their works just as their subject matter broke from tradition. I think of how an artist like Jackson Pollock takes this even further by laying his canvas on the floor and walking on and around it, dropping and splattering the paint.

Close observation of work of art

Interesting details from the literature in notes 4 and 5

CHICAGO ▼ (*Chicago Manual of Style*)

Endnotes (*Chicago* style), beginning on a new page

McCarthy 5

Notes

1. Harry Cooper and Ron Spronk, *Mondrian: The Transatlantic Paintings* (New Haven, Conn.: Yale University Press, 2001), 24.

2. Ibid., 24–25.

3. H. Harvard Arnason and Marla F. Prather, *History of Modern Art* (New York: Abrams, 1998), 393.

4. Cooper and Spronk, 237.

5. Arnason and Prather, 383.

6. Cooper and Spronk, 34.

7. Arnason and Prather, 233.

First line of each note indented

"Ibid" refers to source above

Blue = content issues   Red = format issues

PART 5

Design, Media, and Presentation

21 Document Design   289

22 Visuals   301

23 Online Communication Forums   308

24 Web Site Design   314

25 Portfolios: Hard Copy and Electronic   320

26 Flyers, Brochures, and Newsletters   325

27 Résumés and Letters of Application   329

28 Business Letters and Memos   335

29 Oral and Multimedia Presentations   339

 ONLINE RESOURCES

www.cengage.com/english/raimes

Companion online resources are available for sections throughout this part. We invite you to visit the book's Web site for more information and direct access.

PART 5 DESIGN, MEDIA, AND PRESENTATION

Design, Media, and Presentation

21 **Document Design** 289
21a Formatting a college essay (print) 289
21b Formatting academic writing (online) 292
21c Typefaces 293
21d Color 295
21e Headings and columns 295
21f Lists 296
21g Academic design features in Word 296

22 **Visuals** 301
22a Tables 302
22b Graphs and charts 303
22c Images and copyright issues 306
22d Honesty in visuals 307

23 **Online Communication Forums** 308
23a E-mail in academic and business settings 308
23b E-mail discussion lists, discussion boards, and online communities 309
23c Other forums: Blogs, wikis, and virtual classrooms 312

24 **Web Site Design** 314
24a Planning a Web site 314
24b Making a site map 315
24c Tips for Web site design 316
24d Getting feedback 317
24e A community Web site (a student's project) 318

25 **Portfolios: Hard Copy and Electronic** 320
25a Preparing a portfolio (hard copy) 320

25b Preparing an e-portfolio 321
25c A student's e-portfolio 323

26 **Flyers, Brochures, and Newsletters** 325
26a Design principles for flyers, brochures, newsletters 325
26b Sample student-designed brochure 328

27 **Résumés and Letters of Application** 329
27a How to write a résumé 329
27b Sample print or Web page résumé 331
27c A scannable electronic résumé 332
27d Sample electronic résumé 333
27e Cover letter and sample 334

28 **Business Letters and Memos** 335
28a Features of a business letter 335
28b Sample business letter 335
28c Technical requirements of a business letter 337
28d Basic features of a memo 338

29 **Oral and Multimedia Presentations** 339
29a Preparing an oral presentation 339
29b Speaking from notes or manuscript 340
29c Practicing and presenting 341
29d Preparing a multimedia presentation 342
29e Using PowerPoint 345

There's no getting around it: How we present ourselves to others makes an impression. Your readers will have expectations about what a particular type of document should look like, and to make an impression that inspires their interest and confidence in what you have to say, you will want to fulfill those expectations. Whether it's an English essay or research paper, a business letter or a brochure, a résumé or a post on a community-based blog, the visual design and presentation of your writing communicates to your readers that you understand the conventions required. Equally important, it can help you communicate your message as effectively as possible.

While the design of texts and presentation of information have always been important, the expansion of digital media has enhanced our ability to make strong visual impressions and skillfully convey information to our readers and listeners. Thus, design and presentation play a much more significant role in developing a text. It's not uncommon to see straight text (in words) joined by pictures, photographs, tables, graphs, music, and film to convey information and emotion, often more immediately and dramatically than is possible with words alone. At presentations, audiences have become accustomed to visuals that are digital slides, often with multimedia components to enhance and illustrate what they are hearing. The words of the ancient art of rhetoric (effective communication and persuasion) have been joined by visuals and more.

Whether you are twittering to readers around the globe or sending a message to an older family member who just discovered e-mail, whether you are formatting your English professor's six-page essay assignment or putting the final touches on your e-portfolio before sending the link to a prospective employer, you will want to ask yourself (or your professor) this: What is the best way to meet my audience's expectations, engage their attention, and make my points with the most impact?

21 ⚷

Document Design

21a Formatting a college essay (print)

As you write, revise, and edit your document, you can think about how you'll prepare it for presentation to readers. Guides are available for presenting essays in specific disciplines and media. Frequently used style guides are those published by the Modern Language Association (MLA), American Psychological Association (APA), Council of Science Editors (CSE), and *The Chicago Manual of Style*. The features of these guides are covered in parts 3 and 4 of this handbook. However, commonalities exist among the differences. Basic guidelines are in the Key Points box for preparing your essay on paper, whichever style guide you follow. See 21g for how Word functions can help with formatting academic writing.

KEY POINTS
Guidelines for College Essay Format

- **Paper** White bond, unlined, 8½" × 11"; not erasable or onion-skin paper. Clip or staple the pages.

- **Print** Dark black printing ink—an inkjet or laser printer if possible.

- **Margins** One inch all around. In some styles, one and one-half inches may be acceptable. Lines should have justified left but ragged right margins. In Microsoft Word, go to Format/Paragraph (Word 2003) or to the formatting toolbar (Word 2007) to adjust alignment.

- **Space between lines** Uniformly double-space the entire paper, including any list of works cited. Footnotes (in *Chicago* style) may be single-spaced.

- **Spaces after a period, question mark, or exclamation point** One space, as suggested by most style manuals. Your instructor may prefer two in the text of your essay.

- **Type font and size** Standard type font (such as Times New Roman or Arial), not a fancy font that looks like handwriting. Select a regular size of 10 to 12 points.

- **Page numbers** In the top right margin. (In MLA style, put your last name before the page number. In APA style, put a short version of the title on the left and the page number on the right.) Use Arabic numerals with no period. (See p. 297; 21g shows the header formatting tools available in Word.)

- **Paragraphing** Indent one-half inch (five spaces) from the left.

- **Title and identification** On the first page or on a separate title page. See the examples below and on pages 210 and 252.
- **Parentheses around a source citation** MLA and APA style, for any written source you refer to or quote, including the textbook for your course (for an electronic source, give author only); then add at the end an alphabetical list of works cited.

Note: Your instructor may prefer a separate title page or ask you to include the identification material on the first page of the essay.

Title and identification on the first page The following sample of part of a first page shows one format for identifying a paper and giving it a title. The MLA recommends this format for papers in the humanities.

Croasdale 1

Yulanda Croasdale
Professor Raimes
English 120, Section 13
1 November 2009

Jamaican-American: A New Culture

To outsiders, the emergence of a strong Jamaican-American

Community is probably not a noticeable occurrence, though insiders

are all too well aware of their growing population and spread of

notoriety.

At the top of subsequent pages, write the page number in the upper right corner, preceded by your last name (21g shows you how to make this header). No period or parentheses accompany the page number.

Title and identification on a separate title page In the humanities, include a title page only if your instructor requires one or if you include an outline. (For the social sciences or other academic areas, see chapter 16.) On the title page include the following, all double-spaced:

Title: Centered, about one-third of the way down the page. Do not enclose the title in quotation marks, do not underline it, and do not put a period at the end.

Name: Centered, after the word *by*, on a separate line.

Course information: College course and section, instructor, and date, each centered on a new line, either directly below your name or at the bottom of the title page.

With a title page, you do not need the title and identification on your first page.

21b Formatting academic writing (online)

You may be required to submit an essay for a course online rather than in hard copy. Your instructor may ask you to e-mail an attachment, or in a hybrid or distance-learning course, you may be required to submit your essays in a dropbox or post them on a class online discussion board for the instructor and other students to read and comment on. Alternatively, you may have your own e-portfolio (25b) or Web site (chapter 24) where you display your work. In any of these cases, keep in mind the following general guidelines, and ask your instructor for instructions specific to the course, format, and type of posting.

Guidelines for posting academic writing online Recent versions of word-processing programs can automatically convert a document and save it as an HTML file for the Web. In Word, for example, you simply produce your document in the usual way but then, when you save it, go to "Save As" and change "Save as type" from "Word" to "Web page." The HTML commands are done for you automatically. In addition, Netscape Composer provides an HTML editor that tends to be more efficient in display speed.

KEY POINTS

Posting Academic Writing Online

■ **Structure** Set up a structure with sections and subsections, all with headings, that allows each section to be accessed directly—for example, from your table of contents (see the next point) and from any other part of your paper as well. So instead of saying diffusely, "See above" or "See below," you can provide a specific link allowing readers to jump directly to this part (see the *internal hyperlinks* list entry).

- **Links to sections from a table of contents**   Provide a table of contents, with an internal link to each section. Readers can then click and go directly to any section they are interested in.

- **Internal hyperlinks**   Use internal hyperlinks (Insert/Bookmark) to connect readers directly to relevant sections of your text, content notes, and visuals. Also provide a link from a source cited in the body of your paper to the entry in your list of works cited.

- **External hyperlinks**   Use external hyperlinks (Insert/Hyperlink) to connect to Web documents from references in the body of your paper and from your list of works cited. Useful for the works-cited list, Word has a function that will automatically convert any string starting with <http://> into a hyperlink.

- **No paragraph indentation**   Do not indent new paragraphs. Instead, leave a line space between paragraphs.

- **Attribution of sources**   Make sure that the link you give to an online article in a database is a persistent link, not a link that works for only a few hours or days. It is often difficult to determine at first glance whether a link is persistent or not. Some databases are explicit; others are not. Double-check your links after a few days to see whether they are still working. Some sites such as Thomas at the Library of Congress <http://thomas.loc .gov> and EBSCO databases provide persistent links.

- **List of works cited or list of references**   Give a complete list, with visible hyperlinked URLs, even if you provide some external links to the sources from the body of your paper. If a reader prints your paper, the exact references will then still be available.

21c Typefaces

What's in a typeface? A lot. It's not just what you write but also how it looks when it's read. Fitting the typeface to the content of a public document can be seen as an aesthetic challenge, as it was for the choice of the simple and legible Gotham typeface for the Freedom Tower cornerstone at the site of the former World Trade Center. The silver-leaf letters, with strokes of uniform width with no decorative touches, have been described by David Dunlap in the *New York Times* as conjuring "the exuberant, modernist, midcentury optimism of New York even as they augur the glass and stainless-steel tower to come." That's what's in a typeface. The cornerstone, according to Dunlap, looks "neutral enough so that viewers could impose their own meanings" on a site of profound historical and emotional impact.

Of course, designing the presentation of a college essay is not the same as designing a historic monument. However, you can still make a choice that emphasizes simplicity and legibility.

In his textbook *Contemporary Business Communication*, 7th edition (Boston: Houghton, 2009), Scot Ober recommends using Times New Roman in business correspondence. For college essays in hard copy, consider using the following:

For the body of the text: Times New Roman or some other *serif* font. (A *serif* font has little strokes—serifs—at the top and bottom of individual characters.)

For captions and headings: Arial or some other *sans serif* font. (The word *sans* is French for "without"; a sans serif font does not have the little strokes at the top and bottom of the characters.)

Avoid ornamental fonts such as *Monotype Corsiva* and *Brush Script*. They are distracting and hard to read.

Note that if you are designing a Web page or an online communication, your readers' computer settings determine which fonts can be displayed. The simpler the font you choose (Times, Arial, Georgia, and Verdana all work well on PC and Mac browsers), the more likely readers are to see your chosen font.

For the body of your text in a college essay or a business communication, stick to 10- to 12-point type. Use larger type only for headings and subheadings in business, technical, or Web documents (see 21b and chapters 24 and 29). Never increase or decrease font size to achieve a required page length. You will convey desperation, and you will certainly not fool your instructor.

Note: MLA and APA guidelines do not recommend typeface changes or bold type for titles and headings.

21d Color

Color printers and online publication have made the production of documents an exciting enterprise for both writers and readers. You can include graphs and illustrations in color, and you can highlight headings or parts of your text by using a different color typeface. However, simplicity and readability should prevail. Use color only when its use will enhance your message. Certainly, in the design of business reports, newsletters, brochures, and Web pages, color can play an important and eye-catching role. But for college essays, the leading style manuals ignore and implicitly discourage the use of color. Also keep in mind that many people may not have a color printer, and printing color charts on a black-and-white printer may lead to parts that are difficult to distinguish.

21e Headings and columns

Headings divide text into helpful chunks and give readers a sense of your document's structure. Main divisions are marked by first-level headings, subdivisions by second-level and third-level headings. In the heading structure of chapter 21, for example, the main heading is "Document Design," and the subheadings include "Formatting a college essay (print)," "Formatting academic writing (online)," "Typefaces," "Color," "Headings and columns," "Lists," and "Academic design features in Word."

For headings, bear in mind the following recommendations:

- If you use subheadings, use at least two—not just one.
- Whenever possible, use your word processing program's Style feature to determine the level of heading you need: heading 1, 2, 3, and so on.
- Style manuals, such as the one for APA style, recommend specific formats for typeface and position on the page for levels of headings. Follow these recommended formats. See chapter 16 for an APA paper with headings.
- Keep headings clear, brief, and parallel in grammatical form (for instance, all commands: "Set Up Sales Strategies"; all beginning with *-ing* words: "Setting Up Sales Strategies"; or all noun-plus-modifier phrases: "Sales Strategies").

Columns, as well as headings, are useful for preparing newsletters and brochures (see the example in 26b). In Word 2007 for PC, go to the Page Layout tab to choose the number of columns and the width. Your text will be automatically formatted.

21f Lists

Lists are particularly useful in business reports, proposals, and memos. They direct readers' attention to the outlined points or steps. Decide whether to use numbers, dashes, or bullets to set off the items in a list (21g, item 5). Introduce the list with a sentence ending in a colon (see 21e for an example). Items in the list should be parallel in grammatical form: all commands, all *-ing* phrases, or all noun phrases, for example (see 40j). Listed items should not end with a period unless they are complete sentences.

21g Academic design features in Word

As a college student in the twenty-first century, you probably find it second nature to use the functions of a word processing program to add, delete, move material, and check your spelling. But a word processor can help you readily fulfill the conventions of academic writing and the formatting functions that your instructor may insist on.

This section outlines the features of Word that are most useful in academic writing. (WordPerfect provides similar functions, as does a free alternative to Word, OpenOffice. For full details on the following list of tasks, consult your word processing program's written documentation, built-in "Help" files, or online training and customer support.)

TECH NOTE

Versions of Word for PC and Mac

It is not unusual to find both Mac and PC computers in college computer laboratories, so you may need to become familiar with both Word for PCs and Word for Mac. If you are a PC user and have recently upgraded from Word 2003 to Word 2007, go to Microsoft Office Online's interactive reference guide on converting Word 2003 commands to Word 2007: <http://office.microsoft.com/en-us/word/HA100744321033.aspx>. If you're a Mac user, take advantage of the interactive tutorials for Word features at <http://www.microsoft.com/mac/help.mspx?product=Word&app=4>.

Since you may be writing in one version of Word and sending your document to someone who has a different version, be sure to set the default file format as "Word 97-2003 Document (.doc)" so that your document will be compatible with all versions of Word.

1. Formatting a document using templates and styles   No matter which version you are using—Word 2003, Word 2007 for PC, or Word 2008 for Mac—Word provides useful ready-made design formats called *templates* for an MLA essay, APA paper, and a term paper. It also has templates for many other documents you may need to produce in college and beyond, including résumés, brochures, and newsletters. In addition, you can create and save your own templates. Most word processing programs also use *styles*—a mechanism for setting document format choices that apply to the entire document rather than to individual parts. In Word 2007, the styles feature is easier to use than previous versions. Using the styles feature lets you establish the default look and feel of your document and maintain a consistency of design so you don't have to worry about formatting choices while you are writing or editing.

2. Adding a header or footer on every page   When you open the View menu (Word 2003 and Word 2008 for Mac) or access the Insert tab (Word 2007 for PC), you will see the Header and Footer options. These options allow you to (1) include a page number along with any text, such as your name or a short running head; (2) include the date and time; and (3) toggle between the choice of headers or footers. Headers and footers will adjust automatically to any changes in the pagination of your document. You type the information once only, and it appears in the place you specify on every page, however much material you add or delete.

Word 2007 for PC

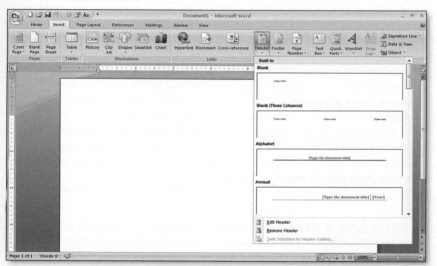

3. Inserting visuals, charts, and graphs   The Insert menu provides access to useful functions. Here, you can insert into your text a page number, a footnote, or a hyperlink to a URL, though you can also set up Word to hyperlink all the URLs automatically (Tools/AutoCorrect/AutoFormat As You Type). You can insert Comments into your own or someone else's document, a useful feature for writing collaboratively and giving feedback. (This feature is on the Review tab/menu in Word 2007.) It is also possible to insert into your text a picture, caption, diagram, or chart. For presentation of data, the chart feature is particularly useful and easy to use: You simply type your data into a data grid and then choose from a wide variety of charts, such as bar, line, pie, doughnut, scatter, and pyramid. One click—and your chart appears. (On pages 305–306 in 22b, Figures 2 and 5 show a graph and a chart made in Word.)

4. Inserting a table   When you click Table/Insert Table in Word 2003 for PC and Word 2008 for Mac, you can then select the numbers of columns and rows you want, as shown below. In Word 2007, simply click Tables on the toolbar.

Word 2008 for Mac

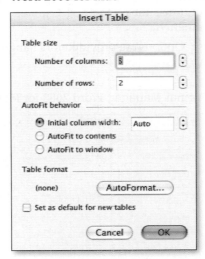

Word 2007 for PC

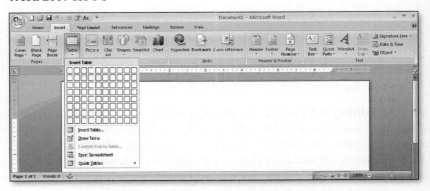

5. Formatting your document As you move toward your final draft, you will want to format your document. The Format menu (Word 2003), Palette (Word for Mac), or Home tab (Word 2007) takes you to the following features:

- **Font** Options are available for changing typeface, styles, and size as well as using superscripts, useful for *Chicago Manual of Style* citations; see also 21c

- **Paragraph** Options are given for line spacing and indenting (see the screen capture on page 300 for how to set the special command for the hanging indents used in an MLA list of works cited)

- **Bullets and Numbering** Options are given for lists, Borders and Shading, Columns, Tabs, Dropped Capitals (just highlight the text to be formatted)
- **Change Case** Options are provided for changing text from capital letters to lowercase, or vice versa

Format Manager, Word 2008 for Mac

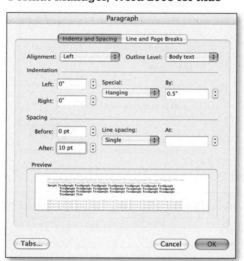

6. Editing with Word: Checking, correcting, and changing The Tools menu (Word 2003 and Word 2008 for Mac) or Review tab (Word 2007) gives you access to a word count, to spelling and grammar checkers and a thesaurus, and to AutoCorrect and AutoFormat functions (such as turning off the automatic hyperlinks when you do not need them underlined for an MLA list of works cited). Note that you can set a grammar checker to look for specific features, such as "Punctuation with quotes" and "Passive sentences." In the Tools menu/Review tab, you will also find the Track Changes feature, a useful tool for adding editing suggestions to your own or somebody else's text.

7. Using Word to format citations Word 2007 will format a citation you include in your paper into MLA, APA, or *Chicago* style and add the source to a list that will be used for your bibliography. Simply select Insert Citation on the References tab. Then Word 2007 will form a bibliography in the style you determine, using only sources you have cited in your paper via the Bibliography command on the References tab.

There are also some tools available that extend the functionality of earlier versions of Word, and other word processors, such as OpenOffice, also include the citation/bibliography feature in their latest versions.

22 ⚷

Visuals

The technology of scanners, photocopiers, digital cameras, and downloaded Web images provides the means of making documents more functional and more attractive by allowing the inclusion of visual material. Frequently, when you are dealing with arguments using complicated data, the best way to get information across to readers is to display it visually.

For a college paper, you can download visuals from the Web (with a source acknowledgment) to strengthen an argument or to present data clearly and efficiently. Alternatively, computers make it easy for you to take data from your own research and present the data as a table, graph, or chart (22a, 22b).

KEY POINTS

On Using Visuals

1. **Plan** Decide which type of visual presentation best fits your data, and determine where to place your visuals; these are usually best within your text. However, APA style for papers to be printed requires visuals in an appendix. See 29d and 29e on using visuals in an oral presentation.

2. **Introduce** Whenever you place a visual in your text, introduce it and discuss it fully before readers come across it. Do not just make a perfunctory comment like "The results are significant, as seen in Figure 1." Rather, say something like "Figure 1 shows an increase in the number of accidents since 2005." In your discussion, indicate where the visual appears ("In the table below" or "In the pie chart on page 8"), and carefully interpret or analyze the visual for readers, using it as an aid that supports your points, not as something that can stand alone. Section 4j shows how a student introduces and discusses a visual in her argument essay.

(Continued)

(Continued)

3. **Compress** When you include a visual in an online document, make sure the image file is not so large that it will take a long time for readers to download.
4. **Identify** Give each visual a title, number each visual if you use more than one of the same type, and credit the source.
5. **Avoid filler** Do not include visuals simply to fill space or make your document look colorful. Every visual addition should enhance your content and provide an interesting and relevant illustration. See 4i for using visuals to enhance an argument.

22a Tables

Tables are useful for presenting data in columns and rows. They can be created easily with word processing programs using figures from large sets of data, as in the following table (see 21g, item 4).

TABLE 1 ▶ Freshmen Pluralistic Orientation for a Diverse Workplace, by Race/Ethnicity (percentages based on self-rating)

Self rating compared to peers	White	African American	American Indian	Asian/PI American	Latina/o	Multi-Racial American
Ability to see the world from someone else's perspective	64.0	62.2	58.5	69.7	66.4	72.9
Tolerance of others with different beliefs	72.6	67.5	60.9	77.9	74.1	79.6
Openness to having my own views challenged	56.3	61.4	51.6	62.6	61.2	64.0
Ability to discuss and negotiate controversial issues	62.8	64.8	52.3	59.3	61.5	71.1
Ability to work cooperatively with diverse people	77.3	80.5	66.8	79.8	80.4	84.9

Note: PI = Pacific Islander
Source: Data are from Sylvia Hurtado and John H. Pryor, *The American Freshman: National Norms for Fall 2008*, Los Angeles, Higher Education Research Institute, University of California, 2009 at <http://www.gseis.ucla.edu/heri/PDFs/pubs/briefs/brief-pr012208-08FreshmanNorms.pdf>; sample size varies over the years; for 2008, data are based on the responses of 240,580 first-time, full-time freshmen at 340 four-year colleges and universities.

22b Graphs and charts

Graphs and charts are useful for presenting data and comparisons of data. Many software products allow you to produce graphs easily, and even standard word processing software gives you several ways to present your numbers in visual form. In Microsoft Office, you can create graphs and charts in Word or Excel. Whether you work in Word for Mac or for PC, you are able to select a type of chart, such as a pie chart or a bar chart, and enter your own details, such as title, labels for the vertical and horizontal axes of a bar chart, numbers, and data labels.

Creating Graphs and Charts in Word for Mac

Simple line graph   Use a line graph to show changes over time. Figure 1 has a clear caption and is self-explanatory.

FIGURE 1 ▶ **Freshmen Keeping Up to Date with Political Affairs**

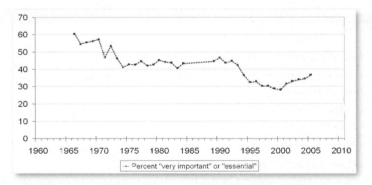

Source: Data are excerpted from Sylvia Hurtado and John H. Pryor, *The American Freshman: National Norms for Fall 2005*, Los Angeles, Higher Education Research Institute, University of California, 2006 at <http://www.gseis.ucla.edu/heri/heri/html>, slide 14; sample size varies over the years; for 2005 data are based on the responses of 26,710 first-time, full-time freshmen at 385 4-year colleges and universities.

Comparative line graph Line graphs are especially useful for comparing data over time. Figure 2, for example, made in Word from raw data, compares childbearing in five countries over a period of fifty-five years, showing large decreases especially in Mexico and China.

FIGURE 2 ▶ Changes in Childbearing in Five Nations

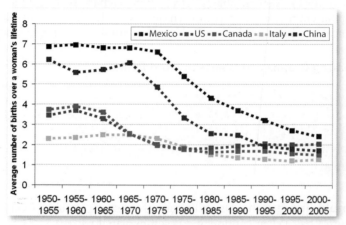

Source: Data from the Population Division of the Department of Economic and Social Affairs of the United Nations Secretariat, World Population Prospects: The 2004 Revision and World Urbanization Prospects: The 2003 Revision, <http://esa .un.org/unpp>

KEY POINTS

Using Graphs and Charts

- Use a graph or chart only to help make a point.
- Set up a graph or chart so that it is self-contained and self-explanatory.
- Make sure that the items on the time axis of a line graph are proportionately spaced.
- Always provide a clear caption.
- Use precise wording for labels.
- Always give details about the source of the data or the chart itself if you download from the Web.
- Choose a value range for the axes of a graph that does not exaggerate or downplay change (see 22d).

Pie chart Use a pie chart to show how fractions and percentages relate to one another and make up a whole. Figure 3 shows petroleum imports in the United States in 2004.

FIGURE 3 ▶ **U.S. Petroleum Import Sources, 2004**

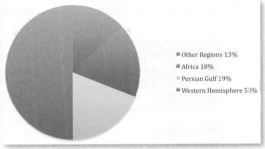

- Other Regions 13%
- Africa 18%
- Persian Gulf 19%
- Western Hemisphere 50%

Source: United States, National Energy Information Center, Department of Energy, June 2005, <http://www.eia.doe.gov/neic/brochure/gas04/gasoline.htm>

Bar chart A bar chart is useful to show comparisons and correlations and to highlight differences among groups. The bar chart in Figure 4, created in MS Word, displays the number of students who frequently or occasionally discussed politics during the presidential election years since 1988. It shows that in 2008 the number of students who frequently discussed politics was at its highest level (35.6%) in twenty years.

FIGURE 4 ▶ **Discussion of Politics among Freshmen during Election Years (vertical bar chart)**

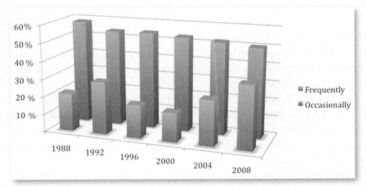

- Frequently
- Occasionally

Source: Data are from Sylvia Hurtado and John H. Pryor, *The American Freshman: National Norms for Fall 2008*, Los Angeles, Higher Education Research Institute, University of California, 2009 at <http://www.gseis.ucla.edu/heri/heri/html>, slide 14; sample size varies over the years; for 2008, data are based on the responses of 240,580 first-time, full-time freshmen at 340 four-year colleges and universities.

A bar chart can also be presented horizontally, which makes it easier to attach labels to the bars. Figure 5 was produced in MS Office using the data from Table 1 on page 302.

FIGURE 5 ▶ Freshmen Pluralistic Orientation for a Diverse Workplace, by Race/Ethnicity (horizontal bar chart)

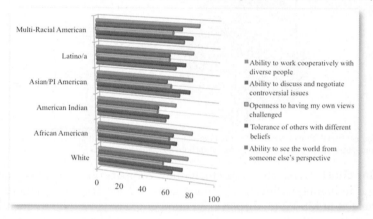

22c Images and copyright issues

Your computer software provides many standard images (clip art) and photographs that you can use free in your documents without any copyright concerns. Web sites offer images to download, either free or at a small cost. Keep in mind, however, that unless the creator of the image has explicitly stated that it is free for noncommercial use (either by a statement on the Web site or by using a Creative Commons license), you should assume that the image is copyrighted and not free for the taking.

Note that if your document is to be posted on the Web, readers who have slow Internet connections may find it time-consuming or even impossible to download images with a large file size. Use a lower quality setting for .jpg files or the .gif or .png format instead (resave if necessary).

Sophisticated and original graphics are usually copyrighted, so if you intend to use an image in a document that you post on the Web or make widely available in print, you must do more than download the image and cite the source. The "fair use" principle of copyright law allows use of a small portion of a source in a noncommercial work, but you may need to write to the originator for permission to use an image or text.

For a college paper intended for your classmates and instructor alone and not posted publicly on the Web, you may want to include an illustration you find on the Web, such as a graph, a map, a photograph of an author or artist, a work of art, or an illustration from an online encyclopedia. You can do so without getting permission, but you must cite the source in your paper.

22d Honesty in visuals

With the ability to use software programs such as Photoshop to crop, combine, juxtapose, erase, and enhance images come attendant dangers and innumerable opportunities for comedy. Late night talk-show hosts show edited photos and video clips from the day's news to hilarious effect. Image manipulation can also be used for political effect (such as Josef Stalin's order to delete Leon Trotsky from photographs that show Lenin). In academic work, the changing of images is never acceptable. Falsifying data can reach the level of fraud, as in the case of a scientist who manipulated images of stem cells to achieve personal ambition. Scientific journals are beginning to check photos that are submitted with research to ensure that they have not been manipulated to remove images, change the contrast, or combine images from several slides into one.

The lesson here is a simple one: Be ethical in your use of visuals.

Charts and graphs can also be manipulated—not by changing the original data but simply by selectively plotting the axes of a graph. Take care when choosing the value range for the axes to avoid exaggerating or downplaying changes over time. For example, for comparative data on population projections ranging between a 50% and 60% increase, a vertical axis of 0% to 100% will show the lines as almost flat, indicating little change over time. However, a vertical axis of 40% to 70% will emphasize and maybe exaggerate the small projected increase—one that could be attributable solely to a sampling fluctuation.

23 ⚏━

Online Communication Forums

23a E-mail in academic and business settings

Communicating online to professors or supervisors in academic or business contexts is different from writing personal e-mail. Observe the following conventions.

Length and readability Be brief, and state your main points clearly at the start. One screen holds about 250 words, and online readers do not want to scroll repeatedly to find out what you are saying. Keep paragraphs short and manageable so that readers can take in the information at a glance. Use numbered or bulleted lists to present a sequence of points as brief items that can be readily seen and absorbed. Avoid multiple colors, fonts, and graphics unless you are certain readers can receive and read these features.

Capitals Avoid using all capital letters in an e-mail message. To readers, it looks as if you are SHOUTING. But do use capitals when appropriate, especially for "I."

URLs Pay attention to the accuracy of punctuation and capital letters. Both matter; one slip can invalidate an address and cause you great frustration. Whenever possible, to avoid having to write out a long URL, simply copy that URL from the relevant Web site page and paste it into your own document (Select/Copy/Paste). If you need to spread an address over two lines, break it after a slash (MLA style) or before a dot, and do not insert any spaces, hyphens, or line breaks.

Accuracy Use a spelling checker and edit your e-mail before sending if you are writing to people you do not know well and if you want them to take your ideas seriously.

Subject headings Subscribers to a list and regular e-mail correspondents are likely to receive a great deal of mail every day. Be clear and concise when composing a subject heading so that readers will know at a glance what your message is about.

Salutations Although e-mail can seem like an informal medium, when communicating with your professor or with individuals that you do not know well, you should begin your e-mail with an appropriate salutation. Unless your instructor tells you otherwise, you should use "Dear Professor [Name]:" to start your e-mail. If you are addressing an individual in an organization, find out and use that person's title.

Signing off Always put your actual name (not just <cutiepie3@aol.com>) at the end of your online message. You can also construct a "signature file," which will appear automatically at the end of every message you send. Find out how to do this from the Help or Tools menu of your e-mail program.

The danger of attachments Attachments can harbor computer viruses, so always be cautious about opening any attachments to an e-mail message. Open attachments only from known senders, and keep your own antivirus software up to date so that you will not spread a virus.

Spam Make sure you add your instructor or business associates to your safe list so that their messages are not classified as spam.

23b E-mail discussion lists, discussion boards, and online communities

E-mail discussion lists, discussion boards on the Web and within course sites such as Blackboard, and online communities provide a forum for a virtual community of people sharing interest in a topic. Thousands of these forums exist—some public, some private—providing opportunities for you to find information and to enter discussions with others and make your own contributions. Since many of the groups and forums may not be moderated or refereed in any way, you must always be careful about evaluating the reliability of a source of information. However, any discussion group can be valuable not only for the information it provides but also for the ideas that emerge as participants discuss an issue and tease out its complexities. As a general rule, e-mail lists to which it is necessary to first subscribe or register tend to be more substantive and professional than lists or boards with no access control.

E-mail discussion lists The administrators of even a public list may screen potential subscribers carefully, although generally there is no fee for subscribing. (To participate in an e-mail list, you need only an e-mail address and a mail program.) Private lists and professionally moderated lists, especially those with a technical focus, can be reliable sources of factual information and informed opinion. When you join an online discussion group, all the messages posted are sent automatically to the e-mail accounts of all those who have registered as subscribers. Subscribing simply means registering, not paying a fee. Lists are managed by specific software programs, such as LISTSERV®, Listproc, and Majordomo, which have similar but not identical procedures.

Caution: Discussion lists often sell e-mail addresses, so you may get huge amounts of spam. Be careful about allowing your e-mail address to be circulated. If there is a box you can check to prohibit giving out your address, be sure to check it.

Finding discussion lists Use the following directories to find the public lists that are available:

- CataList, the official catalog of LISTSERV lists. As of May 24, 2009, it contained 52,411 public lists of a total of 537,434 LISTSERV lists.
- Topica/LISZT, a catalog of e-mail lists of all types
- Yahoo! Groups

KEY POINTS

Guidelines for Participating in Online Discussion Lists

1. **If a Web interface is available for an e-mail discussion list, use it.** Subscription management and posting, each with its own address, will be all in one place and therefore easier to manage.

2. **If you do subscribe via e-mail, remember that a list has two addresses:** the *posting* address (to send messages to all subscribers) and the *subscription* address (to send commands about managing your subscription). To differentiate between them, think of the difference between sending a letter to the editor of a printed newspaper for publication and sending a note to the circulation manager about a vacation suspension of your subscription. Use the subscription address (not the posting address) to subscribe to a list, suspend your subscription, unsubscribe from a list, or make other changes to your subscription details. The wording you use must be exact. Follow the list's directions for the commands, and save a copy.

3. **Lurk before you post!** Spend time reading and browsing in the Web archives to learn the conventions and the types of topics before you start sending messages to everyone on the list.

4. **Manage the volume of mail.** A mailing list may generate thirty, one hundred, or more messages a day, so after a few days away from the list, you may feel overwhelmed. Use the options the list provides to select—for example—Nomail, Digest, or Index. Nomail temporarily suspends the sending of messages to your mailbox; Digest allows you to get only one bundle of mail every day; Index simply lists the messages once a day, and you retrieve the ones you want to read. However, not all options are available for all lists. You can also use filters to put messages into a special folder so that you can read them when you are ready.

5. **Pay close attention to who the actual recipient is.** Is it the whole list or the person who posted the original message? Make sure you know who will actually receive your message. If you want to reply to only the individual sender of a message, do not send your message to the entire list; choose "Reply," not "Reply All." (Don't complain to Manuel about Bob's views and then by mistake send your reply to the whole list, including Bob!) However, some lists automatically send a message to everyone. Find out the policy of your list.

6. **Do not quote the complete original message.** Select only a short passage, the one you immediately refer or reply to. Similarly, if you subscribe to a list in digest form, don't send all of the day's messages back with your reply—edit those out first.

7. **Avoid sending a message like "I agree" to the many subscribers to the list.** Make your postings substantive and considerate so that subscribers find them worth reading.

8. **Do not forward.** Only forward a posting from one list to another if either you ask the sender for permission or the posting is a general informational announcement.

Discussion boards and online communities Now sharing many features with discussion lists, discussion boards are Web pages to which you can post messages directly, but messages are not sent to your e-mail inbox. Sometimes, you post spontaneously; in other instances, you have to register first. Discussion boards are included in many online magazine and media Web sites and in course management software, such as Blackboard, which provides a forum for students' discussions. Many sponsors, including Blackboard, have established "communities," which set up a site for those with similar interests to communicate online. In these public venues, follow the e-mail advice in 23a.

23c Other forums: Blogs, wikis, and virtual classrooms

Blogs   Blogs are publicly posted observations on a topic initiated by the author or authorized group; they cover a range from personal diaries, family photos, and stories about pets to statements of political/religious/cultural views and observations of social issues. Typically open to everyone, they have been called the soapbox of the electronic age; they can be initiated with little technical expertise, thus making contributing to the Web truly democratic.

More and more, blogs such as the *Huffington Post* (<http://www.huffingtonpost.com>) and those hosted by the *New York Times* (<http://www.nytimes.com/ref/topnews/blog-index.html>) provide insight into the state of our society and other societies at a particular point, and they broaden from the personal not only in content but also by including images, videos, and links to other sites. Blogs provide an opportunity to learn how others are thinking and to express your own views for a special audience or for anyone who happens to read your entries. Blogs can be set up so that groups as well as individuals can have posting and discussion rights, so they are useful and affordable discussion venues for student course sites and clubs (for a student's blog for a course, see 1e). Because blogs are often spontaneous, personal, unedited, and written frequently (often daily), they may not be reliable sources of information for researchers. But they serve as a corrective to a self-censoring press, and from them, you can learn about how people view current issues and react to actions taken by individuals, political parties, and governments. Several providers, such as Blogger, Wordpress, and Seedwiki, offer free server space for blogs.

Wikis   The word *wiki* comes from *wiki-wiki*, which means "hurry quick" in Hawaiian. Wikis are Web texts with open access to anyone, demanding no technical expertise and allowing information to be instantaneously added and corrected or otherwise changed. Pages are created as a team or community effort. Some college instructors use wikis in their courses as a venue for student-instructor discussion, to support collaborative writing, or to serve as the platform for course portfolios. As wiki technology has matured, some instructors are switching from commercial course management systems like Blackboard to wikis for the online components of their courses.

One of the best-known wikis is one you are probably familiar with, the collaborative encyclopedia *Wikipedia*. In collaborative writing situations such as a report assigned to a group of students or a team of employees, wikis can be a fast way to work together on generating and editing text. Most wikis can be set up so that contributors have to log in; this is useful for tracking who made specific changes. One of the key features of wikis is that you can easily see what changes have been made and even compare versions throughout the entire history of a document using the "page history" function. In a word processing program, you have to be careful to keep copies of the iterations of your revised work; a wiki will take care of that aspect of composition for you. However, because wikis are server based, it is a good idea to always draft text in your word processor and save it before posting it to the wiki (that way, in the event of a server crash or a network disconnect, you won't lose your work). See 6d for guidelines on using wikis as a research source.

Virtual classrooms   Course management systems such as Blackboard provide virtual classrooms, cyberspaces in which a whole class or a group of students can log in at the same time and communicate in real time in chat rooms. Virtual classrooms exist at different levels of sophistication:

- no more than a chat room, but typically archiving all entries
- adding a "whiteboard," a display/draw space that can be used by both instructor and student (upon permission)
- adding an audio channel to allow verbal exchange
- adding two-way video (including live feed from instructor to students, and vice versa)

Virtual classrooms are used for serious instruction in distance learning, with some providing videoconferencing tools for group projects and opportunities for online discussions.

Note: Whether you participate in discussion lists, communities, blogs, wikis, or virtual classrooms, remember that all are public forums, with their own inherent conventions different from those of personal e-mail or a private journal. When you post messages, pay

attention to the conventions listed in 23a, and avoid chat room abbreviations (CUL8R etc.) and the use of emoticons.

24 ⚷

Web Site Design

A great deal of online help is available for the mechanics of finding a
server for a site (many schools offer space for student Web pages, as
do many Internet service providers) and for the actual creation of a
site. With so much technical help accessible, you don't need to worry
too much about HTML and coding (although there are design and
composition benefits to learning the code, just as knowing the basics
of grammar and usage provides a foundation for effective writing).
Instead, you can focus on adapting what you know about writing for
the page: the important rhetorical considerations of purpose, audience, voice, structure, interaction of text and images, and the design
of your document.

24a Planning a Web site

Purpose   Determine the message you want your site to convey and
what you want your audience to do or learn from your site as a result of viewing it. Do you want to inform, persuade, or entertain—or
all three?

Audience   Try to form a clear idea of the main audience you want
to reach: friends and family, fellow students, colleagues, members of
a club or community, or the general public. Consider what their expectations will be. For a professional or academic audience, choose
fonts and colors that are sober rather than flashy. If you know that
many do not have broadband access, that will make a difference in
the speed of downloading any video or audio clips you may want to
include on the site.

Voice and tone   Visitors to your Web site take away an impression
of you or the institution you represent, so make sure that the content,
language, and images work well to keep readers interested and engaged. Some sites and some audiences enjoy extremes, but for a professional site, play it safe and avoid rants, insults, jargon, terminal
cuteness, and flat attempts at humor.

Structure   Web sites typically consist of several pages and many internal and external links. Your viewers need directions on finding their way and not getting lost. On each page, include a link to the home page on a navigational bar at the top or bottom or in a sidebar. Also consider including an "About" page to explain the purpose of the site. Refer to the structure of sites you like and find easy to navigate to help you devise the structure for your site. Make a site map (see the example in 24b).

Interaction of text and images   Plan the look of each page so that images supplement and complement the text and the site's purpose and draw the audience into the content. In other than personal sites designed for family and friends, avoid using images and animations to add peripheral glitz and clutter. Remember the need to acknowledge text or images from another source, and request permission to use them; the Web is a highly public forum.

Design and presentation   Design and presentation of your work are extremely important in a Web site, as it is open to so many more potential readers than a paper text, even one widely distributed. See 24c for tips on Web site design.

24b Making a site map

Draw a flowchart that shows how the different parts of your site relate to each other. In the *Refugee Resettlement Program* Web site (shown in 24e), the structure is simple. The home page clearly links to the other pages within the site. Here is a map of that site:

Planning Site Map

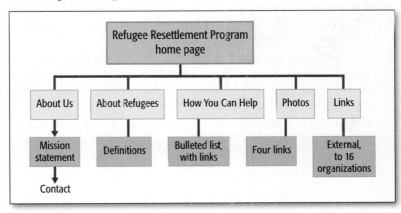

24c Tips for Web site design

Web Site Design Guidelines

- **Keep pages short and simple.** As a general rule, no more than two to three screens, with no fancy fonts.

- **Test first.** To test your page, set your own monitor to a resolution not higher than 800×600, and make sure all the text is visible on your screen without horizontal scrolling. Be sure to test your page in several different browsers (at least Internet Explorer, Firefox, and Safari).

- **Keep sentences short and direct.**

- **Chunk content.** Break text into short passages, and use lists to help readers scan quickly.

- **Provide navigation aids within the content.** Use headings, and provide internal links to the headings. Use a larger point size for the type in headings.

- **Use visuals.** Chosen wisely and used purposefully, visual content (such as pictures, diagrams, photographs, graphs, clip art, or animations) enhances and illustrates ideas. Save photos as .jpg files and graphs or line art as .gif files. Pay attention to the file size of such add-ons. It is often possible to reduce the file size significantly with only a minimal loss of image quality. Position visuals so that they relate clearly to the written text.

- **Use anchors.** Choose descriptive text or images as "anchors" for hyperlinks (not just "Click here"). Check on their reliability and keep them up to date.

- **Use color and background patterns judiciously and consistently.** Choose colors to complement the subject matter: dramatic? subdued? Blue type on a black swirling background may look interesting, but it can be difficult to read.

- **Help to ensure accessibility.** Be sensitive to issues of accessibility for people with disabilities, such as using descriptive text as well as images and offering alternatives to visual and auditory material. You can use WebAIM's web accessibility evaluation tool <http://wave.webaim.org> to check your Web pages for accessibility problems.

- **Avoid clutter.** Keep the site uncluttered for ease of navigation.

- **Provide helpful navigation.** Include relevant navigational links from each page of your site to other pages, such as the home page. Consider the use of a navigation bar that appears on each page of your site. Update your site regularly to maintain the links to external URLs.

- **Make your site transparent.** Include your own e-mail address for comments and questions about your site. State the date of the last page update.

- **Don't plagiarize.** For text and graphics that you download to use in your site, ask for permission and acknowledge the fact that you received permission to use the material. Be aware that you may have to pay a fee to use copyrighted material. Also, provide full documentation for your sources (see 22c).

24d Getting feedback

Before you launch the site, get as much feedback as you can from classmates or colleagues. Ask for feedback on the following:

- the ease of use and of getting to individual pages and back to where you started
- the time it takes for graphics to appear
- page length and width (no horizontal scrolling and little vertical scrolling)
- the legibility and relevance of images (no animations or flashing icons just for effect)
- the sense that everything on the site serves a purpose
- grammatical and mechanical errors (There shouldn't be any!)

TECH NOTE

Getting Help with Web Site Design

A useful resource is Jennifer Niederst Robbins, *Learning Web Design: A Beginner's Guide to HTML, Style Sheets, and Web Graphics*, 3rd edition (Cambridge: O'Reilly, 2007) and the site *Learning Web Design* <http://www.learningwebdesign.com/>.

24e A community Web site: A student's project

The Soling Program at Syracuse University focuses on experiential learning and community involvement (for more on community service writing, see 5d). The program offers a course in Web Design for Novices in which students work with community organizations to design Web sites. While he was a student in the program, Daniel Sauve worked with the Refugee Resettlement Program sponsored by the Interreligious Council of Central New York and by the United Way to develop an informational site containing an appeal for help. Two pages from the site shown next illustrate features of good Web site design.

- The purpose of the site is clear, and the content is succinct and accessible.
- The home page provides a good introduction to the whole site, with no distractions and no vertical scrolling necessary.
- Text does not fill the width of the screen, and no horizontal scrolling is necessary.
- The navigation bar appears on the left side of each page.
- Clicking the title (Refugee Resettlement Program) on each page takes one back to the home page.
- The logos of the two sponsors, linked to their sites, appear on each page, providing instant access to information about the organizations and their purpose.
- The tone is objective, direct, and clear throughout, avoiding hype.
- The content of a hyperlink is made clear in the wording of the text for the link.
- The consistent use of color and the heading format unify the whole site.

Home Page of Site

Refugee Resettlement Program

About Us

About Refugees

How You Can Help

Photos

Links

A United Way Organization

The Refugee Resettlement Program of the InterReligious Council Central New York (RRP-IRC-CNY) fosters inter-religious and intercultural understanding between refugees and asylees of many different religions and cultures and residents of the Central New York, Ithaca, Binghamton and Albany areas. In partnership with Church World Service, Episcopal Migration Ministries, local faith communities and civic groups, we assist refugees from around the world begin their new lives in America. More..

"How You Can Help" Page

Refugee Resettlement Program

How You Can Help Refugees

About Us

About Refugees

How You Can Help

Photos

Links

A United Way Organization

- Invite us to speak to a group about refugees and asylees.
- As a part of a civic group or religious congregation, sponsor a refugee, refugee family, or an asylee.
- Stay informed about world refugee and immigration needs and policies
- Donate household furnishings and goods for newly arrived refugees
- Volunteer your time to help a refugee family or asylee with their life in America.
- Encourage your elected officials to support policies that assist refugees and immigrants.
- Assemble Personal Care Kits
- Assemble Household Care Kits

25

Portfolios: Hard Copy and Electronic

25a Preparing a portfolio (hard copy)

Portfolios are used by artists, writers, and job hunters to demonstrate their range of skills and accomplishments. In your college writing courses, your instructors may ask you to select work to include in a portfolio that allows you and your instructor an opportunity to review and assess your progress over time. If your instructor does not issue specific guidelines for presenting your portfolio, use those in the following Key Points box.

KEY POINTS
Presenting a Course Writing Portfolio

- Number and date drafts; clip or staple all drafts and final copy together.
- To each separate package in your portfolio add a cover sheet describing the contents of the package (for example, "In-class essay" or "Documented paper with three prior drafts").
- Include a brief cover letter to introduce the material and yourself.
- Pay special attention to accuracy and mechanics. Your semester grade may depend on the few pieces of writing that you select for evaluation, so make sure that the ones you include are carefully edited and well presented.

Whether or not a portfolio is required, consider collecting in your own portfolio your academic writing that indicates both the range of topics covered in your courses and the types of writing you have done. To show prospective professors, graduate schools, or employers that you are able to produce several kinds of writing, use the list in the following Key Points box (adapted from Carleton College's writing portfolio requirements for its graduates) as a guideline in preparing your portfolio. Don't leave it up to your readers to deduce what you have accomplished. Be sure to include at the beginning a cover letter, an essay, and/or a table of contents that explicitly states what you have included and why.

KEY POINTS

Preparing an Academic Writing Portfolio

An effective academic writing portfolio will demonstrate to your readers

- your breadth of interests by showing writing that you have produced in multiple courses from a range of departments or disciplines: the humanities, business, education, social sciences, mathematics, and the natural sciences

- your ability to construct, develop, and effectively support an argument

- your ability to observe and report by showing writing such as interviews from a sociology class, field notes from an education class, a laboratory report from the natural sciences, a description of a work of art you observed, or a concert you attended

- your ability to analyze complex information by showing writing that includes, for example, numeric data, multiple texts, or multiple observations

- your ability to interpret, whether it's a film you saw, a poem you read, or a set of data you analyzed

- your ability to conduct effective research by including writing that shows a range of well-identified, integrated, and documented sources

25b Preparing an e-portfolio

Increasingly, individual instructors as well as collegewide programs require or strongly encourage students to construct an e-portfolio. Space is allotted on a server where students can store writing samples, a résumé, information about their experience, and relevant images. Students can also reflect on their work as they present it to Web readers. The specific charges or tasks vary with the course.

While an English instructor will probably focus on writing samples, a social science instructor may ask students to locate primary sources about a specific research topic (like the environment or laws and court cases related to civil unions). In education, e-portfolios have become quite common to document a student's progress through a course of study—for example, to file lesson plans, lesson evaluations, and so on.

TECH NOTE

E-portfolios in Action

For examples of college programs that assign e-portfolios, see the following:

- Penn State includes instructions on building e-portfolios and examples of students' e-portfolios (including video and audio clips) that they used when applying for jobs. See <http://portfolio.psu.edu/>.

- LaGuardia Community College includes a useful e-portfolio flowchart, instructions for developing a portfolio, resources, student samples, and advice about the language to use, the information to provide, and ways to avoid plagiarizing images and sounds found on the Web. See <http://www.eportfolio.lagcc.cuny.edu>.

Whatever software your school may use to support e-portfolios, typically you will have control over the material that goes onto your pages on the (Web) server. In your private storage area, you'll be able to make material available to your instructors and/or other students for review so that these "reviewers" can add their comments to the material. Also, you may have the option of making a document (without the reviewer comments) available to a wider audience ("publish it to the Web") so that future employers or friends and family can also see the work. You can make different documents—aimed at different audiences—available for viewing at any time. One advantage of e-portfolios is that you have the flexibility to remix the materials for different purposes. In addition, you can include a variety of materials that you produce, such as HTML documents, graphics, images, sound, and film clips, rather than simply printed college essays that make up more conventional portfolios.

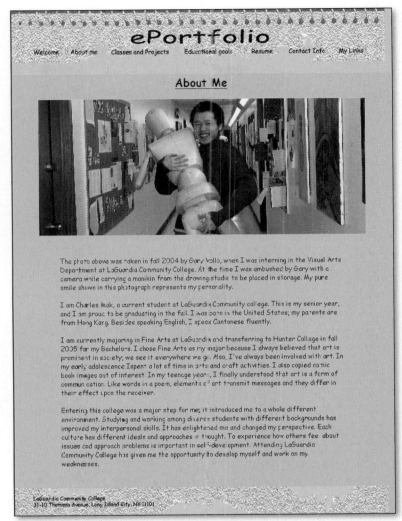

ePortfolio

Welcome   About me   Classes and Projects   Educational goals   Resume   Contact Info   My Links

About Me

The photo above was taken in fall 2004 by Gary Vollo, when I was interning in the Visual Arts Department at LaGuardia Community College. At the time I was ambushed by Gary with a camera while carrying a manikin from the drawing studio to be placed in storage. My pure smile shown in this photograph represents my personality.

I am Charles Mak, a current student at LaGuardia Community college. This is my senior year, and I am proud to be graduating in the fall. I was born in the United States; my parents are from Hong Kong. Besides speaking English, I speak Cantonese fluently.

I am currently majoring in Fine Arts at LaGuardia and transferring to Hunter College in fall 2005 for my Bachelor's. I chose Fine Arts as my major because I always believed that art is prominent in society; we see it everywhere we go. Also, I've always been involved with art. In my early adolescence I spent a lot of time in arts and craft activities. I also copied comic book images out of interest. In my teenage years, I finally understood that art is a form of communication. Like words in a poem, elements of art transmit messages and they differ in their effect upon the receiver.

Entering this college was a major step for me; it introduced me to a whole different environment. Studying and working among diverse students with different backgrounds has improved my interpersonal skills. It has enlightened me and changed my perspective. Each culture has different ideals and approaches or thought. To experience how others feel about issues and approach problems is important in self-development. Attending LaGuardia Community College has given me the opportunity to develop myself and work on my weaknesses.

LaGuardia Community College
31-10 Thomson Avenue, Long Island City, NY 11101

Permission to reprint granted by Charles Mak and the LaGuardia Center for Teaching and Learning, coordinators of the e-portfolio initiative at LaGuardia Community College, CUNY, available at <http://www.lagcc.cuny.edu/ctl>.

25c A student's e-portfolio

Charles Mak prepared an e-portfolio over the course of one semester when he was a student at LaGuardia Community College, City University of New York. The seven-part structure of the portfolio

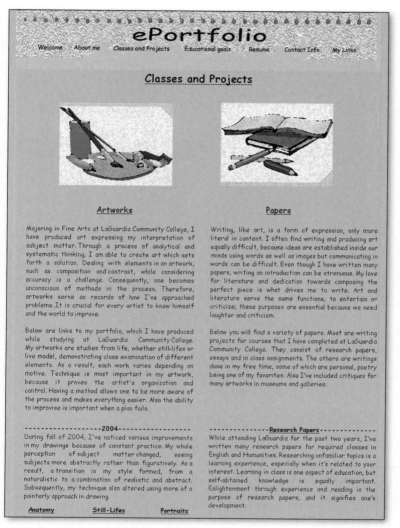

ePortfolio

Welcome   About me   Classes and Projects   Educational goals   Resume   Contact Info   My Links

Classes and Projects

Artworks

Majoring in Fine Arts at LaGuardia Community College, I have produced art expressing my interpretation of subject matter. Through a process of analytical and systematic thinking, I am able to create art which sets forth a solution. Dealing with elements in an artwork, such as composition and contrast, while considering accuracy is a challenge. Consequently, one becomes unconscious of methods in the process. Therefore, artworks serve as records of how I've approached problems. It is crucial for every artist to know himself and the world to improve.

Below are links to my portfolio, which I have produced while studying at LaGuardia Community College. My artworks are studies from life, whether still-lifes or live model, demonstrating close examination of different elements. As a result, each work varies depending on motive. Technique is most important in my artwork, because it proves the artist's organization and control. Having a method allows one to be more aware of the process and makes everything easier. Also the ability to improvise is important when a plan fails.

-------------------2004-------------------
During fall of 2004, I've noticed various improvements in my drawings because of constant practice. My whole perception of subject matter changed, seeing subjects more abstractly rather than figuratively. As a result, a transition in my style formed, from a naturalistic to a combination of realistic and abstract. Subsequently, my technique also altered using more of a painterly approach in drawing.

Anatomy   **Still-Lifes**   **Portraits**

Papers

Writing, like art, is a form of expression, only more literal in content. I often find writing and producing art equally difficult, because ideas are established inside our minds using words as well as images but communicating in words can be difficult. Even though I have written many papers, writing an introduction can be strenuous. My love for literature and dedication towards composing the perfect piece is what drives me to write. Art and literature serve the same functions, to entertain or criticize; these purposes are essential because we need laughter and criticism.

Below you will find a variety of papers. Most are writing projects for courses that I have completed at LaGuardia Community College. They consist of research papers, essays and in class assignments. The others are writings done in my free time, some of which are personal, poetry being one of my favorites. Also I've included critiques for many artworks in museums and galleries.

----------------Research Papers--------------
While attending LaGuardia for the past two years, I've written many research papers for required classes in English and Humanities. Researching unfamiliar topics is a learning experience, especially when it's related to your interest. Learning in class is one aspect of education, but self-obtained knowledge is equally important. Enlightenment through experience and reading is the purpose of research papers, and it signifies one's development.

was provided by templates offered by his college; the actual appearance of the template, with its unifying color scheme throughout the site, is his own design. The screenshots show an excerpt from two pages—About Me and Classes and Projects—both combining text and images and providing internal links to his research papers (on literature, biological sciences, and psychology) and art projects (anatomy, still-life works, and portraits). Note that the links to the home page and all the other pages appear across the top of each screen, allowing easy access to all parts of the site at all times.

26 ⌐━

Flyers, Brochures, and Newsletters

26a Design principles for flyers, brochures, and newsletters

Although it is generally better to use document design software for creating publishable document formats, it is certainly possible to create simple flyers, brochures, and newsletters using word processing software. Templates for flyers, brochures, and newsletters are available on your word processor with a range of design possibilities. Of course, templates only offer the layout. When you are producing material that will be printed or photocopied and then distributed to many people, take extra care to create a document that is attractive and effective. Attention to design increases the chance that your brochure, newsletter, or flyer will be read and have the effect that you intend.

TECH NOTE

Templates in Word

- To find templates in Word 2008 for Mac, go to File/Project Gallery and scroll down the categories column to find several templates for brochures, flyers, and newsletters. Click the category and choose which template to work on.

Word 2008 for Mac

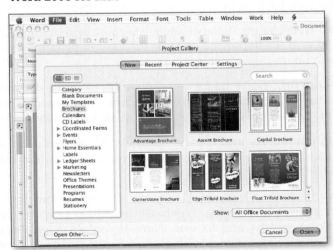

(Continued)

(Continued)

- In Word 2007 for PC, you can select templates from a gallery when starting a new document. You also have the option of connecting to Microsoft's Web site to see user-developed templates in addition to the ones that automatically come with the software. (The interface is very similar to the Word for Mac screen capture shown on the previous page.)

Word 2007 for PC

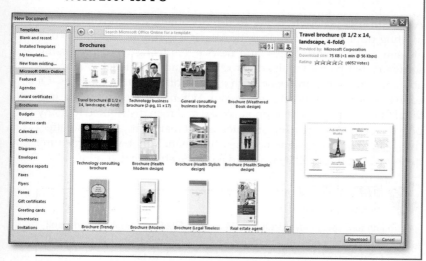

Some basic principles can help you design a successful print communication in academic, community, or business settings.

1. Plan   Consider the audience and the purpose of your document: Who will read the document? What is the most important message you are communicating?

2. Experiment   Leave time to try out variations in the document format. Play with the design—colors, typefaces, images, white space, and so on—and get feedback from sample audience members.

3. Value readability and clarity   Consider the proportion of one element to another within your piece. Give priority to important information.

4. Be consistent   Keep consistency and coherence from page to page in matters of margins, typefaces, headings, captions, borders, column widths, and so forth. *Note:* If you are using a desktop publishing program, set up a grid or template to block out the consistent placement of headings, columns, margins, and boxed features for each document you are designing. The lines of a grid appear on your computer but will not appear when the document is printed.

5. Give careful consideration to the following design variables:

Type size and font Choose a readable type size. Serif typefaces (the ones with little strokes at the top and bottom of each letter) are more readable and are thus the best choice for the main body of a print document. For headlines and headings, use a limited number of other larger type sizes.

Use of white space Allow for a generous amount of white space in your margins and borders and above and below headings. Adequate line spacing is important, too, to make the text easy to read.

End-of-line alignment Justified lines (lines are all the same length to create a squared-off box of text) appear more formal, have a greater type density, and can create a lot of hyphenated words; lines that are ragged right (referred to as left-justified) create a less formal and more open look. Full justification can be more difficult to read unless it is very carefully designed. Most word processing programs are not sophisticated enough to adequately produce full justification; make sure you consider readability when considering alignment.

Column width and line length Shorter columns and shorter lines of type are easier to read (but too many columns on one page may overwhelm your readers).

Rules (printed lines) Horizontal and vertical rules of various thicknesses can be effective in setting off columns, headings, pull-out quotations, photos, and captions.

Boxes and sidebars Boxing a part of your document can give it extra emphasis or attention.

Reversed type With this technique, type appears white against a black or other colored background. However, reversed type becomes hard to read when the type is very small. As with all uses of color, make sure you supply adequate contrast between foreground and background hues.

Screened backgrounds or images If your document is to be printed with black ink and you want a certain section of your document to have a gray background, printers can create that effect by "screening" the section at a certain percentage, which you specify. Ink of any color can be screened.

Bleed images or bleed type This effect makes an image or word appear to be running off the side of the page. It can be used to create a sense of an expanded design space.

26b Sample student-designed brochure

The following brochure was created by students at Baruch College for the college writing center. Note how the design of the logo playfully captures the act of writing and recurs across the front and back of the brochure. The limited color palette effectively draws attention to the words and images, while the display of the black-and-white photos embedded with the words "I write" works as a design motif and also includes images of student writers in the brochure. Finally, note how the number of words is limited and set off for maximum effect.

College Writing Center Brochure Designed by Students: Front

College Writing Center Brochure Designed by Students: Back

Courtesy of Baruch College Writing Center, New York, New York.

27 🔑

Résumés and Letters of Application

Communication in the work world frequently revolves around technology: telephones, faxes, computers, e-mail, presentational software, and spreadsheets. In business, knowing how to prepare documents for the screen and the page is a valuable skill whether you are applying for a job or communicating with colleagues and clients.

27a How to write a résumé

Résumés can be delivered on paper, on the Web, or via e-mail. Designs differ, and no one format works for everybody. However, in all formats, you need to convey to a prospective employer what you have accomplished and when, providing details of your education, work experience, honors or awards, interests, and special skills. Above all, you need to show that your qualifications and experience make you suitable for the job you are applying for.

KEY POINTS
Writing a Résumé

1. Decide how to present your résumé, or follow a prospective employer's instructions: on paper, on the Web, in the body of an e-mail message, as an e-mail attachment—or all of these. Start with a paper version and save it as .rtf or .doc. Convert it to HTML or to PDF to show it on the Web.

2. For a hard-copy version, print on standard-size paper of good quality, white or off-white.

3. Use headings to indicate the main sections.

4. For a hard-copy version, highlight section headings and important information with boldface, italics, bullets, indentation, or different fonts. Use a clear, simple design. Do not use overly elaborate fonts, colors, or design features. Keep a print résumé to one page, if possible. Do not include extraneous information to add length, but do not cram by using single-spacing between sections, a small font, or tiny margins.

5. Include information and experience relevant to the job you are applying for. Use reverse chronological order (begin with your most recent work experience and education).

6. Proofread your résumé several times, and ask someone else to examine it carefully as well. Make sure it contains no errors. Avoid howlers such as "rabid typist" and "responsible for ruining a five-store chain."

7. Accompany your print résumé with a cover letter (27e), also carefully checked to avoid an error such as "Thank you for considering me. I look forward to hearing from you shorty."

Note: Microsoft Word provides résumé templates that set up headings for you—a useful guide.

27b Sample print or Web page résumé

Notice how Aurelia Gomez organized her résumé into clear divisions, using bold headings and a space between sections. This résumé presents the most recent job experience and education first and works backward.*

<table>
<tr>
<td></td>
<td colspan="2">225 West 70th Street
New York, NY 10023
Phone: 212-555-3821
E-mail: agomez@nyu.edu</td>
<td></td>
</tr>
<tr>
<td colspan="3">**Aurelia Gomez**</td>
<td></td>
</tr>
<tr>
<td>**Objective:**</td>
<td colspan="2">Entry-level staff accounting position with a public accounting firm</td>
<td>Provides specific enough objective to be useful</td>
</tr>
<tr>
<td>**Experience:**</td>
<td>Summer 2009</td>
<td>**Accounting Intern:** PricewaterhouseCoopers, New York City
• Assisted in preparing corporate tax returns
• Attended meetings with clients
• Conducted research in corporate tax library and wrote research reports</td>
<td>Places work experience before education because applicant considers it to be her stronger qualification</td>
</tr>
<tr>
<td></td>
<td>Sept. 2005–
Nov. 2008</td>
<td>**Payroll Specialist:** City of New York
• Worked full-time in a civil service position in the Department of Administration
• Used payroll and other accounting software on both DEC 1034 minicomputer and on personal computers
• Represented 28-person work unit on the department's management-labor committee
• Left job to pursue college degree full-time</td>
<td>Uses action words such as *assisted* and *conducted*; uses incomplete sentences to emphasize the action words and to conserve space</td>
</tr>
<tr>
<td>**Education:**</td>
<td>Jan. 2003–
Present</td>
<td>Pursuing a 5-year bachelor of business administration degree (major in accounting) from the Stern School of Business, NYU
• Will graduate June 2010
• Attended part-time from 2003 until 2007 while holding down a full-time job
• Have financed 100% of all college expenses through savings, work, and student loans
• Plan to sit for the CPA exam in May 2011</td>
<td>Provides degree, institution, major, and graduation date

Makes the major section headings parallel in format and in wording

Formats the side headings for the dates in a column for ease of reading</td>
</tr>
<tr>
<td>**Personal Data:**</td>
<td colspan="2">• Helped start the Minority Business Student Association at NYU and served as program director for two years
• Have traveled extensively throughout the Caribbean
• Am a member of the Accounting Society
• Am willing to relocate</td>
<td>Provides additional data to enhance her credentials</td>
</tr>
<tr>
<td>**References**:</td>
<td colspan="2">Available on request</td>
<td>Omits actual names and addresses of references</td>
</tr>
</table>

*Sample documents in 27b–28b are adapted from Scot Ober's *Contemporary Business Communication*, 7th edition (Boston: Houghton, 2009). Used with permission.

27c A scannable electronic résumé

Companies often scan the print résumés they receive to establish a database of prospective employees. They can then use a keyword search to find suitable candidates from those in the database. You may also need to e-mail your résumé to a prospective employer. In either case, you need to adapt a print or formatted résumé to make it easy for users to read and scan. You do not need to limit the length of either a scannable or an e-mail résumé.

KEY POINTS
Preparing a Scannable or an E-mail Résumé

- Check any prospective employer's Web site to find its emphasis and important keywords.
- Use nouns as résumé keywords to enable prospective employers to do effective keyword searches (use "educational programmer," for example, rather than "designed educational programs").
- To transform a formatted MS Word document, such as a résumé, into a plain text format suitable for scannable and electronic résumés, copy your document into Notepad (go to Start, then Accessories). Documents created in or pasted into Notepad are automatically stripped of formatting. On a Mac, cut and paste your document into the Text/Edit application (File/New doc) and choose "Make Plain Text" from the Format menu.
- Use a standard sans serif typeface (such as Arial) and 10- to 12-point type, and for an e-mail document, use "plain text" or ASCII (a file name with a .txt extension).
- Avoid italics, underlining, and graphics.
- Avoid marked lists, or change bullets to + (plus signs) or to * (asterisks).
- Begin each major heading at the left margin.
- Do not include any decorative vertical or horizontal lines or borders.
- E-mail yourself or a friend a copy of your résumé (both as an attachment and within the body of a message) before you send one to an employer so that you can verify that all formatting has been cleared.
- If you feel it is necessary, attach a note saying that a formatted version is available in hard copy, and send one as a backup. Alternatively, you may include the link to a PDF or Web version.

27d Sample electronic résumé

Here is Aurelia Gomez's résumé adapted for e-mailing and scanning.

AURELIA GOMEZ

225 West 70th Street
New York, NY 10023
Phone: 212-555-3821
E-mail: agomez@nyu.edu

OBJECTIVE

Entry-level staff accounting position with a public accounting firm

EXPERIENCE

Summer 2009
Accounting Intern: PricewaterhouseCoopers, New York City
* Assisted in preparing corporate tax returns
* Attended meetings with clients
* Conducted research in corporate tax library and wrote research papers

Sept. 2005–Nov. 2008
Payroll Specialist: City of New York
* Full-time civil service position in the Department of Administration
* Proficiency in payroll and other accounting software on DEC 1034 min computer and on personal computers
* Representative for a 28-person work unit on the department's management-labor committee
* Reason for leaving job: To pursue college degree full-time

EDUCATION

Jan. 2002–Present
Pursuing a 5-year bachelor of business administration degree (major in accounting) from the Stern School of Business, NYU
* Will graduate June 2010
* Attended part-time from 2003 until 2007 while holding down a full-time job
* Have financed 100% of all college expenses through savings, work, and student loans
* Plan to sit for the CPA exam in May 2011

PERSONAL DATA

* Helped start the Minority Business Student Association at New York University and served as program director for two years
* Have traveled extensively throughout the Caribbean
* Am a member of the Accounting Society
* Am willing to relocate

REFERENCES

Available upon request

NOTE

An attractive and fully formatted hard-copy version of this resume is available upon request.

Begins with name at the top, followed immediately by address

Emphasizes, where possible, nouns as keywords

Uses only ASCII characters—one size with no special formatting; no rules, graphics, columns, or tables are used

Uses vertical line spaces (Enter key) and horizontal spacing (space bar) to show relationship of parts

Formats lists with asterisks instead of bullets

Runs longer than one page (acceptable for electronic résumés)

Includes notice of availability of a fully formatted version

27e Cover letter and sample

Accompany your print or e-mail résumé with a cover letter that explains what position you are applying for and why you are a good candidate. Find out as much as you can about the potential employer and type of work; then, in your letter, emphasize the connections between your experience and the job requirements. (Below is an example of a solicited application letter; it accompanies the résumé on p. 331.) Let

March 13, 2010

Mr. David Norman, Partner
Ross, Russell & Weston
452 Fifth Avenue
New York, NY 10018

Addresses the letter to a specific person

Dear Mr. Norman:

Subject: EDP Specialist Position (Reference No. 103-G)

Identifies the job position and source of advertising

My varied work experience in accounting and payroll services, coupled with my accounting degree, has prepared me for the position of EDP specialist that you advertised in the March 9 *New York Times*.

In addition to taking required courses in accounting and management information systems as part of my accounting major at New York University, I took an elective course in EDP auditing and control. The training I received in this course in applications, software, systems, and service-center records would enable me to immediately become a productive member of your EDP consulting staff.

Emphasizes a qualification that might distinguish her from other applicants

My college training has been supplemented by an internship in a large accounting firm. In addition, my two years of experience as a payroll specialist for the city of New York have given me firsthand knowledge of the operation and needs of nonprofit agencies. This experience should help me to contribute to your large consulting practice with government agencies.

Relates her work experience to the specific needs of the employer

After you have reviewed my enclosed résumé, I would appreciate having the opportunity to discuss with you why I believe I have the right qualifications and personality to serve you and your clients. I can be reached by e-mail or phone after 3 p.m. daily.

Sincerely,

Aurelia Gomez

Aurelia Gomez
225 West 70th Street
New York, NY 10023
Phone: 212-555-3821
E-mail: agomez@nyu.edu

Provides a telephone number (may be done either in the body of the letter or at the end of the address block)

Enclosure

the employer see that you understand what type of person he or she is looking for. State when, where, and how you can be contacted. As you do with the résumé itself, proofread the letter carefully.

Once you have had an interview, write a short note to thank the interviewer and emphasize your interest in the position.

28

Business Letters and Memos

28a Features of a business letter

A good business letter usually has the following qualities:

1. It is brief.
2. It clearly conveys to the reader information and expectations for action or response.
3. It lets the reader know how he or she will benefit from or be affected by the proposal or suggestion.
4. It is polite.
5. It is written in relatively formal language.
6. It contains no errors.

28b Sample business letter

LANGUAGE AND CULTURE

Business Letters across Cultures

The basic features of business letters vary from culture to culture. Business letters in English avoid both flowery language and references to religion, elements that are viewed favorably in some other cultures. Do not assume that there are universal conventions. When writing cross-cultural business letters, follow these suggestions:

1. Use a formal style; address correspondents by title and family name.
2. If possible, learn about the writing conventions of your correspondent's culture.
3. Use clear language and a summary to get your point across.
4. Avoid humor; it may fall flat and could offend.

The sample letter uses a block format, with all parts aligned at the left. This format is commonly used with business stationery.

BEN & JERRY'S

November 1, 2006 ↓ 4

> The arrows indicate how many lines to space down before typing the next part. For example, ↓ 4 after the date means to press Enter four times before typing the recipient's name.

Ms. Ella Shore, Professor
Department of Journalism
Burlington College
North Canyon Drive
South Burlington, VT 05403 ↓ 2

Dear Ms. Shore: ↓ 2

Subject: Newspaper Advertising

Thank you for thinking of Ben & Jerry's when you were planning the advertising for the back-to-school edition of your campus newspaper at Burlington College. We appreciate the wide acceptance your students and faculty give our products, and we are proud to be represented in the *Mountain Lark*. We are happy to purchase a quarter-page ad, as follows.

- The ad should include our standard logo and the words "Welcome to Ben & Jerry's." Please note the use of the ampersand instead of the word "and" in our name. Note also that "Jerry's" contains an apostrophe.

- We would prefer that our ad appear in the top right corner of a right-facing page, if possible.

Our logo is enclosed for you to duplicate. I am also enclosing a check for $375 to cover the cost of the ad. Best wishes as you publish this special edition of your newspaper. ↓ 2

Sincerely, ↓ 4

Joseph W. Dye

Joseph W. Dye
Sales Manager ↓ 2

rmt
Enclosures
c: Advertising Supervisor

> **Reference initials:** initials of the person who typed the letter (if other than the signer)
> **Notations:** indications of items being enclosed with the letter, copies of the letter being sent to another person, special-delivery instructions, and the like

30 Community Drive/S. Burlington, VT 05403 tel: 802/846-1500 online: www.benjerry.com

28c Technical requirements of a business letter

Paper and page numbering   Use 8½" × 11" white unlined paper. If your letter is longer than one page, number the pages beginning with page 2 in the top right margin.

Spacing   Type single-spaced, on one side of the page only, and double-space between paragraphs. Quadruple-space below the date. Double-space below the inside address and the salutation. Double-space between the last line of the letter and the closing. Quadruple-space between the closing and the typed name of the writer, and then double-space to *Enclosure* (or *Enc.*) or *c:* (indicating that you are enclosing materials or are sending a copy to another person). See also page 338.

Left and right margins   The sample letter on letterhead in 28b uses a block format: the date, inside address, salutation, paragraphs, closing, and signature begin at the left margin. The right margin should not be justified; it should be ragged (with lines of unequal length) to avoid awkward gaps in the spacing between words. A modified block format places the date, closing, and signature on the right.

Return address   If you are not using business letterhead, give your address as the return address, followed by the date. Do not include your name with the address. (If you are using business letterhead on which an address is printed, you do not have to write a return address.)

Inside address   The inside address gives the name, title, and complete address of the person you are writing to. With a word processing program and certain printers, you can use this part of the letter for addressing the envelope.

Salutation   In the salutation, mention the recipient's name if you know it, with the appropriate title (*Dr., Professor, Mr., Ms.*) or just the recipient's title (*Dear Sales Manager*). If you are writing to a company or institution, use a more general term of address (*Dear Sir or Madam*) or the name of the company or institution (*Dear British Airways*). Use a colon after the salutation in a business letter.

Closing phrase and signature   Capitalize only the first word of a closing phrase, such as *Yours truly* or *Sincerely yours*. Type your name four lines below the closing phrase (omitting *Mr.* or *Ms.*). If you have a title (*Supervisor, Manager*), type it underneath your name. Between the closing phrase and your typed name, sign your name in ink.

Other information Indicate whether you have enclosed materials with the letter (*Enclosure* or *Enc.*) and to whom you have sent copies (*cc: Ms. Amy Ray*). The abbreviation *cc:* previously referred to "carbon copy" but now refers to "courtesy copy" or "computer copy." You may, however, use a single *c:* followed by a name or names to indicate who besides your addressee is receiving the letter.

The envelope Choose an envelope that fits your letter folded from bottom to top in thirds. Use your computer's addressing capability to place the name, title, and full address of the recipient in the middle of the envelope and your own name and address in the top left corner. Remember to include ZIP codes. Word processing programs include a function (Tools) that allows you to create labels for envelopes. (In Word 2007 for PC, these functions appear on the "Mailings" tab.)

28d Basic features of a memo

A memo (from the Latin *memorandum,* meaning "to be remembered") is a message from one person to someone else within an organization. It can be sent on paper or by e-mail. A memo usually reports briefly on an action, raises a question, or asks permission to follow a course of action. It addresses a specific question or issue in a quick, focused way, conveying information in clear paragraphs or numbered points.

Begin what will be a hard-copy memo with headings such as *To, From, Date,* and *Subject*; such headings are frequently capitalized and in boldface type. If you will be sending a memo via e-mail, be sure to fill in the "Subject" field. For both formats, tell readers what your point is in the first sentence. Then briefly explain and give reasons or details. Single-space the memo. If the body of your memo is long, divide it into short paragraphs, or include numbered or bulleted lists and headings (see 21e and 21f) to organize and draw attention to essential points. Most computer programs provide a standard template for memo format. The design and headings are provided; you just fill in what you want to say. Keep in mind that the features of a memo pertaining to considerations such as tone and correctness are essentially the same as for a business letter (28a).

29

Oral and Multimedia Presentations

You may be asked to give oral presentations in writing courses, in other college courses, and in the work world. Usually, you will do some writing as you prepare your talk, and you will deliver your oral report either from notes or from a manuscript text written especially for oral presentation.

29a Preparing an oral presentation

Consider the background and expectations of your audience. Jot down what you know about your listeners and what stance and tone will best convince them of the validity of your views. For example, what effect do you want to have on the members of your audience? Do you want to inform, persuade, move, or entertain them? What do you know about your listeners' age, gender, background, education, occupation, political affiliation, beliefs, and knowledge of your subject? What do listeners need to know? In a college class, your audience will be your classmates and instructor. You can often help build a sense of community with your audience by asking questions and using the inclusive pronoun *we*.

Making an effective oral presentation is largely a matter of having control over your material, deciding what you want to say, and knowing your subject matter well. Preparation and planning are essential.

KEY POINTS

Tips for Preparing an Oral Presentation

1. **Select a topic you are committed to, and decide on a clear focus.** If you are assigned a topic, concentrate on its main points.

2. **Prepare a strong introduction.** Quickly capturing your audience's attention will increase your confidence and help to ensure that your entire talk gets heard.

3. **Make a few strong points.** Back up your ideas with specific details. Have a few points that you can expand on and develop with interesting examples, quotations, and stories.

4. **Provide listening cues.** Include signposts and signal phrases to help your audience follow your ideas (*first, next, finally; the most important point is . . .*).

(Continued)

(Continued)

5. **Structure your talk clearly.** Present the organizational framework of your talk along with illustrative materials in handouts, overhead transparencies, PowerPoint slides (29e), posters, charts, or other visuals (22a and 22b).

6. **Use short sentences, accessible words, memorable phrases, and natural language.** In writing, you can use long sentences with one clause embedded in another, but these are difficult for listeners to follow.

7. **Use repetition.** An audience listening, rather than reading, will appreciate being reminded of the structure of the talk and of points you referred to previously.

8. **Follow the guidelines.** To be effective, you will want to meet the requirements set for the presentation in terms of time available for preparation, length of presentation, and possible questions from the audience.

9. **Prepare a strong ending.** To ensure that you have an impact on the audience, deliver a strong conclusion. Do not simply stop or trail off.

29b Speaking from notes or manuscript

Speaking from notes Speaking from notes allows you to be more spontaneous and to look your audience in the eye. Think of your presentation as a conversation. For this method, notes or a key-word outline must be clear and organized so that you feel secure about which points you will discuss and in what order. Here are a speaker's notes for a presentation on paternity leave.

PATERNITY LEAVE
1. Children's needs
   Benefits
   Bonding
2. Issue of equity
   Equal treatment for men and women
   Cost

Your notes or outline should make reference to specific illustrations and quotations and contain structural signals so that the audience knows when you begin to address a new point (as in Key Points box, page 339, item 4). You can also use either slides prepared with your word processor or PowerPoint slides to guide the direction and structure of your presentation (29e). For a short presentation on a topic that you know very well, use notes with or without the visual aid of slides. Do not read aloud the text on your slides though, especially in front of a small audience.

Speaking from a manuscript Writing out a complete speech may be necessary for a long formal presentation. Still, even if you do this, you should practice and prepare so that you do not have to labor over every word. Remember, too, to build in places to pause and make spontaneous comments. The advantages of speaking from a prepared manuscript are that you can time the presentation exactly and that you will never dry up and wonder what to say next. The disadvantage is that you have to read the text, and reading aloud is not easy, especially if you want to maintain eye contact with your audience. If you prefer to speak from a complete manuscript text, prepare the text for oral presentation as follows:

- Triple-space your text and use a large font.
- When you reach the bottom of a page, begin a new sentence on the next page. Do not start a sentence on one page and finish it on the next.
- Highlight key words in each paragraph so that you will be able to spot them easily.
- Underline words and phrases that you want to stress.
- Use slash marks (/ or //) to remind yourself to pause. Read in "sense groups" (parts of a sentence that are read as a unit—a phrase or clause, for example—often indicated by a pause when spoken and by punctuation when written). Mark your text at the end of a sense group.
- Number your pages so that you can keep them in the proper sequence.

29c Practicing and presenting

Whether you speak from notes or from a manuscript, practice is essential.

- **Practice not just once, but many times.** Try tape-recording yourself, listening to the tape, and asking a friend for comments.
- **Speak at a normal speed and at a good volume.** Speaking too quickly and too softly is a common mistake.

- **Imagine a full audience.** Use gestures, and practice looking up to make eye contact with people in the audience. Practice in front of a mirror and critique yourself, or practice in front of a friend and ask for feedback.

- **Beware of filler words and phrases.** Avoid terms such as *OK, well, you know,* and *like.* The verbal tics, when repeated during a presentation, annoy and distract the audience.

- **Do not punctuate pauses with "er" or "uhm."** These verbalized pauses may undermine your confidence, and they will almost certainly annoy and distract your audience.

It is natural to feel some anxiety before the actual presentation, but most people find that their jitters disappear as soon as they begin talking, especially when they are well prepared.

Look frequently at your listeners. Work the room so that you gaze directly at people in all sections of the audience. In *Secrets of Successful Speakers,* Lilly Walters points out that when you look at one person, all the people in a V behind that person will think you are looking at them. Bear in mind that no matter how well prepared a report is, listeners will not respond well if the presenter reads it too rapidly or in a monotone or without looking up and engaging the audience. If your topic is lighthearted, remember to smile.

29d Preparing a multimedia presentation*

Today, presenters are not limited to using handouts of visuals printed on a page. Thanks to computer technology, they can use digital slides to present a combination of words, drawings, photographs, animation, film, video, and audio to make a point. In fact, today's visually oriented audiences are accustomed to encountering some visual element as part of a presentation, whether it is a flipchart, overhead transparency, photographic or digital slides, film, videotape, actual model, or leave-behind audience handouts. Visual aids can be simple to create and help audiences understand the presentation, especially if they include complex or statistical data. In a review of Al Gore's *An Inconvenient Truth,* film critic A. O. Scott writes, "I can't think of another movie in which the display of a graph elicited gasps of horror, but when the red lines showing the increasing rates of carbon-dioxide emissions and the corresponding rise in temperatures come on screen, the effect is jolting and chilling."

---

*This section has been adapted from Scot Ober's *Contemporary Business Communication,* 7th edition (Boston: Houghton, 2009). Used with permission.

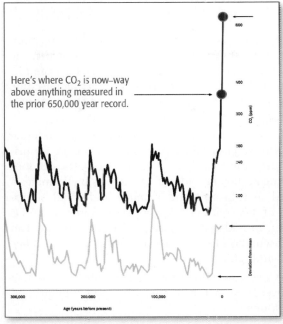

And within 45 years, this is where the CO_2 levels will be if we do not make dramatic changes quickly.

Here's where CO_2 is now–way above anything measured in the prior 650,000 year record.

Current global temperatures

Last ice age

Line graph from Al Gore, *An Inconvenient Truth: The Planetary Emergency of Global Warming and What We Can Do about It* (Emmaus, PA: Rodale, 2006), 66–67. By arrangement with Rodale, Inc.

KEY POINTS
Common Types of Multimedia Aids

- **Electronic presentations** consist of digital slides or video (or both) run directly from a computer and shown on a screen via a digital projector. On the one hand, because the slides come directly from the computer and do not have to be made, they are easy to prepare and easy to update. On the other hand, you are limited by your equipment and the facility where you will be presenting.

- **Transparencies** are easy to use with an overhead projector. You do not need to darken the room and you can face the audience while you speak. They are easy to prepare and easy to update. Thanks to presentation software such as PowerPoint, overhead transparencies easily take advantage of color, designed fonts, charts, artwork, and templates (see 29e).

(Continued)

(Continued)

- **Slides** provide high-quality visuals for a presentation. Non-digital photographic slides are particularly effective when the focus of your presentation is specifically visual—for example, when you want to show reproductions of fine art or architecture. However, they do not provide the flexibility of an electronic presentation and can be relatively expensive to produce.

- **Video clips, audio clips, and DVDs** require a moderate amount of production but can be particularly effective for orientations and training purposes. Presentation software does make integrating audio and video quite easy, as it eliminates a speaker's need to transport and manage additional equipment. Because of their relatively low reproduction cost, DVDs are increasingly provided to audience members so they can review the presentation long after it is over. They are, today, the ultimate "handout."

- **Flipcharts** are best used in informal presentations with a smaller audience. They are easy to prepare, easy to update, and require no equipment.

- **Handouts** can provide the audience with printed copies of notes, tables, or illustrations from your presentation. They can also provide the audience with a permanent record of the presentation's major points. Not only do they help your audience follow your presentation, but they can also provide a review and new information for the audience after the presentation is over.

Including multimedia in oral presentations   When you prepare an oral presentation, think about what multimedia would be appropriate and effective for your purpose, your audience, the length of your presentation, and the media you have available. The goal of your presentation is to effectively communicate to your audience. You want them to leave thinking about *what* you said and not *how* you said it. Use multimedia aids only when they will help your audience grasp an important point and remove them when they are not legitimately needed.

Using multimedia equipment smoothly does not come naturally, so be sure to practice your presentation. And because bulbs can burn out, cords can be forgotten, and computers can crash, always be prepared to give your presentation without visuals if necessary.

TECH NOTE

Multimedia Presentation Design

An excellent online resource that covers a wide range of issues for designers of multimedia presentations is Garr Reynolds's *Presentation Zen* site <http://www.presentationzen.com/>. For examples of compelling multimedia presentations, check out *TED*: "Riveting talks by remarkable people, free to the world" <http://www.ted.com/>.

In preparing a live or online multimedia presentation, consider the effectiveness of positioning images near your words and of conveying emotion and meaning through pictures. Imagine, for instance, how you might present an argument against genetic engineering of food crops to classmates or colleagues. In addition to your well-formed argument, you could show graphs of public opinion data on the issue, pictures of chemicals that are used on crops and how they are applied, and a video clip of interviews with shoppers as they read labels and buy produce. If you use media imaginatively, you can do what writing teachers have long advised for printed essays: Show; don't tell.

29e Using PowerPoint

Using presentation software like PowerPoint gives you access to organizing and design tools. It also allows you to seamlessly integrate audio and visual components to produce a dynamic multimedia presentation.

PowerPoint as an organization tool   PowerPoint allows you to prepare slides that illustrate the logic of your presentation and helps you separate the main points from the supporting details. That way, the slides keep you focused as you give your presentation. Your audience follows your ideas not only because you have established a clear principle of organization but also because the slide on the presentation screen reminds people of where you are in your talk, what point you are addressing, and how that point fits into your total scheme.

PowerPoint slides as visual evidence and support   Many speakers incorporate PowerPoint slides in their presentations as evidence, support, and even as counterpoints to their presentations. Slides containing well-timed quotes, visual images, graphs, and charts can have the same rhetorical effect as well-placed visuals in an argument essay (4i). If you decide to include sound, music, and video clips to illustrate and drive home the points you want to make, be careful not to overdo these effects. PowerPoint features can easily become distracting bells and whistles, and your audience may suspect you have used them to make up for lack of content. They should enhance your work, not dominate it.

Creating PowerPoint slides*   When you create slides, keep in mind the following:

KEY POINTS
Tips for Creating PowerPoint Slides

Using PowerPoint as an Outline	• Make your first or second slide an outline of your presentation. • Follow the order of your outline for the rest of the presentation. • Place only main points on the outline slide.

Slide Structure	• Write in point form, not complete sentences.
	• Include 4–5 points per slide.
	• Consider the 6 × 6 rule:
	  ○ No more than six words across
	  ○ No more than six lines down
	• Avoid wordiness: use key words and phrases only.

Slide Timing	Use one or two slides per minute of your presentation and show one point at a time to • help your audience concentrate on what you are saying • prevent your audience from reading ahead • help you keep your presentation focused

*Adapted from *Making PowerPoint Slides: Avoiding the Pitfalls of Bad Slides* at: <http://www.iasted.org/conferences/formatting/Presentations-Tips.ppt>.

Animation	• Do not use distracting animation.
	• Do not go overboard with the animation.
	• Be consistent with the animation that you use.
Fonts	• Use at least an 18-point font.
	• Use different size fonts for main points and secondary points.
	• Use a standard font like Times New Roman or Arial.
Color	• Use a color of font that contrasts sharply with the background. For example, use a blue font on a white background.
	• Use color to reinforce the logic of your structure. For example, use a dark blue text under a light blue title.
	• Use color to emphasize a point (but only do so occasionally).
Background	• Use backgrounds such as this one that are attractive but simple.
	• Use backgrounds that are light.
	• Use the same background consistently throughout your presentation.
Graphs	• Use graphs rather than just charts and words because
	◦ data in graphs are easier to comprehend and retain than are raw data
	◦ trends are easier to visualize in graph form
	• Always title your graphs.

(Continued)

(Continued)

Spelling and Grammar

- Proof your slides for
  - spelling mistakes
  - the use of repeated words
  - grammatical errors
- If English is not your first language, have someone else check your presentation.

PART 6

Style: The Five C's

30 The First C: Cut   352

31 The Second C: Check for Action   354

32 The Third C: Connect   356

33 The Fourth C: Commit   361

34 The Fifth C: Choose the Best Words   367

35 Revising for Style: A Student's Drafts   378

36 Style Tips   380

 ONLINE RESOURCES
www.cengage.com/english/raimes

Companion online resources are available for sections throughout this part. We invite you to visit the book's Web site for more information and direct access.

PART 6

Style: The Five C's

30 The First C: Cut 352

30a Repetition and wordiness 352
30b Formulaic phrases 353
30c References to your intentions 353
30d Redundancy 353

31 The Second C: Check for Action 354

31a Who's doing what? 354
31b Sentences beginning with *there* or *it* 355
31c Unnecessary passive voice 355

32 The Third C: Connect 356

32a Consistent subjects and topic chains 356
32b Logical connections: Coordination, subordination, and transitions 357
32c Beginning a sentence with *and* or *but* 359
32d Paragraph connections 360

33 The Fourth C: Commit 361

33a Personal presence 361
33b Appropriate and consistent tone 361
33c Confident stance 362
33d Sentence variety 363

34 The Fifth C: Choose the Best Words 367

34a Word choice checklist 367
34b Dictionary and thesaurus 368
34c Exact words and connotations 369
34d Language of speech, region, and workplace 370
34e Figurative language 372
34f Avoiding sexist, biased, and exclusionary language 374
34g Avoiding clichés and pretentious language 376

35 Revising for Style: A Student's Drafts 378

36 Style Tips 380

Readers sometimes suffer from what has been called the MEGO—"My Eyes Glaze Over"—reaction to a piece of writing even when ideas are well organized and there are no grammatical errors. This happens when readers are turned off by a style that obscures meaning—a style characterized by wordiness, flatness, inappropriate word choice, clichés, or sentences constructed without interesting variations. Do your readers a favor. When you read your own draft prior to revision, use the convenient mnemonic of the five C's to remind you what to consider for revision: Cut, Check for Action, Connect, Commit, and Choose the Best Words. Keep clarity and directness in mind as the basics of academic writing. Of course, graceful and elegant writing may ultimately be your aim, but grace and elegance always need an underlay of clarity.

Try this quick test: Read your draft aloud. If you have to pause anywhere to make sense of what you have written (watch out for a stumble, a pause, discomfort, or the occasions when "huh?" flashes through your mind), use the five C's to revise for style and to get rid of the glitch.

LANGUAGE AND CULTURE

Style across Cultures

It is impossible to identify one style as the best. What is considered good (or appropriate) style varies according to the writer's purpose and the expectations of the anticipated readers. Country, culture, region, ethnic heritage, language, gender, class can all play a role in influencing what readers define as *style*. What may please readers in one language and culture in one setting in one part of the world may seem too flat or too adorned in another. Good style is relative and culture-bound. The Japanese novelist Junichuro Tanizaki, for example, gives writers this advice: "Do not try to be too clear: leave some gaps in the meaning." Western cultures, on the other hand, tend to value clarity.

With acknowledgment to Joseph Williams's *Style: Lessons in Clarity and Grace*, 9th edition, chapters 30 to 34 examine five anti-MEGO strategies, called here the "five C's of style": cut, check for action, connect, commit, and choose the best words. Chapters 35 and 36 provide a sample of a passage revised for style and some handy tips for writers.

30 ⚷

The First C: Cut

When you write, do not underdevelop your ideas because you fear taxing readers' patience. Work on developing ideas and presenting material that has substance, persuasive detail, explanation, and original expression, and make sure you don't pad your work to fill an assigned number of pages. However, once you have a draft that has ideas and content you are happy with, scrutinize it for obvious redundancies, fumbling phrases, weak expressions, and obscurities that can easily creep into a first draft.

30a Cut repetition and wordiness

Say something only once and in the best place.

▶ The Lilly Library ~~contains many rare books.~~

~~The books in the library are~~ carefully preserved,ˢ

~~The library also houses a manuscript collection.~~ many rare books and manuscripts.

▶ Steven Spielberg, ~~who has directed~~ director of the movie ~~that has been~~ described as the best war movie ever made, ~~is someone who~~ knows many politicians.

▶ In 1998, California residents voted to abolish bilingual education, ~~The main reason for their voting to abolish bilingual education was that~~ because many children were being

placed indiscriminately into programs and kept there too long.

If your draft says something like "As the first paragraph states" or "As previously stated," beware. Such phrases indicate that you have repeated yourself.

30b Cut formulaic phrases

Replace wordy phrases with shorter and more direct expressions.

Formulaic	Concise
at the present time	now
at this point in time	
in this day and age	
in today's society	
because of the fact that	because
due to the fact that	
are of the opinion that	believe
have the ability to	can
in spite of the fact that	although, despite
last but not least	finally
prior to	before
concerning the matter of	about

Be watchful for the phrase "the fact that." Edit when you can.

▶ **Few people realize ~~the fact~~ that the computer controlling the**
   ***Eagle* lunar module in 1969 had less memory than a cheap**
   wristwatch does today.

30c Cut references to your intentions

Eliminate references to the organization of your text and your own
planning, such as *In this essay, I intend to prove . . .* or *In the next few
paragraphs, I hope to show . . .* or *In conclusion, I have demonstrated. . . .* In
a short essay, there's no need to announce a plan.

However, in the social or physical sciences, information is often
provided in a set order, so such signals are more appropriate and occur
more frequently: *This paper describes three approaches to treating depression.*

30d Cut redundant words and phrases

Trim words that simply repeat an idea expressed by another word in
the same phrase: *basic* essentials, *true* facts, circle *around*, cooperate

together, *final* completion, return *again*, refer *back*, *advance* planning, consensus *of opinion*, *completely* unanimous, *free* gift. Also edit redundant pairs: *various and sundry, hopes and desires, each and every.*

▶ The task took ~~diligence and~~ perseverance.

       has
▶ His surgeon ~~is a doctor with~~ a great deal of clinical experience.
                ^

  Ninety-seven
▶ ~~A total of 97~~ students completed the survey.
      ^

31 🔑

The Second C: Check for Action

Vigorous sentences show clearly who or what is doing the action. Use vivid, expressive verbs when you can. Do not overuse the verb *be* (*be, am, is, are, was, were, being, been*) or verbs in the passive voice.

31a Show "Who's doing what" as subject and verb

In the following sentence, the subject (*approval*) and verb (*was*) tell readers very little:

WORDY   **The mayor's approval of the new law was due to voters' suspicion of the concealment of campaign funds by his deputy.**

The subject and verb of this dull thud of a sentence tell us that "the . . . approval . . . was"—not a very powerful statement! Ask "Who's doing what?" and you come up with a tougher, leaner sentence.

Who's Doing What?

Subject	Verb
the mayor	approved
the voters	suspected
his deputy	had concealed

REVISED   **The mayor approved the new law because voters suspected that his deputy had concealed campaign funds.**

The revision is shorter and more direct; it gets rid of three nouns formed from verbs (*approval, suspicion,* and *concealment*) as well as five phrases using prepositions (words used before nouns and pronouns): *of, to, of, of, by.*

31b Scrutinize sentences beginning with *there* or *it*

For a lean, direct style, rewrite sentences in which *there* or *it* occupies the subject position (as in *there is, there were, it is, it was*). Revise by using verbs that describe an action and subjects that perform the action.

WORDY	**There was a discussion of the health care system by the politicians.** [Who's doing what here?]
REVISED	**The politicians discussed the health care system.**

WORDY	**There is a big gate guarding the entrance to the park.**
REVISED	**A big gate guards the entrance to the park.**

WORDY	**It is a fact that Arnold is proudly displaying a new tattoo.**
REVISED	**Arnold is proudly displaying a new tattoo.**

TECH NOTE

Searching for *There* and *It*

Use the Find function of your computer to find all instances in your draft of *it is, there is,* and *there are* in the initial position in a clause. If you find a filler subject with little purpose, revise.

31c Avoid unnecessary passive voice constructions

The *passive voice* tells what is done to someone or something: "The turkey *was cooked* too long." Extensive use of the passive voice can make your style seem pedantic and wordy, especially if you use a "by . . ." phrase to tell about who is doing the action.

PASSIVE	**The problem will be discussed thoroughly by the committee.**
ACTIVE	**The committee will discuss the problem thoroughly.**

Note: The passive voice occurs frequently in scientific writing because readers are primarily interested in data, procedures, and results, not in who developed or produced them. In a scientific report, you are likely to read, for example, *The rats were fed,* not *The researchers fed the rats.* For other acceptable uses of the passive voice, see section 32a and chapter 42.

32 ⚷

The Third C: Connect

When you read your draft, pay attention to a smooth flow, with clear connections between sentences and paragraphs. Avoid a series of grasshopper-like jumps.

32a Connect with consistent subjects and topic chains

Readers need a way to connect the ideas beginning a sentence with what has gone before. So when you move from one sentence to the next, avoid jarring shifts of subjects by maintaining a topic chain of consistent subjects, as in the revised example that follows.

SHIFT OF SUBJECT	*Memoirs* **are becoming increasingly popular.** *Readers* **all over North America are finding them appealing.**
REVISED	*Memoirs* **are becoming increasingly popular.** *They* **appeal to readers all over North America.**

In the revised version, the subject of the second sentence, *they*, refers to the subject of the previous sentence, *memoirs*; the new information about "readers all over North America" comes at the end, where it receives more emphasis.

Examine your writing for awkward topic switches. Note that preserving a connected topic chain may mean using the passive voice, as in the last sentence of the revision that follows (see also 42d).

FREQUENT TOPIC SWITCHES	*I* **have lived all my life in Brooklyn, New York.** *Park Slope* **is a neighborhood that has many different ethnic cultures.** *Harmony* **exists among the people, even though it does not in many other Brooklyn neighborhoods.** *Many articles in the press* **have praised the Slope for its ethnic variety.**

REVISED
WITH TOPIC
CHAIN

Many different ethnic cultures **flourish in Park Slope, Brooklyn, where I have lived all my life.** *These different cultures* **live together harmoniously, even though they do not in many other Brooklyn neighborhoods. In fact,** *the ethnic variety* **of the Slope has often been praised in the press.**

32b Use logical connections with coordination, subordination, and transitions

When you write sentences containing two or more clauses, consider where you want to place the emphasis.

Coordination   You give two or more clauses equal emphasis when you connect them with one of the following coordinating conjunctions: *and, but, or, nor, so, for,* or *yet.* (For more on coordination, see 32c, 37d, and 47b.)

⎡——independent clause——⎤ ⎡——independent clause——⎤
▶ **The waves were enormous, but the surfers approached them**

⎡——————⎤
with glee.

Subordination   When you use subordinating conjunctions such as *when, if,* or *because* to connect clauses, you give one idea more importance by putting it in the independent clause (37d, p. 391, and 38c).

▶ **We cannot now end our differences. At least we can help make the world safe for diversity.** [Two sentences with equal importance]

⎡————dependent clause————⎤ ⎡—independent clause—⎤
▶ **If we cannot now end our differences, at least we can help**

⎡————————————⎤
make the world safe for diversity.

—John F. Kennedy

[Two clauses connected by *if;* emphasis on the independent clause at the end of the sentence]

Transitional expressions   Use words such as *however, therefore,* and *nevertheless* (known as *conjunctive adverbs*) and phrases such as *in addition, as a result,* and *on the other hand* to signal the logical connection between independent clauses (for a list of transitional expressions, see 2c). A transitional expression can move around in its own clause—yet another stylistic option for you to consider.

▶ He made a lot of money; *however*, his humble roots were always evident.

▶ He made a lot of money; his humble roots, *however*, were always evident.

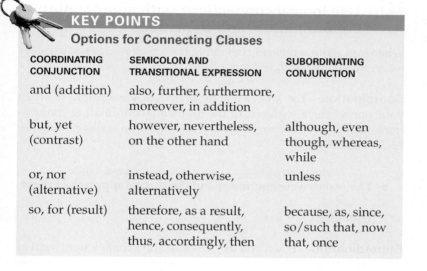

KEY POINTS
Options for Connecting Clauses

COORDINATING CONJUNCTION	SEMICOLON AND TRANSITIONAL EXPRESSION	SUBORDINATING CONJUNCTION
and (addition)	also, further, furthermore, moreover, in addition	
but, yet (contrast)	however, nevertheless, on the other hand	although, even though, whereas, while
or, nor (alternative)	instead, otherwise, alternatively	unless
so, for (result)	therefore, as a result, hence, consequently, thus, accordingly, then	because, as, since, so/such that, now that, once

Know your options   To avoid a series of short, choppy sentences, consider the logical connection between ideas. Frequently, you will have several alternatives: a transition, a coordinator (*and, but, or, nor, so, for,* or *yet*), or a subordinator (a word such as *because, if, although, while, who,* or *which* used to introduce a dependent clause), as in the following examples. Note the punctuation in each.

▶ The flight was long and cramped. The varied entertainment program took our minds off our numb legs.

TRANSITION   The flight was long and cramped; *however*, the varied entertainment program took our minds off our numb legs.

The flight was long and cramped; the varied entertainment program, *however*, took our minds off our numb legs.

COORDINATION   The flight was long and cramped, *but* the varied entertainment program took our minds off our numb legs.

SUBORDINATION   *Although* the flight was long and cramped, the varied entertainment program took our minds off our numb legs.

Avoid excessive coordination or subordination   Too much of any one stylistic feature will become tedious to readers.

EXCESSIVE COORDINATION WITH *AND*   I grew up in a large family, and we lived on a small farm, and every day I had to get up early and do farm work, and I would spend a lot of time cleaning out the stables, and then I would be exhausted in the evening, and I never had the energy to read.

REVISED   Because I grew up in a large family on a small farm, every day I had to get up early to do farm work, mostly cleaning out the stables. I would be so exhausted in the evening that I never had the energy to read.

EXCESSIVE SUBORDINATION   Because the report was weak and poorly written, our boss, who wanted to impress the company president by showing her how efficient his division was, to gain prestige in the company, decided, despite the fact that work projects were piling up, that he would rewrite the report over the weekend.

REVISED   Because the report was weak and poorly written, our boss decided to rewrite it over the weekend, even though work projects were piling up. He wanted to impress the company president by showing her how efficient his division was; that was his way of gaining prestige.

32c Perhaps begin a sentence with *and* or *but*

People who consider *and* and *but* conjunctions that join two or more independent clauses within a sentence may frown when they see these words starting a sentence. Nevertheless, examples of this usage can be found in literature from the tenth century onward. As with any other stylistic device, it is not wise to begin a sentence with *and* or *but* too often. And, given the difference of opinion on this usage, check with your instructor, too.

Sentences Beginning with *And* or *But*

Occasionally, writers choose to start a sentence with *and* or *but*, either for stylistic effect of emphasis or contrast or to make a close connection to the previous sentence:

▶ **You can have wealth concentrated in the hands of a few, or democracy. But you cannot have both.**

—Justice Louis Brandeis

The usage is found often in journalism. Note, though, that the culture of academia is more conservative, and some readers may raise an eyebrow when they see *and* or *but* starting a sentence in an academic paper, especially if it happens often.

32d Connect paragraphs

Just as readers appreciate a smooth flow of information from sentence to sentence, they also look for transitions—word bridges—to move them from paragraph to paragraph. A new paragraph signals a shift in topic, but careful readers will look for transitional words and phrases that tell them *how* a new paragraph relates to the paragraph that precedes it. Provide your readers with steppingstones; don't ask them to leap over chasms.

KEY POINTS
A Checklist for Connecting Paragraphs

☐ **Read your draft aloud.** When you finish a paragraph, make a note of the point you made in the paragraph. Then, check your notes for the flow of ideas and logic.

☐ **Refer to the main idea of the previous paragraph as you begin a new paragraph.** After a paragraph on retirement, the next paragraph could begin like this, moving from the idea of retirement to saving: *Retirement is not the only reason for saving. Saving also provides a nest egg for the unexpected and the pleasurable.*

☐ **Use adjectives like *this* and *these* to provide a link.** After a paragraph discussing urban planning proposals, the next paragraph might begin like this: *These proposals will help. However, . . .*

☐ **Use transition words.** Words and phrases such as *also, too, in addition, however, therefore,* and *as a result* signal the logical connection between ideas (2c).

33

The Fourth C: Commit

E. B. White tells us that William Strunk, Jr., author of *The Elements of Style,* "scorned the vague, the tame, the colorless, the irresolute. He felt it was worse to be irresolute than to be wrong." This chapter focuses on ways to be detailed, bold, colorful, and resolute.

33a Commit to a personal presence

Academic writing is certainly not the same as personal accounts of feelings, events, and opinions. But it is not writing from which you as the writer should fade from sight. The best academic writing reveals personal engagement with the topic and details of what the writer has observed and read, an unmistakable *you.* Always ask yourself: Where am I in this draft? What picture of me and my world do readers get from my writing? Do they see clearly what I base my opinions on? If you use sources, readers should be able to perceive you in conversation with your sources; they should see not just a listing of what sources say but also your responses to and comments on those sources.

Showing a personal presence does not necessarily mean always using *I* or repeatedly saying "in my opinion." It means writing so that readers see *you* in what you write and recognize that you have integrated any research findings into your views on a topic. See 1d for more on voice.

33b Commit to an appropriate and consistent tone

Readers will expect the tone of your document to fit its purpose. The tone of your piece of writing reflects your attitude toward your subject matter and is closely connected to your audience's expectations and your purpose in writing. If you were, for example, writing about a topic such as compensation for posttraumatic stress disorder suffered by soldiers who serve in Iraq or Afghanistan, anything other than a serious, respectful tone would be inappropriate.

For most academic writing, commit resolutely to an objective, serious tone. Avoid sarcasm, colloquial language, name-calling, or pedantic words and structures, even for the sake of variety. Make sure you dedicate a special reading of a draft to examining your tone; if you are reading along and a word or sentence strikes you as unexpected and out of place, flag it for later correction. In formal college essays, watch out especially for sudden switches to a chatty and conversational tone (see 34d), as in "Willy Loman surprises his family and the theater audience when his frustration makes him suddenly become *mad as all hell.*" Since tone is really an indicator of how you anticipate your readers' expectations, ask a tutor or friend to read your document and note any lapses in consistency of tone.

33c Commit to a confident stance

Your background reading, critical thinking, and drafting will help you discover and decide upon a perspective and thesis that seem correct to you (1e, 1f). Once you have made those decisions, commit to that point of view. When you are trying to persuade readers to accept your point of view, avoid the ambivalence and indecisiveness evident in words and phrases like *maybe, perhaps, it could be, it might seem*, and *it would appear.*

Hedging will not heighten readers' confidence in what you say:

▶ **Tough economic times did not stop me from bidding on eBay/but others might have had different experiences.**

Aim for language that reflects accountability and commitment: *as a result, consequently, of course, believe, need, demand, should, must.* It's important, however, to use the language of commitment only after thoroughly researching your topic and satisfying yourself that the evidence is convincing.

In addition, convey to readers an attitude of confidence in your own abilities and judgment. Make an ethical appeal to readers by stressing your evenhanded expertise (4g). Avoid apologies. One student ended a first draft this way:

| TOO APOLOGETIC | I hope I have conveyed something about our cultural differences. I would like my reader to note that this is just my view, even if a unique one. Room for errors and prejudices should be provided. The lack of a total overview, which would take more time and expertise, should also be taken into account. |

If you really have not done an adequate job of making and supporting a point, try to gather more information to improve the draft
instead of adding apologetic notes. The writer revised the ending
after reading section 2e on conclusions.

| REVISED VERSION | The stories I have told and the examples I have given come from my own experience; however, my multicultural background has emphasized that cultural differences do not have to separate people but can bring them closer together. A diverse, multicultural society holds many potential benefits for all its members. |

33d **Commit to sentence variety**

Variety in sentence length   Readers appreciate variety, so aim
for a mix of long and short sentences. If your editing program can
print out your text in a series of single numbered sentences, you will
easily be able to examine the length and structure of each. Academic
writing need not consist solely of long, heavyweight sentences—in
fact, it should not. Short sentences interspersed among longer ones
can have a dramatic effect.

This passage from a student memoir demonstrates the use of
short sentences to great effect:

> When I started high school and Afros became the rage, I immediately decided
> to get one. Now at that time, I had a head full of long, thick, kinky hair, which
> my mother had cultivated for years. When she said to me, "Cut it or perm it,"
> she never for one minute believed I would do either. I cut it. She fainted.
>
> —Denise Dejean, student

**Variety in sentence functions: Statements, questions,
commands, and exclamations**   *Declarative* sentences make statements (Poems are to be read slowly with concentration), *interrogative*

sentences ask questions (What does the author intend?), *imperative* sentences give commands (Forget about trying to understand Barthelme), and *exclamatory* sentences express surprise or some other strong emotion (The ending was a total shock!). Most of the sentences in your college writing will be declarative. However, the occasional question or command provides a sense of contact between writer and reader. Beware, though, of sprinkling an academic text with exclamations.

Variety of sentence types Vary the structure of your sentences throughout any piece of writing. Aim for a mix of simple, compound, complex, and compound-complex sentences.

A *simple sentence* contains one independent clause.

▶ **Kara raised her hand.**

A *compound sentence* contains two or more independent clauses connected with one or more coordinating conjunctions (*and, but, or, nor, so, for, yet*), with a semicolon alone, or with a semicolon and a transitional expression (2c).

   ┌─independent clause─┐   ┌────── independent clause ──────┐
▶ **She raised her hand, and the whole class was surprised.**

   ┌─independent clause─┐   ┌──independent clause──┐
▶ **She raised her hand, but nobody else responded.**

   ┌─independent clause─┐ ┌────independent clause────┐
▶ **She raised her hand; the whole class was surprised.**

   ┌─independent clause─┐   ┌──independent clause──┐
▶ **She raised her hand; as a result, the whole class was**

   ┌──────┐
surprised.

If you read these sentences aloud, you may notice the longer pause in the last two; consider how that pause may affect a reader. Consider, too, how your expectations as a reader change as you move to a comma or a semicolon.

A *complex sentence* contains an independent clause and one or more dependent clauses.

   ┌──────dependent clause──────┐ ┌────── independent clause ──────┐
▶ **When she raised her hand, the whole class was surprised.**

   ┌──────independent clause──────┐ ┌──dependent clause──┐
▶ **The whole class was surprised when she raised her hand.**

When you decide which of the two previous types to write, consider the sentences that precede and follow. Avoiding repetition or following through with a subject or topic chain (see 32a) may help determine which element should come first and which last.

A *compound-complex sentence* contains at least two independent clauses and at least one dependent clause.

┌────── dependent clause ──────┐ ┌────── independent clause ──────┐
▶ **When she raised her hand, the whole class was surprised,**

┌────── independent clause ──────┐ ┌────── dependent clause ──────┐
and the professor waited eagerly as she began to speak.

Sentences like these are common in academic writing. Just make sure that you keep track of where you are in the sentence and check the relationship between dependent and independent clauses.

In addition, be aware of *cumulative* and *periodic sentences*. Cumulative (or loose) sentences begin with the independent clause and add on to it. Periodic sentences begin with words and phrases that lead to the independent clause, giving emphasis to the end of the sentence. The cumulative sentence is the norm in English prose. Use a periodic sentence to make a specific stylistic impact.

CUMULATIVE   *The experienced hunter stood stock still for at least five minutes,* **sweat pouring from his brow, all senses alert, and waiting to hear a twig snap.**

PERIODIC   **Sweat pouring from his brow, all senses alert, and waiting to hear a twig snap,** *the experienced hunter stood stock still for at least five minutes.*

Variety of word order in a sentence   Sometimes, inverted word order of verb followed by subject (v + s) helps achieve coherence, consistent subjects, emphasis, or a smooth transition:

          V   ┌──── S ────┐
▶ **Next to the river runs a superhighway.**

    V   S   V
▶ **Never have I been so tired.**

       V ┌── S ──┐   V
▶ **Not only does the novel entertain, but it also raises our awareness of poverty.**

V   S
▶ **So eager was I to win that I set off before the starter's gun.**

V ┌—S—┐   V
▶ **Rarely has a poem achieved such a grasp on the times.**

Using an occasional rhetorical question will also help drive a point home:

V   S   ┌——V——┐
▶ **How could anyone have thought that war was the answer?**

Variety of sentence beginnings   Consider using some of these variations to begin a sentence, but remember that beginning with the subject will always be clear and direct for readers. Any of the following beginnings repeated too often will seem like a stylistic tic and may annoy readers.

Begin with a dependent or condensed clause

┌————————————dependent clause————————————┐
▶ **While my friends were waiting for the movie to begin, they ate three tubs of popcorn.**

┌————clause condensed to a phrase————┐
▶ **While waiting for the movie to begin, my friends ate three tubs of popcorn.**

Begin with a participle or an adjective   A sentence can begin with a participle or an adjective but only if the word is in a phrase that refers to the subject of the independent clause. If the phrase does not refer to the subject, the result is a *dangling modifier* error (40c).

-ing participle
▶ **Waiting for the movie to begin, my friends ate popcorn.**

past participle
▶ **Forced to work late, they ordered a pepperoni pizza.**

adjective
▶ **Aware of the problems, they nevertheless decided to continue.**

Begin with a prepositional phrase

┌─prepositional phrase─┐
▶ **With immense joy, we watched our team win the pennant.**

You can also occasionally use inverted word order after a prepositional phrase (but see 43d on agreement of subject and verb).

┌──── prepositional phrases ──┐   verb   ┌──── subject ────┐
▶ **At the end of my block stands a deserted building.**

34

The Fifth C: Choose the Best Words

Word choice, or *diction*, contributes a great deal to the effect your
writing has on your readers. Do not give readers puzzles to solve.

34a Word choice checklist

KEY POINTS

Checklist for Word Choice

☐ Underline words whose meaning or spelling you want to
check and words that you might want to replace. Then spend
some time with a dictionary and a thesaurus (34b).

☐ Look for words that might not convey exactly what you mean
(*thrifty* vs. *stingy*, for example), and look for vague words (34c).

☐ Check figurative language for appropriateness, think about
where a simile (a comparison) might help convey your meaning, and find original substitutes for any clichés (34e, 34g).

☐ Check for level of formality and for the appropriateness of any
colloquial, regional, ethnic, or specialized work terms (34d).

☐ Check for gender bias in your use of *he* and *she* and other
gender-related words (34f).

(Continued)

(Continued)

☐ Look for language that might exclude or offend (such as *normal* to mean people similar to you). Build community with your readers by eliminating disrespectful or stereotyping terms referring to race, place, age, politics, religion, abilities, or sexual orientation (34f).

34b Use a dictionary and a thesaurus

Dictionary   The dictionary built into your word processing program informs you about spelling, pronunciation, and definitions. Sometimes, though, you need more than that. Don't forget about the comprehensive dictionaries such as the *Oxford English Dictionary* (OED), available online in many libraries or in print form. In the OED, you can explore the historical development of the meaning and usage of a word (its etymology), find synonyms and antonyms (words of similar and opposite meaning), and learn about grammatical functions and current usage. If you have no easy online access to the OED, invest in a good desk dictionary such as *The American Heritage Dictionary of the English Language*. There, people and places are included, the usage notes make fascinating reading, and the pictures provide instant access to meaning. If you can never remember the three types of columns in Greek architecture (an affliction suffered by the author of this book), you do not have to rely on the written definitions: Each definition (Doric, Ionic, and Corinthian) is accompanied by a color illustration.

Use a dictionary to learn or confirm the *denotation*—the basic meaning—of a word. Some words that appear similar are not interchangeable. For example, *respectable* has a meaning very different from *respectful; emigrant* and *immigrant* have different meanings; and so do *defuse* and *diffuse, uninterested* and *disinterested*, and *principal* and *principle*.

Thesaurus   A thesaurus is useful when you want to find alternatives to words that you know. Exercise caution, however, to make sure that the word you choose fits your context. Suppose you use the word *privacy* a few times and want an alternative in the sentence

"She values the privacy of her own home." You could consult a thesaurus but might find words such as *aloofness, seclusion,* and *isolation* listed. The word *aloofness* would not work as a replacement for *privacy* in the example sentence, and the others do not capture the idea of *privacy*. You might, in the end, want to use two words to convey your meaning: *She values the* safety *and* seclusion *of her own home*, or you might stick with *privacy*.

Thesaurus programs built into word processing programs typically offer lists of synonyms but little guidance on *connotation*—the meaning associated with a word beyond its literal definition. Using a thesaurus alone is not enough. Always check a word in a dictionary that provides examples of usage.

34c Use exact words and connotations

When you write, use words that convey exactly the meaning you intend. Two words that have similar dictionary definitions (*denotation*) can also have additional positive or negative implications and emotional overtones (*connotation*). Readers will not get the impression you intend if you describe a person as *lazy* when the more positive *relaxed* is what you have in mind.

Select words with appropriate connotations. Hurricanes *devastate* neighborhoods; construction workers *demolish* buildings. Writing "Construction workers devastated the building" would be inappropriate. Note how the connotations of words can affect meaning:

VERSION 1   **The crowd consisted of young couples holding their children's hands, students in well-worn clothes, and activist politicians, all voicing support of their cause.**

VERSION 2   **The mob consisted of hard-faced workers dragging children by the hand, students in leather jackets and ragged jeans, and militant politicians, all howling about their cause.**

Some words do little more than fill space because they are so vague. The following oh-so-general words signal the need for revision: *area, aspect, certain, circumstance, factor, kind, manner, nature, seem, situation, thing.*

VAGUE **Our perceptions of women's roles differ as we enter new *areas*. The girl in Kincaid's story did many *things* that are commonly seen as women's work.**

REVISED **Our perceptions of women's roles differ as we learn more from what we *see, hear, read, and experience*. The girl in Kincaid's story did many *household chores* that are commonly seen as women's work. She washed the clothes, cooked, swept the floor, and set the table.**

Some words are abstract and general; other words are concrete and specific. Notice the increasing concreteness and specificity in this list: *tool, cutting instrument, knife, penknife. Tool* is a general term; *penknife* is more specific. If you do not move away from the general and abstract, you will give readers too much imaginative leeway. "Her grandmother was shocked by the clothing she bought" leaves a great deal to readers' imaginations. What kind of clothing do you mean: a low-necked dress, high-heeled platform shoes, and black fishnet stockings or a conservative navy blue wool suit? Choose words that convey exact images and precise information.

34d Monitor the language of speech, region, and workplace

The language of speech   In a formal college essay, avoid colloquial language and slang unless you are quoting someone's words. Use the level of diction appropriate for the academic world, not for the world of hip-hop, Facebook, or IM. Don't enclose a slang expression in quotation marks to signal to readers that you know it is inappropriate. Instead, revise to reach an appropriate level of formality.

▶ The working conditions were "~~gross~~." *disgusting*

▶ The jury returned the verdict that the ~~guy~~ was guilty. *defendant*

▶ Nutrition plays a large part in whether people ~~hang on to~~ *retain* their own teeth as they age.

► The music at the party was ~~dope~~.
excellent

► The reception was boring, so the journalists decided to ~~bounce~~.
leave

In formal writing, avoid colloquial words and expressions, such as *folks, guy, OK, okay, pretty good, hassle, kind of interesting/nice, a ways away, no-brainer*.

Note that the synonyms of the italicized words listed next convey different eras, attitudes, and degrees of formality:

child: kid, offspring, progeny

friend: dog, peeps, buddy, mate, brother/sister, comrade

jail: slammer, cooler, prison, correctional institution

angry: pissed off, ticked off, furious, mad, fuming, wrathful

computer expert: geek, hacker, techie, programmer

threatening: spooky, scary, eerie, menacing

fine: rad, phat, dope, fly, cool, first-rate, excellent

Some of these words—*kid, slammer, ticked off, geek, spooky, rad*—are so informal that they would rarely if ever be appropriate in formal academic writing or business letters, though they would raise no eyebrows in most journalism, advertising, or e-mail. Overuse of formal words—*progeny, comrade, wrathful*—on the other hand, could produce a tone that suggests a stuffy, pedantic attitude (see 34g).

For more on levels of diction and Standard English, see 37c.

Regional and ethnic language Use regional and ethnic dialects in your writing only when you are quoting someone directly (*"Your car needs fixed,"* the mechanic grunted.) or you know that readers will understand why you are using a nonstandard phrase.

► I bought ~~me~~ a backpack.
myself

► He vowed that he wouldn't pay them ~~no never mind~~.
any attention.

► They're here three years already.
have been

► She used to ~~could~~ run two miles, but now she's out of shape.
be able to

LANGUAGE AND CULTURE
Dialect and Dialogue in Formal Writing

Note how Paule Marshall uses Standard English for the narrative thread of her story while reproducing the father's Barbadian dialect and idioms in the dialogue, thus combining the formal and the informal, the academic and the personal into a rich whole:

> She should have leaped up and pirouetted and joined his happiness. But a strange uneasiness kept her seated with her knees drawn tight against her chest. She asked cautiously, "You mean we're rich?"
>
> "We ain rich but we got land."
>
> "Is it a lot?"
>
> "Two acres almost. I know the piece of ground good. You could throw down I-don-know-what on it and it would grow. And we gon have a house there—just like the white people own. A house to end all house!"
>
> "Are you gonna tell Mother?"
>
> His smile faltered and failed; his eyes closed in a kind of weariness.

> —Paule Marshall, *Brown Girl, Brownstones*

The jargon of the workplace People engaged in most areas of specialized work and study use technical words that outsiders perceive as jargon. A sportswriter writing about baseball will refer to *balks*, *ERAs*, *brushbacks*, and *cutters*. A linguist writing about language for an audience of linguists will use terms like *phonemics, sociolinguistics, semantics, kinesics,* and *suprasegmentals*. If you know that your audience is familiar with the technical vocabulary of a field, specialized language is acceptable. Try to avoid jargon when writing for a more general audience; if you must use technical terms, provide definitions that will make sense to your audience.

34e Use figurative language for effect, but don't overuse it

Figures of speech can enhance your writing and add to imaginative descriptions. Particularly useful are similes and metaphors. A simile is a comparison in which both sides are stated explicitly and linked by the words *like* or *as*. A metaphor is an implied comparison in which the two sides are indirectly compared. When figurative language is overused, however, it can become tedious and contrived.

Simile: An explicit comparison with both sides stated

▶ America is *not like a blanket*—one piece of unbroken cloth, the same color, the same texture, the same size. America is more *like a quilt*—many pieces, many colors, many sizes, all woven and held together by a common thread.

—Rev. Jesse Jackson

▶ He was reading, leaning so far back in the chair that it was balanced on its two hind legs *like a dancing dog*.

—Barbara Kingsolver

Metaphor: An implied comparison, without *like* or *as*

▶ A foolish consistency is the hobgoblin of little minds.

—Ralph Waldo Emerson

▶ Some television programs are so much chewing gum for the eyes.

—John Mason Brown

Mixed metaphors Take care not to mix (illogically combine) metaphors.

▶ As she walked onto the tennis court, she was ready to sink or swim. [Swimming on a tennis court?]

▶ He is a snake in the grass with his head in the clouds. [The two metaphors clash.]

▶ He was a whirlwind of activity, trumpeting defiance whenever anyone crossed swords with any of his ideas. [The three metaphors—*whirlwind, trumpet, crossed swords*—obscure rather than illuminate.]

For more examples of figurative language in literature, see 5b.

34f Avoid sexist, biased, and exclusionary language

You cannot avoid writing from perspectives and backgrounds that you know about, but you can avoid divisive terms that reinforce stereotypes or belittle other people. Be sensitive to differences. Consider the feelings of members of the opposite sex, racial or ethnic minorities (now sometimes called "world majorities"), and special-interest groups. Do not emphasize differences by separating society into *we* (people like you) and *they* or *these people* (people different from you). Use *we* only to be truly inclusive of yourself and all your readers. Be aware, too, of terms that are likely to offend. You don't need to be excessive in your zeal to be PC (politically correct), using *underachieve* for *fail*, or *vertically challenged* for *short*, but do your best to avoid alienating readers.

Gender The writer of the following sentence edited to avoid gender bias and sexist language in the perception of women's roles and achievements.

> Andrea
> ▶ ~~Mrs. John~~ Harrison, the ~~attractive~~ chief executive of a successful computer company, has expanded the business overseas.

Choice of words can reveal gender bias, too.

Avoid	Use
chairman	chairperson
female astronaut	astronaut
forefathers	ancestors
foreman	supervisor
mailman	mail carrier
male nurse	nurse
man, mankind (meaning any human being)	person, people, our species, human beings, humanity, humankind
poetess	poet
policeman, policewoman	police officer
salesman	sales representative, salesclerk
veterans and their wives	veterans and their spouses

Pronouns *he* or *she* Pronoun use is especially vulnerable to gender bias. See 44e for more on gender pronouns, the use of the phrase *he or she*, and the use of *they* to avoid tricky decisions.

Race Mention a person's race only when it is relevant. If you write, "Attending the meeting were three doctors and an Asian computer programmer," you reveal more about your own stereotypes than you do about the meeting. When the newly appointed Supreme Court Judge Sonia Sotomayor referred to one of her judicial decisions as made by a "wise Latina," this angered her opponents who saw race as irrelevant in matters of legal precedent. Aside from avoiding gratuitous comments about race, try to use the names that people prefer for their racial or ethnic affiliations. The *Columbia Guide to Standard American English* advises: "It is good manners (and therefore good usage) to call people only by the names they wish to be called." Consider, for example, that *black* and *African American* are preferred terms; *American Indian*, or better still, the particular group (*Sioux* etc.) is now often preferred to *Native American*, though this usage has swung back and forth. *Asian* is preferred to *Oriental*, while *Latino/Latina* vies with *Hispanic* to refer to Americans originating in Latin America.

Place Avoid stereotyping people according to where they come from. Some British people may be stiff and formal, but not all are (the author of this book is from London, so take her word for it). Not all Germans eat sausage and drink beer; not all North Americans carry cameras and chew gum.

Be careful, too, with the way you refer to countries and continents. The Americas include both North and South America, so you need to make the distinction. England, Scotland, Wales, and Northern Ireland make up Great Britain, or the United Kingdom. In addition, shifts in world politics and national borders have resulted in the renaming of many countries. Always consult a current atlas, almanac, or reliable reference Web site.

Age Avoid derogatory or condescending terms associated with age. Refer to a person's age or condition neutrally if at all: not *well-preserved little old lady* but *woman in her eighties* or just *woman*.

Politics Words referring to politics are full of connotations. Consider, for instance, the positive and negative connotations of *liberal* and *conservative* in various election campaigns. Take care when you use words like *radical*, *left-wing*, *right-wing*, and *moderate*. How do you want readers to interpret them? Are you identifying with one group and implicitly criticizing other groups?

Religion   An older edition of an encyclopedia referred to "devout Catholics" and "fanatical Muslims." A newer edition refers to both Catholics and Muslims as "devout," thus eliminating the bias of a sweeping generalization. Examine your use of the following: words that sound derogatory or exclusionary, such as *cult* or *fundamentalist*; expressions, such as *these people*, which emphasize difference; and even the word *we* when it implies that all your readers share your beliefs.

Health and abilities   Avoid expressions such as *confined to a wheelchair* and *AIDS victim* so as not to focus on difference and disability. Instead, write *someone who uses a wheelchair* and *a person with AIDS*, but only if the context makes it necessary to include that information. Do not unnecessarily draw attention to a disability or an illness.

Sexual orientation   Mention a person's sexual orientation only if the information is relevant in context. To write that someone accused of stock market fraud was "defended by a homosexual lawyer" would be to provide gratuitous information. The sexual orientation of the attorney might be more relevant in a case involving discrimination against homosexuals. Since you may not know the sexual orientation of your readers, do not assume it is the same as your own.

The word *normal*   Be especially careful about using the word *normal* when referring to your own health, ability, or sexual orientation. Some readers might justifiably find that usage offensive.

34g Avoid tired expressions (clichés) and pretentious language

Avoid clichés   *Clichés* are tired, overly familiar expressions that anyone can complete: as cool as a _____. Common clichés are *hit the nail on the head, crystal clear, better late than never,* and *easier said than done*. They never contribute anything fresh or original. Avoid or eliminate them as you revise your early drafts.

▶ ~~Last but not least,~~ the article recommends the TeleZapper.
       ^Finally,

▶ My main ambition in life is not to make a fortune, since I know that/ ~~as they say, "money is the root of all evil."~~
       ^having money does not guarantee a good life.

arose
▶ For Baldwin, the problem never ~~reared its ugly head~~ until
one dreadful night in New Jersey.
                               ^

Distinguish the formal from the stuffy *Formal* does not mean
stuffy and pretentious. Writing in a formal situation does not require
you to use obscure words and long sentences. In fact, convoluted
writing is not a sign of brilliance or of a powerful mind. It is usually
just a sign of bad writing. Pretentious language makes reading difficult, as the following example shows:

> ▶ When a female of the species ascertains that a male with
> whom she is acquainted exhibits considerable desire to
> extend their acquaintance, that female customarily will
> first engage in protracted discussion with her close
> confidantes.

Simplify your writing if you find sentences like that in your draft.
Aim for clear, direct expression of ideas. Here are some words to
watch out for:

Stuffy	Direct	Stuffy	Direct
ascertain	find out	optimal	best
commence	begin	prior to	before
deceased	dead	purchase	buy
endeavor	try	reside	live
finalize	finish	terminate	end
implement	carry out	utilize	use

Avoid euphemisms *Euphemisms* are expressions that try to conceal a forthright meaning and make the concept seem more delicate,
such as *change of life* for *menopause* or *downsized* for *fired*. Because euphemisms often sound evasive or are unclear, avoid them in favor
of direct language. Similarly, avoid *doublespeak* (evasive expressions
that seek to conceal the truth, such as *incendiary device* for *firebomb*,
combat situation for *battle*, and *collateral damage* for *civilian casualties*).
Examples of such language are easy to find in advertising, business,
politics, and especially, in war reporting. Do not equate formality
with these indirect expressions.

▶ The building's owners offered the inspectors many

      bribes
~~financial incentives~~ to overlook code violations.
  ^

35

Revising for Style: A Student's Drafts

A student writer's three paragraphs on the topic of books and the Web are shown here as analyzed by a group consisting of the writer and several classmates, with a focus on the style features discussed in this chapter.

Student's passage for peer review	Classmates' analysis, using part 6 on style
Books are becoming obsolete. More and more guys are turning to the Web for both information and entertainment. Web sites are accessed when people need to check a fact or even when they just want to read and relax.	Switch in subject Slang? Or sexist language? Unnecessary passive; switch in subject
In this paragraph, I will turn to explaining the many advantages to the Web. At this point in time, books are losing in popularity due to the fact that they are expensive and not easy to take from place to place. The main reason for the fact that people prefer the Web is that it is there when it's needed. It offers great variety. It also can be informative. A friend of mine reads the news on his iPod. He sends messages to his friends on his iPod. It is very versatile. It's a pretty snazzy tool for everyday life.	Reference to intentions Formulaic phrase Switch in subject Formulaic phrase Wordy No sentence variety in this paragraph Good examples here Tone too conversational
Last but not least, despite the many advantages to the Web, people still	Formulaic cliché

purchase books to endeavor to improve
themselves. There is so much handy and
portable information in books. Books
have passed the test of getting
published, so they can be more reliable.
With books you can move from being an
ignorant numbskull to dissing all your
friends about their ignorance.

There is—action verb better

Good point here

Language of speech

The student worked with his group to revise the paragraphs for style. This is the new version, revised according to the feedback received:

As increasingly more people turn to the Web for information and entertainment, books seem to be fading in popularity. The Web rather than a book is now what we all use to check a fact, communicate with others, or just relax.

Nowadays, the Web wins out over books in several ways. First, books are expensive and not easy to take from place to place. Second, the Web is always there when people need it to answer a question. In addition, it is versatile enough to provide not only information but also entertainment. Many students use their handy little portable iPod to read the news, send messages to friends, make notes for essays, and play video games.

However, in spite of the advantages the Web offers, people are still buying books to improve their skills and knowledge. They know that the information they find on the Web posted by individuals or organizations may be biased, wrong-headed, or even totally inaccurate. They know, though, that with a book, some publisher has been impressed enough by the author and the content to put money behind the publication. So they tuck a handy book into a pocket to read on a bus or train on the way to work. That way, they have instant access to information as well as to entertainment, knowing that a published book will usually offer more reliability than a published Web site.

36 ⦿━

Style Tips

As you write and revise, keep in mind the five C's of style, and aim for sentence variety. For a final quick review of your style, read your draft aloud and use these tips.

KEY POINTS

Tips for Style

1. **Be adaptable.** Consider the style your readers will expect. Don't work on developing a figurative style for short stories and then continue to use the same style in business communications or e-mail. Choose a style as you choose your clothes: the right outfit for the occasion.

2. **When in doubt, favor a plain style.** Be clear and straightforward. Don't search for the big words or the obscure turn of phrase. The following sentences, part of an e-mail message to the author of this book from an online service provider, are decidedly overdressed and stuffed with bureaucratic nothings: "It has been a pleasure assisting you. It is my hope that the information provided would be of great help with regards to your concern."

3. **Less is often better.** Details and descriptions are interesting, but don't overload your writing with adjectives and adverbs: *The perky little redheaded twin sat languidly in the comfortable overstuffed green-striped armchair and bit enthusiastically into a red and yellow fleshy, overripe peach.* Such prose is as overripe as the peach. Also avoid intensifying adverbs such as *very, really, extremely, terribly,* and *enormously.* Find a stronger word to use in place of the two words, such as *terrified* in place of *extremely scared.*

4. **Focus on rhythm, not rules.** Heed the advice of *The New York Times Manual of Style and Usage:* "One measure of skill is exceptions, not rules." And keep in mind this remark by novelist Ford Madox Ford: "Carefully examined, a good—an interesting—style will be found to consist in a constant succession of tiny, unobservable surprises." Ask yourself how you can provide pleasant surprises for your readers.

PART 7

Common Sentence Problems

37 Trouble Spots and Terms 383

38 Fixing a Sentence Fragment 392

39 Run-ons and Comma Splices 396

40 Sentence Snarls 398

41 Verbs 406

42 Passive Voice 423

43 Subject-Verb Agreement 425

44 Pronouns 435

45 Adjectives and Adverbs 446

46 Relative Clauses and Relative Pronouns
(*who, whom, whose, which, that,* etc.) 453

PART 7 COMMON SENTENCE PROBLEMS

@ | **ONLINE RESOURCES**
www.cengage.com/english/raimes

Companion online resources are available for sections throughout this part. We invite you to visit the book's Web site for more information and direct access.

PART 7

Common Sentence Problems

37 Trouble Spots and Terms 383

37a Students' FAQs—and where to find answers 383
37b Grammar-check programs: Uses, dangers, and suggestions 385
37c Standard English/Edited American English 386
37d Terms for the parts of a sentence 387

38 Fixing a Sentence Fragment 392

38a What a sentence needs 392
38b How to fix a phrase fragment with no subject and/or verb 392
38c How to fix a dependent clause fragment 393
38d How to fix a fragment with a missing subject after *and*, *but*, or *or* 395
38e Intentional fragments 395

39 Run-ons and Comma Splices 396

39a How to identify 396
39b Five ways to correct 396
39c How to avoid a run-on or a comma splice when using a transition 397

40 Sentence Snarls 398

40a Tangles: Mixed constructions, confusing comparisons, and convoluted syntax 398
40b Misplaced modifiers: Phrases, *not*, *only*, split infinitives 399
40c Dangling modifiers 401
40d Shifts: Statements/commands, indirect/direct quotation, point of view 401
40e Mismatch of subject and predicate (faulty predication) 402
40f Definitions and reasons 402

40g *Because* and *when* clauses as subject 403
40h Omitted words 403
40i Unnecessary restated subject 404
40j Structures not parallel 404

41 Verbs 406

41a Verb forms: Regular and irregular 406
41b Verbs commonly confused 410
41c Auxiliary verbs 411
41d Tenses: Overview 413
41e Present tenses 414
41f Past tenses 416
41g *-ed* endings: Past tense and past participle forms 417
41h Tense shifts 418
41i Tenses in indirect quotations 419
41j Verbs in conditional sentences, wishes, requests, demands, and recommendations 420

42 Passive Voice 423

42a When to use 423
42b How to form 424
42c Overuse 424
42d As connector 424

43 Subject-Verb Agreement 425

43a Basic principles for an *-s* ending 425
43b What to do when words come between subject and verb 427
43c Agreement with linking verbs (*be*, *seem*, *appear*, etc.) 428
43d What to do when the subject follows the verb 428
43e Eight tricky subjects with singular verbs 429
43f Collective noun as subject 431
43g Subjects containing *and*, *or*, *nor* 431

43h Indefinite pronouns (*anyone*, *nobody*, etc.) 432
43i Quantity words 433
43j Agreement with *this*, *these*, *mine*, *ours*, etc. 434
43k Agreement with subject clauses beginning with *what* 434

44 Pronouns 435
44a Forms of personal pronouns (*I* or *me*, *he* or *him?*) 435
44b Possessive forms (*my* or *mine*, *her* or *hers?*) 438
44c Clear reference 439
44d Agreement with antecedent 440
44e Gender bias 443
44f Consistent point of view 443
44g Use of *you* 444
44h Intensive and reflexive pronouns 444
44i *Who/whom, whoever/whomever* 445

45 Adjectives and Adverbs 446
45a Forms 447
45b When to use 447

45c Adjectives after linking verbs 448
45d Compound adjectives 449
45e Position of adverbs 449
45f Conjunctive adverbs (*however*, *therefore*, etc.) 450
45g Double negatives 450
45h Comparative and superlative forms 451
45i Faulty or incomplete comparisons 453

46 Relative Clauses and Relative Pronouns (*who, whom, whose, which, that*, etc.) 453
46a Relative pronouns 454
46b Restrictive and nonrestrictive clauses 455
46c Agreement of verb 456
46d Clauses with prepositions 457
46e Position of relative clause 458
46f *Where* and *when* 458

37

Trouble Spots and Terms

37a Students' FAQs—and where to find answers

Questions	Short Answer	More Information
Can I begin a sentence with *and* or *but*?	Occasionally, yes	32c, p. 359

(Continued)

Questions	Short Answer	More Information
Can I interchange *but* and *however*?	No. Meanings are similar; usage and punctuation differ.	39c, 47e: pp. 397, 467
Is it *would have drank* or *would have drunk*?	*Drunk*: past participle verb form after *have*	41a, p. 406
How do I know whether to use *I* or *me* with *and*? (The boss promoted *Tom and I* or *Tom and me*?)	Use the "drop the noun in the *and* phrase" test: The boss promoted *me*.	44a, p. 436
When do I use *who*, *whom*, *which*, or *that*?	For people: *who, whom* For things: *which, that* This is a complex issue; turn to the sections in column 3.	46a, 46b, 46d: pp. 454, 455, and 457
What is the difference between *who* and *whom*?	Use *whom* in formal writing as an object form	44i, 46a: pp. 445, 454
When do I use *good* or *well, bad* or *badly*?	*Good* and *bad* modify nouns. *Well* and *badly* modify verbs. But there are tricky exceptions.	45a, 45b, 45c: pp. 447, 448
What are the errors called fragments, run-ons, and comma splices?	A fragment is an incomplete sentence; a run-on or a comma splice is wrongly written as one sentence but needs to be separated or rewritten.	chapters 38 and 39: pp. 392, 396
What is the difference between		
a. *its* and *it's*?	*It's* stands for *it is* or *it has*. *Its* is a possessive adjective.	48f, p. 473
b. *whose* and *who's*?	*Who's* stands for *who is* or *who has*. *Whose* is a possessive relative pronoun.	Glossary of Usage, p. 562
c. *lie* and *lay*?	*Lay* is used only with a direct object, and *lie* with no direct object.	41b, p. 410

37b Grammar-check programs: Uses, dangers, and suggestions

Set aside time for a separate reading of your draft to check for the common problem areas covered in this part of the book and make corrections. Do not rely on computer tools for editing. Spelling checkers and grammar-check programs are not complete or sophisticated enough to cover all the options. Spelling checkers will catch typographical errors, such as *teh* in place of *the*, but they will not catch missing *s* or *-ed* endings, nor will they find a misspelled word that forms another word: *affect/effect, expect/except, then/than,* or *peek/peak/pique,* for example (see section 65, Glossary of Usage, p. 549).

A grammar-check program analyzes sentences and makes suggestions about what might need to be fixed, tightened, or polished. But technology has not advanced enough for it to be able to take context, meaning, and cultural diversity into account.

KEY POINTS
Grammar-Check Programs: Uses, Dangers, and Suggestions

Uses

A grammar-check program provides helpful observations about simple mechanical matters, such as pointing out

- commas and periods that you may need to place inside quotation marks
- quotation marks or parentheses that you may need to close
- passive verbs that you may wish to revise as active
- clichés
- verb problems such as in the sentence, "Can the mayor wins?"

You may find it worthwhile to activate a grammar-check program solely to catch these basic errors. But before you do, be aware of the following dangers.

Dangers

The capabilities of grammar-check programs are limited. They cannot recognize some errors because they do not "understand" the context or your intention. For example, if you wrote "The actors were boring" but meant to write "The actors were bored," a

(Continued)

(Continued)

grammar-check program would not reveal your mistake. Some correct sentences can even be made wrong upon the advice of such a program, as shown in the Note for Multilingual Writers in 3d, p. 46.

Suggestions

If you use a grammar-check program, review all its points of advice before you make any changes based on its recommendations. Never make a suggested change in your draft before verifying that the change is really necessary. Or more radically, consider deactivating the checking feature while you write. Its constant reminders may interrupt your train of thought, introduce errors, and keep you from developing confidence in your own judgment and grammatical expertise.

37c Standard English/Edited American English

Science fiction writer and editor Teresa Neilson Hayden, in *Making Book*, characterizes English as "a generous, expansive, and flexible language" but adds, "a less charitable description would characterize it as drunk and disorderly." The task of editing, she claims, is to try to impose "a degree of regularity on something that is inherently irregular." What can help you move away from irregularities in your writing is a set of conventions referred to as Standard English, or to more directly relate the term to academic writing in the United States, Edited American English.

The American Heritage Dictionary (AHD), 4th edition, defines *Standard English* as "the variety of English that is generally acknowledged as the model for the speech and writing of educated speakers." A Usage Note in the *AHD*, however, continues, "A form that is considered standard in one region may be nonstandard in another" and points out that *standard* and *nonstandard* are relative terms, depending largely on context.

In short, the concept of Standard English is complex. It is entwined with the region, race, class, education, and gender of both the speaker (or writer) and the listener (or reader). Standard English is far from monolithic. It is constantly supplemented and challenged by other ways of speaking and writing, such as those coming from technology, hip-hop, the worlds of gender and sexual politics, popular culture, and conventions in use in different parts of the English-speaking world. (See the Circle of World English in 59a on p. 508.)

Nevertheless, Standard English, with all its quirks, irregularities, rules, and exceptions, is politically and sociologically branded as the language of those in power. Its practices are what most readers still expect in the academic and business worlds. However insightful and original your ideas may be, readers will soon become impatient if those ideas are not expressed in sentences that follow conventions determined by the history of the language and the prescriptive power of its educated users.

Attention to accuracy is important in the business world as well as in college. A study of 120 corporations found that one third of the employees of major companies had poor writing skills, leading an executive to say, "It's not that companies want to hire Tolstoy. But they need people who can write clearly."

To meet readers' expectations in academic and business settings, use the version of Edited American English represented in this book and stressed in parts 7 through 10.

37d Terms for the parts of a sentence

To think about and discuss how sentences work, a shared vocabulary is useful. Here are some of the basic terms covering the parts of speech and the parts of a sentence. The Glossary of Grammatical Terms on page 563 provides further definitions and examples.

Parts of speech   Words are traditionally classified into eight categories called *parts of speech*. Note that the part of speech refers not to the word itself but to its function in a sentence. Some words can function as different parts of speech.

> verb
> ▶ They respect the orchestra manager.

> noun
> ▶ Respect is a large part of a business relationship.

Nouns   Words that name a person, place, thing, or concept—*teacher, valley, furniture, Hinduism*—are called *nouns*. When you use a noun, determine the following: Is it a proper noun, requiring a capital letter? Does it have a plural form? If so, are you using the singular or plural form? See 53b and 60a for more on nouns.

Pronouns   A pronoun represents a noun or a noun phrase. In writing, a pronoun refers to its antecedent—that is, a noun or noun phrase appearing just before it in the text.

▶ My sister loves *her* new car, but *she* dented *it* last week.

Pronouns fall into seven types: personal (44a), possessive (43j, 44b), demonstrative (43j), intensive or reflexive (44h), relative (46a), interrogative (44i), and indefinite (43h). When you use a pronoun, determine the following: What word or words in the sentence does the pronoun refer to? Does the pronoun refer to a noun or pronoun that is singular or plural?

Verbs Words that tell what a person, place, thing, or concept does or is—*smile, throw, think, seem, become, be*—are called *verbs*. Verbs change form, so when you use a verb, determine the following: What time does the verb refer to? What auxiliary or modal verbs are needed for an appropriate tense? Is the subject of the verb singular or plural? Is the verb in the active voice or passive voice? What are the five forms of the verb (*sing, sings, singing, sang, sung*), and are you using the correct form?

Main verbs often need auxiliary verbs (*be, do, have*) or modal auxiliaries (*will, would, can, could, shall, should, may, might, must*) to complete the meaning. For more on verbs, see chapters 41, 42, and 43.

Adjectives Words that describe nouns—*purple, beautiful, big*—are called *adjectives*. An adjective can precede a noun or follow a linking verb:

▶ The speaker was wearing *purple* boots.

▶ Her boots were *purple*.

Descriptive adjectives have comparative and superlative forms: *short, shorter, shortest* (45h). Also functioning as adjectives (before a noun) are *a, an,* and *the,* as well as possessives and demonstratives: *a* cabbage, *an* allegory, *their* poems, *this* book. For more on adjectives, see chapter 45.

Adverbs Words that provide information about verbs, adjectives, adverbs, or clauses are called *adverbs*. Many but not all adverbs end in *-ly: quickly, efficiently*. Adverbs also provide information about how or when: *very, well, sometimes, often, soon, never*. Adverbs modify verbs, adjectives, other adverbs, or clauses.

modifies verb   modifies adverb
▶ Rafael dunked brilliantly. He played spectacularly well.

modifies adjective   modifies whole clause

▶ He is a very energetic player. Undoubtedly, he is a genius.

Conjunctive adverbs—such as *however, therefore, furthermore*—make connections between independent clauses. For more on conjunctive adverbs and other transitional expressions, see 2c, 45f, and 47e.

Conjunctions Words that connect words, phrases, and clauses are called *conjunctions.*

▶ Martin loves ham *and* eggs.

▶ To brighten up her room, she bought a red bowl, a blue jug, *and* yellow cushions.

▶ The magazine was published, *and* his article won acclaim.

The seven coordinating conjunctions—*and, but, or, nor. so, for, yet*—connect ideas of equal importance. Subordinating conjunctions—*because, if, when, although,* for instance (see the list in 38c)—make one clause dependent on another. Consider meaning and style (32b) when deciding whether to use a conjunction or a transition.

Prepositions Words used before nouns and pronouns to form phrases that usually do the work of an adjective or adverb are called *prepositions.*

preposition   preposition

▶ A bird with a red crest flew onto the feeder.

Some common prepositions are *against, around, at, behind, between, except, for, from, in, into, like, on, over, regarding, to,* and *without.* Prepositional phrases are often idiomatic: *on occasion, in love.* To understand their use and meaning, consult a good dictionary. See also chapter 63.

Interjections Words that express emotion and can stand alone—*Ha! Wow! Ugh! Ouch! Say!*—are called *interjections.* Interjections are not used frequently in academic writing. The more formal ones (such as *alas, oh*) are sometimes used in poetry:

> But she is in her grave, and, Oh,
> The difference to me!
>
> —William Wordsworth, "She Dwelt among the Untrodden Ways"

A sentence and its parts You have probably heard various definitions of a *sentence,* the common one being that "a sentence is a complete thought." Sometimes it is. Sometimes it is not, depending on what one expects by "complete." In fact, that definition is not particularly helpful. How complete is this thought?

> ▶ **He did not.**

You probably do not regard it as complete in the traditional sense because it relies on text around it, on other sentences, to tell who he is and what it was he did not do, as in the following example.

> ▶ **Sarah was always competitive with her brother. She studied hard. He did not.**

However, each of these sentences can be said to be *grammatically* complete, containing a subject and verb in an independent clause.

Subject and predicate   A sentence needs at the very least a *subject* (the person or thing doing or receiving the action) and a *predicate* (a comment or assertion about the subject). Only a command (such as "Run!") will not state the subject (*you*). A predicate must contain a complete verb, expressing action or state.

> subject predicate
> ▶ **Babies cry.**
>   verb

> ⎸——— subject ———⎹ ⎸— predicate —⎹
> ▶ **All the babies in the nursery were crying all night.**
>   ⎸— verb —⎹

Direct and indirect object   Some verbs are followed by a *direct object*, a word that receives the action of a verb.

> direct object
> ▶ **Many people wear glasses.** [A verb that is followed by a direct object is known as a *transitive verb*. *Intransitive verbs* such as *sit, happen, occur,* and *rise* are never followed by a direct object.]

Verbs such as *give, send,* and *offer* can be followed by both a direct and an *indirect object* (see 62c).

> ⎸— indirect object —⎹ ⎸— direct object —⎹
> ▶ **He gave his leading lady one exquisite rose.**

Complement   Verbs such as *be, seem, look,* and *appear* are not action verbs but *linking verbs*. They are followed by a *subject complement* that renames or describes the subject.

subject complement

▶ **The singers in the choir look happy.**

An *object complement* renames or describes the direct object.

direct object ————object complement————

▶ **We appointed a student the chairperson of the committee.**

Phrase   A *phrase* is a group of words that lacks a subject, a verb, or both. A phrase is only a part of a sentence. It cannot be punctuated as a sentence.

an elegant evening gown

singing in the rain

on the corner

worried by the news

with her thoughts in turmoil

to travel around the world

See 38b for more on phrase fragments.

Clause   Clauses can be independent or dependent. A sentence must contain a *main clause*, also called an *independent clause*, which is one that can stand alone. A clause introduced by a word such as *because, when, if,* or *although* is a *dependent clause*. Every independent clause and dependent clause needs its own subject and predicate.

————independent clause————

▶ **Her eyesight is deteriorating.**

————dependent (subordinate) clause———— ——independent clause——

▶ **Because her eyesight is deteriorating, she wears glasses.**

Dependent clauses can function as adverbs, adjectives, or nouns.

▶ *When the sun shines,* **the strawberries ripen.** [Adverb clause expressing time]

▶ **The berries** *that we picked yesterday* **were delicious.** [Adjective clause modifying *berries*]

▶ **The farmers know** *what they should do.* [Noun clause functioning as a direct object]

See 38c for more on dependent clause fragments.

38 🔑

Fixing a Sentence Fragment

A *fragment* is a group of words incorrectly punctuated as if it were a complete sentence.

38a What a sentence needs

Check that your sentences contain the following:

1. a **capital letter** at the beginning
2. an **independent (main) clause**—one that can stand alone—containing both a **subject** and a **complete verb** and not introduced by a word such as *when, because, although, which,* or *until* (such words, known as *subordinators* or *subordinating conjunctions,* introduce dependent clauses and are common culprits in fragments)
3. appropriate **end punctuation:** period, question mark, exclamation point, or semicolon

Note that a semicolon indicates the end of one independent clause with a close meaning attachment to another independent clause: *The senator explained the budget items; her assistants helped by displaying explanatory charts.*

　　Most problems occur when what is presented as a sentence has no complete independent clause.

> ⌐a phrase fragment: no subject or verb⌐
▶ He wanted to make a point. **To prove his competence.**

> ⌐─────────── not an independent clause ───────────
▶ The audience left. **Because the film was too long and too**

confusing.

(*Because* is a subordinating conjunction connecting to an idea in the previous sentence.)

38b How to fix a phrase fragment with no subject and/or verb

1. Connect the fragment to what comes before or after, removing a period and the following capital letter:

> *to*
> ▶ Architects recommend solar panels/~~To~~ save on heating bills.
>   ^

> *, the*
> ▶ In a valiant attempt to save some money/~~The~~ family moved
>   into their RV and rented their house.   ^

> *a*
> ▶ Rossellini was diagnosed with scoliosis/~~A~~ disease of the spine.
>   ^ ^

> ▶ The sculptor described his ~~proposal. An~~ innovative plan for
>   an abstract fountain in the middle of the town square.

> *the*
> ▶ A prize was awarded to Ed/~~The~~ best worker in the company.
>   ^ ^

2. Revise so that each group of words between a capital letter and a
   period contains a subject and a verb.

> *he valued*
> ▶ Nature held many attractions for Thoreau. Especially, the
>   solitude in the countryside.   ^

> *It is*
> ▶ Many people try to lose weight. ~~Is~~ wise for them to avoid
>   sugary snacks.   ^

38c How to fix a dependent clause fragment

A *dependent clause* begins with a word that makes the clause subordinate and dependent upon another clause. Unable to stand alone, a
subordinate clause must be attached to an independent clause. Here
are the words that introduce subordinate adverb clauses:

Subordinating Conjunctions
---

time: when, whenever, until, till, before, after, while, once, as
   soon as, as long as

place: where, wherever

cause: because, as, since

condition: if, even if, unless, provided that

contrast: although, though, even though, whereas, while

comparison: than, as, as if, as though

purpose: so that, in order that

result: so . . . that, such . . . that

Whenever you begin a sentence with one of these words, make sure you see a comma at the end of the clause and then the subject and verb of the independent clause:

▶ **When** Jane Austen describes people, she emphasizes all their little foibles.

Words introducing other types of dependent clauses (adjective or noun clauses) include *who, whom, whose, which, that, what, when,* and *whoever.*

Methods of correcting a dependent clause fragment   Two methods are available:

1. Connect the fragment to an independent clause before or after it.

   ▶ **Lars wants to be a stand-up comic/~~Because~~ he likes to make people laugh.**   *because*

   ▶ **The family set out for a new country/~~In~~ which they could practice their culture and religion.**   *in*

   ▶ **She made many promises to her family/~~That~~ she would write to them every day.**   *that*

   ▶ **The name** *Google* **comes from the word** *googol*/~~Which~~ **is the mathematical term for a one followed by a hundred zeros.**   *which*

For the use of commas before clauses beginning with *who, whom,* or *which,* see 46b and 47d.

2. Delete the subordinating conjunction. The dependent clause then becomes an independent clause, which can stand alone.

   ▶ **Lars plans to become a stand-up comic. ~~Because~~ ~~he~~ likes to make people laugh.**   *He*

Note: It is a myth that a sentence should never begin with *because.* A word like *because* at the beginning of a sentence does not always signal a fragment. The following sentence is perfectly grammatical, beginning with a dependent clause and ending with an independent clause.

▶ **Because Lars likes to make people laugh, he plans to become a stand-up comic.**

38d How to fix a fragment with a missing subject after *and*, *but*, or *or*

Two separate sentences need two separate subjects. In academic English, one subject is enough for a compound predicate (two verbs after the subject in the same sentence), but it cannot do the work of a subject across two sentences.

Fragment

▶ After an hour, the dancers changed partners. And easily
——————fragment: no subject of *adapted*——————
adapted from rock and roll to the tango.

Possible revisions

▶ After an hour, the dancers changed partners and easily adapted from rock and roll to the tango.

▶ After an hour, the dancers changed partners. They easily adapted from rock and roll to the tango.

▶ After an hour, the dancers changed partners, adapting easily from rock and roll to the tango.

▶ After an hour, the dancers changed partners. And they adapted easily from rock and roll to the tango. [See the Language and Culture box in 32c for more on sentences beginning with *and* or *but*.]

38e Intentional fragments

Fragments are used frequently in advertisements to keep the text short. In academic writing, you will sometimes see a fragment used intentionally for emphasis, after a question, as an explanation, or at a point of transition.

▶ Did Virginia know that Tom was writing frequently at this time to Leonard asking for advice? Probably.

—Hermione Lee, *Virginia Woolf*

▶ He [Dylan Thomas] lived twenty-four years after he began to be a poet. Twenty-four years of poetry, dwindling rapidly in the last decade.

—Donald Hall, *Remembering Poets*

By all means, use fragments to achieve a specific effect. However, edit fragments that serve no identifiable rhetorical purpose.

39 ⚷

Run-ons and Comma Splices

39a How to identify run-on (or *fused*) sentences and comma splices

A writer who takes two independent clauses and rams them up against each other, end to end, creates the error of a *run-on sentence*, also known as a *fused sentence*. Academic readers expect two independent clauses to be separated by more than a comma alone.

Run-on error

► ┌──────────── independent clause ────────────┐
  Blue jeans were originally made as tough work clothes

  ┌─────────── independent clause ──────────┐
  they became a fashion statement in the 1970s.

Inserting a comma between the two clauses is no help. That would then be a *comma splice* error.

Comma splice error

► **Blue jeans were originally made as tough work clothes, they became a fashion statement in the 1970s.**

Note: Comma splices are often used in advertising and journalism for stylistic effect to emphasize a contrast: *Obama and Hillary Clinton campaigned on different issues. He looked for ways to create change in the future, she looked back to her husband's presidency.* Take this stylistic risk only if you are sure of the effect you want to achieve.

39b Five ways to correct run-on sentences and comma splices

You can correct run-ons and comma splices in the following five ways. Select the one that works best for the sentence you are editing.

> ### KEY POINTS
> **Options for Editing a Run-on or Comma Splice**
>
> **1.** When the two clauses are quite long, simply separate them.
>
> ► **Blue jeans were originally made as tough work clothes.**
>   ***They* became a fashion statement in the 1970s.**

> ▶ Blue jeans were originally made as tough work clothes; *they* became a fashion statement in the 1970s.

2. Include a comma, but make sure it is followed by *and, but, or, nor, so, for,* or *yet.*

> ▶ Blue jeans were originally made as tough work clothes, *but* they became a fashion statement in the 1970s.

3. If you are switching direction or want to stress the second clause, separate the clauses with a period or a semicolon, followed by a transitional expression such as *however* or *therefore,* followed by a comma (see also 39c and 45f).

> ▶ Blue jeans were originally made as tough work clothes; *however,* they became a fashion statement in the 1970s.

4. Rewrite the sentences as one sentence by using, for example, *because, although,* or *when* to make one clause introduce or set up the clause containing the important point.

> ▶ *Although* blue jeans were originally made as tough work clothes, they became a fashion statement in the 1970s.

5. Condense or restructure the sentence.

> ▶ Blue jeans, *originally* made as tough work clothes, became a fashion statement in the 1970s.

39c How to avoid a run-on or a comma splice when using a transition

Run-ons and comma splices often occur with transitional expressions such as *in addition, however, therefore, for example,* and *moreover* (see the list in 2c). When one of these expressions precedes the subject of its own clause, end the previous sentence with a period or a semicolon. Put a comma after the transitional expression, not before it.

CORRECTED
RUN-ON ERROR
Martha cleaned her closets ~~in~~ In addition she reorganized the kitchen.

CORRECTED
COMMA SPLICE ERROR
The doctor prescribed new pills ; however she did not alert the patient to the side effects.

Note: You can use the coordinating conjunctions *and, but,* and *so* after a comma to connect two independent clauses, but *in addition, however,* and *therefore* do not follow the same punctuation pattern.

▶ **The stock market was falling, so he decided not to invest his savings.**

▶ **The stock market was falling; therefore, he decided not to invest his savings.**

Commas should both precede and follow a transitional expression that does not appear at the beginning of its own clause:

▶ **The doctor prescribed some medicine. She did not, however, alert the patient to the side effects.**

40 ⚷

Sentence Snarls

Snarls, tangles, and knots are as difficult to deal with on a bad writing day as on a bad hair day, though they may not be as painful. Sentences with structural inconsistencies give readers trouble. They make readers work to untangle the meaning.

40a Tangles: Mixed constructions, confusing comparisons, and convoluted syntax

Mixed constructions   A mixed construction is a sentence with parts that do not match grammatically. The sentence begins one way and then veers off in an unexpected direction. Check to ensure that the subject and verb in your sentence are clear and work together, and note that a phrase beginning with *by* can never be the subject of a sentence. Do not use a pronoun to restate the subject as shown in the third example that follows.

                The
▶ ~~In the~~ excerpt by Heilbrun and the story by Gould are similar.
      ʌ

                Working
▶ ~~By working~~ at night can create tension with family members.
      ʌ

▶ Dinah Macy ~~she~~ got Lyme disease when she was ten.

When you start a sentence with a dependent clause (beginning with a word like *when, if, because,* and *since*), make sure you follow that clause with an independent clause. A dependent clause cannot serve as the subject of a verb.

Swimming
▶ ~~Because she swims~~ every day does not guarantee she is healthy.
^

Trading
▶ ~~When~~ a baseball player ~~is traded~~ every few years causes
^

family problems.

Confusing comparisons   When you make comparisons, readers need to know clearly what you are comparing. See also 44a for faulty comparisons with personal pronouns.

CONFUSING COMPARISON	**Like Wallace Stevens, her job strikes readers as unexpected for a poet.** [Her job is not like the poet Wallace Stevens; her job is like his job.]
REVISED	**Like Wallace Stevens, she holds a job that strikes readers as unexpected for a poet.**

Convoluted syntax   Revise sentences that ramble on to such an extent that they become tangled. Make sure they have clear subjects, verbs, and connections between clauses.

TANGLED	**The way I feel about getting what you want is that when there is a particular position or item that you want to try to get to do your best and not give up because if you give up you have probably missed your chance of succeeding.**
POSSIBLE REVISION	**To get what you want, keep trying.**

40b Misplaced modifiers: Phrases, *not, only*, split infinitives

A modifier is a word or words describing a noun, verb, or clause. A misplaced modifier is a word, phrase, or clause that is wrongly placed so that it appears to modify the incorrect word or words.

Place a phrase or clause close to the word it modifies

MISPLACED   **She proudly showed the BlackBerry to her colleagues that her boss had given her.**

REVISED   **She proudly showed her colleagues the BlackBerry that her boss had given her.**

Take care with modifiers such as *only* and *not*   Place a word such as *only*, *even*, *just*, *nearly*, *not*, *merely*, or *simply* immediately before the word it modifies. The meaning of a sentence can change significantly as the position of a modifier changes, so careful placement is important.

▶ Next year, *not* everyone in the company will ~~not~~ get a raise. [The unrevised sentence says that nobody at all will get a raise. If you move *not*, the sentence now says that although not all workers will get a raise, some will.]

▶ *Only* the journalist began to investigate the forgery. [no one else]

▶ The journalist *only* began to investigate the forgery. [but didn't finish]

▶ The journalist began to investigate *only* the forgery. [and nothing else]

What you need to know about splitting an infinitive   When you place a word or phrase between *to* and the verb (the infinitive), the result can be awkward. Avoid splitting an infinitive when the split is unnecessary or clumsy, as in the following:

▶ They waited for the sun ~~to brightly shine.~~ *to shine brightly.*

▶ We want ~~to honestly and in confidence inform~~ *to inform* you of our plans *honestly and in confidence.*

Traditionally, a split infinitive was frowned upon, but it is now acceptable, as in the *Star Trek* motto "To boldly go where no man has gone before. . . ." Sometimes, however, splitting may be necessary to avoid ambiguity.

▶ We had *to stop* them from talking *quickly*. [Were they talking too quickly? Did we have to stop them quickly? The meaning is ambiguous.]

    ▶ We had *to quickly stop* them from talking. [The split infinitive clearly says that we were the ones who had to do something quickly.]

40c Dangling modifiers

When a modifier beginning with *-ing* or *-ed* is not grammatically connected to the noun or phrase it is intended to describe, it is said to *dangle*.

DANGLING   *Driving* across the desert, the saguaro *cactus* appeared eerily human. [Who or what was driving? The cactus?]

Usually, you can fix a dangling modifier by either (1) making the modifier refer to the person or thing performing the action or (2) rewriting the modifier as a dependent clause.

POSSIBLE   *Driving* across the desert, *the naturalists* thought the
REVISIONS saguaro cactus appeared eerily human.

    When the naturalists were driving across the desert, the saguaro cactus appeared eerily human.

40d Shifts: From statements to commands, from indirect to direct quotation, and in point of view

Sudden shifts in your sentences can disconcert readers. See also 41h on avoiding unnecessary shifts in verb tense.

Do not shift abruptly from statements to commands

                    They should demand
▶ Consumers need to be more aggressive. ~~Demand~~ refunds for
    defective merchandise.   ^

Do not shift from indirect to direct quotation   See 41i and 62d for more on tenses in indirect quotations.

    ▶ The client told us that he wanted to sign the lease and
      asked us to
      ~~would we~~ prepare the papers.
      ^

▶ She wanted to find out whether any interest had accumulated

whether she was
on her account and ~~was she~~ receiving any money.
            ^

Do not shift point of view in pronouns Be consistent in using first, second, or third person pronouns. For example, if you begin by referring to *one*, do not switch to *you* or *we*. Also avoid shifting unnecessarily between third person singular and plural forms.

SHIFT *One* needs a high salary to live in a city because *you* have to spend so much on rent and transportation.

POSSIBLE
REVISIONS *One* needs a high salary to live in a city because *one* has to spend so much on rent and transportation.

We all need a high salary to live in a city because we have to spend so much on rent and transportation.

A high salary is necessary in a city because rent and transportation cost so much.

40e Mismatch of subject and predicate

To avoid confusing readers, never use a subject and predicate that do not make logical sense together (see 37d, p. 390, for the definition of a predicate). This error is known as *faulty predication.*

       Building
▶ ~~The decision to build~~ an elaborate extension onto the train
     ^
station made all the trains arrive late. [It was not the decision that delayed the trains; building the extension did.]

▶ According to the guidelines, ~~people in~~ dilapidated public housing will be demolished this year. [Surely the housing, not people, will be demolished!]

40f Definitions and reasons ("is when" and "is because")

When you write a definition of a term, use parallel structures on either side of the verb *be.* In formal writing, avoid defining a term by using *is when* or *is where* (or *was when, was where*).

▶ A tiebreaker in tennis *is* ~~*when there is*~~ a final game to decide a set.

In giving reasons in both speech and writing, the expression *the reason is because* is becoming common. However, many readers of formal prose traditionally prefer *the reason is that* or simply *because* by itself. Decide what your readers may expect, and consider your options.

▶ *The reason* Roger Federer lost *is* ~~because~~ his opponent won the big points.
                  that (above "because")

▶ ~~The reason~~ Roger Federer lost ~~is~~ *because* his opponent won the big points.

40g *Because* and *when* clauses as subject

A dependent adverb clause (37d) beginning with *because* or *when* cannot function as the subject of a sentence.

▶ ~~Just because she swims~~ every day does not mean she is
       Swimming (above)

healthy. [The subject is now a noun phrase, *Swimming every day,* instead of a clause, *Because she swims every day.*]

▶ When people eat too much fat increases their cholesterol.
                              , *they* (above)

[The dependent clause *When people eat too much fat* is now attached to an independent clause with its own subject, *they.*]

40h Omitted words

Include necessary words in compound structures   If you omit a verb form from a compound verb, the main verb form must fit into each part of the compound; otherwise, you must use the complete verb form (see 40j on parallelism).

▶ He has always and will always try to preserve his father's good
        tried (above)

name in the community. [*Try* fits only with *will,* not with *has.*]

Include necessary words in comparisons

▶ The volleyball captain is as competitive or even more
                                   as (above)

competitive than her teammates. [The comparative structures are *as competitive as* and *more competitive than.* Do not merge them.]

If you omit the verb in the second part of a comparison, ambiguity may occur.

▶ He liked baseball more than his son~~/~~ ^did^ [Omitting *did* implies he liked baseball more than he liked his son.]

For more on faulty comparisons, see 45i. For sentence snarls caused by omitting an apostrophe, see 48c.

40i Unnecessary restated subject

Do not insert a pronoun between the subject and the verb to restate the subject (see also 62f).

            subject   verb
▶ The businessmen who supported the candidate ~~they~~ felt betrayed when he lost the election. [The stated subject is "The businessmen."]

                      — subject —   verb
▶ What may seem funny to some ~~it~~ can be deadly serious to others. [The subject is the clause "What may seem funny to some."]

40j Structures not parallel

Parallel structures are words, phrases, or clauses that use similar grammatical form. Balance your sentences by using similar grammatical constructions in each part.

NOT PARALLEL   **The results of reform were that class size decreased, more multicultural courses, and being allowed to choose a pass/fail option.**

PARALLEL CLAUSES AFTER *THAT*   **The results of reform were that class size decreased, more multicultural courses were offered, and students were allowed to choose a pass/fail option.**

PARALLEL NOUN PHRASES   **The results of reform were a decrease in class size, an increase in the number of multicultural courses, and the introduction of a pass/fail option for students.**

The use of parallel structures helps produce cohesion and coherence in a text. Aim for parallelism in sentences and in longer passages, too. The structures can be clauses or phrases, as shown in the following passages from "Maintenance" by Naomi Shihab Nye.

Parallel structures: clauses

We saw one house *where walls and windows had been sheathed in various patterns of gloomy brocade*. We visited another *where the kitchen had been removed* because the owners only ate in restaurants.

Parallel structures: verb phrases

Sometimes I'd come home to find her *lounging* in the bamboo chair on the back porch, *eating* melon, or *lying* on the couch with a bowl of half-melted ice cream balanced on her chest.

Use parallel structures with paired (correlative) conjunctions

When your sentence contains *correlative conjunctions*—pairs such as *either . . . or, neither . . . nor, not only . . . but also, both . . . and, whether . . . or,* and *as . . . as*—the structure after the second part of the pair should be exactly parallel in form to the structure after the first part.

▶ He made up his mind *either* to paint the van *or* ^to sell it to

another buyer. [*To paint* follows *either*; therefore, *to sell* should follow *or*.]

▶ She loves *both* swimming competitively *and* ~~to play~~ ^playing golf.

[An *-ing* form follows *both*; therefore, an *-ing* form should also follow *and*.]

▶ The drive to Cuernavaca was *not only* too expensive *but also* ~~was~~ too tiring to do alone. [*Too expensive* follows *not only*; therefore, *too tiring* should follow *but also*.]

Use parallel structures in comparisons with *as* or *than* and in lists

▶ ~~Driving~~ ^To drive to Cuernavaca is as expensive as to take the bus.

▶ ~~To find~~ ^Finding a life partner is infinitely more complex than

choosing a new pair of shoes.

▶ Writing well demands the following: (1) planning your time, (2) paying attention to details, (3) ~~the need for revision,~~ ^revising, and (4) proofreading.

41

Verbs

A verb expresses what the subject of the sentence is or does. Verbs may change form according to person, number, and tense; can be regular or irregular; and may require auxiliary verbs (forms of *be, do,* or *have*) or modal verbs (*will, would, can, could, shall, should, may, might,* and *must*) to complete their meaning.

A verb will fit into all four of the following:

1. They want to _____.   3. It is going to _____.
2. They will _____.   4. It might _____.

Identify a verb by checking that the *base form* (that is, the form listed as a dictionary entry) fits these sentences. Note, however, that modal verbs (see 41c) follow a different pattern. Although you may use a variety of verb forms when you speak, readers generally expect verbs in formal writing to follow predictable patterns.

41a Regular and irregular verb forms in Edited American English

Regular Verbs   Regular verbs follow a predictable pattern. From the base form—that is, the dictionary form—you can construct all the forms.

Regular Verbs

Base	-s	*-ing* Present Participle	Past Tense	Past Participle
paint	paints	painting	painted	painted
smile	smiles	smiling	smiled	smiled

Irregular verbs   Irregular verbs also have the *-s* and the present participle (*-ing*) forms, but they do not use *-ed* to form the past tense and the past participle. (For *be, do,* and *have,* see 41c; for *rise, lie,* and *sit/set,* see 41b.) However, there are many more verbs, so use a dictionary or the complete list of irregular verbs on our Web site to check irregular past tense and past participle forms if you are unsure. Always refer to 41c for help in deciding which form to use in tenses after auxiliary verbs (such as *has swam* or *has swum*?—the latter is correct).

Note, too, that verbs such as *bet, burst, cost, cut, hit, hurt, let, put, quit, set, slit, split, spread,* and *upset* are irregular only in that they make no change for their past tense or past participle form.

Common Irregular Verbs

Base Form	Past Tense	Past Participle
arise	arose	arisen
be	was/were	been
bear	bore	born, borne
beat	beat	beaten
become	became	become
begin	began	begun
bend	bent	bent
bind	bound	bound
bite	bit	bitten
bleed	bled	bled
blow	blew	blown
break	broke	broken
bring	brought	brought
build	built	built
buy	bought	bought
catch	caught	caught
choose	chose	chosen
cling	clung	clung
come	came	come
creep	crept	crept
deal	dealt	dealt
dig	dug	dug
do	did	done
draw	drew	drawn
drink	drank	drunk
drive	drove	driven
eat	ate	eaten
fall	fell	fallen
feed	fed	fed
feel	felt	felt
fight	fought	fought
find	found	found
flee	fled	fled
fly	flew	flown
forbid	forbad(e)	forbidden
forget	forgot	forgotten
forgive	forgave	forgiven

(Continued)

(Continued)

Base Form	Past Tense	Past Participle
freeze	froze	frozen
get	got	gotten, got
give	gave	given
go	went	gone
grind	ground	ground
grow	grew	grown
hang*	hung	hung
have	had	had
hear	heard	heard
hide	hid	hidden
hold	held	held
keep	kept	kept
know	knew	known
lay	laid	laid (41b)
lead	led	led
leave	left	left
lend	lent	lent
lie	lay	lain (41b)
light	lit, lighted	lit, lighted
lose	lost	lost
make	made	made
mean	meant	meant
meet	met	met
ride	rode	ridden
ring	rang	rung
rise	rose	risen (41b)
run	ran	run
say	said	said
see	saw	seen
seek	sought	sought
sell	sold	sold
send	sent	sent
shake	shook	shaken
shine	shone, shined	shone, shined
shoot	shot	shot

* *Hang* meaning "put to death" is regular: *hang, hanged, hanged.*

Base Form	Past Tense	Past Participle
shrink	shrank	shrunk
sing	sang	sung
sink	sank	sunk
sit	sat	sat (41b)
sleep	slept	slept
slide	slid	slid
speak	spoke	spoken
spend	spent	spent
spin	spun	spun
spit	spit, spat	spit
spring	sprang	sprung
stand	stood	stood
steal	stole	stolen
stick	stuck	stuck
sting	stung	stung
stink	stank, stunk	stunk
strike	struck	struck, stricken
swear	swore	sworn
sweep	swept	swept
swim	swam	swum
swing	swung	swung
take	took	taken
teach	taught	taught
tear	tore	torn
tell	told	told
think	thought	thought
throw	threw	thrown
tread	trod	trodden, trod
understand	understood	understood
wake	woke	waked, woken
wear	wore	worn
weave	wove	woven
weep	wept	wept
win	won	won
wind	wound	wound
wring	wrung	wrung
write	wrote	written

41b Verbs commonly confused

Give special attention to verbs that are similar in form but different in meaning. Some of them, called *transitive verbs,* can take a direct object. Others, called *intransitive verbs,* never take a direct object (see 62c).

1. *rise:* to get up, to ascend (intransitive; irregular)
   raise: to lift, to cause to rise (transitive; regular)

Base	-s	-ing	Past Tense	Past Participle
rise	rises	rising	rose	risen
raise	raises	raising	raised	raised

▶ The sun *rose* at 5:55 a.m. today.

▶ The historian *raised* the issue of accuracy. [The direct object answers the question "raised what?"]

2. *sit:* to occupy a seat (intransitive; irregular)
   set: to put or place (transitive; irregular)

Base	-s	-ing	Past Tense	Past Participle
sit	sits	sitting	sat	set
set	sets	setting	sat	set

▶ The audience *sat* on hard wooden seats.

▶ The artist *set* his "Squashed Clock" sculpture in the middle of the shelf.

3. *lie:* to recline (intransitive; irregular)
   lay: to put or place (transitive; regular)

Base	-s	-ing	Past Tense	Past Participle
lie	lies	lying	lay	lain
lay	lays	laying	laid	laid

▶ She ~~laid~~ lay down for an hour after her oral presentation.

▶ She was ~~laying~~ lying down when you called.

▶ ~~Lie~~ Lay the map on the floor.

In addition, note the verb *lie* ("to say something untrue"), which is intransitive and regular.

Base	-s	-ing	Past Tense	Past Participle
lie	lies	lying	lied	lied

▶ He *lied* when he said he had won three trophies.

41c Auxiliary verbs

An auxiliary verb is used with a main verb and sometimes with other auxiliaries. The auxiliary verbs are *do, have,* and *be,* and the nine modal verbs are *will, would, can, could, shall, should, may, might,* and *must* (61b). Note the irregular forms of *do, have,* and *be.*

Base	Present Tense Forms	-ing	Past	Past Participle
do	do, does	doing	did	done
have	have, has	having	had	had
be	am, is, are	being	was, were	been

See 43a for agreement with present tense forms of *do, have,* and *be.*

 LANGUAGE AND CULTURE

Language and Dialect Variation with *Be*

In some languages (Chinese and Russian, for example), forms of *be* used as an auxiliary ("She *is* singing") or as a linking verb ("He *is* happy") can be omitted. In some spoken dialects of English (African American Vernacular, for example), subtle linguistic distinctions not possible in Standard English can be achieved: The omission of a form of *be* and the use of the base form in place of an inflected form (a form that shows number, person, mood, or tense) signal entirely different meanings.

VERNACULAR		STANDARD
He busy.	(temporarily)	He is busy now.
She be busy.	(habitually)	She is busy all the time.

Edited American English always requires the inclusion of a form of *be.*

are
▶ Latecomers always at a disadvantage.
　　　　　　　^

Auxiliary verbs can be used in combination. Whatever the combination, the form of the main verb is determined by the auxiliary that precedes it.

Verb Forms Following Auxiliaries

Last Auxiliary and Its Forms	+ base	+ *ing*	+ past participle
do modals (*can, could, will, would, shall, should, must, might, may*)	*did* write *might* go *would* fall		
have			*has/have/had* written should *have* seen would *have* gone
be (active)		*is* writing *were* singing might *be* driving has *been* running should have *been* thinking	
be (passive)			*are* grown *was* taken was *being* stolen would *be* eaten has *been* written might have *been* worn

Pay careful attention to the tricky editing points here:

1. Make sure you use a past participle form after *have*. In speech, we run sounds together, and the pronunciation may be mistakenly carried over into writing.

   ▶ He could ~~of~~ run faster.
      ^{have}

   ▶ She should ~~of~~ left that job a long time ago.
      ^{have}

   The contracted forms *could've, should've, would've,* and so on are probably responsible for the nonstandard substitution of the word *of* in place of *have*. Watch out for this as you edit.

2. With modal verbs and the verbs *do* and *have,* the verb form following is fixed. It is only with *be* that a conscious choice of active or passive voice comes into play.

▶ Laura *is taking* her driving test. [active]

▶ Laura *was taken* to the hospital last night. [passive]

NOTE FOR MULTILINGUAL WRITERS

What Comes before *Be, Been,* and *Being*

Be requires a modal auxiliary before it to form a complete verb (*could be jogging; will be closed*). *Been* requires *have, has,* or *had* (*have been driving; has been eaten*). *Being* must be preceded by *am, is, are, was,* or *were* to form a complete verb and must be followed by an adjective or a past participle: *You are being silly. He was being followed.*

41d Verb tenses: Overview

Tenses indicate time as perceived by the speaker or writer. The following examples show active voice verbs referring to past, present, and future time. For passive voice verbs, see chapter 42.

Past Time

Simple past	They *arrived* yesterday./They *did* not *arrive* today.
Past progressive	They *were leaving* when the phone rang.
Past perfect	Everyone *had left* when I called.
Past perfect progressive	We *had been sleeping* for an hour before you arrived.

Present Time

Simple present	He *eats* Wheaties every morning./ He *does* not *eat* eggs.
Present progressive	They *are working* today.
Present perfect	She *has* never *read* Melville.
Present perfect progressive	He *has been living* here for five years.

Future Time (using *will*)

Simple future	She *will arrive* soon.
Future progressive	They *will be playing* baseball at noon tomorrow.
Future perfect	He *will have finished* the project by Friday.
Future perfect progressive	By the year 2014, they *will have been running* the company for twenty-five years.

Other modal auxiliaries can substitute for *will* and thus change the meaning: *must arrive, might be playing, may have finished, should have been running* (see also 61b).

NOTE FOR MULTILINGUAL WRITERS

Verbs Not Using *-ing* Forms for Progressive Tenses

Use simple tenses, not progressive forms, with verbs expressing mental activity referring to the senses, preference, or thought, as well as with verbs of possession, appearance, and inclusion (for example, *smell, prefer, understand, own, seem, contain*).

▶ The fish in the showcase is smelling bad.
$\qquad\qquad\qquad\qquad\qquad\qquad$ smells $\wedge$

▶ They are possessing different behavior patterns.
$\qquad$ possess $\wedge$

41e Present tenses

Simple present   Use the simple present tense for the following purposes:

1. To make a generalization

   ▶ Gardening *nourishes* the spirit.

2. To indicate a permanent or habitual activity

   ▶ The poet *uses* rhyme and meter in an innovative way.

   ▶ The directors *distribute* a financial report every six months.

3. To express future time in dependent clauses (clauses beginning with words such as *if, when, before, after, until, as soon as*) when *will* is used in the independent clause

   ▶ When the newt colony *dies* in the cold weather, building construction will begin.

4. To discuss literature and the arts (called the *literary present*) even if the work was written in the past or the author is no longer alive

   ▶ In *Zami*, Audre Lorde *describes* how a librarian *introduces* her to the joys of reading.

However, when you write a narrative of your own, use past tenses to tell about past actions.

   ▶ Then the candidate ~~walks~~ up to the crowd and ~~kisses~~ all the babies.

   (walked / kissed)

 NOTE FOR MULTILINGUAL WRITERS

No *Will* in Time Clause

In a dependent clause beginning with a conjunction such as *if, when, before, after, until,* or *as soon as,* do not use *will* to express future time. Use *will* only in the independent clause. Use the simple present in the dependent clause.

   ▶ When they ~~will~~ arrive, the meeting will begin.

Present progressive   Use the present progressive to indicate an action in progress at the moment of speaking or writing.

   ▶ Publishers *are getting* nervous about Internet copyright issues.

However, do not use progressive forms with intransitive verbs such as *believe, know, like, prefer, want, smell, own, seem, appear,* and *contain.*

   ▶ Many people ~~are believing~~ that there may be life on other planets.

   (believe)

Present perfect and present perfect progressive   Use the present perfect in the following instances:

1. To indicate that an action occurring at some unstated time in the past is related to present time

   ▶ They *have worked* in New Mexico, so they know its laws.

2. To indicate that an action beginning in the past continues to the present

   ▶ She *has worked* for the same company since I *have known* her.

If you state the exact time when something occurred, use the simple past tense, not the present perfect.

> worked
> ▶ They ~~have worked~~ in Arizona three years ago.

3. To report research results in APA style

> ▶ Feynmann *has shown* that science can be fun.

Use the present perfect progressive when you indicate the length of time an action has been in progress up to the present time.

> ▶ Researchers *have been searching* for a cure for arthritis for many years. [This implies that they are still searching.]

41f Past tenses

Use past tenses consistently. Do not switch from past to present or future for no reason (see 41h).

Simple past   Use the simple past tense when you specify a past time or event.

> ▶ World War I soldiers *suffered* in the trenches.

When the sequence of past events is indicated with words like *before* or *after,* use the simple past for both events.

> ▶ She *knew* how to write her name before she went to school.

Use past tenses in an indirect quotation (a reported quotation, not in quotation marks) introduced by a past tense verb.

> ▶ His chiropractor *told* him that the adjustments *were* over.

Past progressive   Use the past progressive for an activity in progress over time or at a specified point in the past.

> ▶ Abraham Lincoln *was attending* the theater when he was assassinated.

Past perfect and past perfect progressive   Use the past perfect or the past perfect progressive only when one past event was completed before another past event or stated past time.

> ▶ Ben *had cooked* the whole meal by the time Sam arrived.
> [Two events occurred: Ben cooked the meal; then Sam arrived.]

▶ He *had been cooking* for three hours when his sister finally offered to help. [An event in progress—cooking—was interrupted in the past.]

Make sure that the past tense form you choose expresses your exact meaning.

▶ When the student protesters marched into the building at noon, the administrators *were leaving*. [The administrators were in the process of leaving. They began to leave at, say, 11:57 a.m.]

▶ When the student protesters marched into the building at noon, the administrators *had left*. [There was no sign of the administrators. They had already left at 11 a.m.]

▶ When the student protesters marched into the building at noon, the administrators *left*. [The administrators saw the protesters and then left at 12:01 p.m.]

41g *-ed* endings: Past tense and past participle forms

Both the past tense form and the past participle of regular verbs end in *-ed*. Edited American English (see 37c) requires the *-ed* ending in the following instances:

1. To form the past tense of a regular verb.

   ▶ The new trainee ask$\overset{ed}{\wedge}$ to take on more responsibility.

2. To form the expression *used to*, indicating past habit

   ▶ Computers use$\overset{d}{\wedge}$ to be more expensive than they are now.

3. To form the past participle of a regular verb after the auxiliary *has*, *have*, or *had* in the active voice or after forms of *be* (*am, is, are, was, were, be, being, been*) in the passive voice (see chapter 42)

   ▶ The Kennedy family has work$\overset{ed}{\wedge}$ in politics for a long time. [active]

   ▶ Their work will not be finish$\overset{ed}{\wedge}$ soon. [passive]

4. To form a past participle used as an adjective

   ▶ The nurses rushed to help the injure$\overset{d}{\wedge}$ toddler.

   ▶ I was surprise$\overset{d}{\wedge}$ to read how many awards he had won.

NOTE FOR MULTILINGUAL WRITERS

The *-ed* Ending

The *-ed* ending is particularly troublesome for learners of English because in speech the ending is difficult to hear and may seem to be dropped—particularly when it blends into the next sound.

> ► They wash ^*ed* two baskets of laundry last night.

This is an area that will always need careful editing.

The following *-ed* forms are used with *be: concerned, confused, depressed, divorced, embarrassed, married, prejudiced, satisfied, scared, supposed (to), surprised, used (to), worried.* Some can also be used with *get, seem, appear,* and *look.* Do not omit the *-d* ending.

> ► People are often confuse^*d* when driving around a rotary in England.

> ► They were suppose^*d* to call their parents.

Do not confuse the past tense and past participle forms of an irregular verb (41a). A past tense form occurs alone as a complete verb, and a past participle form must be used with a *have* or *be* auxiliary.

> ► He ~~drunk~~ ^*drank* the liquid before his medical tests.

> ► She ~~done~~ ^*did* her best to learn how to count in Japanese.

> ► The explorers could have ~~went~~ ^*gone* alone.

> ► A chime is ~~rang~~ ^*rung* to conclude the yoga session.

41h Tense shifts

If you use tenses consistently throughout a piece of writing, you help readers understand what is happening and when. Check that your verbs consistently express present or past time, both within a sentence and from one sentence to the next. Avoid unnecessary tense shifts.

TENSE SHIFTS **Selecting a jury *was* very difficult. The lawyers *ask* many questions to discover bias and prejudice;**

sometimes, the prospective jurors *had* the idea they *are acting* in a play.

REVISED **Selecting a jury *was* very difficult. The lawyers *asked* many questions to discover bias and prejudice; sometimes, the prospective jurors *had* the idea they *were acting* in a play.**

When you write about events or ideas presented by another writer, use the literary present consistently (see 41e).

illustrates
▶ **The author ~~illustrated~~ the images of women in two shows using advertisements and dramas on TV. One way shows women who advanced their careers by themselves, and the other shows those who used beauty to gain recognition.**

Tense shifts are appropriate in the following instances:

1. When you signal a time change with a time word or phrase

signal for switch from past to present
▶ **Harold *was* my late grandfather's name, and *now* it *is* mine.**

2. When you follow a generalization (present tense) with a specific example of a past incident

generalization
▶ **Some bilingual schools *offer* intensive instruction in English.**

specific example
▶ **My sister, for example, *went* to a bilingual school where she *studied* English for two hours every day.**

41i Tenses in indirect quotations

An indirect quotation reports what someone said. It does not use quotation marks, and it follows the tense of the introductory verb. For example, when the verb introducing an indirect quotation is in a present tense, the indirect quotation should preserve the tense of the original direct quotation (see also 62d).

DIRECT **"The economic outlook has improved."**

present   indirect quotation
INDIRECT **The reporter *says* that the economic outlook has improved.**

When the introductory verb is in a past tense, use forms that express past time in the indirect quotation.

DIRECT   "The banks are lending and the economic outlook has improved."

                              past   ┌──────── indirect quotation ────────
INDIRECT   The reporter *announced* that the banks were lending
           ──┐
           and the economic outlook *had improved.*

In a passage of more than one sentence, preserve the sequence of tenses showing past time throughout the whole passage.

▶ The reporter announced that the banks were lending and the economic outlook *had improved.* His newspaper *had reassigned* him to another case, so he *was ending* his daily reports on the crisis.

Note: Use a present tense after a past tense introductory verb only if the statement is a general statement that holds true in present time.

▶ The reporter *announced* that he *is* happy with his new assignment.

41j Verbs in conditional sentences, wishes, requests, demands, and recommendations

Conditions   When *if* or *unless* introduces a dependent clause, the sentence expresses a condition. There are four types of conditional sentences: two refer to actual or possible situations, and two refer to speculative or hypothetical situations.

KEY POINTS
Verb Tenses in Conditional Sentences

MEANING EXPRESSED	*IF* CLAUSE	INDEPENDENT CLAUSE
1. Fact	Simple present	Simple present

▶ If mortgage rates *go* down, house sales *increase.*

MEANING EXPRESSED	*IF* CLAUSE	INDEPENDENT CLAUSE
2. Prediction/ possibility	Simple present	*will, can, should, might* + base form

> ► If you *turn* left here, you *will end up* in Mississippi.

> ► If we *don't speak* ill of the dead, who *will*?
>
> —Harold Bloom

3. Speculation about present or future	Simple past or subjunctive *were*	*would, could, should, might* + base form

> ► If he *had* an iPhone, he *would download* music. [But he does not have one.]

> ► If she *were* my lawyer, I *might win* the case. [But she is not.]

4. Speculation about past	Past perfect (*had* + past participle)	*would have could have should have might have* + past participle

> ► If they *had saved* the diaries, they *could have sold* them. [But they did not save them.]

Use of subjunctive *were* in place of *was* With speculative conditions about the present and future using the verb *be, were* is used in place of *was* in the dependent *if* clause. This use of *were* to indicate hypothetical situations involves what is called the *subjunctive mood*.

> ► If my aunt *were* sixty-five, she *could get* a discount airfare. [My aunt is sixty.]

Blending Some blending of time and tenses can occur, as in the case of a condition that speculates about the past in relation to the effect on the present.

> ► If I *had bought* a new car instead of this old wreck, I *would feel* a lot safer today.

Use of *would* When writing in an academic setting, use *would* only in the independent clause, not in the conditional clause. However, *would* occurs frequently in the conditional clause in speech and in informal writing.

> *showed*
> ► If the fish-fry committee ~~would show~~ more initiative, people
> might attend their events more regularly.

> *had*
> ► If the driver ~~would have~~ heard what the pedestrian said, he
> would have been angry.

***Would, could,* and *might* with conditional clause understood** *Would, could,* and *might* are used in independent clauses when no conditional clause is present. These are situations that are contrary to fact, and the conditional clause is understood.

> ► I *would* never *advise* her to leave college without a degree. She *might come back* later and blame me for her lack of direction.

Wishes Like some conditions, wishes deal with speculation. For a present wish—about something that has not happened and is therefore hypothetical and imaginary—use the past tense or subjunctive *were* in the dependent clause. For a wish about the past, use the past perfect: *had* + past participle.

A wish about the present

> ► I wish I *had* your attitude.

> ► I wish that Shakespeare *were* still alive.

A wish about the past

> ► Some union members wish that the strike *had* never *occurred.*

Requests, demands, and recommendations The subjunctive also appears after certain verbs, such as *request, command, insist, demand, move* (meaning "propose"), *propose,* and *urge.* In these cases, the verb in the dependent clause is the base form regardless of the person and number of the subject.

> ► The dean suggested that students *be* allowed to vote.

> ► He insisted that she *submit* the report.

> ► I move that the treasurer *revise* the budget.

Some idiomatic expressions preserve the use of the subjunctive, for example, *far* be *it from me, if need* be, *as it* were.

42

Passive Voice

In the active voice, the grammatical subject is the doer of the action, and the sentence tells "who's doing what." The passive voice tells what "is done to" the subject of the sentence. The person or thing doing the action may or may not be mentioned but is always implied: "My car was repaired" (by somebody at the garage).

Active

    ┌── subject ──┐ active voice verb ┌── direct object ──┐
▶ **Alice Walker**   **wrote**   *The Color Purple.*

Passive

                     passive
   ┌────── subject ──────┐ ┌─ voice verb ─┐ ┌── doer or agent ──┐
▶ *The Color Purple* **was written** **by Alice Walker.**

42a When to use the passive voice

Use the passive voice sparingly. A general rule is to use the passive voice only when the doer or agent in your sentence (the person or thing acting) is unknown or is unimportant or when you want to connect the topics of two clauses (see 32a and 42d).

> ▶ The pandas are rare. Two of them *will be returned* to the wild.

> ▶ He had a lot of people working for him, maybe sixty, and most of them liked him most of the time. Three of them *will be* seriously *considered* for his job.
>
> —Ellen Goodman, "The Company Man"

However, in scientific writing, the passive voice is often preferred to indicate objective procedures. Scientists and engineers are interested in analyzing data and in performing studies that other researchers can replicate. The individual doing the experiment is therefore relatively unimportant and usually is not the subject of the sentence.

> ▶ The experiment *was conducted* in a classroom. Participants *were instructed* to remove their watches prior to the experiment.

NOTE FOR MULTILINGUAL WRITERS

Passive Voice with Transitive Verbs

Use the passive voice only with verbs that are transitive in English (that is, they can be followed by a direct object). Intransitive verbs such as *happen*, *occur*, and *try* (*to*) are not used in the passive voice.

▶ The ceremony ~~was~~ happened yesterday.

▶ Morality is an issue that ~~was~~ tried to explain ~~by~~ *have*
   (many philosophers)

42b How to form the passive voice

The complete verb of a passive voice sentence consists of a form of the verb *be* followed by a past participle.

receiver as subject   verb: *be* + past participle   doer omitted or named after *by*

▶ The windows *are cleaned* [by someone] every month.

▶ The windows *were being cleaned* yesterday afternoon.

▶ The windows *will have been cleaned* by the end of the workday.

Auxiliaries such as *would, can, could, should, may, might,* and *must* can also replace *will* when the meaning demands it.

▶ The windows *might be cleaned* next month.

42c Overuse of the passive voice

In the humanities, your writing will generally be clearer and stronger if you name the subject and use verbs in the active voice to explain who is doing what. If you overuse the passive voice, the effect will be heavy and impersonal (see 31a).

UNNECESSARY PASSIVE   He *was alerted* to the danger of drugs by his doctor and *was persuaded* by her to enroll in a treatment program.

REVISED   His doctor alerted him to the danger of drugs and persuaded him to enroll in a treatment program.

42d The passive voice as connector

In the following passage, notice how the passive voice preserves the topic chain of *I* subjects (see also 32a):

▶ **I remember to start with that day in Sacramento . . . when I first entered a classroom, able to understand some fifty stray English words. The third of four children, I** *had been preceded* **to a Roman Catholic school by an older brother and sister.**

—Richard Rodriguez, *Hunger of Memory*

Subject-Verb Agreement

The principle of agreement means that when you use the present tense of any verb or the past tense of the verb *be* in academic writing, you must make the subject and verb agree in person (first, second, or third) and number (singular or plural): *A baby cries. Babies cry.*

43a Basic principles for an -s ending

The ending -s is added to both nouns and verbs but for very different reasons.

1. An -s ending on a noun is a plural signal: *her brothers* (more than one).

2. An -s ending on a verb is a singular signal; -s is added to a third person singular verb in the present tense: *Her plumber wears gold jewelry.*

> ### KEY POINTS
> #### Two Key Points about Agreement
>
> **1.** Follow the "one -s rule" in the present tense. Generally, you can put an -s on a noun to make it plural, or you can put an -s on a verb to make it singular. (But see the irregular forms *is* and *has* on p. 426.) Do not add an -s to both subject and verb.
>
> NO   The articles explains the controversy. [Violates the "one -s rule"]
>
> POSSIBLE   The article explains the controversy.
> REVISIONS
>   The articles explain the controversy.
>
> *(Continued)*

(Continued)

2. Do not omit a necessary -*s*.

> deals
> Whitehead's novel ~~deal~~ with issues of race and morality.
> ^

> reports
> The ~~report~~ in the files describe the housing project in detail.
> ^

Most simple present verbs show agreement with an -*s* ending. The verb *be,* however, has three instead of two present tense forms. In addition, *be* is the only verb to show agreement in the past tense, where it has two forms: *were* and the third person singular *was.* The table shows agreement forms for a regular verb and for the three auxiliary verbs *have, be,* and *do.*

Subject-Verb Agreement

Base Form	like (regular)	have	be	do
Simple Present: Singular				
First person: I	like	have	am	do
Second person: you	like	have	are	do
Third person: he, she, it	likes	has	is	does
Simple Present: Plural				
First person: we	like	have	are	do
Second person: you	like	have	are	do
Third person: they	like	have	are	do

LANGUAGE AND CULTURE

Issues of Subject-Verb Agreement

Many languages make no change in the verb form to indicate number and person, and several spoken versions of English, such as African American Vernacular (AAV), Caribbean Creole, and London Cockney, do not observe the standard rules of agreement.

> AAV: She *have* a lot of work experience.

> ▶ Cockney: He *don't* never wear that brown whistle. [The standard form is *doesn't*; other nonstandard forms in this sentence are *don't never* (a double negative) and *whistle*— short for *whistle and flute*, rhyming slang for *suit*.]

Use authentic forms like these when quoting direct speech; for your formal academic writing, though, follow the subject-verb agreement conventions used in academic English.

43b What to do when words come between the subject and verb

When words separate the subject and verb, find the verb and ask "who?" or "what?" about it to determine the subject. Ignore any intervening words.

> ▶ The general discussing the attacks looks tired. [Who looks tired? The subject, *general*, is singular.]

> ▶ Her collection of baseball cards is valuable. [What is valuable? The subject, *collection*, is singular.]

> ▶ The government's proposals about preserving the
>
> environment cause controversy. [What things cause controversy? The subject, *proposals*, is plural.]

Do not be confused by intervening words ending in -s, such as *always* and *sometimes*. The -s ending still must appear on a present tense verb if the subject is singular.

> ▶ A school play always get the parents involved.
>   s

Phrases introduced by *as well as, along with, together with*, and *in addition to* that come between the subject and the verb do not change the number of the verb.

> ▶ His daughter, as well as his two sons, want him to move nearby.
>   s

> ▶ The article, together with the books, make a significant
>   s
> contribution to the topic.

43c Agreement with linking verbs (*be, seem, appear*)

Linking verbs such as *be, become, look,* and *appear* are followed by what is called a *complement*, and a subject complement should not be confused with a subject (see 37d). Make the verb agree with the subject.

> plural
> ┌── subject ──┐
> **Rare books *are* her passion.**
> plural verb
> singular
> ┌ complement ┐

> singular
> ┌── subject ──┐
> **Her passion *is* rare books.**
> singular verb
> plural
> ┌ complement ┐

▶ **My favorite part of dorm life *has become* the parties.**

▶ **Parties *have become* my favorite part of dorm life.**

43d What to do when the subject follows the verb

When the subject follows the verb in the sentence, you must still make the subject and verb agree.

1. Questions In a question, make the auxiliary verb agree with the subject, which follows the verb.

> singular
> ┌ subject ┐
▶ *Does* **the editor agree to the changes?**

> plural subject
▶ *Do* **the editor and the production manager agree to the changes?**

2. Initial *here* or *there* When a sentence begins with *here* or *there*, make the verb agree with the subject.

> singular
> ┌ subject ┐
▶ **There *is* a reason to rejoice.**

> plural subject
▶ **There *are* many reasons to rejoice.**

However, avoid excessive use of an initial *there* (see 31b): *We have a reason to rejoice.*

NOTE FOR MULTILINGUAL WRITERS

Singular Verb after *It*

It does not follow the same pattern as *here* and *there*. The verb attached to an *it* subject is always singular.

▶ It *is* hundreds of miles away.

---

3. Inverted word order When a sentence begins not with the subject but with a phrase placed before the verb, the verb still agrees with the subject (see also 33d, p. 365).

plural
verb
┌──prepositional phrase──┐ │ ┌─ plural subject ─┐
▶ **In front of the library sit two stone lions.** [Who or what performs the action of the verb? Two stone lions do.]

43e Eight tricky subjects with singular verbs

1. *Each* and *every* *Each* and *every* may seem to indicate more than one, but grammatically, they are singular words. Use them with a singular verb, even if they are parts of a compound subject (43g) using *and* or *or*.

▶ *Each* of the poems *employs* a different rhyme scheme.

▶ *Every* change in procedures *causes* problems.

▶ *Every* essay and quiz *counts* in the grade.

2. *-ing* or infinitive form as subject With a subject beginning with the *-ing* verb form used as a noun (a *gerund*) or with an infinitive, always use a singular verb form.

singular
┌─ subject ─┐
▶ *Speaking* in public *causes* many people as much fear as death.

▶ *To keep* our air clean *takes* careful planning.

3. Singular nouns ending in *-s* Some names of disciplines that end in *-s* (*economics, physics, politics, mathematics, statistics*) are not plural. Use them and the noun *news* with a singular verb.

▶ The news *has* been bad lately.

▶ Politics *is* dirty business.

4. Phrases of time, money, and weight When the subject is regarded as one unit, use a singular verb.

▶ Five hundred dollars *seems* too much to pay.

▶ Seven years *was* a long time to spend at college.

But

▶ Seven years *have* passed.

5. Uncountable nouns An uncountable noun (such as *furniture, jewelry, equipment, advice, happiness, honesty, information,* and *knowledge*) encompasses all the items in its class. An uncountable noun does not have a plural form and is always followed by a singular verb (60b).

▶ That advice *makes* me nervous.

▶ The information found in the press *is* not always accurate.

6. *One of* *One of* is followed by a plural noun (the object of the preposition *of*) and a singular verb form. The verb agrees with the subject *one*.

▶ *One* of her friends *loves* to tango.

▶ *One* of the reasons for his difficulties *is* that he spends too much money.

For agreement with *one of* and *the only one of* followed by a relative clause, see 46c, page 457.

7. *The number of/a number of* The phrase *the number of* is followed by a plural noun (the object of the preposition *of*) and a singular verb form.

▶ The number of reasons *is* growing.

However, with the phrase *a number of,* meaning "several," use a plural verb.

▶ A number of reasons *are* listed in the letter.

8. The title of a long work or a word referred to as the word itself Use a singular verb with the title of a long, whole work or a word referred to as the word itself. Use a singular verb even if the title or word is plural in form (see also 52a and 52d).

▶ *Cats was* based on a poem by T. S. Eliot.

▶ In her story, the *word* "dudes" *appears* five times.

43f Collective noun as subject

A collective noun names a collection of people or things: *class, government, family, jury, committee, group, couple,* or *team.* If you refer to the group as a whole, use a singular verb.

▶ The family *returns* to Mexico every other year.

Use a plural verb if you wish to emphasize differences among the individuals or if members of the group are thought of as individuals.

▶ His family *are* mostly artists and musicians.

▶ The jury *are* from every walk of life.

If that seems awkward to you, revise the sentence.

▶ His close relatives *are* mostly artists and musicians.

▶ The members of the jury *are* from every walk of life.

However, with the collective nouns *police, poor, elderly,* and *young,* always use plural verbs.

▶ The elderly *deserve* our respect.

43g Subjects containing *and, or,* or *nor*

Subjects with *and* When a subject consists of two or more parts joined by *and,* treat the subject as plural and use a plural verb.

```
         ┌────── plural subject ──────┐   ↗ plural verb
```
▶ His instructor and his advisor *want* him to change his major.

However, if the parts of the compound subject refer to a single person or thing, use a singular verb.

```
         ┌── singular subject (one person) ──┐  ↗ singular verb
```
▶ The restaurant's chef and owner *makes* good fajitas.

—singular subject—   ^singular verb

▶ **Fish and chips** *is* **a popular dish in England, but it is no longer served wrapped in newspaper.**

Also use a singular verb with a subject beginning with *each* or *every*.

▶ **Every claim and conclusion** *deserves* **consideration.**

With *or* or *nor*   When the parts of a compound subject are joined by *or* or *nor*, the verb agrees with the part nearer to it.

▶ **Her sister or her parents** *look* **after her children every Friday.**

▶ **Neither her parents nor her sister** *drives* **a station wagon.**

43h   Indefinite pronouns (*anyone, everybody, nobody*, etc.)

Words that refer to nonspecific people or things (indefinite pronouns) can be tricky. Most of them take a singular verb. Usage may differ in speech and writing, so when you write, it is important to pay attention to the conventions of agreement between subject and verb.

Indefinite pronouns used with a singular verb

> someone, somebody, something
>
> anyone, anybody, anything
>
> one, no one, nobody, nothing
>
> everyone, everybody, everything
>
> each, either, neither

▶ **Nobody** *knows* **the answer.**

▶ **Everyone** *agrees* **on the author's intention.**

▶ **Everything about the results** *was* **questioned in the review.**

▶ **Both films are popular; neither** *contains* **gratuitous violence.**

▶ **Each of the chess games** *promises* **to be exciting.**

See 44d, page 442, on the personal pronouns to use (*he*? *she*? *they*?) to refer to indefinite pronouns.

A note on *none* and *neither*

None Some writers prefer to use a singular verb after *none* (of) because *none* means "not one": *None of the contestants has smiled.* However, as *The American Heritage Dictionary* (4th ed.) points out, a singular or a plural verb is technically acceptable: *None of the authorities has (or have) greater tolerance on this point than H. W. Fowler.* Check to see if your instructor prefers the literal singular usage.

Neither The pronoun *neither* is, like *none*, technically singular: *The partners have made a decision; neither wants to change the product.* In informal writing, however, you may come across *neither* with a plural verb, especially when followed by an *of* phrase: *Neither of the novels reveal a polished style.*

43i Quantity words

Some quantity words are singular, and some are plural. Others can be used to indicate either singular or plural depending on the noun they refer to.

Words Expressing Quantity

With Singular Nouns and Verbs	With Plural Nouns and Verbs
much	many
(a) little	(a) few
a great deal (of)	several
a large amount of	a large number of
less	fewer
another	both

See 64c for more on the difference between *few* and *a few*.

▶ Much *has* been accomplished.

▶ Much of the machinery *needs* to be repaired.

▶ Many *have* gained from the recent economic swings.

▶ Fewer electronic gadgets *are* sold during a recession.

You will see and hear *less* used in place of *fewer*, especially with numbers ("5 items or less"), but in formal writing, use *fewer* to refer to a plural word.

▶ More *movies* have been made this year than last, but *fewer have* made a large profit.

Quantity words used with both singular and plural nouns and verbs The following quantity words take their cue from the number (singular or plural) of the noun they refer to: *all, any, half (of), more, most, no, other, part (of), some.*

▶ You gave me *some information. More is* **necessary.**

▶ You gave me *some facts. More are* **needed.**

▶ *All the furniture is* **old.**

▶ *All the students look* **healthy.**

43j Agreement with *this, that, these, those, mine, ours*, etc.

Demonstratives agree in number with a noun: *this solution, these solutions; that problem, those problems.*

plural

▶ **The mayor is planning changes. These will be controversial.**

Singular	Plural
this	these
that	those

Possessives such as *mine, his, hers, ours, yours,* and *theirs* can refer to both singular and plural antecedents (see 44d).

singular
subject   singular verb
▶ **Her average is good, but *mine is* better.**

plural
subject   plural verb
▶ **His grades are good, but *mine are* better.**

43k Agreement with subject clauses beginning with *what* or other question words

When a clause introduced by *what* or other question words, such as *how, who,* and *why,* functions as the subject of an independent clause, use a third person singular verb in the independent clause.

subject
▶ **What they are proposing *concerns* us all.**

subject
▶ **How the players train *makes* all the difference.**

When the verb is followed by the linking verb *be* and a plural complement, some writers use a plural verb. However, some readers may object.

▶ What I need *are* black pants and an orange shirt.

You can avoid the issue by revising the sentence to eliminate the *what*
clause.

▶ I need black pants and an orange shirt.

44

Pronouns

A pronoun is a word that substitutes for a noun, a noun phrase, or
another pronoun.

▶ Jack's hair is so long that *it* hangs over *his* collar.

44a Forms of personal pronouns (*I* or *me*, *he* or *him*?)

Personal pronouns change form to indicate person (first, second, or
third), number (singular or plural), and function in a clause.

KEY POINTS

Forms of Personal Pronouns

PERSON	SUBJECT	OBJECT	POSSESSIVE (+ NOUN)	POSSESSIVE (STANDS ALONE)	INTENSIVE AND REFLEXIVE
1st person singular	I	me	my	mine	myself
2nd person singular and plural	you	you	your	yours	yourself/ yourselves
3rd person singular	he	him	his	his	himself
	she	her	her	hers	herself
	it	it	its	its [rare]	itself

(Continued)

(Continued)

PERSON	SUBJECT	OBJECT	POSSESSIVE (+ NOUN)	POSSESSIVE (STANDS ALONE)	INTENSIVE AND REFLEXIVE
1st person plural	we	us	our	ours	ourselves
3rd person plural	they	them	their	theirs	themselves

In a compound subject or compound object with *and*: *I* or *me*; *he* or *him*?   In speech, the forms *I* and *me, he* and *him, she* and *her* are often interchanged even by educated people (the fourth example sentence below was said by President Obama in an impromptu interview), but you should take care to edit them in formal writing. To decide which pronoun form to use with a compound subject or compound object, mentally recast the sentence with only one pronoun in the subject or object position.

► Jenny and ~~me~~ ^I^ volunteer in a soup kitchen. [Drop the words

    Jenny and. Then you will have *I volunteer,* not *me volunteer.* Here you need the subject form, *I.*]

► ~~Him~~ ^He^ and his whole family decided to move to Oregon. [He

    decided to move.]

► ~~Her~~ ^She^ and ~~me~~ ^I^ tried to solve the problem. [She tried. I tried.]

► The ambassador invited Michelle and ~~I~~ ^me^ to join the celebration.

    [If the word *Michelle* is dropped, the sentence would be *The ambassador invited me,* not *The ambassador invited I.* The object form is needed here. He invited *me,* not "He invited I."]

After a preposition   After a preposition, you need an object form.

► Between you and ~~I~~ ^me^, the company is in serious trouble.

► Rachid stared at my colleague and ~~I~~ ^me^. [He stared at my colleague. He stared at me.]

After a linking verb   In formal academic writing, use the subject form of a personal pronoun after a linking verb, such as *be*, *seem*, *look*, or *appear*.

▶ **Was that Oprah Winfrey? It was *she*.** [Informal: "It was her."]

▶ **It was *she* who gave away cars.** [Many writers would revise this sentence to sound less formal: "She was the one who gave away cars" or simply "She gave away cars."]

After a verb and before an infinitive   Use the object form of a personal pronoun after a verb and before an infinitive. When a sentence has only one object, this principle is easy to apply.

▶ **The dean wanted *him* to lead the procession.**

Difficulties occur with compound objects.

  him and me
▶ **The dean wanted ~~he and I~~ to lead the procession.**
            ^

In appositive phrases and with *we* or *us* before a noun   When using a personal pronoun in an appositive phrase (a phrase that gives additional information about a preceding noun), determine whether the noun that the pronoun refers to functions as subject or as object in its own clause.

                                                      appositive
                    ┌── direct object ◄──┐ ┌── phrase ──┐
▶ **The supervisor praised only two employees, Ramon and me.**
    [She praised me.]

                    ┌── subject ◄──┐ _appositive phrase_
                                   ┌──────────────┐
▶ **Only two employees, Ramon and I, received a bonus.** [I received a bonus.]

Similarly, when you consider whether to use *we* or *us* before a noun, use *us* when the pronoun is the direct object of a verb or preposition; use *we* when it is the subject.

                    object of preposition
                              /
▶ **LL Cool J waved to us fans.**
    subject
        /
▶ **We fans have decided to form a club.**

In comparisons   In comparisons with *than* and *as*, decide when to use the subject or object form of the personal pronoun by mentally completing the meaning of the comparison.

▶ **She is certainly not more intelligent than I.** [. . . than I am.]

▶ **Matt and Juanita work in the same office; Matt criticizes his boss more than she.** [. . . more than Juanita does.]

▶ **Matt and Juanita work in the same office; Matt criticizes his boss more than her.** [. . . more than he criticizes Juanita.]

44b Possessive forms of pronouns (*my* or *mine*, *her* or *hers*?)

Distinguish between adjective and pronoun forms (*her* and *hers*)

▶ **The large room with three windows is *her* office.** [*Her* is an adjective.]

▶ **The office is *hers*.** [*Hers*, the possessive pronoun, can stand alone.]

When a possessive pronoun functions as a subject, the word it refers to (its antecedent) determines singular or plural agreement for the verb (see 43j).

▶ **My shirt is cotton; hers *is* silk.** [*shirt* is singular; it needs a singular verb.]

▶ **My gloves are black; hers *are* yellow.** [plural antecedent and plural verb]

Note: The word *mine* does not follow the pattern of *hers, theirs, yours,* and *ours*. The form *mines* is nonstandard.

▶ **The little room on the left is *mine*.**

No apostrophe with possessive personal pronouns Even though possessive in meaning, the pronouns *yours, ours, theirs, his,* and *hers* should never be spelled with an apostrophe. Use an apostrophe only with the possessive form of a noun.

▶ **That essay is *Maria's*.**

▶ **That is *her* essay.**

▶ **That essay is *hers*.**

▶ **Those conclusions were *ours*, too.**

▶ **These books are the *twins'*.** (48c)

▶ These are *their* books.

▶ These books are *theirs*.

No apostrophe with *its* as a possessive pronoun   The word *it's* is not a pronoun; it is the contraction of *it is* or *it has*. An apostrophe is never used with *its*, the possessive form of the pronoun *it* (see also 48f).

▶ The paint has lost *its* gloss.

▶ *It's* not as glossy as it used to be. [It is not as glossy . . .]

Possessive pronoun before an *-ing* form   Generally, use a possessive personal pronoun before an *-ing* verb form used as a noun.

▶ We appreciate *your* participating in the auction.

▶ *Their* winning the marathon surprised us all.

Sometimes, the *-ing* form is a participle functioning as an adjective. In that case, the pronoun preceding the *-ing* form should be in the object form.

▶ We saw *them* giving the runners foil wraps.

Comparisons using possessive forms   Note how using *them* in place of *theirs* in the following sentence would change the meaning by comparing suitcases to roommates, not suitcases to suitcases.

▶ It's really hard to be roommates with people if your suitcases are much better than *theirs*.

—J. D. Salinger, *The Catcher in the Rye*

Forgetting to use the appropriate possessive form in the next example, too, could create a misunderstanding. Is the writer comparing a house to a person or his house to her house?

▶ I like his house more than I like her͜s͕/

44c Pronoun reference to a clear antecedent

A pronoun substitutes for a noun, a noun phrase, or a pronoun already mentioned. The word or phrase that a pronoun refers to is known as the pronoun's *antecedent*. Antecedents should always be clear and explicit.

▶ Because the Canadian skater practiced daily with *her* trainers,

she won the championship.

State a specific antecedent Be sure to give a pronoun such as *they, this,* or *it* an explicit antecedent.

NO SPECIFIC
ANTECEDENT

When Mr. Rivera applied for a loan, they outlined the procedures for him. [The pronoun *they* lacks an explicit antecedent.]

REVISED

When Mr. Rivera applied to bank officials for a loan, *they* outlined the procedures for him.

When you use a pronoun, make sure it does not refer to a possessive noun or to a noun within a prepositional phrase.

George Orwell

▶ In ~~George Orwell's~~ "Shooting an Elephant," ~~he~~ reports an

incident that shows the evil effects of imperialism. [The pronoun *he* cannot refer to the possessive noun *Orwell's*.]

Lance Morrow's essay

▶ ~~In the essay by Lance Morrow, it~~ points out the problems of

choosing a name. [*It* refers to *essay*, which functions as the object of the preposition *in* and therefore cannot function as an antecedent.]

Avoid ambiguous pronoun reference Your readers should never be left wondering which *this, they,* or *it* is being discussed.

AMBIGUOUS

My husband told my father that he should choose the baby's name. [Does *he* refer to *husband* or *father*?]

REVISED

My husband told my father to choose the baby's name.

REVISED

My husband wanted to choose the baby's name and told my father so.

44d Making a pronoun agree with its antecedent

A plural antecedent needs a plural pronoun; a singular antecedent needs a singular pronoun.

▶ Listeners heard *they* could win free tickets. The ninth caller learned *she* was the winner.

Make a demonstrative pronoun agree with its antecedent   The demonstrative pronouns *this* and *that* refer to singular nouns; *these* and *those* refer to plural nouns: *this/that house, these/those houses* (43j).

singular antecedent

▶ He published his autobiography two years ago. This was his first book.

plural antecedent

▶ One reviewer praised his honesty and directness. These were qualities he had worked hard to develop.

Make a pronoun agree with a generalized (generic) antecedent Generic nouns name a class or type of person or object, such as *a student* meaning "all students" or *a company* meaning "any company" or "all companies." Sometimes, writers use *they* to refer to a singular generic noun, but the singular/plural mismatch annoys some readers.

singular antecedent   plural pronoun

MISMATCH   When a student is educated, they can go far in the world.

singular antecedent   singular pronoun

REVISED BUT SOMEWHAT STILTED   When a student is educated, he or she can go far in the world.

plural antecedent   plural pronoun

BEST   When students are educated, they can go far in the world.

Increasingly, you see in advertising, journalism, and informal writing (and you will certainly hear this usage in speech, too) a plural pronoun referring to a singular antecedent, as in the following station wagon advertisement:

▶ One day *your child* turns sixteen, and you let *them* borrow the keys to the wagon.

However, in formal academic writing, many readers may still expect a pronoun to agree with its antecedent. Even though usage may be changing, you can avoid problems by making the antecedent plural.

people

▶ We should judge ~~a person~~ by who they are, not by the color of their skin.

Make a pronoun agree with an indefinite pronoun   Indefinite pronouns, such as *everyone, somebody, each*, and *nothing* (see the list in 43h), are singular in form. A singular antecedent traditionally needs a singular pronoun to refer to it, but which one: *he, she,* or *he or she*? The *Oxford English Dictionary* points out that for centuries, *they* has often been used "in reference to a singular noun made universal by *every, any, no*, etc., or applicable to one of either sex (= 'he or she')."

   Despite the increasingly widespread use of *they*, some readers may still object to it, so revising the sentence is a good idea.

SINGULAR PRONOUN
: *Everyone* **picked up** *his* **assignments and raced off to write** *his* **parts of the report.** [Sentence needs revision because of the sexist bias.]

REVISED BUT CLUMSY
: *Everyone* **picked up** *his or her* **assignments and raced off to write** *his or her* **parts of the report.**

REVISED BUT SOME MAY OBJECT
: *Everyone* **picked up** *their assignments* **and raced off to write** *their* **parts of the report.** [The plural pronoun *their* refers to a singular antecedent, *everyone*.]

PROBABLY BEST
: **The lawyers all picked up** *their* **assignments and raced off to write** *their* **parts of the report.**

Make a pronoun agree with the nearer antecedent when you use *or* or *nor*   When an antecedent includes *or* or *nor*, a pronoun agrees with the element that is nearer to it. If one part of the compound is singular and the other part is plural, put the plural antecedent closer to the pronoun and have the pronoun agree with it.

▶ **Either my tutor or my professor has left** *his* **wallet on the table.**

▶ **Neither Bill nor the campers could find** *their* **soap.**

Make a pronoun agree with a collective noun   Use a singular pronoun to refer to a collective noun (*class, family, jury, committee, couple, team*) if you are referring to the group as a whole.

▶ **The class revised** *its* **examination schedule.**

▶ **The committee has not yet completed** *its* **report.**

Use a plural pronoun if members of the group named by the collective noun are considered to be acting individually.

▶ **The committee began to cast** *their* **ballots in a formal vote.**

44e Gender bias

For many years, the pronoun *he* was used routinely in generic references to unspecified individuals in certain roles or professions, such as student, teacher, doctor, lawyer, and banker, and *she* was used routinely in generic references to individuals in roles such as nurse, secretary, or typist. This usage is now considered sexist language.

NOT
APPROPRIATE
When an accountant learns a foreign language, *he* gains access to an expanded job market.

To revise such sentences that make general statements about people, roles, and professions, use one of the following methods:

1. Use a plural antecedent plus *they* (see also 34f and 44d).

   ▶ **When accountants learn a foreign language, *they* gain access to an expanded job market.**

2. Avoid the issue by rewriting the sentence to eliminate the pronoun.

   ▶ **An accountant who learns a foreign language gains access to an expanded job market.**

3. Use a singular antecedent and the phrase *he or she*.

   ▶ **When an accountant learns a foreign language, *he or she* gains access to an expanded job market.**

The problem with option 3 is that awkward and repetitive structures can result when such a sentence is expanded.

   ▶ **When an accountant learns a foreign language, *he or she* gains access to an expanded job market once *he or she* has decided on *his or her* specialty.**

That's clumsy. Use the *he or she* option only when a sentence is relatively short and does not repeat the pronouns. On the whole, though, revision is usually the best:

   ▶ **Accountants who learn a foreign language gain access to expanded job markets once they choose a specialty.**

   See also pronoun agreement with indefinite pronouns (p. 442).

44f Consistent point of view

Always write from a consistent perspective. Pronouns can help maintain consistency. Consider the person and number of the pronouns you use:

- Are you emphasizing the perspective of the first person (*I* or *we*)?
- Are you primarily addressing the reader as the second person (*you*)?
- Are you, as is most common in formal academic writing, writing about the third person (*he, she, it, one,* or *they*)?

Avoid confusing readers by switching from one perspective to another.

INCONSISTENT   *The company* decided to promote only three midlevel managers. *You* had to have worked there for ten years to qualify.

REVISED   *The company* decided to promote only three midlevel managers. *The employees* had to have worked there for ten years to qualify.

44g The use of the pronoun *you*

In formal writing, do not use the pronoun *you* when you mean "people generally." Use *you* only to address readers directly and to give instructions.

NOT APPROPRIATE   **Credit card companies should educate students about how to handle credit. *You* should not have to find out the problems the hard way.** [A reader addressed directly in this way might think, "Who, me? I don't need to be educated about credit, and I have no problems."]

APPROPRIATE   **Turn to the next page, where *you* will find an excerpt from Edith Wharton's novel that will help *you* appreciate the accuracy of the details in this film.**

Edit uses of *you* if you are making a generalization about a group or if using *you* entails a switch from the third person.

▶ While growing up, ~~you~~ teenagers face arguments with ~~your~~ their parents.

▶ It doesn't matter if young professionals are avid music admirers or comedy fans; ~~you~~ they can find anything ~~you~~ they want in the city.

44h Intensive and reflexive pronouns

Intensive pronouns emphasize a previously mentioned noun or pronoun. Reflexive pronouns identify a previously mentioned noun or pronoun as the person or thing receiving the action (see the Key Points box in 44a).

INTENSIVE   **The president *himself* appeared at the gates.**

REFLEXIVE   **He introduced *himself*.**

Do not use an intensive pronoun in place of a personal pronoun in a compound subject:

▶ **Joe and ~~myself~~ will design the brochure.**

Forms such as *hisself, theirself,* and *theirselves* occur in spoken dialects but are not Standard English.

44i *Who/whom, whoever/whomever*

In all formal writing situations, distinguish between the subject and object forms of the pronouns used to form questions (interrogative pronouns) or to introduce a dependent noun clause.

Subject	Object
who	whom (or informally, *who*)
whoever	whomever

In questions In a question, ask yourself whether the pronoun is the subject of its clause or the object of the verb. Test the pronoun's function by rephrasing the question as a statement, substituting a personal pronoun for *who* or *whom*.

▶ **Who wrote that enthusiastic letter?** [*He* wrote that enthusiastic letter. Subject: use *who*.]

▶ **Whoever could have written it?** [*She* could have written it. Subject: use *whoever*.]

▶ **Who[m] were they describing?** [*They* were describing *him*. Object: *whom* (formal), though *who* is common in such contexts both in speech and in writing.]

When introducing a dependent clause with a pronoun, determine whether to use the subject or object form by examining the pronoun's function in the clause. Ignore expressions such as *I think* or *I know* when they follow the pronoun; they have no effect on the form of the pronoun.

subject of clause

▶ **They want to know who runs the business.**

subject of clause (who runs the business)

▶ **They want to know who I think runs the business.**

object of *to* [the manager reports to him or her]

▶ They want to know whom the manager reports to.

subject of clause

▶ I will hire whoever is qualified.

object of *recommends*

▶ I will hire whomever my boss recommends.

For uses of *who* and *whom* in relative clauses, see 46a.

45

Adjectives and Adverbs

Adjectives describe, or modify, nouns or pronouns. They do not add -*s* or change form to reflect number or gender. For the order of adjectives, see 62g.

▶ Analysts acknowledge the *beneficial* effects of TV.

▶ The director tried a *different* approach to a documentary.

▶ The depiction of rural life is *accurate*.

▶ The reporter keeps her desk *tidy*.

 NOTE FOR MULTILINGUAL WRITERS

No Plural Form for Adjectives

Do not add -*s* to an adjective that modifies a plural noun.

▶ Mr. Lee tried three *differents* approaches.

Adverbs modify verbs, adjectives, and other adverbs, as well as whole clauses.

▶ The financial analyst settled down *comfortably* in her new job.

▶ The patient is demanding a *theoretically* impossible treatment.

▶ *Apparently*, the experiment was a success.

45a Forms of adjectives and adverbs

No single rule indicates the correct form of all adjectives and adverbs.

Adverb: adjective + -ly   Many adverbs are formed by adding -ly to an adjective: *soft/softly; intelligent/intelligently*. Sometimes, when -ly is added, a spelling change occurs: *easy/easily; terrible/terribly*.

Adjectives ending in -ic   To form an adverb from an adjective ending in -ic, add -ally (*basic/basically; artistic/artistically*), except for *public*, whose adverb form is *publicly*.

Adjectives ending in -ly   Some adjectives, such as *friendly, lovely, timely*, and *masterly*, already end in -ly and have no distinctive adverb form.

adjective

► She is a friendly person.

┌── adverbial phrase ──┐
► She spoke to me in a friendly way.

Irregular adverb forms   Certain adjectives do not add -ly to form an adverb:

Adjective	Adverb
good	well
fast	fast
hard	hard

adjective

► He is a hard worker.

adverb

► He works hard. [*Hardly* is not the adverb form of *hard*. Rather, it means "barely," "scarcely," or "almost not at all": *I could hardly breathe in that stuffy room.*]

Note: Well can also function as an adjective, meaning "healthy" or "satisfactory": *A* well *baby smiles often. She feels* well.

45b When to use adjectives and adverbs

In speech, adjectives (particularly, *good, bad*, and *real*) are often used to modify verbs, adjectives, or adverbs. This is nonstandard usage. Use an adverb to modify a verb or an adverb.

▶ The webmaster fixed the link ~~good~~. *well.*

▶ The chorus sings ~~real good~~. *really well.*

▶ The guide speaks very ~~clear~~. *clearly.*

▶ They dance ~~bad~~. *badly.*

45c Adjectives after linking verbs

After linking verbs (*be, seem, appear, become*), use an adjective to modify the subject.

▶ Sharon Olds's poems are *lyrical.*

▶ The book seems *repetitive.*

Some verbs (*appear, look, feel, smell, taste*) are sometimes used as linking verbs and sometimes as action verbs. If the modifier tells about the subject, use an adjective. If the modifier tells about the action of the verb, use an adverb.

ADJECTIVE   The analyst looks *confident* in her new job.

ADVERB   The lawyer looked *confidently* at all the assembled partners.

ADJECTIVE   The waiter feels *bad.*

The steak smells *bad.*

ADVERB   The chef smelled the lobster *appreciatively.*

Note: Use a hyphen to connect two words used as an adjective when they appear before a noun. Do not use a hyphen when the words follow a linking verb with no noun complement.

▶ Sonny Rollins is a *well-known* saxophonist.

▶ Sonny Rollins is *well known.*

45d Compound adjectives

A compound adjective consists of two or more words used as a unit to describe a noun. Many compound adjectives contain the past participle *-ed* verb form: *flat-footed, barrel-chested, broad-shouldered, old-fashioned, well-dressed, left-handed.* Note the form when a compound adjective is used before a noun: hyphen, past participle (*-ed*) form where necessary, and no noun plural (*-s*) ending.

▶ They have a *five-year-old* daughter. [Their daughter is five years old.]

▶ She gave me a *five-dollar* bill. [She gave me five dollars.]

▶ He is a *left-handed* pitcher. [He pitches with his left hand.]

For more on hyphenation with compound adjectives, see 56b.

45e Position of adverbs

An adverb can be placed in various positions in a sentence.

▶ *Enthusiastically,* she ate the sushi.

▶ She *enthusiastically* ate the sushi.

▶ She ate the sushi *enthusiastically.*

NOTE FOR MULTILINGUAL WRITERS

Adverb Placement

Do not place an adverb between a verb and a short direct object (62b).

▶ She ate ⌐*enthusiastically*⌐ the sushi.

Put adverbs that show frequency (*always, usually, frequently, often, sometimes, seldom, rarely, never*) in one of four positions:

1. At the beginning of a sentence

▶ *Sometimes,* I just sit and daydream instead of writing.

When *never, seldom,* or *rarely* occurs at the beginning of the sentence, word order is inverted (see also 43d).

▶ *Never* will I let that happen.

2. Between the subject and the main verb

   ▶ They *always* arrive half an hour late.

3. After a form of *be* or any auxiliary verb (such as *do, have, can, will, must*)

   ▶ The writing center is *always* open in the evening.

   ▶ The tutors are *seldom* late for training.

   ▶ There has *never* been an available computer during exam week.

4. In the final position

   ▶ Amira checks her e-mail *frequently.*

Note: Don't place the adverb *never* in the final position.

45f   Conjunctive adverbs (*however, therefore, etc.*)

There are two important points to remember about conjunctive adverbs such as *however, therefore,* and *moreover.*

1. When a conjunctive adverb occurs in the middle of a clause, set it off with commas.

   ▶ The mayor's course of action has, therefore, been severely criticized.

2. When it occurs between independent clauses, use a semicolon to end the first clause and put a comma after the adverb.

   ▶ The hearings were contentious; however, the Supreme Court justice was approved.

   See also 2c, 32b, 39c, and 47e.

45g   No double negatives

Adverbs like *hardly, scarcely,* and *barely* are considered negatives, and the contraction *-n't* stands for the adverb *not.* Some languages and dialects allow the use of more than one negative to emphasize an idea, but the standard form is for only one negative in a clause. Avoid double negatives.

DOUBLE NEGATIVE	We do*n't* have *no* excuses.
REVISED	We do*n't* have *any* excuses. [or] We have *no* excuses.

DOUBLE NEGATIVE	She did*n't* say *nothing.*
REVISED	She did*n't* say *anything.* [or] She said *nothing.*

DOUBLE NEGATIVE	City residents ca*n't hardly* afford the sales tax.
REVISED	City residents can *hardly* afford the sales tax.

45h Comparative and superlative forms of adjectives and adverbs

Adjectives and adverbs have three forms: positive, comparative, and superlative. Use the comparative form when comparing two people, places, things, or ideas; use the superlative form when comparing more than two.

Regular forms Add the ending -*er* (or just -*r* for an adjective already ending in -*e*, such as *feeble*) to form the comparative and -*(e)st* to form the superlative of both short adjectives (those that have one syllable or those that have two syllables and end in -*y* or -*le*) and one-syllable adverbs. (Change -*y* to -*i* if -*y* is preceded by a consonant: *icy, icier, iciest*.) Generally, a superlative form is preceded by *the* (*the shortest distance*).

Positive	Comparative (Comparing two)	Superlative (Comparing more than two)
short	shorter	shortest
pretty	prettier	prettiest
simple	simpler	simplest
fast	faster	fastest

With longer adjectives and with adverbs ending in -*ly*, use *more* (for the comparative) and *most* (for the superlative). Note that *less* (comparative) and *least* (superlative) are used with adjectives of any length (*less bright, least bright; less effective, least effective*).

Positive	Comparative	Superlative
intelligent	more intelligent	most intelligent
carefully	more carefully	most carefully
dangerous	less dangerous	least dangerous

If you cannot decide whether to use *-er/-est* or *more/most*, consult a dictionary. If there is an *-er/-est* form, the dictionary will say so.

Note: Do not use the *-er* form along with *more* or the *-est* form along with *most*.

▶ The first poem was ~~more~~ better than the second.

▶ Boris is the ~~most~~ fittest person I know.

Irregular forms   The following common adjectives and adverbs have irregular comparative and superlative forms:

Positive	Comparative	Superlative
good	better	best
bad	worse	worst
much/many	more	most
little	less	least
well	better	best
badly	worse	worst

***Than* with comparative forms**   To compare two people, places, things, or ideas, use the comparative form and the word *than*. If you use a comparative form in your sentence, you need the word *than* to let readers know what you are comparing with what.

▶ This course of action is more efficient. than the previous one.

Comparative forms are also used without *than* in an idiomatic way.

▶ The *harder* he tries, the *more satisfied* he feels.

▶ The *more*, the *merrier*.

Absolute adjectives   Do not use comparative and superlative forms of adjectives that imply absolutes: *complete, empty, full, equal, perfect, priceless,* or *unique.* In addition, do not add intensifying adverbs such as *very, totally, completely,* or *absolutely* to these adjectives. To say that something is "perfect" implies an absolute rather than something measured in degrees.

▶ He has the most perfect view of the ocean.
^a (above "the most")

▶ They bought a totally unique quilt at an auction.

45i Faulty or incomplete comparisons

Make sure that you state clearly what items you are comparing. Some faulty comparisons can give readers the wrong idea (see 40h and 44b).

INCOMPLETE   **He likes the parrot better than his wife.**

Do you really want to suggest that he prefers the parrot to his wife? If not, clarify the comparison by completing the second clause.

REVISED   **He likes the parrot better *than his wife does.***

Edit sentences like the following:

▶ My essay got a higher grade than Maria's. [Compare the two essays, not your essay and Maria.]

▶ Williams's poem gives a more objective depiction of the painting than Auden's. [To compare Williams's poem with Auden's poem, you need to include an apostrophe; otherwise, you compare a poem to the poet W. H. Auden.]

Comparisons must also be complete. If you say that something is "more efficient," your reader wonders, "More efficient than what?"

▶ Didion shows us a home that makes her feel more tied to her roots, than her home in Los Angeles does. [Include the other part of the comparison.]

46 🔑

Relative Clauses and Relative Pronouns (*who, whom, whose, which, that,* etc.)

A relative clause relates to an antecedent in a nearby clause.

relative clause
▶ The girl *who* can't dance says the band can't play.

—Yiddish proverb

46a Relative pronouns

When deciding whether to use *who, whom, which,* or *that,* use the following table as a guide. Your choice of pronoun will depend on these three factors:

1. The function of the relative pronoun in its clause
2. Whether the relative pronoun refers to a human or nonhuman antecedent
3. Whether the clause is restrictive or nonrestrictive (see 46b for this distinction)

Relative Pronouns and Antecedents

	Function of Relative Pronoun		
Antecedent	Subject	Object	Possessive
Human antecedent	*who*	*whom* (can be omitted)	*whose*
Nonhuman antecedent	*that* or *which* (see 46b)	*that* (can be omitted) or *which* (see 46b)	*of which* (formal) *whose* (informal)

Human

SUBJECT   **The teachers *who* challenge us are the ones we remember.**

OBJECT   **The players [*whom*] the spectators boo often end up in the minor leagues.**

POSSESSIVE **Spectators *whose* cell phones ring will be asked to leave.**

Nonhuman

SUBJECT   **The dog *that* kept barking all night drove the neighbors crazy.**

OBJECT   **They stayed at a hotel [*that*] their friends had recommended.**

POSSESSIVE **We stayed in a picturesque town the name *of which* I can't remember.**

We stayed in a picturesque town *whose* name I can't remember.

Watch out! Do not rename the subject in the independent clause.

▶ The teachers who challenge us ~~they~~ are the ones we remember.

Remember that an inserted phrase does not affect the function of a pronoun.

▶ Let's reward contestants who we realize have not been coached.

Do not use *what* as a relative pronoun.

that
▶ The deal ~~what~~ the CEO was trying to make turned out to be crooked.
        ^

46b Restrictive and nonrestrictive relative clauses

The two types of relative clauses, restrictive and nonrestrictive, fulfill different functions and need different punctuation (47d).

RESTRICTIVE   **The people *who live in the apartment above mine* make a lot of noise at night.**

NONRESTRICTIVE   **The Sullivans, *who live in the apartment above mine,* make a lot of noise at night.**

Restrictive relative clause   A restrictive relative clause provides information essential for identifying the antecedent and restricting its scope.

Features

1. The clause is not set off with commas. It is needed to understand what the subject is.
2. An object relative pronoun can be omitted.
3. *That* (rather than *which*) is used for reference to nonhuman antecedents.

   ▶ The teachers *who challenge us* are the ones we remember.
   [The independent clause—"The teachers are the ones we remember"—leads us to ask, "Which teachers?" The relative clause provides information that is essential to completing the meaning of the subject; it restricts the meaning from "all teachers" to "the teachers who challenge us."]

▶ **The book** [*that*] *you gave me* **was fascinating.** [The relative pronoun *that* is the direct object in its clause ("You gave me the book") and can be omitted.]

Nonrestrictive relative clause   A nonrestrictive relative clause provides information that merely adds descriptive information.

Features

1. The antecedent is a unique, designated person or thing.
2. The clause is set off by commas; it provides additional nonessential information, a kind of aside. It could be omitted, and the sentence would make sense without it.
3. *Which* (not *that*) is used to refer to a nonhuman antecedent.
4. An object relative pronoun cannot be omitted.

▶ **The book** *War and Peace,* **which you gave me, was fascinating.** [The independent clause—"The book *War and Peace* was fascinating"—does not promote further questions, such as "Which book?" The information in the relative clause ("which you gave me") is almost an aside and not essential for understanding the independent clause.]

A nonrestrictive relative clause with a quantity word   Relative clauses beginning with a quantity word such as *some, none, many, much, most,* or *one* followed by *of which* or *of whom* are always nonrestrictive.

▶ **They selected five candidates,** *one of whom* **would get the job.**

▶ **The report mentioned five names,** *none of which* **I recognized.**

   NOTE FOR MULTILINGUAL WRITERS

Relative versus Personal Pronouns

Do not add a personal pronoun in addition to the relative pronoun.

                    most of whom
▶ **I tutored some students,** ~~which most of them~~ **were my classmates.**

46c   Agreement of verb with relative pronoun

Determine subject-verb agreement within a relative clause by asking whether the antecedent of a subject relative pronoun is singular or plural.

────── relative clause ──────
▶ **The book that *is* at the top of the bestseller list gives advice about health.** [The singular noun *book* is the antecedent of *that*, the subject of the singular verb *is* in the relative clause.]

────── relative clause ──────
▶ **The books that *are* at the top of the bestseller list give advice about health, success, and making money.** [The plural noun *books* is the antecedent of *that*, the subject of the plural verb *are* in the relative clause.]

Note: The phrase *one of* is followed by a plural noun phrase. However, the verb can be singular or plural depending on the meaning.

▶ **Juan is one of the employees who *work* long hours.** [Several employees work long hours. Juan is one of them. The plural noun *employees* is the antecedent of *who*, the subject of the plural verb *work* in the relative clause.]

─ antecedent ─   singular verb
▶ **Juan is the only one of the employees who *works* long hours.** [Only Juan works long hours.]

46d Relative clauses with prepositions

When a relative clause contains a relative pronoun within a prepositional phrase, do not omit the preposition. Keep in mind these three points:

1. Directly after the preposition, use *whom* or *which*, never *that*.

────── relative clause ──────
▶ **The man *for whom* we worked last year has just retired.**

2. If you place the preposition after the verb, use *that* (or you can omit *that*), but do not use *whom* or *which*.

[that]
▶ **The security measures ~~which~~ the mayor had insisted on made him unpopular.**

3. Do not add an extra personal pronoun object after the preposition at the end of the relative clause.

▶ **The theater company [that] they are devoted to ~~it~~ has produced six new plays this season.**

46e Position of relative clause

To avoid ambiguity, place a relative clause as close as possible to its antecedent (see also 40b on misplaced modifiers).

AMBIGUOUS **He searched for the notebook all over the house that his friend had forgotten.** [Had his friend forgotten the house?]

REVISED **He searched all over the house for the notebook that his friend had forgotten.**

46f *Where* and *when* as relative pronouns

When you refer to actual or metaphoric places and times, you can use *where* to replace *in which, at which,* or *to which,* and you can use *when* to replace *at which, in which,* or *on which.* Do not use a preposition with *where* or *when.*

▶ **The morning on which she graduated was warm and sunny.**

▶ **The morning *when* she graduated was warm and sunny.**

▶ **The village in which he was born honored him last year.**

▶ **The village *where* he was born honored him last year.**

Use *where* or *when* only if actual time or physical location is involved.

                                                   according to which
▶ **The influence of the Sapir-Whorf hypothesis, ~~where~~ behavior
   is regarded as influenced by language, has declined.**

Punctuation, Mechanics, and Spelling

47 Commas 462

48 Apostrophes 470

49 Quotation Marks 474

50 Semicolons and Colons 478

51 Other Punctuation Marks 482

52 Italics/Underlining 488

53 Capitalization 489

54 Abbreviations 492

55 Numbers 495

56 Hyphens 496

57 Online Guidelines 497

58 Spelling 499

 **ONLINE RESOURCES**

www.cengage.com/english/raimes

Companion online resources are available for sections throughout this part. We invite you to visit the book's Web site for more information and direct access.

PART 8

Punctuation, Mechanics, and Spelling

47 Commas 462

47a Comma: Yes and no 462
47b Before *and*, *but*, etc., between independent clauses 465
47c After introductory phrase or clause 465
47d With extra (nonrestrictive) elements 466
47e With transitional expressions and insertions 467
47f With items in a series 467
47g With certain adjectives 468
47h With direct quotations 468
47i Special uses 469

48 Apostrophes 470

48a Apostrophe: Yes and no 470
48b When to use -'s to signal possession 471
48c With plural nouns ending in -s 472
48d In contractions 472
48e Two occasions to use -'s to form a plural 473
48f *It's* versus *its* 473

49 Quotation Marks 474

49a Guidelines 474
49b Punctuation introducing and ending a quotation 474
49c Dialogue 476
49d Quotation within a quotation 476
49e With titles, definitions, and translations 476
49f When not to use 477

50 Semicolons and Colons 478

50a Semicolon: Yes and no 478
50b Colon: Yes and no 480

51 Other Punctuation Marks 482

51a Periods 482
51b Question marks, exclamation points 483
51c Dashes 484
51d Parentheses 485
51e Brackets 485
51f Slashes 486
51g Ellipsis dots 486

52 Italics/Underlining 488

52a Titles of long, whole works 488
52b When not to italicize titles 488
52c Transportation 489
52d Letters, numerals, and words as words 489
52e Words from other languages not adopted in English 489
52f Not for emphasis 489

53 Capitalization 489

53a *I* and first word of sentence 489
53b Proper nouns and proper adjectives 490
53c Title before a name 491
53d Major words in a title 492
53e Capitals with colons and quotations 492

54 Abbreviations 492

54a Titles with people's names 493
54b Certain types of familiar names 493
54c Terms used with numbers 493
54d Common Latin terms 494
54e When not to abbreviate 494
54f Plurals of abbreviations 494

55 Numbers 495

55a Conventions 495
55b Beginning a sentence 495
55c When to use numerals 496
55d Plurals of numerals 496

56 Hyphens 496

56a With prefixes 496
56b In compound words 497
56c In spelled-out numbers 497
56d At end of line 497

57 Online Guidelines 497

57a Punctuation in URLs 497
57b Capital letters online 498

57c Hyphens online 498
57d Abbreviations online 499
57e Italics online 499

58 Spelling 499

58a Plurals of nouns 499
58b Doubling consonants 500
58c Spelling with -y or -i 501
58d Internal ie or ei 502
58e Adding a suffix 502
58f Multinational characters:
     Accents, umlauts, tildes,
     and cedillas 503

P unctuation serves to regulate the flow of information through a sentence, showing readers how to read your ideas. The following headline from the *New York Times*, "Stock Fraud Is Easier, and Easier to Spot," says that stock fraud is not only easy to engage in but also easy to detect. Without the comma, however, the sentence would send a different message: It would say that detecting stock fraud is becoming increasingly easy.

Try reading the following without the benefit of the signals a reader usually expects.

> When active viruses especially those transmitted by contact can spread easily within the world health organization hard working doctors are continually collaborating to find treatments for several infectious diseases sars avian flu and hepatitis.

Conventional punctuation and mechanics clarify the meaning:

> When active, viruses—especially those transmitted by contact—can spread easily; within the World Health Organization, hard-working doctors are continually collaborating to find treatments for several infectious diseases: SARS, avian flu, and hepatitis.

47 ⚿

Commas

A comma separates parts of a sentence. It does not separate one sentence from another. When readers see a comma, they know that the parts of the sentence are separated for a reason. When you really can't decide whether to use commas, follow this general principle: "When in doubt, leave them out." Readers find excessive use of commas more distracting than a few missing ones.

47a Checklists: Comma yes and comma no

Use the following guidelines, but note that variations can occur. Details and more examples follow in the rest of the chapter. Throughout chapter 47, note the comma where there is blue shading.

KEY POINTS

Comma Yes

1. Between two independent clauses connected by a coordinating conjunction: *and, but, or, nor, so, for,* or *yet,* but optional in British English (47b)

   ▶ **The talks failed, but the union leaders held their ground.**

   A comma is optional if the clauses are short.

   ▶ **He offered to help and he did.**

2. After most introductory words, phrases, or clauses (47c)

   ▶ **After the noisy party, the neighbors complained. When the police came, the guests left.**

3. To set off extra (nonrestrictive) information included in a sentence ("extra commas with extra information"—see 47d)

   ▶ **Her husband, a computer programmer, works late at night.**

4. To set off a transitional expression or an explanatory insert (47e)

   ▶ **The ending of the film, however, is disappointing. In fact, it is totally predictable.**

5. To separate three or more items in a series (47f)

   ▶ **The robot vacuums, makes toast, and plays chess.**

6. Between adjectives that can be reversed and connected with *and* (coordinate adjectives—47g)

   ▶ **When people move, they often discard their worn, dilapidated furniture.**

7. Before or after a quotation (47h)

   ▶ **"I intend to win an Oscar," she announced. He replied, "Good luck."**

In the following box and in 47b–i, yellow shading indicates "no comma here."

KEY POINTS

Comma No

1. Not between subject and verb

   ▶ **Interviews with women helped the CEO understand the need for child care.**

Note: Use paired commas, however, to set off any extra information inserted between the subject and verb (see 47d).

   ▶ **The fund manager, a billionaire, has been married five times.**

2. Not before the word *and* that connects two verbs to the same subject

   ▶ **She won the trophy and accepted it graciously.**

3. Not *after* a coordinating conjunction (*and, but, or, nor, so, for, yet*) connecting two independent clauses, but *before* it (see 47b)

   ▶ **The movie tried to be engaging, but it failed miserably.**

4. Not between two independent clauses without any coordinating conjunction such as *and* or *but* (use either a period or a semicolon instead)

   ▶ **The writing had faded; it was hard to decipher.**

(Continued)

(Continued)

Some writers, however, use a comma between two independent clauses when the clauses use parallel structures (40j) to point out a contrast.

▶ **She never insults, she just criticizes.**

5. Not between an independent clause and a following dependent clause introduced by *after, before, because, if, since, unless, until,* or *when* (no comma before the subordinating conjunction)

▶ **Test results tend to be good when students study in groups.**

6. Not before a clause beginning with *that*

▶ **The dean warned the students that the speech would be long.**

Note: A comma can appear before a *that* clause when it is the second comma of a pair before and after extra information inserted as a nonrestrictive phrase.

▶ **He skates so fast, despite his size, that he will probably break the world record.**

7. Not before or after essential, restrictive information (see 47d)

▶ **Alice Walker's essay "Beauty: When the Other Dancer Is the Self" discusses coping with a physical disfigurement.** [Walker has written more than one essay. The title restricts the noun *essay* to one specific essay.]

Similarly, a restrictive relative clause introduced by *who, whom, whose, which,* or *that* is never set off by commas. The clause provides essential, identifying information (see 47b and 47d).

▶ **The teachers praised the children who finished on time.** [The teachers didn't praise all the children. The clause "who finished on time" restricts the meaning to only those who finished on time.]

8. Not between a verb and its object or complement

▶ **The best gifts are food and clothes.**

9. Not after *such as*

> ▶ **Popular fast-food items, such as hamburgers and hot dogs, tend to be high in cholesterol.**

10. Not separating cumulative adjectives (adjectives that cannot be connected by *and* and whose order cannot be reversed— see 47g for more examples)

> ▶ **many little white ivory buttons**

47b Use a comma before a coordinating conjunction (*and, but,* etc.) that connects independent clauses

When you connect independent clauses with a coordinating conjunction (*and, but, or, nor, so, for, yet*), place a comma before the conjunction.

> ▶ **The managers are efficient, but personnel turnover is high.**

> ▶ **The juggler juggled seven plates, and we all cheered.**

However, when the clauses are short, many writers omit the comma.

47c Use a comma after most introductory phrases and clauses

The comma signals to readers that the introductory part of the sentence has ended. It says, in effect, "Now wait for the main point in the independent clause."

> ▶ **If you blow out all the candles, your wishes will come true.**

> ▶ **As recently as twenty years ago, very few students had computers or cell phones.**

The comma after the introductory material tells readers to expect the subject and verb of the independent clause. After one word or a short phrase, the comma can be omitted: *Immediately the fun began.* However, in some sentences, omitting the comma can lead to a serious or humorous misreading:

> ▶ **While the guests were eating a mouse ran across the floor.**
>   ^,

47d Use commas to set off an extra (nonrestrictive) phrase or clause

A phrase or clause may provide extra information that can be omitted without changing the meaning of the independent clause by restricting its meaning. Such information may be included almost as an aside—a "by the way." If the insertion comes in midsentence, think of the commas as handles that can lift the extra information out without inconveniencing your reader.

NONRESTRICTIVE   **We'll attend, even though we'd rather not.** [We will definitely attend. The *even though* clause does not restrict the meaning of the independent clause.]

RESTRICTIVE   **We'll attend if we have time.** [We will attend only if circumstances permit. The *if* clause restricts the meaning.]

Commas around appositive phrases   Use commas to set off a descriptive or explanatory phrase, called an *appositive phrase*. If the phrase were omitted, readers might lose some interesting details but would still be able to understand the message.

appositive
┌── phrase ──┐
▶ **She loves her car, a red Toyota.**

┌── appositive phrase ──┐
▶ **His dog, a big Labrador retriever, is afraid of mice.**

▶ **Salinger's first novel, *The Catcher in the Rye*, captures the language and thoughts of teenagers.** [The commas are used because the title provides supplementary information about the first novel, not information that identifies which novel the writer means.]

Commas around nonrestrictive participle phrases   Nonrestrictive participle phrases add extra descriptive, but not essential, information.

▶ **My boss, wearing a red tie and a green shirt, radiated the holiday spirit.** [The participle phrase does not restrict the meaning of *boss* by distinguishing one boss from another.]

Commas around extra information in nonrestrictive relative clauses   When you give nonessential information in a relative clause introduced by *who, whom*, or *which* (never *that*), set off the clause with commas.

▶ **My boss, who wears bright colors, is a cheerful person.** [The independent clause "My boss is a cheerful person" does not lead readers to ask "Which boss?" The relative clause does not restrict the meaning of *boss*.]

Note: Do not use commas to set off essential, restrictive information.

┌restricts *people* to a subgroup┐
▶ **People who wear bright colors send an optimistic message.** [The relative clause, beginning with *who*, restricts "people" to a subgroup: Not all people send an optimistic message; those who wear bright colors do.]

47e Use commas to set off transitional expressions and explanatory insertions

Transitional expressions and conjunctive adverbs connect or weave together the ideas in your writing and act as signposts for readers. See 2c for a list of these expressions. Use commas to set off a transitional expression from the rest of the sentence.

▶ **Most Labrador retrievers, however, are courageous.**

Note: When you use a transitional expression such as *however, therefore, nevertheless, above all, of course,* or *in fact* at the beginning of an independent clause, end the previous clause with a period or a semicolon. Then place a comma after the transitional expression.

▶ **The party was a success. In fact, it was still going on at 2 a.m.**

You may sometimes choose to insert a phrase or a clause to make a comment, offer an explanation, drive a point home, or indicate a contrast. Insertions used for these purposes are set off by commas.

▶ **The consequences will be dire, I think.**

▶ **The best, if not the only, solution is to apologize and start over.**

▶ **Seasonal allergies, such as those caused by ragweed, are common.**

▶ **Unlike SUVs, compact cars do not guzzle gas.**

47f Use commas to separate three or more items in a series

Readers see the commas between items in a series (words, phrases, or clauses) and realize "this is a list." If you said the sentence aloud, you would pause between items; when writing, you use commas to separate them. However, journalists and British writers often omit a comma before the final *and*.

> ▶ **Searching through the drawer, the detective found a key, a stamp, three coins, and a photograph.**

See also 50a for when to use semicolons in place of commas in a list.

47g Use commas to separate certain (coordinate) adjectives

Adjectives are *coordinate* when their order can be reversed and the word *and* can be inserted between them without any change in meaning. Coordinate adjectives (such as *beautiful, delicious, exciting, noisy*) make subjective and evaluative judgments rather than provide objectively verifiable information about, for instance, size, shape, color, or nationality. Separate coordinate adjectives with commas.

> ▶ **Buyers like to deal with energetic, efficient, and polite salespeople.**

Do not, however, put a comma between the final adjective of a series and the noun it modifies.

> ▶ **Energetic, efficient, and polite salespeople are in demand.**

Note that no comma is necessary to separate adjectives that are cumulative, modifying the whole noun phrase that follows (see 62g for the order of these adjectives).

> ▶ **Entering the little old stone house brought back memories of her childhood.**

47h Use a comma between a direct quotation and the preceding or following clause

The independent clause may come either before or after the quotation.

> ▶ **When asked what she wanted to be later in life, she replied, "An Olympic swimmer."**

> ▶ **"I want to be an Olympic swimmer," she announced confidently.** [The comma is inside the quotation marks.]

However, omit the comma if the quotation is a question or exclamation.

> ▶ **"Do you want to be a swimmer?" she asked.**

In addition, do not insert a comma before a quotation that is integrated into your sentence:

▶ The advertisers are promoting "a healthier lifestyle."

47i Special uses of commas

To prevent misreading Use a comma to separate elements in a sentence that may otherwise be confusing.

▶ He who can, does. He who cannot, teaches.

—George Bernard Shaw, *Man and Superman*

[Usually, a comma is not used to separate a subject from the verb. Here, the comma is necessary to prevent confusion.]

With an absolute phrase Use a comma to set off a phrase that modifies the whole sentence (an absolute phrase).

```
                  ──── absolute phrase ────
```
▶ The audience looking on in amusement, the valedictorian blew kisses to all her favorite instructors.

With a date Use a comma to separate the day from the year in a date.

▶ On May 14, 1998, the legendary singer Frank Sinatra died.
[Do not use a comma before the year when the day precedes the month: 14 May 1998.]

With numbers Use a comma (never a period) to divide numbers into thousands.

▶ 1,200   ▶ 515,000   ▶ 34,000,000

No commas are necessary in years (*2012*), numbers in addresses (*3501 East 10th Street*), or page numbers (*page 1008*).

With titles Use commas around a person's title or degree when it follows the name.

▶ Stephen L. Carter, PhD, gave the commencement speech.

With the parts of an address

▶ Alice Walker was born in Eatonton, Georgia, in 1944.

However, do not use a comma before a ZIP code: Newton, MA 02159.

With a conversational tag, tag question, or insert

▶ Yes, Salinger's daughter, like others before her, has produced a memoir.

▶ She has not won a Pulitzer Prize, has she?

▶ The show dwelt on tasteless, not educational, details.

With a direct address or salutation

▶ Whatever you build next, Mr. Trump, will cause controversy.

48

Apostrophes

An apostrophe indicates ownership or possession: *Fred's books, the government's plans, a year's pay* (the books belonging to Fred, the plans of the government, the pay for a year). It can also signal omitted letters in contractions.

48a Checklists: Apostrophe yes and apostrophe no

KEY POINTS

Apostrophe Yes

1. Use *-'s* for the possessive form of all nouns except plural nouns that end with *-s*: *the hero's misfortunes, the boss's plans, the people's advocate.*

2. Use an apostrophe alone for the possessive form of plural nouns that end with *-s*: *the heroes' misfortunes, the bosses' plans, liberal politicians' efforts.*

3. Use an apostrophe to indicate the omission of letters in contracted forms such as *didn't, they're, can't,* and *let's.* However, some readers of formal academic writing may object to such contractions.

Note: If you do use a contraction, use *it's* only for "it is" or "it has": *It's a good idea; it's been a long time* (see 48f).

KEY POINTS

Apostrophe No

1. Generally, do not use an apostrophe to form the plurals of nouns (see 48e for rare exceptions).

2. Never use an apostrophe before an -s ending on a verb. Note that *let's* is a contracted form for *let us*; the -s is not a verb ending.

3. Do not write possessive pronouns (*hers, its, ours, yours, theirs*) with an apostrophe.

4. Do not use an apostrophe to form the plural of names: *the Browns.*

5. With inanimate objects and concepts, *of* is often preferred to an apostrophe: *the cost of service, the roof of the hotel, the back of the desk.*

48b When to use -'s to signal possession

As a general rule, to signal possession, use -'s with singular nouns, with indefinite pronouns (43h), with names, and with plural nouns that do not form the plural with -s: *the child's books, anybody's opinion, the children's toys, today's world, this month's budget, Mr. Jackson's voice, someone else's idea, their money's worth.* Also note the following uses:

With individual and joint ownership To indicate individual ownership, make each owner possessive.

▶ **Updike's and Roth's recent works received glowing reviews.**

To show joint ownership, make only the last owner possessive: *Sam and Pat's house.*

With compound nouns Add -'s to the last word in a compound noun.

▶ **his brother-in-law's car**

With singular proper nouns ending in -s When a name ends in -s, add -'s as usual for the possessive.

▶ **Dylan Thomas's imagery conjures up the Welsh landscape.**

When a name has more than one syllable and ends in *-s* with a *z* pronunciation, you can use an apostrophe alone: *Moses'* law, *Euripides'* dramas.

In all words that need an apostrophe to signal possession

▶ **My mother's expectations differed from Jing Mei's mother.**
   [meaning the expectations of the mother of Jing Mei]

48c Use only an apostrophe to signal possession in plural nouns already ending in *-s*

Add only an apostrophe when a plural noun already ends in *-s*.

▶ **the students' suggestions**   ▶ **my friends' ambitions**
   [more than one student]   [more than one friend]

Remember to include an apostrophe in comparisons with a plural noun understood:

▶ **His views are different from other professors'.** [. . . from other professors' views]

48d Use an apostrophe in contractions

In a contraction (*shouldn't, don't, haven't*), the apostrophe appears where letters have been omitted. To test whether an apostrophe is in the correct place, mentally replace the missing letters. The replacement test, however, will not help with the following:

won't   will not

Note: Some readers may object to contractions in formal academic writing, especially scientific writing, because they view them as colloquial and informal. It is safer not to use contractions unless you know the conventions of the genre and your readers' preferences.

can't	cannot	they'd	they had *or* they would
didn't	did not		
he's	he is *or* he has	they're	they are
's	is, has, *or* does (How's it taste?)	it's	it is *or* it has
		let's	let us (as in "Let's go.")

Never place an apostrophe before the *-s* ending of a verb:

▶ **The author let's his characters take over.**

An apostrophe can also take the place of the first part of a year or decade.

▶ **the radical rebellion of the '60s** [the 1960s]

▶ **the Spirit of '76** [the year 1776]

Note: Fixed forms spelled with an apostrophe, such as *o'clock* and the poetic *o'er*, are contractions ("of the clock," "over").

48e Two occasions to use -'s to form a plural

1. Use -'s for the plural form of letters of the alphabet Italicize only the letter, not the plural ending (52d).

▶ **Maria picked all the *M*'s out of her alphabet soup.**

▶ **Georges Perec's novel called *A Void* has no *e*'s in it at all.**

2. Use -'s for the plural form of a word referred to as the word itself Italicize the word named as a word, but do not italicize the -'s ending (52d).

▶ **You have too many *but*'s in that sentence.**

MLA and APA prefer no apostrophe in the plural form of numbers, acronyms, and abbreviations (54f).

the 1900s   the terrible twos   CDs   FAQs   BAs

However, you may see such plurals spelled with -'s. In all cases, be consistent in your usage.

Never use an apostrophe to signal the plural of common nouns or personal names: *big bargains, the Jacksons.*

48f Distinguish between *it's* and *its*

Its is the possessive form of the pronoun *it* and means "belonging to it." Use the apostrophe only if you intend *it is* or *it has* (see also 44b, p. 439).

▶ **It's a good idea.**   ▶   **The committee took its time.**

Many writers slip up with these forms. Use your spell checker to search your entire document for both *its* and *it's*. Then check each one by asking "Am I saying *it is* or *it has* here?" If the answer is yes, use *it's* or *it is*. If the answer is no, use *its*.

49 ⚷

Quotation Marks

In American English, double quotation marks indicate where some-one's exact words begin and end. (British English, however, uses single quotation marks.) For long quotations, see 49f.

49a Guidelines for using quotation marks

> ### KEY POINTS
> **Quotation Marks: Basic Guidelines**
> 1. Quote exactly the words used by the original speaker or writer.
> 2. Pair opening quotation marks with closing quotation marks to indicate where the quotation ends and your ideas begin.
> 3. Use correct punctuation to introduce and end a quotation, and place other marks of punctuation carefully in relation to the quotation marks.
> 4. Enclose the titles of articles, short stories, songs, and poems in quotation marks.
> 5. Enclose any added or changed material in square brackets (51e); indicate omitted material with ellipsis dots (51g).

49b Punctuation introducing and ending a quotation

After an introductory verb, such as *say, state,* or *write,* use a comma followed by a capital letter to introduce a direct quotation

> ▶ It was Erma Bombeck who said, "Families aren't dying. They're merging into conglomerates."
>
> —"Empty Fridge, Empty Nest"

Use a colon after a complete sentence introducing a quotation, and begin the quotation with a capital letter

▶ Woody Allen always tries to make us laugh even about serious issues like wealth and poverty: "Money is better than poverty, if only for financial reasons."

—Without Feathers

When a quotation is integrated into the structure of your own sentence, use no special introductory punctuation other than the quotation marks

▶ Phyllis Grosskurth says of Lord Byron that "anxiety over money was driving him over the brink."

—Byron

Put periods and commas inside quotation marks, even if these punctuation marks do not appear in the original quotation

▶ When Henry Rosovsky characterizes Bloom's ideas as "mind-boggling," he is not offering praise.

—The University

In a documented paper, when you use parenthetical citations after a short quotation at the end of a sentence, put the period at the end of the citation, not within the quotation. See 10e and 49f for how to handle long quotations.

▶ Geoffrey Wolff observes that when his father died, there was nothing to indicate "that he had ever known another human being" (11).

—The Duke of Deception

Put question marks and exclamation points inside the quotation marks if they are part of the original source, with no additional period When your sentence is a statement, do not use a comma or period in addition to a question mark or exclamation point.

▶ She asked, "Where's my mama?"

Put a question mark, exclamation point, semicolon, or colon outside the closing quotation marks If your sentence contains punctuation that is your own, not part of the original quotation, do not include it within the quotation marks.

▶ The chapter focuses on this question: Who are "the new American dreamers"?

49c   Quotation marks in dialogue

Do not add closing quotation marks until the speaker changes or you interrupt the quotation. Begin each new speaker's words with a new paragraph.

interruption
of quotation

▶ "I'm not going to work today," he announced. "Why should I? I worked all weekend. My boss is away on vacation. And I have a headache."

change of speaker

▶ "Honey, your boss is on the phone," his wife called from the bedroom.

If a quotation from one speaker continues for more than one paragraph, place *closing* quotation marks at the end of only the *final* paragraph of the quotation. However, place *opening* quotation marks at the beginning of every paragraph so that readers realize that the quotation is continuing.

49d   A quotation within a quotation

Enclose quotations in double quotation marks. Use single quotation marks to enclose a quotation or a title of a short work within a quotation. (The reverse is the case in British English.)

▶ Margaret announced, "I have read 'The Lottery' already."

▶ The comedian Steven Wright once said, "I have an existential map. It has 'You are here' written all over it."

49e   Quotation marks with titles, definitions, and translations

For a translation or definition, use quotation marks:

▶ The abbreviation *p.m.* means "after midday."

KEY POINTS
Titles: Quotation Marks or Italics/Underlining?

1. **Quotation marks** with the title of an article, short story, poem, song, or chapter: "Kubla Khan"; "Lucy in the Sky with Diamonds"; "The Yellow Wallpaper"; "America: The Multinational Society"

2. **Italics** (or underlining in a handwritten manuscript) with the title of a book, journal, magazine, newspaper, film, play, or long poem published alone: *The Anthologist, Newsweek, District 9, Beowulf* (52a)

3. **No quotation marks and no italics or underlining** with the title of your own essay

For more on capital letters with titles, see 53d.

49f When not to use quotation marks

In the sample sentences, yellow shading means "no quotation marks here."

1. Do not put quotation marks around indirect quotations

▶ One woman I interviewed said that her husband argued like a lawyer.

2. Do not put quotation marks around clichés, slang, or trite expressions Instead, revise. See also 34d and 34g.

involvement.
▶ All they want is "a piece of the action."
                     ^

3. Do not put quotation marks at the beginning and end of long indented quotations When you use MLA style to quote more than three lines of poetry or more than four typed lines of prose, indent the whole passage one inch from the left margin. For 40 or more words in APA style or for 100 words (eight lines or two or more paragraphs) in *Chicago* style, indent the passage one-half inch. Do not enclose the quoted passage in quotation marks, but retain any internal quotation marks. See 10e and chapter 13 for examples.

4. On the title page of your own paper, do not put quotation marks around your essay title   Use quotation marks in your title only when your title contains a quotation or the title of a short work.

▶  Charles Baxter's "Gryphon" as an Educational Warning

50 ⚷

Semicolons and Colons

A colon (:) looks somewhat like a semicolon (;). A colon is two dots; the semicolon, a dot above a comma. However, they are used in different ways, and they are not interchangeable.

50a Checklists: Semicolon yes and semicolon no

A period separates independent clauses with finality; a semicolon, such as the one you just saw in this sentence, provides a less distinct separation and indicates that an additional related thought or item will follow immediately. As essayist Lewis Thomas comments in his "Notes on Punctuation":

> The period tells you that that is that; if you didn't get all the meaning you wanted or expected, anyway you got all the writer intended to parcel out and now you have to move along. But with a semicolon there you get a pleasant little feeling of expectancy; there is more to come.

KEY POINTS
Semicolon Yes

1. Between closely connected independent clauses when no coordinating conjunction (*and, but, or, nor, so, for, yet*) is used

▶ **Biography tells us about the subject; biographers also tell us about themselves.**

Do not overuse semicolons in this way. They are more effective when used sparingly. Do not use a capital letter to begin a clause after a semicolon.

2. Between independent clauses connected with a transitional expression like *however, moreover, in fact, nevertheless, above all,* or *therefore* (see the list in 2c)

▶ **The results of the study support the hypothesis; however, further research with a variety of tasks is necessary.**

(If the transitional expression is in the middle or at the end of its clause, the semicolon still appears between the clauses: *The results support the hypothesis; further research, however, is necessary.*)

3. To separate items in a list containing internal commas

▶ **When I cleaned out the refrigerator, I found a chocolate cake, half-eaten; some canned tomato paste, which had a blue fungus growing on the top; and some possibly edible meat loaf.**

KEY POINTS
Semicolon No

1. Not in place of a colon to introduce a list or an explanation

▶ **Ellsworth Kelly has produced a variety of works of art; drawings, paintings, prints, and sculptures.**

2. Not after an introductory phrase or dependent clause, even if the phrase or clause is long. A semicolon would produce a fragment. Use a comma instead.

▶ **Because the training period was so long and arduous for all the players; the manager allowed one visit by family and friends.**

3. Not before an appositive phrase

▶ **The audience cheered the Oscar winner; Sean Penn.**

4. Not in place of a comma before *and, but, or, nor, so, for,* or *yet* joining independent clauses

▶ **The thrift shop in the church basement needed a name; and the volunteers chose Attic Treasures.**

50b Checklists: Colon yes and colon no

A colon signals anticipation. It follows an independent clause and introduces information that readers will need. A colon tells readers, "What comes next will define, illustrate, or explain what you have just read." Use one space after a colon.

> ### KEY POINTS
> #### Colon Yes

1. After an independent clause to introduce a list

   ▶ **The students included three pieces of writing in their portfolios: a narrative, an argument, and a documented paper.**

2. After an independent clause to introduce an explanation, expansion, or elaboration

   ▶ **After an alarming cancer diagnosis and years of treatment, Lance Armstrong was victorious: He won the Tour de France seven times.**

   Some writers prefer to use a lowercase letter after a colon introducing an independent clause. Whatever you choose to do, be consistent in your usage.

3. To introduce a rule or principle, which may begin with a capital letter

   ▶ **The main principle of public speaking is simple: Look at the audience.**

4. To introduce a quotation not integrated into your sentence and not introduced by a verb such as *say*

   ▶ **Emily Post has provided an alternative to attempting to outdo others: "To do *exactly as your neighbors do* is the only sensible rule."**

   A colon also introduces a long quotation set off from your text (see 10e).

5. In salutations, precise time notations, titles, and biblical citations of chapter and verse

- Dear Chancellor Witkin:
- To: The Chancellor
- 7:20 p.m.
- *Backlash: The Undeclared War against American Women*
- Genesis 37:31–35 [In MLA style, a period is used in place of the colon.]

KEY POINTS

Colon No

(Note that in the sample sentences, yellow shading means "no colon here.")

1. Not directly after a verb (such as a form of *be* or *include*)

- The two main effects were the improvement of registration and an increase in the numbers of advisers.

- The book includes a preface, an introduction, an appendix, and an index.

2. Not after a preposition (such as *of, except,* and *regarding*) or the phrase *such as*

- The essay consisted of a clear beginning, middle, and end.

- The novel will please many readers except linguists and lawyers.

- They packed many different items for the picnic, such as taco chips, salsa, bean salad, pita bread, and egg rolls.

3. Not after *for example, especially,* or *including*

- His varied taste is shown by his living room furnishings, including antiques, modern art, and art deco lighting fixtures.

51 🔑

Other Punctuation Marks

51a Periods

In British English, a period is descriptively called a "full stop." The stop at the end of a sentence is indeed full—more of a stop than a comma provides. Periods are also used with abbreviations, decimals, and amounts of money, as in items 3 and 4 below.

1. Use a period to end a sentence that makes a statement or gives a command

▶ The interviewer asked the manager about the company's finances.

▶ Note the use of metaphor in the last paragraph.

The Web site of the Modern Language Association (MLA), in its list of Frequently Asked Questions about the *MLA Handbook*, recommends leaving one space after a concluding punctuation mark but sees "nothing wrong with using two spaces" if your instructor approves. For periods used with sentences within parentheses, see 53a.

2. Use a period, not a question mark, to end a sentence concluding with an indirect question

▶ The interviewer asked the manager how much the company made last year. [See also 40d and 62d.]

3. Use a period to signal an abbreviation

Mr.   Dr.   Rev.   Tues.   etc.

Use only one space after the period: Mr. Lomax. When abbreviations contain internal periods, do not insert a space after any internal periods.

e.g.   i.e.   a.m.   p.m.   (or A.M.   P.M.)

Note: For some abbreviations with capital letters, you can use periods or not. Just be consistent.

A.M. or AM   P.M. or PM   U.S.A. or USA

When ending a sentence with an abbreviation, do not add an extra period: *The plane left at 7 a.m.*

However, MLA style recommends that no periods be used with initials of names of government agencies (HUD) or other organizations (ACLU), acronyms (abbreviations pronounced as words: NASA, AIDS), Internet abbreviations (URL), abbreviations for states (CA, NJ), or common time indicators (BC, AD) (54c).

4. Use a period with decimals and with amounts of money over a dollar

▶ 3.7, $7.50

51b Question marks and exclamation points

Question marks (?)   A question mark at the end of a sentence signals a direct question. Do not use a period in addition to a question mark.

▶ **What is he writing?**

If questions in a series are not complete sentences, you still need question marks. A question fragment may begin with a capital letter or not. Just make your usage consistent.

▶ **Are the characters in the play involved in the disaster? Indifferent to it? Unaware of it?**

▶ **Are the characters in the play involved in the disaster? indifferent to it? unaware of it?**

However, after an indirect question, use a period, not a question mark (51a, item 2).

▶ **I wonder what he is writing.**

Questions are useful devices to engage readers' attention. You ask a question and then provide an answer.

▶ **Many cooks nowadays are making healthier dishes. How do they do this? For the most part, they use unsaturated oil.**

A question mark is sometimes used to express uncertainty about a date or to indicate a query.

▶ **"She jumped in?" he wondered.** [Note that no comma is needed after a question mark that is part of a quotation.]

▶ **Plato (427?–347 BC) founded the Academy at Athens.**

Exclamation points (!) An exclamation point at the end of a sentence indicates that the writer considers the statement amazing, surprising, or extraordinary. As novelist F. Scott Fitzgerald said, "An exclamation point is like laughing at your own joke." Let your words and ideas carry the force of any emphasis you want to communicate.

NO   **The last act of her play is really impressive!**

YES   **The last act of her play resolves the crisis in an unexpected and dramatic way.**

If you feel you absolutely have to include an exclamation point to get your point across in dialogue or with an emphatic command or statement, do not use it along with an additional comma or period.

▶ **"Just watch the ball!" the coach yelled.**

Note: An exclamation point (or a question mark) *can* be used with a period that signals an abbreviation:

▶ **The match didn't end until 1 a.m.!**

Avoid using a question mark or an exclamation point enclosed in parentheses to convey irony or sarcasm.

NO   **The principal, that great historian (?), has proposed a new plan for the history curriculum.**

YES   **The principal, who admits he is no historian, has proposed a new plan for the history curriculum.**

51c Dashes

A dash (—) alerts readers to an explanation, to something unexpected, or to an interruption. Form a dash by typing two hyphens with no extra space before, between, or after them. Some word processing software will transform the two hyphens into one continuous dash. Dashes should enclose a phrase, not a clause.

▶ **Armed with one weapon—his wit—he faced the crowd.**

▶ **The accused gasped, "But I never—" and fainted.**

▶ **In America there are two classes of travel—first class and with children.**

                 —Robert Benchley, in Robert E. Drennan, *The Algonquin Wits*

Commas can be used to set off an appositive phrase, but a pair of dashes is preferable when appositive phrases form a list already containing commas.

▶ **The contents of his closet—torn jeans, frayed jackets, and suits shiny on the seat and elbows—made him reassess his priorities.**

Overusing the dash may produce a staccato effect. Use it sparingly.

51d Parentheses

Use parentheses to mark an aside or provide additional information.

▶ **Everyone admires Rafael Nadal's feat (winning Grand Slam finals on all court surfaces).**

Also use parentheses to enclose citations in a documented paper and to enclose numbers or letters preceding items in a list.

▶ **(3) A journalist reports that in the course of many interviews, he met very few people who were cynical about the future of the country (Lamb 5).**

At the end of a sentence, place the period inside the last parenthesis only when a separate new sentence is enclosed (see examples in 53a).

▶ **Lance Armstrong's feat led to greater visibility for competitive cycling in the United States. (He won the Tour de France in seven consecutive years.)**

51e Brackets

Square brackets ([ ])   When you insert words or comments or make changes to words within a quotation, enclose the inserted or changed material in square brackets. Be careful to insert only words that help the quotation fit into your sentence grammatically or that offer a necessary explanation. Do not insert words that substantially change the meaning.

▶ **According to Ridley, "the key to both of these features of life [the ability to reproduce and to create order] is information."**

On occasion, you may need to use brackets to insert the Latin word *sic* (meaning "thus") into a quoted passage in which an error occurs. Using *sic* tells readers that the word or words that it follows were present in the original source and are not your own.

▶ **Richard Lederer tells of a man who did "exercises to strengthen his abominable [sic] muscles."**

Square brackets can also be used in MLA style around ellipsis dots that you add to signal an omission from a source that itself contains ellipsis dots (51g).

Angle brackets (< >) Use angle brackets to enclose e-mail addresses and URLs when you need to include them in an MLA works-cited list (see 12a, 12f, and 57a).

51f Slashes

Use a slash (/) to separate two or three lines of poetry quoted within your own text. For quoting more than three lines of poetry, see 10e.

▶ **Philip Larkin asks a question that many of us relate to: "Why should I let the toad *work* / Squat on my life?"**

Slashes are also used in expressions such as *and/or* and *he/she* to indicate options. Be careful not to overuse these expressions.

51g Ellipsis dots

When you omit material from a quotation, indicate the omission—the ellipsis—by three dots with a space between each dot (. . .). (MLA style recommends using square brackets around ellipsis dots if the passage you quote from itself contains an ellipsis.) The following passage by Ruth Sidel, on page 27 of *On Her Own*, is used in the examples that follow.

> These women have a commitment to career, to material well-being, to success, and to independence. To many of them, an affluent lifestyle is central to their dreams; they often describe their goals in terms of cars, homes, travel to Europe. In short, they want their piece of the American Dream.

Words omitted from the middle of a quotation Use three ellipsis dots when you omit material from the middle of a quotation.

▶ **Ruth Sidel reports that the women in her interviews "have a commitment to career . . . and to independence" (27).**

Words omitted at the end of your sentence When you omit part of a quotation and the omission occurs at the end of your own sentence, insert ellipsis dots after the sentence period, followed by the closing quotation marks, making four dots in all.

▶ **Ruth Sidel presents interesting findings about jobs and money: "These women have a commitment to career, to material well-being. . . ."**

When a parenthetical reference follows the quoted passage, put the final sentence period after the parenthetical reference:

▶ **Ruth Sidel presents interesting findings about jobs and money: "These women have a commitment to career, to material well-being . . ." (27).**

Complete sentence omitted   When you omit a complete sentence or more, insert three ellipsis dots.

▶ **Sidel tells us how "an affluent lifestyle is central to their dreams; . . . they want their piece of the American Dream" (27).**

Line of poetry omitted   When you omit one or more lines of poetry from a long, indented quotation, indicate the omission with a line of dots.

▶ **This poem is for the hunger of my mother**
. . . .
who read the Blackwell's catalogue
like a menu of delights
and when we moved from Puerto Rico to the States
we packed 100 boxes of books and 40 of everything else.

—Aurora Levins Morales, *Class Poem*

When not to use ellipsis dots   Do not use ellipsis dots when you quote only a word or a phrase because it will be obvious that material has been omitted:

▶ **The women Sidel interviewed see an "affluent lifestyle" in their future.**

Note: Use three dots to indicate a pause in speech or an interruption.

▶ **The doctor said, "The good news is . . ." and then turned to take a phone call.**

52 ⚷

Italics/Underlining

Italics and underlining serve the same function: to highlight a word, phrase, or title. Use underlining only in a handwritten or typed manuscript. In all other material written with a word processor or online, use italics. In some e-mail postings and discussion lists, you may need to indicate italics by a single underscore at the beginning and end of the passage you would usually italicize.

52a When to italicize the titles of long, whole works

In the body of an essay, italicize the titles of books, journals, magazines, newspapers, plays, films, TV series, long poems, musical compositions, Web sites, online databases, and works of art.

▶ *The Sun Also Rises*	▶ *Mona Lisa*
▶ *The Daily Show*	▶ *Newsweek*
▶ *The Wire*	▶ *About.com*

52b When not to italicize titles

- In the body of your text, do not italicize the names of sacred works such as the Bible and the Koran (Qur'an). Note, though, that these will be italicized in an MLA citation (11b, item T) and in an MLA works-cited list (12c, item 19).

- Do not italicize the books of the Bible (Genesis, Psalms) or the titles of documents and laws, such as the Declaration of Independence, the Constitution, and the Americans with Disabilities Act. However, follow style guides for the use of italics for titles of works in bibliographical lists or notes: CSE, for example, does not use italics for titles.

- Do not italicize the titles of short works, such as poems, short stories, essays, and articles. (MLA and *Chicago* styles use quotation marks for short works in their list of works cited or notes.)

- Do not italicize the title of your own essay (see 49e).

- See MLA, APA, CSE, and *Chicago* styles for the conventions of using italics and quotation marks in a list of references (chapters 12–20).

52c Italicize names of ships, trains, airplanes, and spacecraft

▶ *Mayflower*   ▶ *Silver Meteor*   ▶ *Mir*   ▶ *Columbia*

However, do not italicize any abbreviation preceding the name: USS *Constitution*.

52d Italicize letters, numerals, and words referring to the words themselves, not to what they represent

▶ The sign had a large *P* in black marker and a *3* in red.

▶ *Zarf* is a useful word for some board games.

52e Italicize words from other languages not yet adopted in English

Expressions not commonly used in English should be italicized. Do not overuse such expressions because they tend to sound pretentious.

▶ The Marshall Plan was instrumental in creating the *Wirtschaftswunder* in West Germany after World War II.

Do not italicize common expressions: et al., croissant, film noir, etc.

52f Do not use italics for emphasis

Select a word that better conveys the idea you want to express.

       hair-raising.
▶ The climb was ~~so scary~~.

53 🔑

Capitalization

53a Capitalize *I* and the first word of a sentence

Always use a capital letter for the pronoun *I* and for the first letter of the first word of a sentence. E-mail correspondence without any capitals may look sloppy and annoy some readers (see also 57b). However, do not use a capital letter for the first word after a semi-colon even when it begins a complete sentence. In addition, use no capital letter if you insert a complete sentence into another sentence using parentheses:

▶ **The Web site provides further historical information (just click the icon).**

If you want to give the material within the parentheses a little more emphasis, make it a sentence with a capital letter and place the period before the closing parenthesis.

▶ **The Web site provides further historical information. (Just click the icon.)**

53b Capitalize proper nouns and proper adjectives

Begin the names of specific people, places, and things with a capital letter. For the use of *the* with proper nouns, see 60f.

Types of Proper Nouns and Adjectives	Examples
People	Albert Einstein, P. Diddy, T. S. Eliot, Bill Gates (but bell hooks), Sarah Palin
Nations, continents, planets, stars, and galaxies	Hungary, Asia, Mercury, the North Star, the Milky Way
Mountains, rivers, and oceans	Mount Everest, the Thames, the Pacific Ocean
Public places and regions	Golden Gate Park, the Great Plains, the Midwest, the South (but no capital for direction, as in "Drive south on the turnpike")
Streets, buildings, and monuments	Rodeo Drive, the Empire State Building, the Roosevelt Memorial
Cities, states, and provinces	Toledo, Kansas, Nova Scotia
Days of the week and months	Wednesday, March
Holidays	Labor Day, the Fourth of July

Types of Proper Nouns and Adjectives	Examples
Organizations, companies, and search engines	the Red Cross, Microsoft Corporation, eBay (internal capital), Yahoo!
Institutions (including colleges, departments, schools, government offices, and courts of law)	University of Texas, Department of English, School of Business, Department of Defense, Florida Supreme Court
Historical events, named periods, and documents	the Civil War, the Renaissance, the Roaring Twenties, the Declaration of Independence
Religions, deities, revered persons, and sacred texts	Buddhism, Islam, Muslim, Baptist, Jehovah, Mohammed, the Torah, the Koran (Qur'an)
Races, tribes, nations, nationalities, and languages	the Navajo, Greece, Greek, Spain, Spanish, Syrian, Farsi
Registered trademarks	Kleenex, Apple, Bic, Nike, Xerox
Names of ships, planes, and spacecraft	the USS *Kearsarge*, the *Spirit of St. Louis*, the *Challenger*
Titles of courses	English Composition, Introduction to Sociology

Note: Do not capitalize nouns naming general classes or types of people, places, things, or ideas: *government, jury, mall, prairie, utopia, traffic court, the twentieth century, goodness, reason.* Also, do not capitalize the names of seasons (*next spring*) or subjects of study, except for languages (*She is interested in geology and Spanish.*). For the use of capital letters in online writing, see 57b.

53c Capitalize a title before a person's name

▶ The reporter interviewed Senator McCain.

▶ The residents cheered Grandma Jones.

Do not use a capital letter when a title is not attached to a person's name.

▶ Each state elects two senators.

▶ My grandmother is ninety years old.

When a title substitutes for the name of a known person, a capital letter is often used.

▶ **Have you spoken with the Senator [senator] yet?**

53d Capitalize major words in a title

In titles of published books, journals, magazines, essays, articles, films, poems, and songs, use a capital letter at the beginning of all words. Exceptions: articles (*the, a, an*), coordinating conjunctions (*and, but, or, nor, so, for, yet*), *to* in an infinitive (*to stay*), and prepositions unless they begin or end the title or subtitle.

▶ **"With a Little Help from My Friends"**

▶ *Reflections from the Keyboard: The World of the Concert Pianist*

For more on titles, see the Key Points box in 49e, p. 477.

53e Capitals with colons and quotations

Writers often ask how to use capital letters with colons and quotations.

Should a capital letter be used at the beginning of a clause after a colon? Usage varies. Usually, a capital letter is used if the clause states a rule or principle (p. 480, item 3). Make your usage consistent.

Should a capital letter be used at the beginning of a quotation? Capitalize the first word of a quoted sentence if it is capitalized in the original passage.

▶ **Quindlen says, "This is a story about a name," and thus tells us the topic of her article.**

Do not capitalize when you quote part of a sentence.

▶ **When Quindlen says that she is writing "a story about a name," she is telling us the topic of her article.**

54 🔑

Abbreviations

For abbreviations commonly used in online writing, see 57d.

54a Abbreviate titles used with people's names

Use an abbreviation, followed by a period, for titles before or after names. The following abbreviated titles precede names: *Mr., Mrs., Ms., Prof., Dr., Gen.,* and *Sen.* The following abbreviated titles follow names: *Sr., Jr., PhD, MD, BA,* and *DDS.* Do not use a title both before and after a name: *Dr. Benjamin Spock* or *Benjamin Spock, MD.* Do not abbreviate a title if it is not attached to a specific name.

doctor
▶ Pat Murphy, Sr., went to the ~~dr.~~ twice last week.

54b Abbreviate the names of familiar institutions, countries, tests, diseases, diplomas, individuals, and objects

Use capitalized abbreviations of the names of well-known institutions (*UCLA, YWCA, FBI, UN*), countries (*USA* or *U.S.A.*), tests and diplomas (*SAT, GED*), diseases (*MS, HIV*), individuals (*FDR*), TV and radio networks and stations (*PBS, WQXR*), and objects (*DVD*). If you use a specialized abbreviation, first use the term in full followed by the abbreviation in parentheses; then use the abbreviation.

▶ The Graduate Record Examination (GRE) is required by many graduate schools. GRE preparation is therefore big business.

54c Abbreviate terms used with numbers

Use abbreviations such as *BC, AD, a.m., p.m., $, mph, wpm, mg, kg,* and other units of measure only when they occur with specific numbers.

▶ **35 BC** [meaning "before Christ," now often replaced with *BCE,* "before the Common Era"]

▶ **AD 1776** [*anno domini,* "in the year of the Lord," now often replaced with *CE,* "Common Era," used after the date: 1776 CE]

▶ **2:00 a.m./p.m.** [*ante* or *post meridiem,* Latin for "before or after midday"] Alternatives are A.M./P.M. or AM/PM. Be consistent.

Do not use these abbreviations and other units of measure when no number is attached to them.

money
▶ His family gave him a wallet full of $ to spend on vacation.

afternoon.
▶ They arrived late in the ~~p.m.~~

54d Abbreviate common Latin terms

In notes, parentheses, and source citations, use abbreviations for common Latin terms. In the body of your text, use the English meaning.

Abbreviation	Latin	English Meaning
etc.	et cetera	and so on
i.e.	id est	that is
e.g.	exempli gratia	for example
cf.	confer	compare
NB	nota bene	note well
et al.	et alii	and others

54e Do not abbreviate familiar words to save time and space

In formal writing, write in full expressions such as the following:

&	and
bros.	brothers [Use "Bros." only if it is part of the official name of a business.]
chap.	chapter
lb.	pound
Mon.	Monday
nite	night
NJ	New Jersey [Abbreviate the name of a state only in an address, a note, or a reference.]
no.	number [Use the abbreviation only with a specific number: "No. 17 on the list was deleted."]
Oct.	October [Write names of days and months in full, except in some works-cited lists, such as in MLA format.]
soc.	sociology [Write names of academic subjects in full.]
thru	through
w/	with

54f Use -*s* (not -'*s*) for the plural form of an abbreviation

Do not use an apostrophe to make an abbreviation plural (48e).

► **She has over a thousand CDs.**

► **Both his SUVs are at the repair shop.**

55

Numbers

Conventions for using numerals (actual figures) or words vary across the disciplines.

55a Use the conventions of the discipline in which you are writing

In the humanities and in business letters

Use words for numbers expressible in one or two words and for fractions (*nineteen, fifty-six, two hundred, one-half*).

Use numerals for longer numbers (*326; 5,625; 7,642,000*).

Use a combination of words and numerals for whole millions, billions, and so on (*45 million, 1 billion*).

In scientific and technical writing

Use numerals for all numbers above nine.

Use numerals for numbers below ten only when they show precise measurement, as when they are grouped and compared with other larger numbers (*5 of the 39 participants*) or when they precede a unit of measurement (*6 cm*), indicate a mathematical function (*8%; 0.4*), or represent a specific time, date, age, score, or number in a series.

Use words for fractions: *two-thirds.*

55b Spell out numbers that begin a sentence

▶ One hundred twenty-five members voted for the new bylaws.

▶ Six thousand fans have already bought tickets.

 NOTE FOR MULTILINGUAL WRITERS

Number before *Hundred, Thousand,* and *Million*

Even after plural numbers, use the singular form of *hundred, thousand,* and *million.* Add *-s* only when there is no preceding number.

▶ Five *hundred* books were damaged in the flood.

▶ *Hundreds* of books were damaged in the flood.

55c Use numerals for giving the time and dates and in other special instances

In nonscientific writing, use numerals for the following:

Time and dates	6 p.m. on 31 May 2009
Decimals	20.89
Statistics	median score 35
Addresses	16 East 93rd Street
Chapter, page, scene, and line numbers	chapter 5, page 97
Quantities appearing with abbreviations or symbols	6°C (for temperature Celsius), $21, 6′ 7″
Scores	The Yankees beat the Phillies 7–3 to win the World Series.

For percentages and money, numerals and the symbol (*75%, $24.67*) are usually acceptable, or you can spell out the expression if it is fewer than four words (*seventy-five percent, twenty-four dollars*).

55d Use *-s* (not *-'s*) for the plural form of numerals

▶ **in the 1980s**

▶ **They scored in the 700s on the SATs.**

56 ⚷

Hyphens

Use hyphens to divide a word or to form a compound. For the use of hyphens online, see 57c.

56a Hyphens with prefixes

Many words with prefixes are spelled without hyphens: *cooperate, nonrestrictive, unnatural*. Others are hyphenated: *all-inclusive, anti-intellectual, self-effacing*. Always use a hyphen when the main word is a number or a proper noun: *all-American, post-2010*. If you are unsure about whether to insert a hyphen after a prefix, check a big dictionary to see if it lists the word as hyphenated.

56b Hyphens in compound words

Some compound nouns are written as one word (*toothbrush*), others as two words (*coffee shop*), and still others with one or more hyphens (*role-playing, father-in-law*). Always check an up-to-date dictionary. Similarly, check a dictionary for compound verbs (*cross-examine, overemphasize*).

Hyphenate compound adjectives preceding a noun: *a well-organized party, a law-abiding citizen, a ten-page essay*. When the modifier follows the noun, no hyphen is necessary: *The party was well organized. Most citizens try to be law abiding. The essay was ten pages long.*

Do not insert a hyphen between an *-ly* adverb and the word it modifies or after an adjective in its comparative (*-er*) or superlative (*-est*) form: *a tightly fitting suit, an expertly written essay, a sweeter sounding melody*.

Treat a series of hyphenated prefixes like this:

▶ **Many second- and third-generation Americans celebrate their origins.**

56c Hyphens in spelled-out numbers

Use hyphens when spelling out two-word numbers from twenty-one to ninety-nine. (See chapter 55 for more on spelling out numbers.)

▶ **Twenty-two applicants arrived early in the morning.**

Also use a hyphen in spelled-out fractions: *two-thirds of a cup.*

56d End-of-line hyphens

Most word processors either automatically hyphenate words or automatically wrap words around to the next line. Choose the latter option to avoid the strange and unacceptable word division that sometimes appears with automatic hyphenation. Do not insert a hyphen into a URL to split it across lines (see 57a).

57 🔑

Online Guidelines

57a Punctuation in URLs

Punctuation marks communicate essential information in Web site addresses—uniform resource locators (URLs)—and in e-mail addresses.

Be sure to include all marks when you write an address, and if you need to spread a URL over more than one line in your text, split it after a slash (MLA, CSE, and *Chicago* styles) or before a punctuation mark such as a period (APA and *Chicago* styles). Do not split the protocol (<http://>). In a print source in MLA style, use angle brackets to enclose e-mail and Web addresses.

> ▶ **The Modern Language Association, whose Web site is at <http://www.mla.org>, provides examples of documenting Web sources.**

Do not include any additional punctuation within the angle brackets.

When you write an online paper, URLs are hyperlinked and therefore appear as underlined on the screen. Do not use angle brackets for a paper published online.

57b Capital letters online

Don't let the speed and informal nature of e-mail delude you into thinking that no rules or conventions matter anymore. Especially in academic and business settings, e-mail messages written with no capitals for the first letter of the first word of a sentence, for proper nouns, or for *I* will send readers the somewhat insulting signal that you have not bothered to check what you send them.

Overdoing capitals is as bad as (maybe worse than) including none at all. Writing a whole message in capital letters can be perceived by readers as the online equivalent of shouting. In order not to offend readers in e-mail communications and online discussion groups, avoid the prolonged use of capital letters.

57c Hyphens online

Some e-mail addresses and URLs include hyphens, so never add a hyphen to indicate that you have split an address between lines. When an online address includes a hyphen, do not break the line at a hyphen because readers will not know whether the hyphen is part of the address. Break the line after @ or after a slash.

Technological vocabulary changes quickly. You will find both *e-mail* and *email*. The MLA prefers the hyphenated spelling, *e-mail* (as does the author of this book), but the tendency is for common words like this to move toward closing up. Whichever form you use, use it consistently.

57d Abbreviations online

Many abbreviations in the electronic world have become standard fare: CD-ROM, RAM, PIN, and more. In addition, the informal world of online communication leads to informal abbreviations, at least in personal e-mail messages. Abbreviations such as *BTW* ("by the way"), *IMHO* ("in my humble opinion"), and *TTYTT* ("to tell you the truth") are used in informal e-mail, but you should avoid them in formal contexts.

57e Italics online

If you are using a basic e-mail system that provides no italics, you can indicate a title and other types of words usually italicized by inserting an underscore before and after the words to be italicized:

▶ **I was surprised by the ending of _The Great Gatsby_.**

58 🔑

Spelling

Get into the habit of using a dictionary and a word processor with a spelling-check program. Even if you check your spelling with computer software, you still need to proofread. A program will not alert you to a correctly spelled word used in the wrong place (such as *cite* used in place of *sight* or *site*). However, you may be called upon to write spontaneously without access to a spelling program or a dictionary, so learn the basic rules in this chapter.

58a Plurals of nouns

Regular plural forms   The regular plural of nouns is formed by adding -*s* or -*es* to the singular word.

essay, essays   match, matches

To form the plural of a compound noun, attach the -*s* to the main noun in the phrase.

mothers-in-law   passersby

Proofread carefully for words that form the plural with *-s* but make other changes, too, such as the following:

-f or *-fe* ⟶ *-ves*
thief, thieves
wife, wives
Exceptions: beliefs, roofs, chiefs

-o ⟶ *-oes*	*-o* ⟶ *-os*
potato, potatoes	hero (sandwich), heros
tomato, tomatoes	photo, photos
hero (human), heroes	piano, pianos

Consonant + *-y* ⟶ *-ies*	**Vowel + *-y*** ⟶ *-ys*
family, families	toy, toys
party, parties	monkey, monkeys

Irregular plural forms (no *-s* ending)

man, men	foot, feet
woman, women	tooth, teeth
child, children	mouse, mice

Plural forms borrowed from other languages   Words borrowed from other languages, particularly Greek and Latin, frequently borrow the plural form of the language, too.

basis, bases	nucleus, nuclei
thesis, theses	vertebra, vertebrae
hypothesis, hypotheses	alumnus (m.), alumni
criterion, criteria	alumna (f.), alumnae

Plural forms with no change   Some words have the same form in singular and plural: *moose, deer, sheep, species.*

58b   Doubling consonants

Doubled consonants form a link between spelling and pronunciation because the doubling of a consonant signals a short vowel sound.

Double the consonant when the verb stem contains one vowel plus one consonant in one syllable

slip, slipping, slipped   hop, hopping, hopped

The doubled consonant preserves the short vowel sound. Compare the pronunciation of *hop, hopping, hopped* with *hope, hoping, hoped.* Compare the vowel sounds in *write, writing,* and *written.*

Double the consonant when the verb stem contains two or more syllables with one vowel plus one consonant in the final stressed syllable

refer, referring, referred   control, controlling, controlled

Compare *traveling* and *traveled* with the stress on the first syllable. (British English usage, however, is *travelling* and *travelled*.)

Double the consonant when the suffix -*er* or -*est* is added to one-syllable adjectives ending in one vowel plus one consonant

big, bigger, biggest   hot, hotter, hottest

Double the *l* when adding -*ly* to an adjective that ends in one -*l*

careful, carefully   successful, successfully

58c Spelling with -*y* or -*i*

Verb Ends in Consonant + -*y*	-*ies*	-*ying*	-*ied*
cry	cries	crying	cried
study	studies	studying	studied

Verb Ends in Vowel + -*y*	-*ys*	-*ying*	-*yed*
play	plays	playing	played

Exceptions: pay/paid, say/said, lay/laid

Verb Ends in Vowel + -*e*	-*ies*	-*ying*	-*ied*
die	dies	dying	died

Two-Syllable Adjective Ends in -y	-i with a Suffix
happy	happier, happily, happiness

Two-Syllable Adjective Ends in -ly	-lier	-liest
friendly	friendlier	friendliest

58d Internal *ie* or *ei*

This traditional rhyme helps with the decision about whether to use *ie* or *ei*: "I before *e* / Except after *c* / Or when sounded like *ay* / As in *neighbor* and *weigh*." The following examples illustrate those guidelines:

i before *e*	*e* before *i* after *c*	*e* before *i* when sounded like *ay*
believe	receive	vein
relief	ceiling	reign
niece	deceive	sleigh

But note the exceptions:

i before *e* even after *c*	*e* before *i*, not after *c*	
conscience	height	seize
science	either/neither	foreign
species	leisure	weird

58e Adding a suffix

Keep a silent -*e* before an -*ly* suffix

immediate, immediately   sure, surely
Exceptions: true, truly; whole, wholly; due, duly

Keep a silent -*e* before a suffix beginning with a consonant

state, statement   force, forceful   rude, rudeness
Exceptions: acknowledge, acknowledgment; judge, judgment; argue, argument

Drop a silent -*e* before a suffix beginning with a vowel

hope, hoping   observe, observant
write, writing   remove, removable

>*Exceptions:* enforce, enforceable, change, changeable. Retaining the *-e* preserves the soft sound of the preceding consonant.

With adjectives ending in *-le*, drop the *-le* when adding *-ly*

sensible, sensibly

With adjectives ending in *-ic*, add *-ally* to form the adverb

basic, basically   characteristic, characteristically

Exception: public, publicly

Pay attention to the suffixes *-able*, *-ible*, *-ant*, *-ent*, *-ify*, and *-efy* More words end in *-able* than in *-ible*. Here are some of the most common *-ible* words:

eligible	incredible	irresistible	legible
permissible	responsible	terrible	visible

Unfortunately, there are no rules of thumb to help you decide whether to use the suffix *-ant* or *-ent*. Learn common words with these suffixes, and have your dictionary handy for others.

-ant	*-ent*
defiant	confident
observant	convenient
relevant	existent
reluctant	imminent
resistant	independent

The suffix *-ify* is more common than *-efy*. Learn the four *-efy* words:

liquefy   putrefy   rarefy   stupefy

58f Multinational characters: Accents, umlauts, tildes, and cedillas

Words and names in languages other than English may be spelled with special marks over or under a letter, such as an accent (é or è), an umlaut or dieresis (ö), a tilde (ñ), or a cedilla (ç). Your word processing program probably provides these characters (in Microsoft Word, go to Insert/Symbol). If it does not, insert them by hand.

TECH NOTE

A Useful Web Site for Writing in Other Languages

International Accents and Diacriticals: Theory, Charts, and Tips, prepared by Irene Starr of the Foreign Language Resource Center at the University of Massachusetts, is a useful site that provides charts of how to produce multinational characters; instructions on accessing and using the International English keyboard; and links to sites useful for those writing non-Roman alphabets.

PART 9

Writing across Cultures

59 Diversity and Edited American English: Challenges for Multilingual Writers 507

60 Nouns and Articles 520

61 Verbs and Verb Forms 526

62 Sentence Structure and Word Order 533

63 Prepositions and Idioms 539

64 Language Learners' FAQs 542

PART 9 WRITING ACROSS CULTURES

© | **ONLINE RESOURCES**
www.cengage.com/english/raimes

Companion online resources are available for sections throughout this part. We invite you to visit the book's Web site for more information and direct access.

PART 9

Writing across Cultures

59 Diversity and Edited American English: Challenges for Multilingual Writers 507

59a Englishes and other languages 507
59b Difference, not deficit 509
59c Learning about difference as you write 510
59d Editing guide to multilingual transfer patterns 510
59e Editing guide to vernacular Englishes 517
59f Tips for multilingual writers 518

60 Nouns and Articles 520

60a Categories of nouns 520
60b Uncountable nouns 521
60c Basic rules for *a*, *an*, and *the* 523
60d *The* for a specific reference 523
60e Which article? Four basic questions to ask 524
60f Proper nouns and articles 525

61 Verbs and Verb Forms 526

61a The *be* auxiliary 526
61b Modal auxiliary verbs 527
61c Infinitive after verbs and adjectives 529
61d Verbs followed by *-ing* 531
61e Verbs followed by an infinitive or *-ing* 531
61f *-ing* and *-ed* forms as adjectives 532

62 Sentence Structure and Word Order 533

62a A subject in every clause 533
62b Order of sentence elements 533
62c Direct and indirect objects 534
62d Direct and indirect quotations and questions 534
62e Dependent clauses (*although* and *because*) 538
62f Unnecessary pronouns 538
62g Order of adjectives 539

63 Prepositions and Idioms 539

63a Expressions with three common prepositions 539
63b Adjective + preposition 540
63c Verb + preposition 540
63d Phrasal verbs 540
63e Preposition + *-ing* 542

64 Language Learners' FAQs 542

64a *No* and *not* 542
64b *Too* and *very* 543
64c *Few* and *a few* 543
64d *Most, most of*, and *the most* 544
64e *Easy, hard*, and *difficult* 544
64f *It* and *there* 544
64g *His* and *her* 545
64h *Get used to* and *used to* 546

59 🔑

Diversity and Edited American English: Challenges for Multilingual Writers

College students in North America are a linguistically diverse group: monolingual English-speaking students who have little experience with other cultures and who may speak a local dialect of English; students who grew up in North America among family and friends with their own languages and cultures; students who learned English in formal or informal situations either in their own countries or after they immigrated from other countries; students who speak several languages fluently; and various mixes and remixes of these categories. Use the chapters in this part of the book to help you with the particular language issues that concern you as you write.

59a Englishes and other languages

At the same time as travel and the Internet make us more aware of diversity and other countries' languages and cultures, we are also experiencing a spread in the use of English. Worldwide estimates now show three nonnative speakers of English for every native speaker. More than 400 million people speak English as their native language, and more than a billion use English as a common language for special communicative, educational, and business purposes within their own communities. And by 2017, the estimated number of people speaking English will be about three billion—that is, half the world.

But languages are not fixed and static, and the users of English in their various locations adapt the language for their own purposes.

The concept of one English or a "standard" language is becoming more fluid; it is more focused on the situation and the readers of any one particular piece of writing rather than on one set of rules. Consequently, the English regarded as standard in North America is not necessarily standard in Australia, the United Kingdom, Hong Kong, Singapore, Indonesia, India, or Pakistan. Scholars see Englishes—varieties of English—in place of one monolithic language, and these

The Circle of World English (used with permission)

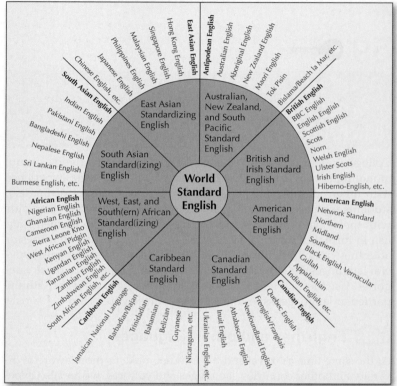

Source: Tom McArthur, "The English Languages?" *English Today* (July 1987), p. 11.

Englishes claim their own names, such as Spanglish, Singlish, Hindlish, and Taglish. English is constantly being reinvented around the world, sometimes to the dismay of academics and government officials and sometimes with the approval of individuals who see the adaptation as an act of freedom, even rebellion. The Filipino poet Gemino Abad has gone so far as to make this claim: "The English language is now ours. We have colonized it."

In the United States, too, the Conference on College Composition and Communication as early as 1974 passed a resolution on "Students' Right to Their Own Language" <http://www.ncte.org/library/NCTEFiles/Groups/CCCC/NewSRTOL.pdf>. The report on this resolution stresses the differences between speech and writing, affirming the viability of spoken dialects. However, the report makes the point that students "who want to write EAE [Edited American English] will have to learn the forms identified with that dialect as additional options to the forms they already control." The concept of *addition* and not *replacement* is important.

Therefore, despite the complexity and fluidity of varieties of English, with all their quirks, irregularities, rules, and exceptions, in the academic and business worlds the conventions of what is often called Edited American English remain relatively constant in grammar, syntax, and vocabulary (though not in spelling), with only subtle variations from country to country, region to region. Whether you are monolingual—familiar only with American English—or grew up multilingual or learned English in classes designated for English as a Second Language (ESL) students, in everyday life you, too, constantly switch the Englishes you use depending on whether you are texting a friend, Twittering, writing a report for a supervisor, or writing a research paper in college. In all instances, it is *you* in the writing, but they are different *yous*, different voices of you. The formal voice of Standard English is the one to use in academic contexts.

59b Difference, not deficit

Students in colleges in North America who grew up speaking another language are often called students of English as a Second Language, and the ESL abbreviation is commonly used in college curricula, professional literature, and the press. However, this term is not broad enough. Many so-called second-language students speak three or four languages depending on their life and educational circumstances and the languages spoken at home. Along with being bilingual or multilingual, such students frequently are multicultural, equipped with all the knowledge and experience that those terms imply.

Whether your first language is a variety of English or a totally different language, it is a good idea to see your knowledge of language and culture as an advantage rather than a problem. Unlike many monolingual writers (individuals who know only one version of one language), you are able to know different cultures in depth and to switch at will among varied linguistic and rhetorical codes. Rather than having only one language, one culture, and one culturally bound type of writing, you have a broader perspective—more to think about, more to write about, more resources to draw on as you write, and far more comparisons to make among languages, writers, writing, and culture. You bring your culture with you into your writing, and as you do so, you help shape and reshape the culture of North America.

Remember, too, that in many situations, the readers you write for will be culturally and linguistically diverse, not all emerging from one educational background. In formal settings, always aim to make your ideas clear to *all* readers by using standard forms of edited English, avoiding slang and jargon, and choosing a style appropriate to your subject matter.

59c Learning about difference as you write

Even for students who have been learning a new language or the conventions of academic writing for some time, departures from the standard language forms are inevitable. Welcome and embrace what others describe as errors. Study them and learn from them. Having errors pointed out can help you become aware of differences among languages. In fact, errors show learning in progress. If you make no errors while you are learning to speak or write a new language or a standard version of English, perhaps you are being too careful and using only what you know is correct. Be willing to take risks and try new words, new expressions, new combinations. Expand your repertoire.

TECH NOTE

Web Sites on Language and Writing

The Web sites listed here provide useful information.

■ ESL Resources, Handouts, and Exercises from Purdue University's Online Writing Lab at <http://owl.english.purdue.edu/handouts/esl/index.html>.

■ Guide to Grammar and Writing at <http://grammar.ccc.commnet.edu/grammar>. On this Capital Community College site, you will find information and quizzes on words, paragraphs, and essays. The Grammar Logs in "Ask Grammar" contain people's questions and answers and cover interesting points.

When somebody points out an error in your writing, write a note about it. Consider why you made the error—was it, for example, a transfer from your home language, a guess, a careless mistake? Or was it the employment of a logical but erroneous hypothesis about the rules of edited English (such as "many verbs form the past tense with *-ed*; therefore, the past tense form of *swear* is probably *sweared*")? Analyzing the causes of errors will help you understand how to edit them and avoid them in the future. (By the way, the past tense form of *swear* is *swore*.)

59d Editing guide to multilingual transfer patterns

Nonstandard forms can occur while you are writing in a new language, especially when you are grappling with new subject matter and difficult subjects. You concentrate on ideas and clarity, but because no writer can do everything at once, you fail to concentrate on editing.

The editing guide that follows identifies several problem areas for multilingual writers. It shows grammatical features (column 1) of specific languages (column 2) and features that lead to an error when transferred to English (column 3). An Edited American English version appears in column 4. Of course, the guide covers neither all linguistic problem areas nor all languages. Rather, it lists a selection, with the goal of being useful and practical. Use the guide to raise your awareness about your own and other languages.

Editing Guide

Language Features	Languages	Sample Transfer Errors in English	Edited Version
ARTICLES (60c–60f)			
No articles	Chinese, Japanese, Russian, Swahili, Thai, Urdu	*Sun is hot.* *I bought book.* *Computer has changed our lives.*	*The sun is hot.* *I bought a book.* *The computer has changed our lives.*
No indefinite article with profession	Arabic, French, Japanese, Korean, Vietnamese	*He is student.* *She lawyer.*	*He is a student.* *She is a lawyer.*
Definite article with days, months, places, idioms	Arabic	*She is in the bed.* *He lives in the Peru.*	*She is in bed.* *He lives in Peru.*
Definite article used for generalization	Farsi, French, German, Greek, Portuguese, Spanish	*The photography is an art.* *The books are more expensive than the disks.*	*Photography is an art.* *Books are more expensive than disks.*
Definite article used with proper noun	French, German, Portuguese, Spanish	*The Professor Brackert teaches in Frankfurt.*	*Professor Brackert teaches in Frankfurt.*

(Continued)

(Continued)

Language Features	Languages	Sample Transfer Errors in English	Edited Version
No definite article	Hindi, Turkish	*Store on corner is closed.*	*The store on the corner is closed.*
No indefinite article	Korean (uses *one* for *a*; depends on context)	*He ran into one tree.*	*He ran into a tree.*
VERBS AND VERB FORMS (chapter 61)			
A form of the verb *be* can be omitted	Arabic, Chinese, Greek, Russian	*India hotter than Britain.* *They working now.* *He cheerful.*	*India is hotter than Britain.* *They are working now.* *He is cheerful.*
No progressive forms	French, German, Greek, Russian	*They still discuss the problem.* *When I walked in, she slept.*	*They are still discussing the problem.* *When I walked in, she was sleeping.*
No tense inflections	Chinese, Thai, Vietnamese	*He arrive yesterday.* *When I was little, I always walk to school.*	*He arrived yesterday.* *When I was little, I always walked to school.*
No inflection for third person singular	Chinese, Japanese, Korean, Russian, Thai	*The singer have a big band.* *She work hard.*	*The singer has a big band.* *She works hard.*
Past perfect formed with *be*	Arabic	*They were arrived when I called.*	*They had arrived when I called.*
Different tense boundaries from English	Arabic, Chinese, Farsi, French	*I study here for a year.* *He has left yesterday.*	*I have been studying here for a year.* *He left yesterday.*

Language Features	Languages	Sample Transfer Errors in English	Edited Version
Different limits for passive voice	Japanese, Korean, Russian, Thai, Vietnamese	*They were stolen their luggage.*	*Their luggage was stolen.*
		My name base on Chinese characters.	*My name is based on Chinese characters.*
		The mess clean up quick.	*The mess was cleaned up quickly.*
		A miracle was happened.	*A miracle (has) happened.*
No -*ing* (gerund)/ infinitive distinction	Arabic, Chinese, Farsi, French, Greek, Portuguese, Spanish, Vietnamese	*She avoids to go.*	*She avoids going.*
		I enjoy to play tennis.	*I enjoy playing tennis.*
Infinitive not used to express purpose	Korean	*People exercise for losing weight.*	*People exercise to lose weight.*
Overuse of progressive forms	Hindi, Urdu	*I am wanting to leave now.*	*I want to leave now.*
SENTENCE STRUCTURE AND WORD ORDER (chapter 62)			
Verb precedes subject	Arabic, Hebrew, Russian, Spanish (optional), Tagalog	*Good grades received every student in the class.*	*Every student in the class received good grades.*
Verb-subject order in dependent clause	French	*I knew what would propose the committee.*	*I knew what the committee would propose.*

(Continued)

(Continued)

Language Features	Languages	Sample Transfer Errors in English	Edited Version
Verb after subject and object	Bengali, German (in dependent clause), Hindi, Japanese, Korean, Turkish	*. . . (when) the teacher the money collected.*	*. . . (when) the teacher collected the money.*
Coordination favored over subordination	Arabic	Frequent use of *and* and *so*	
Relative clause or restrictive phrase precedes noun it modifies	Chinese, Japanese, Korean, Russian	*The enrolled in college student . . .*	*The student (who was) enrolled in college . . .*
		A nine-meter-high impressive monument . . .	*An impressive monument that is nine meters high . . .*
		He gave me a too difficult for me book.	*He gave me a book that was too difficult for me.*
Adverb can occur between verb and object or before verb	French, Spanish, Urdu (before verb)	*I like very much clam chowder.*	*I like clam chowder very much.*
		They efficiently organized the work.	*They organized the work efficiently.*
That clause rather than an infinitive	Arabic, French, Hindi, Russian, Spanish	*I want that you stay.*	*I want you to stay.*
		I want that they try harder.	*I want them to try harder.*
Inversion of subject and verb (rare)	Chinese	*She is leaving, and so I am.*	*She is leaving, and so am I.*

Language Features	Languages	Sample Transfer Errors in English	Edited Version
Conjunctions occur in pairs	Chinese, Farsi, Vietnamese	*Although she is rich, but she wears simple clothes.* *Even if I had money, I would also not buy that car.*	*Although she is rich, she wears simple clothes.* *Even if I had money, I would not buy that car.*
Subject (especially *it* pronoun) can be omitted	Chinese, Italian, Japanese, Portuguese, Spanish, Thai	*Is raining.*	*It is raining.*
Commas set off a dependent clause	German, Russian	*He knows, that we are right.*	*He knows that we are right.*
No exact equivalent of *there is/there are*	Japanese, Korean, Portuguese, Russian, Thai (adverb of place and *have*)	*This article says four reasons to eat beans.* *In the garden has many trees.*	*This article says [that] there are four reasons to eat beans.* *There are many trees in the garden.*
NOUNS, PRONOUNS, ADJECTIVES, ADVERBS (chapters 44, 45, 60)			
Personal pronouns restate subject	Arabic, Gujarati, Spanish (optional)	*My father he lives in California.*	*My father lives in California.*
No human/ nonhuman distinction for relative pronoun (*who/which*)	Arabic, Farsi, French, Russian, Spanish, Thai	*Here is the student which you met her last week.* *The people which arrived . . .*	*Here is the student [whom] you met last week.* *The people who arrived . . .*
Pronoun object included in relative clause	Arabic, Chinese, Farsi, Hebrew	*The house [that] I used to live in it is big.*	*The house that I used to live in is big.*

(Continued)

(Continued)

Language Features	Languages	Sample Transfer Errors in English	Edited Version
No distinction between subject and object forms of some pronouns	Chinese, Gujarati, Korean, Thai	*I gave the forms to she.*	*I gave the forms to her.* Or *I gave her the forms.*
Nouns and adjectives have same form	Chinese, Japanese	*She is beauty woman.* *They felt very safety on the train.*	*She is a beautiful woman.* *They felt very safe on the train.*
No distinction between *he* and *she*, *his* and *her*	Bengali, Farsi, Gujarati, Spanish (*his* and *her* only), Thai	*My sister dropped his purse.*	*My sister dropped her purse.*
No plural form after a number	Creole, Farsi	*He has two dog.*	*He has two dogs.*
No plural (or optional) forms of nouns	Chinese, Japanese, Korean, Thai	*Several good book . . .*	*Several good books . . .*
No relative pronouns	Korean	*The book is on the table is mine.*	*The book that is on the table is mine.*
Different perception of countable/ uncountable	Japanese, Russian, Spanish	*I bought three furnitures.* *She has red hairs.*	*I bought three pieces of furniture.* Or *I bought three chairs.* *She has red hair.*
Adjectives show number	Russian, Spanish	*I have helpfuls friends.*	*I have helpful friends.*
Negative before verb	Spanish	*Jack no like meat.*	*Jack does not like meat.*
Double negatives used routinely	Spanish	*They don't know nothing.*	*They don't know anything.* Or *They know nothing.*

59e Editing guide to vernacular Englishes

Many of the varieties of English shown in the Circle of English in section 59a differ from what is known as a standard form of the language in their use of words and grammatical conventions. Speakers of these Englishes have to do a kind of translating, called *code switching*, when they speak or write, just as we all switch codes between levels of formality when we interact with different audiences. Consider, for example, situations when you might say, "'Sup?" ("What's up?") rather than "Good morning." As David Crystal, author of *The Stories of English*, points out, "We need to be very sure of our ground (or very drunk) before we say, 'Yo, Officer.'"

The following table shows some of the common language features that confront speakers of African American Vernacular (AAV), Creole, and other varieties of English in North America when they move back and forth between their home culture and the academic world.

Vernaculars and Standard English

Linguistic Feature of Vernacular	Example (Nonstandard)	Edited for Standard English
Omitted form of *be*	*Maxine studying.*	*Maxine is studying.*
Use of *be* for habitual action	*Ray be working at home.*	*Ray usually works at home.*
Use of *been* without *have*	*I been sleeping all day.*	*I have (I've) been sleeping all day.*
Omitted *-ed*	*The books arrive this morning.*	*The books arrived this morning.*
No *-s* ending for third person singular present tense verb	*That model have a big smile.*	*That model has a big smile.*
No plural form after a plural number	*Jake own two dog.*	*Jake owns two dogs.*
Verb inversion before indefinite pronoun subject	*Can't nobody do that.*	*Nobody can do that.*
They instead of possessive *their*	*The players grabbed they gear.*	*The players grabbed their gear.*

(Continued)

(Continued)

Linguistic Feature of Vernacular	Example (Nonstandard)	Edited for Standard English
Hisself instead of *himself*	*That musician promote hisself too much.*	*That musician promotes himself too much.*
Personal pronoun restates subject	*His instructor, she strict.*	*His instructor is strict.*
No apostrophe + *-s* for possessive	*She my brother wife.*	*She is my brother's wife.*
It used in place of *there*	*It's a gate at the entrance.*	*There is (There's) a gate at the entrance.*
Double negative	*You don't know nothing.*	*You don't know anything.* Or *You know nothing.*

59f Tips for multilingual writers

Get help   Use the help available at your college. Librarians and Writing Center tutors are there to help you. Don't be afraid to ask. And make sure that you go to your instructor during assigned office hours to get advice and clarification on any of the assignments and on your progress in the course.

Participate in class   It isn't always easy to join a discussion with a group of students who speak English fluently, but if you prepare well for class, you will find that your fellow students will be eager to hear the comments and observations of somebody who knows more than one language and more than one country. In class or in a group, listen attentively to others and offer informative responses. Your instructor and classmates will be delighted to hear comments from a cross-cultural perspective.

Follow the conventions   Be aware of the conventions associated with writing papers in North America. Readers expect you to take a stand on a controversial issue, and they value direct expression of your opinions, authoritatively backed up by evidence. Academic readers will expect you to express your point of view clearly in a thesis statement somewhere close to the beginning of your paper and back up your claim with concrete points of evidence. Some students find that making an outline helps with organizing a paper. See section 1h for sample outlines.

Don't lapse into informality and slang It is often difficult for learners of a language to decide exactly how and when to use the new language forms they hear and read. By all means, try out new words and expressions, but try them in safe situations before you use them in an academic setting where they might be inappropriate or even cause offense. When you are in doubt about whether you should use a new expression, check its connotations first with a friend, tutor, or your instructor.

Keep a learning log In a notebook or a computer file, keep a log of language errors that your instructor or peer editors comment on. If you enter in your log a sentence with an error and then correct the error there on the page, you will create a record of your own editing and learning. In addition, keep special logs of prepositions (rely *on*, afraid *of*) and of idioms, those expressions that defy rules and follow no patterns, such as *burn up* and *burn down*.

Consult learners' dictionaries Make use of an English dictionary specifically designed for multilingual writers, such as *Cambridge Advanced Learner's Dictionary* or *Oxford ESL Dictionary for Students of American English*. Such dictionaries provide useful information to language learners, including example sentences.

Learn from Web sites Use sites specially designed for language learners, such as the ones listed on page 510. In addition, go to *Activities for ESL Students* at <http://a4esl.org>, which includes quizzes and crossword puzzles in English as well as bilingual quizzes in more than forty languages.

Acknowledge sources In some cultures, the citing of classic, often memorized texts without acknowledgment of the exact source is accepted and common. However, academic conventions in North America require citing all sources of information other than the common knowledge of dates and events in the lives of public figures. Whatever you do, avoid plagiarism, and cite your sources (9a–9c).

60

Nouns and Articles

60a Categories of nouns

Nouns in English fall into two categories: proper nouns and common nouns. A *proper noun* names a unique person, place, or thing and begins with a capital letter: *Walt Whitman, Lake Superior, Grand Canyon, Vietnam Veterans Memorial, Tuesday* (53b, 60f).

    A *common noun* names a general class of persons, places, or things and begins with a lowercase letter: *bicycle, furniture, plan, daughter, home, happiness.* Common nouns can be further categorized as countable and uncountable.

- A *countable noun* has a plural form. Countable nouns frequently add -*s* to indicate the plural: *picture, pictures; plan, plans.* Singular countable nouns are used after *a, an, the, this, that, each, every.* Plural countable nouns are used after *the, these, those, many, a few, both, all, some, several.*

- An *uncountable noun* cannot be directly counted. It has no plural form: *furniture, advice, information.* Uncountable nouns are used after *the, this, that, much, some,* and other singular expressions of quantity.

Common Nouns

Countable	Uncountable
tool, hammer (tools, hammers)	equipment
chair, desk (chairs, desks)	furniture
necklace, earring (necklaces, earrings)	jewelry
view, scene (views, scenes)	scenery
tip, suggestion (tips, suggestions)	advice

The concept of countability varies across languages. Japanese, for example, makes no distinction between countable and uncountable nouns. In French, Spanish, and Chinese, the word for *furniture* is a countable noun; in English, it is not. In Russian, the word for *hair* is countable and used in the plural.

60b Uncountable nouns

Some nouns are usually uncountable in English and are commonly listed as such in a language learners' dictionary such as *The American Heritage English as a Second Language Dictionary*. Learn the most common uncountable nouns, and note the ones that end in -*s* but are nevertheless singular:

> *A mass made up of parts:* clothing, equipment, furniture, garbage, homework, information, jewelry, luggage, machinery, money, scenery, traffic, transportation
>
> *Abstract concepts:* advice, courage, education, fun, happiness, health, honesty, information, knowledge
>
> *Natural substances:* air, blood, cotton, heat, ice, sunshine, water, wood, wool
>
> *Diseases:* diabetes, influenza, measles
>
> *Games:* checkers, chess, soccer, tennis
>
> *Subjects of study:* biology, economics, history, physics

Note the following features of uncountable nouns.

1. An uncountable noun has no plural form:

   >   some
   > ▶ She gave me ~~several~~ information*s̸*.
   >   ^

   > ▶ The couple bought a lot of new furniture*s̸*.
   >   ^

2. An uncountable noun subject is always followed by a singular verb:

   >   is
   > ▶ Their advice ~~are~~ useful.
   >   ^

3. You can give an uncountable noun a countable sense—that is, indicate a quantity of it—by adding a word or phrase that indicates quantity. The noun itself will always remain singular: three pieces of *furniture*, two items of *information*, many pieces of *advice*.

4. Some nouns can be countable in one context and uncountable in another. Always examine the context.

General class (uncountable)

> ▶ He loves *chocolate*. [all chocolate, in whatever form]
>
> ▶ *Time* flies.

▶ He has red *hair.*

A countable item or items

▶ She gave him a *chocolate.* [one piece of candy from a box of many chocolates]

▶ They are having *a good time.*

▶ There is a *long gray hair* on her pillow.

KEY POINTS

What to Use before an Uncountable Noun

Use

The zero article (generalization)	Furniture is expensive.
The (specific reference)	*The* furniture in the new office is hideous.
This, that	*This* furniture is tacky.
A possessive pronoun: *my, his, their*, etc.	*Their* furniture is modern.
A quantity word: *some, any, much, less, more, most, a little, a great deal (of), all, other* (43i)	She has bought *some* new furniture.

Do not use

A/an (except in phrases *a little* or *a great deal of*)	The room needs a~~ ~~new furniture.
Each, every, another	All furniture ~~Every furniture~~ should be ⌃ practical.
These, those	That furniture is ~~Those furnitures are~~ elegant. ⌃
Numerals: *one, two, three*, etc.	two pieces of furniture. They bought ~~two furnitures.~~ ⌃
A plural quantity word: *several, many, a few*	a little furniture She took only a ~~few furniture~~ ⌃ with her to her new apartment.

60c Basic rules for *a, an,* and *the*

1. Use *the* whenever a reference to a common noun is specific and unique for writer and reader (see 60d).

   > the
   > ▶ He loves museum that Rem Koolhaas designed.
   >   ^

2. Do not use *a* or *an* with a plural countable noun.

   > ▶ They cited a̸ reliable surveys.

3. Do not use *a* or *an* with an uncountable noun.

   > ▶ He gave a̸ helpful advice.

4. Use *a* before a consonant sound: *a bird, a house, a sonnet.* Use *an* before a vowel sound: *an egg, an ostrich, an hour, an ugly vase.* Take special care with the sounds associated with the letters *h* and *u,* which can have either a consonant or a vowel sound: *a housing project, an honest man; a unicorn, an uprising.*

5. To make a generalization about a countable noun, do one of the following:

   - Use the plural form: *Lions are majestic.*
   - Use the singular with *a* or *an: A lion is a majestic animal.*
   - Use the singular with *the* to denote a classification: *The lion is a majestic animal.*

6. Make sure that a countable singular noun is preceded by an article or by a demonstrative pronoun (*this, that*), a number, a singular word expressing quantity, or a possessive.

   > A (Every, That, One, Her) nurse
   > ▶ ~~Nurse~~ has a difficult job.
   >   ^

7. In general, though note that there are exceptions, use no article with a singular proper noun (*Mount Everest*), and use *the* with a plural proper noun (*the Himalayas*) (see 60f).

60d *The* for a specific reference

When you write a common noun that both you and your readers know refers to one or more specific persons, places, things, or concepts, use the article *the.*

► **I study** *the* **earth,** *the* **sun, and** *the* **moon.** [the ones in our solar system]

► **She closed** *the* **door.** [of the room she was in]

► **Her husband took** *the* **dog out for a walk.** [the dog belonging to the couple]

► *The* **kitten that her daughter brought home had a distinctive black patch above one eye.** [a specific kitten—one that her daughter brought home]

► **Her daughter found** *a* **kitten. When they were writing a lost-and-found ad that night, they realized that** *the* **kitten had a distinctive black patch above one eye.** [The second mention is of a specific kitten identified earlier—the one her daughter had found.]

► **He bought** *the most expensive* **bicycle in the store.** [A superlative makes a reference to one specific item.]

60e Which article? Four basic questions to ask

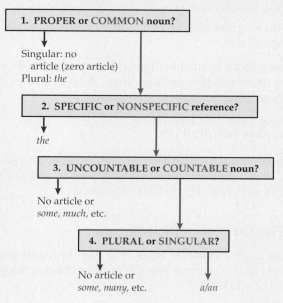

KEY POINTS

Articles at a Glance: Four Basic Questions about a Noun

1. **PROPER or COMMON noun?**

Singular: no
    article (zero article)
Plural: *the*

2. **SPECIFIC or NONSPECIFIC reference?**

the

3. **UNCOUNTABLE or COUNTABLE noun?**

No article or
some, much, etc.

4. **PLURAL or SINGULAR?**

No article or
some, many, etc.   *a/an*

Multilingual writers often have difficulty choosing among the articles *a, an,* and *the* and the *zero article* (no article at all). Languages vary greatly in their representation of the concepts conveyed by English articles (see the Editing Guide to Multilingual Transfer Patterns in 59d). The Key Points box on page 524 should help you.

You can use the questions to decide which article, if any, to use with the noun *poem* as you consider the following sentence:

▶ **Milton wrote ___?___ moving poem about the blindness that afflicted him before he wrote some of his greatest works.**

1. Is the noun (*poem*) a proper noun or a common noun?

COMMON   **Go to question 2.**

2. Does the common noun refer to a specific person, place, thing, or idea known to both writer and reader as unique, or is the reference nonspecific?

NON-SPECIFIC   [*Poem* is not identified to the reader in the same way that *blindness* is. We know the reference is to the blindness that afflicted Milton before he wrote some of his greatest works. However, there is more than one "moving poem" in literature. The reference would be specific for readers only if the poem had been previously discussed.] **Go to question 3.**

3. Is the noun uncountable or countable?

COUNTABLE   [We can say *one poem, two poems.*] **Go to question 4.**

4. Is the noun plural or singular?

SINGULAR   [The first letter in the noun phrase *moving poem* is *m*, a consonant sound.] **Use *a* as the article.**

▶ **Milton wrote *a* moving poem about the blindness that afflicted him before he wrote some of his greatest works.**

60f Proper nouns and articles

Singular proper nouns: Use no article   As a general rule, capitalize singular proper nouns and use no article: *Stephen King, Central America, Africa, Islam, Golden Gate Park, Hollywood Boulevard, Cornell University, Lake Temagami, Mount St. Helens, Thursday, July.* However, note the many exceptions.

Exceptions: Singular Proper Nouns with *The*

Proper nouns with a common noun and *of* as part of the name: *the University of Texas, the Fourth of July, the Museum of Modern Art, the Statue of Liberty*

Highways: *the New Jersey Turnpike, the Long Island Expressway*

Buildings: *the Eiffel Tower, the Prudential Building*

Bridges: *the Golden Gate Bridge*

Hotels and museums: *the Hilton Hotel, the Guggenheim Museum*

Countries named with a phrase: *the United Kingdom, the Dominican Republic, the People's Republic of China*

Parts of the globe: *the North Pole, the West, the East, the Riviera*

Seas, oceans, gulfs, rivers, and deserts: *the Dead Sea, the Atlantic Ocean, the Persian Gulf, the Yangtze River, the Mojave Desert*

Historical periods and events: *the Enlightenment, the October Revolution, the Cold War*

Groups: *the Taliban, the Chicago Seven*

Plural proper nouns: Use *the*   Examples are *the United States, the Great Lakes, the Himalayas, the Philippines, the Chinese* (people) (53b).

61 ⚷

Verbs and Verb Forms

A clause needs a complete verb consisting of one of the five verb forms (41a) and any necessary auxiliaries. Forms derived from a verb (*verbals*) cannot serve as the main verb of a clause; such forms are an *-ing* form, a past participle (ending in *-ed* for a regular verb), or an infinitive (*to* + base form). Because readers get so much information from verbs, they have a relatively low level of tolerance for error, so make sure you edit with care and use auxiliary verbs whenever necessary.

61a The *be* auxiliary

Inclusion   The *be* auxiliary must be included in a verb phrase in English, though in languages such as Chinese, Russian, and Arabic it can be omitted (see also 41c).

> *are*
> ► They studying this evening.
>   ^

▶ They have been studying since dinner.

Sequence   What comes after a *be* auxiliary? (see also 41c)

- The *-ing* form follows a verb in the active voice: He *is sweeping* the floor.
- The past participle follows a verb in the passive voice: The floor *was swept* yesterday.

61b Modal auxiliary verbs: Form and meaning

The nine modal auxiliary verbs are *will, would, can, could, shall, should, may, might,* and *must.* Note the following three important points.

1. The modals do not change form.
2. The modals never add an *-s* ending.
3. The form immediately following a modal is always a base form of a verb without *to: could go, should ask, must arrive, might have seen, would be* sleeping.

   ▶ The committee must ~~to~~ vote tomorrow.

   ▶ The proposal might improve~~s~~ the city.

   ▶ The residents could disapprove~~d~~.

Meanings of Modal Verbs

Meaning	Present and Future	Past
1. Intention	*will, shall*	*would*
	She *will* explain. [*Shall* is used mostly in questions: *Shall I buy that big green ceramic horse?*]	She said that she *would* explain.
2. Ability	*can (am/is/are able to)*	*could (was/were able to)*
	He *can* cook well. [Do not use *can* and *able to* together: *He is able to cook well.*]	He *could* not read until he was eight. [He was not able to read until he was eight.]

(Continued)

(Continued)

Meaning	Present and Future	Past
3. Permission	*may, might, can, could*	*might, could*
	May I refer to Auden again? [*Might* or *could* is more tentative.]	Her instructor said she *could* use a dictionary.
4. Polite question	*would, could*	
	Would readers please indulge me for a moment?	
	Could you try not to read ahead?	
5. Speculation	*would, could, might*	*would* or *could* or *might* + *have* + past participle
	If he had more talent, he *could* become a professional pianist. [See also 41j.]	If I had studied, I *might have* passed the test.
6. Advisability	*should*	*should* + *have* + past participle
	You *should* go home and rest.	You *should have* taken your medication. [Implied here is "but you did not."]
7. Necessity (stronger than *should*)	*must* (or *have to*)	*had to* + base form
	Applicants *must* apply for a mortgage.	Theo van Gogh *had to* support his brother.
8. Prohibition	*must* + *not*	
	Participants *must not* leave until all the questions have been answered.	

Meaning	Present and Future	Past
9. Expectation	*should*	*should* + *have* + past participle
	The author *should* receive a check soon.	You *should have* received your check a week ago.
10. Possibility	*may, might*	*might* + *have* + past participle
	The technician *may* be working on the problem now.	She *might* already *have* revised the ending.
11. Logical assumption	*must*	*must* + *have* + past participle
	She's late; she *must* be stuck in traffic.	She *must have* taken the wrong route.
12. Repeated past action		*would* (or *used to*) + base form
		When I was a child, I *would* spend hours drawing.

61c Infinitive after verbs and adjectives

Some verbs are followed by an infinitive (*to* + base form) or a base form alone. Some adjectives also occur with an infinitive. Such combinations are highly idiomatic. You need to learn each one individually as you come across it in your reading.

Verb + infinitive These verbs are commonly followed by an infinitive (*to* + base form):

agree	choose	fail	offer	refuse
ask	claim	hope	plan	venture
beg	decide	manage	pretend	want
bother	expect	need	promise	wish

Note any differences between English and your native language. For example, in Spanish, the word for *refuse* is followed by the equivalent of an *-ing* form. In English, you need *to* + the base form.

> ► He refused ~~criticizing~~ the system.
>   *to criticize*

Position of a negative In a verb + infinitive pattern, the position of the negative affects meaning. Note the difference in meaning that the position of a negative (*not, never*) can create.

> ► He did *not* decide to buy a new car. His wife did.

> ► He decided *not* to buy a new car. His wife was disappointed.

Verb + noun or pronoun + infinitive Some verbs are followed by a noun or pronoun and then an infinitive. See also 44a (p. 437) for a pronoun used before an infinitive.

>   V   pron. ┌─inf.─┐
> ► The librarian *advised them to use* a better database.

Verbs that follow this pattern are *advise, allow, ask, cause, command, convince, encourage, expect, force, help, need, order, persuade, remind, require, tell, urge, want, warn.*

Spanish and Russian use a *that* clause after verbs like *want.* In English, however, *want* is followed by an infinitive.

> ► Rose wanted ~~that~~ her son ~~would~~ become a doctor.
>   *to*

Make, let, and _have_ After these verbs, use a noun or pronoun and a base form of the verb (without *to*).

> ► He *made his son practice* for an hour.

> ► They *let us leave* early.

> ► She *had her daughter wash* the car.

Note the corresponding passive voice structure with *have:*

> ► She usually *has the car washed* once a month.

Adjective + infinitive Some adjectives are followed by an infinitive. The filler subject *it* often occurs with this structure.

infinitive

▶ It is dangerous to hike alone in the woods.

These are some of the adjectives that can be followed by an infinitive: *anxious, correct, dangerous, eager, essential, foolish, happy, (im)possible, (in)advisable, likely, lucky, powerless, proud, right, silly, sorry, (un)fair, (un)just, (un)kind, (un)necessary, wrong.*

▶ They were foolish to think they could climb to the top of the mountain.

61d Verbs followed by an -*ing* verb form used as a noun

▶ I can't help *laughing* at Jon Stewart.

The verbs that are systematically followed by an -*ing* form (known as a *gerund*) make up a relatively short and learnable list.

admit	consider	enjoy	miss	resist
appreciate	delay	finish	postpone	risk
avoid	deny	imagine	practice	suggest
be worth	discuss	keep	recall	tolerate
can't help	dislike			

inviting

▶ We considered to invite his parents.

hearing

▶ Most people dislike to hear cell phones at concerts.

Note that a negation comes between the verb and the -*ing* form:

▶ During their vacation, they enjoy *not* getting up early every day.

61e Verbs followed by an infinitive or an -*ing* verb form

Some verbs can be followed by either an infinitive or an -*ing* verb form (a gerund) with almost no discernible difference in meaning: *begin, continue, hate, like, love, start.*

▶ **She loves** *cooking.*   ▶ **She loves** *to cook.*

The infinitive and the *-ing* form of a few verbs (*forget, remember, try, stop*), however, signal different meanings:

> ▶ **He remembered** *to mail* **the letter.** [an intention]

> ▶ **He remembered** *mailing* **the letter.** [a past act]

61f *-ing* and *-ed* forms used as adjectives

Both the present participle (*-ing* verb form) and the past participle (ending in *-ed* in regular verbs) can function as adjectives (see 41a and 41g). Each form has a different meaning: The *-ing* adjective indicates that the word modified produces an effect; the past participle adjective indicates that the word modified has an effect produced on it.

> ▶ **The** *boring* **cook served baked beans yet again.** [The cook produces boredom. Everyone is tired of baked beans.]

> ▶ **The** *bored* **cook yawned as she scrambled eggs.** [The cook felt the emotion of boredom as she did the cooking, but the eggs could still be appreciated.]

Produces an Effect	Has an Effect Produced on It
amazing	amazed
amusing	amused
annoying	annoyed
confusing	confused
depressing	depressed
disappointing	disappointed
embarrassing	embarrassed
exciting	excited
interesting	interested
satisfying	satisfied
shocking	shocked
surprising	surprised
worrying	worried

Note: Do not drop the *-ed* ending from a past participle. Sometimes in speech, it blends with a following *t* or *d* sound, but in writing, the *-ed* ending must be included.

► I was surprise to see her wild outfit.
     d

► The researchers were ~~worry~~ that the results were contaminated.
    worried

62 🔑

Sentence Structure and Word Order

62a A subject in every clause

In some languages, a subject can be omitted. In English, you must include a subject in every clause, even just a filler subject such as *there* or *it*.

► When the director's business partners lost money, were immediate effects on the share prices.
     there

► The critics hated the movie because was too sentimental.
     it

Do not use *it* to point to a long subject that follows. Put the long subject in the subject position before the verb.

► We can say that it does not matter the historical period of the society.

62b Order of sentence elements

Subject, verb, object Languages vary in their basic word order for the sentence elements of subject (S), verb (V), and direct object (DO). In English, the most commonly occurring sentence pattern is S + V + DO ("Children like candy") (see also 37d).

► ~~Good grades received every~~ student in the class.
   Every   *received good grades.*

Expressions of time and place Do not put an adverb or a phrase between the verb and its direct object.

► The quiz show host congratulated ~~many times~~ the winner.
                             many times.

Descriptive adjective phrases   Put a descriptive adjective phrase after, not before, the noun it modifies.

▶ I would go to ⟨known only to me⟩ places.

62c   Direct and indirect objects

Some verbs—such as *give, send, show, tell, teach, find, sell, ask, offer, pay, pass,* and *hand*—can be followed by both a direct object and an indirect object. The indirect object is the person or thing to whom or to which, or for whom or for which, something is done. It follows the verb and precedes the direct object (37d).

      ⌐—— IO ——⌐ ⌐—— DO ——⌐
▶ He gave his mother some flowers.

       IO ⌐—— DO ——⌐
▶ He gave her some flowers.

An indirect object can be replaced with a prepositional phrase that *follows* the direct object:

      ⌐—— DO ——⌐ prepositional phrase
▶ He gave some flowers to his mother.

Some verbs—such as *explain, describe, say, mention,* and *open*—are never followed by an indirect object. Rather, they are followed by a direct object and a prepositional phrase with *to* or *for:*

               to me.
▶ She explained ~~me~~ the election process/

Note that *tell*, but not *say*, can take an indirect object.

     told
▶ She ~~said~~ him the secret.

62d   Direct and indirect quotations and questions

In a direct quotation or direct question, the exact words used by the speaker are enclosed in quotation marks. In an indirect quotation or indirect question, the writer reports what the speaker said, and quotation marks are not used. Changes also occur in pronouns, time expressions, and verb tenses (41i).

      ⌐——— direct quotation ———⌐
▶ He said, "I have lost my notebook."

┌──────── indirect quotation ────────┐
▶ He said that he had lost his notebook.

┌──── direct question ────┐
▶ He asked, "Have you seen it?"

┌──── indirect question ────┐
▶ He asked if we had seen it.

Direct and indirect quotations Usually, you must make several changes when you use an introductory verb in the past tense to report a direct quotation as an indirect quotation. You will do this often when you write college papers and report the views of others. Avoid shifts from direct to indirect quotations (40d).

Direct and Indirect Quotations

Change	Direct/ Indirect Quotation	Example	Explanation
Punctuation and tense	Direct	The young couple said, "The price *is* too high."	Exact words within quotation marks
	Indirect	The young couple said that the price *was* too high.	No quotation marks; tense change (41i)
Pronoun and tense	Direct	He insisted, "*I understand* the figures."	First person pronoun and present tense
	Indirect	He insisted that *he understood* the figures.	Change to third person pronoun; tense change
Command to statement	Direct	"Cancel the payment," her husband said.	
	Indirect	Her husband *told* her *to* cancel the payment.	Verb (*tell, instruct*) + *to*

(Continued)

(Continued)

Change	Direct/Indirect Quotation	Example	Explanation
Expressions of time, place, and tense	Direct	The bankers said, "We *will* work on *this* deal *tomorrow*."	
	Indirect	The bankers said *they would* work on *that* deal *the next day*.	Expressions of time and place not related to speaker's perspective; tense change (41i); change to third person pronoun
Colloquial to formal	Direct	The clients said, "Well, no thanks; *we won't* wait."	
	Indirect	The clients thanked the bankers but said *they would not* wait.	Spoken words and phrases omitted or rephrased; also a tense change

Direct and indirect questions   When a direct question is reported indirectly, it loses the word order of a question (V + S) and the question mark. Sometimes, changes in tense are necessary (see also 41i).

DIRECT QUESTION
The buyer asked, "*Are* the goods ready to be shipped?"
<small>V   S</small>

INDIRECT QUESTION
The buyer asked if the goods *were* ready to be shipped.
<small>S   V</small>

DIRECT QUESTION
The boss asked, "What *are* they doing?"
<small>V   S</small>

INDIRECT QUESTION
The boss asked what they *were* doing.
<small>S   V</small>

DIRECT QUESTION	V S V "Why *did* they *send* a letter instead of a fax?" her secretary asked.

INDIRECT QUESTION	S V V Her secretary asked why they [*had*] *sent* a letter instead of a fax.

Use only a question word such as *why* or the word *if* or *whether* to introduce an indirect question. Do not use *that* as well.

▶ Her secretary asked ~~that~~ why they had sent a letter instead of a fax.

Direct and Indirect Questions

	Introductory Words	Auxiliary Verb	Subject	Auxiliary Verb(s)	Main Verb and Rest of Clause
DIRECT	What	are	they		thinking?
INDIRECT	Nobody knows what		they	are	thinking.
DIRECT	Where	does	he		work?
INDIRECT	I can't remember where		he		works.
DIRECT	Why	did	she		write that poem?
INDIRECT	The poet does not reveal why		she		wrote that poem.
DIRECT		Have	the diaries	been	published yet?
INDIRECT	The Web site does not say if (whether)		the diaries	have been	published yet.

(Continued)

(Continued)

	Introductory Words	Auxiliary Verb	Subject	Auxiliary Verb(s)	Main Verb and Rest of Clause
DIRECT		Did	the space program		succeed?
INDIRECT	It is not clear if		the space program		succeeded.

62e Clauses beginning with *although* and *because*

In some languages, a subordinating conjunction (such as *although* or *because*) can be used along with a coordinating conjunction (*but, so*) or a transitional expression (*however, therefore*) in the same sentence. In English, only one is used.

NO	*Although* he loved his father, *but* he did not have much opportunity to spend time with him.
POSSIBLE REVISIONS	*Although* he loved his father, he did not have much opportunity to spend time with him.
	He loved his father, *but* he did not have much opportunity to spend time with him.

NO	*Because* she had been trained in the church, *therefore* she was sensitive to the idea of audience.
POSSIBLE REVISIONS	*Because* she had been trained in the church, she was sensitive to the idea of audience.
	She had been trained in the church, *so* she was sensitive to the idea of audience.
	She had been trained in the church; *therefore*, she was sensitive to the idea of audience.

See 47e for punctuation with transitional expressions.

62f Unnecessary pronouns

Do not restate the simple subject of a sentence as a pronoun (see also 40i).

▶ Visitors to the Statue of Liberty ~~they~~ have worn the steps down.

▶ The counselor who told me about dyslexia ~~he~~ is a man I will never forget.

In a relative clause introduced by *whom*, *which*, or *that*, do not include a pronoun that the relative pronoun has replaced (see also 46d).

▶ The house that I lived in ~~it~~ for ten years has been sold.

62g Order of adjectives

Cumulative adjectives cannot have the word *and* inserted between them as each modifies the whole noun phrase that follows it. With cumulative adjectives, follow the conventional sequence before the head noun: (1) size, (2) shape, (3) age, (4) color, (5) region or geographical origin, (6) architectural style or religion, (7) material, (8) noun used as adjective to modify the head noun.

```
        1    3    5    7    head noun
```
▶ the big old Italian stone house

```
        2       4       6       8    head noun
```
▶ our rectangular green Art Deco storage chest

Do not use commas between cumulative adjectives. For punctuation with other types of adjectives (coordinate adjectives), see 47g.

63 ⌖

Prepositions and Idioms

Prepositions appear in phrases with nouns and pronouns, and they also combine with adjectives and verbs in various ways. Learn the idioms one by one as you come across them.

63a Expressions with three common prepositions

Learn the uses of prepositions by writing them in lists when you come across them in your reading. Here is a start:

In + year, month, part of day, state, country, city, language, etc.

in 2009, in July, in the morning, in Ohio, in the United States, in Milwaukee, in Spanish, in the drawer, in the closet, in the cookie jar, in the library stacks, in a book, in the rain, in his pocket, in bed, in school, in class, in time (to participate in an activity), in the envelope, in the newspaper, in love

---

On + day, date, street name, etc.

---

on Saturday, on 9 September 2009, on Union Street, on the weekend, on the moon, on Earth, on the menu, on the library shelf, on the roof, a ring on her finger, an article on education, on occasion, on time (punctual), on foot, on the couch, knock on the door, the address on the envelope

---

At + time, etc.

---

at eight o'clock, at home, at a party, at night, at work

63b Adjective + preposition

When you are writing, use a dictionary to check the specific prepositions used with an adjective.

▶ The botanist is *afraid of* spiders.

▶ E. O. Wilson was *interested in* ants.

Some idiomatic adjective + preposition combinations are *afraid of, ashamed of, aware of, fond of, full of, jealous of, proud of, suspicious of, tired of, interested in, grateful to* (someone), *grateful for* (something), *responsible to* (someone), *responsible for* (something), *anxious about, content with,* and *satisfied with.*

63c Verb + preposition

Some idiomatic verb + preposition combinations are *apologize to* (someone), *apologize for* (an offense or error), *arrive in* (a country or city), *arrive at* (a building or an event), *blame* (someone) *for* (an offense or error), *complain about, concentrate on, congratulate* (someone) *on* (success or good fortune), *consist of, depend on, explain* (facts) *to* (someone), *insist on, laugh at, rely on, smile at, take care of, thank* (someone) *for* (a gift or favor), *throw* (an object) *to* (someone waiting to catch it), *throw* (an object) *at* (someone not expecting it), and *worry about.* Keep a list of others you notice.

63d Phrasal verbs

Prepositions and a few adverbs (such as *away* and *forward*) can combine with verbs in such a way that they no longer function as prepositions or ordinary adverbs. They are then known as *particles*. Only a few languages other than English—Dutch, German, and Swedish, for example—have this verb + particle (preposition or adverb) combination, which is called a *phrasal verb*.

The meaning of a phrasal verb is entirely different from the meaning of the verb alone. Note the idiomatic meanings of some common phrasal verbs.

break down [stop functioning]	get over [recover from]
put off [postpone]	put up with [tolerate, endure]
run out [become used up]	run across [meet unexpectedly]
look into [examine]	take after [resemble]

Always check the meanings of such verbs in a specialized dictionary such as *The American Heritage English as a Second Language Dictionary.*

A particle can be followed by a preposition to make a three-word combination:

▶ She *gets along with* **everybody**. [She is friendly toward everybody.]

Other three-word verb combinations are

catch up with [draw level with]	lock up to [admire]
look down on [despise]	put up with [endure]
look forward to [anticipate]	stand up for [defend]

Position of direct objects with two-word phrasal verbs   Some two-word transitive phrasal verbs are separable. The direct object of these verbs can come between the verb and the accompanying particle.

▶ She *put off* **her dinner party**. [She postponed her dinner party.]

▶ She *put* **her dinner party** *off.*

When the direct object is a pronoun, however, always place the pronoun between the verb and the particle.

▶ She *put* **it** *off.*

Some commonly used phrasal verbs that follow that principle are listed here. They can be separated by a noun as a direct object; they must be separated when the direct object is a pronoun.

call off [cancel]	give up [surrender]	make up [invent]
fill out [complete]	leave out [omit]	turn down [reject]
find out [discover]	look up [locate]	turn off [stop]

Most dictionaries list phrasal verbs that are associated with a particular verb along with their meanings and examples. Develop your own list of such verbs from your reading.

63e Preposition + -*ing* verb form used as a noun

The -*ing* verb form that functions as a noun (the *gerund*) frequently occurs after a preposition.

▶ They congratulated him *on winning* the prize.

▶ The school principal expressed interest *in participating* in the fundraiser.

▶ He ran three miles *without stopping*.

▶ The cheese is the right consistency *for spreading*.

Note: Take care not to confuse *to* when used as a preposition with *to* used in an infinitive. When *to* is a preposition, it is followed by an object—a noun, a pronoun, a noun phrase, or an -*ing* verb form, not by the base form of a verb.

              ┌ infinitive ┐
▶ They want *to adopt* a child.

              preposition + -*ing* form (gerund)
▶ They are looking forward *to adopting* a child.

Check which to use by testing whether a noun replacement fits the sentence:

▶ They are looking forward to *parenthood*.

Note also *be devoted to, be/get used to* (see 64h).

64 ⚷

Language Learners' FAQs

64a When do I use *no* and *not*?

Not is an adverb that negates a verb, an adjective, or another adverb. *No* is an adjective and therefore modifies a noun.

▶ She is *not* wealthy.

▶ She is *not* really poor.

▶ The author does *not* intend to deceive the reader.

▶ The author has *no* intention of deceiving the reader.

64b What is the difference between *too* and *very*?

Both *too* and *very* intensify an adjective or adverb, but they are not interchangeable. *Too* indicates excess. *Very* indicates degree and means "extremely."

▶ It was *very* hot.

▶ It was *too* hot to sit outside. [*Too* occurs frequently in the pattern *too* + adjective or adverb + *to* + base form of verb.]

▶ The Volvo was *very* expensive, but he bought it anyway.

▶ The Volvo was *too* expensive, so he bought a Ford instead.

64c Does *few* mean the same as *a few*?

A few is the equivalent of *some*. *Few* is the equivalent of *hardly any*; it has more negative connotations than *a few*. Both expressions are used with countable plural nouns. Although *a* is not generally used with plural nouns, the expression *a few* is an exception.

some
▶ She feels fortunate because she has *a few* helpful colleagues.

hardly any
▶ She feels depressed because she has *few* helpful colleagues.

You might prefer to use only the more common *a few* and use *hardly any* in sentences where the context demands *few*. Similar expressions used with uncountable nouns are *little* and *a little*.

some
▶ She has *a little* time to spend on work-related projects.

hardly any
▶ She has *little* time to spend on recreation.

64d How do I distinguish *most, most of,* and *the most*?

Most expresses a generalization, meaning "nearly all."

▶ *Most* young children like ice cream.

When a word like *the, this, these, that,* or *those* or a possessive pronoun (such as *my, their*) precedes the noun to make it specific, *most of* is used. The meaning is "nearly all of."

▶ I did *most of* this needlework.

▶ *Most of* his colleagues work long hours.

The most is used to compare more than two people or items.

▶ Bill is *the most* efficient of all the technicians.

64e What structures are used with *easy, hard,* and *difficult*?

The adjectives *easy, hard,* and *difficult* cause problems for speakers of Japanese and Chinese. All of the following patterns are acceptable in English.

▶ It is *easy* for me to change a fuse.

▶ It is *easy* to change a fuse.

▶ To change a fuse is *easy* for me.

▶ To change a fuse is *easy.*

▶ Changing a fuse is *hard* for him.

▶ Changing a fuse is *difficult.*

▶ He finds it *difficult* to change a fuse.

However, a sentence like the following needs to be edited in English into one of the patterns listed above or as follows:

> think it is
▶ I ~~am~~ *easy* to change a fuse.
    ^

64f How do I use *it* and *there* to begin a sentence?

Use *there* to indicate that something exists (or existed) or happens (or happened) (see also 31b).

There
► ~~It~~ was a royal wedding in my country several years

ago.

There
► ~~It~~ is a tree on the corner of my block.

Use *it* for weather, distance, time, and surroundings.

► It is a long way to Tipperary.

► It is hot.

Use *it* also in expressions such as *it is important, it is necessary*, and *it is obvious*, emphasizing the details that come next (see also 31b).

► It is essential for all of you to sign your application forms.

It or *there* cannot be omitted as a filler subject.

it
► As you can see, is dark out already.

64g Which possessive adjective do I use: *His* or *her*?

In some languages, the form of the adjective used to indicate possession changes according to the gender of the noun that follows it, not according to its antecedent. In French, for instance, *son* or *sa* means "his" or "her," and in Spanish, *su* means *his* or *her*. The form is determined by the noun the adjective modifies.

► Marie et sa mère [Marie and her mother]

► Pierre et sa mère [Pierre and his mother]

► Pierre et son père [Pierre and his father]

In English, however, the gender of a possessive (*his, her*, or *its*) is always determined by the antecedent.

► I met Marie and her mother.

► I met Pierre and his mother.

64h What is the difference between *be/get used to* and *used to*?

For multilingual writers of English, the distinction between *used to* + base form and *be/get used to* + *-ing* (gerund) is difficult.

▶ The bankers *used to eat* lunch at a fancy restaurant. [They don't any more.]

▶ Now they are *getting used to eating* lunch in the cafeteria. [They are getting accustomed to it.]

PART 10

Glossaries

65 Words to Watch For: Glossary of Usage   549

66 Glossary of Grammatical Terms   563

Glossaries

65   **Words to Watch For:**
Glossary of Usage   549

66   **Glossary of Grammatical**
Terms   563

65

Words to Watch For: Glossary of Usage

Listed in this glossary are words that are often confused (*affect/effect*, *elicit/illicit*) or misspelled (*it's/its*). Also listed are nonstandard words (*irregardless*, *theirself*) and colloquial expressions (*OK*) that should be avoided in formal writing.

a, an   Use *an* before words that begin with a vowel sound (the vowels are *a, e, i, o,* and *u*): *an apple, an hour* (*h* silent). Use *a* before words that begin with a consonant sound: *a planet, a yam, a ukulele, a house* (*h* pronounced).

accept, except, expect   *Accept* is a verb: *She accepted the salary offer. Except* is usually a preposition: *Everyone has gone home except my boss. Expect* is a verb: *They expect to visit New Mexico on vacation.*

adapt, adopt   *Adapt* means "to adjust" and is used with the preposition *to: It takes people some time to adapt to the work routine after college. Adopt* means "to take into a family" or "to take up and follow": *The couple adopted a three-year-old child. The company adopted a more aggressive policy.*

adverse, averse   *Adverse* is an adjective describing something as hostile, unfavorable, or difficult. *Averse* indicates opposition to something and usually takes the preposition *to: The bus driver was averse to driving in the adverse traffic conditions.*

advice, advise   *Advice* is a noun: *Take my advice and don't start smoking. Advise* is a verb: *He advised his brother to stop smoking.*

affect, effect   In their most common uses, *affect* is a verb, and *effect* is a noun. To *affect* is to have an *effect* on something: *Pesticides can affect health. Pesticides have a bad effect on health. Effect,* however, can be used as a verb meaning "to bring about": *The administration hopes to effect new health care legislation. Affect* can also be used as a noun in psychology, meaning "a feeling or emotion."

aisle, isle   You'll walk down an *aisle* in a supermarket or a church. An *isle* is an island.

all ready, already   *All ready* means "totally prepared": *The students were all ready for their final examination. Already* is an adverb meaning "by this time": *He has already written the report.*

all right, alright   *All right* (meaning "satisfactory") is standard. *Alright* is nonstandard. However, *alright* is used in popular culture to mean "wonderful."

all together, altogether   *All together* is used to describe acting simultaneously: *As soon as the boss had presented the plan, the managers spoke up all together. Altogether* is an adverb meaning "totally," often used before an adjective: *His presentation was altogether impressive.*

allude, elude   *Allude* means "to refer to": *She alluded to his height. Elude* means "to avoid": *He eluded her criticism by leaving the room.*

allusion, illusion   The noun *allusion* means "reference to": *Her allusion to his height made him uncomfortable.* The noun *illusion* means "false idea": *He had no illusions about being Mr. Universe.*

almost, most   Do not use *most* to mean a*lmost: Almost* [not *Most*] *all my friends are computer literate.*

alot, a lot of, lots of   *Alot* is nonstandard. *A lot of* and *lots of* are regarded by some as informal for *many* or *a great deal of: Students send lots of text messages.*

aloud, allowed   *Aloud* is an adverb meaning "out loud": *She read her critique aloud. Allowed* is a form of the verb *allow: Employees are not allowed to participate in the competition.*

ambiguous, ambivalent   *Ambiguous* is used to describe a phrase or act with more than one meaning: *The ending of the movie is ambiguous; we don't know if the butler really committed the murder. Ambivalent* describes uncertainty and the coexistence of opposing attitudes and feelings: *The committee is ambivalent about the proposal for restructuring the company.*

among, between   Use *between* for two items, *among* for three or more: *I couldn't decide between red or blue. I couldn't decide among red, blue, or green.*

amoral, immoral   *Amoral* can mean "neither moral nor immoral" or "not caring about right or wrong," whereas *immoral* means "morally wrong": *Some consider vegetarianism an amoral issue, but others believe eating meat is immoral.*

amount, number   *Amount* is used with uncountable expressions: *a large amount of money, work, or effort. Number* is used with countable plural expressions: *a large number of people, a number of attempts.* See 60b.

an   See *a*.

ante-, anti-   *Ante-* is a prefix meaning "before," as in *anteroom*. *Anti-* means "against" or "opposite," as in *antiseptic* or *antifreeze*.

anyone, any one   *Anyone* is a singular indefinite pronoun meaning "anybody": *Can anyone help me? Any one* refers to one from a group and is usually followed by *of* + plural noun: *Any one* [as opposed to any two] *of the suggestions will be acceptable.*

anyplace   The standard *anywhere* is preferable.

anyway, anywhere, nowhere; anyways, anywheres, nowheres   *Anyway, anywhere,* and *nowhere* are standard forms. The others, ending in *-s*, are not.

apart, a part   *Apart* is an adverb: *The old book fell apart. A part* is a noun phrase: *I'd like to be a part of that project.*

as, as if, like   See *like*.

as regards   See *in regard to*.

assure, ensure, insure   All three words mean "to make secure or certain," but only *assure* is used in the sense of making a promise: *He assured us everything would be fine. Ensure* and *insure* are interchangeable, but only *insure* is commonly used in the commercial or financial sense: *We wanted to ensure that the rate we paid to insure our car against theft would not change.*

awful   Avoid using *awful* to mean "bad" or "extremely": not *He's awful late,* but *He's extremely late.*

a while, awhile   *A while* is a noun phrase: *a while ago; for a while. Awhile* is an adverb meaning "for some time": *They lived awhile in the wilderness.*

bad, badly   *Bad* is an adjective, *badly* an adverb. Use *bad* after linking verbs (such as *am, is, become, seem*): *They felt bad after losing the match.* Use *badly* to modify a verb: *They played badly.*

bare, bear   *Bare* is an adjective meaning "naked": the *bare facts,* a *bare-faced lie. Bear* is a noun (the animal) or a verb meaning "to carry" or "to endure": *He could not bear the pressure of losing.*

barely   Avoid creating a double negative (such as *can't barely type*). *Barely* should always take a positive verb: *She can barely type. They could barely keep their eyes open.* See *hardly*.

because, because of   *Because* is a subordinating conjunction used to introduce a dependent clause: *Because it was raining, we left early. Because of* is a two-word preposition: *We left early because of the rain.*

being as, being that   Avoid. Use *because* instead: *Because* [not *Being as*] *I was tired, I didn't go to class.*

belief, believe   *Belief* is a noun: *She has radical beliefs. Believe* is a verb: *He believes in an afterlife.*

beside, besides   *Beside* is a preposition meaning "next to": *Sit beside me. Besides* is a preposition meaning "except for": *He has no assistants besides us. Besides* is also an adverb meaning "in addition": *I hate horror movies. Besides, there's a long line.*

better   See *had better.*

between   See *among.*

brake, break   To slow down, we *brake* by applying the *brake(s)* in a car. We can *break* a window or even get a bad *break.*

breath, breathe   *Breath* is a noun, *breathe* a verb: *Take three deep breaths. Breathe in deeply.*

bring, take   Use *bring* to suggest carrying something from a farther place to a nearer one and *take* for any other transportation: *First bring me a cake from the store, and then we can take it to the party.*

can't hardly   This expression is nonstandard. See *hardly.*

censor, censure   The verb *censor* refers to editing or removing from public view. *Censure* means to criticize harshly. *The new film was censored for graphic content, and the director was censured by critics for his irresponsibility.*

cite, site, sight   *Cite* means "to quote or mention"; *site* is a noun meaning "location"; *sight* is a noun meaning "view": *She cited the page number in her paper. They visited the original site of the abbey. The sight of the skyline from the plane produced applause from the passengers.*

compare to, compare with   Use *compare to* when implying similarity: *They compared the director to Alfred Hitchcock.* Use *compare with* when examining similarities or differences: *She wrote an essay comparing Hitchcock with Orson Welles.*

complement, compliment   As verbs, *complement* means "to complete or add to something," and *compliment* means "to make a flattering comment about someone or something": *The wine complemented the meal. The guests complimented the hostess on the fine dinner.* As nouns, the words have meanings associated with the verbs: *The wine was a fine complement to the meal. The guests paid the hostess a compliment.*

compose, comprise *Compose* means "to make up"; *comprise* means "to include." *The conference center is composed of twenty-five rooms. The conference center comprises twenty-five rooms.*

conscience, conscious *Conscience* is a noun meaning "awareness of right and wrong": *Conscious* is an adjective meaning "awake" or "aware." *Her conscience troubled her after the accident. The victim was still not conscious.*

continual, continuous *Continual* implies repetition; *continuous* implies lack of a pause: *The continual interruptions made the lecturer angry. Continuous rain for two hours stopped play.*

could care less This expression is often used but is regarded by some as nonstandard. In formal English, use it only with a negative: *They could not care less about their work.*

council, counsel A *council* is a group formed to consult, deliberate, or make decisions. *Counsel* is advice or guidance. *The council was called together to help give counsel to the people.* Counsel can also be a verb: *We counseled the students to withdraw from the course.*

credible, creditable, credulous *Credible* means "believable": *The jury found the accused's alibi to be credible and so acquitted her. Creditable* means "deserving of credit": *A B+ grade attests to a creditable performance. Credulous* means "easily taken in or deceived": *Only a child would be so credulous as to believe that the streets are paved with gold.* See also *incredible, incredulous.*

criteria, criterion *Criteria* is the plural form of the singular noun *criterion: There are many criteria for a successful essay. One criterion is sentence clarity.*

curricula, curriculum *Curricula* is the plural form of *curriculum. All the departments have well-thought-out curricula, but the English Department has the best curriculum.*

custom, customs, costume All three words are nouns. *Custom* means "habitual practice or tradition": *a family custom. Customs* refers to taxes on imports or to the procedures for inspecting items entering a country: *go through customs at the airport.* A *costume* is "a style of dress": *a Halloween costume.*

dairy, diary *Dairy* is associated with cows and milk, *diary* with a daily journal.

decease, disease *Decease* is a verb or noun meaning "die" or "death." *Disease* is an illness: *The disease caused an early decease.*

decent, descent, dissent *Decent* is an adjective meaning "good" or "respectable": *decent clothes, a decent salary. Descent* is a noun meaning "way down" or "lineage": *She is of Scottish descent. Dissent,* used both as a noun and a verb, refers to disagreement: *The dissent about freedom led to civil war.*

desert, dessert *Desert* can be pronounced two ways and can be a noun with the stress on the first syllable (*the Mojave Desert*) or a verb with the stress on the second syllable: *When did he desert his family?* The noun *desert* means "a dry, often sandy, environment." The verb *desert* means "to abandon." *Dessert* (with stress on the second syllable) is the sweet course at the end of a meal.

device, devise *Device* is a noun: *He said they needed a device that could lift a car. Devise* is a verb: *She began to devise a solution to the problem.*

different from, different than Standard usage is *different from: She looks different from her sister.* However, *different than* appears frequently in speech and informal writing, particularly when *different from* would require more words: *My writing is different than* [in place of *different from what*] *it was last semester.*

differ from, differ with To *differ from* means "to be unlike": *Lions differ from tigers in several ways, despite being closely related.* To *differ with* means to "disagree with": *They differ with each other on many topics but are still good friends.*

discreet, discrete *Discreet* means "tactful": *Be discreet when you talk about your boss. Discrete* means "separate": *He writes on five discrete topics.*

disease See *decease.*

disinterested, uninterested *Disinterested* means "impartial or unbiased": *The mediator was hired to make a disinterested settlement. Uninterested* means "lacking in interest": *He seemed uninterested in his job.*

dissent See *decent.*

do, due *Do* is a verb. Do not write "*Do* to his absences, he lost his job"; instead use the two-word preposition *due to* or *because of. Due* is also an adjective meaning "expected at a certain time": *When will the final payment be due?*

drag, dragged Use *dragged* for the past tense of the verb *drag. Drug* is nonstandard.

drown, drowned The past tense of the verb *drown* is *drowned; drownded* is not a word: *He almost drowned yesterday.*

due to the fact that, owing to the fact that Wordy. Use *because* instead: *They stopped the game because* [not *due to the fact that*] *it was raining.*

each, every These are singular pronouns; use them with a singular verb. See also 43h and 44d.

each other, one another Use *each other* with two; use *one another* with more than two: *The twins love each other. The triplets all love one another.*

effect See *affect.*

e.g. Use *for example* or *for instance* in place of this Latin abbreviation.

elicit, illicit *Elicit* means "to get or draw out": *The police tried in vain to elicit information from the suspect's accomplice. Illicit* is an adjective meaning "illegal": *Their illicit deals landed them in prison.*

elude See *allude.*

emigrate, immigrate *Emigrate from* means "to leave a country"; *immigrate to* means "to move to another country": *They emigrated from Ukraine and immigrated to the United States.* The noun forms *emigrant* and *immigrant* are derived from the verbs.

eminent, imminent *Eminent* means "well known and noteworthy": *an eminent lawyer. Imminent* means "about to happen": *an imminent disaster.*

ensure See *assure.*

etc. This abbreviation for the Latin *et cetera* means "and so on." Do not let a list trail off with *etc.* Rather than *They took a tent, a sleeping bag, etc.,* write *They took a tent, a sleeping bag, cooking utensils, and a stove.*

every, each See *each.*

everyday, every day *Everyday* (one word) is an adjective meaning "usual": *Their everyday routine is to break for lunch at 12:30. Every day* (two words) is an adverbial expression of frequency: *I get up early every day.*

except, expect See *accept.*

explicit, implicit *Explicit* means "direct": *She gave explicit instructions. Implicit* means "implied": *A tax increase is implicit in the proposal.*

farther, further Both words can refer to distance: *She lives farther (further) from the campus than I do. Further* also means "additional" or "additionally": *The management offered further incentives. Further, the union proposed new work rules.*

female, male Use these words as adjectives, not as nouns in place of *man* and *woman: There are only three women* [not *females*] *in my class. We are discussing female conversational traits.*

few, a few   *Few* means "hardly any": *She feels depressed because she has few helpful colleagues. A few* means "some"; it has more positive connotations than *few*: *She feels fortunate because she has a few helpful colleagues.* See 64c.

fewer, less   Formal usage demands *fewer* with plural countable nouns (*fewer holidays*), *less* with uncountable nouns (*less sunshine*). However, in informal usage, *less* with plural nouns commonly occurs, especially with *than: less than six items, less than ten miles, fifty words or less.* In formal usage, *fewer* is preferred.

first, firstly   Avoid *firstly, secondly,* and so on, when listing reasons or examples. Instead, use *first, second.*

flammable, inflammable, nonflammable   Both *flammable* and *inflammable* mean the same thing: able to be ignited easily. *Nonflammable* means "unable to be ignited easily." *Dry wood is flammable,* or *Dry wood is inflammable. Asbestos is nonflammable.*

flaunt, flout   *Flaunt* means "to show [something] off" or "to display in a proud or boastful manner." *Flout* means "to defy or to show scorn for." *When she flaunted her jewels, she flouted good taste.*

former, latter   These terms should be used only in reference to a list of two people or things: *We bought lasagna and rhubarb, the former for dinner and the latter for dessert.* For more than two items, use *first* and *last: I had some pasta, a salad, and rhubarb; though the first was very filling, I still had room for the last.*

get married to, marry   These expressions can be used interchangeably: *He will get married to his fiancée next week. She will marry her childhood friend next month.* The noun form is *marriage: Their marriage has lasted thirty years.*

go, say   Avoid replacing the verb *say* with *go,* as this is nonstandard usage: *Jane says* [not *goes*], *"I'm tired of this game."*

good, well   *Good* is an adjective; *well* is an adverb: *If you want to write well, you must use good grammar.* See 45a.

had better   Include *had* in Standard English, although it is often omitted in advertising and in speech: *You had better* [not *You better*] *try harder.*

hardly   This is a negative word. Do not use it with another negative: not *He couldn't hardly walk,* but *He could hardly walk.*

have, of   Use *have,* not *of,* after *should, could, might,* and *must: They should have* [not *should of*] *appealed.*

height   Note the spelling and pronunciation: not *heighth.*

heroin, heroine Do not confuse these words. *Heroin* is a drug; *heroine* is a brave woman. *Hero* may be used for an admirable person of either sex.

hisself Nonstandard; instead, use *himself.*

hopefully This word is an adverb meaning "in a hopeful manner" or "with a hopeful attitude": *Hopefully, she e-mailed her résumé.* Avoid using *hopefully* in place of *I hope that:* not *Hopefully, she will get the job,* but *I hope that she will get the job.* The former usage is, however, quite common.

I, me Do not confuse *I* and *me.* Use *I* only in the subject position, and use *me* only in the object position. To check subjects and objects using *and,* simply drop any additional subject or object so that only the pronoun remains: not *The CFO and me were sent to the conference,* but *The CFO and I were sent* (I was sent); not *Please send copies to my secretary and I,* but *Please send copies to my secretary and me* (send copies to me). See 44a.

illicit See *elicit.*

illusion See *allusion.*

immigrate See *emigrate.*

imminent See *eminent.*

implicit See *explicit.*

imply, infer *Imply* means "to suggest in an indirect way": *He implied that further layoffs were unlikely. Infer* means "to guess" or "to draw a conclusion": *I inferred that the company was doing well.*

incredible, incredulous *Incredible* means "difficult to believe": *The violence of the storm was incredible. Incredulous* means "skeptical, unable to believe": *They were incredulous when he told them about his daring exploits in the whitewater rapids.*

infamous *Infamous* is an adjective meaning "notorious": *Blackbeard's many exploits as a pirate made him infamous along the American coast.* Avoid using it as a synonym for "not famous."

inflammable See *flammable.*

in regard to, as regards Use one or the other. Do not use the nonstandard *in regards to.*

insure See *assure.*

irregardless Nonstandard; instead, use *regardless: He selected a major regardless of the preparation it would give him for a career.*

it's, its   The apostrophe in *it's* signals not a possessive but a contraction of *it is* or *it has*. *Its* is the possessive form of the pronoun *it*: *The city government agency has produced its final report. It's available upon request.* See also 48f.

kind, sort, type   In the singular, use each of these nouns with *this* and a singular noun: *this type of book.* Use in the plural with *these* and a plural noun: *these kinds of books.*

kind of, sort of   Do not use these to mean "somewhat" or "a little." *The pace of the baseball game was somewhat* [not *kind of*] *slow.*

knew, new   *Knew* is the past tense of the verb *know*. *New* is an adjective meaning "not old": *He knew that the book was new.*

lend, loan   *Lend* is a verb, and *loan* is ordinarily used as a noun: *Our cousins offered to lend us some money, but we refused the loan.*

less   See *fewer*.

lie, lay   Be sure not to confuse these verbs. *Lie* does not take a direct object; *lay* does. See 41b.

like, as, as if   In formal usage, *as* and *as if* are subordinating conjunctions and introduce dependent clauses: *She walks as her father does. She looks as if she could eat a big meal. Like* is a preposition and is followed by a noun or pronoun, not by a clause: *She looks like her father.* In speech, however, and increasingly in writing, *like* is often used where formal usage dictates *as* or *as if: She walks like her father does. He looks like he needs a new suit.* Know your audience's expectations.

likely, liable   *Likely* means "probably going to," while *liable* means "at risk of" and is generally used to describe something negative: *Eddie plays the guitar so well he's likely to start a band. If he keeps playing that way, he's liable to break a string. Liable* also means "responsible": *The guitar manufacturer cannot be held liable.*

literally   Avoid overuse: *literally* is an adverb meaning "actually" or "word for word" and should not be used in conjunction with figurative expressions such as *my jaw literally hit the floor* or *he was literally bouncing off the walls. Literally* should be used only when the words describe exactly what is happening: *He was so scared his face literally went white.*

loan   See *lend*.

loose, lose   *Loose* is an adjective meaning "not tight": *This jacket is comfortable because it is so loose. Lose* is a verb (the past tense form and past participle are *lost*): *Many people lose their jobs in a recession.*

lots of   See *alot*.

man, mankind   Avoid using these terms, as they are gender-specific. Instead, use *people, human beings, humankind, humanity,* or *men and women.*

marital, martial   *Marital* is associated with marriage, *martial* with war: *Their marital relationship was sometimes martial.*

may be, maybe   *May be* consists of a modal verb followed by the base form of the verb *be; maybe* is an adverb meaning "perhaps." If you can replace the expression with *perhaps,* make it one word: *They may be there already, or maybe they got caught in traffic.*

me, I   See *I.*

media, medium   *Media* is the plural form of *medium: Television and radio are both useful communication media, but his favorite medium is the written word.*

most   See *almost.*

myself   Use only as a reflexive pronoun (*I told them myself*) or as an intensive pronoun (*I myself told them*). Do not use *myself* as a subject pronoun: not *My sister and myself won,* but *My sister and I won.*

no, not   *No* modifies a noun: *The author has no intention of deceiving the reader. Not* modifies a verb, adjective, or adverb: *She is not wealthy. He does not intend to deceive.*

nonflammable   See *flammable.*

nowadays   All one word. Be sure to include the final *-s.*

nowhere, nowheres   See *anyway.*

number   See *amount.*

off, off of   Use only *off,* not *off of: She drove the car off* [not *off of*] *the road.*

oftentimes   Do not use. Prefer *often.*

OK, O.K., okay   Reserve these forms for informal speech and writing. Choose another word in a formal context: not *Her performance was OK,* but *Her performance was satisfactory.*

one another   See *each other.*

owing to the fact that   See *due to the fact that.*

passed, past   *Passed* is a past tense verb form: *They passed the deli on the way to work. He passed his exam. Past* can be a noun (*in the past*), an adjective (*in past years*), or a preposition (*She walked past the bakery.*).

peak, peek, pique   *Peak* is the top of a summit: *She has reached the peak of her performance. Peek* (noun or verb) means "glance": *A peek through the* *window is enough. Pique* (also a noun or a verb) has to do with being indignant: *Feeling insulted, he stormed out in a fit of pique.*

personal, personnel *Personal* is an adjective meaning "individual," while *personnel* is a noun referring to employees or staff: *It is my personal belief that a company's personnel should be treated like family.*

phenomena, phenomenon *Phenomena* is the plural form of the noun *phenomenon: Outer space is full of celestial phenomena, one spectacular phenomenon being the Milky Way.*

plus Do not use *plus* as a coordinating conjunction or a transitional expression. Use *and* or *moreover* instead: *He was promoted, and* [not *plus*] *he received a bonus.* Use *plus* as a preposition meaning "in addition to": *His salary plus his dividends placed him in a high tax bracket.*

pore, pour To *pore* is to read carefully or to ponder: *I saw him poring over the want ads before he poured himself a drink.*

precede, proceed *Precede* means "to go or occur before": *The Roaring Twenties preceded the Great Depression. Proceed* means "to go ahead": *After you pay the fee, proceed to the examination room.*

prejudice, prejudiced *Prejudice* can be a noun (*Prejudice is harmful to society.*) or a verb with *prejudiced* as its past participle: *He is prejudiced against ethnic minorities.*

pretty Avoid using *pretty* as an intensifying adverb. Use *really, very, rather,* or *quite: The stew tastes very* [not *pretty*] *good.*

principal, principle *Principal* is a noun (*the principal of a school*) or an adjective meaning "main" or "most important": *His principal motive was monetary gain. Principle* is a noun meaning "standard or rule": *He always acts on his principles.*

quite, quiet Do not confuse the adverb *quite,* meaning "very," with the adjective *quiet* ("still" or "silent"): *We were all quite relieved when the audience became quiet.*

quote, quotation *Quote* is a verb. Do not use it as a noun; use *quotation: The quotation* [not *quote*] *from Walker tells the reader a great deal.*

real, really *Real* is an adjective; *really* is an adverb. Do not use *real* as an intensifying adverb: *She acted really* [not *real*] *well.*

reason is because Avoid *the reason is because.* Instead, use *the reason is that* or rewrite the sentence. See 40f.

regardless Use this to mean "in spite" or "anyway": *They finished the game regardless of the weather. It rained, but they finished the game regardless.* See also the nonstandard *irregardless.*

respectable, respectful, respective *Respectable* means "presentable, worthy of respect": *Wear some respectable shoes to your interview.* *Respectful* means "polite or deferential": *Parents want their children to be respectful to adults.* *Respective* means "particular" or "individual": *The friends of the bride and the groom sat in their respective seats in the church.*

respectfully, respectively *Respectfully* means "showing respect": *He bowed respectfully when the queen entered.* *Respectively* refers to items in a list and means "in the order mentioned": *Horses and birds gallop and fly, respectively.*

rise, raise *Rise* is an intransitive verb: *She rises early every day.* *Raise* is a transitive verb: *We raised alfalfa last summer.* See 41b.

sale, sell *Sale* is a noun: *The sale of the house has been postponed.* *Sell* is a verb: *They are still trying to sell their house.*

should (could, might) of Nonstandard; instead use *should have*: *You should have paid.* See 41c.

since Use this subordinating conjunction only when time or reason is clear: *Since you insist on helping, I'll let you paint this bookcase.* Unclear: *Since he got a new job, he has been happy.* *Since* here may refer to time or to reason (*because*).

site, sight See *cite.*

sometimes, sometime, some time The adverb *sometimes* means "occasionally": *He sometimes prefers to eat lunch at his desk.* The adverb *sometime* means "at an indefinite time": *I read that book sometime last year.* The noun phrase *some time* consists of the noun *time* modified by the quantity word *some*: *After working for Honda, I spent some time in Brazil.*

sort, type See *kind.*

sort of See *kind of.*

stationary, stationery *Stationary* is an adjective meaning "not moving" (*a stationary vehicle*); *stationery* is a noun referring to writing paper.

supposedly Use this, not *supposably: She is supposedly a great athlete.*

taught, thought Do not confuse these verb forms. *Taught* is the past tense and past participle form of *teach*; *thought* is the past tense and past participle form of *think: The students thought that their professor had not taught essay organization.*

than, then *Then* is a time word; *than* must be preceded by a comparative form: *bigger than, more interesting than.*

their, there, they're *Their* is a pronoun indicating possession; *there* indicates place or is used as a filler in the subject position in a sentence;

they're is the contracted form of *they are*: *They're over there, guarding their luggage.*

theirself, theirselves, themself Nonstandard; instead, use *themselves.*

threat, treat A *threat* is a "possible danger": *The threat of an earthquake was alarming.* A *treat* is a "source of pleasure": *She gave the children some cookies as a treat.*

thusly Incorrect form of *thus.*

to, too, two Do not confuse these words. *To* is a sign of the infinitive and a common preposition; *too* is an adverb meaning *also*; *two* is the number: *She is too smart to agree to report to two bosses.*

undoubtedly This is the correct word, not *undoubtably.*

uninterested See *disinterested.*

unique The adjective *unique* means "the only one of its kind" and therefore should not be used with qualifying adjectives like *very* or *most*: *His recipe for chowder is unique* [not *most unique* or *quite unique*]. See 45h.

used to, get (become) used to These expressions share the common form *used to.* But the first, expressing a past habit that no longer exists, is followed by the base form of a verb: *He used to wear his hair long.* (Note that after *not*, the form is *use to*: *He did not use to have a beard.*) In the expression *get (become) used to, used to* means "accustomed to" and is followed by a noun or an *-ing* verb form: *She couldn't get used to driving on the left when she was in England.* See also 64h.

way, ways Use *way* to mean "distance": *He has a way to go. Ways* in this context is nonstandard.

wear, were, we're *Wear* is a verb meaning "to have on as covering adornment or protection" (*wearing a helmet*); *were* is a past tense form of *be*; *we're* is a contraction for *we are.*

weather, whether *Weather* is a noun; *whether* is a conjunction: *The weather will determine whether we go on the picnic.*

whose, who's *Whose* is a possessive pronoun: *Whose goal was that? Who's* is a contraction of *who is* or *who has*: *Who's the player whose pass was caught? Who's got the ball?*

your, you're *Your* is a pronoun used to show possession. *You're* is a contraction for *you are*: *You're wearing your new shoes today, aren't you?*

66

Glossary of Grammatical Terms

absolute phrase A phrase consisting of a noun phrase followed by a verbal or a prepositional phrase and modifying an entire sentence: *Flags flapping in the wind*, the stadium looked bleak. 47i.

acronym A pronounceable word formed from the initials of an abbreviation: *NATO, MADD, NOW*. 51a.

active voice The attribute of a verb when its grammatical subject performs the action: The dog *ate* the cake. See also 42a on the passive voice.

adjective The part of speech that modifies a noun or pronoun: She wears *flamboyant* clothes. His cap is *orange*. 37d, 45a, 62g. See also *comparative; coordinate adjective; cumulative adjective; superlative; parts of speech.*

adjective clause A dependent clause beginning with a relative pronoun (*who, whom, whose, which,* or *that*) and modifying a noun or pronoun: The writer *who won the prize* was elated. Also called a *relative clause*. 37d, 46a.

adverb The part of speech that modifies a verb, an adjective, another adverb, or a clause: She ran *quickly*. He will *inevitably* become a success. The children were *well* liked. Many adverbs end in *-ly*. 37d, 45a, 45b. See also *comparative; conjunctive adverb; frequency adverb; parts of speech; superlative.*

adverb clause A dependent clause that modifies a verb, an adjective, or an adverb and begins with a subordinating conjunction: He left early *because he was tired*. 37d.

agent The person or thing doing the action described by a verb: *His sister* won the marathon. The marathon was won by *his sister*. 42a.

agreement The grammatical match in person, number, and gender between a verb and its subject or between a pronoun and its antecedent (the word the pronoun refers to): The *benefits continue; they are* pleasing. The *benefit continues; it is* pleasing. 43a, 44d.

antecedent The noun that a pronoun refers to: My son who lives nearby found a *kitten*. *It* was black and white. 44c, 44d, 46a.

appositive phrase A phrase occurring next to a noun and used to describe it: His father, *a factory worker*, is running for office. 47d.

article   *A, an* (indefinite articles), or *the* (definite article). Also called a *determiner*. 60c–60e.

auxiliary verb   A verb that joins with another verb to form a complete verb. Auxiliary verbs are forms of *do, be,* and *have,* as well as the modal auxiliary verbs. 37d, 41c. See also *modal auxiliary verb.*

base form   The dictionary form of a verb, used in an infinitive after *to: see, eat, go, be.* 41, 41a.

clause   A group of words that includes a subject and a verb. 37d. See also *dependent clause; independent clause.*

cliché   An overused, predictable expression: *as cool as a cucumber.* 34g.

collective noun   A noun naming a collection of people or things that are regarded as a unit: *team, jury, family.* For agreement with collective nouns, see 43f, 44d.

comma splice   The error that results when two independent clauses are incorrectly joined with only a comma. 39a–39c.

common noun   A noun that does not name a unique person, place, or thing. 60a, 60b. See also *proper noun.*

comparative   The form of an adjective or adverb used to compare two people or things: *bigger, more interesting.* 45h. See also *superlative.*

complement   A *subject complement* is a word or group of words used after a linking verb to refer to and describe the subject: Harry looks *happy.* An *object complement* is a word or group of words used after a direct object to complete its meaning: They call him a *liar.* 37d, 43c.

complete verb   A verb that shows tense. Some verb forms, such as *-ing* (present) participles and past participles, require auxiliary verbs to make them complete verbs. *Going* and *seen* are not complete verbs; *are going* and *has been seen* are complete. 38a, 41c.

complex sentence   A sentence that has one independent clause and one or more dependent clauses: *He wept when he won the marathon.* 33d.

compound adjective   An adjective formed of two or more words often connected with hyphens: a *well-constructed* house. 45d, 56b.

compound-complex sentence   A sentence that has at least two independent clauses and one or more dependent clauses: *She works in Los Angeles, but her husband works in San Diego, where they both live.* 33d.

compound noun   A noun formed of two or more words: *toothbrush, merry-go-round.* 56b.

compound predicate A predicate consisting of two or more verbs and their objects, complements, and modifiers: He *whistles and sings in the morning.* 38d, 40h.

compound sentence A sentence that has two or more independent clauses: *She works in Los Angeles, but her husband works in San Diego.* 33d.

compound subject A subject consisting of two or more nouns or pronouns and their modifiers: *My uncle and my aunt* are leaving soon. 43g, 44a.

conditional clause A clause introduced by *if* or *unless* expressing conditions of fact, prediction, or speculation: *If we earned more, we would spend more.* 41j.

conjunction The part of speech used to link words, phrases, or clauses. 37d, 38c. See also *coordinating conjunction; correlative conjunctions; parts of speech; subordinating conjunction.*

conjunctive adverb A transitional expression used to link two independent clauses. Some common conjunctive adverbs are *moreover, however,* and *furthermore.* 2c, 37d.

connotation The meanings and associations suggested by a word, as distinct from the word's denotation, or dictionary meaning. 34c.

contraction The shortened form that results when an apostrophe replaces one or more letters: *can't* (for *cannot*), *he's* (for *he is* or *he has*), *they're* (for *they are*). 48d.

coordinate adjective An evaluative adjective modifying a noun. When coordinate adjectives appear in a series, their order can be reversed, and they can be separated by *and.* Commas are used between coordinate adjectives: the *comfortable, expensive car.* 47g.

coordinating conjunction The seven coordinating conjunctions are *and, but, or, nor, so, for,* and *yet.* They connect sentence elements that are parallel in structure: He couldn't call, *but* he sent an e-mail. 32b, 37d, 47b.

coordination The connection of two or more ideas to give each one equal emphasis: *Sue worked after school, so she didn't have time to jog.* 32b.

correlative conjunctions A pair of conjunctions joining equivalent elements. The most common correlative conjunctions are *either . . . or, neither . . . nor, both . . . and,* and *not only . . . but also: Neither* my sister *nor* I could find the concert hall. 40j.

countable noun A common noun that has a plural form and can be used after a plural quantity word (such as *many* or *three*): one *book,* three *stores,* many *children.* 60a, 60e.

cumulative adjective An adjective that modifies a noun and occurs in a conventional order with no comma between adjectives: a *new red plastic* bench. 62g.

cumulative sentence A sentence that adds elements after the independent clause. 33d.

dangling modifier A modifier that fails to modify the noun or pronoun it is intended to modify: not *Turning the corner,* the lights went out, but *Turning the corner, we* saw the lights go out. 40c.

demonstrative pronoun The four demonstrative pronouns are *this, that, these,* and *those: That* is my glass. 43j.

denotation A word's dictionary meaning. See also *connotation.* 34b, 34c.

dependent clause A clause that cannot stand alone as a complete sentence and needs to be attached to an independent clause. A dependent clause begins with a subordinating word such as *because, if, when, although, who, which,* or *that: When it rains,* we can't take the children outside. 37d, 38c.

diction The choice of appropriate words and tone. 34a–34g.

direct object The person or thing that receives the action of a verb: They ate *cake* and *ice cream.* 37d, 62c.

direct quotation A person's words reproduced exactly and placed in quotation marks: *"I won't be home until noon,"* she said. 10e, 40d, 62d.

double negative The use of two negative words in the same sentence: He does *not* know *nothing.* This usage is nonstandard and needs to be avoided: *He does not know anything. He knows nothing.* 45g.

Edited American English The variety of English to use in formal academic writing. 37c, 59a.

ellipsis The omission of words from a quotation, indicated by three dots: "I pledge allegiance to the flag . . . and to the republic for which it stands . . ." 51g.

etymology The origin of a word. 34b.

euphemism A word or phrase used to disguise literal meaning: She *is in the family way* [meaning "pregnant"]. 34g.

faulty predication The error that results when subject and verb do not match logically: not The *decrease* in stolen cars *has diminished* in the past year, but The *number* of stolen cars *has decreased* in the past year. 40e.

figurative language The use of unusual comparisons or other devices to draw attention to a specific meaning. See *metaphor; simile.* 5b, 34e.

filler subject   *it* or *there* used in the subject position of a clause, followed by a form of *be*: *There are* two elm trees on the corner. 31b, 43d, 64f.

first person   The person speaking or writing: *I* or *we*. 44a.

fragment   A group of words that is punctuated as if it were a sentence but is grammatically incomplete because it lacks a subject or a predicate or begins with a subordinating word: *Because it was a sunny day.* 38a–38e.

frequency adverb   An adverb that expresses time (such as *often, always,* or *sometimes*). It can be the first word in a sentence or be used between the subject and the main verb, after an auxiliary verb, or as the last word in a sentence. 45e.

fused sentence   See *run-on sentence.*

gender   The classification of a noun or pronoun as masculine (*Uncle John, he*), feminine (*Ms. Torez, she*), or neuter (*book, it*). 44e, 64g.

generic noun   A noun referring to a general class or type of person or object: *A student* has to write many papers. 44d.

gerund   The *-ing* verb form used as a noun: *Walking* is good for your health. 43e, 61d–61e, 63e. See also *verbal.*

helping verb   See *auxiliary verb.*

imperative mood   The verb mood used to give a command: *Follow* me. 33d.

indefinite pronoun   A pronoun that refers to a nonspecific person or thing: *anybody, something.* 43h, 44d.

independent clause   A clause that has a subject and predicate and is not introduced by a subordinating word. An independent clause can function as a complete sentence. *Birds sing. The old man was singing a song.* Hailing a cab, *the woman used a silver whistle.* 32b, 37d.

indicative mood   The verb mood used to ask questions or make statements. It is the most common mood, used for declarative statements and questions. See also *subjunctive mood.*

indirect object   The person or thing to whom or to which, or for whom or for which, an action is performed. It comes between the verb and the direct object: He gave his *sister* some flowers. 37d, 62c.

indirect question   A question reported by a speaker or writer, not enclosed in quotation marks: They asked *if we would help them.* 62d.

indirect quotation   A description or paraphrase of the words of another speaker or writer, integrated into a writer's own sentence and not enclosed in quotation marks: He said *that they were making money.* 40d, 62d.

infinitive The base form, or dictionary form, of a verb, preceded by *to*: *to see, to smile.* 41a, 61c, 61e.

infinitive phrase An infinitive with its objects, complements, or modifiers: *To wait for hours* is unpleasant. He tries hard *to be punctual.* 38b, 43e.

intensive pronoun A pronoun ending in *-self* or *-selves* and used to emphasize its antecedent: They *themselves* will not attend. 44h.

interjection The part of speech that expresses emotion and is able to stand alone: *Aha! Wow!* Interjections are seldom appropriate in academic writing. 37d.

interrogative pronoun A pronoun that introduces a direct or indirect question: *Who* is that? I don't know *what* you want. 44i.

intransitive verb A verb that does not take a direct object: Exciting events *have occurred.* He *fell.* 37d, 42a. See also *transitive verb.*

inverted word order The presence of the verb before the subject in a sentence; used in questions or for emphasis: *Do you expect* an award? Not only *does she do* gymnastics, she also wins awards. 31b, 43d.

irregular verb A verb that does not form its past tense and past participle with *-ed: sing, sang, sung; grow, grew, grown.* 41a.

linking verb A verb connecting a subject to its complement. Typical linking verbs are *be, become, seem,* and *appear:* He *seems* angry. A linking verb is intransitive; it does not take a direct object. 37d, 41c, 44a, 45c.

mental activity verb A verb not used in a tense showing progressive aspect: *prefer, want, understand:* not He *is wanting to leave,* but He *wants* to leave. 41d.

metaphor A figure of speech implying a comparison but not stating it directly: a *gale* of laughter. 5b, 34e.

misplaced modifier An adverb (particularly *only* and *even*) or a descriptive phrase or clause positioned in such a way that it modifies the wrong word or words: She showed the ring to her sister *that her aunt gave her.* 40b.

mixed structure A sentence with two or more types of structures that clash grammatically: *By doing* her homework at the last minute *caused* Meg to make many mistakes. 40a, 40e, 40f.

modal auxiliary verb The nine modal auxiliaries are *will, would, can, could, shall, should, may, might,* and *must.* They are followed by the base form of a verb: *will go, would believe.* Modal auxiliaries do not change form. 41c, 61b.

modifier   A word or words that describe another noun, adverb, verb, phrase, or clause: He is a *happy* man. He is smiling *happily*. 45a–45e.

mood   The mood of a verb tells whether the verb states a fact (*indicative:* She *goes* to school); gives a command (*imperative: Come* back soon); or expresses a condition, wish, or request (*subjunctive:* I wish you *were* not leaving). 41j. See also *imperative mood; indicative mood; subjunctive mood.*

nonrestrictive phrase or clause   A phrase or clause that adds extra or nonessential information to a sentence and is set off with commas: His report, *which he gave to his boss yesterday,* received enthusiastic praise. 46b, 47d.

noun   The part of speech that names a person, place, thing, or idea. Nouns are proper or common and, if common, countable or uncountable. 37d, 60a, 60b. See also *collective noun; common noun; compound noun; countable noun; generic noun; noun clause; parts of speech; proper noun; uncountable noun.*

noun clause   A dependent clause that functions as a noun: I like *what you do. Whoever scores a goal* will be a hero. 37d.

noun phrase   A noun with its accompanying modifiers and articles: *a brilliant, hard-working student.* 37d.

number   The indication of a noun or pronoun as singular (one person, place, thing, or idea) or plural (more than one). 43a, 44d.

object of preposition   The noun or pronoun (along with its modifiers) that follows a preposition: on *the beach.* 37d.

paragraph   A group of sentences set off in a text, usually on one topic. 2a, 2b, 2d.

parallelism   The use of coordinate structures that have the same grammatical form: She likes *swimming* and *playing* tennis. 40j.

participle phrase   A phrase beginning with an *-ing* verb form or a past participle: The woman *wearing a green skirt* is my sister. *Baffled by the puzzle,* he gave up. 33d. See also *verbal.*

particle   A word (frequently a preposition or adverb) that combines with a verb to form a phrasal verb, a verb with an idiomatic meaning: get *over,* take *after.* 63d.

parts of speech   Eight traditional categories of words used to form sentences: noun, pronoun, verb, adjective, adverb, conjunction, preposition, and interjection. See 37d and the entry for each in this glossary.

passive voice   The attribute of a verb when its grammatical subject is the receiver of the action that the verb describes: The book *was written* by my professor. 31c, 42a–42d. See also *active voice.*

past participle   A verb form that in regular verbs ends with -*ed*. The past participle needs an auxiliary verb to function as the complete verb of a clause: *has chosen, was cleaned, might have been told.* The past participle can function alone as an adjective. 41a, 41c, 41d, 41g, 61f.

perfect progressive tense forms   The verb tenses that show actions in progress up to a specific point in present, past, or future time. For active voice verbs, use forms of the auxiliary *have been* followed by the -*ing* form of the verb: *has/have been living, had been living, will have been living.* 41d.

perfect tense forms   The verb tenses that show actions completed by present, past, or future time. For active voice verbs, use forms of the auxiliary *have* followed by the past participle of the verb: *has/have arrived, had arrived, will have arrived.* 41d.

periodic sentence   A sentence that uses words and phrases to build up to the independent clause. 33d.

person   The form of a pronoun or verb that indicates whether the subject is doing the speaking (first person, *I* or *we*), is spoken to (second person, *you*), or is spoken about (third person, *he, she, it,* or *they*). 43a, 44a.

phrasal verb   An idiomatic verb phrase consisting of a verb and a preposition or adverb called a *particle: put off, put on.* 63d.

phrase   A group of words that lacks a subject or predicate and functions as a noun, verb, adjective, or adverb: *under the tree, has been singing, amazingly simple.* 37d. See also *absolute phrase; appositive phrase; infinitive phrase; participle phrase; prepositional phrase.*

possessive   The form of a noun or pronoun that indicates ownership. Possessive pronouns include *my, his, her, their, theirs,* and *whose: my* boat, *your* socks. The possessive form of a noun is indicated by an apostrophe or an apostrophe and -*s: Mario's* car, the *children's* nanny, the *birds'* nests. 43j, 44b, 48a, 48b, 48c.

predicate   The part of a sentence that contains the verb and its modifiers and that comments on or makes an assertion about the subject. To be complete, a sentence needs a subject and a predicate. 37d.

prefix   The letters attached to the beginning of a word that change the word's meaning: *un*necessary, *re*organize, *non*stop. 56a.

preposition   The part of speech used with a noun or pronoun in a phrase to indicate time, space, or some other relationship. 37d, 46d, 63a–63e. The noun or pronoun is the object of the preposition: *on the table, after dinner, to her.*

prepositional phrase A phrase beginning with a preposition and including the object of the preposition and its modifiers: The head *of the electronics company* was waiting *for an hour.* 33d (p. 367), 37d, 46d.

present participle The *-ing* form of a verb, showing an action as being in progress or continuous: They are *sleeping.* Without an auxiliary, the *-ing* form cannot function as a complete verb but can be used as an adjective: *searing* heat. When the *-ing* form is used as a noun, it is called a *gerund*: *Skiing* can be dangerous. 41a, 43e, 61d, 61f. See also *verbal.*

progressive tense forms The verb tenses that show actions in progress at a point or over a period of time in past, present, or future time. They use a form of *be* + the *-ing* form of the verb: They *are working;* he *will be writing.* 41d–41f.

pronoun The part of speech that takes the place of a noun, a noun phrase, or another pronoun. 37d, 43h, 44a, 44b. See *parts of speech.*

pronoun reference The connection between a pronoun and its antecedent. Reference should be clear and unambiguous: Mr. Estern picked up *his* hat and left. 44c.

proper noun The capitalized name of a specific person, place, or thing: *Golden Gate Park, University of Kansas.* 37d, 53b, 60f. See also *common noun.*

quantity word A word expressing the idea of quantity, such as *each, every, several, many,* and *much.* Subject-verb agreement is tricky with quantity words: *Each* of the students *has* a different assignment. 43i. See also *agreement.*

reflexive pronoun A pronoun ending in *-self* or *-selves* and referring to the subject of a clause: They incriminated *themselves.* 44h.

regular verb A verb that ends with *-ed* in its past tense and past participle forms. 41a.

relative clause See *adjective clause.*

relative pronoun A pronoun that introduces a relative clause: *who, whom, whose, which, that.* 46a.

restrictive phrase or clause A phrase or clause that provides information essential for identifying the word or phrase it modifies. A restrictive phrase or clause is not set off with commas: The book *that is first on the bestseller list* is a memoir. 46b, 47d.

run-on sentence The error that results when two independent clauses are not separated by a conjunction or by any punctuation: not *The dog ate the meat the cat ate the fish,* but *The dog ate the meat; the cat ate the fish.* Also called a *fused sentence.* 39a–39c.

second person   The person addressed: *you.* 44a, 44g.

shifts   The inappropriate switches in grammatical structure such as from one tense to another or from statement to command or from indirect to direct quotation: not *Joan asked whether I was warm enough and did I sleep well,* but *Joan asked whether I was warm enough and had slept well.* 40d, 41h.

simile   A figure of speech that makes a direct comparison: She has a laugh *like a fire siren.* 5b, 34e.

simple tense forms   The verb tenses that show present, past, or future time with no perfect or progressive aspects: they *work,* we *worked,* she *will work.* 41d–41g.

split infinitive   An infinitive with a word or words separating *to* from the base verb form: *to successfully complete.* This structure has become acceptable. 40b.

Standard English   "The variety of English that is generally acknowledged as the model for the speech and writing of educated speakers." This *American Heritage Dictionary,* 4th edition, definition warns that the use of the term is "highly elastic and variable" and confers no "absolute positive evaluation." 34d, 37c, 59a. See also *Edited American English.*

subject   The noun or pronoun that performs the action of the verb in an active voice sentence or receives the action of the verb in a passive voice sentence. To be complete, a sentence needs a subject and a verb. 37d, 38d, 40i, 62a.

subjunctive mood   The verb mood used in conditions and in wishes, requests, and demands: I wish he *were* here. She demanded that he *be* present. 41j.

subordinate clause   See *dependent clause.*

subordinating conjunction   A conjunction used to introduce a dependent adverb clause: *because, if, when, although, since, while.* 32b, 37d, 38c.

suffix   The letters attached to the end of a word that change the word's function or meaning: gentle*ness,* humor*ist,* slow*er,* sing*ing.* 58e.

superlative   The form of an adjective or adverb used to compare three or more people or things: *biggest; most unusual; least effectively.* 45h, 60d. See also *comparative.*

synonym   A word that has the same or nearly the same meaning as another word.

tense   The form of a verb that indicates time. Verbs change form to distinguish present and past time: he *goes;* he *went.* Various structures are used to express future time, mainly *will* + the base form, or *going to* + the base form. 41d. See also *perfect progressive tense forms; perfect tense forms; progressive tense forms; simple tense forms.*

third person The person or thing spoken about: *he, she, it, they,* or nouns. 43a, 44a.

topic chain The repetition of key words or related words throughout a passage to aid cohesion. 32a, 42d.

transitional expression A word or phrase used to connect two independent clauses, such as *for example, however,* and *similarly.* 2c, 47e, 50a.

transitive verb A verb that takes an object—the person or thing that receives the action (in the active voice): Dogs *chase* cats. When transitive verbs are used in the passive voice, the subject receives the action of the verb: Cats *are chased* by dogs. 37d, 41b, 42a. See also *intransitive verb.*

uncountable noun A common noun that cannot follow a plural quantity word (such as *several* or *many*) is never used with *a* or *an*, is used with a singular third person verb, and has no plural form: *furniture, happiness, information.* 43e, 60b.

verb The part of speech that expresses action or being and tells (in the active voice) what the subject of the clause is or does. The complete verb in a clause might require auxiliary or modal auxiliary verbs to complete its meaning. 37d, 41a–41j, 61a–61f.

verbal A form, derived from a verb, that cannot function as the main verb of a clause. The three types of verbals are the infinitive, the *-ing* participle, and the past participle (for example, *to try, singing, stolen*). A verbal can function in a phrase as a noun, adjective, or adverb. 61c–61f, 63e.

verb chain The combination of an auxiliary verb, a main verb, and verbals: She *might have promised to leave;* they *should deny having helped* him. 61a–61e.

verb phrase A complete verb formed by auxiliaries and the main verb: *should have waited.* 37d.

voice The transitive verbs (verbs that take an object) can be used in the active voice (*He is painting the door*) or the passive voice (*The door is being painted*). 42a, 42b.

zero article The lack of an article (*a, an,* or *the*) before a noun. Uncountable nouns are used with the zero article when they make no specific reference. 60b, 60d, 60e.

Index

Note: An asterisk (*) refers to a page number in the Glossary of Grammatical Terms.

a, an, 388, 523–526, 549. *See also* articles (parts of speech)
AAV (African American Vernacular), 411, 517
Abad, Gemino, 508
abbreviations, 177, 492–494, 499
absolute phrases, 469, 563*
abstracts
  APA reference list style for, 240, 248
  in experimental papers, 93–94
  MLA citation style for, 190, 196
academic disciplines, 91
Academic Info, 12
Academic Search Premier database, 113, 118, 191, 193
academic writing
  everyday writing *versus*, 4–5
  I in, 10
  online design of, 292–293
  social networking sites and, 20–21
  thesis in, 21
  unified paragraphs in, 28
accents, 503–504
accept, except, expect, 549
accessibility, 9, 316–317
ACQWEB's *Directory of Publishers and Vendors*, 130
acronyms, 483, 563*
active voice, 563*
Activities for ESL Students Web site, 519
adapt, adopt, 549
Adbusters.com Web site, 70
addresses
  in business letters, 337
  commas in, 469–470

MLA documentation style for, 207–208
ad hominem attack, 68
adjective clause, 388, 454, 563*
adjectives
  commas to separate, 468
  comparative, 451–453
  compound, 449–450
  coordinate, 468, 565*
  cumulative, 539, 565*
  definition of, 388, 563*
  forms of, 446–448
  infinitives after, 529–531
  -ing and *-ed* verb forms as, 532–533
  linking verbs before, 448
  order of, 539
  prepositions and, 540
  proper, 490–491
  sentences beginning with, 366
  superlative, 451–453
  in writing across cultures, 515–516
advanced searches, 116–118
adverb clause, 388, 563*
adverbs
  comparative, 451–453
  conjunctive, 450
  definition of, 388–389, 563*
  forms of, 446–448
  frequency, 449, 567*
  superlative, 451–453
  in writing across cultures, 515–516
adverse, averse, 549
advertisements, 130, 205
advice, advise, 549
affect, effect, 385, 549
affirming, as transition, 29
African American Biographies, 106
African American Vernacular (AAV), 411, 517
after, 415

afterwords
APA reference list style for, 239
Chicago Manual of Style style for, 278
MLA citation style for, 185
age, stereotyping by, 375
agent, 423, 563*
agreement, 563*. *See also* subject-verb agreement
aisle, isle, 549
alerts, online, 116–118
alignment, end-of-line, 327
a little, 558
all, 433–434
Alliance for Childhood, 64
alliteration, 86
all ready, already, 550
all right, alright, 550
all together, altogether, 550
allude, elude, 550
allusion, illusion, 550
almanacs, 106
almost, most, 550
alot, a lot of, lots of, 550
aloud, allowed, 550
AltaVista.com, 125
alternative transitions, 29
although, 538
ambiguous, ambivalent, 550
American English, 386–387, 406–409. *See also* Standard English
American Film Institute, 124
American Heritage Dictionary of the English Language, The, 106, 368, 386
American Heritage English as a Second Language Dictionary, 521
American Men and Women of Science, 106
American Psychological Association (APA). *See* APA (American Psychological Association)
among, between, 550
amoral, immoral, 550
amount, number, 550
anchors, for Web sites, 316

and
fragments after, 395
sentences starting with, 359–360
in subject, 431–432
angle brackets, 486
animation, in PowerPoint, 347
annotated bibliographies, 142–143
annotating
drafts, 46–49
example of, 209
sources, 145–146
ante-, anti-, 551
antecedents to pronouns, 439–442, 454, 563*
anthologies
Chicago Manual of Style style for, 277–278
MLA citation style for, 169, 182–183
anyone, 432–433
anyone, any one, 551
anyplace, 551
anyway, anywhere, nowhere, anyways, anywheres, nowheres, 551
APA (American Psychological Association), 225–261
author name-year style of, 157, 227–231
authors in reference list of, 234–235
books and pamphlets in reference list of, 235–240
documentation style of, 137
formatting guidelines of, 290
notes, tables, figures and headings style of, 232
online sources in reference list of, 243–249
periodicals in reference list of, 240–243
quotation citing style of, 153
reference list style of, 232–234
sample paper in style of, 251–261
style features of, 225–227
visual, multimedia, and miscellaneous sources in reference list of, 250–251

visual documentation style of, 125, 137

Web site documentation style of, 157–160

APA Publication Manual, 96, 232

apart, a part, 551

apostrophes, 470–473

-'s, possession as, 471–472

appeals

in arguments, 62–65

to senses, 32–33

appear, 428

Applied Science and Technology Index, 107

appositive phrases, 466, 563*

archives. *See* sources

argumentative writing, 8

arguments, 51–80

appeals in, 62–65

common ground in, 65

constructing, 52–53

in essays, 53–55

example of, 73–80

four questions for, 61–62

logical fallacies and, 67–69

logical reasoning in, 66–67

opposing views in, 65–66

reasons and evidence to support, 58–61

thinking critically about, 52

topics and claims for, 55–58

visual, 69–73

Arial font, 294

Aristotle, 63

articles (parts of speech)

as adjectives, 388

definition of, 564*

using, 549

in writing across cultures, 511–512, 523–526

zero, 522, 524, 573*

articles (published works)

APA reference list style for, 240–243, 245–247

Chicago Manual of Style style for, 277–281

CSE reference list style for, 266–267

evaluating, 129–130

MLA citation style for, 187–191

as sources, 120–123

Art Index database, 107, 112

arts, writing on, 92

ARTstore database, 112

as, as if, like, 551, 558

asides, as transitions, 29

Ask.com, 113

as regards, in regard to, 551, 557

assigned topics, adapting to, 12–13

assonance, 86

as soon as, 415

assumptions, in arguments, 52, 62

assure, ensure, insure, 551

at, 540

Atlantic Monthly, 129

atlases, 106

attachments, to e-mail, 309

audiences

appeals to, 63–65

for Web sites, 314

writing about literature for, 82

writing for, 8–9

audio recordings

Chicago Manual of Style style for, 283

MLA documentation style for, 206–207

in presentations, 344

author/page, as MLA citation style, 167–170

authors

APA reference list style for, 234–235, 248

Chicago Manual of Style style for, 276, 278

of literature, 84

MLA citation style for, 165, 178–179, 194

none named, 170–172, 184, 194–195, 230

in writing about literature, 87

AutoCorrect function, 25, 300

AutoFormat function, 300
auxiliary verbs, 388, 412–413, 564*
averse, adverse, 549
awful, 551
a while, awhile, 551

backgrounds, in PowerPoint slides, 347
bad, badly, 551
bar charts, 305–306
bare, bear, 551
barely, 551
Bartlett's Familiar Quotations, 106
base form of verbs, 406–409, 564*
be, 411, 413, 428, 526–527
be, get used to, used to, 546
bear, bare, 551
because, 538, 551, 554, 560
because clauses, 403
because of, 551
become used to, get used to, used to, 562
been and *being,* 413
before, 415
being as, being that, 552
belief, believe, 552
Berkshire Encyclopedia of World History, 105
beside, besides, 552
better, 552
betterwhois.com Web site, 131
between, among, 550
biased language, 367, 374–376, 444
Bible, MLA citation style for, 174, 186
bibliographical software, 143–145
bibliographies, 105
    annotated, 142–143
    in *Chicago Manual of Style* style, 275, 283–284
    working, 139–143
bilingual education, 57, 67. *See also* Language and Culture feature; writing across cultures
biographies, 105

Biography Index: A Cumulative Index to Biographic Material in Books and Magazines, 105
Blackboard course Web sites, 309, 312–313
bleeding images, 327
blending, 421
blogs
    APA reference list style for, 249, 251
    evaluating, 131
    in MLA list of works cited, 199
    as online forums, 312–314
    topics from, 13–14
boards, discussion, 249–250, 311–312. *See also* groups, online discussion
Bobby Web site, to test accessibility, 9
Bookmark feature, 139
books
    APA reference list style for, 235–240, 249
    Chicago Manual of Style style for, 277–279, 281–283
    CSE reference list style for, 265–266
    evaluating, 129
    MLA citation style for, 179–187
    in MLA list of works cited, 198
    as sources, 120–123
Book Search, 113
Books in Print, 105, 122, 130
Boolean searches, 114
boxes, design of, 327
brackets, 485–486
brainstorming, 15–16, 38, 55
brake, break, 552
breath, breathe, 552
bring, take, 552
broadband connections, to Internet, 9
brochures, 205, 325–329
Brockman, John, 51
Brown v. Board of Education (1954), 57
bullets, in document design, 300
business letters, 335–338
business writing, 4
but, 359–360, 395

call numbers, for books, 121
*Cambridge Advanced Learner's
    Dictionary,* 519
can, 411, 527–529
can't hardly, 552
capitalization
    in APA reference list, 233
    in e-mail, 308
    of first word in sentence, 489–492
    of letters, 392
    online, 498
captions, for graphs, 304
Carleton College, 320
cartoons, MLA documentation style
    for, 204
catalogs, library, 121–122
causal fallacy, 68
cause-and-effect structure, 17, 55
CDs and CD-ROM
    APA reference list style for, 251
    Chicago Manual of Style style for,
        282–283
    CSE reference list style for, 268
    MLA documentation style for, 202,
        208–209
cedillas, 503–504
censor, censure, 552
characters, 83, 85
charts
    in document design, 298
    MLA documentation style for, 205
    types of, 303–306
Chicago Manual of Style, 273–286
    articles in style of, 279–280
    books in style of, 277–279
    citing sources by, 274–275
    documentation style of, 92, 137
    endnote-footnote system of, 156,
        175, 276
    features of, 274
    formatting guidelines of, 290
    online sources in style of, 280–282
    quotation citing style of, 153
    sample bibliography in style of,
        283–284
    sample paper in style of, 285–286

visual, multimedia, and
    miscellaneous sources in style
    of, 282–283
Web site documentation style of,
    157–160
Chicano Scholars and Writers, 106
CIA World Factbook, 106
circular reasoning, 68
citations. *See also* APA (American
    Psychological Association);
    Chicago Manual of Style; CSE
    (Council of Science Editors);
    MLA (Modern Language
    Association)
    boundaries of, 154–155
    parenthetical, 151
    for research papers, 101
    rules for, 136–138
    Word 2007 to format, 300–301
citation-sequence and citation-name
    styles, CSE, 264–265
cite, site, sight, 552
cite while you write (CWYW)
    feature, 143–144, 167
City University of New York, 209,
    322–323
claims, in arguments, 55–58. *See also*
    thesis
classical works
    APA citation style for, 231
    Chicago Manual of Style style for,
        278–279
    MLA citation style for, 174
classification, 35
classrooms, virtual, 313–314
clauses
    adjective, 563*
    adverb, 563*
    although and *because* to begin, 538
    because, 403
    in complex sentences, 364–365
    condensed, 366
    conditional, 420–422, 565*
    connecting, 357–359
    definition of, 391, 564*
    dependent, 366, 393–394, 415, 566*

clauses (cont'd)
 direct quotations and, 468
 as fragments, 393–394
 independent, 392
 nonrestrictive, 455–456, 466
 relative, 453–458, 457–458
 restrictive, 455–456
 subjects in, 533
 when, 403
clichés, 376–377, 564*
close readings, 6
closing, in business letters, 337
clustering, 16
clutter, avoiding, 317
CNN.com, 123
code switchings, 120
collaborative writing, 23
collective nouns, 431, 564*
College Board, 125
*College Composition and
 Communication* (Shen), 22
college courses, writing in. *See
 writing in college courses*
colloquial expressions, 549
colons, 480–481, 492
color
 in document design, 295
 online, 9
 in PowerPoint slides, 347
 on Web sites, 316
Columbia Encyclopedia, 34, 105
*Columbia Guide to Standard American
 English*, 375
*Columbia-Lippincott Gazetteer of the
 World*, 106
Columbia World of Quotations, 106
columns, 295–296, 327
commands, statements to, 401
commas
 absolute phrases and, 469
 adjectives separated by, 468
 in conversation, 470
 coordinating conjunctions and, 465
 in dates, 469
 direct quotations and, 468–469
 explanatory insertions and, 467

introductory phrases and, 465
nonrestrictive phrases and,
 466–467
numbers and, 469
to prevent misreading, 469
in quotation marks, 475
in series of items, 467–468
transitional expressions and, 467
using, 462–465
comma splices, 396–398, 564*
Comment function, in word
 processing programs, 25
common ground, 65
common ground, finding, 7
common nouns, 520, 564*
*Communication Media in Higher
 Education: A Directory of
 Academic Programs and Faculty in
 Radio-Television-Film and Related
 Media*, 106
communities, online, 311–312. *See
 also* groups, online discussion
community service, 90–91
comparative adjectives and adverbs,
 388, 451–453, 564*
comparative line graphs, 304
compare to, compare with, 552
comparisons
 confusing, 399
 incomplete, 453
 in paragraphs, 35
 as prompts, 17
complement, compliment, 552
complement, of sentences, 390–391,
 564*
complete verbs, 392, 415, 564*
complex sentences, 364, 564*
component parts, analyzing, 34
compose, comprise, 553
compound adjectives, 449–450, 564*
compound-complex sentences, 365,
 564*
compound nouns, 497, 564*
compound objects, 436
compound predicate, 395, 403, 565*
compound sentences, 364, 403, 565*

compound subjects, 431, 436, 565*
compound words, 497
compression, of visuals, 302
computer tools, for editing, 42, 46
conclusions, 39–40, 67, 94
condensed clauses, 366
conditional clauses, 420–422, 565*
conditional sentences, 420–423
Conference on College Composition
    and Communication, 508
conference papers, APA style for, 250
conjunctions
    coordinating, 358, 465
    correlative, 405, 565*
    definition of, 389, 565*
    subordinating, 358, 572*
conjunctive adverbs, 450, 565*
connotations, 369–370, 565*
Connotes software, 144
conscience, conscious, 553
consonants, doubling, 500–501
constructions, mixed, 398–399, 568*
Contemporary Authors, 106
Contemporary Literary Criticism
    database, 107, 191
context links, 29
continual, continuous, 553
contractions, 472–473, 565*
contrasting, 29, 35
conventions, 8, 87, 100
conversations
    APA citation style for, 231
    APA reference list style for, 250
    MLA citation style for, 173
    online, 13–14
convoluted syntax, 399
coordinate adjectives, 468, 565*
coordinating conjunctions, 465, 565*
coordination of clauses, 357–359,
    565*
Copy and Paste function, 24, 42, 140
copyright regulations, 306–307. *See
    also* plagiarism
Cornell University, 128
corporations, citing, 170, 230,
    238–239

correlative conjunctions, 405, 565*
costume, custom, customs, 553
costumes, in plays, 85
could, 411, 527–529
could care less, 553
could of, 561
council, counsel, 553
Council of Science Editors (CSE). *See*
    CSE (Council of Science Editors)
countable nouns, 520, 565*
Countries of the World, 106
courses, in MLA list of works cited,
    199
cover letters, 334–335
CQ (Congressional Quarterly), 106
creative nonfiction, 5–8
creative writing, as genre, 4
credible, creditable, credulous, 553
Creole vernacular English, 517
criteria, criterion, 553
critical reading, 53, 126–127
critical thinking, 52
cross-references, 183
Crystal, David, 517
CSE (Council of Science Editors),
    262–272
    articles in reference list of, 266
    books in reference list of,
        265–266
    citation-sequence system of,
        156–157
    citation style of, 264
    documentation style of, 137
    electronic sources in reference list
        of, 266–268
    formatting guidelines of, 290
    reference list style of, 264–265
    sample paper in style of, 268–272
    style features of, 263–264
    visuals documentation style of,
        125
    Web site documentation style of,
        157–160
culture. *See* Language and Culture
    feature; writing across cultures
cumulative adjectives, 539, 566*

cumulative sentences, 365, 566*
curiosity, thesis to stimulate, 21
Current Index to Statistics, 106
curricula, curriculum, 553
custom, customs, costume, 553
cutting wordiness, 352–354
CWYW (cite while you write)
    feature. *See* cite while you write
    (CWYW) feature

daily journal, 13
dairy, diary, 553
dangling modifiers, 401, 566*
Dartmouth College, 92
dashes, 484–485
databases
    APA reference list style for,
        245–248
    Chicago Manual of Style style for,
        281
    CSE reference list style for, 267
    MLA citation style for, 191–193
    for record keeping, 143–145
    of scholarly journals, 128
    as sources, 112, 118–119
dates, 469, 496
debates, *Chicago Manual of Style* style
    for, 283
decease, disease, 553
decent, descent, dissent, 554
declarative sentences, 363
deductive organization, 31
deductive reasoning, 66
definitions, quotation marks with,
    476–477
demands, in sentences, 420–423
demonstrative pronouns, 434, 566*
denotation, 368–369, 566*
dependent clauses, 366, 393–394, 415,
    566*
descent, dissent, decent, 554
descriptions, as prompts, 17
descriptive adjectives, 388
desert, dessert, 554
design. *See* document design; Web
    site design

determiners. *See* articles (parts of
    speech)
device, devise, 554
diacritical marks, 503–504
dialects and dialogue, 372, 411, 476
dialup connections, to Internet, 9
diary, dairy, 553
dichotomy, false, 68
diction, 367–377, 566*
dictionaries, 106
    MLA citation style for, 171, 197
    for multilingual writers, 519
    for word choices, 368–369
Dictionary of American Biography, 105
Dictionary of Literary Biography, 106
different from, different than, 554
differ from, differ with, 554
difficult, easy, hard, 544
Digest of Education Statistics, 106
digital files, MLA documentation
    style for, 209
digital object identifier (DOI),
    244–246
dilemma, false, 68
direct objects, 534, 541, 566*
directories, 106, 111–112
Directory of Publishers and Vendors,
    130
direct questions, 536–537
direct quotations, 401–402, 566*
disabilities, 9
discreet, discrete, 554
discussion, in experimental papers,
    94
discussion groups. *See also* groups,
    online discussion
    APA citation style for, 231
    APA reference list style for,
        249–250
    CSE reference list style for,
        267–268
    in MLA list of works cited, 199
    as sources, 131
disease, decease, 553
disinterested, uninterested, 554
dissent, decent, descent, 554

dissertations, citing, 186–187, 240
Distinguishing Scholarly Journals from Other Periodicals Web site (Cornell University), 128
do, 411
do, due, 554
documentation, 101, 135. *See also* APA (American Psychological Association); *Chicago Manual of Style*; CSE (Council of Science Editors): MLA (Modern Language Association); sources, integrating and documenting
document design, 289–301
    academic writing online, 292–293
    color in, 295
    essay formatting for print, 289–292
    headings and columns in, 295–296
    lists in, 296
    typefaces in, 293–295
    Word features for, 296–301
Dogpile.com, 113
DOI (digital object identifier), 244–246
domain names, 131
double-entry journal, 13
double negatives, 450–451, 566*
doubling consonants, 500–501
drafting. *See also* editing; proofreading; revising
    annotations in, 46–49
    file names in, 42
    outlining and, 23–27
    reading aloud in, 42
    research papers, 101
    titles, 45
drag, dragged, 554
drama, 85
drown, drowned, 554
due, do, 554
due to the fact that, owing to the fact that, 554
Dunlap, David, 294
DVDs and DVD-ROM
    APA reference list style for, 251

Chicago Manual of Style style for, 282–283
CSE reference list style for, 268
MLA documentation style for, 203, 208–209
in presentations, 344

each, every, 429, 555
each other, one another, 555
easy, hard, difficult, 544
Ebony magazine, 129
e-books, 123, 282–283
EBSCO *Academic Search Premier*, 112
Economist, The, 128–129
-ed endings, 385, 417–418, 532–533
Edited American English (EAE), 386, 508, 566*
edited works, APA reference list style for, 238
editing. *See also* drafting; proofreading; revising; writing across cultures
    example of, 46–49
    overview of, 45–46
    research papers, 109–110
    run-on sentences and comma splices, 396–397
editions of books, MLA citation style for, 185
editorials
    APA reference list style for, 242–243, 248
    Chicago Manual of Style style for, 280
    MLA citation style for, 190, 196
editors
    Chicago Manual of Style style for, 277
    CSE reference list style for, 266
    in MLA lists of works cited, 182
.edu domain extensions, 131–132
effect, affect, 549
e.g., 555
ei or *ie*, 502
electronic presentations, 343

Elements of Style, The (Strunk and White), 361
elicit, illicit, 555
ellipsis dots, 151, 486–487, 566*
elude, allude, 550
e-mail. *See also* groups, online discussion
　APA citation style for, 231
　APA reference list style for, 250
　in business and academic settings, 308–309
　Chicago Manual of Style style for, 282
　discussion lists via, 309–312
　MLA citation style for, 173, 200
　in MLA list of works cited, 199
emigrate, immigrate, 555
eminent, imminent, 555
emotional appeals (*pathos*), 64
Encyclopaedia Britannica, 105
Encyclopedia of Religion, 91
Encyclopedia of Sociology, 91
encyclopedias, 92, 105, 171, 197
endings, of presentations, 340
endnotes and footnotes, 175–176, 274, 276
EndNote software, 143–144, 164, 166
end-of-line alignment, 327
end-of-line hyphens, 497
end punctuation, 392
Engineering Index, 107
English. *See also* dictionaries; writing across cultures
　American, 386–387, 406–409
　other languages *versus,* 507–510
　Standard, 45, 386–387
　vernacular, 517–518
English as a Second Language (ESL), 509–510
ensure, insure, assure, 551
envelopes, for business letters, 338
ERIC (Educational Resources Information Center), 107, 112, 131, 191
ESL (English as a Second Language), 509–510

essays
　arguments in, 53–55
　Chicago Manual of Style style for, 277–278
　everyday writing *versus,* 4–5
　in exams, 81–82
　formatting, 289–292
　organized by ideas, 146–147
　thesis in, 21
et al., in citations, 228
etc., 555
ethical appeals (*ethos*), 64
ethics, visuals manipulation and, 307
ethnic language, 371
ethnographic studies, 95
ethos (ethical appeals), 64
etymology, 368, 5668
euphemisms, 377, 566*
every, each, 429, 555
everybody, 432–433
everyday, every day, 555
everyday writing, 4–5
evidence, 61, 152
exact words, 369–370
examples, 17, 29, 31–32
exams, essays in, 81–82
Excel 2007, graphs created in, 303
except, expect, accept, 549
exclamation points, 475, 484
exclamatory sentences, 364
exclusionary language, 374–376
Expanded Academic ASAP, 112
expect, except, accept, 385, 549
experimental papers, 93
explanations, as transitions, 29
explanatory insertions, 467
explicit, implicit, 555
"Export to Bibliographic Manager" feature, 144
expressions, 376–377, 467
external hyperlinks, 293

Facebook, 4, 19–21
facts and statistics, 33
"fair use" principle, 135, 307

fallacies, logical, 55, 67–69
false dichotomy or dilemma, 68
farther, further, 555
faulty predication, 402, 566*
Favorites feature, 139
feedback, 43–45, 317–318
female, male, 555
few, a few, 543, 556
fewer, less, 433–434, 556
figurative language, 85–86, 367, 372–373, 566*
figures, APA style for, 232
filenames, conventions for, 42, 100
fillers, visuals used as, 302
filler subject, 355, 428, 545, 567*
films
    APA reference list style for, 250
    Chicago Manual of Style style for, 283
    MLA documentation style for, 205–206
"Find" feature, 42
first, firstly, 556
first person, 435, 567*
FirstSearch, 112
flammable, inflammable, nonflammable, 556
flaunt, flout, 556
Flickr.com, 125
flipcharts, 344
flout, flaunt, 556
flowcharts, 315
flyers, design of, 325–328
Follow the Money, 124
fonts
    for college essays, 290
    for flyers, brochures, and newsletters, 327
    options for, 299
    in PowerPoint slides, 347
    serif *versus* sans serif, 294
foot, in poetry, 85
footnotes. *See* endnotes and footnotes
Foreign Language Institute Center, University of Massachusetts, 504

forewords
    APA reference list style for, 239
    Chicago Manual of Style style for, 278
    MLA citation style for, 185
for example, 555
for instance, 555
formality, in language, 367
formal outlining, 25–27
formal writing, dialects and dialogue in, 372
formatting. *See also* document design
    documents, 299–301
    essay for print, 289–292
former, latter, 556
formulaic phrases, 353
forums, online discussion
    blogs, wikis, and virtual classrooms as, 312–314
    in business and academic settings, 308–309
    e-mail in, 309–312
fragments
    after *and, but,* or *or,* 395
    definition of, 567*
    as dependent clauses, 393–394
    intentional, 395
    phrase, 392–393
Freedom Tower, New York, 294
freewriting, 15
frequency adverbs, 449, 567*
further, farther, 555
fused sentences. *See* run-on sentences
Fussell, Paul, 15–16, 46

gazetteers, 106
Genamics JournalSeek database, 128
gender bias, 367, 374–375, 443, 567*
generalizations, 21, 43, 67
general-to-specific structure, 53–54
generic nouns, 441, 567*
genres, 4, 83, 177
George Mason University, 92
gerunds, 429, 531–532, 542, 567*
get married to, marry, 556

get used to, become used to, used to, 562
get used to, used to, be, 546
Globe, 129
go, say, 556
good, well, 556
Google Book Search, 116
Google.com
    advanced searches on, 116–118
    directories of, 12
    image searches on, 125
    "sponsored links" on, 113
GoogleDocs.com, 23, 45, 117
Google Earth, 116
Google Notebook, 117, 140
Google Reader Alerts, 116, 118
Google Scholar, 113, 116, 128
Gore, Al, 342
gossip, 130
Gotham typeface, 294
government publications, 106
    APA citation style for, 230
    APA reference list style for,
        238–239, 249
    Chicago Manual of Style style for,
        278, 282
    MLA citation style for, 198,
        200–201
    no author named for, 170
GPO Access, 106
grammar check programs, 46, 300,
    348, 385–386
graphic novels, MLA citation style
    for, 186
graphs
    in document design, 298
    in PowerPoint slides, 347
    types of, 303–306
"grasshopper prose," 29
grouping words, in searches, 115
groups, classification into, 35
groups, online discussion
    APA citation style for, 231
    APA reference list style for,
        249–250
    blogs, wikis, and virtual
        classrooms as, 312–314

in business and academic settings,
    308–309
CSE reference list style for,
    267–268
e-mail in, 309–312
evaluating, 124, 131
MLA list of works cited style for,
    199

had better, 556
Handbook of Labor Statistics, 106
handouts, in presentations, 344
hard, difficult, easy, 544
hardly, 556
have, 411, 530–531
have, of, 556
Hayden, Theresa Neilson, 386
headers and footers, 297–298
headings, 232, 295–296, 308
health and wellness, language of,
    376
height, 556
helping verbs, 388, 412–413, 564*
her, his, 545
heroin, heroine, 557
her or *hers*, 438–439
highlighting, for source tracking,
    140
his, her, 545
hisself, 557
hopefully, 557
however, 450
Huffington Post blog, 312
human beings, 559
humanities, writing on, 92
humanity, 559
humankind, 559
Hunter College, City University of
    New York, 209
hyperlinks, 124, 293
hyphens, 496–498
hypothesis, for research papers,
    101

I, me, 10, 557
IBM's Many Eyes project, 72

ideas, organizing by, 146–147
identification, 291–292, 302
identity. *See* Language and Culture
  feature
idiomatic expressions, 540–542
ie or *ei*, 502
if, 415
illicit, elicit, 555
illusion, allusion, 550
images. *See also* visuals
  bleeding, 328
  critically reading, 5–8
  in prose, 84
  screened, 327
  on Web sites, 69, 315
"imagination economy," 64
immigrate, emigrate, 555
imminent, eminent, 555
immoral, amoral, 550
imperative sentences, 364, 567*
implicit, explicit, 555
imply, infer, 557
in, 539
Inconvenient Truth, An (Gore), 342
incredible, incredulous, 557
indefinite pronouns, 432–433, 441,
  567*
indentation
  in APA reference list, 233
  in *Chicago Manual of Style* style, 276
  in MLA list of works cited, 176
independent clauses, 365–366, 392,
  567*
indexes, 107, 122
indicative mood, 365, 567*
indirect objects, 534, 567*
indirect questions, 536–537, 567*
indirect quotations, 401–402,
  535–536, 567*
inductive reasoning, 66–67
infamous, 557
infer, imply, 557
infinitive phrases, 392, 429, 568*
infinitives, 529–532, 568*
inflammable, flammable, nonflammable,
  556

inflected form of verbs, 411
INFOMINE (University of California,
  Riverside), 111
Information Please, 105
InfoTrac College Edition, 112–113
InfoTrac database, 130, 191
-ing verb form, 531–532, 542
in regard to, as regards, 557
"Insert Comment" feature, 42
insertions, explanatory, 467
inside address, in business letters,
  337
insure, assure, ensure, 551
intensive pronouns, 444–445, 568*
intentional fragments, 395
intentions, references to, 353
interjections, 389, 563*
internal hyperlinks, 293
*International Accents and Diacriticals:
  Theory, Charts, and Tips* (Starr),
  504
International Medieval Bibliography,
  105
Internet, 9, 12, 13, 250. *See also* Web
  sites
Internet Archive, The, 112, 123
Internet Encyclopedia of Philosophy,
  105
Internet Public Library, 111
interpretive material, MLA
  documentation style for, 205
Interreligious Council of Central
  New York, 318–319
interrogative pronouns, 445–446,
  563*
interrogative sentences, 363–364
interviews
  APA citation style for, 231
  APA reference list style for, 241,
    250
  Chicago Manual of Style style for,
    283
  MLA citation style for, 173
  MLA documentation style for,
    207
  for research papers, 104

intransitive verbs, 410, 568*
introductions
   APA reference list style for, 239
   Chicago Manual of Style style for, 278
   commas and, 465
   MLA citation style for, 185
   of source materials, 155–156
   writing, 36–39
Intute database, 112
inverted word order, 429, 568*
-i or *-y* as verb endings, 501–502
irregardless, 557
irregular verbs, 406–409, 568*
is because, 402–403
ISI Web of Science database, 112
isle, aisle, 549
ISTOR database, 191
is when, 402–403
it, 355, 429
it, there, as sentence beginning, 544–545
italicizing
   in APA reference list, 233
   in MLA list of works cited, 177
   online, 499
   quotation marks *versus*, 477
   titles, 87
   when to use and when not to use, 488–489
items in series, 467–468
it's, its, 473, 558

Jane's Space Directory, 106
jargon, 372
journalists' questions, 17
journals, 10, 13–14. *See also* articles (published works); scholarly journals
JournalSeek database, 128
JSTOR databases, 112, 118

key words
   defining, 17, 33–34
   searching by, 113–116
kind, sort, type, 558

kind of, sort of, 558
knew, new, 558
Kornberg, Mara Lee, 58

LaGuardia Community College, City University of New York, 322–323
language
   biased, 367
   figurative, 85–86, 367, 372–373, 566*
   formality in, 367
   in literature, 84
   natural, 340
   pretentious, 376–377
   sexist, biased, and exclusionary, 374–376
   speech, region, and workplace, 370–372
   stuffy, 377
Language and Culture feature. *See also* writing across cultures
   academic discipline cultures, 91
   and or *but* to begin sentences, 360
   arguments, 58, 61
   be, dialect forms of, 411
   business letters, 335–336
   dialect and dialogue, 372
   identity and thesis statement, 22
   I in academic writing, 10
   ownership rights, 135
   reader expectations, 9
   style, 351
   subject-verb agreement, 426
Latin terms, 494
latter, former, 556
lay, lie, 410, 558
Learning Web Design: A Beginner's Guide to HTML, Style Sheets, and Graphics (Robbins), 318
lectures, citation style for, 173, 207–208, 283
legal documents, citation style for, 174–175, 208
lend, loan, 558

less, fewer, 556
let, 530–531
letters, capital, 392
letters (documents)
    APA citation style for, 231
    APA reference list style for, 248,
      250
    business, 335–338
    Chicago Manual of Style style for,
      277–278
    cover, 334–335
    to the editor, 190, 280
    as everyday writing, 4–5
    memos, 338
    MLA citation style for, 173, 196
    MLA documentation style for,
      208
LexisNexis database, 112–113, 118,
    123, 130, 191
liable, likely, 558
Librarians' Index to the Internet, The,
    12, 112, 123
Library of Congress, 112, 120–121
Library of Congress Subject Headings,
    12, 120
LibWeb, 120
lie, lay, 410, 558
lighting, in plays, 85
like, 551
like, as, as if, 558
likely, liable, 558
line graphs, 303–304
line length, 327
line spacing, 290
linguistic conventions, 8
linking verbs, 428, 448, 568*
links, in writing, 29–31, 293
listening cues, 339
list of works cited, MLA style, 166,
    176–209
    authors in, 178–179
    books and pamphlets in,
      179–187
    databases in, 191–193
    example of, 209–220
    in online posts, 293

    organization of, 176–178
    periodicals in, 187–191
    visual, performance, multimedia,
      and miscellaneous sources in,
      201–209
    Web sites in, 194–201
Listproc software, 310
lists, 4–5, 296
LISTSERV software, 310
literally, 558
Literary Market Place, 130
literature
    MLA citation style for, 173–175
    overview of, 82–87
    writing on, 87–90
live performances, citation style for,
    203, 206–207
Lives of the Painters, 106
loaded terms, 57
loan, lend, 558
logical fallacies, 55, 67–69
logical reasoning, 66–67
logos (rational appeals), 63–64
loose, lose, 558
Los Angeles Times, 130
lots of, a lot of, alot, 550
LP records, citation style for, 202
lurking, on discussion lists, 311
lyrics, citation style for, 202–203

magazines
    APA reference list style for,
      240–241
    Chicago Manual of Style style for,
      279–281
    CSE reference list style for, 266
    MLA citation style for, 187, 195
    online, 123
mailing lists, citation style for, 199,
    249
Majordomo software, 310
make, 530–531
Making Book (Hayden), 386
male, female, 555
man, mankind, 559
manipulation of visuals, 307

many, 433–434

Many Eyes project, IBM, 72

mapping, 16

maps, citation style for, 205

margins, on documents, 290, 337

marital, martial, 559

marry, get married to, 556

martial, marital, 559

may, 411, 527–529

may be, maybe, 559

me, I, 557

media

  CSE reference list style for, 268

  documenting across, 201–203

  writing, 11

media, medium, 559

memos, 338

men and women, 559

mental activity verbs, 414, 568*

messages, online, 4–5

MetaCrawler.com, 113

metaphor, 85, 373, 568*

meta-search engines, 113

meter, in poetry, 84–85

method, in experimental papers, 93

metonymy, 86

Michigan Electronic Library (MeL.,
  University of Michigan), 111

microform, articles on, 190–191

might, 411, 527–529

might of, 561

mine, 434, 438–439

misplaced modifiers, 399–401, 568*

mixed constructions, 398–399, 568*

mixed metaphor, 373

*MLA Handbook for Writers of Research
  Papers,* 164, 175, 209

*MLA International Bibliography of
  Books and Articles on the Modern
  Languages and Literature,* 105,
  112

MLA (Modern Language
  Association)

  author/page style of, 167–170

  authors in list of works cited,
    178–179

  books in list of works cited,
    179–187

  documentation style of, 92, 137,
    156–157

  endnotes and footnotes style of,
    175–176

  final draft format of, 88

  formatting guidelines of, 290

  identification format of, 46

  list of works cited organization,
    176–178

  literary works citation style of,
    173–175

  multimedia citation style of, 172

  no author named style of,
    170–172

  online databases in list of works
    cited, 191–193

  periodicals in list of works cited,
    187–191

  personal communication, lecture,
    and speech style of, 173

  quotation citing style of, 150,
    153

  research paper example, 209–220

  style features of, 165–167

  visuals, performance, multimedia,
    and miscellaneous sources in
    list of works cited, 201–209

  visuals documentation style of,
    125, 137

  Web site documentation style of,
    142, 157–160

  Web sites in list of works cited,
    194–201

modal auxiliary verbs, 527–529,
  568*

modal verbs, 411

modifiers

  dangling, 401

  definition of, 569*

  misplaced, 399–401

money, 430

mood, 420–422, 569*

most, almost, 550

most, most of, the most, 544

MP3 files
  APA reference list style for, 250–251
  Chicago Manual of Style style for, 283
  MLA documentation style for, 202
much, 433–434
Multilingual Writing feature. *See also* writing across cultures
  adverb placement, 449
  be, *been*, and *being*, 413
  -ed endings, 418
  grammar check programs, 46
  numbers, 495
  passive voice, 424
  plural form for adjectives, 446
  progressive tenses, 414
  relative *versus* personal pronouns, 456
  verbs after *it*, 429
  will, 415
multimedia
  APA citation style for, 230
  APA reference list style for, 250–251
  Chicago Manual of Style style for, 282–283
  MLA citation style for, 172, 201–209
  presentations using, 342–345
multimedia arguments, 72–73
multivolume work, citation style for, 184
multivolume works
  APA citation style for, 231
  APA reference list style for, 239
  Chicago Manual of Style style for, 279
  MLA citation style for, 172–173
museum interpretive material, citation style for, 205
music, in plays, 85
must, 411, 527–529
my, 438–439
myself, 559
MySpace, 20–21

names, capitalizing, 491–492
names of authors, citation style for, 165
narrative devices, 84
narrators, 84, 87
Nation, The, 129
National Enquirer, 129
National Telecommunications and Information Administration, 125
natural language, 340
natural sciences, writing on, 92–95
navigation, Web site, 317
nearly all, 544
negatives, double, 450–451
neither, 432–433
new, *knew*, 558
New Books on Women and Feminism, 105
Newsbank, 106
newsgroups, citation style for, 249
newsletters, design of, 325–328
newspapers
  APA reference list style for, 241, 248
  Chicago Manual of Style style for, 280, 282
  CSE reference list style for, 266
  MLA citation style for, 188, 193, 195
news sites, online, 123
Newsweek magazine, 128, 129
New Yorker magazine, 71
New York Public Library, 120
New York Review of Books, 129
New York Times, 71, 123, 130, 148, 294, 312
New York Times Magazine, 63–64
New York Times Manual of Style and Usage, 380
no, *not*, 400, 542–543, 559
nobody, 432–433
none, 432–433
nonfiction, creative, 5–8
nonflammable, *flammable*, *inflammable*, 556

nonprint sources, citation style for, 230–231
nonrestrictive clauses, 455–456, 569*
nonrestrictive phrases, 466–467, 569*
non sequitors, 67
nonstandard words, 549
nor, 431–432, 442
notes, citation style for, 232, 274–275
note taking, 100, 145–146
noun clauses, 391, 569*
noun phrases, 391, 569*
nouns
  articles and, 526–527
  collective, 431
  compound, 497, 564*
  definition of, 387, 569*
  generic, 441, 567*
  infinitives after, 530–531
  plural, 472–473, 499–500
  preposition and *-ing* verb form as, 542
  proper, 490–491
  uncountable, 430–431
  verbs as, 531
  in writing across cultures, 515–516, 520–522, 525–526
novels, citation style for, 173
nowadays, 559
nowhere, nowheres, 551
NPR (National Public Radio), 54
number, amount, 550
number of, a number of, 430
numbers
  abbreviations with, 493
  Chicago Manual of Style style for, 276
  commas in, 469
  in document design, 300
  hyphens in, 497
  spelling out, 495
  in time and dates, 496
number (singular or plural), 435, 569*

objects
  compound, 436

  direct and indirect, 534
  order of, 533–534
  phrasal verbs and, 541
  of prepositions, 430, 541, 569*
Occupational Outlook Handbook, 106
of, have, 556
off, off of, 559
oftentimes, 559
OK, O.K., okay, 559
omitted words, 403–404
on, 540
one another, each other, 555
one of, 430
online communities, 311–312. *See also* groups, online discussion
online conversations, 13–14
online magazines, 123
online messages, 4–5, 497–499
online sources
  APA reference list style for, 234, 243–249
  Chicago Manual of Style style for, 276, 280–282
  CSE reference list style for, 266–268
only, 400
onomatopoeia, 86
open-access databases, 119
Open Office word processing software, 296
opposing views, in arguments, 54, 65–66
or, 395, 431–432, 442
oral presentations, 339–342, 344
organizations, citing, 170, 230, 238–239
organizing by ideas, 146–147
ours, 434
outlining
  arguments, 59–60
  drafting and, 23–27
  in essay exams, 82
owing to the fact that, 554
ownership, -s' for, 471–472
ownership rights, 135. *See also* plagiarism
Oxford Companion, 107

Oxford English Dictionary (OED), 106, 368
Oxford ESL Dictionary for Students of American English, 519
Oxford Text Archive, 112
oxymoron, 86

page numbers
    in APA reference list, 234
    for business letters, 337
    for college essays, 290
    in MLA citation style, 165
    in MLA list of works cited, 177, 191
paired conjunctions, 405
PAIS database, 112
pamphlets, 235–240
papers, conference, 250
paper type, 290
paragraphs, 27–40
    for college essays, 290
    conclusions as, 39–40
    connections between, 360–361
    definition of, 569*
    examples of, 31–36
    introductions as, 36–39
    in online posts, 293
    topic sentences in, 28–29
    transitions and links in, 29–31
    unified, 28–29
parallel sentence structure, 404–405, 569*
paraphrasing
    APA citation style for, 227
    in note-taking, 100
    sources, 147–150
parentheses, 485
    in APA citation style, 227
    in MLA citation style, 167
    in source citations, 291
parenthetical citations, 151
Parents magazine, 129
participle phrases, 466, 569*
participles, 366, 406–409
particles (phrasal verbs), 540–542, 569*

parts of speech, 387–389, 569*
passed, past, 559
passive voice
    avoidance of, 355–356
    definition of, 570*
    in social sciences writing, 96
    using, 423–425
past participles, 406–409, 570*
past tense, 416–418
pathos (emotional appeals), 64
patterns, on Web sites, 316
PDF print sources, 247
peak, peek, pique, 385, 559–560
Penn State University, 322
pentameter, in poetry, 85
people, 559
perfect progressive tenses, 413–414, 570*
perfect tense forms, 413–414, 570*
performances, citation style for, 201–209
periodicals
    APA reference list style for, 240–243
    MLA citation style for, 187–191
periodic sentences, 365, 570*
periods, 475, 482–483
personal, personnel, 560
personal communication
    APA citation style for, 231
    APA reference list style for, 250
    Chicago Manual of Style style for, 282
    MLA citation style for, 173, 200
    MLA documentation style for, 208
personal presence, 361
personal pronouns, 435–438, 456, 570*
personification, 86
persuasion, arguments and, 52
persuasive writing, 8
phenomena, phenomenon, 560
photographs
    APA reference list style for, 251
    Chicago Manual of Style style for, 283

photographs (cont'd)
  MLA documentation style for,
    203–204
phrasal verbs, 540–542, 570*
phrases
  absolute, 469, 563*
  appositive, 466
  definition of, 391, 570*
  formulaic, 353
  as fragments, 392–393
  infinitive, 392, 429, 568*
  introductory, 465
  misplaced modifiers in,
    399–400
  nonrestrictive, 466–467
  participle, 466
  prepositional, 367
  redundant, 353–354
  of time, money, and weight,
    430
  verb, 388, 573*
pie charts, 305
Pink, Daniel, 64
pique, peek, peak, 559–560
plagiarism, 133–145
  avoidance of, 135–136
  citation rules and, 136–138
  multilingual writers and, 519
  paraphrasing to avoid, 149
  passage on, 145
  penalties for, 24
  "seven sins" of, 134–135
  source tracking and, 138–140
  on Web sites, 317
  Word 2007 and database software
    to avoid, 143–145
  working bibliography and,
    140–143
plays, citation style for, 174
Plessy v. Ferguson, 57
plot, in plays, 85
plural nouns, 472–473, 499–500
plural pronouns, 435
plus, 560
podcasts, citation style for, 207,
  250

poetry
  Chicago Manual of Style style for,
    277–278
  description of, 84–85
  MLA citation style for, 173
  in MLA list of works cited, 198
point of view, 83, 402, 443–444
Political Science Bibliographies, 105
politics, language of, 375–376
Population Index, 106
pore, pour, 560
portfolios
  electronic, 321–324
  example of, 323–324
  hard copy, 320–321
possession, *-s'* for, 471–472
possessive pronouns, 438–439, 545,
    570*
poster sessions, conference, citation
    style for, 250
PowerPoint software, 345–348
precede, proceed, 560
predicate
  compound, 395, 403, 565*
  definition of, 570*
  mismatched with subjects, 402
  subject and, 390
predication, faulty, 402, 566*
prefaces
  APA reference list style for, 239
  Chicago Manual of Style style for, 278
  MLA citation style for, 185
prefixes, hyphens with, 496, 570*
prejudice, prejudiced, 560
prepositional phrases, 367, 571*
prepositions, 457
  definition of, 389, 570*
  objects of, 430
  uses of, 539–542
presence, personal, 361
presentations
  APA reference list style for, 251
  multimedia, 342–345
  oral, 339–342
  in plays, 85
  PowerPoint software for, 345–348

Presentation Zen Web site (Reynolds), 345
present participle, 406–409, 532–533, 571*
present progressive tense, 420–423
present tense. 414–416
pretentious language, 376–377
pretty, 560
primary sources, 104–105
principal, principle, 560
printing college essays, 290
print sources
    CSE reference list style for, 266–267
    evaluating, 129–130
    searching, 120–123
proceed, precede, 560
proceedings, conference, citation style for. 250
ProCite software, 144
progressive tenses, 413–414, 420–423, 571*
Project Bartleby, 112, 123
Project Gutenberg, 112, 123
Project Muse database, 191
prompts for writing topics, 17–18
pronoun reference, 439–440, 571*
pronouns
    antecedents to, 439–442
    definition of, 387–388, 571*
    demonstrative, 434, 566*
    indefinite, 432–433, 441, 567*
    infinitives after, 530–531
    intensive, 444–445
    interrogative, 445–446, 568*
    personal, 435–438, 456
    point of view of, 402
    possessive, 438–439, 545
    reflexive, 444–445
    relative, 453–458, 456–457
    unnecessary, 538–539
    in writing across cultures, 515–516
proofreading, 50. *See also* drafting; editing; revising

propaganda, 130
proper nouns and adjectives, 490–491, 520, 526–527, 571*
proposals, for research papers, 108–109
props, in plays, 85
prose, writing about. 84
Psychology Today, 129
PsycINFO database, 112
Public Agenda Online, 124
publication medium, citation style for, 178
publisher's imprint, 185
publishing information, citation style for, 276
punctuation. *See* apostrophes; brackets; colons: commas; dashes; ellipsis dots; exclamation points; parentheses; periods; question marks; quotation marks; semicolons; URLs (Uniform Resource Locators)
purpose statement, 108–109

quantity words, 433–434, 571*
question, research, 100, 107–108
question marks, 475, 483
questionnaires, 104
questions, 434–435, 536–538
quite, quiet, 560
quotation marks, 474–478
quotations
    APA citation style for, 231
    capitalizing, 492
    Chicago Manual of Style style for, 276, 278
    commas to set off, 468–469
    dictionaries of, 106
    direct and indirect, 401–402, 534–536
    to integrate and document sources, 150–154
    integrating, 87
    MLA citation style for, 175

quotations (cont'd)
  qtd. in references for, 169
  tenses in, 419–420
quote, quotation, 560

radio programs, citation style for,
    206, 250
raise, rise, 561
rational appeals (*logos*), 63–64
readability, 308, 326
readers
  appeals to, 63–65
  expectations of, 9
  writing for, 3–4
Readers' Guide to Periodical Literature,
    107, 112, 118
reading
  aloud, 42
  commas to prevent misreading
    in, 469
  critically, 5–8, 53, 126–127
  responding to, 17–18
readings, documentation style for,
    207–208
real, really, 560
reasoning, logical, 66–67
reason is because, 560
reasons, arguments supported by,
    59–60
recommendations, 94, 420–423
recordings
  APA reference list style for,
    250
  Chicago Manual of Style style for,
    283
  MLA documentation style for,
    206–207
  in presentations, 344
redundant words, 353–354
reference list, APA style
  authors in, 234–235
  books and pamphlets in, 235–240
  in online posts, 293
  online sources in, 243–249
  overview of, 225, 232–234
  periodicals in, 240–243

visual, multimedia, and
    miscellaneous sources in,
    250–251
reference list, CSE style
  articles in, 266
  books in, 265–266
  online sources in, 266–268
  overview of, 264–265
references
  APA reference list style for, 238,
    249
  books as, 183
  Chicago Manual of Style style for,
    276, 278, 281
  in experimental papers, 94
  to intentions, 353
  MLA citation style for, 197
  types of, 105–107, 111
reflective reports, 90
reflexive pronouns, 444–445, 571*
Refugee Resettlement Program,
    Interreligious Council of Central
    New York, 318–319
RefWorks software, 144, 164, 166
regardless, 560
regional language, 370–372
regular verbs, 406, 571*
relative clauses, 453–458, 466, 571*
relative pronouns, 456–457, 571*
religious works, 231, 376
repetition, 340, 352–354
reports, 4–5
reprinted works, citation style for,
    239
republished books, citation style for,
    185
reputation, of publications, 130
requests, in sentences, 420–423
research papers, 99–110
  components of, 99–102
  everyday writing *versus,* 4–5
  in MLA style, 209–220
  primary and secondary sources
    for, 104–105
  proposals for, 108–109
  reference works for, 105–107

research question to working thesis for, 107–108
revising and editing, 109–110
schedule for, 102–103
writing, 91–92, 109–110
Research Quickstart (University of Minnesota), 111
respectable, respectful, respective, 561
respectfully, respectively, 561
restrictive clauses, 455–456, 571*
results, writing about, 29, 94
résumés
    example of, 331, 333
    scannable, 332
    writing, 329–330
return address, in business letters, 337
reversed type, 327
reviews, citation style for, 196, 241, 248
revised works, citation style for, 239
revising, 40–49. *See also* drafting; editing; proofreading
    big-picture and little-picture concerns in, 41–42
    example of, 46–49
    feedback for, 43–45
    research papers, 100, 109–110
    strategies for, 42–43
    for style, 378–379
    titles, 45
Reynolds, Garr, 345
rhetorical conventions, 8
rhyme scheme, in poetry, 84
rhythm, in writing style, 380
rise, raise, 410, 561
Robbins, Jennifer Niederst, 318
RSS (Really Simply Syndication), 118
rules (printed lines), 327
run-on sentences, 396–398, 571*

-s
    in plural abbreviations, 494
    in plural numerals, 496
    as verb ending, 425–427
-'s, possession as, 471–473

sacred texts, citation style for, 174, 186, 231
sale, sell, 561
salutations, 309, 337
San Diego State University, 10
San Francisco Bay Bird Observatory, 124
sans serif fonts, 294
sarcasm, 65
say, go, 556
scenery, in plays, 85
schedule, writing, 24, 99, 102–103
scholarly journals, 10
    APA reference list style for, 240–241
    Chicago Manual of Style style for, 279, 281
    CSE reference list style for, 266–267
    databases of, 128
    evaluating articles of, 127–128
    MLA citation style for, 187–189, 192–193
    in MLA list of works cited, 178, 195, 198
    online, 123
ScienceDirect database, 112
sciences, writing on, 92–95
Scientific American, 129
scientific journals, visuals manipulation and, 307
Scientific Style and Format: The CSE Manual for Authors, Editors, and Publishers (Council of Science Editors), 262–272
scientific writing, 10, 423, 495
Scott, A. O., 342
scratch outlines, 59–60, 82
scratch outlining, 25–26
screened backgrounds, 327
sculptures, citation style for, 278–279
search engines, 113–116. *See also* specific named search engines
secondary sources, 92, 104–105, 229
second person, 435, 572*
Secrets of Successful Speakers (Walters), 342

seem, 428
sell, sale, 561
semicolons, 358, 478–479
-*s* endings, 385, 425–427
sensationalism, 130
senses, details appealing to, 32–33
sentences
  adjectives after linking verbs in,
    448
  adjectives and adverb forms in,
    446–448
  and or *but* to start, 359–360
  antecedents to pronouns in,
    439–442
  auxiliary verbs in, 412–413
  basics of, 392
  because and *when* clauses as
    subjects of, 403
  capitalizing first letter of, 489–490
  comma splices and run-on,
    396–398
  comparative and superlative
    adjectives and adverbs in,
    451–453
  compound adjectives in, 449–450
  conditional, 420–423
  confusing comparisons in, 399
  conjunctive adverbs in, 450
  convoluted syntax in, 399
  dangling modifiers in, 401
  definitions and reasons in, 402–403
  dependent clause fragments
    versus, 393–394
  double negatives in, 450–451
  fragments after *and, but,* or *or,* 395
  gender bias in, 444
  grammar check programs for,
    385–386
  incomplete comparisons in, 453
  intensive and reflexive pronouns
    in, 444–445
  intentional fragments of, 395
  mismatched subjects and
    predicates in, 402
  misplaced modifiers in, 399–401
  mixed constructions in, 398–399

numbers to begin, 495
omitted words in, 403–404
parts of, 387–391
passive voice in, 423–425
periods to end, 482–483
personal pronoun forms in,
  435–438
phrase fragments *versus,* 392–393
point of view in, 443–444
possessive pronoun forms in,
  438–439
questions about, 383–384
relative clauses and pronouns in,
  453–458
shifts in, 401–402
Standard English *versus* American
  English in, 386–387
subject-verb agreement in, 425–435
there or *it* to begin, 355, 544–545
topic, 28–29
unparallel structures in, 404–405
variety in, 363–367
verb forms in, 406–409
verbs confused in, 410–411
verbs in conditional, 420–422
verb tenses in, 413–420
who/whom, whoever/whomever in,
  445–446
word order in, 533–539
you in, 444
sequential references, citation style
  for, 169
serif fonts, 294
service learning projects, 90
Seton Hill University, 13
setting, 83, 85
"seven sins" of plagiarism, 134–135
sexist language, 374–376
sexual orientation, language of, 376
shall, 411, 527–529
shifts
  definition of, 572*
  in sentences, 401–402
  in tenses, 418–419
short-answer tests, writing in, 81–82
should, 411, 527–529

should of, 561
sidebars, 327
sight, cite, site, 552
signature, in business letters, 337
signing off, in e-mail, 309
similes, 85, 373, 572*
simple line graphs, 303
simple sentences, 364
simple tenses, 413–416, 572*
since, 561
singular pronouns, 435
singular verbs, 429–431
SIRS (Social Issues Resources Series),
    106, 118
sit, set, 410
site, sight, cite, 552
site maps, 315
slang, 519
slashes, 486
slides, for presentations, 344
Smithsonian Institution Libraries, 120
Social Explorer database, 112
social networking sites, 19–21
social sciences, writing on, 95–96
Sociology Collection database, 112
software, citation style for, 251
Soling Program, Syracuse
    University, 318
some, 433–434, 543
sometimes, sometime, some time, 561
somewhat, 558
sort, type, kind, 558
sort of, kind of, 558
sound recordings
    Chicago Manual of Style style for,
        283
    MLA documentation style for,
        206–207
    in presentations, 344
sources, 110–126
    advanced searches and alerts for,
        116–118
    databases of, 118–119
    documenting, 101
    for humanities and arts papers, 92
    print, 120–123

for research papers, 104–105
searching for, 111–116
tracking, 138–140
visual, 124–125
Web, 123–124
sources, evaluating, 126–133
    critical reading for, 126–127
    print, 129–130
    scholarly articles, 127–128
    Web, 130–133
sources, integrating and
        documenting, 145–160
    annotating for, 145–146
    citation boundaries for, 154–155
    discipline requirements for,
        156–157
    introductions for, 155–156
    organizing by ideas for, 146–147
    quotations for, 150–154
    summarizing and paraphrasing
        for, 147–150
    synthesizing for, 146
    systems for, 157–160
spacing, line, 290, 327
spam, 309
special effects, in plays, 85
specific-to-general structure, 54–55
speeches
    Chicago Manual of Style style for,
        283
    language of, 370–372
    manuscript for, 341
    MLA citation style for, 173
    MLA documentation style for,
        207–208
    notes for, 340–341
spelling, 499–504
    accents, umlauts, tildes, and
        cedillas, 503–504
    doubling consonants, 500–501
    ie or *ei,* 502
    plurals of nouns, 499–500
    suffixes, 502–503
    -y or *-i* as verb endings, 501–502
spelling checkers, 46, 300, 308, 348
split infinitives, 400–401, 572*

"sponsored links," on search
   engines, 113
square brackets, 485–486
stage directions, in plays, 85
stance, as style, 362–363
Standard English, 45, 386–387, 572*
stanzas, in poetry, 84
Star, 129
Starr, Irene, 504
statements to commands, 401
stationary, stationery, 561
Statistical Abstract of the United States,
   106
statistics, 33, 106
stereotyping, 375
Stories of English, The (Crystal), 517
structure
   cause-and-effect, 55
   general-to-specific, 53–54
   in literature, 83
   of oral presentations, 340
   of plays, 85
   specific-to-general, 54–55
   unparallel sentence, 404–405
   Web site, 315
Strunk, William, Jr., 361
style, 350–380. *See also* APA
   (American Psychological
   Association); *Chicago Manual of
   Style;* CSE (Council of Science
   Editors); MLA (Modern
   Language Association)
   and or *but* to start sentences,
      359–360
   connotations, 369–370
   consistent subjects, 356–357
   cutting, 352–354
   dictionary and thesaurus, 368–369
   figurative language, 372–373
   formatting for, 297
   logical connections, 357–359
   paragraph connections, 360–361
   passive voice avoidance, 355–356
   personal presence, 361
   in prose, 84
   revising for, 378–379

sentence variety, 363–367
sexist, biased, and exclusionary
   language, 374–376
speech, region, and workplace
   language, 370–372
stance, 362–363
subjects and verbs, 354–355
tips for, 380
tired expressions and pretentious
   language, 376–377
tone, 361–362
word choices, 367–368
subjects
   in clauses, 533
   compound, 431, 436, 565*
   consistent, 356–357
   definition of, 572*
   as e-mail headings, 308
   filler, 355, 428, 545, 567*
   order of, 533–534
   predicates and, 390, 402
   searches for, 120
   in sentences, 392
   unnecessary to restate, 404
   verbs connected to, 354–355
subject-verb agreement, 425–435
   and, or, or *nor* in subject and,
      431–432
   collective nouns and, 431
   if subject follows verb, 428–429
   for indefinite pronouns, 432–433
   in independent clauses, 392
   for linking verbs, 428
   for quantity words, 433–434
   -s endings for, 425–427
   singular verbs and, 429–431
   with *this, that, these, those, mine,
      ours,* 434
   with *what* and other question
      words, 434–435
   words between, 427
subjunctive mood, 421–422, 572*
subordinate clauses, 357–359, 572*
subordinating conjunctions, 358,
   572*
subscription databases, 112

subsequent references, citation style for, 275
suffixes, 502–503, 572*
summarizing
   news, 106
   sources, 147–150
   as transition, 29
superlative adjectives and adverbs, 388, 451–453, 572*
supposedly, 561
surveys, 104
sweeping generalizations, 67
symbols, 84
synecdoche, 86
synonyms, 572*
syntax, convoluted, 399
synthesizing sources, 146
Syracuse University, 318

table of contents, 93, 293
tables
   citation style for, 232
   in experimental papers, 94
   inserting, 298–299
   as visuals, 302
take, bring, 552
taught, thought, 561
technical reports, citation style for, 240
technical writing, 495
Tech Note feature
   accessibility and disabilities, 9
   annotated bibliographies, 142–143
   collaborative writing, 23
   Comment and AutoCorrect, 25
   editing, computer tools for, 46
   electronic portfolios, 322
   ESL (English as a Second Language), 510
   GoogleDocs, 45
   journal databases, 128
   logical fallacies, 69
   multimedia presentations, 345
   online lists of works cited, 178
   revising, computer tools for, 42

there and *it*, searching for, 355
track changes feature, 45
visualization tools, 72
Web directories, 12
Web site design, 318
Wikipedia, 105
Word 2007 to 2003 converter, 297
Writing Across the Curriculum Web sites, 92
writing in other languages, 504
www.betterwhois.com, 131
telephone conversations, citation style for, 250
television programs, citation style for, 206, 250
templates, 297, 325, 338
tenses
   in conditional sentences, 420–423
   definition of, 572–573*
   in indirect quotations, 419–420
   past, 416–418
   present, 414–416
   shifts in, 418–419
   in writing about literature, 87
tests, writing in, 81–82
tetrameter, in poetry, 84
text, Web site, 315
than, then, 561
that, 453–456
the, 388, 523–526
their, there, they're, 561–562
theirself, theirselves, themself, 562
theme, in literature, 83
the most, most of, most, 544
themselves, 562
then, than, 385, 561
there, it, 355, 544–545
there, they're, their, 561–562
therefore, 450
thesaurus, 46, 368–369
these, 434
thesis. *See also* arguments
   presentation of, 18–22
   for research papers, 101, 107–108
   for writing about literature, 82
thinking critically, 5, 52

third person, 435, 573*
this, that, these, those, 434
thought, taught, 561
threat, treat, 562
thusly, 562
tildes, 503–504
time, 85, 415, 430, 496
Time magazine, 128, 129
Times New Roman font, 294
tired expressions, 376–377
titles
  abbreviating, 493
  in APA reference list, 233
  capitalizing, 491–492
  Chicago Manual of Style style for, 276
  for college essays, 291–292
  of experimental papers, 93
  italicizing, 488
  quotation marks with, 476–478
  revising, 45
  singular verbs with, 430
  underline or italicize, 87
to, too, two, 562
tone
  in literature, 83
  as style, 361–362
  Web site, 314
too, very, 543
topic chain, 356, 424, 573*
topics, 11–18
  for arguments, 55–58
  assigned, 12–13
  brainstorming for, 15–16
  freewriting for, 15
  journals, blogs, and online conversations for, 13–14
  mapping for, 16
  prompts for, 17–18
  for research papers, 100
  subject and thesis *versus,* 19–20
topic sentences, 28–29
Toulmin, Stephen, 61
Track Changes feature, 45
transitional expressions, 467, 479, 573*

transitions
  for logical connections, 357–358
  in paragraphs, 29–31
  run-on sentences and comma splices and, 397–398
transitive verbs, 410, 424, 573*
translations
  APA reference list style for, 239
  Chicago Manual of Style style for, 277–278
  MLA citation style for, 184
  quotation marks with, 476–477
transparencies, for presentations, 343
transparency, of Web sites, 317
treat, threat, 562
trimeter, in poetry, 84
Twitter, 4
two, too, to, 562
type, bleeding, 327
type, kind, sort, 558
typefaces, 293–295, 299

UCLA Higher Education Research Institute, 125
umlauts, 503–504
uncountable nouns, 430–431, 520–522, 573*
UN Demographic Yearbook, 106
underlining, 87, 477, 488
undoubtedly, 562
unified paragraphs, 28–29
Uniforms: Why We Are What We Wear (Pussell), 15–16, 46
uninterested, disinterested, 554
unique, 562
University Microfilms International (UMI), 186
University of California, Riverside, 111
University of California, Santa Barbara, 12, 112
University of Connecticut, 69
University of Massachusetts, 504
University of Michigan, 111
University of Minnesota, 111

University of Southern California, 72
University of Virginia Electronic Text Center, 112, 123
university publications, citation style for, 249
unparallel sentence structure, 404–405
until, 415
URLs (Uniform Resource Locators)
  abbreviations in, 499
  APA reference list style for, 244–245
  capital letters in, 498
  documenting, 140, 158
  evaluating, 131
  hyphens in, 498
  in MLA list of works cited, 178
  precision of, 308
  punctuation in, 497–499
  to search for sources, 124
U.S. Bureau of the Census, 106, 125
used to, get used to, be. 546
used to, get used to, become used to, 562
Uses of Argument, The (Toulmin), 61

verbals, 529–533, 542, 573*
verb chains, 526–532. 573*
verb phrases. 388, 573*
verbs. *See also* subject-verb agreement
  action, 354–355
  auxiliary, 412–413
  in conditional sentences, 420–422
  confused, 410–411
  definition of, 388, 573*
  forms of, 406–409
  infinitives after, 529–532
  ing form of, 531–532, 542
  -i or *-y* as endings of, 501–502
  it and, 429
  linking, 428, 448
  mental activity, 414, 568*
  modal auxiliary, 527–529, 568*
  as nouns, 531
  order of, 533–534

phrasal, 540–542
prepositions and, 540
relative pronoun agreement with, 456–457
subjects following. 428–429
tenses of, 413–420
transitive, 424
in writing across cultures, 512–513, 525–526, 526–533
very, too, 543
video
  APA reference list style for, 250–251
  Chicago Manual of Style style for, 283
  MLA documentation style for, 203, 205–206
  in presentations, 344
virtual classrooms, 313–314
vision-impaired audience, 9
visual arguments, 69–73
visuals
  APA citation style for, 230
  APA reference list style for, 250–251
  Chicago Manual of Style style for, 282–283
  copyright of, 306–307
  in document design, 298
  graphs and charts as, 303–306
  manipulation of, 307
  MLA citation style for, 201–209
  as sources, 124–125
  tables as, 302
  using, 301–302
  on Web sites, 316
Vogue magazine, 129
voice
  active, 563*
  definition of, 573*
  passive, 423–425
  Web site, 314
  in writing. 10–11
Voice of the Shuttle (University of California at Santa Barbara), 12, 112

Walters, Lilly, 342
was, 421
Washington Post, 130
way, ways, 562
wear, were, we're, 562
weather, whether, 562
WebAim Web site, to test
    accessibility, 9
Web directories, 12
Weblog postings, 251
Web site design, 314–319
    example of, 318–319
    feedback on, 317–318
    guidelines for, 316–317
    planning, 314–315
    site map for, 315
Web sites
    Adbusters.com, 70
    APA reference list style for, 234,
        243–249
    Chicago Manual of Style style for,
        276, 280–282
    citing, 139
    CSE reference list style for,
        266–268
    directories on, 111–112
    for discussion lists, 310
    documenting, 157–160
    evaluating, 130–133
    images on, 69
    on logical fallacies, 69
    lyrics on, 203
    MLA citation style for, 171–172,
        194–201
    for multilingual writers, 519
    Presentation Zen (Reynolds), 345
    as sources, 123–124, 124
    videos on, 203
    Writing Across the Curriculum, 92
weight, 430
well, good, 556
were, 421
were, wear, we're, 562
what, 434–435
*What Have You Changed Your Mind
    About?* (Brockman), 51

when, 403, 415, 458
where, 458
whether, weather, 562
which, 453–456
White, E. B., 361
white space, 327
whose, who's, 562
Who's Who, 105
who/whom, whoever/whomever,
    445–446, 453–456
Wikipedia, 105, 124, 313
wikis, 131, 199, 249, 312–313
wildcard characters, in searches, 115
will, 411, 415, 527–529
wishes, in sentences, 420–423
Word 2007
    citation formatting by, 300–301
    document design in, 296–301
    flyer, brochure, and newsletter
        templates of, 325–326
    graphs created in, 303
    for record keeping, 143–145
    Review tab functions of, 300
    to Word 2003 converter, 297
Word Count feature, 46
wordiness, cutting, 352–354
word links, 30
WordPerfect word processing
    software, 296
words
    choosing, 367–368
    connotations of, 369–370
    dictionaries and thesaurus for,
        368–369
    exact, 369–370
    hyphens in compound, 497
    inverted order of, 429, 568*
    nonstandard, 549
    omitted, 403–404
    order of, 365–366, 513–515,
        533–539
    quantity, 433–434
    question, 434–435
    redundant, 353–354
    between subjects and verbs, 427
working bibliography, 139–143

working thesis, 107–108. *See also* thesis
workplace language, 370–372
works cited. *See* list of works cited, MLA style
World Almanac, The, 106
World Trade Center, New York, 294
would, 411, 527–529
writer's block, 24
writing, 3–27
  audience for, 8–9
  critically reading, 5–8
  dialects and dialogue in, 372
  drafting and outlining in, 23–27
  everyday *versus* college, 4–5
  grammar check programs for, 46
  media for, 11
  in other languages, 504
  with others, 23
  purpose of, 8
  for readers, 3–4
  research papers, 109–110
  thesis presentation for, 18–22
  topics for, 11–18
  voice in, 10–11
writing across cultures, 505–546
  adjectives, 515–516
  adverbs, 515–516
  articles (*a, an, the*), 511–512, 523–526
  be, get used to, used to, 546
  easy, hard, difficult, 544
  English *versus* other languages, 507–510
  few, a few, 543

  it, there as sentence beginning, 544–545
  most, most of, the most, 544
  multilingual writers and, 518–519
  no, not, 542–543
  nouns, 515–516, 520–522, 525–526
  possessive pronouns, 545
  prepositions, 539–542
  pronouns, 515–516
  too, very, 543
  verb forms, 512–513, 525–526, 526–533
  vernacular English, 517–518
  word order, 513–515, 533–539
Writing Across the Curriculum (WAC), 80–81, 91–92
writing in college courses, 80–96
  on community service, 90–91
  everyday writing *versus*, 4–5
  example of, 87–90
  on humanities and arts, 92
  on literature, 82–87
  on natural sciences, 92–95
  researching and, 91–92
  on social sciences, 95–96
  in tests, 81–82
WWW Virtual Library, 112

Yahoo!.com, 12, 125
-*y* or -*i* as verb endings, 501–502
you, 444
your, you're, 562

zero article, 522, 524, 573*
zeugma, 86
Zotero software, 144

TEXT CREDITS

LIST OF BOXES AND SOURCE SHOTS

 Key Points

How to Be a Critical Reader of Text and Images 6

Subject, Topic, Question, Thesis: A Continuum 18

A Good Working Thesis 21

Tips for Writing Drafts 24

When to Begin a New Paragraph 28

Transitional Expressions 30

How to Write a Good Introduction 37

How to Write a Good Conclusion 39

Triggers for Revision 43

Giving Feedback to Others 44

Proofreading Tips 50

The Features of a Good Argument 53

Basic Structure for a General-to-Specific Argument 54

Four Questions to Ask about Your Argument 61

Ways to Establish Common Ground with Readers 65

Using Visuals 70

Guidelines for Essay Exams 82

Ten Ways to Analyze a Work of Literature 83

Common Conventions in Writing about Literature 87

A Model for the Organization of an Experimental Paper in the Sciences 93

Writing a Working Thesis 108

Tips on Using Search Engines 113

What Google Can Do for You 116

Reading Sources Critically 126

How to Recognize a Scholarly Article in Print 127

Questions to Evaluate a Print Source 129

Developing Your Junk Antennae: How to Evaluate Web Sites 131

Plagiarism's Seven Sins 134

How to Avoid Plagiarizing 136

Sources to Cite or Not to Cite 138

What Bibliographical Software Can Do 143

How to Paraphrase 149

How to Cite and List Sources in MLA Style 165

Guidelines for the MLA List of Works Cited 176

MLA Guidelines for Listing Works in Online Databases 191

Nine Ways to Document a Jay-Z Song 202

How to Cite and List Sources in APA Style 225

Guidelines for the APA List of References 233

Working with DOIs and URLs 244

How to Number and List Sources in the CSE Citation-Sequence or Citation-Name Style 263

Setting Up the CSE List of Cited References 264

How to Number and Document Sources in the *Chicago* Endnote/Footnote Style 274

Guidelines for *Chicago* Endnotes and Footnotes 276

Guidelines for College Essay Format 290

Posting Academic Writing Online 292

On Using Visuals 301

Using Graphs and Charts 304

Guidelines for Participating in Online Discussion Lists 310

Web Site Design Guidelines 316

Presenting a Course Writing Portfolio 320

Preparing an Academic Writing Portfolio 321

Writing a Résumé 330

Preparing a Scannable or an E-mail Résumé 332

Tips for Preparing an Oral Presentation 339

Common Types of Multimedia Aids 343

Tips for Creating PowerPoint Slides 346

Options for Connecting Clauses 358

A Checklist for Connecting Paragraphs 360

Checklist for Word Choice 367

Tips for Style 380

Grammar-Check Programs: Uses, Dangers, and Suggestions 385

Options for Editing a Run-on or Comma Splice 396

Verb Tenses in Conditional Sentences 420

Two Key Points about Agreement 425

Forms of Personal Pronouns 435

Comma Yes 462

Comma No 463

608

Apostrophe Yes 470
Apostrophe No 471
Quotation Marks: Basic Guidelines 474
Titles: Quotation Marks or
   Italics/Underlining? 477
Semicolon Yes 478
Semicolon No 479
Colon Yes 480
Colon No 481
What to Use before an Uncountable
   Noun 522
Articles at a Glance: Four Basic Questions
   about a Noun 524

Language and Culture

Assessing Your Readers' Expectations 9
Using "I" in Academic Writing 10
Language, Identity, and the Thesis
   Statement 22
Arguments across Cultures: Making a
   Claim and Staking a Position 58
Evidence Used to Support an Argument 61
The Cultures of the Academic
   Disciplines 91
Ownership Rights across Cultures 135
Business Letters across Cultures 335
Style across Cultures 351
Sentences Beginning with *And* or *But* 360
Dialect and Dialogue in Formal Writing 372
Language and Dialect Variation with *Be* 411
Issues of Subject-Verb Agreement 426

Note for Multilingual Writers

Beware of Grammar-Check Programs 45
What Comes before *Be, Been,* and *Being* 413
Verbs Not Using *-ing* Forms for Progressive
   Tenses 414
No *Will* in Time Clause 415
The *-ed* Ending 418
Passive Voice with Transitive Verbs 424
Singular Verb after *It* 429
No Plural Form for Adjectives 446
Adverb Placement 449
Relative versus Personal Pronouns 456
Number before *Hundred, Thousand,* and
   Million 495

Tech Note

Taking Accessibility Issues and Disabilities
   into Account 9
Using Web Directories to Find a Topic 12
Web Sites for Generating Ideas and
   Planning 13
Writing Collaboratively on the
   Computer 23
Using Comment and AutoCorrect 25
Computer Tools for Revising an Essay 42
Using Track Changes or GoogleDocs 45
Computer Tools for Editing 46
Logical Fallacies on the Web 69
Images on the World Wide Web 69
Exploring Data Visualization Tools 72
Useful Sites for Writing Across the
   Curriculum 92
Using *Wikipedia* 105
Databases of Journal Information 128
Finding Out about a Site 131
A Web Site on Plagiarism 135
Annotated Bibliographies 143
Posting Your Paper Online 178
Versions of Word for PC and Mac 297
Getting Help with Web Site Design 318
E-portfolios in Action 322
Templates in Word 325
Multimedia Presentation Design 345
Searching for *There* and *It* 355
A Useful Web Site for Writing in Other
   Languages 504
Web Sites on Language and Writing 510

Source Shot

Listing a Book in MLA Style 180
Listing a Scholarly Article in MLA
   Style 188
Listing a Magazine Article in an Online
   Database (MLA) 192
Listing a Web Source (MLA) 196
Listing an Online Government Publication
   (MLA) 200
Listing a Book (APA) 236
Listing a Periodical Article (APA) 242
Listing an Article (with a DOI) in an Online
   Database 246

Symbol	Example (change marked)	Example (change made)
`⌃o`	Correct a typo.	Correct a typo.
`⌃r·/m⌃/⌃o`	Correct more than one typo.	Correct more than one typo.
`t`	Insert a leter.	Insert a letter.
`or words`	Insert a word.	Insert a word or words.
	Make a deletion.	Make a deletion.
	Delete and close up space.	Delete and close up space.
`⊂`	Close up extra space.	Close up extra space.
`#`	Insert proper spacing.	Insert proper spacing.
`#/⊂`	Insert space and close up.	Insert space and close up.
`tr`	Transpose letters indcated.	Transpose letters indicated.
`tr`	Transpose as words indicated.	Transpose words as indicated.
`tr`	Reorder shown as words several.	Reorder several words as shown.
`⊏`	⊏ Move text to left.	Move text to left.
`⊐`	⊐ Move text to right.	Move text to right.
`⊓`	⌊Indent for paragraph.	Indent for paragraph.
`no ⊓`	⊏ No paragraph indent.	No paragraph indent.
`run in`	Run back turnover lines.	Run back turnover lines.
`⌐`	Break line when it runs far too long.	Break line when it runs far too long.
`⊙`	Insert period here.	Insert period here.
`⌃`	Commas commas everywhere.	Commas, commas everywhere.
`⌄`	Its in need of an apostrophe.	It's in need of an apostrophe.
`⌄ / ⌄`	Add quotation marks he begged.	"Add quotation marks," he begged.
`;`	Add a semicolon don't hesitate.	Add a semicolon; don't hesitate.
`:`	She advised "You need a colon."	She advised: "You need a colon."
`?`	How about a question mark.	How about a question mark?
`⌐=⌐`	Add a hyphen to a bill like receipt.	Add a hyphen to a bill-like receipt.
`⟨/⟩`	Add parentheses as they say.	Add parentheses (as they say).
`lc`	Sometimes you want Lowercase.	Sometimes you want lowercase.
`caps`	Sometimes you want upperCASE.	Sometimes you want UPPERCASE.
`ital`	Add italics instantly.	Add italics *instantly*.
`rom`	But use *roman* in the main.	But use roman in the main.
`bf`	Add boldface if necessary.	Add **boldface** if necessary.
`sp`	Spell out all 3 terms.	Spell out all three terms.
`stet`	Let stand as is.	Let stand as is. (This retracts a change already marked.)

CORRECTION GUIDE

Note: Numbers refer to chapters and sections in the book.

Abbreviation	Meaning/Error
ab or abbr	abbreviation, 54, 57d
adj	adjective, 37d, 45
adv	adverb, 37d, 45
agr	agreement. 43, 44d
apos	apostrophe, 48
arg	argument error, 4e–4i
art	articles, 60
awk	awkward, 30, 31, 40
bias	biased or sexist language, 33f, 44e
ca or case	case, 44a
cap (ʈom)	use capital letter, 53, 57b, 60f
coh	coherence, 2c
comp	comparative, 45h, 45i
coord	coordination, 2b, 32c, 47b
cs	comma splice, 39
d	diction, 34
db neg	double negative, 45g
dev	development, 2d
dm	dangling modifier, 40c
doc	documentation, 11–20
-ed	error with -ed ending, 41g
exact	exactness, 34c
frag	sentence fragment, 38
fs	fused sentence, 39
gen	gender bias, 34f, 44e
hyph	hyphenation, 56, 57d
id	idiom, 63
inc	incomplete sentence or construction, 40h, 62a
ind quot	indirect quotation, 41i, 62d
-ing	error with -ing ending, 61
ital	italics/underlining, 12a, 15a, 19c, 52
jar	jargon, 34d
lc (Ɱe)	use a lowercase letter, 53
log	logic, 4h, 4j

Abbreviation	Meaning/Error
mix or mixed	mixed construction, 40a
mm	misplaced modifier, 40b
ms	manuscript form, 21, 25, 26, 27
nonst	nonstandard usage, 37c, 38–46
num	faulty use of numbers, 55
//	parallelism, 40j
p	punctuation, 47–51, 57a
pass	passive voice, 31c, 42
prep	preposition, 37d, 63
pron	pronoun, 37d, 44
quot	quotation, 10f, 49
ref	pronoun reference, 44c
rel cl	relative clause, 46
rep or red	repetitive or redundant, 30a, 30d
-s	error with -s ending, 43
shift	needless shift, 40d, 41h
sp	spelling, 58
s/pl	singular/plural, 43a, 43h, 58a
sub	subordination, 32b, 62e
sup	superlative, 45h
s-v agr	subject-verb agreement, 43
t	verb tense, 41d
trans	transition, 2c, 47e
und	underlining/italics, 52
us	usage, 65
v or vb	error with verb, 41
var	[sentence] variety, 33d
w	wordy, 30
wc	word choice, 34
wo	word order, 33d, 62b, 62g
ww	wrong word, 34

CONTENTS

1 The Writing Process
1. **Ways into Writing** 3
2. **Developing Paragraphs and Essays** 27
3. **Revising, Editing, and Proofreading** 40
4. **Writing and Analyzing Arguments** 51
5. **Writing in All Your Courses** 80

2 Research/Sources
6. **The Research Process** 99
a What's involved
b Set a schedule
c Use primary and secondary sources
d Consult reference works
e Move from research question to working thesis
f Write a purpose statement or a proposal
g Tips for the process
7. **Searching for Sources** 110
a Starting the search
b Search engines and keyword searching
c Getting the most out of online searches
d Databases
e Print sources
f Web sources
g Visual sources
8. **How to Evaluate Sources** 126
a Read sources critically
b Recognize a scholarly article in print
c Recognize a scholarly article online
d Evaluate print works
e Evaluate Web sources
9. **How to Avoid Plagiarizing** 133
a The seven sins of plagiarism
b How to avoid even the suspicion of plagiarism
c Know why, how, and what to cite
d Keep track of sources
e Annotated bibliographies Student's sample
f Use software and databases
10. **How to Use, Integrate, and Document Sources** 145
a Annotate and make notes Student's sample
b Put yourself in your paper, and synthesize sources
c Organize by ideas, not sources
d Summarize and paraphrase
e Quote accurately
f Indicate boundaries
g Introduce and integrate source material
h Document to fit the discipline
i One source, four systems of documentation

3 MLA Style
AT A GLANCE: MLA Style 162
11. **MLA: Citing Sources** 165
12. **List of Works Cited** 176
13. **MLA: Sample Paper** 209

4 APA, CSE, and *Chicago* Style
AT A GLANCE: APA Style 223
14. **APA: Citing Sources** 225
15. **APA: List of References** 232
16. **APA: Sample Paper** 251
17. **CSE Style** 262
AT A GLANCE: CSE Citation 262
18. **CSE: Sample Paper** 268
19. ***Chicago* Style** 273
AT A GLANCE: Sample *Chicago* Endnotes and Footnotes 273
20. ***Chicago:* Sample Paper** 285

5 Design, Media, and Presentation
21. **Document Design** 289
22. **Visuals** 301
23. **Online Communication Forums** 308
24. **Web Site Design** 314
25. **Portfolios** 320
26. **Flyers, Brochures, and Newsletters** 325
27. **Résumés, Letters** 329
28. **Business Letters** 335
29. **Presentations** 339

6 Style: The Five C's
30. **Cut** 352
31. **Check for Action** 354
32. **Connect** 356
33. **Commit** 361
34. **Choose the Best Words** 367
35. **Revising for Style: A Student's Drafts** 378
36. **Style Tips** 380

7 Common Sentence Problems
37. **Trouble Spots/Terms** 383
a Students' FAQs
b Grammar-check programs
c Standard English/Edited American English
d The parts of a sentence
38. **Sentence Fragments** 392
a What a sentence needs
b Missing subject and/or verb
c Dependent clause fragment
d Missing subject after *and, but,* or *or*
e Intentional fragments
39. **Run-ons and Comma Splices** 396
a How to identify
b Five ways to correct
c Comma splices with transitions
40. **Sentence Snarls** 398
a Types of tangles
b Misplaced modifiers
c Dangling modifiers
d Types of shifts
e Mismatched subjects and predicates
f Definitions and reasons
g *Because* and *when* clauses as subject
h Omitted words
i Unnecessary restated subject
j Structures not parallel
41. **Verbs** 406
a Verb forms: regular and irregular
b Verbs commonly confused
c Auxiliary verbs
d Tenses: Overview
e Present tenses
f Past tenses
g *-ed* endings
h Unnecessary tense shifts
i Tenses in indirect quotations
j Conditional sentences, wishes, requests, demands, and recommendations
42. **Passive Voice** 423
a When to use
b How to form
c Overuse
d As connector